Reading Medical Records

Reading Medical Records

Second Edition

J. Stanley McQuade

Carolina Academic Press
Durham, North Carolina

Libary of Congress Cataloging in Publication Data
McQuade, J. Stanley (James Stanley), 1929-
Reading medical records / Stanley McQuade.—2nd ed.
p. cm.
Includes bibliographical references and index.
ISBN 978-1-61163-109-8 (alk. paper)
1. Medical records--Evaluation. 2. Evidence, Expert. 3. Medical jurisprudence. I. Title.

RA1056.M37 2012
651.5'04261--dc23 2012016495

Carolina Academic Press
700 Kent Street
Durham, NC 27701
Telephone (919) 489-7486
Fax (919) 493-5668
www.cap-press.com

Printed in the United States of America
2026 Printing

Contents

Introduction

This book is designed to enable a lawyer or paralegal or any other compensation professional to read and work with a medical record and to converse with medical consultants.

The items which it contains are simple. The first three chapters provide a general introduction to medical records and their use in the legal context. Chapter two contains a brief description of the basic documents which make up a medical record, showing how they come into being, where they may be found and the kinds of information that they are likely to contain. A fairly complete set of illustrative documents is appended to this chapter. Chapter three discusses how the materials in a medical record can be organized and presented efficiently by means of a flow-chart. Chapter four deals with the basic template that lies behind most medical documents, the history and physical examination.

The remaining five chapters deal with important terms and concepts in clinical medicine. This is not medicine as it is taught to doctors, but specially selected and interpreted to meet the needs and purposes of compensation lawyers. The topics treated here are:

1. Head injuries and the related topic of mental impairments
2. Musculoskeletal problems
3. Cardiac disability and
4. Lung disability heart and lung disability.

These topics (brains, bones, hearts and lungs) cover most of the medical problems raised in personal injury and compensation evaluation. The items presented even within these topics have been further selected out, for much of the information that is important to doctors is more or less irrelevant to lawyers. Other items, e.g. intervertebral disc disease or minimal brain damage, are treated in some detail since they are common injuries and, moreover, give lawyers handling head injuries and back cases a good deal of difficulty.

Some special tools have been added.

1. **Short working glossaries.** A very short glossary (just a few pages) has been appended to each of the five medical chapters. These are not intended as reference dictionaries, but rather as a list of the basic terms which must be understood in order to work efficiently in these areas. These terms should, if possible, be learned off: the time and effort involved will be repaid many times over in saving the reader from the chore of constant reference to a medical dictionary.

2. **Model handwritten notes** have also been added to each of the four medical chapters. Each represents the history and physical examination in an appropriate case. These

are intended to teach the reader the common terms and especially the abbreviations which are used by doctors in handwritten progress notes etc. They are ,of course, accompanied by translations. The use of symbols and especially letter abbreviations (acronyms) is increasing in medicine as elsewhere, and quite large dictionaries of abbreviations can be needed to cover them all. For the most part, however, only a (relative) few are in common use and most of these will be found in these model notes.

These two items, the model handwritten notes and the short wworking glosssaries, should be studied very seriously. They are the key to handling medical information efficiently. They should be committed to memory in the interests of efficiency and not just treated as reference works. It should very seldom be necessary to go beyond these simple resources.

3. **A short additional glossary of abbreviations and symbols** has also been appended to the book. This is taken from the list of officially recognized acronyms published by a small hospital. It was compiled by a very intelligent nurse and is , I think, superior to the published lists of many large referral hospitals. The reader should become as familiar as possible with this list, but it is a short reference work not intended to be memorized in advance.

4. **Illustrative drawings.** More than eighty computer drawn illustrations and diagrams have been provided on the principle that one picture is worth a thousand words. These have been interpolated into the medical chapters at appropriate points in the text for the convenience of the reader.

This book is the fruit of more than two decades of experience in teaching law students, lawyers, and paralegals how to read and work with medical records. This experience is the foundation of my belief that a considerable degree of competence in this area is well within the ability of any one who wishes to acquire it. This book is particularly designed for the young lawyer or legal assistant who is just beginning to do personal injury or disability work. It is short and (I hope) clear and readable, but it contains more than enough information for most legal purposes. A lawyer does not have to know how to diagnose and treat diseases, only to evaluate them for compensation purposes. Fortunately this does not require a vast amount of medical learning. Indeed all that is needed, at least in the initial reading of a medical record, is to be sufficiently familiar with basic terms and concepts to form some idea of what was happening in the case. Detailed and more accurate understanding can be supplied later by further reading and discussion with medical consultants. The latter is extremely important. To be able to communicate meaningfully and efficiently with doctors and other medical personnel is indeed the basic prerequisite for anyone working in the compensation area. Ignorance of basic terms and notions on the part of the lawyer leads to long and frustrating conferences, with prolonged explanations by the doctor which are as often as not misunderstood by the lawyer. The very basic level of familiarity with things medical which is contained in these pages is more than is ordinarily required to facilitate useful communication between the two professions.

One last point. There is more information in this little book than is absolutely required for an elementary course in medical records. For instance, I do not normally in my course deal with the autonomic nerves, or with eye ear nose and throat matters. But, as I say to my law students, don't throw the book away or leave it to gather dust on your bookshelves.

Keep working with it. Take it down in the odd spare moment and read a chapter or even a few sections; you will be surprised how much better you will perform and how much more understanding of cases you will achieve.

Reading Medical Records

Chapter One

Mastering the Medical Record

§ 1:1 The significance of medical records

Many of the cases that come to a general-practice lawyer's office involve a medical record. Consider the following:

- Automobile accidents
- Workers' compensation
- Social Security or insurance disability
- Medical malpractice
- Transactional or legal competence

Some might think that it is not necessary for lawyers to learn to read a medical record, since a medical consultant might be obtained who would translate it and explain it to them. Unfortunately, total reliance on medical consultants is not very satisfactory for the following reasons.

1. Medicine and law are quite different disciplines. They view the same facts in quite different ways, even though they use the same words, for example, "cause" and "future complications."
2. Doctors and lawyers pursue quite different objectives; the one is concerned with treatment and the other with compensation. What is interesting and significant to a doctor then, may be irrelevant to a lawyer, and vice versa.
3. The medical facts must be adapted into the language and categories of compensation law and presented to insurance adjusters or courts in those terms. No one can do this except the lawyer who is handling the case. A doctor may consult and advise, but in the last analysis the case must filter through the mind of the attorney handling it.

It is possible then, and even likely, that unless the doctors can be made to understand something of what is the lawyer's mind, important facts may be missed (unknown to the lawyer and not deemed relevant by the doctor), or concepts may not be properly transposed into legal terms. In short, the case may not be properly presented. However, what is more likely is that the medical consultation will be slow and difficult for both parties. Doctors become frustrated with having to explain what they consider to be simple things over and over again, and even then they are not properly grasped by the lawyer. Lawyers too complain that doctors do not explain things well. The only hope is that either the doctor should know exactly what is required by the lawyer, or the lawyer should know enough about medicine to put the right questions to the consultant and understand the answers well enough to adapt the medical materials for legal purposes. So either the doctor or the lawyer must cross over to understand the other side. Even when the doctor is experienced and aware of legal issues, the lawyer needs to be aware of the medical perspective, if for no other reason than the final product is legal, not medical.

§ 1:2 What is needed to understand a medical record

The following are the basic essentials needed to read a medical record for legal purposes:

1. *A general knowledge of hospital affairs,* especially things relating to documentation and procedures. One cannot really understand medical records without some awareness of the environment in which they are produced, any more than one can read a statute in ignorance of the legislative process or a case report with no knowledge of procedure.

2. *An acquaintance with the various documents which make up a medical record.* It is important to know what items are contained in each of them, or (to put it the other way round) where one would go to find certain kinds of information. Conversely, it is equally important to know what one will *not* find in a document. One should not expect to find detailed information about the events of an automobile accident in an admission history, nor think that the discharge summary contains all the relevant information required for compensation purposes. It would likewise be a mistake to conclude that reports of any untoward incidents in the hospital will be found in the spaces provided in the medical reports for this purpose.

3. *Some knowledge about clinical medicine and medical science*. It is impossible to read medical documents with any degree of understanding without some information about common diseases and the ways in which they are diagnosed and treated. This may seem an impossible task, but one must remember that there are fundamental differences between the knowledge required to diagnose and treat diseases and that needed to evaluate injuries and disabilities for compensation purposes. The knowledge required by present day clinicians is indeed daunting. Specialists and subspecialists have difficulty keeping up with the information reaching them in the medical journals, and keeping current with new findings and new treatments. When one moves from the clinical area to the compensation field, most of this knowledge shrinks down to very manageable proportions. The reason for this is that much of the material that makes up the bulk of medical books is irrelevant in compensation evaluation. A large part of an orthopedic textbook will be devoted to the subject of fractures, which is seldom of any importance to compensationists. Even if fractures do not heal normally with the initial treatment, they can usually be fixed at a second attempt. Similarly, much of the material in a textbook on neurosurgery will be concerned with malignant brain tumors or massive head trauma, both of which will commonly leave the surviving patients with severe impairments. In such cases, virtually no medical knowledge on the part of the compensationist is required; their task is essentially legal. The general knowledge required for initial comprehension of a compensation/disability case is probably a good deal less than that of an average nurse. The information contained in this handbook is in fact much more than most lawyers normally require. This is not so, of course, in complex medical malpractice cases, where detailed information about medical conditions and their proper management may be needed.

4. *A basic medical vocabulary.* It is not necessary to know all the terms in a medical dictionary. Medical terms can be looked up in glossaries and dictionaries, but it is inefficient and exhausting to be constantly reaching for a reference book. A reasonable working vocabulary (perhaps 100–200 terms) will take one a long way, but these should be in memory and familiar. Similarly, a vast knowledge of medical abbreviations (acronyms) is not required. Those found in the specimen handwritten records following the medical chapters of this book will explain most of the items that one is likely to encounter in any given medical record. It should be emphasized, of course, that these items should be learned and not treated as reference materials.

5. *Some skill in reading handwritten medical notes*, especially the ones with poor handwriting and obscure abbreviations. Handwritten specimens are appended to the medical chapters, and a number of handwritten notes are to be found in the appendix following Chapter 2.

6. *A good method of organizing* the mass of apparently unconnected materials, which make up the usual medical record, into an orderly systematic form which can be used to understand and present the case. This topic will be taken up in Chapter 3.

§ 1:3 The reference library

Large *medical text books* (beloved of lawyers) are probably the least helpful reference works that one can purchase. They are expensive and are at least two years out of date on the day of publication. Furthermore, they tend to be incomprehensible to lawyers because the authors do not trouble to explain essential concepts and terms (these are presumed to be understood by the doctors reading them). A visit to a medical library to consult medical texts may be necessary on occasion, and it does not hurt to have one of these tomes on the shelf in the office, but they are unlikely to be helpful in the initial stages, when a lawyer is trying to understand a cardiac or a low back case.

1. *Nursing text books* or text books intended for medical technicians, physical therapists, and other medical professionals are very valuable to lawyers who wish to become familiar with medical topics for the following reasons:

   i. They are generally written by teachers rather than researchers;

   ii. They are intended to make things clear to people who have not much background in scientific medicine;

   iii. They are usually very well illustrated; and finally,

   iv. They are generally less expensive than medical text books.

There is an abundance of such books, and a student nurse or recent graduate can often recommend one which has acquired a good reputation in the profession.

2. *Texts on physical examination* are useful. These are the first books read by medical students when they begin their clinical rotations in hospital, and they are most useful works so far as lawyers are concerned. The "patient history and physical examination" is the basic template for a great many documents in the medical record. [See Chapter 4.] It is the basis for the initial admitting notes or the doctors' progress notes, and a number of the nurses' notes are essentially reports of what was said by the patient and

found by the nurse on examination. Nursing evaluations are indeed becoming more and more like the history and physical of the physicians. It is most important then that anyone reading such notes should know something about the questions that are asked, and the clinical tests and procedures that are carried out in such examinations. Knowing what was probably said and done is often the vital clue that renders intelligible and interprets some mysterious squiggle in a handwritten medical note. When you are not sure what is there, it helps to know what is usually there.

3. *Medical dictionaries* are necessary reference books and usually contain glossaries of abbreviations and symbols. These are useful, but it is difficult to keep such materials current, so that those found in medical dictionaries may be decades out of date.

4. *Hospital lists of acceptable abbreviations* are also available. Medical schools and hospitals have long been attempting to deal with the problem of letter abbreviations (acronyms). The current policy is to curb the creative urges of the physicians by issuing lists of acceptable standard abbreviations. If a physician wishes to introduce a new acronym, it must be submitted to, and approved by the medical records committee of the hospital. The hospital medical records department can and will refuse to sign off on a medical record which is not properly written (e.g., contains unapproved acronyms), and they can make this decision stick. Medical records policies are reviewed carefully by inspection teams from the American Hospitals Association who, along with the insurers, will support the medical informatics department. The doctor and the hospital will not be reimbursed until the record is properly completed. The little booklets containing the list of approved acronyms for the hospital are modest in length, cost only a few dollars, and can prove most useful to lawyers. The glossary of acronyms at the end of this handbook is adapted from the approved list of a local hospital. It was put together by a smart nurse and is indeed superior to those promulgated by many large referral hospitals.

5. *Medical informatics textbooks* have always been helpful to lawyers. These are primarily intended for the personnel in the Medical Records Department (now called Medical Informatics) who must transcribe the dictated medical notes. They thus concentrate on the meaning (and spelling) of medical terms, and so these works generally have a good list of acceptable medical abbreviations and symbols. Those which discuss the origin and derivation of terms are likely to be especially helpful. This kind of information can also be found in medical dictionaries; however, the medical informatics texts tend to be more in line with current usage. They also contain information about the rapidly expanding use of computers in medical informatics departments. The basic workhorse of the compensation lawyer is still the ordinary patient medical file. The computerized version can be printed out for the lawyers, and they do not differ fundamentally from the older hard copy medical files.

§ 1:4 Some other valuable books

There are three other books that can be valuable additions to the medical library of the practicing lawyer. These are:

1. The Merck Medical Handbook *produced by the drug company Merck, Sharpe and Dohme.* It contains a brief description of virtually every known disease, covering un-

derlying pathology (where known), diagnosis, treatment and usual outcomes. The most recent edition of this useful work was produced in 1993, and, unfortunately, it will be the last (MS&D is discontinuing its publication). This is bad news for physicians, but not quite so terrible for compensation professionals, since its main use for them is to provide a little background information about disease conditions. In fact, even an older version of this handbook will be adequate for most legal purposes.

2. *The most recent version of the Diagnostic and Statistical Manual of Mental Disorders* (DSM-IV) costs around $95 and may be money well spent. Mental disabilities have become much more important in recent years, and DSM-IV is a most valuable tool, both for understanding them and for a number of specific legal purposes.

3. *Any edition of Lawrence Weed's book* THE PROBLEM ORIENTED MEDICAL RECORD is useful. Electronic medical records are already here in some form or other, and the complete computerization of the medical record is nearing completion. This movement has been driven by the medical informatics association, and has been backed by payor agencies (such as Medicare and major health insurance carriers) since it allows them much easier access to the medical information they require to monitor reimbursement for services rendered. The informatics authorities have adopted the Weed system of medical record keeping as the only one suitable for their computerization project. This little book, discussed further in Chapter 4, is worth adding to the lawyer's medical library.

§ 1:5 Learning to read medical records by practice

Doctors do not usually receive formal instruction in medical record keeping. They learn by doing. The best teacher is practice. A full medical record has not been included in this handbook for reasons of space, but the materials provided in the Supplement to Chapter 2 of this book should make it possible for even a beginner to tackle a real medical record. There are also short vocabularies attached to each of the five major medical chapters. Short handwritten records have also been added as practice materials. These cover the basic topics of central nervous system examination, the psychiatric evaluation, musculoskeletal examination, cardiovascular examination and examination of the respiratory system. Students who work through these materials can usually read 90 percent or more of handwritten records, thus they only occasionally have to look up a word or ask a question.

§ 1:6 Reading medical records—the importance of a methodical approach

There are no doubt many ways to go about reading medical records and organizing the information contained in them, but the necessity of some systematic method could hardly be overemphasized. Floundering around for several weeks in a medical record is neither efficient nor enjoyable. The flow-sheet approach described in Chapter 3 is a simple method of arranging complex data that is often used by engineers, intensive care doctors, and other such persons who must keep track of an overabundant flow of information. It is also a very easy and apt way to manage a large or complicated set of medical documents.

§ 1:7 Electronic medical records

This topic has been briefly mentioned earlier (§ 1:4) but a further word is needed here. The medical branch of the American Informatics Association announced several years ago that all medical records would be required to be electronic by the year 2005. This was not an idle boast. All the governmental and private payor agencies were behind this move, and doctors, nurses and everyone else in the medical business have had to come on board for financial reasons. The hardware and software had been available for a number of years, and the only serious obstacle was the training and motivation of the medical staff. The project is now virtually complete, although a little merciful allowance to the medical staff has been allowed here and there. Electronic records tend to be bulky, but otherwise they will not differ substantially from the older hard-copy format. The focus of attention here will therefore be on the ordinary medical file, and anything said here should apply equally well to an electronic record.

Chapter Two

The Documents

Part I.
General Observations—The Big Three

§ 2:1 General description of a medical record

The traditional medical record consists of a patient file containing pages of reports and documents, produced by many departments and many people. Some of these are administrative materials, such as the admission sheet prepared by the admitting clerks when the patient is admitted to hospital. However, most of them relate to patient care. The most important of these will be considered in the following paragraphs.

Traditionally all of these documents were handwritten and many of them (e.g., nurses' notes and doctors' progress notes) may still be in this form. Many are dictated and transcribed and, increasingly, they are produced bed-side on small computers. Electronic records are steadily taking over, but generally the information remains the same, and the same management principles apply. Electronic records will not, therefore, be separately discussed in this chapter. Another development, the *Problem Oriented Medical Record* (POMR), will likewise not be considered here, but discussed briefly in Chapter 4, which deals with the routine history and physical examination.

§ 2:2 The doctors' discharge summary

The most obvious document in a medical record is the discharge summary, because it is usually at the front of the chart as assembled by the Medical Records Department (Medical Information Services). It is also the best place to begin, as it gives a bird's-eye view of the case through the eyes of a doctor, and is, in a sense, a free medical consultation. It must normally (by hospital regulation) be dictated and transcribed, not handwritten, and this is an additional advantage. There are, however, a number of drawbacks to the discharge summary which should be remembered.

1. The discharge summary is supposed to be dictated when the patient is discharged from the hospital. But busy (or tardy) doctors may put off their dictation, and may find themselves with a pile of medical charts to complete at the end of each month—the deadline if they are to continue to have admission privileges to the hospital. In teaching hospitals, the duty of dictating discharge summaries may be delegated by the

treating physician to residents or interns, who are also very busy people, and may likewise be late and pressed for time in dealing with their medical records. In this kind of situation, working in a hurry, important items may be omitted or incorrectly recorded.

2. If the physician is aware, at the time of dictation, of the possibility that legal action may be associated with the case, this knowledge may affect the discharge summary. The likelihood of a medical malpractice suit against the doctor in question or a colleague is one example, but not the only one. Doctors are aware that they may become involved in disability and compensation proceedings, and this knowledge can make them very careful about what they say. They may, therefore, leave out items which they think might lead to questioning, and perhaps rough handling, by adverse lawyers. They may even suppress items which they think might encourage someone to consider a law suit, in order to stay out of legal proceedings altogether.

3. But the most serious drawback to the discharge summary is simply the difference between the medical and the legal points of view (mentioned in the previous chapter). Information which is vital for compensation purposes (such as the mental competence of the patient to make a statement or a will) will normally be irrelevant to the doctor. Lawyers, therefore, commonly find themselves obliged to hunt through the entire chart for relevant information, and sometimes they must look in vain.

Despite these drawbacks, the overall benefits of reading the discharge summary first, before looking at the other documents, are considerable. It allows the reader to develop a broad picture of the patient's problems and hospital course, which helps to make sense of all the individual items which will be read later. It is especially valuable in providing an overview of the test reports which make up much of the bulk in the larger medical records. There is probably no need to examine three hundred pages filled with X-ray and lab reports when the results are summed up in a few paragraphs, or perhaps even in a sentence.

§ 2:3 The nurses' notes

At least one nurse's note must be entered in each of the three eight-hour shifts that make up the day. If the patient's condition merits it, more frequent notes will, of course, be required. These are normally handwritten, and it has, until recently, been customary to use a different colored pen for each shift (commonly red, green and blue/black). A number of hospitals now require all nurses' notes to be written with a black pen, since it is easier to read and photocopy them. The nurses' notes are the lawyers' friend for the following reasons:

1. The handwriting is usually good and they supply information that is often not found elsewhere.

2. They are the only place in the medical record where there is a round-the-clock account of the patient's general condition. Nurses are trained to record what they see and hear. They will, for example, note how well the patient was eating or whether they were complaining much about pain.

3. They represent a broader perspective on the patient's condition than will usually be found in the notes made by physicians, and thus contain information not readily available elsewhere. They will, for example, note how well the patient was eating and sleeping and whether the patient's mood was depressed or anxious.

4. They are probably the best place to go to evaluate pain and suffering in any patient. Nurses administer most of the medications given for pain and will often comment on the frequency and severity of patients' complaints about pain, and the effectiveness, or lack thereof, of the medications given to relieve it. Even if the pain medications are administered by the patients themselves, the nurses may need to recommend increase or reduction of the dosage.

5. An injury which has been missed by the attending physicians (which sometimes happens in severe multiple trauma cases) can sometimes be evidenced for insurance purposes by entries in the nurses' notes.

§ 2:4 The doctors' progress notes—the medical perspective

Doctors' progress notes (DPNs) come in one of two types as a rule, very long or very short. Medical students, interns and residents tend to write longer notes. Consultant physicians on the other hand write terse notes, fewer notes, or no notes at all. The DPNs can be the most difficult parts of the chart to read. To begin with, they are normally handwritten, if they are not computer derived, and so can be difficult to decipher, especially the notes written by consultants who, for some reason or other, tend to scribble. Residents, interns and medical students write reasonably legibly as a rule, but their notes tend to feature letter abbreviations and hieroglyphics. The greatest difficulty, however, in reading progress notes is that here, more than in any other part of the medical chart, medical knowledge is vital in order to understand what is going on. Medical consultation may be needed at times to make sense of them.

A comment should be made at this point about the progress notes of medical students. It might be supposed that these, being the product of mere beginners, are not worth reading, but this is far from being the case. Medical students as a rule take the patient's history very painstakingly. They ask all the proper questions without shortcuts, and record the answers in very long notes filled with detailed information. Much of this material can be useful to the treating physicians, who may miss an important point that the more thorough inquiries of the student will elicit. They can also be important for lawyers, who may find their particular questions answered, or partly answered, here, rather than in the more cryptic notes of the experienced physicians.

Part II.
Documents Relating to Surgery

§ 2:5 The surgical summary

The surgical summary is normally made by the surgeon performing the operation, though occasionally, in a teaching hospital, the task may be assigned to a senior surgical resident. It is normally dictated immediately following surgery, in the doctors' changing room in the operating room suite. It is therefore normally contemporaneous and, of course, since it is dictated and transcribed, it is legible.

The surgical summary generally includes the following items of information and usually in the order shown.

1. The preoperative diagnosis (e.g., acute appendicitis)
2. The postoperative diagnosis (hopefully the same)
3. The skin incision (precisely and fully described)
4. The approach to the operating site (in detail, tissue by tissue and cut by cut)
5. What was done (the appendix removed)
6. Description of the closure (layer by layer and stitch by stitch)
7. A comment on the patient's condition going to the recovery room

This kind of format is followed so rigidly that any departure from it merits at least a question. Additions, such as reiterating that something was done at once or in a timely manner, may be significant, since such expressions are not usually found in the surgical summary—one might be wise to enquire if there was delay in getting the patient to the operating suite. Also, some items in the list may be omitted in cases where there is some likelihood of a malpractice action being brought, even though the recording doctor is not likely to be a party to the suit.

§ 2:6 The anesthesia records

There are three parts to the anesthesia record:

- the preanesthetic evaluation,
- the anesthesia record itself, and
- the postanesthetic evaluation.

The anesthesia record is normally the hardest part to interpret. It is commonly a mass of entries that can be difficult if not impossible to disentangle, but it can be made manageable. It should be divided into its constituent parts (see example on page 13). These are:

1. **Patient information** (labeled **A** in the sample). This includes the patient's name, room number, name of physician, the proposed operation and anything else that may help to identify the patient accurately. The main purpose of all this is to avoid mix-ups, e.g., where one patient gets an operation intended for someone else.

2. **Preanesthetic data** (labeled **B** in the sample). There may be very little information here. Anyone looking for clinical information about the patient will then have to look elsewhere, e.g., in the preanesthetic evaluation. If clinical information is given directly on the anesthetic sheet, it will commonly include a complete blood count (CBC) which makes sure that the patient is not anemic or developing an infection. It also normally includes an EKG and (over a certain age) a chest X-ray. Any allergies (especially to drugs) and any continuing medications (e.g., heart medications) would also be noted here. This part of the record can be important, since any anesthesiologist who might have to take over the case unexpectedly can look at this section and quickly apprise themselves of important points in the patient's medical history.

3. **The numbered record of events** (labeled **C** in the example opposite). Each event in the anesthetic (e.g., that the patient was put asleep or intubated) is noted in this space and the item is numbered. Corresponding numbers are written just below the time frame at the top of the graphic chart. Comparison of these two sets of numbers tell the reader what happened and when.

4. **The drug record** (labeled **D** in the sample). The names of the drugs are usually entered in the appropriate place (usually on the upper left border of the graphic chart)

Breakdown of the Anesthetic Record into Its Basic Units

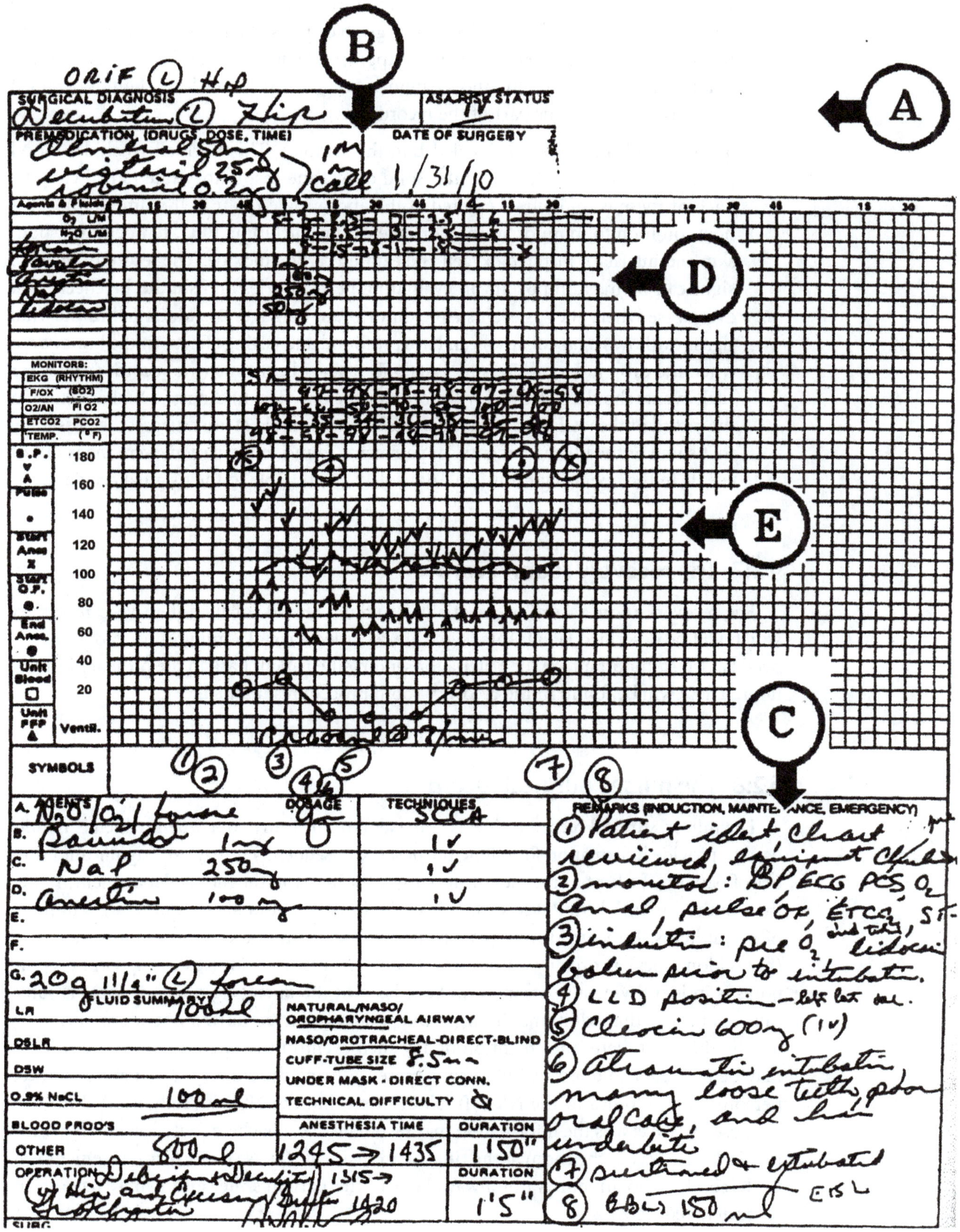

along with the units of measurement, e.g., in milligrams (mg) in the case of Pentothal, or in liters/min (L/min) in the case of any gases or intravenous fluids which are being given to the patient. The actual amounts given or rates of administration are then entered across the graphic chart under the appropriate time slot. The amounts and times of administration of all substances administered to the patient (drugs, liquids or gases) can thus be read in this part of the record.

5. **The monitoring record** (labeled **E** in the sample). This normally includes blood pressures (inverted Vs), heart rate (solid dots), and respiratory rate (small circles). Each of these is, of course, entered at the appropriate point in the time frame. It is now common to monitor all sorts of other things including EKG, temperature (both skin and internal), inspired oxygen and expired carbon dioxide. The record of the vital signs can be most important in evaluating head injuries and should be checked in every case where they is even suspicion of brain damage. A sudden fall in the vital signs (cardiovascular collapse) can have profound and lasting effects on the brain, even when the drop in blood pressure lasts only a very short time (the recorded times for such events should be treated with some suspicion). The finding of a V-shaped dip in the record of the vital signs in the anesthesia record should at least suggest the possibility that some of the ultimate mental impairments found in the patient were the result of events in the operating room, and not solely attributable to the original accident.

§ 2:7 The recovery room record

The recovery room record is essentially a nursing record (of the intensive-care variety which will be described later). Vital signs are recorded every 15 minutes, or more often if need be. Most important are the criteria for sending the patient back to the ordinary nursing floor. These will be found in the recovery room procedures manual.

§ 2:8 The nurses' surgical record

The nurses' surgical record (NSR) is really an administrative document which is mainly used to provide information for billing purposes. Consequently it may, in a significant number of patients, be kept in the files of the surgical suite, or in the billing department, rather than in the patient's hospital record. It is in the form of a flow sheet containing a number of useful items. It records times, persons present, sometimes the drugs given, and should (but seldom does) record any untoward incidents. Its main use for legal compensation purposes is in identifying all persons who have been in the operating room. If there is some cause to believe that additional harm to the patient occurred during operation and (as is usually the case) there is no mention of any such event in the operating room records, it may be necessary to question all persons present during the surgery. The names of these persons will be found in the NSR. It is not often that the NSR is really needed for this purpose by lawyers, as the information may be obtainable elsewhere, but if one really wishes to check who was in the room at the time of an incident, the NSR is a very convenient way to do so. This document is not always kept in the patient's file, and it may have to be separately requested.

§ 2:9 The sponge and instrument count

The sponge and instrument count is carried out at least twice and usually three times: once before the operation begins, once just before closure, and again after closure. It is made by the circulating nurse, commonly the charge nurse in the operating room, but from time to time student nurses may make the NSR (under supervision) as part of their training. Like the nurses' surgical record, it is not always a part of the patient's chart and may be kept in the operating room files. It is only occasionally important in compensation settings, for example in malpractice cases where a sponge or surgical instrument has been left behind in a surgical patient. Even here it is only really important on those rare occasions when the surgeon has chosen to disregard the discrepancy in the instrument count reported by the operating room nurses and proceeded to close the wound anyway. But this must be a very rare event.

Part III.
Various Other Documents

§ 2:10 Other nursing records

There are a number of nursing records, besides the actual nurses' notes, including:

1. *The nurses' graphic chart* contains a continuous record of the patient's vital signs (temperature, blood pressures, heart rate etc.), and usually some other kinds of information as well (how the patient ate, whether the patient had a bowel movement, etc.). Such information can usually be found in the nurses' notes, but the graphic chart is a convenient summary of these things, and it is particularly useful, since it is a pictogram which shows the trend of the vital signs at a glance. The graphic chart is mainly used in clinical medicine to indicate infections and to monitor their treatment (temperatures tend to return to normal as the infection comes under control). In the compensation setting, it can be used to show storming (the *diencephalic syndrome*) where the vital signs oscillate wildly up and down following a severe whiplash injury involving the brain stem. The duration of storming is not a good indicator of the prognosis in a head injury case, unless it persists for two weeks or more, but its presence is a clear sign that the brain has suffered a significant impact. It is, therefore, a useful finding in those marginal cases where one is not sure whether there are residual impairments or not. If significant storming was present, the patient should be evaluated very carefully before concluding that their problems are imaginary or factitious.

2. The *nurses' medication sheet* is prepared from the doctor's orders by the nursing service. It is a flow sheet, which notes in the first column the drugs to be administered to the patient; the next column shows the time at which each dose should be given; and the remaining columns record when (and by whom) the medications were dispensed (the nurse's initials appear in the appropriate space). Finally, when the drug has been discontinued (for whatever reason), the remaining spaces are crossed out to prevent the patient getting any further doses of that medication by mistake.

3. The *input-output chart* (*I/O chart*) notes the amounts of fluids given to the patient and also the quantities put out by the body. This kind of record is only appropriate

in critically ill patients who must receive enough intravenous fluids, but should not be overloaded. Making and recording these measurements is a time-consuming business, and these records will not be kept up-to-date unless the doctor makes it clear to the nursing staff that they are important. Many hospitals have a regulation which makes I/O orders void after 24 hours unless they are renewed.

4. The *nursing plan* is commonly a "problem oriented" medical record (POMR) in the form of a flow sheet. It lists the patient's problems one at a time, states what the nurses hope to do about them (objectives) and how they expect to achieve these goals (methods). The last column is for evaluating how well the desired goals have been achieved. This is considered an in-service document aimed at improving the quality of care and so may not be included in the patient's record; it may even be destroyed after the patient is discharged.

§ 2:11 Lab work and other diagnostic data

The lab reports contain the results of biochemical and microscopic testing on blood and other body fluids, as well as bacteriology studies and pathology reports on biopsy and other tissue specimens. They were formerly delivered as separate lab slips, and in this form constituted much of the bulk of a medical record. They are now much smaller in size, since they are for the most part computer generated and can show many test results on each page. Nevertheless, they still make up a considerable part of the patient record; the number of tests carried out on patients and the amount of information produced by these tests seem to become greater each year. The commonest of these (ordered on every patient who is admitted to hospital) are the complete blood count (CBC) and the urinalysis (U/A). The CBC (see sample following this chapter) quantifies every kind of cell found in blood, i.e., red cells, white cells and platelets. With regard to the red cells, the CBC gives the hemoglobin (Hb), the hematocrit (Ht), the red cell count (RCC), and a number of measurements of red cell size known as "indices." The hemoglobin estimation measures the number of grams of this pigment contained in 100ml of blood, e.g., 14G% (14 grams per deciliter). The hematocrit is measured by putting blood in a glass tube, centrifuging it, and seeing what percentage of the blood column is composed of the spun down red cells (normal value approximately 45%). The red cell count is the number of red cells in 1 ml of blood , normally about 5 million. The indices are calculated by the computer from the other measurements and include such things as the mean cell volume (MCV), the mean corpuscular hemoglobin (MCH), and the mean corpuscular hemoglobin concentration (MCHC). The report on the red cells also usually includes the observations of the lab technician on the appearance and size of the cells. They may thus be described as *microcytic* (small cells), *macrocytic* (large cells), or *poikilocytic* (varying a good deal in shape and size). Special shapes such as *sickle cells* or *reticulocytes* (immature red cells) may also be described. With the aid of all this information, it is usually possible not only to say that a patient is anemic, but to determine the type of anemia (e.g., iron deficiency anemia) and have a good idea as to the probable cause. A *sedimentation rate* (sed rate) notes the amount of RBCs that have spun down in one minute (it is a timed hematocrit). It is a non-specific indicator that there is something wrong in the body, but does not say what it is. It is commonly used in rheumatic diseases to show that there is a problem and to measure its severity.

The *white cell count* (WCC) or white blood count (WBC) measures the total number of white cells in 100 ml of blood and is usually 5–8,000. It will usually rise above 12,000 in even a mild infection and may approach and even exceed 60,000 in a leukemia. The *differential white cell count* (DWCC) gives the percentage of each type of white blood cell present. Most of these (65% or more) should be *polymorphonuclear cells* (polys) and 25–35% should be *lymphocytes* (small round cells). There should also be some *monocytes* (large round phagocytic cells), a few *eosinophils* (pink staining cells found in allergic conditions), and one or two dark staining cells called *basophils.* In acute bacterial infections, immature polymorphic cells known as *band cells* may be found in large numbers. The white cell count is normally included in the complete blood count. The DWCC usually has to be separately ordered. From these two, the WCC and the DWCC, the presence of an infection and even the type of infection can usually be determined. In viral infections, the white cell count first rises, but then drops quickly below normal levels (e.g., 2–3,000) and the DWCC shows a preponderance of lymphocytes (lymphs). A high white cell count and a preponderance of polys suggests a bacterial infection. The presence of a lot of immature polys (band cells), even when the white cell count is normal, suggests an acute bacterial infection, as in the early stages of appendicitis.

Platelets are tiny particles which function in the clotting mechanisms of the blood. They can be seen with the ordinary light microscope, and the CBC report will normally contain a comment by the technician as to whether they were present in adequate numbers or not. In specially important circumstances, e.g., where the patient has or is suspected of having a bleeding disorder, a special platelet count may be ordered. This is normally in the range of 150–450,000 platelets /ml of blood. Counts of 50,000/ml or less would be considered dangerously low. Such counts can occur in ITP (*idiopathic thrombocytopenic purpura*).

Studies of substances other than cells in the blood are commonly called *blood chemistries.* They were formerly done as individual evaluations, but are nowadays normally carried out by multianalyzers, which carry out a number of tests on a single specimen of blood. The term *serum multianalyzer* (SMA) is often used to describe these machines, and standard batteries of tests can be set up, e.g., SMA-12 or SMA-6. The SMA-6 will commonly include sodium (Na), potassium (K), chloride (Cl), and bicarbonate (HCO^3) determinations, plus a blood sugar and the *blood urea nitrogen* (BUN). The BUN rises as the kidneys begin to malfunction. An SMA-12 will usually include all of these plus a number of other items such as the *serum creatinine* (a more specific measure of renal function than the BUN), *serum bilirubin* (to check liver function), the *serum cholesterols,* and some cardiac enzymes such as the *creatinine phosphokinase* (CPK) and *lactose dehydrogenase* (LDH). These act as screening measures for a number of conditions, and may be followed up with more specific tests. An elevated CPK suggests heart trouble and a raised LDH (appropriate fraction) and bilirubin might create suspicion of a liver problem.

§ 2:12 Imaging reports

Radiology is often called imaging nowadays, since it includes ultrasound (U/S) and magnetic resonance imaging (MRI) which involve no roentgen rays. Ultrasound is becoming particularly important in the evaluation of the heart and the abdomen (especially the pelvis).

It is considered essential nowadays for obstetrics. There are many other diagnostic imaging modalities currently available at most hospitals, and the number increases all the time.

1. *Computerized tomography* (CT scanning) can "focus" on a thin section through an organ and distinguish the tissues in it. A section of the brain may thus show a subdural hematoma (SDH) or a brain tumor, while a section across the vertebral spine may show a herniated nucleus pulposus (HNP), a slipped disc. In very sophisticated machines, the various sections can be put together by the computer to produce a three dimensional image. Very rapid sequence pictures can even be produced to give a "movie" effect, and so enable imaging of moving things, such as the circulation of blood through the heart, to be made. *Magnetic resonance imaging* (MRI) does not use X-rays, but places the body or body part in a strong magnetic field that lines up ionized body particles (such as proteins) that spin around their linear axes. They are then bombarded with intermittent pulsed radio waves. This knocks the spinning particles off their linear axes, and then allows them to return again—like tapping on a spinning top. The movement of these charged particles in the magnetic field creates small electrical currents that are detected on the surface of the body and analyzed by the computer. The source of the electrical charge and the size of the protein (large proteins oscillate more slowly) can both be determined, and the information can be processed to produce sectional or even three dimensional images of the body tissues under investigation. MRI is more sensitive in distinguishing different tissues than CT, (especially when a contrast agent is used). Many new uses for MRI and CT are emerging all the time. Fast MRI which can image moving tissues, such as blood, is being developed and is available at research hospitals. MRI is becoming increasingly available, as well as much more affordable, and is present in virtually every major medical center and large hospital. Mobile units are now bringing this modality to local hospitals on a weekly basis.

2. *Contrast imaging* is a term used to describe procedures where special substances are introduced into the body to highlight tissues. Examples include barium introduced into the stomach or colon in bowel contrast studies, and contrast dyes injected intravenously to outline the kidneys and ureters (called an intravenous pyelogram or IVP). Contrast dyes have also been developed for CT scanning, and *paramagnetic substances* (which rotate in the opposite direction in a magnetic field) shorten the relaxation time for the moving proteins and greatly improve the already considerable ability of MRI to distinguish one tissue from another.

3. *Radionuclear imaging* (RNI) is the term used to describe studies where radiolabeled substances (such as Technetium 99m) are introduced into the body and the resulting radioactivity detected with a scintillation counter or a gamma camera. Computer analysis of the data is becoming very sophisticated. Antibodies and white cells, which attach themselves to tissues, can be radiolabeled, allowing clinicians to diagnose and localize such things as tumors and abscesses deep in the body (e.g., in the bone marrow or retroperitoneal space).

4. *Functional imaging* indicates the activity of tissues (structural imaging only reveals their shape). Several forms of functional imaging are available, including *positron emission tomography* (PET), *magnetic resonance spectroscopy* (MRS), *single photon emission computerized tomography* (SPECT) and *brain electrical activity mapping* (BEAM).

These can distinguish metabolically inactive areas in the brain, heart or other organs from normally functioning tissue. Functional imaging is being increasingly used both for clinical and compensation purposes. It is particularly useful in showing mild cortical impairments in marginal brain damage cases, where it is difficult to be sure whether the claimant is significantly harmed or not.

§ 2:13 Reports of electrodiagnostic studies

These tests detect and interpret electrical activity in some part of the body. The *electrocardiogram* (EKG), the *electroencephalogram* (EEG), and the *electromyogram* (EMG) are all electrodiagnostic tests. They can be used in special studies, such as *exercise stress testing* (EST), which uses the exercise treadmill along with the EKG, or *evoked potential studies,* which note the effects of sensory stimulation on the EEG, or *nerve conduction studies* which study the rate at which impulses travel in nerves. Nerve conduction studies often operate by linking electrical stimulation of a nerve to electromyographic (EMG) studies of the associated muscle. Computer-assisted interpretation of these tests has also become common, and in many cases is considered very reliable. *Brain electrical activity monitoring* (BEAM), for instance, is a computerized interpretation of evoked potential EEG studies which can be used to study brain damage. *Visual EEGs* are brain electrical activity studies where a video camera also observes the patient. The two are synchronized so that abnormal activity on the EEG can be matched up with twitches or seizure-like activity seen on the videotape. This allows more reliable diagnosis of seizures.

As far as lawyers are concerned, it is important to know that such test modalities exist and to appreciate how they can help in the compensation process. It is not necessary, as a rule, to know much about how these tests work or how the results are interpreted, because they come already accompanied by a computer printout which gives both the results and their interpretation. An exception is *exercise stress testing,* which is crucial to the determination of cardiac disability, and which therefore requires a little more knowledge on the part of the compensation lawyer. This topic will be taken up in Chapter Eight, which deals with cardiac disability.

§ 2:14 Respiratory function tests

The term *pulmonary function tests* (PFTs) is sometimes used to include *arterial blood gas studies* (ABGs) as well as the evaluation of breathing. Strictly speaking, however, the term should be confined to the study of ventilation, *spirometry.* The basic investigative tool here is the *respirometer* (spirometer) where the breathing of the patient is recorded. There are two main kinds of spirometry available.

1. The *traditional spirometer* uses a pen to produce a trace on a moving strip of paper. First to be noted, before starting the roller, is the *vital capacity* (VC), the full amount of air that the patient can get out of the lung after a maximal inspiration. Then the pen is allowed to make a trace on the moving roll of paper. The *tidal volume* (TV) found in ordinary breathing appears as a sine wave; then a forced expiratory breath (measuring the *FEV/1second%*) is noted; and finally rapid maximal breathing (the

maximum ventilatory volume or MVV), which shows the amount of air that a patient breathing maximally and rapidly can move in one minute

2. The more modern *computerized spirogram* requires only a single maximal inspiration and expiration. The result is recorded as a single trace in the form of a loop, where each point on the trace represents the rate of the air flowing in or out of the lungs at that particular volume of air being exhaled from the lungs. These traces are called *flow-volume (F/V) loops*. The computer analyzes this trace and derives from it all the needed information. Respiratory therapy departments favor the flow-volume loop system since it is simpler, faster and more economical to operate than the older spirometers. Flow volume loops are, however, unacceptable for purposes of Social Security disability determination, as there are concerns about the possibility of someone tampering with the computer. Most respiratory therapy departments, therefore, carry out both kinds of test, using the F/V loops for clinical purposes and carrying out traditional spirometry for Social Security determinations.

§ 2:15 The importance of pictograms and traces

The trend towards using computer printouts in test reports has already been noted. It should also be noted that there is an increasing tendency to represent data by pictograms as well as by numbers. For example, cardiac isoenzyme studies are often in the form of little graphs. [See Fig. 8-13.] Respiratory function tests are also commonly in this form. These little pictures and graphs are quite easy to interpret once their meaning is grasped. They are particularly valuable to lawyers, and time spent in understanding them will be well repaid.

§ 2:16 Departmental records

Physical therapy, respiratory therapy, occupational therapy, and other such departments keep records of their own that can be valuable. These records can be quite detailed and very helpful in documenting disability. Departmental records are not usually part of the patient's chart, though the departmental staff may enter notes into the patient's medical chart. Lawyers can obtain them just like any other record, but commonly, though not always, they must be requested directly from the department in question.

1. The records of the *physical therapy department* can be very important in personal injury cases. Physical therapists supervise and carry out exercises and other treatments for patients, such as whirlpool baths, and *transdermal electrical nerve stimulation* (TENS) which helps alleviate postoperative pain. They also examine and evaluate patients and record their findings, such as the range of movement (ROM) of various joints. Sometimes quantitative measurements of movement and strength, such as the weight that the patient can lift and the amount of work that can be carried out before fatigue sets in, are performed. Computerized versions of this kind of testing are commonly available. One such system is known as *functional capacity assessment* (FCA). In this, the mechanical stresses of particular jobs can be simulated, the performance of the patient is evaluated by the computer, and the findings expressed as

a percentile of normal performance. Thus, one performing in the upper 25th percentile will be considered normal, one in the lowest quarter totally disabled, and those in between will be assigned some percentage of total disability. FCA centers exist in most cities, or larger hospitals, and are commonly used in evaluating workers' compensation claims.

2. Most *pharmacies*, even in small hospitals, do not merely supply drugs to the nursing stations; they make up the medications (including the IVs) for each patient individually. To do this, they make out medication sheets of their own that are kept in the *pharmacy records*. These are not usually considered patient records. The pharmacy records contain information about the costs of the medication and, like the nurses' medication sheet, can be used to provide a useful summary of the patient's drug treatments, for example, pain medications.

3. The *psychiatry* department should not be forgotten. Psychiatric social workers, psychologists, and psychiatrists from this department commonly visit patients all over the hospital to provide psychiatric consultations. There will normally be an entry in the patient's progress notes recording these consults, but a fuller note may well be filed in the departmental records of the psychiatry department (the information may be considered too sensitive to put in the regular medical record). The patient may also, upon beginning recovery from physical illness or injury, be taken to the psychiatry department for interview or testing. Again the fullest report will normally be filed in departmental records. After discharge, patients may return to the department for further evaluation and treatment on an outpatient basis. These latter reports will almost certainly be departmental.

4. *Respiratory therapy* and *cardiac therapy* departments may also keep their own records of visits they have made to patients in their hospital rooms, or when the patients were brought to the department for evaluation and treatment. Perhaps more important are the records of return visits of patients after they have been discharged home or even home visits by the staff. These evaluations, made when the patients have recovered as fully as could be expected, are the records that are mainly used to determine whether they have residual impairments or not. The disabilities noted during their hospital stay with an acute illness may be irrelevant. It is the patient's condition when as fully recovered as can be expected that determines disability.

§ 2:17 Documents relating to the standard of care

These are not true medical records, but can be important, not only in establishing the standard of care, but also in explaining why certain things were done during the course of the patient's treatment. A great many documents relate to the standard of care.

1. The most important of these are probably *procedures manuals*. Every department in a hospital (nursing, radiology, anesthesia, respiratory therapy, etc.,) has a procedures manual which regulates all that goes on in the department. In radiology, for example, female patients must be asked if they are pregnant (to avoid irradiating an unborn child). If an iodine-based dye is being used, the patient must be asked questions concerning their allergies. Most procedures manuals include requirements about keeping

records to show that the procedures mandated by the manuals have been carried out. Procedures manuals are usually located in the department in question. The Joint Commission for the Accreditation of Health Care Organizations (JCAHO), formerly the JCAH, has a publication which contains, among other things, models for procedures manuals. Most hospital manuals are essentially versions of these model regulations. The JCAHO book is now a rather large multivolume work, but it can be obtained and consulted through most library services if need be.

2. *Utilization reviews* and *quality of care audits* are constantly carried out in hospitals. Reviews of the hospital as a whole, of hospital departments and even of individual professionals, are also carried out from time to time, e.g., by state-authorized peer review organizations. The reports of such reviews are generally privileged, that is, they cannot be obtained by lawyers. But even were this not the case, they tend nowadays to be very non-committal in their language, due to fear on the part of those writing the reports that they might end up in the hands of adverse parties.

3. *Incident reports* record things like the patient falling out of bed, or getting the wrong medicines. They contain potentially incriminating material and are not included in the patient record. Lawyers seeking, by devious means, to obtain the information contained in them, may occasionally succeed. Nowadays, however, they generally only contain innocuous materials that are not worth having. If they were sure to be privileged they might do something about improving patient care.

4. The *morbidity/mortality* reports are made by a hospital committee that considers all deaths and unexpected bad results that have occurred during the previous month. In a small hospital, the committee may consist of the entire medical staff. In a larger one, it may comprise all, or a select few, of the physicians who work in a particular department. The morbidity/mortality committee is supposed to pick out correctable faults and make suggestions as to improvement of care. Unfortunately, the thought that their comments and suggestions might end up on the desk of an unfriendly lawyer has often made these reports, like the incident report, innocuous documents.

§ 2:18 Patient records obtainable outside the hospital

Besides their hospital records, patients may have medical charts in other places. These include records from the offices of family physicians, reports from specialists to whom they have been referred for consultation, and the records of various kinds of clinics. The patients may have been referred, or gone on their own initiative, to an urgent care facility, a mental health clinic, a pain clinic, a chiropractic clinic, or even been evaluated for return to work in a functional capacity assessment (FCA) clinic. These records may need to be sought out in appropriate cases.

Medical records from the family doctor are particularly important to lawyers since:

1. They may contain copies of the discharge summaries of all the patient's admissions, both in local and in distant hospitals.

2. It is usual for consulting physicians to send a copy of their report, in the form of a letter, to the family physician.

All such documents are commonly kept in the patient's chart in the family doctor's office and provide a most useful summary of hospital admissions and consultations which might otherwise be very difficult to trace and obtain. But they may sometimes need to be specially requested when asking for the patient's medical records.

Appendix to Chapter Two

A selection of illustrative documents from medical records

The following set of medical documents comprising standard forms, handwritten notes, and dictated notes is not, nor is it intended to be, the continuous medical record of a single patient. I have supplied such in the past but currently feel that it is better to represent a greater variety of situations than to focus on a single type of case. Included are:

Doctors' Records

Standard patient admission history and physical examination forms
Handwritten doctors' progress notes
Physician's order sheet
Doctor's discharge summary (transfer summary)
A neurosurgical resident's handwritten admission note (with translation)

Nursing Records

Nursing service admission form
Handwritten nurses' notes
A nursing care plan
Intake/output forms
Nurses' medication form
A graphic chart
A nursing service transfer accompanying a patient to an extended care facility

Operating Room Records

Doctor's operative note
Operating nurse's surgical summary
Instrument and sponge count
Handwritten note of anesthetist's pre-op and recovery room score system

Also included are:

Emergency department records, including doctors' handwritten notes (with translations)
Pathology lab and radiology department reports on various imaging procedures
Departmental records from the respiratory therapy and physical therapy departments

Doctor's Records

Standard Hospital H&P Admission Form — The History

CLEMENT AIRDREE
P. O. Box 2350
Rural Route 16
Harnett County

Date: 1/1/10
Hospital No: 248863

HISTORY:

Chief Complaint LBP.

Present Illness Hurt his back when lifting furniture at work. At home in bed x 3 days.

Past History Episodes of back pain once in a while – none serious

Family History Father died of heart attack aged 53. Mother A & W. No other FH of disease

James Daughtry M.D.

Standard Hospital H&P Admission Form — The Physical Exam

AIRDREE, CLEMENT T.
Patient's Name | Admitted | Discharged | S.S. No. | M.D.

PHYSICAL EXAMINATION

Head and Neck:

Eyes: VA 20/20 EOMI Nose: nl. Throat: nl.

Ears: TM intact bilat. Neck: supple

Chest:

Lungs: Clear to IPPA Heart: HS✓ ō (m) B.P. 135/85

Abdomen: Obese ++ soft ō scars ō masses LKKS = 0

Pelvic: //

Rectal: Normal tone ō masses. Prostate not ↑

Spine: Spasm of paraspinals + scholiosis cx → (L)

~~Extremities~~: Tender L5 S1 SLR · R 75° L 66°

Reflexes: DTRs ++ x+ for 1+ (L) AJ. ? some

Local Examination: numbness (L) foot

Skin: nl. Texture: nl.

Impression: HNP L5 S1

James Daughtry M.D.

Doctor's Progress Note (1)

RECORD SHEET

(Discharge Summary, History, Physical, Progress Notes)

Last Name	First Name	Attending Physician	Room No.	Hosp. No.
AIRDREE	CLEMENT T.	J. DAUGHTRY, M.D.	421	2607563

Date	Notes Should Be Signed by Physician
1/5/10	S. Pt states he had the best night's sleep since he hurt his back. No parenteral analgesics required. Relieved by PO meds. Has been OOB and to BR c̄ help.
	O. Still c/o pain on SLR > 65° on LLE.
	AJ ? ++ on (L)
	No finding of anesthesia on foot
	A. Improving on conservative Tx.
	P. Continue c̄ hip Txn + HP's.
	James Daughtry MD
1/6/10	S: Hurting worse today. Experienced a "shooting pain" in back and LLE on way back from BR last PM.
	O. Definite leg pain on SLR of LLE > 45°.
	AJ ?+ on (L) — Dull to pinprick
	Sens:

	A. Definite HNP now.
	P:- Will ask Dr. McBrayne neurosurgery to see and advise re surgical intervention.
	James Daughtry MD

Form 185 TWYFORD PRINTING CO., DUNN, N.C. PROGRESS NOTES

Doctor's Progress Note (2)

RECORD SHEET
(Discharge Summary, History, Physical, Progress Notes)

Last Name	First Name	Attending Physician	Room No.	Hosp. No.

Date	Notes Should Be Signed by Physician
1/7/10	S Pt states he had a better night
	pain relieved by po meds at HS.
	O. Still tender on elevating (L) LE
	AJ still ↓ on (L)
	Sens:-  dull to pinprick
	(L)
	P. Continue hip traction
	HP's to back.
	Will evaluate again in a.m.
	If not much improvement neurosurg:
	consult may need to be
	considered.
	James Daughtry MD.
1/8/10	Transferred to services of Dr McBrayne
	& Dr Black, neurosurgeons
	James Daughtry MD

Form 185 TWYFORD PRINTING CO., DUNN, N.C. PROGRESS NOTES

Physician's Order Sheet

PHYSICIAN'S ORDER SHEET

ORDERS: Another brand of a generically equivalent product identical in dosage form and content of active ingredient may be administered unless checked.

WRITE OR IMPRINT PATIENT INFORMATION BELOW

DATE 1/1/10 START

#1 Complete bed rest OOB to BR c̄ help only

#2 1500 Cal diet.

TIME A.M. P.M.

#3 Pelvic traction @ 30 lbs.

#4 Percocet i tab q 4–6H PRN for pain p.o.

#5 Flexeril 10 mg t.i.d. p.o.

Imprint Patient Name Here

START NEW ORDERS BELOW

Be sure No. shows before WRITING

DATE START

#6 Nubain 10 mg / Vistaril 50 mg } IM q 4–6h for pain not relieved by Percocet

#7. CBC

TIME A.M. P.M.

#8 Panel 12

#9 U/A

#10 CXR.

Imprint Patient Name Here

START NEW ORDERS BELOW

Be sure No. shows before WRITING

DATE START

#11 EKG

#12 XR Lumbar Spine in AM

#13. Book for CT scan L Spine L5 S1.

TIME A.M. P.M.

#14 Halcion 0.25 p.o. HS only if really needed for sleep

#15. Metamucil 1 tbsp in H_2O q am

J Daughtry M.D.

Imprint Patient Name Here

DRUG ALLERGIES

Be sure No. shows before WRITING

▲ DO NOT WRITE BELOW THIS LINE ▲

To remove orders from set, lift face sheet & tear at proper perforation

ADHS-0895 (3/85)

PHYSICIAN'S ORDERS

Transfer Summary Accompanying Patient to Referral Hospital (1)

ADMITTING DIAGNOSES:

1. Abdominal pain – origin unknown
2. R/O adynamic ileus
3.R/O Intestinal obstruction
4. R/O Recurring myocardialinfarction
5. S/P myocardial infarction
6. Generalized atherosclerotic disease

DISHARGE DIAGNOSES

1. Adynamic ileus
2. Possible intestinal obstruction
3. Esophageal ulcer with esophageal stenosis
4, S/P recent endothelial MI
5. Atherosclerotic cardiovascular disease
6. S/P Surgical repair of hiatus hernia

CONSULTATIONS: Surgical consultation re abdominal pain

SURGERY: None

PROCEDURE: Esophagoscopy

HISTORY: This is a 70 year old white female who was discharged from this hospital o 4/2/99 where she had been admitted one week earlier for a subendothelial myocardial infarction. She was doing reasonably well at home until the day of admission when she developed severe abdominal pain, mainly in the mid abdomen with some radiation into the epigastrium. It was associated with some nausea and vomiting. When she arrived in the E.R she was evaluated and EKG did show incomplete RBBB that was not present during the previous admission. X-ray of the abdomen showed some air fluid levels consistent with adynamic ileus. She was subsequently admitted for further evaluation and treatment of this problem,

PHYSICAL EXAMINATION: Temperature 98.6^{0}F. Pulse 78, Respirations 20, B/P 150/80. This was an alert, cooperative, elderly white female who appeared to be chronically ill and in some degree of acute distress. Neck was supple without thyromegaly or jugulovenous distention. Heart beat regular without murmurs, rubs or gallop. Chest showed normal A/P diameter. Lungs clear to P&A. Abdomen soft without masses or organomegaly but there was generalized abdominal tenderness without rebound tenderness. Bowel sounds normal and active. The was unable to walk due to her various pains and other problems. She has some hardness of hearing,

LAB DATA: Glucose 143, BUN 19, serum amylase 74, electrolytes normal on admission. Initial CPK was 32 with M.B. fraction 0. Follow up CPK was 34 with MB fraction 0 and follow up blood glucose was 150, BUN and creatinine on 4/29/99 were 21 an 0.9 respectively. Electrolytes on that date were all normal with potassium 5.1, sodium 140, chloride 106 , bicarb 28. Third set of cardiac enzymes were normal. On 5/1/99, glucose was 160. Total protein 5.5, albumin 2.9, calcium 8.4, sodium 129, potassium 5.1, chloride 96, bicarb 31,. On 5/2/99 BUN was 11.8, creatinine was 0.9, sodium 128, potassium 4.2, chloride 96 ,bicarb 27. Initial CBC showed WBC 10,000 with 67 segs, 2 stabs, 29 lymphs, 2 monos, hct

Transfer Summary Accompanying Patient to Referral Hospital (2)

40.5, hbg. 40.5, hgb 13, platelets 334,000. On 5/2/99 WBC was 15,800 with 19 segs 59 stabs 11 lymphs, 10 monos, 1 meta, hct 38.2, hbg 12.7, platelet count 365,000. Urinalysis was normal. Initial EKG showed incomplete RBBB which was new with T-wave inversion in V 1-3 and V5. Follow up EKG showed incomplete RBBB and sinus tachycardia. Third EKG showed occasional PVC and continued to show incomplete RBBB and sinus tachycardia. Initial abdominal X-ray showed fin most likely consistent with adynamic ileus with a number of flat air-fluid levels. There was marked lumbar scoliosis with degenerative changes. Chest X-ray was negative. Abdominal ultrasound on 4/29/99 showed no evidence of gallstones. The pancreas was not identified due to overlying gas shadows. Abdominal X-ray on 4/30/99 showed more gaseous distention in the small bowel with a little more gas in he large intestine, probably due to intestinal obstruction at the level of the proximal ileum. Telemetry pattern was basically negative except for occasional PVC.

HOSPITAL COURSE: The patient was admitted and put on bed rest. Once it was determined that she did not have any cardiac damage on this particular admission, nasogastric aspiration was scaried out whih showed some blood in the aspirate. She was having persistent vomiting and was placed on intermittent suction per nasogastric tube. Ultrasound was carried out the day after admission and surgical consult was obtained to check for possible intestinal obstruction. By 4/30/99 the patient was feeling somewhat better, her abdomen was soft and she had good bowel sounds. She was alaert but attempts to feed her produced recurrence of vomiting. By 5/1/99 in the morning she was tolerating clear liquids but complained of abdominal pain and ht afternoon developed abdominal distention and a nasogastric tube had to be reinserted. On 5/2/99 it was noted that the N/G tube was not draining well. Attempted reinsertions were not successful in improving drainage and the surgeons recommended esophagoscopy which was carried out by me at approximately 1.45 pm. An ulcer was found in the lower esophagus and esophageal stenosis was present. Some bile was returning but the endoscope could not bepassed into the gastric antrum. On the recommendation of the local surgeons, especially in view of her generally poor condition, she was transferred to the service of Dr. Creedmore in Megapolis Metropolitan Hospital, who was consulted by telephone and agreed to accept her on transfer She travelled to MMH by ambulance without incident. On the recommendation of Dr. Creedmore intravenous antibiotics were started prior to transfer

Handwritten Progress Note by Neurosurgical Resident

Last Name	First Name	Attending Physician	Room No.	Hosp. No.

Date	Notes Should Be Signed by Physician
1/2/10	JAR Neurosurg
	pt admit 24° prior following AA c̄ LOC.
	Clearing of mentation through the night
	pt c/o's H/A, facial pains — facial lacerations
	repaired in ER, skull and c-spine films neg in ER
	On exam pt is awake, alert, Ox3,
	memory - 2/4 items at 5 min. Repeats 5 digits
	forward and backward. CN's - VA 20/20 OU by
	card, optic disc Nl, EOMI + VF's intact,
	Nl sens and facial movements, hearing grossly
	Nl to voice. Motor - strength 5/5 throughout
	except some difficulty picking up pennies c̄ (R) hand
	Rhomberg neg, rapid tapping difficult on (R) -
	Sens ~ intact throughout to light touch, pain,
	vibration, Reflexes
	Gait Nl —

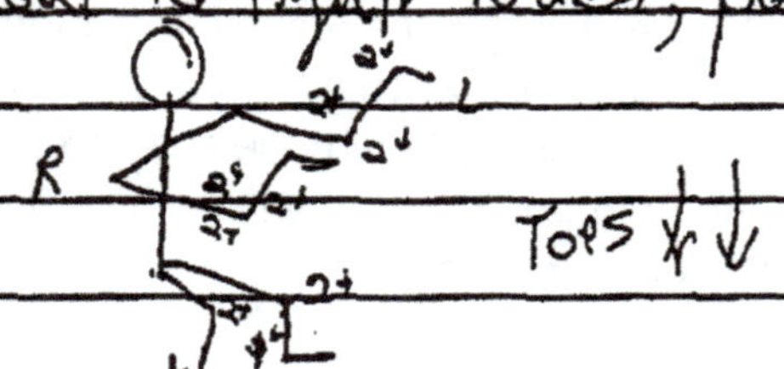

	HEENT - several sutured
	lacerations, s̄ excessive
	drainage
	neck — AFROM, non tender
	Ht+lungs — clear Abd benign
	Ext's — scattered contusions, previously noted.
	Impression — ↑MS, persistent mild deficit on R
	Plan continued observation for improvement
	M. Scully, MD

Translation of Neurosurgical Resident's Note

1/2/87 (by) Junior Admitting Resident in Neurosurgery.

Patient admitted 24 hours ago following an automobile accident with loss of consciousness. Clearing of mentation through the night. Patient's complaints - headache, facial pains and facial laceration (which was) repaired in the Emergency Room. Skull and cervical spine (X-ray) films negative in the ER.

On examination patient is awake, alert, oriented x 3 (i.e. as to time, place and circumstances)

Memory - (remembers 2/4 items at 5 minutes (i.e.50%) - repeats 5 digits forward and backward

Cranial nerves - Visual acuity 20/20 in both eyes - (test carried out) by card - optic disc(s) normal, extraocular muscles intact and visual fields intact.

Normal sensation and facial movements, hearing grossly normal to voice. (testing cranial nerves vii and viii)

Motor - strengths 5/5 throughout except some difficulty in picking up pennies with right hand.

Romberg test - negative, rapid tapping (diadochokinesia) difficult on the right.

Sensation - intact throughout to light touch, pain, vibration

Reflexes - Diagram shows normal deep tendon reflexes and indicates (by arrows) that the plantar reflexes (TOPS) are downgoing and symmetrical (i.e. normal)

Head,eyes ear, nose and throat - Several sutured lacerations without excessive drainage

Neck - Active and full range of motion, non tender

Heart and lungs - clear

Abdomen - benign

Extremities - Scattered contusions, previously noted

Impression - Impaired mental status, persistent mild deficit on the right (side of the body)

Plan - Continued observation for improvement.

(signed) M. Sculley, M.D.

Nurses' Hospital Records

Nursing Service Patient Admission Form (1)

NURSING SERVICE ADMISSION HISTORY AND ASSESSMENT

ADMISSION TIME 0700 (AM) PM

T 101^E P 104 R 24 BP L 144/92 R 146/92 HT 6' WT 180

ADMITTED PER:
__ AMBULATORY
X WHEELCHAIR
__ STRETCHER

FROM:
__ ADMITTING OFFICE
X EMERGENCY DEPT.
__ EXTENDED CARE FACILITY
__

ORIENTATION TO ROOM AND UNIT
X CALL LIGHT
X BED OPERATION
X PHONE
X TELEVISION
X BATHROOM
X MEALS
X VISITING HOURS

X PATIENT I.D. BRACELET ON

VALUABLES

1 WATCHES 1 RINGS __ JEWELRY
__ OTHER
DESCRIPTION
__ VALUABLES PLACED IN BUSINESS OFFICE
X VALUABLES SENT HOME WITH
NAME
RELATIONSHIP Wife
X PT. WANTS TO KEEP AT OWN RISK. HOSPITAL NOT RESPONSIBLE.

PATIENT'S SIGNATURE

X SMOKING POLICY REVIEWED
X ELECTRICAL APPLIANCE POLICY REVIEWED
X GLASSES
__ CONTACT LENS __ R __ L
__ LENS IMPLANT __ R __ L
__ HEARING AID __ R __ L
__ DENTURES
__ UPPER __ LOWER
__ BRIDGE
__ WHEELCHAIR
__ BRACE(S)
__ WALKER
__ ARTIFICAL LIMB(S)
__ OTHER

D. Gauch RN
EMPLOYEE SIGNATURE

CALL IF NEEDED
NAME M. Hetrick
TELEPHONE NO. 876-5432
RELATIONSHIP Wife

NEEDS ASSISTANCE WITH:
__ FEEDING __ WALKING __ HIGH RISK FOR FALLS
__ BATHING __ DRESSING
__ TURNING __ OTHER

RN NURSING ASSESSMENT
SOURCE OF INFORMATION
X PATIENT __ RELATIVE __ FRIEND
REASONS FOR HOSPITALIZATION (PATIENT'S WORDS)
"I feel terrible"
"My back is sore"
"I can't stand up straight"
EXISTING HEALTH PROBLEMS
None
PREVIOUS SURGERIES
None

CURRENT MEDICATIONS

PRESCRIPTIONS WITH DOSAGE	LAST DOSE	RETAINED	HOME
NONE			

SOCIAL ASSESSMENT

OCCUPATION: Public Relations Exec
HOME SITUATION: Married c̄ children
EMOTIONAL REACTION TO ADMISSION:
__ ANGER __ CRYING
X ACCEPTANCE __ FRIGHTENED
POTENTIAL DIFFICULTIES AT HOME DUE TO ILLNESS
None foreseeable
HOW CAN WE ASSIST YOU:

PREVIOUS SERVICES PROVIDED BY:
__ HOME HEALTH __ HEALTH DEPT.
__ SOCIAL SERVICES __ OTHER

EDUCATIONAL NEEDS
__ DISEASE PROCESS SPECIFY:
__ DIET
__ MEDICATIONS TYPE
X ACTIVITY LEVELS
X DIAGNOSTIC STUDIES
__ PRE/POST OP TEACHING
__ PEDIATRIC CARE
__ OTHER:

R.N. SIGNATURE D. Gauch RN

ALLERGIES (DRUG) NKA
(FOOD) NKA
HOW PATIENT REACTS: N/A
ALLERGY BAND ON: N/A
MARK DRAWING WITH APPROPRIATE LETTER:

A —AMPUTATION
B —BURN
BR —BRUISE
D —DEFORMITY
DC —DECUBITUS
L —LACERATION
R —RASH
S —SCAR

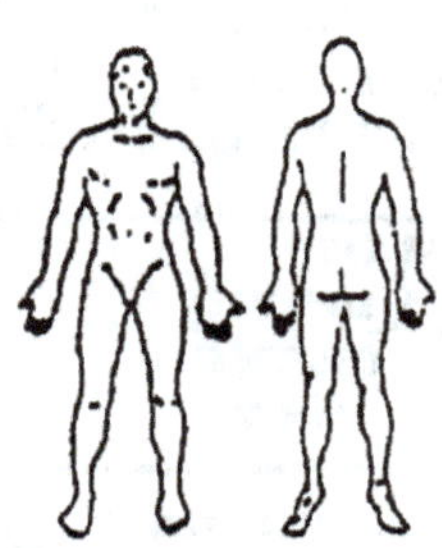

DESCRIBE:

Nursing Service Patient Admission Form (2)

NURSING DEPARTMENT — NURSING SYSTEMS CHECK

MUSCULOSKELETAL

___ FULL ROM
X PAIN
___ WEAKNESS
___ GAIT:
X STEADY ___ UNSTEADY

___ CONTRACTURES
___ JOINT STIFFNESS
___ FRACTURES
___ PARALYSIS
___ ARTHRITIS

COMMENTS: ___

CARDIOVASCULAR

PULSES: PRESENT -
RADIAL X R X L APICAL RATE 104
PEDAL X R X L
RHYTHM: X REGULAR ___ IRREGULAR ___ PACEMAKER
___ GROSS MURMURS
___ HYPERTENSIVE

___ PAIN — EXPLAIN: ___

COMMENTS: ___

INTEGUMENTARY

COLORING:
SKIN
X PINK
___ CYANOTIC
___ JAUNDICE
___ OTHER ___

NAIL BEDS
X PINK
___ PALE
___ CYANOTIC

TEXTURE/TURGOR
X ELASTIC ___ INELASTIC
___ MOIST ___ OTHER
___ VERY DRY ___

ORAL MUCOSA
X PINK
___ OTHER ___
___ MOIST
X DRY

SCLERA
X WHITE
___ JAUNDICE
___ OTHER ___

EDEMA
X ABSENT
___ PEDAL
___ SACRAL

COMMENTS: ___

ENDOCRINE

___ DIABETES
INSULIN DOSAGE ___
THROID GOITER
___ PRESENT
X ABSENT
___ BIRTH CONTROL PILLS
X WEIGHT LOSS
___ WEIGHT GAIN
COMMENTS: ___

RENAL/UROLOGICAL

URINE FLOW:
___ NO PROBLEM
___ URGENCY
___ INCONTINENT
X BURNING

___ HESITANCY
___ DYSURIA
___ HEMATURIA
X FREQUENCY

FOLEY
___ YES
X NO
TYPE ___

APPEARANCE/COLOR: CLOUDY
COMMENTS: ___

NEUROPSYCHOLOGICAL

MENTAL STATUS
X ORIENTED
X PERSON
X PLACE
X TIME
X ALERT
X DULL AFFECT

MOTOR SKILL
X VISION ___ BLIND
X HEARING ___ DEAF
X SPEECH

STIMULUS RESPONSE
X VERBAL
X TOUCH
X PAIN

GENERAL
___ NO PROBLEM
___ SYNCOPE
___ DIZZINESS
X MALAISE
___ SEIZURES
___ MEMORY LOSS
___ INSOMNIA
___ OTHER

BEHAVIOR
X CO-OPERATIVE
___ UN-COOPERATIVE
___ COMBATIVE
___ ANXIOUS
___ DEPRESSED
X RESTLESS
___ UNRESPONSIVE
___ OTHER ___
___ CONFUSED (EXPLAIN) ___

PUPILS: X EQUAL
___ UNEQUAL

MOVEMENT OF EXTREMITIES:
X LL X RL
X LA X RA

SENSATION OF EXTREMITIES:
X LL X RL
X LA X RA

COMMENTS: ___

RESPIRATORY

RESPIRATIONS:
X NORMAL
___ SHALLOW
___ WHEEZING
___ DYSPNEA

___ APNEIC PERIODS
___ ORTHOPNEA
___ PAINFUL

COUGH
___ PRODUCTIVE (describe)
___ NON-PRODUCTIVE

LUNG SOUNDS: CLEAR: X R X L
RALES: ___ R ___ L
RHONCHI ___ R ___ L

RHYTHM: X REGULAR ___ IRREGULAR
COMMENTS: ___

GASTROINTESTINAL

INTAKE/APPETITE
___ ADEQUATE
X POOR
___ DYSPHAGIA

___ TROUBLE CHEWING
X NAUSEA
X VOMITING
___ OTHER ___

FOOD INTOLERANCES: ___

BOWEL HABITS:
FREQUENCY: ___
___ DIARRHEA
___ CONSTIPATION
DATE LAST BM 7/31/10
AIDS FOR ELIMINATION: ___

COLOR:
X BROWN
___ BLACK
___ BLOODY
___ OTHER ___

ABDOMEN:
X SOFT
___ DISTENDED
___ PAINFUL

BOWEL SOUNDS: ___ YES X NO
OTHER: ___
COMMENTS: ___

R.N. SIGNATURE: [signature]
DATE: 8/1/10 TIME DONE: 0700

Neurosurgical Intensive Care Nursing Notes

NURSES NOTES

	Room No.	Hosp. No.
	ICU	1379

Date	
9/20/10	0750 – Neuro – Alert, moaning but unresponsive to commands ē will occasionally nod yes to questions. Spont. MOE x4 ē equal strength & coord. PERRL – midsize. CV: Ht. sds. S_1S_2 audible s̄ (m). Card. mon. Sinus tach ē occas. PAC & rare PVC. Undertones pink. Skin w/d. All pulses palpable. Thigh High TED support stockings on. Ø edema noted. Pulm/Resp.: Resps. reg/ unlabored; rate 16. Equal bilat chest expansion (R) CT → 20cm Pleur-Evac yields sm. amt. brick col. thin fluid – Lung sds. ē scattered rales, rhonchi all lung zones. NTS ē sterile NaCl soln for sm.-mod. amt. thick white mucoid secretions slightly blood-tinged. Good gag & cough reflexes present. O_2 @ 4l per N.C. GI: Abd. flat ē active BS x4 quads & soft. 50% Isocal/50% H_2O inf. well → NG 50° per Kangaroo pump. 20 ml aspirated from NG Ø Guaiac Neg partially digested feeding soln. OTHER – D_5 ½ NS ē 40 mEq KCl/l inf. well → (R) periph @ 50° per NAC – 1 l D_5½NS ē 40 mEq KCl/hung to replace presently depleting bag @ 50° per NAC – Foley → SD yields dr. amber col. fluid; Specific gravity 1.016. VS – T100° R, BP (L)(AL) 128/80, P114 irreg. @ times, R 16 reg/unlabored. Bilat. hand restraints on. SRs ↑ x2. ——— D. Gouch RN 0850 – Pt. restless. Valium 2mg given IV. Pt. turned & repositioned. Dr. ___ in. (cont'd next pg.) D Gouch RN

Form 185 TWYFORD PRINTING CO., DUNN, N.C.

Nursing Notes on Nephrolithiasis (Kidney Stones) Patient

NURSES NOTES

	Attending Physician	Room No.	Hosp. No.
	D. Gauch	305 B	

Date	
8/1/10	Admitted 45 yo caucasian ♂ to Rm 305 bed B. Pt.
0700	accompanied by wife. Pt. admitted per services of
	Dr. Gauch MD. Admission diagnosis ① UTI ② R/O
	Nephrolithiasis. Pt. states "I feel terrible" "My
	back hurts" "I can't stand up straight" "I
	feel very sick to my stomach and I've been
	vomiting alot". Pt seen in ER immediately
	prior to being admitted. Initial lab work
	obtained in ER see chart. Pt. denies any
	allergies to medication or food. Pt. is alert
	and oriented x 3. VS: T-101^{8} BP-146/92 R-24
	P-108 Pt. states he has been ill for 3 days
	prior to coming to the hospital. Nursing assessment
	completed, see chart. Pt instructed as to hospital
	facilities, visiting hours, safety pre-cautions
	and general routines. Valuables not kept by Pt.
	given to Pt's wife. Pt states he has had some
	relief of pain & N&V since receiving medication
	in ER approx. 1° ago. Dr Gauch notified — JAR
0800	Pt medicated as per orders. Pt tolerated well. Pt
	resting in bed, wife c̄ him in room. No emesis
	since 0600 8/1 —— JAR
1200	Pt resting in bed T-100^{6} BP-140/88 R-20 P-96 JAR
1300	Pt given Phenergan Supp 25mg c/o N&V. Pt states
	he ate small amount of lunch approx 30' ago
	then felt nauseous —— JAR
1330	Pt states nausea relieved, resting quietly — JAR

Nursing Care Plan

NURSING CARE PLAN

DIAGNOSIS: R/O CVA.

LONG TERM GOAL: to return home to ADL ē adjustments as needed, ē understanding of disease, prescribed medications, diet understanding + F/u medical care importance.

DATE INITIALS & TITLE	PATIENT NEEDS/ PROBLEMS	EXPECTED GOAL	NURSING INTERVENTION OR ACTION	ACTUAL OUTCOM EVALUATION / DATE
10/2/10 ER RN	Disorientation	Pt to be oriented x3 prior to discharge	1. Orient pt freq. to person, place + time. 2. Place calendar + clock in room 3. Neurological checks q̄ 2 hrs. for changes. 4. Document findings on neuro flow sheet.	10/2 · Disoriente x3. 10/3 Oriented - name onl 10/4 Oriented - name + pl
10/3/10 ER RN.	Lt sided weakness	Pt will accept handi-cap and will perform exercises to ↑ strength of Lt side.	1. Teach patient about disease process, causes, course of treatment. 2. Physical therapy treatments per physician's orders. 3. Assess patient's understanding of exercise and prognosis. 4. Explain importance of safety i.e., using hand rails, walker, etc.	10/6 Pt depres 10/7 Patient ask questions re stroke + prognosis 10/8 Pt eager-begin PT 10/9. Pt amb. ē walker + usi squeeze ball in Lt hand freq.
	Difficulty swallowing	Pt will be able to swallow proper diet to provide sufficient caloric intake.	1. Assess gag reflex 2. Stay ē pt while drinking liquids 3. Encourage patient to chew well, slowly and small amts. 4. Teach patient proper dietary needs, options, etc. 5. Have dietician discuss diet ē pt prior to discharge.	10/2 NPO 10/3. Taking fewer liquid 10/5 - swallow soft fo 10/7 - chewing improving 10/9. Dietician vs pt.

Intake-Output Nursing Records

Intake: Time	Intake: Type	Intake: Amount	Output: Time	Output: Type	Output: Amount
8:00 am	juice	100cc	2:00pm	urine	400cc
	milk	240cc			
10:00 am	water	30cc			
12: NOON	tea	250cc			
7-3 Total		620cc			400cc

3: P.M. - 11 P.M.

Time	Type	Amount	Time	Type	Amount
			10:00p	urine	300cc
coffee		250cc			
juice		100cc			
3-11 Total		350cc			300cc

11: P.M. - 7: A.M.

Time	Type	Amount	Time	Type	Amount
12:mN	water	150cc	6:00Am	urine	120cc

Grand Total Intake 150 Grand Total Output 120

Balance Difference

Flow Sheet For Turning Patients

Position

	R. Side	Back	L. Side	R. Side	Back	L.Side
Time						
Time						

Patient's Name Doe, Jane Rm 102

Date 10/8/10

Final Patient Chart Version of Input/Output

Rm 102

10/8/10

ACCURATE INTAKE AND OUTPUT RECORD

Date and Time	INTAKE						OUTPUT						
Date 10/8/10	ORAL	PARENTERAL	TUBE FEEDING	PACKED CELLS	OTHER	TOTAL	URINE	EMESIS	STOOL	SUCTION	OTHER	TOTAL	DAILY WEIGHTS
7 a.m.-3 p.m.	620					620	400		+			400	
3 p.m.-11 p.m.	350					350	300					300	
11 p.m.-7 a.m.	150					150	120					120	
24 Hr. Total						1120						820	
Date 10/9/10 7 a.m.-3 p.m.	540	800				1340	1200					1200	
3 p.m.-11 p.m.	300	750				1050	1250	50				1300	
11 p.m.-7 a.m.	100	850				950	1000					1000	
24 Hr. Total	940	2400				3340	3450	50				3500	
Date 7 a.m.-3 p.m.													
3 p.m.-11 p.m.													
11 p.m.-7 a.m.													
24 Hr. Total													
Date 7 a.m.-3 p.m.													
3 p.m.-11 p.m.													
11 p.m.-7 a.m.													
24 Hr. Total													
Date 7 a.m.-3 p.m.													
3 p.m.-11 p.m.													
11 p.m.-7 a.m.													
24 Hr. Total													

CHART

Nurses' Medication Sheet

NAME PLATE

MEDICATION ADMINISTRATION RECORD

Enter Here IN PENCIL Number of Forms in Use

DIAGNOSES: ① UTI
② R/O Nephrolithiasis

DIET Regular

LOCATION CODES	ANT. THIGH	GLUTEAL REGION	DELTOID	VENTRAL GLUTEAL	ABDOMEN	LAT. THIGH
	Right - Code A Left - Code B	Right - Code C Left - Code D	Right - Code E Left - Code F	Right - Code G Left - Code H	Right - Code I Left - Code J	Right - Code Left - Code

DATES GIVEN

OR DATE INITIALS	EXP DATE TIME	MEDICATION-DOSAGE-FREQUENCY-RT. OF ADM.	HR.	8/1	8/2	8/3	8/4	8/5	8/6	8/7	8/8	8/9	8/10	8/11	8/12	8/13	8/14
		Bacitracin DS ↑ P.O.	0800	AG	AG	AG	AG	AG	AG	AG	—	—	—	—	—	—	—
		BID X 7 days	2000	RN	RN	FM	FM	FM	RN	RN	—	—	—	—	—	—	—
		Pyridium 100mg.	0800	AG	AG	AG	X	AG	X	X	X	X	X	X	X	X	X
		↑ P.O. BID PRN	2000	RN	RN	FM	FM	X	X	X	X	X	X	X	X	X	X
		Phenergan Supp. ↑	1300	AG	X	X	X	X	X	X	X	X	X	X	X	X	X
		25 mg Q4-6° PRN		X	X	X	X	X	X	X	X	X	X	X	X	X	X
		Tylenol 650mg	800	AG	AG	X	X	X	X	X	X	X	—	—	—	—	—
		Q4° PRN	1200	AG	AG	X	X	X	X	X	X	X	—	—	—	—	—
			1600	AG	AG	X	X	X	X	X	X	X	—	—	—	—	—
			2000	RN	RN	X	X	X	X	X	X	X	—	—	—	—	—
			2400	FR	RN	X	X	X	X	X	X	X	—	—	—	—	—
			0400	FR	—	X	X	X	X	X	X	X	—	—	—	—	—

Single Orders + Pre-Operatives

ENTER HERE IN PENCIL NO. OF FORMS IN USE

OR DATE INITIALS	MEDICATION-DOSAGE-RT. OF ADM.	TO BE GIVEN DATE	TO BE GIVEN TIME	NURSE INITIAL	OR DATE INITIALS	MEDICATION-DOSAGE-RT. OF ADM.	TO BE GIVEN DATE	TO BE GIVEN TIME	NURSE INITIAL
8/1/10	Demerol 75 mg IM Ⓒ	8/1	0600	AG					
MW	Phenergan 25mg IM Ⓒ	8/1	0600	AG					

AGE 45 RELIGION ______ DOCTOR D. GOUCH ______ DATE/TIME ADMITTED 8/1/10/0700

ROOM NO. – Allergic To: NKA

Graphic Chart

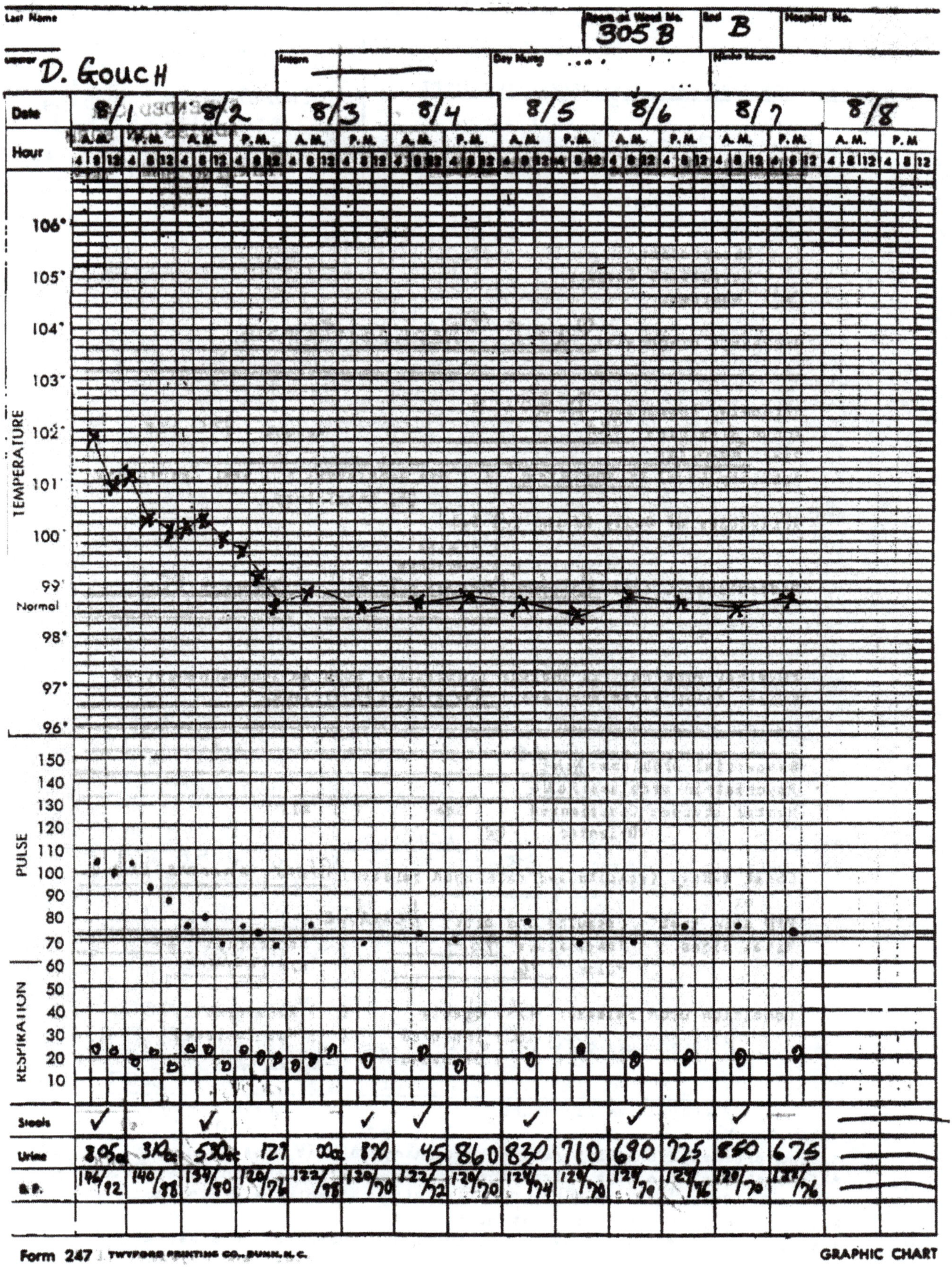

Nursing Home (Extended Care) Admission Form

EXTENDED CARE
ADMISSION FORM

[NURSING HOME RECORDS]

EXTENDED CARE FACILITY INFORMATION SHEET

( ) Observation
( ) Outpatient Surgery
(X) Inpatient

Discharge Diagnosis: ① UTI ② Nephrolithiasis

Attending Physician D. GOUCH
Known Allergies NKA Weight 180 lbs.
Diet Regular
Activity Level as tolerated ( ) Non Ambulatory ( ) Semi Ambulatory
(X) Ambulatory

Activities of Daily Living (X) Self
( ) Assist
( ) Complete

Medications (list) Rx for Percocet * given to Pt.

Physical Problems (to include limitations such as incontinence, NG tubes, foley catheters, etc.) Strain all urine

Behavorial problems: NONE
Psychiatric problems: NONE
Mental status: Disoriented ( ) Some ( ) All
Oriented (X)

Chest X-Ray: (results and date upon release) Clear, unremarkable
or
PPD skin test : (results and date) Negative
Vital Signs : Temperature 98⁶ Repiration 20
Pulse 76 B/P 122/76

Condition upon release: (X) Stable ( ) Recovered
(X) Improved ( ) Not Improved
( ) Deceased

(Signature & Title) 2000 (Date & Time)

8-7-07 2000

(Physician Signature) (Date & Time)

* Send prescriptions with patient returning to rest home.
* Send physician orders, discharge summary, history and physical (E.R. sheet for Observation and Day-Op only) with patients returning to a Nursing Home, or Care More Rest Home.
* Send copies of Lab & X-Ray for Outpatients (Observation & Day-OP).

Operating Room Records

Doctor's Surgical Summary (1)

OPERATIVE REPORT

Doe, Jane
MR# 1111
SURGEON: Dr. Hacker
ASSISTANT: Dr. Small
REFERRING PHYSICIAN: Dr. Shipley
TYPE OF ANESTHESIA : General, endotracheal
ANESTHETIST: Martha Nettles CRNA
PREOP DIAGNOSIS: Chronic cholecysitis with cholelithiasis
POSTOP DIAGNOSIS: Same
SURGERY: Cholecystitis with intraoperative cholangiography
ESTIMATED BLOOD LOSS: 250cc
SPECIMEN: Gall bladder and 5 small stones

The patient was taken to the E.R. and placed on the table in supine position. After satisfactory induction of endotracheal anesthesia, the skin of the abdomen and lower chest was washed thoroughly with Betadine scrub solution and dried with sterile towels. The skin was reprepped with Betadine solution and the surgical area was draped in a sterile fashion. A transverse incision was performed in the right upper quadrant following the lines of the skin. The incision was carried through the subcutaneous tissue and anterior fascia of the abdomen. Several bleeders were clamped with small Kelly forceps and tied with 2-0 chromic catgut. The peritoneum and posterior fascial sheath were opened between hemotsats. Exploration of the abdominal cavity revealed a normal sized uterus with no abnormalities. The ovaries and fallopian tubes were benign. The sigmoid colon and caecum were normal to palpation and inspection. The stomach and pylorus were within normal limits. The liver was of normal appearance in structure, size, color and consistency. The pancreas, and kidneys were unremarkable. The gall-bladder was enlarged and somewhat distended with easily palpable gall stones. A Balfour retractor was placed in the incision and the bowels were packed away with exposure of the gall bladder and common bile duct. The common duct and cystic duct were normal in size. The fundus of the gall bladder was grasped with large Kelly forceps and sharp dissection of the gall bladder was initiated from the fundus toward the neck with separation of the gall bladder from the hepatic bed. The cystic artery was identified, clamped, divided and ligated with 2-0 silk. The cystic duct was dissected to its junction with the common duct. The cystic duct was clamped with long right angle forceps and divided. A #16 catheter was placed into the cystic duct stump and secured in place with a cystic duct clamp. The dye was injected through the catheter and two X-rays taken that showed a benign biliary tree with no signs of common duct stones or obstruction of the biliary tree. The intracatheter was removed and the cystic duct was reclamped closer to the junction with the common duct, trimmed and tied with 2-0 silk. The hepatic bed was checked for hemostasis and no active bleeding was observed. A Jackson-Pratt drain was placed in Morrison's pouch through the foramen of Winslow and passed through a separate stab wound of the anterior abdominal wall. The drain was anchored to the skin with a 3-0 silk suture. Sponge count was correct.

Doctor's Surgical Summary (2)

Instrument and needle count were correct. The peritoneum and posterior fascial sheath were closed with running suture of O-vicryl suture. Subcutaneous tissue was closed with metal clips. Safety pin was put in the drain and the drain connected to a suction bulb. Dressing applied and secured with tape. General anesthesia was discontinued and the endotracheal tube was removed. The patient tolerated the procedure and anesthesia well and was stable when she left the O.R. to go to the recovery room.

CJL/ja
Dictated: 8-7-06
Transcribed 8-7-06

Nurse's Surgical Summary Form

NURSE'S OPERATIVE NOTE

Pre-Op Diagnosis: Decubitus left hip

Operation: Debridement and Excision of ulcer of left greater trochanter

Post-Op Diagnosis: same

Complications: none

Surgeon: Assistant:

Anesthesia: General Anesthetist: Hal Lambdin

Scrub Nurse(s): Todi Pelham RN Hazel Tait, LPN

Circulating Nurse: Lorma Spears, RN

Other Authorized Personnel: none

O.R. Times: 12:30 Anesthesia: 12:45P Incision: 1:15P Finish: 2:25P.M.

Instrument Count: NA Final Status: NA

Needle Count: Final Status:

Sponge Count: Final Status:

Pt. Identified: Yes Chart Checked: Yes Physical & Mental Status Pre-op: Stable

Blood Available: Yes Amt. Blood Ordered in O.R.

Catheterized By: NA Type Cath: Cath in Amt. Urine Output: Color:

Position: Supine [ ] Prone [ ] Lithotomy [ ] Lateral [✓] Sitting [ ]

Special Position: c̄ arms right arm on padded board - legs positioned

Electrocautery Position: Back Settings: 1 Coagulation: 3 Cutting: 3

Tourniquet Position: NA Applied By: Start Time: Release:

Operative Site: left hip Skin Condition: Clean Shaved: Yes [ ] No [✓]

Culture: NA Routine [ ] Aerobic [ ] Anaerobic [ ] Other [ ]

Drains: JACKSON Pratt Type: Site: left hip Open [✓] Connected to:

Packing: NA Type: Site:

X-Rays Taken: Yes [ ] No [✓] Area:

Specimen: Yes Frozen Sect. Yes [ ] No [ ] w/Pathologist [ ] To Lab. [✓]

Dressing: Yes Type: Fluff X2 ABD X2

Prosthesis Used: NA

Serial No. NA

Discharged from O.R. by: Stretcher [✓] Wheelchair [ ] To: RR [✓] ICU [ ] Floor [ ]

Nursing Post-op Assessment Pt. Condition: STABLE

Special Information: Coccyx decubitus dressed c̄ 4X4 + ABD sponges Class III

Pre-Closure Sponge and Instrument Count

INSTRUMENTS

6✓	Needleholders
18✓	Hemostats
6✓	Mosquitos
—	Tonsil Hemostats
8✓	Kellys
8✓	Allis
4✓	Babcocks
6✓	Kockers
4✓	Right Angles
3✓	Sponge Sticks
—	Laheys
12✓	Towel Clips
3✓	Knife Handles

FORCEPS

10✓	Forceps

SCISSORS

6✓	Scissors

SUCTION TIPS

—	T & A Suction w/Tip
1✓	Abdominal w/Guard
—	Frazier
—	Other

SCREWS ON RETRACTORS

1✓	Balfour
	Other

OTHER INSTRUMENTS

6✓	Hemoclip Appliers
—	Tenaculums
—	Intestinal Clamps
—	Gallbladder Inst.
—	Haney Clamps
1✓	Thompson Retractor
12✓	Joints
2✓	Adj wrenches
6✓	Extra Long Kellys
6✓	Extra Long Rt. Angles

Correct: 1. yes ✓ 2. yes ✓

OPERATION Exploratory Laparotomy – Excision of mass right pelvic

SURGEON: DR. John Doe ASSISTANT DR. JACK, Doe

CIRCULATING PERSON L. Doe Spear, RN

SCRUB PERSON(S) H. Doe, LPN / J. Smooth, CST

DATE 10/10/10

NEEDLES

ATRALOC	FREE	[illegible]
2✓ +2 = 4 +2 = 6 +2 = 8✓	0	2✓

INJECTION NEEDLES: 2 +1 = 3✓

KNIFE BLADE: 3✓

Correct: 1. yes ✓ 2. yes ✓ 3. yes ✓

SPONGE COUNT

FLATS	LAPS	PEANUTS	TONSIL
10✓ +10✓ = 20✓ +10✓ = 30✓	5✓ +5✓ = 10 +5✓ = 15✓	0	0

Correct: 1. yes ✓ 2. yes ✓ 3. yes ✓

ORIGINAL COUNT BY: L. Doe Spear R.N. H. D. Doe, LPN

FINAL COUNT BY: L. Doe Spear R.N. H. D. Doe, LPN

CORRECT yes (✓) INCORRECT ____

Pre-Op and Post-Op Anesthesia Notes

PROGRESS NOTES

Last Name	First Name	Attending Physician	Room No.	Hosp. No.
pts. name				

Date	Notes Should Be Signed by Physician
9/11/10 745A	pre-op evaluation
	(1) pt's condition has improved since admission to hospital p̄ colonoscopy - pt. adm due to inability to void & embarrassed respiration - pt required as post-op p̄ Versed 1mg IV & pentothal 100mg IUDD for IV sedation
	(2) NKA - see pre-op evaluation prior to colonoscopy on 9-9-89 for med. listing
	(3) spinal anesthesia c̄ IV sedation & full monitoring
	William CRNA / [signature]
9/11/10 12 NOON	Post-op note
	pt's condition stable post-op; pt on O_2 @ 4LM via nasal prongs - unsuccessful spinal attempts x4 & proceeded to endotracheal gen c̄ no appar anest complications during O.R or in RR - will vigorously treat prior respiratory condition as pre-op - will follow carefully - pt. to sit up this afternoon & ambulate c̄ help this PM.
	Pt- anest well William CRNA

Form 185 TWYFORD PRINTING CO.-DUNN, N.C. PROGRESS NOTES

Anesthesia Record

PATIENT IDENTIFICATION

OR# I Time 8:00A Consent signed
Date 9/18/?0 P.A.M. ck ✓
Postop. Dx. LEFT ventral hernia
Operation Repair of LEFT ventral hernia
Surgeons Dr. John Doe

PREMEDICATION (DRUG, DOSE, TIME, EFFECT) VERSED 3 mg + Robinul 0.3 mg IM 7:00A / at 8:00A calm, dry
ANTIBIOTIC 0
NPO p̄ 12MN IV #18 angio c̄ 1000cc D5RL x1 LEFT hand by J.W. CRNA

BP 140/?0 T 97.6° P 100 R 2?
PNS Lt facial Art. Line 0 CVP 0 Pa. Line 0
Anes. 7:45A Op. Start 8:44A Op. Finish 9:23A Anes. Finish 9:50A

Code ASA III
CFPRE iv block NRB
Regional Blockade ①
Local Stand By

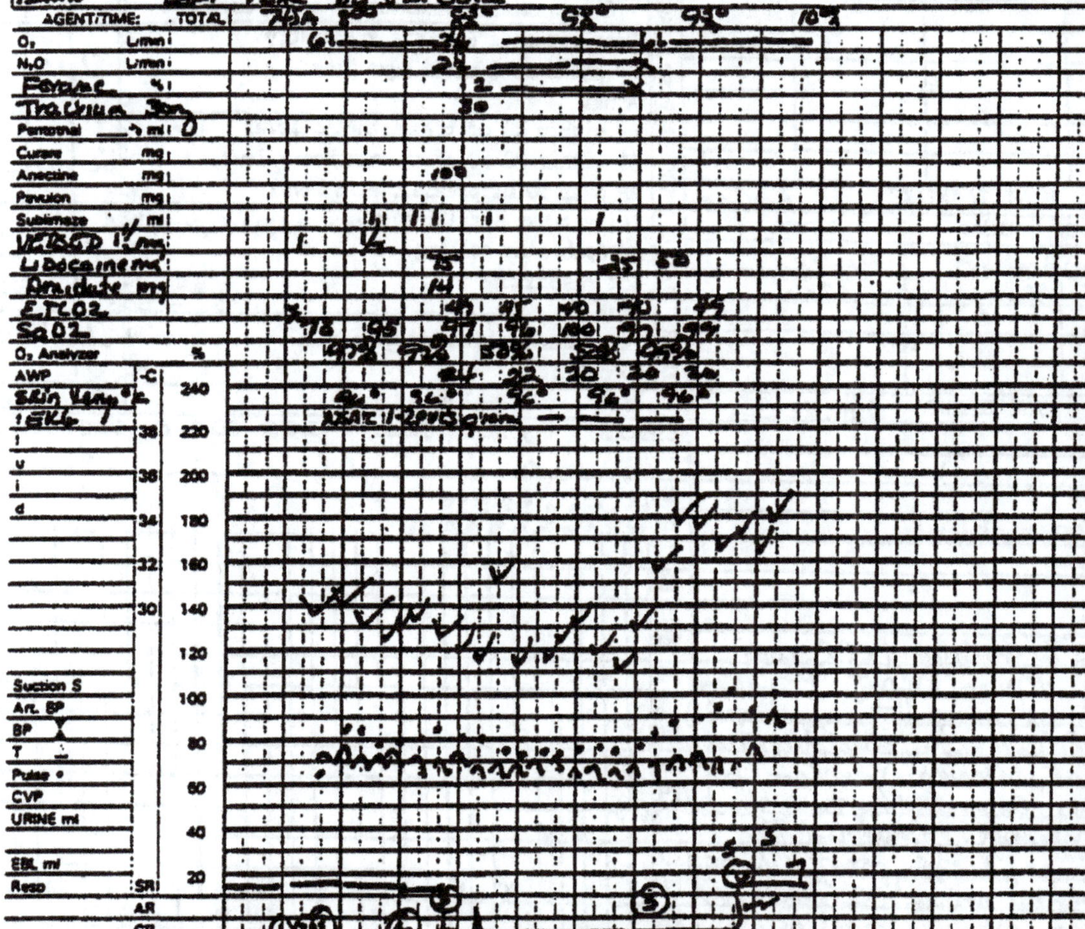

Spinal/Epidural
Agent Attempts x 4 unsuccessful due to spinal deformity
Needle due to
CSP: clear bloody none attempts
Time
Anes. Level
Brand
Exp. date
Lot #

Induction
Pre O₂ Smooth
Crash Excitement
Mask OAW NAW
Endotracheal Naso
Direct Blind
Ease c̄ difficulty
c̄ cuff w/o cuff
Xylo jelly c̄ stylet
n-dec. oint.
Size 7.0 Time 8:?? A
Ventilator: Vt 800cc
Rate 10 AWP 24
Intubation per 1
BSBE p̄ int. = Bil
teeth + gums p̄ int same
tooth guard

Position
Supine prone
sitting lithotomy
Rev. trendelenburg
Lateral R.L.
Kidney R.L.
Arms/Legs:
Positioned padded
Secured
Cont. EKG
Precord Steth
Esoph. Steth
T Monitor
O₂ Monitor
Eyes: taped closed padded-taped

Fluids
D₅RL 1050cc
RL
Subtotal
WB
PRBC
FFP
Albumin
Plasmanate
Total 1050 ml
Tourniquet 0
EBL <50cc ml
URINE 300 ml

REMARKS:
1. pt. received in holding area - ID c̄ armband checked - chart reviewed
2. Atropine 0.3mg IV - IV sedation
3. pt. to OR #1 - monitors applied - pre O₂ oximeter c̄ 78 - increased to 97 c̄ O₂ by mask - prehydration 300cc D5RL
4. pt. turned on left side positioned for spinal - unable to insert needle due to bony resistance - attempts x4 including paramedian approach
5. pt turned supine - induction c̄ no difficulty - foley cath as pt stated he needed to void prior to induction - and taken away
6. Prostigmin 2.5 mg + Atropine 1.2 mg 10:00
7. extubation - airway out
8. RR - awake - responding to verbal stimulation 1??/?0 - 100 - 24 O² sat 97%

701-005 Rev. 1/86 Anesthetist J. Williams CRNA Surgeon Dr. J. Doe

Recovery Room Record

Date:	1/31/[illegible]	O2 Therapy			Operation:	Debridement decubitus & Excision of Greater Trochanter (L) hip
Time In:	2:39 p	Route:	O/G Time On	Time Off		
Adm. Nurse:		Face Shield/100%	2:39 p	3:00 p	Pre-OP B/P:	140/90, 140/86, 137/90
Time Out:	3:?? p	ET Tube				
Dischg. Nurse	R Grinder RN	Ventilator			OR B/P:	140/90, 150/86
Reported To:	B. Smith, LPN					

ER IV's	Time Started	Time Ended	Amt. Rec.
	OR	RR	700
	RR	Floor	150
Blood RN			
	TOTAL IV INTAKE		850cc

Drainage - Types	Color	Amount
Urine (Foley)	Amber	225cc
Jackson Pratt	Bloody	30cc
	TOTAL OUTPUT	255cc

POST ANESTHESIA SCORE		IN	30	60
ACTIVITY	Moves 4 extremities voluntarily or on command =2 2 extremities voluntarily or on command =1 0 extremities voluntarily or on command =0	1	2	2
RESP.	Deep breathes & coughs frequently =2 Dyspneic or limited breathing =1 Apnea =0	2	2	2
CIRC.	BP within 20 of preanesthetic level =2 BP within 20-50 of preanesthetic level =1 BP over 50 of preanesthetic level =0	2	2	2
L.O.C.	Fully awake & talking *Same as pre-operatively* =2 Arousable on calling =1 Not responding =0	1	2	2
COLOR	Pink =2 Pale; dusky; blotchy; jaundice =1 Cyanotic =0	2	2	2
	TOTALS	8	10	10

SYMBOLS: ∨ B.P. ∧ · - Pulse * - SPONT. RESP. o - CONT. RESP.

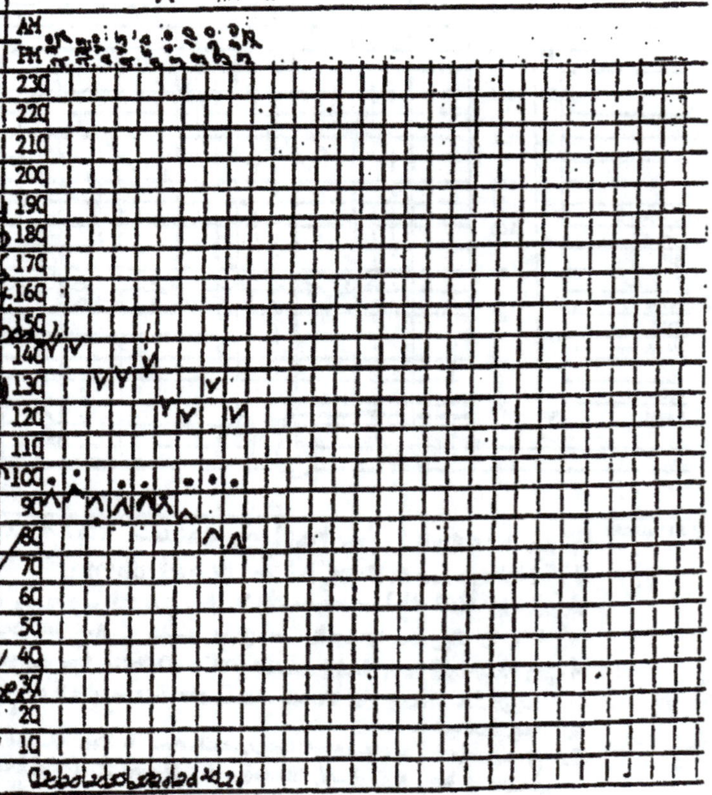

Medications:

Type of Anesthesia: General

Anesthesia Orders:

Nurse's Notes: 2:39 p Admitted to RR via stretcher. Moves (L) foot. Pt is blind & non-verbal per-operatively. Resp 20 & easy. Oral airway intact. O2 @ 100% via mask. Good air exchange bilat. (L) hip dsg clean, dry & intact. Jackson pratt compressed c̄ [illegible] ant. [illegible] bloody drainage. Foley patent & emptied of 225cc Amber urine. R Grinder RN

2:40 p Moving arms & feet. Oral airway out. Deep breathes on command. [illegible] (L) hip dsg remains clean, dry & intact. Jackson pratt changed. R Grinder RN

2:50 p Moving around. Non-verbal. Responds to verbal commands. Foley patent. (L) hip dsg clean & dry. Jackson pratt changed. R Grinder RN

3:00 p Resp 20 & easy. Deep breathes @ intervals. O2 off. IV [illegible] (L) hand. Foley patent. (L) [illegible]

ADDRESSOGRAPH (cont) R Grinder RN

Recovery Room Score System

	SCORE	AT ARRIVAL	HOUR 1	HOUR 2	HOUR 3
ACTIVITY					
Able to move 4 extremities	2	0	✓2	✓2	
Able to move 2 extremities	1				
Able to move 0 extremities	0	✓0			
RESPIRATION					
Able to deep-breathe & cough freely	2			✓2	
Dyspnea or limited breathing	1		✓1		
Apneic	0	✓0			
CIRCULATION					
BP ± 20% of preanesthetic level	2		✓2	✓2	
BP ± 20–50% of preanesthetic level	1	✓1			
BP ± 50% or more of preanesthetic level	0				
CONSCIOUSNESS					
Fully awake	2				
Arousable on calling	1		✓1	✓1	
Not responding	0	✓0			
COLOR					
Pink	2	✓2	✓2	✓2	
Pale, dusky, blotchy, jaundiced, other	1				
Cyanotic	0				
TOTALS		3	8	9	

SCORE MUST BE AT LEAST 7–8
FOR PATIENT'S RELEASE

JANE DOE

PATIENT

*Adapted, by permission of the authors and publisher, from Aldrete JA, Kroulik D: *Anesth Analg* 49:924-934, Nov-Dec 1970.

PLEASE NOTE: This Recovery-Room Scorecard is one example of the kind of postsurgical charts in current use. Roche Products Inc. and Hoffmann-La Roche Inc. are not responsible for any decisions based on information provided by its use.

ROCHE

Emergency Department Records

Single-Page Type of Emergency Room Form

IMMEDIATE CARE REPORT

MORE CONDENSED AND ABBREVIATED FORM WHERE NURSES NOTES, DOCTORS NOTES, ORDERS AND PATIENT DATA ARE ALL CONTAINED IN ONE PAGE

MEDICAL RECORD/ACCOUNT NO. | INIT | SOCIAL SECURITY NO. | ADMISSION DATE

PATIENT: NAME (LAST, FIRST, MIDDLE, M) | AGE | BIRTHDATE
MAILING ADDRESS (STREET, CITY, STATE) | ZIP | PHONE
EMPLOYER - PATIENT | SPOUSE/RESP. PARTY EMPLOYER

GUAR.: GUAR. NAME | SOCIAL SECURITY NO. | FIN. CLASS
MAILING ADDRESS(STREET, CITY, STATE) | ZIP | PHONE

INSURANCE:

PLAN NO.	INSURANCE CO. NAME	INS. CO. CODE	POLICYHOLDER NAME	REL.	CERTIFICATE NO.	GROUP NO.
(A)	BCBS					
(B)						
(C)						

COMPANY ADDRESSES — NO 10 DAYS — ICD-9 CODES
(A)
(B)
(C)

FAMILY DR. | ATTENDING DR. | DR. NO. | DATE OF ONSET INJURY/ILLNESS

ALLERGIES ☐ NO ☐ YES - SPECIFY: NKA
DR. NOTIFIED: TIME 10:00 M
PT. SEEN BY DR: 10:10 M
LAST TETANUS <1 yr ago

NURSING ASSESSMENT/TREATMENT

TIME	TEMP	PULSE	RESP	B/P
10:00	98.3	76	20	126/7.

Involved in MVA 1 hr ago. 45 yr old white male states hit head on roof of car. Denies LOC, nausea or vomiting. PERRLA. Swollen area noted top of head. c/o pain in neck. no other injuries noted. States was wearing seat belt. ETON

NURSE'S SIGNATURE

X-RAY | LAB | MEDS/IV'S | TIME | ROUTE | SITE | IN.

noted on arrival. Good neuro function in all extremities. D Barnes RN (etc.) NC NP

Skull films, C-spine

HX-PHYSICAL-CLINICAL FINDINGS

S: 45 y.o. WM involved in AA ~1 hr PTA
c/o Head and neck pain
Struck head on roof of car
s̄ LOC, s̄ numbness or weakness of Ext's — No Home Meds
Denies other injuries
PH NKDA, ∅ meds, s̄ chronic d/s, Last Td <1 yr
O: VS's WNL, in NAD, Head - tender area at top of scalp, minimal swelling, PERRLA, EOMI, fundi-benign, ENT clear,
DX: Neck - Tender R para cerv muscles, AFROM s̄ films,
TREATMENT: Lungs clear, COR-RRR s̄m, Abd Benign — Skull films
A: Closed head injury s̄ LOC, Ext's s̄ CCorE, Neuro - awake, alert C-spine
② cervical strain — of 3, M+S grossly intact, gait NL — v.o. Dr Sloan, D Barnes
DISPOSITION P: Skull + spine Xray → neg.
CONDITION OF DISCHARGE cerv. collar,
TIME OUT:
PATIENT INSTRUCTIONS & FOLLOW-UP CARE Head injury instruction sheet, F/U as needed.
See Dr on call for recheck ~ 5-7 d, Tylenol for pain
I HAVE READ AND UNDERSTAND THE FOLLOW-UP CARE INSTRUCTIONS GIVEN

E. M. Service M.D.
PHYSICIAN'S SIGNATURE — PATIENT'S SIGNATURE

Single-Page Type of Emergency Room Form

Nursing assessment

Involved in motor vehicle accident 1 hour ago. 45 year old whit male. States hit head on roof of car. Denies loss of consciousness, nausea or vomiting. Pupils equal, round, react to light and accommodate. Swollen area noted (on) top of head. complaining of pain in neck, no other injuries noted. States was wearing seat belts. Alcohol noted on person. Good neurological functions in all extremities. D. Barnes R.N. [two further nurses' notes written in the doctor's part of the record state "no home meds" and "skull films and Cervical spine (films) verbal order Dr. Glaser]

X-rays etc. ordered are skull films and X-rays of the cervical spine.

History -physical-clinical findings

Subjective - 45 year old white male involved in automobile accident one our prior to admission. complaining of head and neck pain. Struck head on roof of car without loss of consciousness, without numbness or weakness of extremities. Denies other injuries.

Past history - No known drug allergies,no medications, no chronic complaints, last to a doctor less than 1 year ago.

Objective - Vital signs within normal limits, in no acute distress, Head - tender area a top of scalp, minimal swelling, Pupils equal, round, react to light and accommodate, extraocular muscles intact, fundi benign, Ear nose and throat - clear, without discharge. Neck - Tender right paracervical muscles, active full range of movement after films (i.e. the neck movements were deferred until after X-ray films were taken to avoid injuring the spinal cord should an unstable fracture of the neck be present). Lungs clear Heart regular rate and rhythm no murmurs Abdomen benign Extremities without clubbing, cyanosis or edema Neurological (exam) - awake, alert, oriented x three (to time, place and circumstance) Musculoskeletal grossly intact, gait normal.

Diagnosis and treatment section.

Assess - #1 Closed head injury without loss of consciousness
#2 Cervical strain.

Plan - Skull and cervical spine X-rays ---negative
Cervical collar
Head injury instruction sheet
Follow up as needed
See doctor on call for recheck in 5-7 days
Tylenol for pain

E.M. Service M.D.

Attending Physician's Emergency Room Note

SINGLE ER SHEET WITH NURSES NOTES,
DOCTORS NOTES AND DOCTORS' VERBAL ORDERS (VO)
WRITTEN OUT BY NURSE

EDICAL RECORD/ACCOUNT NO.

SECURITY NO. | ADMISSION DAT

NAME (LAST, FIRST, MIDD

BIRTHDATE

MAILING ADDRESS (STRE

PHONE

EMPLOYER - PATIENT | SPOUSE/RESP. PARTY EMPLOYER

GUAR. NAME | SOCIAL SECURITY NO. | FIN. CLASS

MAILING ADDRESS(STREET, CITY, STATE) | ZIP | PHONE

PLAN NO.	INSURANCE CO. NAME	INS. CO. CODE	POLICYHOLDER NAME	REL.	CERTIFICATE NO.	GROUP NO.
(A)						
(B)						
(C)						

COMPANY ADDRESSES | ICD-9 CODES

(A)
(B)
(C)

AMILY DR. | ATTENDING DR. | DR. NO. | DATE OF ONSET INJURY/ILLNE

LLERGIES
☐ NO ☐ YES - SPECIFY:

DR. NOTIFIED: TIME M | LAST TETANUS
PT. SEEN BY DR: M

NURSING ASSESSMENT/TREATMENT | TIME | TEMP | PULSE | RESP | B/P

See flowsheet

NURSE'S SIGNATURE Cleepste

X-RAY | LAB | MEDS/IV'S | TIME | ROUTE | SITE | INI

HX-PHYSICAL CLINICAL FINDINGS

S: 60 y.o. WF brought by rescue
c̄ C/O C/P × ~1 hr. Onset
shovelling snow. c̄ SOB,
radiates to (L) arm, some nausea, s̄ vomiting
Hx of recent C/P's when out walking, relieved c̄ rest —
s̄ PH AMI, (−) HTN, (+) DM, (+) FH — fr c̄ MI
PH — NKDA, meds — Insulin 40 u NPH Q AM, Naprosyn for "N
DMI — AODM, arthritis

DX: O: P 100, 110/70, R 20, T 98, skin moist, lungs clear
TREATMENT: cor — s̄ JVD, RRR s̄ m, Abd — BS's active, soft, NT
Ext's — s̄ C/C/E. EKG — R~100, RSR,
A: acute Inf MI peaking T's — II, III, F
DISPOSITION P: O2 @ 4L CXR — neg
CONDITION OF DISCHARGE Monitor — RSR TIME OUT
PATIENT INSTRUCTIONS & FOLLOW-UP CARE IV D5W KVO MS ~4 mg IV — improving
I HAVE READ AND UNDERSTAND THE FOLLOW-UP CARE INSTRUCTIONS GIVEN
NTG 1/150 SL — s̄ relief Admit — Discussed c̄ Dr. Lary

PHYSICIAN'S SIGNATURE A. Paul MD M.D. 47 PATIENT'S SIGNATURE

MEDICAL RECORDS

Translation of Attending Physician's Emergency Room Note

Subjective. 60 year old white female brought by rescue (squad) with complaints of chest pain for ?two hours. Onset (while) shovelling snow with shortness of breath and (pain) radiates to the left arm, some nausea (pain was) without remission. History of recent chest pains when out walking, relieved with rest. Without (no) past history of myocardial infarction, no hypertension, history of (positive for) diabetes mellitus. Positive family history, father had myocardial infarction.

Personal history: No known drug allergies. Medications: Insulin 40 units of NPH (insulin) each morning, Naprosyn (a non steroidal antiinflammatory drug) for arthritis. Past medical illnesses - adult onset diabetes mellitus, arthritis.

Objective: Pulse 100 (beats per minute), (blood pressure) 110/70, respirations 20 (per minute), temperature 98° (Fahrenheit), skin moist, lungs clear.

Heart: No (without) jugular venous distension, regular rate and rhythm, no (without) murmurs.

Abdomen: Bowel sounds active, soft, non tender.

Extremities: No (without) clubbing, cyanosis or edema.

EKG: Rate 100 (complexes per minute) regular sinus rhythm, peaking (tall) T-waves in (leads) II,III and VF (the inferior leads).

Chest X-ray: Negative

Assess: Acute inferior myocardial infarction.

Plan: Oxygen at 4 liters (per minute)

Monitor - Regular sinus rhythm (at present)

Intravenous (administration of) 5% dextrose in water at sufficient rate to keep the vein open

Morphine sulphate 4 milligrams intravenously - (patient is) improving

Nitroglycerin (tablet) 1/150th (mg) sublingually - without relief (of pain), to be delivered (given in IV.

(case) discussed with Dr. Cary

(signed) J.Paul M.D.

Emergency Department Nurses' Flow Sheet

EMERGENCY DEPARTMENT FLOW SHEET

DATE & TIME: 8/1/10 7AM

TRIAGE CATEGORY

EMERGENT	URGENT	NON-URGENT	PRIVATE PHYSICIAN	
	✓			TIME M.D. NOTIFIED: 703am TIME PATIENT SEEN: 703am

NAME:	AGE	SEX	RACE	TX. PTA:	MEDICAL/SURGICAL HX:
Doe, Jane.	54.	F	W	O2 → N/C 6LPM.	Hx: MI – 3yrs ago.

CHIEF COMPLAINT:	ONSET OF SX	ALLERGIES	PRESENT MEDS:
chest pain.	30 mins ago	Codeine.	(1) NPH Insulin 10u SQ daily; (2) Lasix 40mg ī daily (3) nitroglycerin gr 1/150 SL prn (4) Isordil 10mg po qid.

BP	PULSE	RESP.	TEMP.	L.O.C.	TETANUS	LMP:	BC?
90/60 (R)/L	120	32	98.6 (O)/Ax/R	alert + oriented	NA	NA	NA

ARRIVED: (Rescue) (Stretcher) w/c Walk Carried Triage Nurse

INITIAL ASSESSMENT: Arrived in SF position grasping chest c/o substernal pain Color - dusky. Skin - cool & moist. O2 continued @ 6LPM via N/C. Monitor applied showing Sinus Tachycardia s̄ ectopy. Hx: as above. - pt took NTG ī SL prior to arrival at ~~home @ approx~~ ~~mor~~ at hospital at approx 6:00am s̄ relief. Dr Closer examined pt. EKG done @ 7:15Am. IV started as charted below. Medicated for pain as below. Labwork drawn @ 7:25am. Portable CXR done @ 7:35Am. Relief in chest pain noted @ 7:35Am. Dr Make notified of pt's condition + orders recieved to admit. Transferred to CCU-01 via stretcher - cond. guarded. C. Legister RN

RECORD OF I.V. FLUIDS AND BLOOD ADMINISTRATION (cont)

TIME UP	BY	SOLUTION	AMT. UP	MEDICATION ~~ADDED~~ given	TIME	BY	TIME DOWN	AMT. GIVEN
7:15A	CL	D5W. @KVO — #18 gauge Lt AC spare	1000cc	NTG gr 1/150 SL	7:16A	CL		

INTAKE		OUTPUT						
			ORAL		URINE			
TIME	ORAL	TIME	Vomitus	Suction	Voided	Cath	Stools	Other
7:20A	H2O – 50cc	7:25A			150cc			
TOTAL ORAL		50cc			150cc			
TOTAL I.V.		TOTALS						
TOTAL INTAKE		TOTAL OUTPUT						

Patient Transfer Form

PATIENT TRANSFER FORM

1. Dispositon of Case

Patient Transferred:

[ ] Based on a weighing of risks and benefits.

[ ] At request of patient or his/her legal representative. (*Transfer for this reason requires patient or guardian signature below.)

[✓] Treatment received. CONDITION STABLE.

2. Transfer Information

Name of Receiving Facility: Wake Medical Center

Name of Contact at Receiving Facility: DR. T. Smith.

Space Available? yes ✓ no ____ other CCU-05

Will facility accept transfer? yes ✓ no ____

Name of person authorizing acceptance: D. Norris CCU charge Nurse.

Are treatment records being sent? yes ✓ no ____ LIST: copy of ER record, copy of lab work, EKG, ABG's + chest xray films

Name of Transfer Agent: Harnett Co. EMS

Medicare # ____________

DX: Chest Pain R/O MI

Medicaid # ____________

VS: 97⁴ - 110 - 28 110/60

Signature of Patient or Legal Representative, if required: Jack Adams (husband)

I have reviewed the information above and it is correct: Fred Jones, MD

M.D. or R.N.

NOTE: THIS FORM COMPLIES WITH PATIENT TRANSFER PROVISIONS OF SECTION 1967 OF THE MEDICARE AC

Nursing Notes Accompanying Transfer Patient

PATIENT TRANSFER – NURSES NOTES

Transfer to: Wake CCU

Date: 7/28/10

Transfer from: Good Hope CCU

Departure Time: 9:00pm

Accompanied by: Ima Good, RN; Rexie Que, EMT-I; Savle Driver, EMT-I

Arrival Time: 9:45pm

Condition on Departure: stable

Equipment used: O2, IV, monitor suction,

Condition on Arrival: stable

Time	Vital Signs	Medications	Comments
9:00pm	100/60 - 90 irreg - 24	IV - D5W @ 100cc/Hr	—— 72 y/o F being transported in SF position alert + oriented. Denies chest pain @ present: Hx: MI ̄c sudden onset of chest pain approx 3 hrs ago. Treated ̄c NTG SL x2 ̄c relief and being transported to Dr. Newman for cardiac catheterization. Skin w/D. Color - pink. C/o slight nausea. Monitor → Sinus Rhythm ̄c occas PVC. IV ̄c D5W 1000cc bag infusing via Lt AC space @ KVO ̄s abnormalities. Lungs clear. Denies any other complaints. —— C. Ready RN
9:10pm	100/60 100 irreg - 28		Vomited approx 50cc stomach contents. Denies any chest pain. Monitor ̄s change
9:13pm		Phenergan 25mg	given [illegible] IV push slow — for vomiting per order of Dr. Happy at GHH medical control —— C. Ready RN
9:20pm	110/60 98 irreg - 26		Resting quiet. No c/o pain ——
9:30pm	110/60 96 irreg - 26		No change in condition or monitor ——
9:40pm			Arrived at Wake CCU - condition unchanged since departure from GHH. Denies any chest pain. Occas PVC on monitor ̄c Sinus Rhythm. IV infusing well. Transport uneventful except for vomiting episode x1. —— C. Ready RN

Ira Tate, RN 7/28/10 9:58 pm

SIGNATURE AND TITLE OF PERSON RECEIVING PATIENT Date Time

Instruction Sheet for Patients Being Discharged from the E.R.

Emergency Room Physician's Discharge Instructions / Medical Record # 137604 0

Patient's Name __________ Age 12 Date 7/31/10

HEAD INJURY

[✓] Clear liquid diet for 24 hrs.
[✓] Limit activity for next 24 hrs.
[✓] Awaken patient every 1-2 hrs during night & evaluate patient's condition.
[✓] Contact your physician if any of the following occur:

1. Frequent, forceful vomiting.
2. Increasing drowsiness, irritability, confusion or severe headache.
3. Double or blurred vision
4. Abnormally deep sleep or difficulty arousing or convulsions.
5. Changes in behavior.
6. Inequality of pupils (black part of eye, should be equal).
7. Blood or clear fluid coming from ears, or nose.

CAST PRECAUTIONS

1. Prevent swelling by exercising fingers or toes and by keeping the extremity elevated when inactive. Important - elevation must be higher than the heart.
2. Keep all casts clean and dry, moisture of any kind causes casts to fall apart.
3. Do not stick anything, whatsoever, or pour anything, either wet or dry, into your cast. Itching underneath the cast must be endured, not scratched.
4. If your cast becomes soft, cracked, broken or feels loose, please call the office for further instructions.
5. Do not walk on a cast intended for bearing weight until 48 hours after it is applied.
6. Wear your cast boot at all times when up and walking, whether indoors or outdoors.
7. The following list of conditions are considered emergencies:
   - A. Excessive swelling that persists in spite of elevation and exercise.
   - B. Fingers or toes turning blue or cold.
   - C. Numbness in fingers or toes
   - D. Excessive burning or places feeling raw or sore under the cast.
   - E. Loss of motion of joints.
   - F. Fever
   - G. Foul odor or drainage.

   Should any of these conditions persist, you should call your physician for further instructions.

IF X-RAYED

[ ] The results of the x-rays given you today are the preliminary readings. If the final results should be read differently, you will be notified.

SPRAINS

[ ] Elevate the injured part.
[ ] Apply ice packs.
[ ] If you have an elastic bandage, rewrap it if too tight or too loose. Do not wear elastic bandage to bed.
[ ] Use crutches and do not bear weight: [ ] while painful to step. [ ] until seen by physician for follow-up.

CUTS, PUNCTURES, SUTURE WOUNDS

[ ] Keep the injured part elevated.
[ ] Keep wound clean and dry.
[ ] Change dressing if it becomes soiled or wet or contact your physician for dressing change.
[ ] Change dressing in ___ hours and every ___ days thereafter.
[ ] See your physician in ___ hours for a dressing change and recheck
[ ] Contact your physician if you notice any of the following:

1. increasing redness or red streaks.
2. excessive swelling.
3. excessive drainage.
4. persistent bleeding.
5. increasing or persistent pain.

[ ] Call your physician and arrange to have your stitches removed in _____ days.

TETANUS IMMUNIZATION

[ ] Tetanus Toxoid [ ] D.T.
[ ] D.P.T. [ ] Hypertet
[ ] You have been started on a tetanus immunization series today please complete the series with your private M.D.

DIET

[ ] Nothing by mouth for __________
[ ] Clear Liquids for __________
[ ] Soft for __________
[ ] Normal

ACTIVITY

[ ] Bedrest except for bathroom.
[ ] Rest as much as possible.
[ ] Light activity.
[ ] Normal.

1. The on-call physician is Dr Hoot
   His/Her office number is 465-68[illegible]
2. Please see the on-call physician or your family physician within 24 hrs. ~~days~~ for followup care. Call His/Her office for an appointment within 24 - 48 hrs.
3. If your condition worses, or new symptoms appear, contact your on-call physician, family physician, or return to this emergency department.
4. Your signature below indicates you have received and understand instructions for followup care.

X __________
Patient or Responsible Party
(Father)
Relationship to Patient

PEDIATRIC INSTRUCTIONS

NAUSEA AND VOMITING

1. Nothing by mouth for 6 hours.
2. Start sips of water or 1/2 ounce pedialyte every hour.
3. Advance to clear liquids.
4. Return slowly to regular diet, adding milk products last.
5. Call the child's doctor if there is not rapid improvement.

FEVER

1. For flu-like symptoms or fever associated with chicken pox, DO NOT GIVE ASPIRIN.
2. For fever associated with teething, ear or throat infections, give aspirin or tylenol every 4 hours. Before giving either, check temperature with thermometer. Do not continue giving after temperature has returned to normal.
3. Do not awaken to give aspirin or tylenol if child is resting comfortably.
4. For temperature of 103 F and above tepid (room temperature) water sponging will help reduce, fever never sponge off child with alcohol.
5. Do not wrap child up in blankets or coats. They will keep the fever high.
6. Give clear liquids by mouth - coke, water, tea, kool-ade, gingerale, pedialyte, or gatoradid. Shake the fizz out of carbonated drinks.

SPECIAL INSTRUCTIONS

____

TREATMENT CERTIFICATE

Was treated at Good Hope Hospital Emergency Room on __________.
[ ] May not return to work until seen by Dr. __________ on __________.
[ ] May return to light work on __________.
[ ] Is able to return to work/school on __________.
[ ] Excused from physical ed. until __________.

Date: 7/31/10

B. Everyready RN
Nurse

Medical Record Copy

Pathology Lab Reports

Reports of Routing Admission Lab Work

©1987 COULTER ELECTRONICS, INC., HIALEAH, FLORIDA

TEST: ☐ CBC PROFILE: ☐ WBC ☐ RBC ☐ PLT ☐ PLOT

REQ'D BY: DATE 8/1/10

PERFORMED BY: [signature] DATE 8-1-10

- 6.3
- 4.73
- 14.7
- 44.1
- 93.2
- 31.1
- 33.3
- 14.1
- 212.
- 7.7
- 15.4
- 1.3
- 83.3

COMMENTS

URINALYSIS—STOOL

Room: | Doctor:

☐ Routine

☐ Preop Date Requested

☐ Stat

☐ Outpatient Requested By

☐ Voided ☐ Catheterized ☐ Clean Catch | Time Collected | Collected By

ROUTINE						
Appearance	cloudy	Nitrite	pos	RBC's	2-3	—PREGNANCY TESTS—
Color	yellow	Bilirubin	0	WBC's	8-10	UCG Slide
Sp Gravity	1.010	Urobilin- 0.1-1.0		Bacteria	1+	UCG (2 Hr. Tube)
Ph	6	ogen Units	1.0	Crystals	—	—STOOL—
Protein	trace			Mucus	trace	Occult Blood
Glucose	neg	—SEDIMENT—				Ova & Parasites
Ketones	neg	Casts				
Occult Blood	trace	Epithelial Cells	4-5	Tech [initials]		Date 8-1-10

CHEMISTRY I

Room: | Doctor:

☐ Routine

☐ Preop Date Requested

☐ STAT

☐ Outpatient Requested By

✓	Test	Result	✓	Test	Result	✓	Test	Result	✓ Electrolyte Panel	
	Amylase		✓	Glucose	108	✓	Total Bilirubin	1.1	Sodium (138-146)	1
	Lipase			SGOT			Direct Bilirubin		Potassium (3.8-5.1)	3.
✓	BUN	8		LDH			Acid Phosphatase		Chloride (100-108)	1
✓	Creatinine	0.8		CPK			Alk. Phosphatase		CO2 (23-30)	2
	Uric Acid			Total Protein			Phosphorus			
	Cholesterol			Albumin			Glucose 4 PM		Tech [initials]	
	Triglycerides			Calcium			Glucose 2 hr P.P.		Date 8/1/10 Reported	

Radiology Reports

Reports on Diagnostic Imaging (1)

NAME: Wallace, Elizabeth AGE: 64 WF

DOCTOR: Daniels

DATE: 3/18/10

EXAM: Portable chest

Single AP supine portable examination of the chest at 0530 hours on 3/15/89 shows both lungs to be well expanded and free of active areas of consolidation. The heart size is normal. Endotracheal tube tip is at the T-6 level. Right subclavian catheter tip is in the superior vena cava. No active disease is noted.

NAME: Brady, William James X-RAY NO: A 26311

DOCTOR: Masterson/Brown LOCATION: ER

CLINICAL HISTORY: Right flank pain radiating to right testicle R/O stone

DICTATED: 8/11/10

TRANSCRIBED: 8/11/10

INTRAVENOUS UROGRAM:

100cc of contrast was administered intravenously without immediate complication. After approximately 3 minutes the patient began to experience difficulties in breathing which increased over the next one to two minutes. At this point approximately 1/10cc of 1/1000 epinephrine was administered intravenously and the patient was transferred to the ER for further treatment.

CT BRAIN SCAN: NO PREVIOUS FILMS.

20 YR OLD FEMALE TO R/O BLEED.

TRANSAXIAL CUTS THROUGH THE BRAIN PERFORMED PRE AND POST CONTRAST ENHANCEMENT DEMONSTRATE NORMAL VENTRICLE, SULCI AND SUBARACHNOID SPACES FOR AGE. BRAIN PARENCHYMA IS NORMAL AND NO ENHANCEMENT IS SEEN. NO EXTRACEREBRAL FLUID COLLECTION OR MASS SHIFT IS SEEN. NO ABNORMAL CALCIFICATIONS. CALVARIUM, SKULL BASE AND FACIAL STRUCTURES APPEAR NORMAL.

IMP. NEGATIVE PRE AND POST CONTRAST BRAIN CT SCAN.

Reports on Diagnostic Imaging (2)

PATIENT: Strong, Charles **AGE: 26 YO WM**

DOCTOR:

DATE: 7/10/10

CLINICAL DIAGNOSIS OR DIAGNOSTIC PROBLEM: Head trauma with LOC and subdural hematoma in the right frontal area evacuated surgically

EXAMINATION: CT brain

CT BRAIN SCAN: MULTIPLE CONTIGUOUS COMPUTER ASSISTED TOMOGRAPHIC IMAGES OF THE BRAIN ARE OBTAINED UTILIZING A 20 DEGREE ANGLE TO THE ORBITAL-MEATAL LINE. THERE IS A RIGHT FRONTAL CRANIOTOMY PRESENT WITH A SMALL AREA OF DECREASED RADIODENSITY IN THE RIGHT FRONTAL REGION AND MILD ENLARGEMENT OF THE FRONTAL HORN OF THE RIGHT LATERAL VENTRICLE. REPORTEDLY, THE PATIENT HAS HAD RECENT RIGHT FRONTAL SUB-DURAL HEMATOMA EVACUATED. THERE IS SOME MILD PROMINENCE OF THE TEMPORAL HORN OF THE LEFT LATERAL VENTRICLE AND MILD CORTICAL PROMINENCE IN THE LEFT TEMPORAL REGION. NO INTRACEREBRAL HEMORRHAGE, MASS EFFECT OR MIDLINE DISPLACEMENT IS NOTED. VENTRICULAR SYSTEM OTHERWISE NORMAL IN SIZE AND SHAPE.
INCIDENTAL NOTE IS MADE OF SOME DEFORMITY OF THE ZYGOMATIC ARCH ON THE LEFT AND MILD MUCOSAL THICKENING IN THE LEFT MAXILLARY SINUS. AFTER THE IV INJECTION OF 100CC OF OMNIPAQUE 300, THERE IS NO CHANGE WITH THE CONTRAST ENHANCEMENT. NO ABNORMAL BLUSH NOTED.

CONCLUSION: POST-OPERATIVE CHANGE IN THE FRONTAL REGION WITH EVIDENCE OF FOCAL ATROPHY IN THE RIGHT FRONTAL AND LEFT TEMPORAL PORTIONS OF THE BRAIN, PRESUMABLY DUE TO PREVIOUS TRAUMA.

Respiratory Services Report

Serial Blood Gas Studies on a Patient in Respiratory Distress

BLOOD GAS ANALYSIS

NORMAL ARTERIAL VALUES

pH	7.35–7.45
pO_2	85–100mm/Hg
pCO_2	35–45mm/Hg
HCO_3^-	24–29meq/L
BASE EXCESS	0±2

SAMP	DATE	DRAW TIME	SOUR.	RUN TIME		INIT	FIO_2	COMMENTS	pH	pCO_2	pO_2	%SAT	HCO_3		B.E.
1	9/27	1044	LRA	1046		Bg	2L	Pos. Allen test	7.521	44	66.9	94.8	36		12.6
2	9/28	0705	RRA	0710		T.W	2L	+ Allen Test	7.344	50.3	66.7	92	27.3		2
3	9/29	0505	LRA	0508		TW	2L	AT +	7.392	51.5	44.6	79.4	31.3		5.8
4	9/29	0630	RRA	0633		TW	2L	AT +	7.44	45.6	57.8	90.8	30.9		6.6
5	9/29	0710	LRA	0713		Bgd	2L	pos. Allen test	7.478	31.4	58.2	92.2	23.3		0
6	9/30	0742	RRA	0749		Bgd	2L	pos. Allen test	7.436	43.7	54.1	88.9	29.2		4.9
7	9/30	2350	LRA	2355		Bg	2L	Pos. Allen test	7.362	53.5	60.5	89.9	30.3		5.0
8	10/1	0412	RRA	0416		Bg	IMV 12 30%	V_T 700	7.479	40.7	74.2	97	30.2		6.7
9	10/1	0453	LRA	0456		Bg	IMV 12 35%		7.472	40.5	65.5	94	29.6		5.9
10	10/1	0621	RRA	0629		Bg	IMV 10 35%		7.477	40.7	101	97	30.1		6.6
11	10/1	0727	LRA	0732		Bg	IMV 10 35%		7.415	47	85.3	96.5	30.1		5.8
12	10/1	0938	RRA	0943		TW	IMV 30%	10 V_T 700	7.392	49.5	85.7	96.3	30.1		5.4
								Pt transferring							
								to Megapolis Gen. Hosp.							
								to Services of							
								Dr Huffin							

Departmental Records

Physical Therapy Departmental Progress Notes

Date

Patient Age 72 Sex F

Address 16 RIVER ROAD, PORTADOWN Phone 4-2591 Attending Physician Brown

DIAGNOSIS low bk pain c̄ degenerative changes

Med./ BC/BS

Date	PROGRESS NOTES
4/5/10	Pt. is a 72 y.o. white F. who was D/c'd from hosp. yesterday after having had a myelogram + CT scan run. It showed extensive degenerative changes in her bk. refer to x-ray reports in pts. chart. Pt. has had 2 previous surgeries to remove spurs from her lower bk. which the surgeries were done by Dr. Alan Burch. She states one of the things she has problems c̄ is housekeeping but it's like this several years. Referred to PT for evaluation + Rx x 6 days. Pt. says she had a stroke last Oct. c̄ (L) hemiparesis
	O: Oriented x3.
	Rom: UE has 75% of shoulder mobility + functional mobility of hand + wrist (L)
	LE has limited use due to stroke last yr
	(R) LE functional
	Strength UE fair – overall (R) LE fair, (L) LE poor
	Sensation: Pain at base of spine
	Musculoskeltal · Some tightness at pelvis area
	scar is present thru length of lumbar vertebrae

RECORD OF TREATMENTS

Month	1	2	3	4	5	6	7	8	9	10	11	12	13	14	15	16	17	18	19	20	21	22	23	24	25	26	27	28	29	30	31	Total
Sept 2000					[illegible]				[illegible]																							

Physical Therapy Record

Date

Patient Age Sex

Address Phone Attending Physician

DIAGNOSIS

Date	PROGRESS NOTES
	A: Pt. has severe osteo changes in her low bk.
	STG: ↓ pain, ↓ spasms
	LTG: ↓ pain by 80% activities
	P: To see x 6 days for above Rx. Eval. at end of Rx.
	Anne Franks PT
9/9/10	Rx. for today was HP x 20 min. to the back followed by US/S in sitting. May try TNS mid wk. next wk.
	Anne Franks, PT
9/10/10	S: Pt says bk is "no better, no worse"
	O: Rx: HP to bk x 20 mins. Followed by US/S
	A: No change in pt. status
	P: Cont. c̄ Rx gd.
	Anne Franks PT

RECORD OF TREATMENTS

Month	1	2	3	4	5	6	7	8	9	10	11	12	13	14	15	16	17	18	19	20	21	22	23	24	25	26	27	28	29	30	31	Total

Chapter 3

Organizing Medical Data for Legal Purposes

§ 3:1 Introduction—preliminary organization of the medical record

The patient's medical record in a compensation case can be very simple, but in some instances it is very large or, even when the number of pages is small, the data contained in it can be complicated and confusing. It is these bulky and complex cases that require some attention to method.

A medical record, as it arrives from the informatics department of a hospital, is usually in order; but it is not the kind of order that a lawyer needs. Medical records grow naturally from back to front; the second day's documents are laid on top of the previous ones, and so on. When a patient is discharged, the staff of the informatics department takes the file apart and puts the documents in the proper order, with page one at the front and the others following behind it in due sequence. There may be minor errors from time to time in this rearrangement, for the informatics staff are only human, but they perform this task many times every day and usually do it properly. When a medical record becomes disordered it is generally because someone else, for instance a lawyer or a doctor going through it, has dropped it on the floor or otherwise interfered with it. The medical ordering of the patient file is nevertheless unsuitable for the lawyers' purposes. Each set of documents, for example the doctor's progress notes or the nurses' notes, is arranged in a proper time sequence, but the time relations between the items of information described in the various sets of documents is not made clear. For a lawyer's purposes, it is necessary to integrate these various sets into a single unified system where all of the events of each day, and sometimes of each hour, can be seen in their proper order.

This process of turning a discontinuous time sequence into a continuous one can be approached in an orderly or a disorderly manner. Both will probably reach the desired end point, but an orderly approach is likely to be quicker, less frustrating and, above all, less expensive. There is more than one way to skin a cat, and more than one way to organize a medical chart. I have chosen the flow chart method, which will be described in the following paragraphs. It is widely used in other professions and has been found to be convenient, time saving, and systematic so that few errors or omissions will be made.

§ 3:2 The initial reading

The steps involved in creating a flow chart representing a medical case are simple:

1. The pages of the chart should be numbered with a pencil if this has not already been done by medical informatics (which is often the case). This sounds like laboring the obvious, and it is; but if every note and every quote is not accompanied by a page reference, hours and even days can be spent searching for some dimly remembered, but important, item. It is best then, right from the outset, to form the habit of numbering the pages of the medical record before looking at it, *and referring all notes and observations to the relevant page*. In some law offices there is a standing arrangement whereby the pages are numbered before any of the lawyers see the chart. It should even be possible to check that the pages are in order at that point or, in the rare instance where this is not the case, they should if possible be put in order before numbering. This can normally be done by someone without any great expertise by comparing the last words on one page with the first ones on the next. If it is not possible to put the pages in order, they should be numbered anyway. The initial page numbering can be deleted and corrected later. In the meanwhile the page numbering will perform its main function; the reader will always be able to find the reference on page 99 even if page 99 really ought to be page 88.

2. The next step is to try to get some idea of what the case is about, which is best done by reading the discharge summary (DS). This does not mean that the discharge summary is an adequate representation of the relevant facts in the case; it does not even mean that it is a truthful account of the matter. Yet even if, in the lawyer's opinion, the discharge summary is a self-serving document intended to cover up or distort the actual events described, it nevertheless gives a general background picture which is useful in reading the chart as a whole. [See Chapter 2.]

3. The general picture obtained from the discharge summary can then be filled in by reading the nurses' notes. These are usually legible, with fewer hieroglyphics or abbreviations, and may tell the story of the patient's hospital course more fully and more accurately than any other part of the chart.

4. The doctors' progress notes should now be examined. When these are reasonably comprehensive (which is not always the case) they mirror to some extent the picture painted by the nurses' notes, but from a different perspective. The doctors' progress notes should record the clinical thinking of treating physicians, their day-to-day assessment of the patient's medical problems and their plans to deal with them.

5. The other relevant parts of the medical record may now be read in any order. It may not be necessary to go thorough every set of documents. It is true that any item may turn out to be important, but it is probably more efficient, at least in the initial evaluation of a medical case, to focus on the items that relate to the legal issues and to pick these up, by and large, from the three most important sets of documents already studied (DS, NNs and DPNs). Lab data, for example, can usually be evaluated by looking at the overview of the test results in the discharge summary.

Steps 1–5 above should have been performed with a pen, pencil, colored marker or some other such implement in hand. The significant, or seemingly significant, passages can be circled or marked in some way. Some prefer the pencil or erasable colored markers so that marks or comments may be deleted if they should change their minds during a later reading of the chart.

6. Items in the chart are marked or circled because they are thought to be relevant. The reasons why they are deemed relevant are also important and these usually take the form, in the initial evaluation of the case, of *questions* and *comments*. These should be noted down at once as they occur to the reader. It does not matter that the questions may later be irrelevant or the comments inappropriate; they can be deleted or amended later. If not recorded, they may be forgotten or overlooked. Some like to record them separately (with page references, of course) in a notebook to secure them from prying eyes, or directly enter them into a computer. The simplest method is to write them opposite the text on the blank reverse side of the previous page. The ways in which these questions and comments (Q&Cs) can be used will be discussed later. They are, of course, important to the evaluating lawyer, but they can later be invaluable in enabling a consultant to understand the point of view and the needs of the lawyer.

The whole process described above should probably be repeated at least twice to make sure that nothing important has been overlooked. The chart can be read 20 times if one wishes, but probably two or three times are sufficient for the initial reading. Further studies should be reserved until after the medical consultation, when understanding will hopefully have been improved.

The marked chart is now ready to be organized. This can be done by the person evaluating the case but it is probably more efficient to delegate it to secretarial staff. It is a routine matter and relatively inexperienced secretarial staff can be quickly trained to transcribe the marked passages (with accompanying questions and comments) into a flow sheet.

§ 3:3 Making the flow sheet

A flow sheet is simply a legal application of the marine engineer's flow sheet, which organizes all the information about temperatures, pressures and shaft rotation speed in columns so that someone coming on duty can see right away how matters stand with the ship's engines. In its simplest and crudest form (computerized versions will be discussed later), all that is required is an ordinary legal pad and a pencil. In essence, the flow sheet has time (in days) indicated on the left-hand margin of the page and the titles of the various types of information (nurses' notes, progress notes, lab reports, etc.) are written across the top. As each column is filled in, the day-by-day, hour-by-hour story can be read across in chronological sequence. And it is most important that each entry should be accompanied by its page reference in the medical chart.

The *discharge summary* is a good place to start. The salient points of the case can be extracted from this form. They need not be entered in a separate column but written down in summary form at the top of the chart or simply kept in mind. Occasionally the discharge summary will contain information and observations not supplied elsewhere in the medical record, and a separate column for these materials may be needed, but this is not often the case.

The first column is usually assigned to the *nurses' notes*. This is likely to contain a great many items and so should be assigned a fairly wide column (one third to one half of the width of the page). The first page is marked A1. When the first column in this page is filled, another page is added and labeled A2. Further pages (A3, A4, etc.,) are added until all the passages from the nurses' notes that are deemed important have been entered into the first column.

The same procedure is then followed with the next set of documents (e.g., the *doctors' progress notes*), entering them into the second column on pages A1, A2, and so on, until all the relevant statements have been recorded. Lab reports, X-ray reports, and other reports can then be treated in the same way. Each item of interest is entered in a column opposite the appropriate day. When the space across the A page is exhausted (which normally happens after the second column has been entered, a second series of pages (B1, B2, etc.) is begun. The ultimate result is a chart made up of these pages reading A, B, C, etc., from side to side and 1, 2, 3, etc., from top to bottom (as illustrated below).

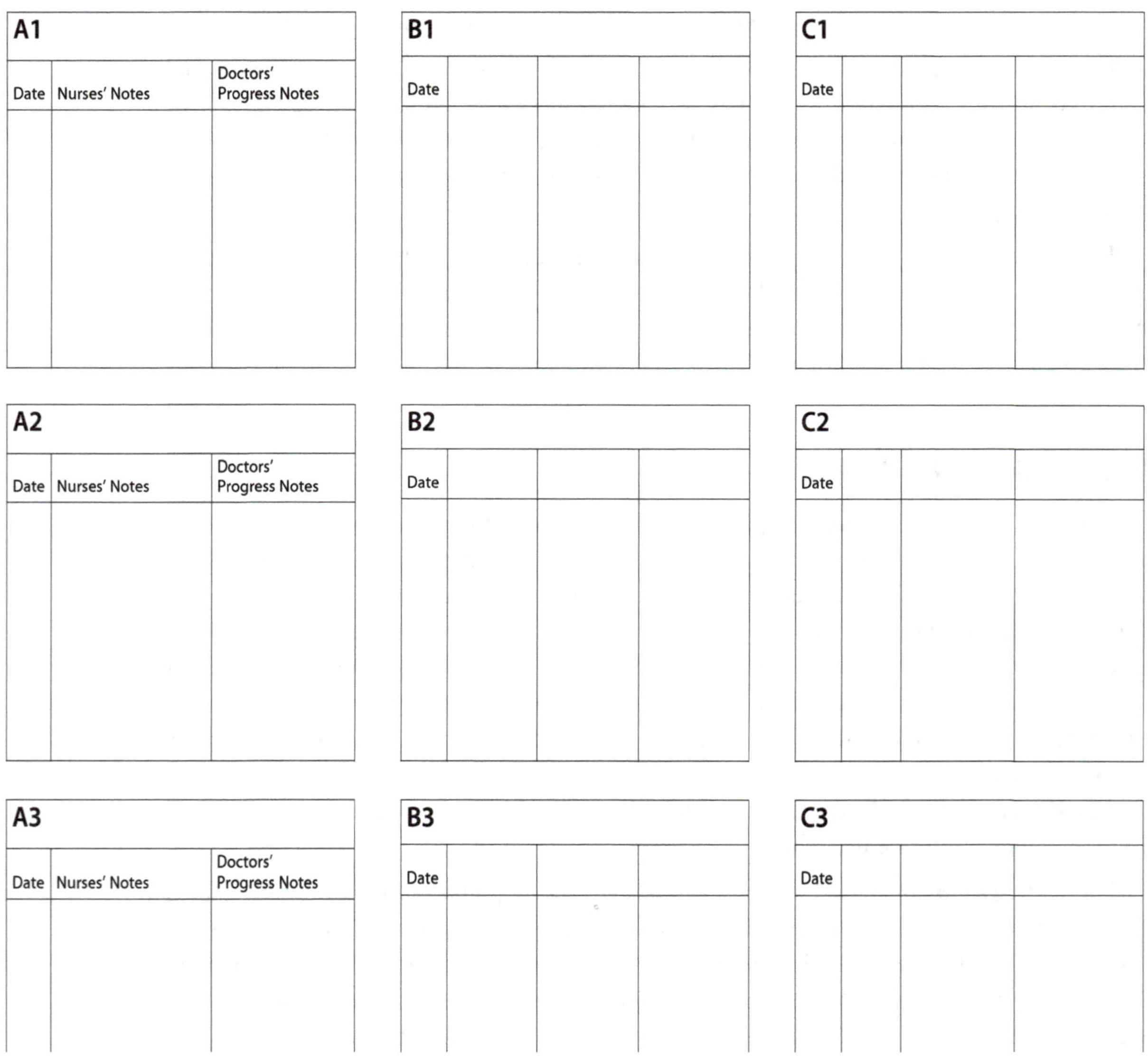

Figure 3-1. The final arrangement of the flow sheet

The last column on the right-hand side can be reserved for the *Questions and Comments*, but some prefer to keep these separate and confidential, for they can be sensitive. But whether they are included in the flow sheet or kept separately, it is most important that these should be page referenced also.

§ 3:4 Using a computer to make the flow sheet

When law office practice is computerized, which is now almost universally the case, the process of making a flow sheet, and especially of altering and revising it, is very simple. The columns are made using the column feature of a word processor or in a spreadsheet. The circled items are entered in the columns, either manually on a blank printed copy or directly into the computer. Changes and corrections are easily made. They can be noted on the blank reverse side of a printed copy, with perhaps a colored paper clip to guide the secretarial staff to the affected page for entry into the computer. The chart can be printed out at any time.

§ 3:5 Uses of a flow sheet

The completed flow sheet, described in the previous paragraphs, consists of separately numbered pages (written or printed out), which is a very convenient arrangement from several points of view. The individual pages are not large and so can be easily copied; they can be inserted into an ordinary envelope and mailed to a consultant; or they can be put together and assembled into a wall chart. The flow sheet has a number of other advantages as well.

1. Approaching a medical record using the flow-sheet method is a systematic, economical way of working. Nothing is wasted. Every time something of interest is noticed, it is highlighted or circled with a pencil or identified in some other way. It may be that, when the file is read through a second time, different things will be noticed, but this does not matter; corrections can be made, a second flow sheet arises from the ashes of the first and nothing is lost. It is like using a winch—every move advances the process by another notch, and there is no retrograde movement.

2. The flow sheet is extremely effective as a communication device. It can be copied and mailed to a medical consultant or a colleague who can see at a glance the lawyer's understanding of the case. The selection of items and the accompanying *questions and comments* will make that clear. Consultants can communicate in these circumstances much more easily and more adequately than if they simply received the medical record and a request to advise. Consultants can even add their own comments to the flow sheet and return a copy to the sender. The consulting parties can indeed talk back and forth to one another in this way until each is satisfied that they have given (and received) all the relevant information and advice. The doctor has learned how the lawyer sees the case and what is needed, while the lawyer has presumably extracted from the doctor any relevant medical opinions. Doctors complain that consultation with lawyers is a long and frustrating chore. A flow sheet makes this communication efficient and rapid. It is also impressive to a physician. It conveys the idea that the lawyer is a systematic

and well organized person. The result may well be a more effective and cordial consultation. The end result should be that the lawyer is more likely to really understand the medical aspects of the case and, more important, that this understanding is captured within the four corners of the flow sheet.

3. A flow sheet can be used in the settlement and trial process. The flow sheet, properly constructed, is a simplification and clarification of the facts in a complex case. It can be helpful, then, to include it in a settlement brochure, or it can be given to a judge and jury (without the questions and comments, of course). It is impressive to insurance adjusters to see a thorough analysis of the chart, and they in turn can present the chart to their medical advisers for evaluation. Judge and jury will almost certainly find a flow sheet helpful, and are likely to be impressed also. It is very difficult for them to keep track of all the facets and facts of a medical case, and even harder to keep them in temporal sequence. However, it is most important to note that a different type of flow sheet is normally necessary for such purposes. This is so because what is appropriate for analysis is not necessarily suited for purposes of presentation. The analytical version of the flow sheet should be *comprehensive*, including all relevant items. The persuasive version should be more *selective*, including only the more important items. This is not a recommendation to exclude anything that does not advance the lawyer's case; the flow sheet should honestly reflect all the relevant materials. The point that is being made is that the most telling facts should not be lost in a mass of details. Special flow sheets, like those outlined in the next section, are normally better suited for presentation to other parties in the case.

§ 3:6 More selective ways of presenting medical information

When a flow-chart is in a developed state and is being revised for presentation to a claims adjuster or to a court, some refinements may be in order.

1. First *the original flow sheet should be drastically pruned and shortened.* Only the essential items should remain. The simpler a presentation flow sheet can be made, the more effective it is likely to be.

2. Certain items may be selected out of the nurses' notes or some other part of the chart and presented as *special columns.* For instance, in a case concerning pneumonia, items representing the patient's temperature, white-cell counts, arterial blood gases (ABGs), and chest X-rays might each be located a separate column.

3. The chart may be made more effective, and certainly more convenient to read, by *locating related items side by side with one another.* In a diabetes case, for instance, the blood sugar and urinary sugar estimations obviously belong together. The reader should not have to jump around in the chart to find items that are closely related to one another. Which columns are juxtaposed to one another depends on the arguments or points that are being made. By proper selection and placement of the columns, the flow sheet can be made to tell its own story, and tell it very effectively.

4. The *relevant items can be circled in red or highlighted* in some other way to indicate their importance. This is particularly useful when only a few points are really crucial. To represent the case with a flow sheet or chart containing only those items looks suspicious, suggesting that all contrary information has been suppressed. Allowing the

flow sheet to outline the whole story but highlighting the essential and most telling points will help to avoid this criticism.

5. *Symbols can be substituted for words.* Many items in a chart can be represented graphically or highlighted or labeled by an accompanying symbol.

6. *Data can be processed into graphs or charts.* Graphs are particularly useful to represent the changes in a problem or a finding over a period of time. The worsening or improving of a back problem, or changes in mental problems relating to a head injury, can be represented by a set of graphs that effectively demonstrate the trend. Spreadsheet programs such as Excel or Lotus 1-2-3 make it relatively easy to take a set of figures and turn it into virtually any kind of chart or graph.

7. *Imagination and creativity are important* in selecting and processing information in order to make a case. One ingenious lawyer in a malpractice case used an empty column (labeled doctor visits) to make the point that his client had been almost abandoned by the physician. The contrast of this with a very full column containing the nurses' notes on the patient's condition was very telling. This is perhaps an unusual example, but it makes the point that the presentations should suit the case and make the appropriate points as clearly and effectively as possible.

§ 3:7 Summary and conclusion—is the flow-chart method energy efficient?

The flow-chart method of analyzing and presenting medical information is orderly and systematic. As the medical record is reviewed, a flow chart may have to be remade, perhaps several times, but each version derives from and improves on the previous one, incorporating its valuable parts in a fresh understanding of the case. It might seem, looking at the process, that a lot of work is involved, and it might likewise appear that it would be simpler just to sit down with a yellow pad and pencil and make notes. But what could be simpler than to take the record itself and mark it (adding questions and comments on the blank side of the previous page); the rest of the work can be carried out by support staff. When the other benefits of the system are considered, the matter is, in my opinion, beyond dispute. The flow-chart method is uniquely adapted for communication with other persons, especially with medical consultants. The back and forth process of consultation using a flow sheet as a medium of communication is more efficient, less tiring, and ultimately less time-consuming than any alternative of which I am aware. When, as is usually the case, a face-to-face interview with a consultant is arranged, the conference will be much more fruitful because mutual understanding has already been well advanced by the previous exchanges of opinion via the flow sheet. To be (or even to seem to be) brief, efficient, comprehending and non-wearisome are important qualities when dealing with practicing physicians.

In critical cases, especially malpractice cases, a very careful lawyer will copy the record as it arrives in the hospital and put the sealed original in the office safe. This sealed text will later act as the gold standard should any question of tampering with the record arise during litigation.

Chapter Four

The History and Physical Examination

§ 4:1 The importance of the history and physical (H&P)

The most basic procedure in clinical medicine is the patient interview, where the clinician talks to the patient, asks questions (taking the history) and then observes, touches, listens to heart and lungs, and generally examines the patient (the physical examination). In former times the H&P was the entire diagnostic armamentarium of the physicians, and they made good use of it, especially the history, which is the most important part. Diagnostic tests have become increasingly important and they appear, in public perception at any rate, to be the primary means of finding out what a patient's problems may be. Yet technological advances have not diminished the importance of the H&P. Weak diagnosticians rush to order a battery of tests. The competent take a history and examine the patient first.

§ 4:2 Locations in a medical record where the H&P may appear

From the beginning of a hospital admission and continuing through to final discharge, the patient will be interviewed and examined. The H&P will appear then in various parts of the patient's medical record, including:

- The admitting note of the admitting physician
- The discharge summary of the attending physician (dictated and transcribed)
- Doctors' progress notes (usually handwritten)
- Reports of consultants (handwritten or dictated)

The history and physical was essentially developed by doctors, but nurses, physical therapists, and medical professionals of all kinds also interview their patients, and they tend nowadays to record their findings in much the same way as the physicians. H&Ps will therefore be found in the records made by most of the ancillary staff. Some of these will be quite detailed. The nurse, conducting an admission interview, has a different perspective from that of the doctor, but the nurse's admitting note is often a fairly full one, and generally follows the outlines of the physicians' H&P. Physical therapists also tend to conduct a reasonably comprehensive initial interview and to organize their findings in the H&P format. The notes of the physical therapist, indeed, can be more helpful for compensation purposes in a musculoskeletal case than those of physicians.

§ 4:3 The outline of the history

The good clinician allows patients to describe their complaints in their own words. Some interjected questions may be required to elicit details and to keep the patient from wandering, but these should be as few as possible and never be leading questions. Later, however, this material must be organized in a suitable format:

1. *Chief complaints* (CC). These will be numbered and each entered on a separate line, with an added note indicating how long the condition had been present. For example:

   #1 HA x 3/12 [headaches for three months]

   #2 LBP X 5/52 [low back pain for five weeks]

2. *The history of the chief complaints* (HCC). Here the complaints are described in detail one by one in the numbered order. Important items here are the date when symptoms first appeared; the nature of the symptoms; the diurnal timing of the symptoms (e.g., starting in the morning and getting better as the day wears on); anything that seemed to bring on the problem; anything that made it worse; and anything that made it better. For example:

   #1 Headache began 3/12 ago; severe, continuous ache felt mainly at the top and back of the head; begins late afternoon or early evening and may be precipitated by stress; is not helped by ASA (aspirin)

3. *Past medical history* (PMH). This will list previous surgeries and serious illnesses and indicate their present status. For example:

   PMH: Gall bladder surgery 1999, no continuing or recurrent problems; adult onset diabetes mellitus (ADOM) diagnosed 2004, controlled by diet and hypoglycemic medications.

Included under this heading, or perhaps presented as separate categories, are such things as allergies (especially to drugs or to iodine) and continuing medications.

4. *Family history*. This lists any diseases which tend to occur in the family, such as diabetes, heart disease, mental disorders and cancer.

5. *Personal history.* This should include anything in the lifestyle of the patient which is relevant to the condition. Alcohol, tobacco or other drug use are usually noted here. For example:

   PH: ETOH = 0 PY = 20 [does not use alcohol at all but smokes cigarettes equivalent to 20 pack year, i.e., has smoked one pack a day for twenty years]

6. *Occupational history*. This notes the employment of the patient when this may be relevant to the condition, such as an allergic dermatitis, which may be caused by something they are encountering in their working environment.

7. *Menstrual history and obstetrical/gynecological history* may be added in female patients. The menstrual history would note the age at which menses first began (or ended in an elderly patient), and whether and how they were abnormal. The obstetrical history would note the number of children born alive, the number of miscarriages, and the number of stillborn children, if any. Any complications of pregnancy or childbirth should also be given. For example:

MH: Menses began aged 14, nil abnormal.

OB/GYN G3 P2 A=1 [gravida (pregnant) three times, parous (delivered) twice, one abortion].

8. *The review of systems* (ROS) which is sometimes called the systematic questions(S/Q). This is simply a safety net, a set of questions asked to makes sure that focusing on the main problems has not led to overlooking others. The ROS can be carried out in a number of ways, but is commonly approached by asking a series of questions covering possible complaints in each body system. The information elicited by the responses might then be arranged as follows:

CNS [central nervous system]:- *No-complaints other than the above*

EENT [Eyes, ears, nose and throat]:- *N/C* [non-contributory]

RSS [respiratory system]:-*frequent chest colds*

CVS [cardiovascular system]:- *N/C*

MSS [musculoskeletal system]:- *N/C*

GIS [gastrointestinal system]:- *N/C*

GU [genitourinary system]:- *Past history of kidney stones*

Endocrine:- AODM as above, otherwise N/C

IS [integumentary system or skin]:- *N/C*

§ 4:4 The report of the physical examination

The physical examination (PE) can be organized in either of two ways. It can proceed (like the review of systems) through the various body systems (CNS, CVS, MSS, etc.), or it can be arranged around body parts such as head and neck, chest, abdomen and extremities. Commonly it is a mix of the two. For example:

Head and Neck:- PERRLA, EOMI, fundi benign, ears nl; neck supple

Chest:- Clear to IPPA [inspection, palpation, percussion & auscultation]

Cor [heart]:- *BP* [blood pressure] *120/80 HR* [heart rate] *80/min & regular, HS nl 2AA 0 m* [heart sounds normal, two in all areas, no murmurs]

ABD:- soft, LKKS = 0 [liver, both kidneys and spleen not enlarged] *0 hernias, 0 masses*

Ext [arms and legs] *MAEs nl* [moves all extremities normally]

CNS:- A&O x 3 [alert and oriented to place, time and circumstances] *cn ii—xii GI* [cranial nerves 2–12 grossly intact]. *PTCS nl* [power, tone, coordination and sensation normal]

DTRs [deep tendon reflexes]:- *BR., TR., KJ & AJ ++/++++ & =* [biceps reflex, triceps reflex, knee jerk and ankle jerk present normally and equal]

§ 4:5 Assessment and Plan

Assessment (A) is the current term for what used to be termed the diagnosis (*Dx*). It a less threatening notion, and does not carry the implication that one knows the patient's diagnosis or diagnoses with any degree of certainty. It merely states what the clinician's best opinion may be as to the underlying cause or causes of the patient's problems. If the clinician has no idea what the diagnoses may be, it is perfectly legitimate to simply say so. It is more usual, however, to list a few possibilities as working hypotheses (the differential diagnosis). These may be accompanied by a question mark to indicate that they are tentative suggestions, not established or even probable diagnoses. The list should be headed by the more serious possibilities (diagnoses of exclusion). These will commonly be designated *R/O* (rule out). for example:

> *Assess #1 Headaches. Probably tension headaches but R/O brain tumor; R/O Post herpetic neuralgia.*

The plan (P) represents what the clinician proposes to do about the perceived problems of the patient. If no clear plan suggests itself, it is perfectly proper to acknowledge the fact. It is usual, however, to offer some suggestions, either in the form of proposed tests or possible consultations which might help to establish a diagnosis and begin appropriate treatment. For example:

> *Plan: #1 CT scan of brain*
> *#2 Psychiatric consult to Dr. Brain*
> *#3 Fluorescent antibody testing for herpes virus*

§ 4:6 The problem-oriented medical record

The problem-oriented medical record, mentioned earlier, was devised by Dr. Lawrence Weed, an internist in Vermont. It is a very logical system and was influential for a time, until doctors and nurses discovered that it took a considerable amount of time and effort to construct and maintain it. It then largely fell into disuse, although two of its items remained popular. These are:

1. The use of the flow sheet in intensive care units, to make it easy for incoming staff to quickly become aware of a critically ill patient's condition.
2. The use of the SOAP mnemonic to organize the information obtained in the H&P. SOAP stands for: *S* is subjective (what the patient tells you); *O* is objective (what you find out by examining the patient); *A* is assessment (what you think is wrong with the patient); and *P* is plan (how you propose to treat the patient's problems). *A* (assessment) in the Weed system replaces *Dx* (diagnosis) in the older format; it allows for the possibility that the examiner does not know what the diagnosis is, and can therefore more modestly give a list of possibilities (the differential diagnosis). *P* (plan) replaces the older term *Tx* (treatment), again recognizing that the examiner may not know how to treat the patient. The Weed system allows for this and the examiner may simply give a list of possibilities or even suggest a consultation to someone who might be able to make a more definite diagnosis.

It would seem, however, that the POMR, more or less in its original form, will come back into general use, since the Medical Informatics organization in Chicago has indicated that it is the only system of medical record keeping which is suited for the computer age.

Chapter Five

Low Back and Neck Injuries

Introduction

§ 5:1 The prevalence and significance of back and neck injuries

The numbers that are bandied about for diseases and conditions vary a good deal. To some extent this is due to whether we are talking about prevalence or incidence. Prevalence refers to the number of people (usually in 100,000) who will be found to have had a condition within a given time frame and area. Incidence usually refers to the number of new cases of any condition appearing in a given year. Figures given for either the prevalence or the incidence of any condition will also vary depending on how the condition is defined. If we are considering the number of people who complain of low back pain (LBP) at any time during their lifetimes, the number will be large, perhaps approaching 90%. If, on the other hand, we only consider those who see a doctor for a back condition, both the incidence and the prevalence will be much lower. Nevertheless, however defined, low back pain (LBP) is a common condition, probably the commonest occupational medical problem that comes to the attention of lawyers. Neck pain, deriving from a whiplash type of injury, is also a very common complaint following an automobile accident. Any disorder affecting the musculoskeletal system can turn up in a legal claim, but these two, neck and low back injuries, are the most common, and, moreover, the ones that lawyers find most difficult to evaluate. Thus a chapter on musculoskeletal problems designed for lawyers should focus on these issues, and treat other matters as somewhat peripheral. So, while some explanation of the musculoskeletal system and its diseases will be given here, the discussion of neck and low back injuries will loom large, and other matters will be treated somewhat cursorily.

§ 5:2 The importance of bones for lawyers

Besides the fact that they get injured in accidents, bones have another very important function for lawyers (and doctors too, for that matter). They are important anatomical markers, which can be used to indicate the position of all sorts of other things. An injury will be located, if possible, in relation to the nearest bone. Long bones are conventionally divided into three parts for this very purpose: the part farthest from the midline of the body (median) being termed the *distal* third, the one nearest the body the *proximal* third, and the remaining one the *middle* third. A laceration of the forearm might thus be described as being at the junction of the middle third (M/3) and the distal third (D/3) of the ulna.

A great many other body parts, e.g., arteries, veins and nerves, are likewise located by an adjacent bone. For example, the common iliac artery in the pelvis is named for the nearby iliac bone. The common iliac artery divides into the internal and external iliac arteries. As the internal iliac artery passes beneath the inguinal ligament into the leg, next to the femur, it is called the femoral artery. In the lower leg it again divides into the anterior (front) and posterior (rear) tibial arteries, the one passing before and the other behind the tibia. The bottom line, then, is that a knowledge of the principal bones and their names is useful in order to know where many body parts are located. A brief review of the principal bones of the body, and of their locations, is therefore a necessary prelude to the discussion of musculoskeletal injuries.

Part I.
Anatomy and Physiology

§ 5:3 The constituents of the musculoskeletal system—bony and soft tissues

The musculoskeletal system does not consist only of muscles and bones, as the name might suggest. The system also includes other tissues, including ligaments, tendons, cartilage, and fibroelastic tissue. The components of the M/S system are often classified into bony and soft tissues, and this arrangement, while not really satisfactory medically, has advantages so far as lawyers are concerned. For compensation purposes, this crude division is generally sufficient, since bony and non-bony injuries tend to present different legal problems. Bony injuries (fractures) are generally easier to prove, and calculation of damages is also simpler; whereas with soft tissues, proof is more difficult and the deficits may be less obvious. Nevertheless, since bones are the central tissue around which the others are arranged, it is important that lawyers should know something about them. We will begin here then, as purely medical texts normally do, by describing the nature and functions of bones.

§ 5:4 The basic anatomical structure of bones

Bone is astonishingly light. This is because it is not a solid tissue. Under a thin solid *cortical* layer lies a maze of tiny tunnels separated by thin walls called *trabeculae.* This trabecular arrangement, like the geodesic framework used by aeronautical engineers, provides maximum strength with minimum weight. The trabecular walls are lined by two kinds of living cells; *osteoclasts* which are continually breaking them down and *osteoblasts* which are rebuilding them again. The net result of these two activities, destructive and constructive, is that the tunnels are constantly being realigned in the direction of the lines of force applied to the bone. Bone has indeed been described as a very viscous fluid, constantly flowing into new shapes to meet new circumstances.

The central part of a bone is known as the medulla (bone marrow). In infancy, the marrow of virtually all bones is busy producing red cells and other blood components. As we grow older, most of this red marrow is replaced by fatty tissue (yellow marrow), but some active areas remain, mostly near the ends of long bones. It is important to remember that bones do not merely act as the structural support of our bodies. Besides producing red

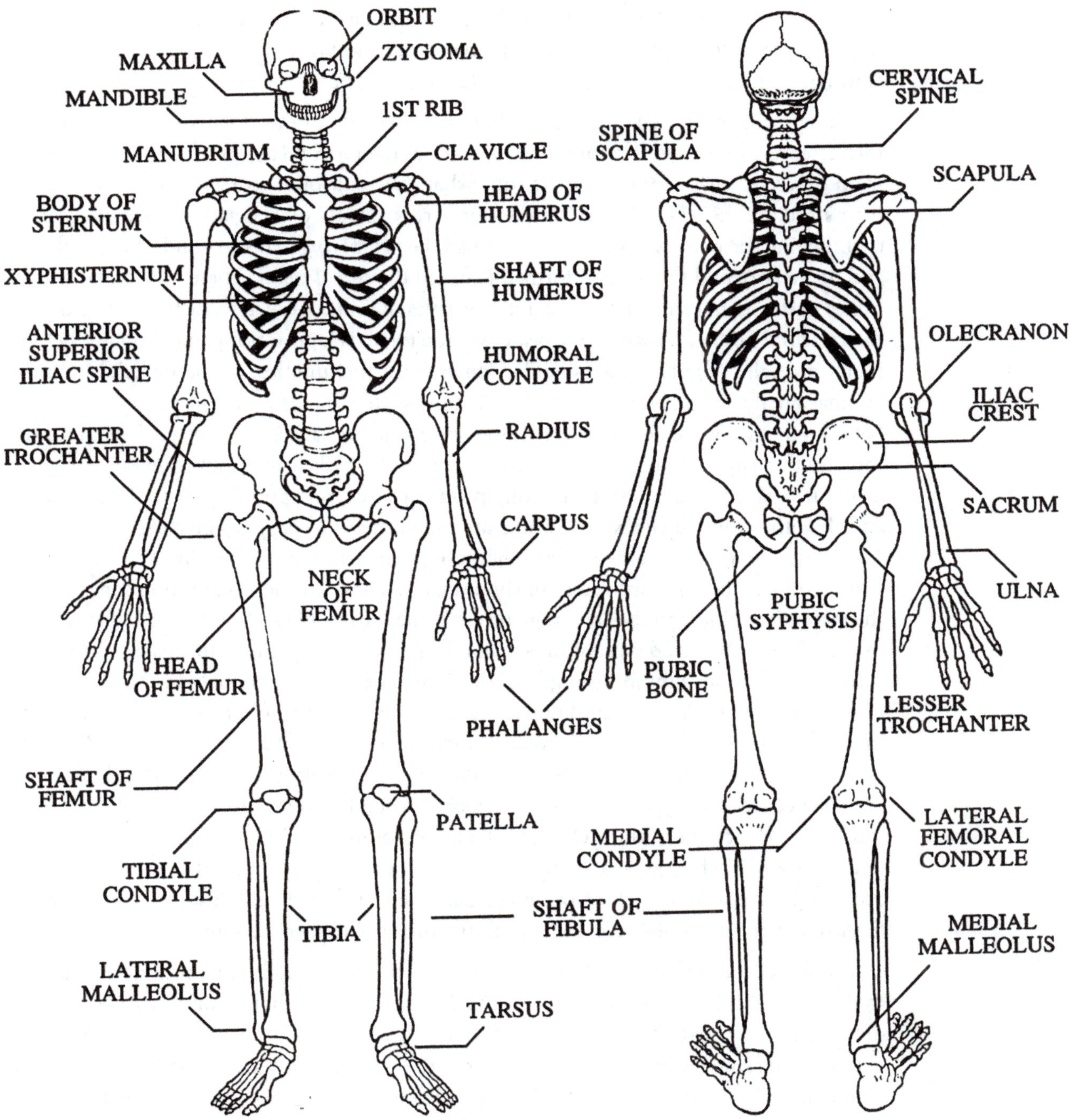

Fig. 5-1 Anterior and posterior views of the human skeleton

cells, already noted, they are the site for the production of a great many immune proteins that are important in host defense against infection and cancer. The bones also act as a reservoir of a number of minerals, notably calcium.

§ 5:5 Structure of the axial skeleton

The spinal column (axial skeleton) is the central part of the skeleton. It is particularly important from the legal perspective, since two of the most common compensation problems (low back pain and neck sprains) are located in this area.

The spine is composed of a series of bones, one on top of the other, which are known as the vertebral bones, and is commonly described as the *vertebral column*. The vertebral bones from different parts of the spine are somewhat different, but there is a general likeness in their structure. [See Fig. 5-16.] The anterior part is a solid body (*soma*), the weight-bearing part. Behind the body is a ring of bone termed the *neural ring* that surrounds the spinal cord and the nerves, and the tube so formed is called the *spinal canal*. There are several named bones in the neural ring. The most anterior pairs of bones, directly attached posteriorly to the vertebral bodies, are called the *pedicles* (little feet). The posterior pairs of bones, behind them, are called the *laminae* (singular *lamina*). At the junction of the pedicles with the laminae are the *lateral processes,* which function as attachments for muscles. At the junction between the two laminae posteriorly is the *dorsal process*. This acts as an attachment for the muscles that support the spine. At the junction of the pedicle and the lamina on each side of the neural ring, there are small bony protuberances, one pointing rostrad (headward) and the other caudad (tailward). These are called the *articular processes* (joint processes). They articulate with the joint processes of the adjacent vertebrae at tiny joint surfaces (facets) which connect the bone above and the bone below. These little joints are commonly termed the *facet joints,* although they are more properly the *zygoapophyseal joints*. Each of these little joints allows only a modicum of movement, but cumulatively, they can rotate or otherwise move the vertebral column through 18° or more. The bony part in between the upper and lower facet joint surfaces on each bone is called the *pars interarticularis* (the part in between the joints). It is congenitally defective in a sizeable percentage of the population (1% among males of Irish extraction). Bone begins in the foetus as cartilage, which is first calcified and then turned into bone by the action of osteoblasts (building bone) and osteoclasts (breaking it down). The actions of these cells give it a honeycomb appearance, in effect creating a geodesic structure which is very strong and very light. When this process stops short of true bone in the zygoapophyseal region, it is weak, and the weak area, known as a *pars interarticularis defect*, or simply a *pars defect,* can fracture and render the spine unstable.

The spinal cord occupies the *neural canal* (spinal canal), and it remains a solid structure to the L1 level (*first lumbar vertebra*). Caudal to this point, it divides up into a series of individual cords, known descriptively as the *cauda equina* (horse's tail). The peripheral nerves exit from the spinal canal into the body through openings between the pedicles, called the *neural foramina* (*foramen* means "window"). There is also a space at the back between one neural ring and the next. A needle can be inserted at this point into the spinal canal to give a spinal anesthetic or to draw fluid off in a spinal tap. [See Fig. 5-19.]

The axial skeleton contains one of the important shock-absorbing systems of the body (another being the muscles of the legs). In between the vertebral bodies there are *intervertebral discs*. These are, in effect, fibrous bags with a jelly-like center. The tough fibro-elastic outer covering is called the *anulus fibrosus,* and the central part is known as the *nucleus pulposus*. The outer part is called a ring (*anulus*), because the early anatomists only saw the edges of it poking out between the vertebral bodies. They did not realize that it was a complete sac.

Each time we jump, take a step, or even stand up, force is transmitted downwards onto the intervertebral discs, which flatten down and spread outward. The energy of the impact is absorbed by the anulus fibrosus and also by the anterior and posterior *longitudinal ligaments* that run down anterior and posterior to the discs all the way from the skull to the sacrum. These ligaments contain a good deal of elastic tissue. The posterior longitudinal ligament not only absorbs force, it also protects the spinal cord and the nerve roots as the discs flatten and expand backward under pressure. When these protective mechanisms are impaired by injury or disease, the nucleus pulposus can push through and past the ligament to touch on the nerves and cause nerve root irritation. This radicular pain shooting down the back of the leg is the classical presenting symptom of an *acute intervertebral disc* problem or (in popular terms) a ruptured disc. There are, of course, other presentations of disc disease.

§ 5:6 The main divisions of the vertebral column

The spinal column is conventionally divided into four (or five) sections. [See Fig. 5-2.] The seven bones above the rib cage (in the neck) are called the *cervical spine* (*cervix* means "neck"). The twelve vertebrae below this—each of them having ribs attached—comprise the *dorsal spine* (thoracic spine). Caudal (tailward) to this are five bones without ribs called the *lumbar spine*. Lower again are five bones, which are usually fused together at birth, and so are usually called the *sacrum* rather than the sacral spine. A significant percentage of people have an opening or defect in the back of the sacrum that can be felt with the finger that can be used to inject local anesthetic into the CSF. This procedure is called a *caudal block*, and it was formerly in common use in obstetrical practice. The tailbone, still further caudal, properly consists of five bones and is called the *coccyx*. However, the coccygeal bones, like the sacral bones, are usually fused together into a single bone before birth, or sometimes into two or three units. They can project into the birth canal during delivery and hinder the descent of the baby's head.

§ 5:7 The spinal curvatures

A curvature which is concave (hollowed out) posteriorly is called a *lordosis*, and there are two normal lordoses, one in the cervical region and the other, much more noticeable, in the lumbar region. A curvature which is concave anteriorly is called a *kyphosis*. The dorsal (thoracic) spine has a normal kyphosis. A sideways curvature is called a *scoliosis* and it is always abnormal. Tuberculosis of the spine, if untreated, can result in spinal deformities, typically a marked scoliosis and increased dorsal curvature of the thoracic spine, the hunchback deformity, which was common in former times.

§ 5:8 Skeletal appendages—the costal bones (ribs)

There are 12 pairs of ribs. The first six sets of ribs come around to meet the sternum (breast bone) on the front. The remaining six do not. Four of the last six ribs attach to costal cartilage which connects them indirectly both to the adjacent ribs and also to the sternum. The last two ribs are floating ribs. They do not attach to anything but "hang free." The junctions between ribs and cartilages are called *costochondral junctions* (*costa* means rib and *chondron* means cartilage). Sometimes these costochondral joints, or *C-C joints* as

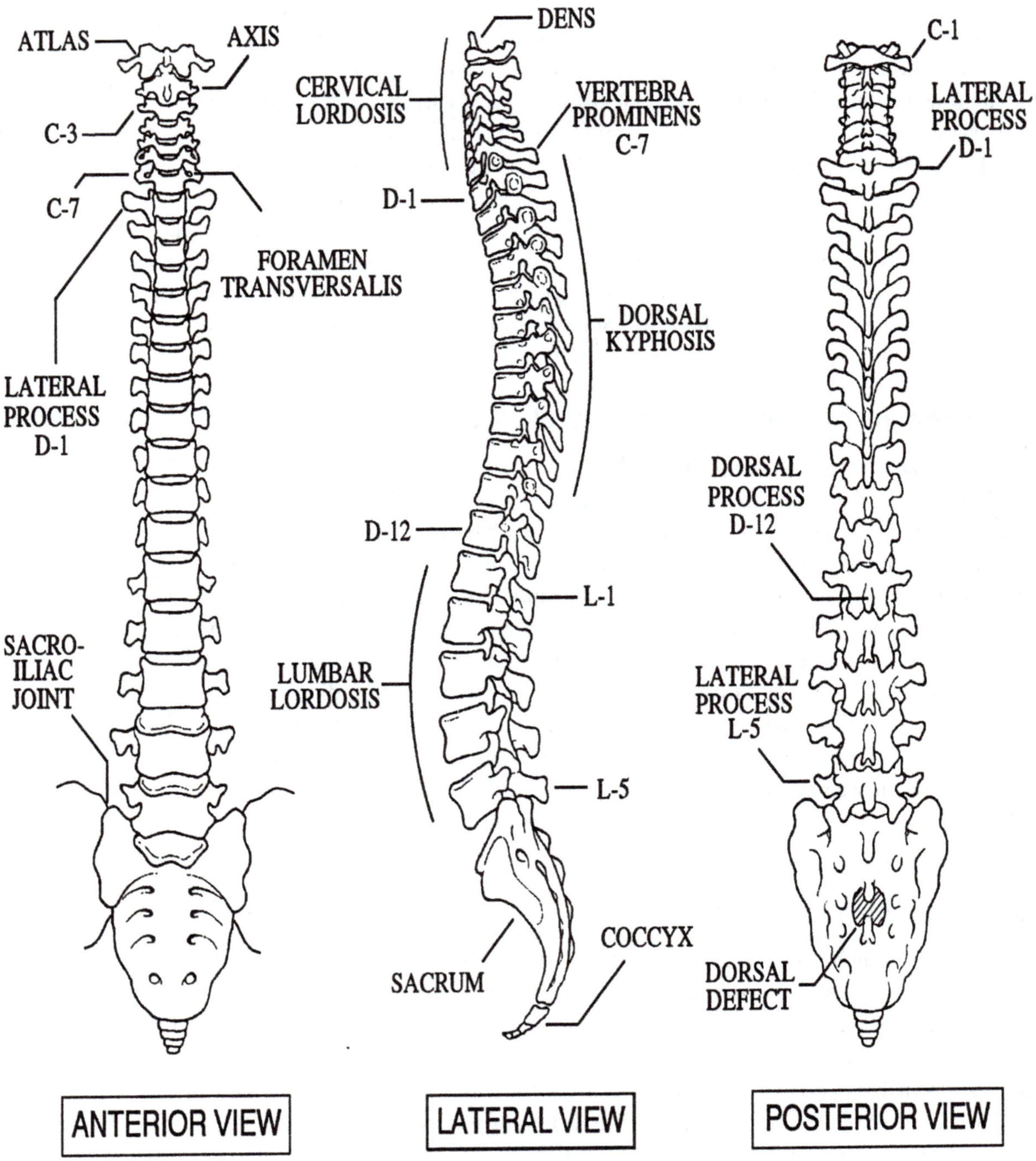

Fig. 5-2 Anterior, lateral, and posterior views of the vertebral column

they are called, become irritated or inflamed and can cause considerable pain. This is *costochondritis* or inflammation of the costochondral joints, and it is a fairly common cause of chest pain. Patients with pain coming from these joints often need to be checked out with cardiac tests to make sure that the pain is not coming from the heart.

The ribs protect the important contents of the chest, the heart and the lungs. They also take part in breathing and do so in two ways. First of all they form an expandable box which

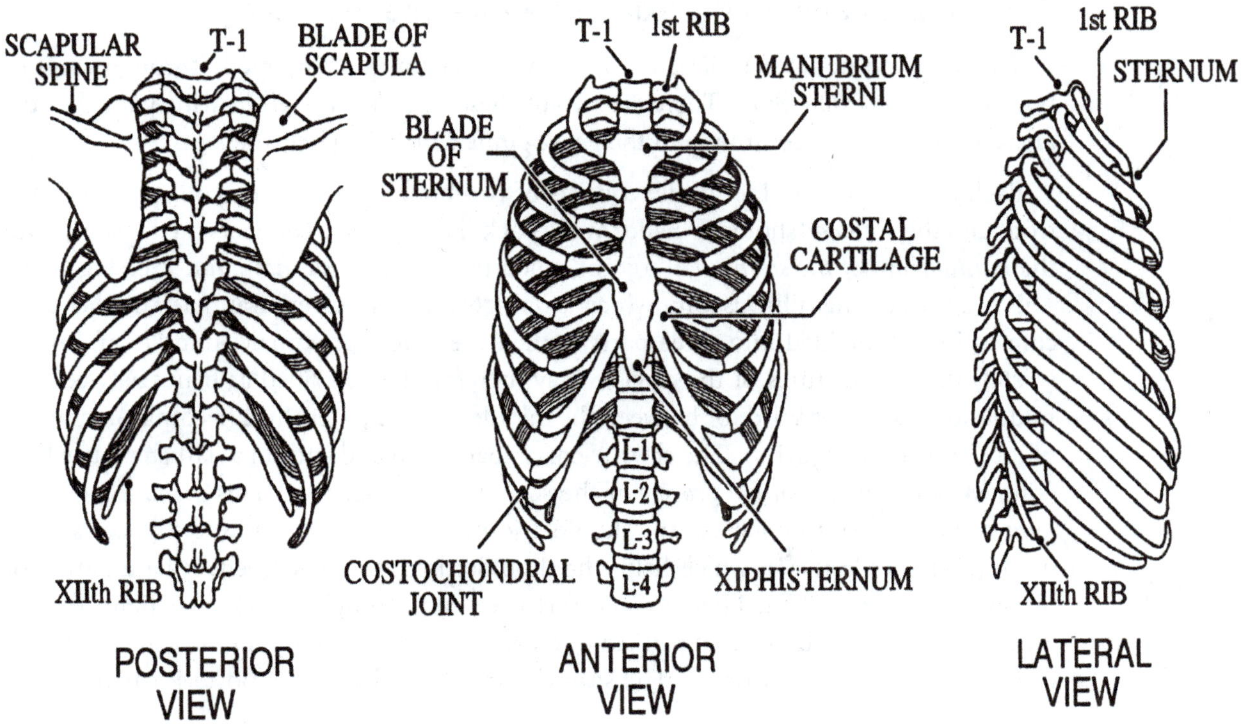

Fig. 5-3 The rib cage: posterior, anterior, and lateral views

is sealed airtight by the *pleural membranes* which surround the lungs. Thus when the diaphragm is pulled downward, the box becomes larger, a vacuum is created and air is sucked through the nose and mouth into the lungs. If there is a penetrating wound to the chest, this mechanism will not work. Air is sucked in through the hole in the chest into the space surrounding the lungs (the *pleural cavity*) where it is useless, and the lung (being an elastic tissue) will collapse in on itself. If several ribs are broken in two places so that part of the chest wall flaps free, the free flap simply moves in and out with respiration (flail chest) and very little air is pulled into the lungs. It is therefore very important in automobile accidents that penetrating wounds are sealed immediately, and that ultimately a drain be inserted to take the air out. It is also important to stabilize a flail chest so that the ribs may function normally in respiration.

The ribs can take an active part in respiration when required. Their joints and movements are cunningly contrived so that they move both sideways and forwards when the ribs are pulled upward by the intercostal muscles. The sideways movement is called bucket-handle movement, as the ribs lift outward like the handles of a bucket. The anterior displacement is called pump-handle movement, as the sternum slips forward and backward like the handle of a pump. Together the movements increase the volume of the chest and so extra air will be pulled in. This mechanism is not used in quiet respiration, but only when we exercise. People with chronic lung disease (COPD) have lungs that are already fully expanded due to the loss of elastic tissue. On chest X-rays their ribs can be seen to be already lifted upward and outward at rest in a manner only found in normal people during strenuous exercise. People with advanced emphysema, therefore, cannot breathe with their ribs at all, but only with their diaphragms. It is obvious from this that their exercise capacity will be very limited.

§ 5:9 Appendages to the axial skeleton—the shoulder girdle

The limbs do not attach directly to the axial skeleton, but indirectly through rings of bone called the *limb girdles*. There are two of these, the *shoulder girdle* which attaches the arms to the vertebral column, and the *pelvic girdle* which supports the legs.

Each half of the shoulder girdle consists of two bones, the *clavicle* (collar bone) at the front and the *scapula* (shoulder blade) at the back. Each clavicle connects (articulates) with the *manubrium of the sternum* at a joint called the *manubriosternal joint.* [See Fig. 5-4.] This is a very strong, fibrous joint which is only torn in very severe trauma. The clavicle is conventionally divided into three parts termed the inner (proximal), middle, and outer (distal) thirds. Fractures of the clavicle may therefore be described as being between the middle and the inner third, or between the middle and the outer third (a common method of localizing bony injuries). The clavicle curves backward and ends in a flattish plate which connects with the *acromion process* of the scapula. [See Fig. 5-4.] This *acromioclavicular joint* is the roof, so to speak, of the shoulder joint. Just under it is a little slippery sac, or *bursa* (Latin for "purse"), which helps the shoulder joint to move freely. Inflammation of the shoulder bursa is called *bursitis,* and it is a common complaint. These patients cannot lift their arms above 90° without pain, and sometimes a creaking (*crepitation*) can be palpated or even heard when they do so. The scapula (shoulder blade), the posterior bone of the

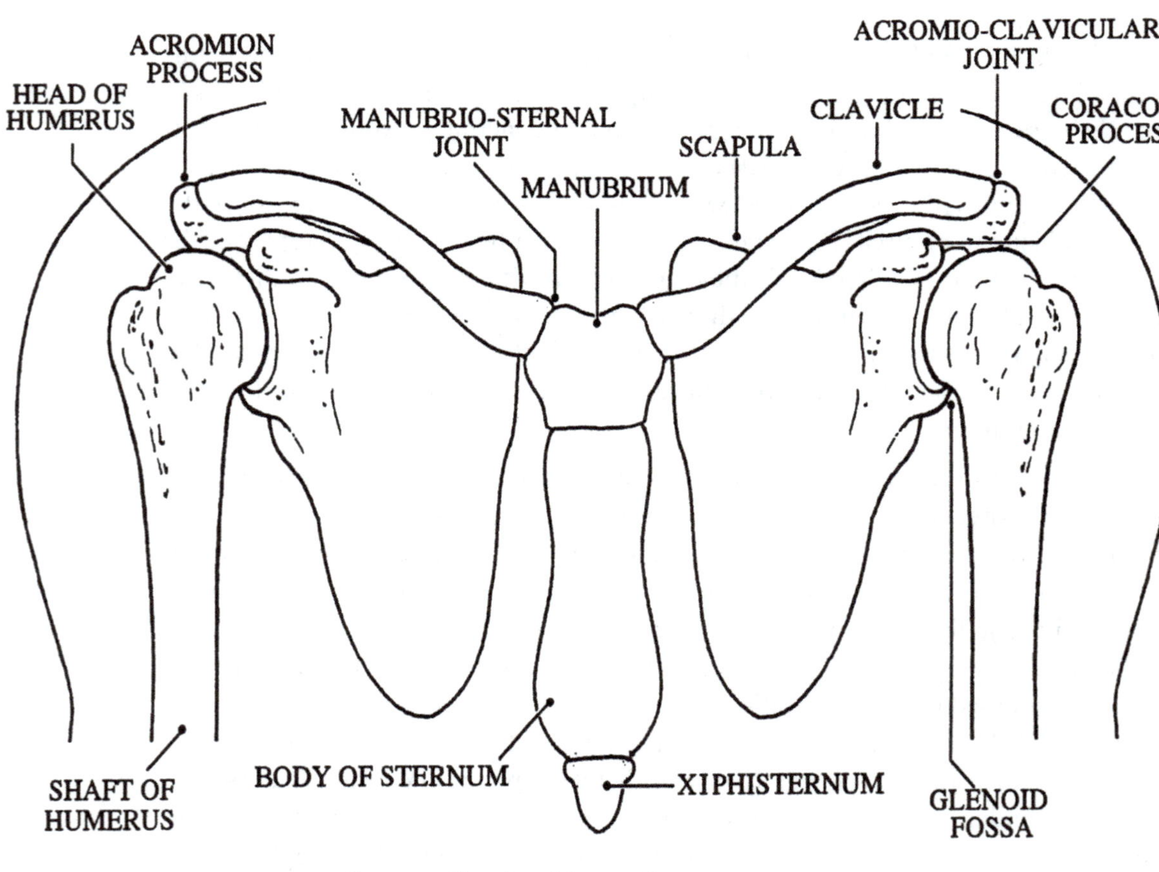

Fig. 5-4 The shoulder girdle, anterior view

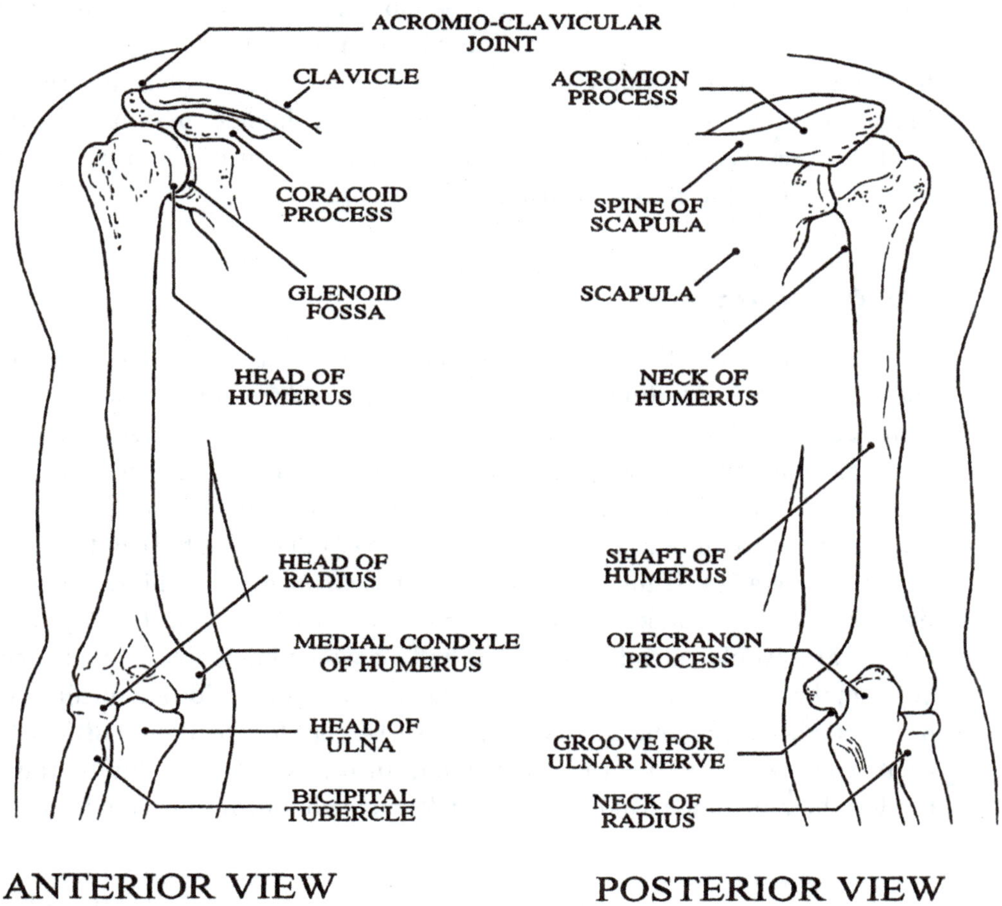

Fig. 5-5 The arm and elbow

shoulder girdle, is a flat bone which slides over the rib cage posteriorly to allow arm movement. It is divided into two parts—an upper and a lower—by a bony ridge called the scapular spine (*spine of the scapula*). Strong muscles attach above and below this spine and they are naturally called the *supraspinatus* and the *infraspinatus* muscles. These muscles help to stabilize the shoulder joint. The acromion process of the scapula, already mentioned, is an anterior projection from the scapular spine that articulates with the clavicle at the acromio-clavicular joint, thus forming a roof over the shoulder joint. There is another little process pointing forwards on the scapula [see Fig. 5-4] which looks like a crow's beak. The Greek word for "crow" is *corax*, and this process is called the *coracoid process*. It is the attachment for one of the muscles of the arm, appropriately called the *coracobrachialis* (*brachium* is Latin for "arm"). The scapula does not connect directly with the rib cage. It is mainly attached to the chest wall by the *rhomboid muscles*. This gives it a great deal of freedom to move, which is necessary in order that our arms may reach forward and in various directions freely. The *glenoid fossa* of the scapula, lying under the acromion, is the articulating surface for the head of the humerus. [See Fig. 5-5.] The fossa is decidedly shallow. This makes for great mobility of the arm, but not too much stability. Stability is largely maintained by several muscles that come from the chest wall (the shoulder girdle) and attach to the top of the *humerus* (or arm bone). The tendons of these muscles fuse together and are called the *rotator cuff*, which overlies and protects the shoulder joint. Also important is a little ring of cartilage (the *glenoid cartilage*) that sits out from the margins of the glenoid fossa and helps to keep the head of the humerus in place in the joint. This cartilaginous ring can be torn in a dislocation injury, which usually means that the shoulder may dislocate more readily the next time. When the shoulder joint dislocates too easily, too often, an operation is needed to repair the glenoid cartilage.

§ 5:10 The arm

The upper bone of the arm is called the *humerus*. It has a head, a neck, a shaft and two enlargements on the bottom, termed the *humoral condyles* (*condylos* is the Greek word for "knuckle"). [See Fig. 5-5.] A fracture above these condyles is called a *supracondylar fracture*. It is difficult to stabilize and generally a very nasty fracture indeed. The bony fragments can press on and endanger the brachial artery, so it is important with such a fracture to feel the pulse at the wrist and make sure it is still palpable. In between the condyles at the back of the humerus is a *fossa* (Latin for "ditch") called the *olecranon fossa*. This receives the olecranon process of the ulnar bone and limits extension of the elbow joint. If this process were cut off, the arm would extend beyond 180° and we would be double-jointed. There are two bones in the forearm. [See Fig. 5-6.] The *radius* on the outer side is a turning bone, and so has a little head (proximal end) with a flat surface apt for rotation; it articulates with the lateral condyle of the humerus. As the radius turns, its distal end travels around the ulna to allow the palm of the hand to be turned down, a movement which is known as *pronation*.

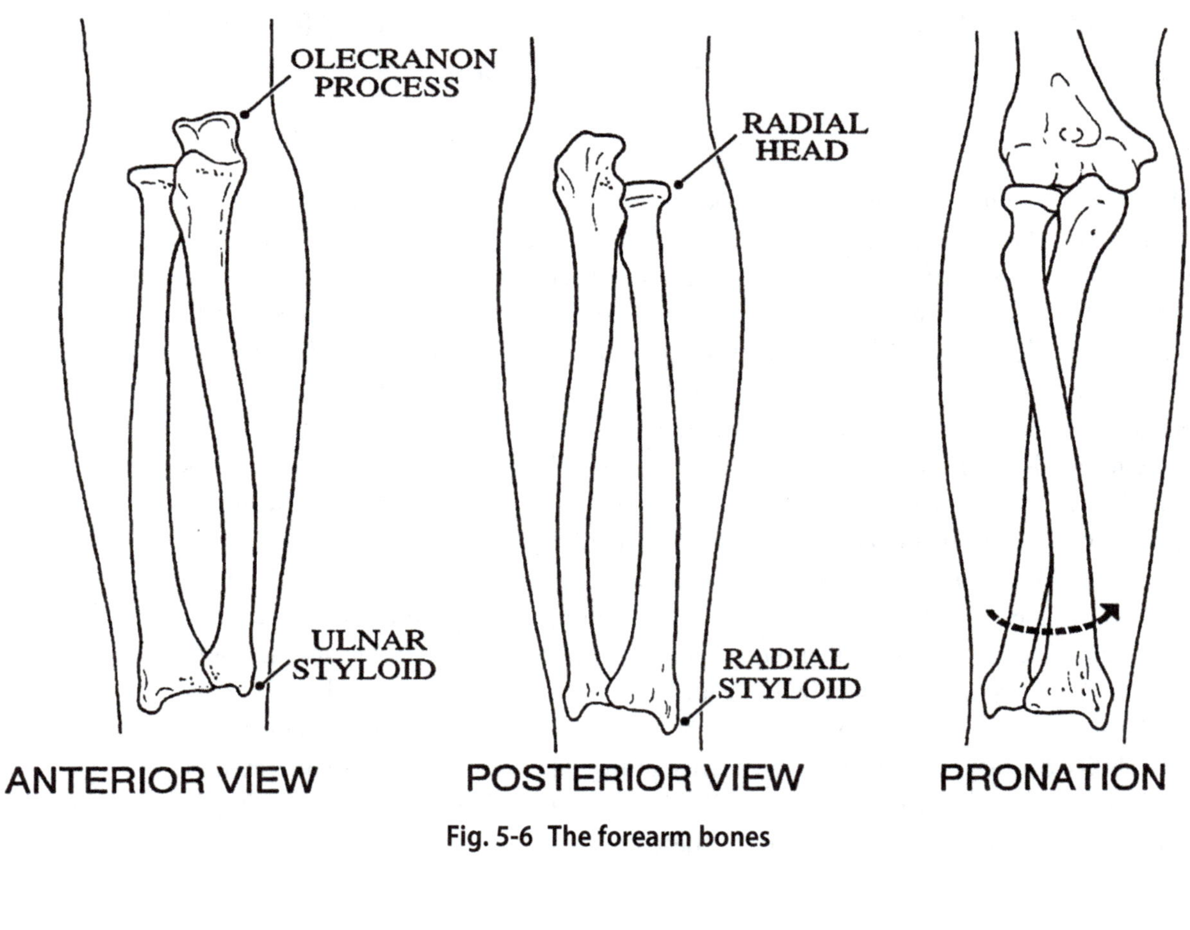

Fig. 5-6 The forearm bones

The reverse movement is called *supination*. Needless to say, the artery which runs by this bone is called the *radial artery*, and the accompanying nerve is called the *radial nerve*. The medial bone of the forearm is called the *ulna*, and it functions in flexion and extension of the forearm. The olecranon process, already mentioned, is its proximal end. As one would expect, the *ulnar artery* and *ulnar nerve* travel alongside the ulna. This side of the forearm (medial in the anatomical position) is also called its ulnar side, just as the opposite side is called the radial side.

§ 5:11 Appendages to the axial skeleton—the pelvic girdle

The pelvic girdle is divided into two halves, each attached to the skeleton. [See Fig. 5-7.] The large bones on each side are the *iliac bones* (*ilium* means "wing"). The broad top of each of these is called the *iliac crest*, and the bumps (tuberosities) on the anterior and posterior ends of this flattish area (*the iliac spines*) are important surface landmarks. The *anterior superior iliac spines* are two bony knobs which can easily be palpated on either side at the lower end of the abdomen. The *posterior superior iliac spines* appear in most people as two dimples low down on the back, and they can also be palpated through the skin. The two sacroiliac joints run downward and medially from a point just medial to each posterior superior iliac crest, and they are also palpable. The lower bones of the pelvis are

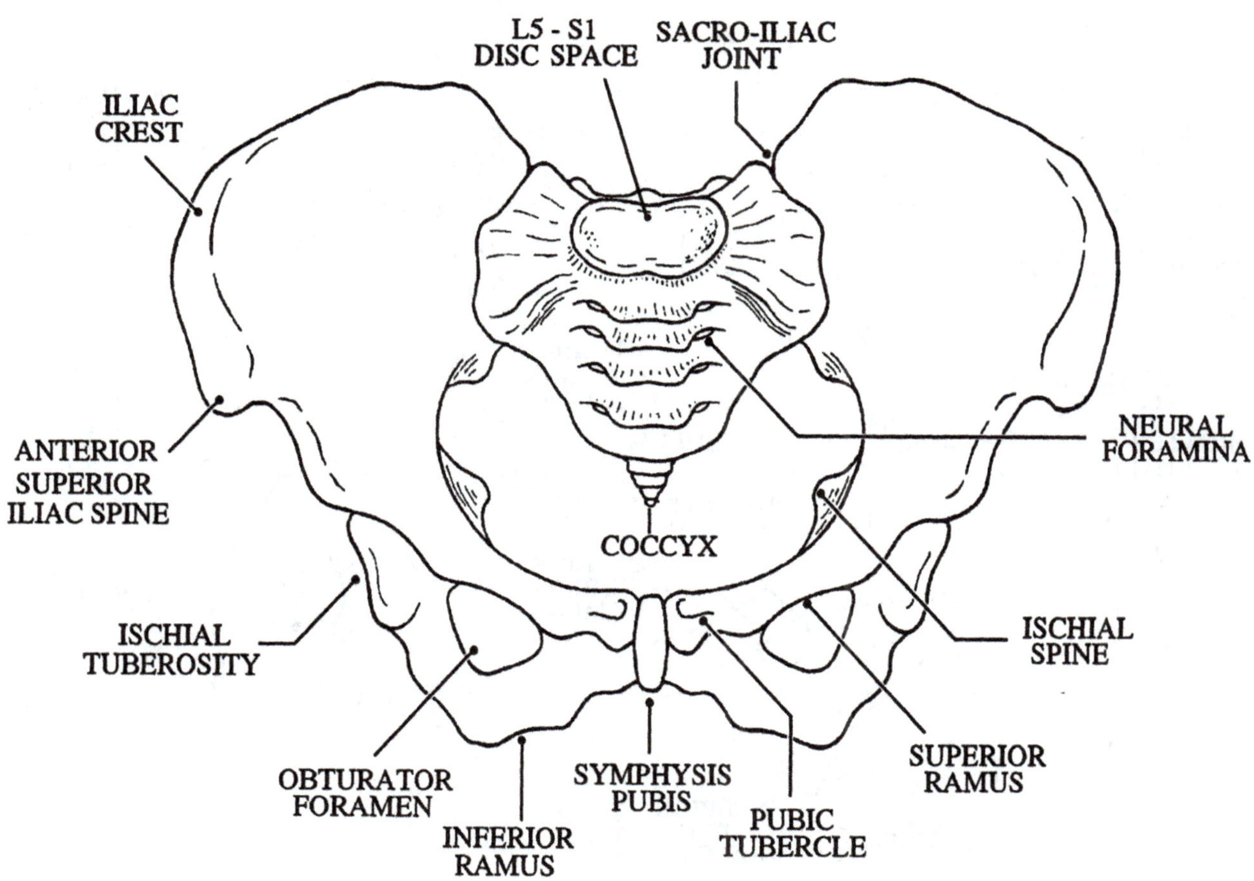

Fig. 5-7 The pelvic girdle, anterior view

called the *ischia* (ischial bones). Each ischium has two important landmarks, the *ischial spine* and the *ischial tuberosity.* The ischial spine can be felt on rectal or vaginal examination. This is a very important anatomical marker in obstetrics, because the progress of a baby's head in the birth canal during labor is measured by whether it has reached or passed the ischial spines. Nerve blocks are also put in at this point, since the pudendal nerve curls around the tip of the ischial spine. The ischial tuberosities are the bony prominences which support our weight when we sit. Patients who are paralyzed tend to sink down very heavily onto them in the sitting position. Continuous pressure by the ischial tuberosities in this manner produces ulceration of the overlying skin. These unfortunate people sometimes need to have the ischial tuberosities removed surgically to get rid of this pressure and allow the ulcers to heal.

The anterior bones of the pelvis are called the *pubic bones* (or collectively the *pubis*). [See Fig. 5-8.] Each of these bones has a central space called the *obturator foramen* which is covered by a sheet of connective tissue called the *obturator membrane.* The function of this opening is that it makes the pelvic ring lighter; nothing much comes through it. The upper arm of the pubic bone above the opening is called the *superior ramus* of the pubic bone, and the one below is called the *inferior pubic ramus* (*ramus* means "branch" or "arm"). The medial part of the pubic bone is called the body. The joint between the two pubic bodies is called the *symphysis pubis,* and it is an important anatomical landmark. It can easily be felt as the uppermost part of the pelvis anteriorly near the midline. So an incision may be described as beginning at the symphysis pubis and proceeding to the umbilicus (belly button).

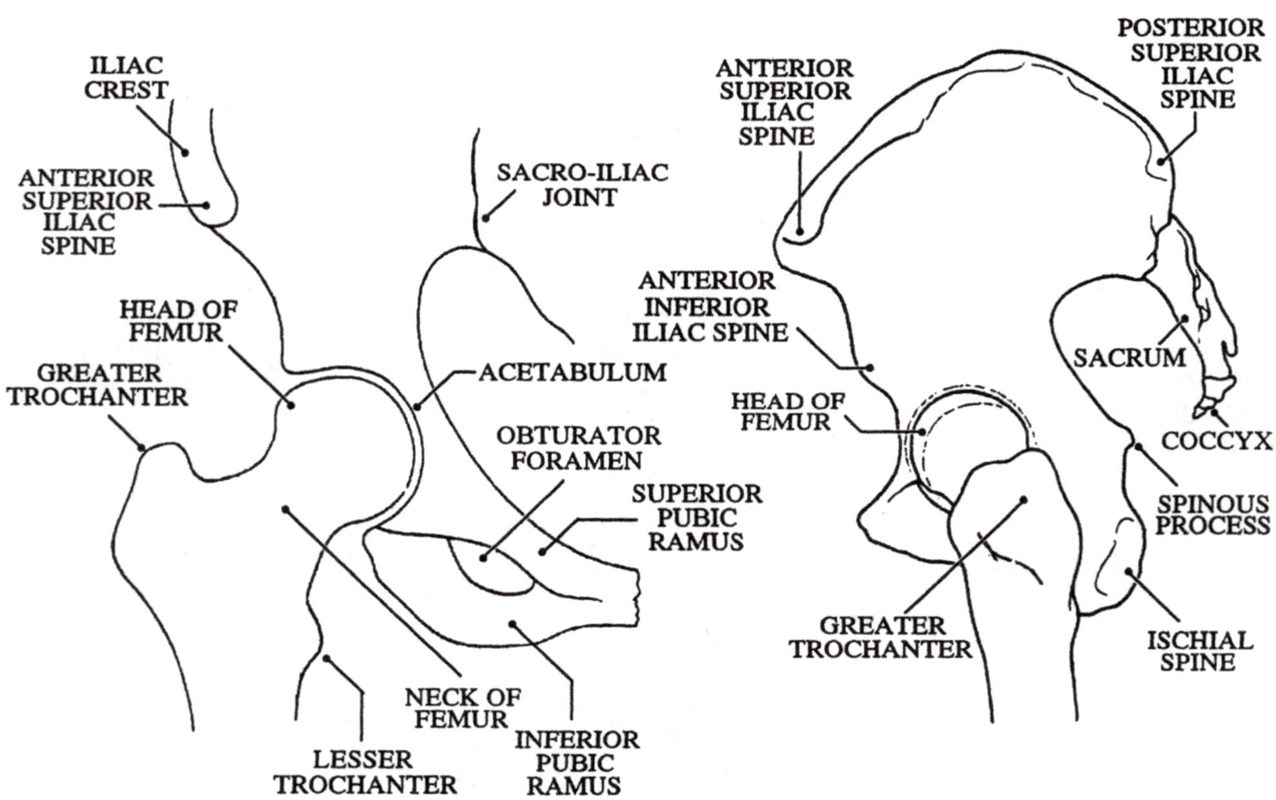

Fig. 5-8 The hip joint, anterior and lateral views

Likewise a bullet wound may be described as entering three inches above and two inches to the right of the symphysis pubis.

The deep articulating surface that receives the head of the femur is called the *acetabulum* and it receives a contribution from all three pelvic bones—the ilium, the pubis and the ischium. Sometimes the acetabulum is fractured in automobile accidents by the upward thrust of the femur. Acetabular fractures can cause arthritic problems later on, generally requiring joint replacement, which means that these are very nasty fractures in a young person.

§ 5:12 The leg

The *femur* has a head, a neck, and two large bumps on the upper end called the trochanters. There is the *greater trochanter* on the outside and the *lesser trochanter* on the inside. [See Fig. 5-10.] These act as bony attachments for muscles. Fractures frequently occur in elderly people in the *neck of the femur*. [See Fig. 5-9.] The management of femoral neck fractures depends mainly on the site of the break and so they are described rather precisely by various names. One just under the head of the femur is called a *subcapital fracture*. A fracture of the neck distal to this point will be described as a *high* or *low neck fracture*. A fracture that runs across between the trochanters is appropriately called an *intertrochanteric fracture*. A fracture between the trochanters may be immobilized by putting a pin (really a stout triangular nail) through the upper shaft and into the neck of the femur, where there is sufficient bone to fix it firmly. A subcapital fracture cannot be easily treated in this way because there is not enough bone to hold the nail. Also, the head of the femur may lose an important part of its blood supply, which travels from the acetabulum into the bone along with the *ligamentum teres*, which holds the head of the femur in place in its socket. [See Fig. 5-10.] Nasty fractures in this area and dislocations of the hip are therefore liable to result in tears to this ligament and ischemic damage to the head of the femur (known as *aseptic necrosis*). Subcapital fractures are therefore treated, as a rule, by surgically removing the head and replacing it with an artificial head such as an *Austin-Moore prosthesis*. Below the neck is the shaft of the femur, which, like the humerus, has enlargements at the distal end (*condyles*).

The lower leg, like the lower arm, has two bones. [See Fig. 5-12.] The *tibia* is a large weight-bearing bone. The top of it is rather flat and is called the *tibial plateau*. Fractures just below this area are called *plateau fractures*. They tend to be nasty fractures, difficult to reduce and immobilize. Lateral to the tibia is the *fibula*. The fibula is more or less a bony strut; it does not primarily bear weight but rather functions as an attachment site for muscles. The lower part of the fibula and of the tibia are expanded into *malleoli* (knuckles). These are the ankle bones. They function by keeping the ankles stable. The uppermost bone of the ankle (the *talus*) fits between these two expansions, and together they form a carpenter's mortise joint: indeed this arrangement is described as the *ankle mortise*. Ankle fractures are usually described by the number of malleoli involved, so that if both malleoli are broken it is called a bimalleolar fracture. There is also a little process on the dorsum of the tibia called the *posterior malleolus*. If this becomes broken off, the fracture is sometimes called a *trimalleolar fracture*. Ankle fractures tend to be unstable and commonly need to be surgically immobilized by pinning. They are also commonly accompanied by injuries to the ligaments

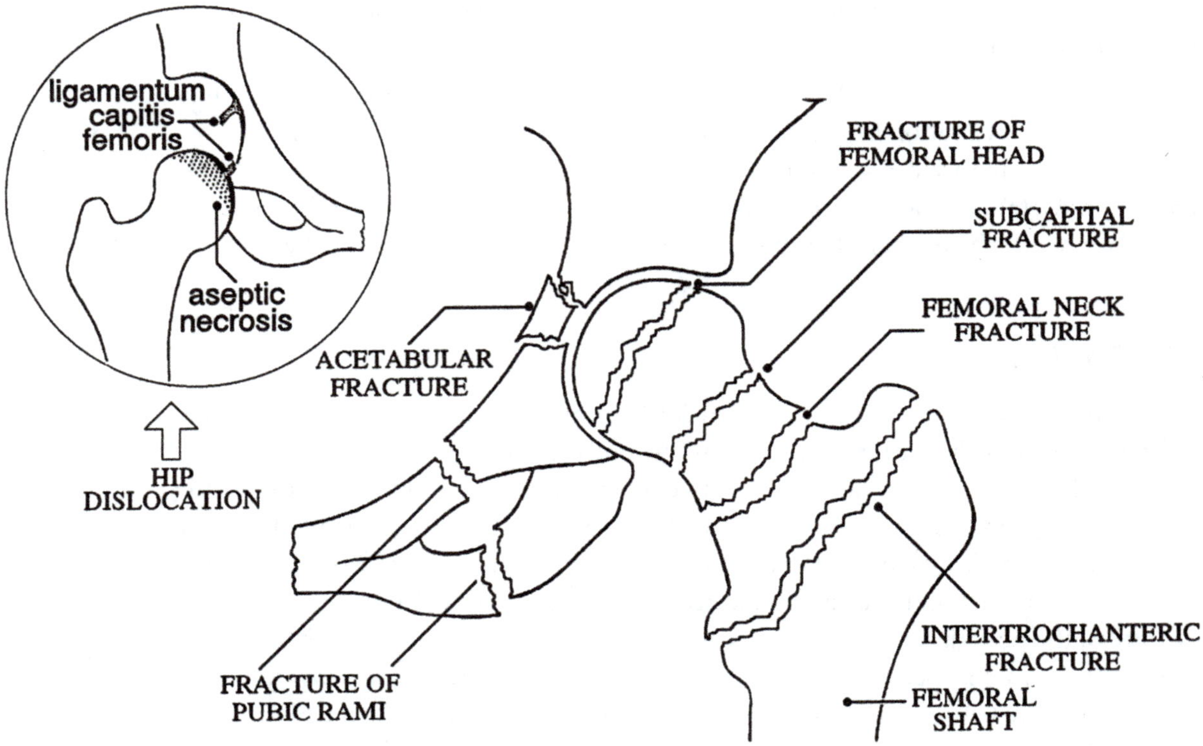

Fig. 5-9 Hip fractures, anterior view

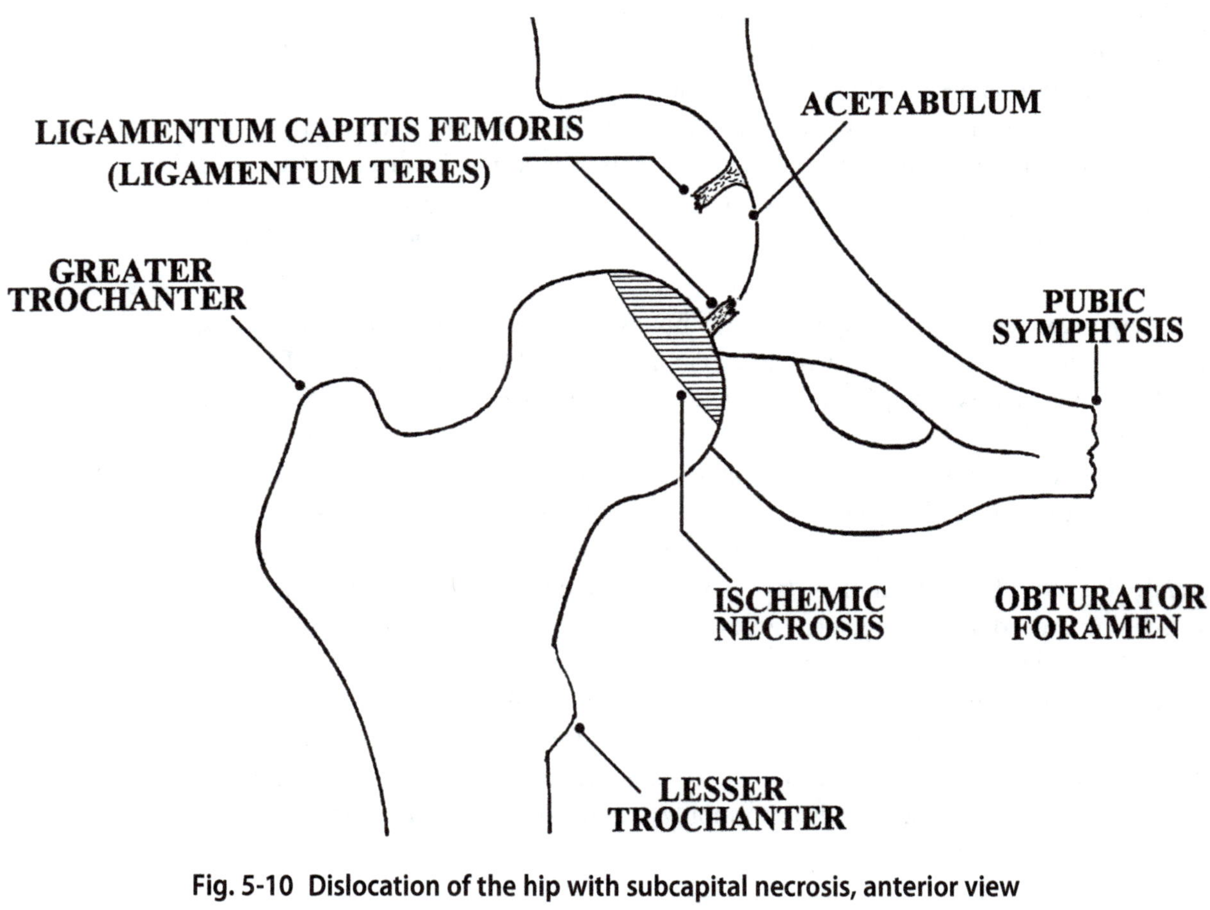

Fig. 5-10 Dislocation of the hip with subcapital necrosis, anterior view

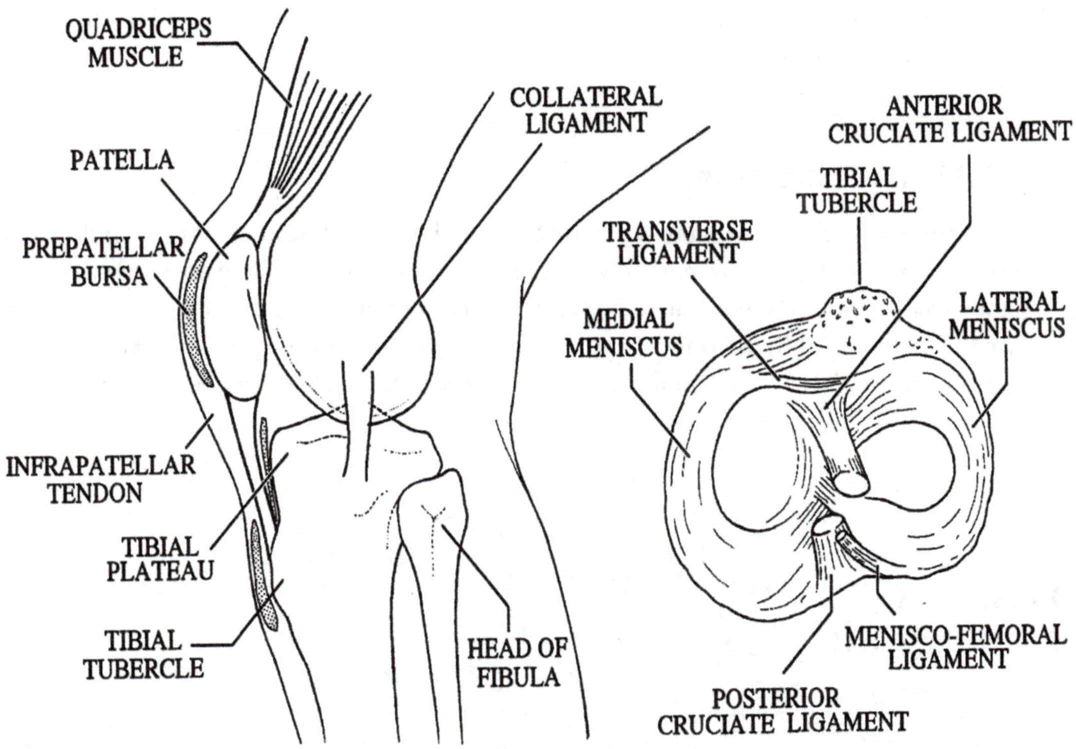

Fig. 5-11 The knee joint, lateral and superior views

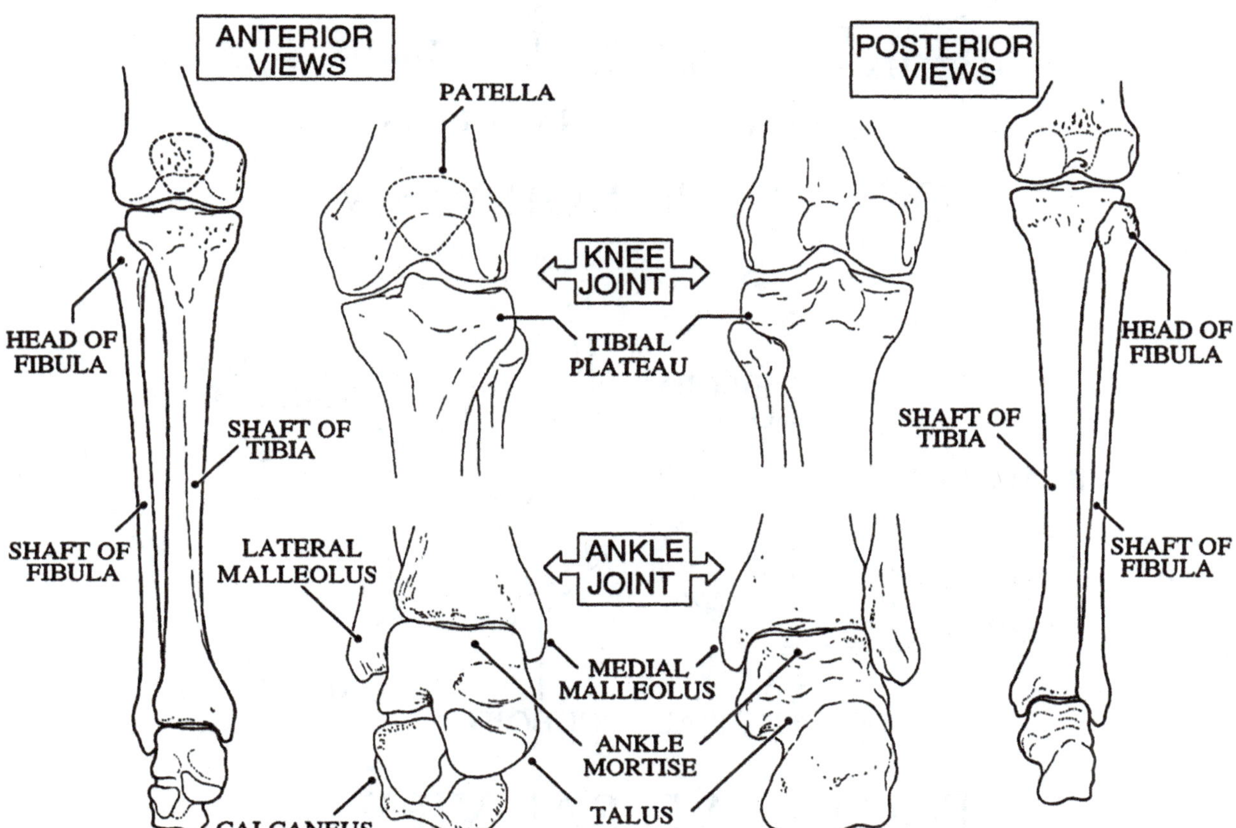

Fig. 5-12 The lower leg and ankle joint, anterior and posterior views

which hold the ankle together. These ligamentous injuries can be long lasting and may require surgical repair.

§ 5:13 The extremities

At the end of each arm is the wrist (*carpus*) and below each lower leg is the ankle (*tarsus*). [See Fig. 5-13] These are remarkably similar in general outline. There are seven wrist bones (the *carpal bones*). The equivalent bones in the foot are called the *tarsal bones*. Beyond these are the *metacarpals* (hand bones) and *metatarsals* (foot bones) respectively (*meta* is a Greek word meaning "after"). Beyond the metacarpals are the digits or *phalanges* (*phalanx* is the

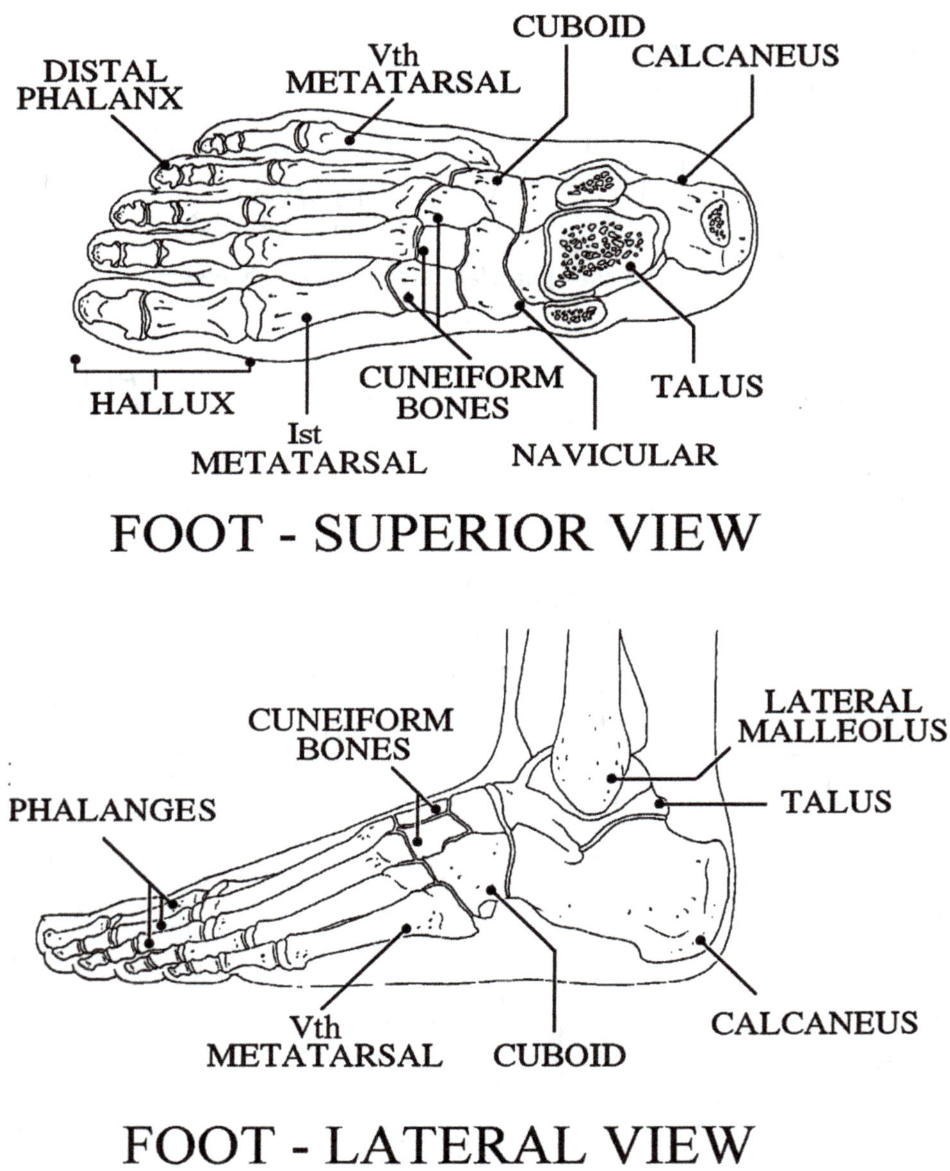

Fig. 5-13 The foot and ankle joint, superior and lateral views

Greek word for "finger"). The thumb and great toe are rather important digits, and each has a special name. The thumb is called the *pollex*, so the muscle which flexes it is called *flexor pollicis longus* (the long flexor of the thumb). The toe is called the *hallux*. Thus, the proper name for a bunion (when the big toe is deformed and points inward) is *hallux valgus*. This means a valgus (or inturning) deformity of the great toe. When the lower bone points outward, this is described as a *varus deformity*. The proper term for "knock knees" is therefore *genu varus*. The joints of the fingers are usually described in medical records by their letter abbreviations, which are therefore worth learning. They are the *metacarpophalangeal joints* (MP joints), the *proximal interphalangeal joints* (PIP joints), and the *distal interphalangeal joints* (DIP joints). Notice that the thumb only has a proximal and distal interphalangeal joint, (no interphalangeal joint) as does the great toe.

§ 5:14 The anatomical position—planes and movements

The anatomical position is the way in which the body is viewed by anatomists for purposes of description. Very simply it is represented by someone standing with the feet apart, the hands by the sides, the palms pointing forwards, and the thumbs directed outward (laterally). [See Fig. 5-14] A line drawn straight down the middle of the body and ending just between the two feet is called the *median*. Any movement in towards this line is called *medial* and any movement away from this is called *lateral*. There are also traditional planes which are

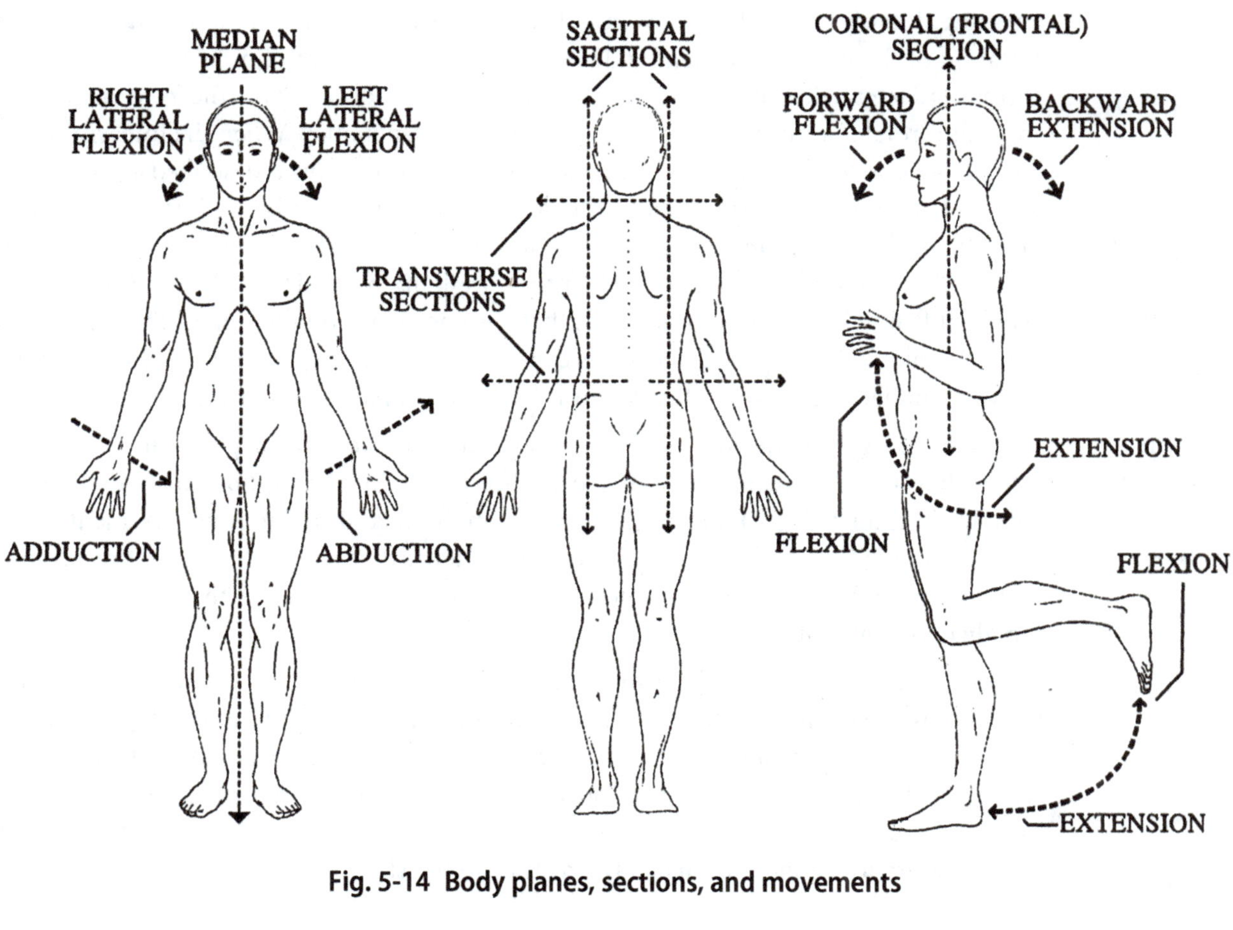

Fig. 5-14 Body planes, sections, and movements

thin sections through the body. The term section means "a cut," and they can indeed be considered as slices through the body made with an imaginary blade. Sections from the front to back are in fact called *sagittal sections* (*sagitta* is late Latin for "lancet" or "scalpel"). Sections made by a horizontal sweep of the imaginary blade, as in cutting off the head, are *transverse sections.* Sections made by a downward sweep of the blade from the side are *coronal sections* (usually *frontal sections*). A coronal section, for example, would lift the front of the chest off to expose the lungs and heart, or the front of the abdomen off to expose the abdominal contents.

§ 5:15 Formal description of movements and positions

Medial and lateral movement have already been defined. Lateral movement of a limb away from the midline is called *abduction*; medial movement in the opposite direction is termed *adduction.* [See Fig. 5-14.] Rotation of a bone or limb in a joint (e.g., the rotation of the radius) is also described as being medial or lateral. If the anterior part of the limb moves inward, the movement will be described as *medial rotation,* and if it moves outward, the movement will be considered *lateral rotation. Flexion* is formally defined as narrowing of the angle of a joint. Conversely, *extension* is increasing the angle of a joint. The angle of a joint is normally its anterior aspect, but there are a few exceptions. In the knee, the angle of the joint is its posterior aspect, so that the knee flexes and extends by narrowing and opening up its posterior angle. The neck is also peculiar. In addition to flexing and extending in the ordinary sense of the term, by moving the head forward and backward, the neck can also flex sideways, and these movements are described as left (or right) *lateral flexion.* Rotation of the neck is also right and left. Since the neck is a midline structure, the terms medial and lateral do not properly apply to it. Rotatory movements of the lower arm (when the radius rotates around the ulna) are also given special names. When the forearm rotates laterally so as to leave the palm of the hand pointing forward, this is described as *supination.* The reverse movement, which leaves the dorsum of the hand pointing forward, is termed *pronation.* The term *prone* literally means "face-down" (as when someone is lying on their stomach) and *supine* is "face-up" (when they are lying on their back). Medical students avoid confusion by using the mnemonic that "supine means on the spine." These terms are applied analogically to the hand which is considered to be face up when the palm is pointing forward and face down when the dorsum (back) of the hand is anterior.

There are some anatomical terms which describe movement or position on the body rather than movements of the body parts. [See Fig. 5-15.] The limbs must be viewed as completely abducted (sticking out sideways) from the axial skeleton. Any movement or position on the limbs which is towards the trunk is termed *proximal.* Movement or position away from the trunk is termed *distal.* So the humerus is proximal to the elbow joint, and the ulna is distal to it.

Movement or position on the trunk is described as being *cephalad* (or rostral) and *caudad.* (*cephalos* is "head" in Greek, *rostrum* is "beak" or "snout" in Latin, and *cauda* is "tail" in both languages). Thus any movement or position towards the head is described as being rostral (rostrad) or cephalad, while movement and position towards the tail is said to be caudal or caudad. So the lumbar spine is caudal in relation to the chest, and, on the other hand, the cervical spine is cephalad (or rostral) to the chest.

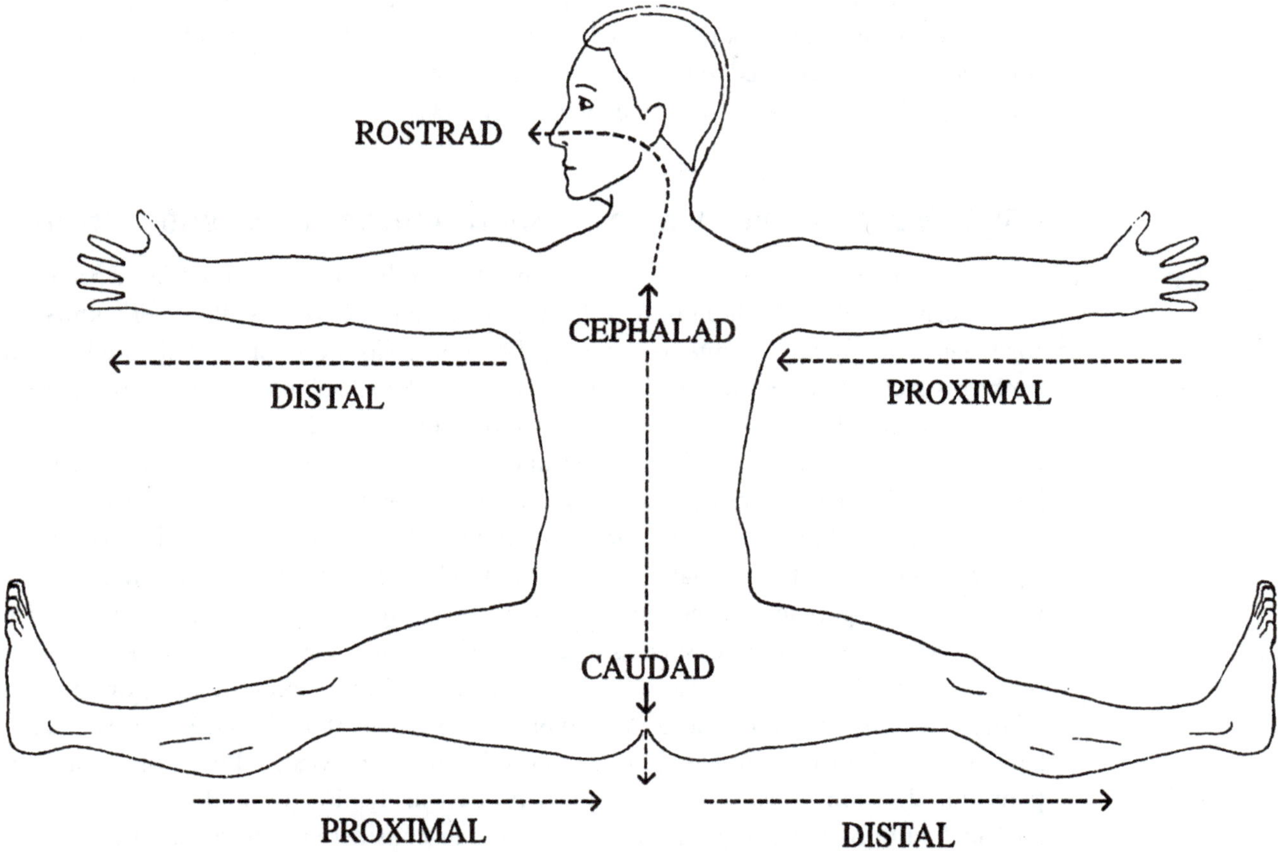

Fig. 5-15 Position and movement in relation to the spine

Part II.
Musculoskeletal Disorders

§ 5:16 The legal viewpoint on musculoskeletal disorders and diseases

Soft tissues, bones and joints can be affected by metabolic diseases, genetic abnormalities, infections, inflammatory diseases and cancers. Detailed knowledge about many of these diseases is not, however, of much importance to lawyers. They do require the attention of compensationists at times, since they may feature in a disability case, as when someone is claiming Social Security disability based on a systemic arthritis such as rheumatoid arthritis (RA) or systemic lupus erythematosus (SLE). Yet even in such cases the diagnosis is not usually in question and the disability is clear, so that very little medical knowledge is required in order to handle the legal aspects of the claim. Similarly traumatic fractures, which take up a good deal of the time and attention of orthopedists, are not usually difficult so far as lawyers are concerned. Fractures generally heal with little or no disability. Even if they do not heal properly, the problem can be repaired, and if not, the deformity will usually be obvious, so that compensation is a legal rather than a medical matter. If the complications are allegedly due to medical malpractice, a great deal of medical knowledge may of course be needed, so much so that no book intended for the use of lawyers, and especially a small work such as this one, would be adequate to meet the needs of the lawyers.

So far as lawyers are concerned, two topics (mentioned earlier) are of preeminent interest and importance—low back problems and neck sprains. Most of the attention in the rest of this chapter will be devoted to these two topics, although something will be said about other musculoskeletal diseases for the sake of completeness.

§ 5:17 Musculoskeletal trauma—short-term and long-term problems

Trauma to the musculoskeletal system can produce both immediate and delayed problems. Short-term problems include immobilization and pain incurred while a bone knits, the torn edges of a muscle reunite, or a repaired tendon heals. Sometimes there are lingering problems even following successful treatment of musculoskeletal injuries. Muscles are wasted and must be built up, joints are stiff and must be exercised and made limber again, and so forth. All these can be shown by a lawyer, and no great knowledge of medicine is required (provided the problem is not overlooked). Wasting is normally demonstrated by measuring the diameter of a limb; anything more than an inch of difference between the girth of two legs at the same point will usually be considered to be evidence of significant wasting. In a young fairly fit person, muscle bulk can be restored by exercise; in older persons or in patients who cannot exercise, such as severe arthritics, muscle weakness may be prolonged or even permanent. Shortening of a limb, destruction and fusion of a joint, or complete failure of a tendon to heal are also likely to produce permanent disabilities. However, claims based on such injuries require little in the way of medical knowledge. By the time that compensation decisions must be made, the deficits are usually obvious, and presumably every attempt to improve them has already been made or considered. The remaining questions revolve around the limitations imposed by such injuries and the amounts of money proper to compensate them.

Future complications such as the possibility of developing osteomyelitis at a later date in a badly fractured bone, or the possibility of delayed onset arthritis in an injured joint, are problems which may be difficult or even impossible to provide for in compensation. They are like the possibility of future epileptic seizures, mentioned in connection with head injuries.

§ 5:18 Compensation problems—percentage disability systems

The principal problem which lawyers have with obvious orthopedic injuries is translating the disability into a money sum. Statutory schemes, such as Workers' Compensation, use percentage disability tables in these circumstances. Permanent losses can be translated into compensable sums by consulting these tables, which convert every injury ultimately into a percentage of the total disability for the entire person. It is quite common for doctors to cite such systems (or similar ones published by medical groups to facilitate percentage disability determinations by doctors) in private personal injury cases, where they do not, strictly speaking, apply. There is no harm in this provided it is done simply to provide a ball-park figure as a starting point for negotiations. It should be remembered, however, that these are simply mathematical games applied for special purposes (statutory compensation systems) where certainty and predictability of the amounts to be paid in compensation are very important. No one should think that disability can be reduced to numbers in such a simple manner in the real world. Evaluating injuries for compensation purposes should take into account all the circumstances of the injured person, including age, occupation, and leisure activities.

§ 5:19 Mechanisms protecting the spine from injury

The anatomy of the spine and the intervertebral discs has already been mentioned [§ 5:5]. Each time a disc is compressed vertically, it flattens and spreads horizontally. Normally the *anulus fibrosis* and *posterior longitudinal ligament* contain the spreading of the disc and prevent it from pressing on the cord or the spinal nerve roots. The anulus and the posterior ligament are both very strong, and normally it would be impossible for any of the disc structures to reach and impinge on the nerve roots or the cord. The amount of force necessary to rupture an intact annulus can be calculated, and it exceeds by far the force generated by any imaginable trauma that one could encounter and survive. Yet discs do rupture; the nucleus pulposus does extrude from the disc to press on the cord and nerve roots; and these events occur sometimes with minimal trauma, such as bending over to open a window or pick up a pencil. The reason for this is that very few discs in adult persons are normal. Degenerative processes set in as early as the third decade of life (the mid-twenties), and are far advanced before most of us reach middle age. These degenerative changes need to be understood in order to appreciate intervertebral disc syndromes.

§ 5:20 Degenerative disc disease (DDD)

Autopsy studies on soldiers killed in action have shown that pathological changes in the intervertebral discs are common, if not universal, even in young healthy adults, who often show the beginnings of the degenerative process. Advanced changes are so common in persons over 40 years of age that their presence excites almost no comment when they are seen on routine X-rays of the spine.

These changes involve both the nucleus pulposus and the anulus fibrosus. The normal nucleus has active cells which lay down a jelly-like matrix containing only a few fibrocytes (scar cells). This matrix has the ability to absorb water, thus expanding to increase the volume of the disc and by this means maintaining its proper shape. The pressure of standing and sitting all day increases hydrostatic pressure on the discs and forces some of this water out of them, so that we may be half an inch or even one inch shorter in the evening than we were in the morning. With degenerative change, the nucleus seems to produce less jelly, to have more fibrous tissue, and to lose some of its ability to retain water. As a result, the disc is not fully distended and so, not being firmly fixed in the intervertebral space, can wobble around and permit movement of the adjacent vertebral bones. The anulus also becomes altered by degenerative forces. Its fibers become shorter, more fragmented and generally less elastic. Consequently, it is less able to absorb and contain the forces applied to it by the nucleus pulposus. The nucleus may, therefore, begin to erode through the anulus and can eventually rupture through it. Anterior rupture creates few problems since only the great vessels lie on that side of the spine. Superior and inferior ruptures of the nucleus are common and can be seen on routine X-rays of the spine (*Shmorl's nodes*). These too create few problems. However, a posterior rupture through the anulus and past the posterior

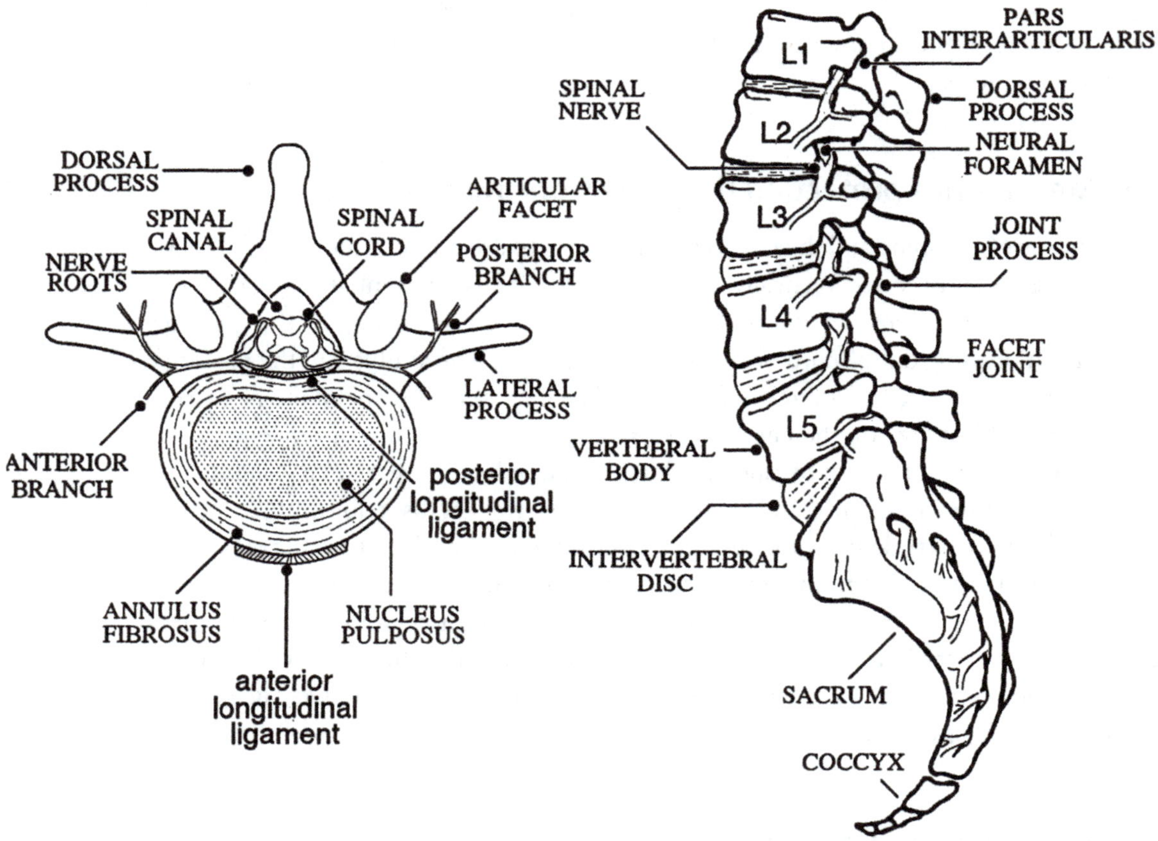

Fig. 5-16 The lumbosacral spine, superior and lateral views

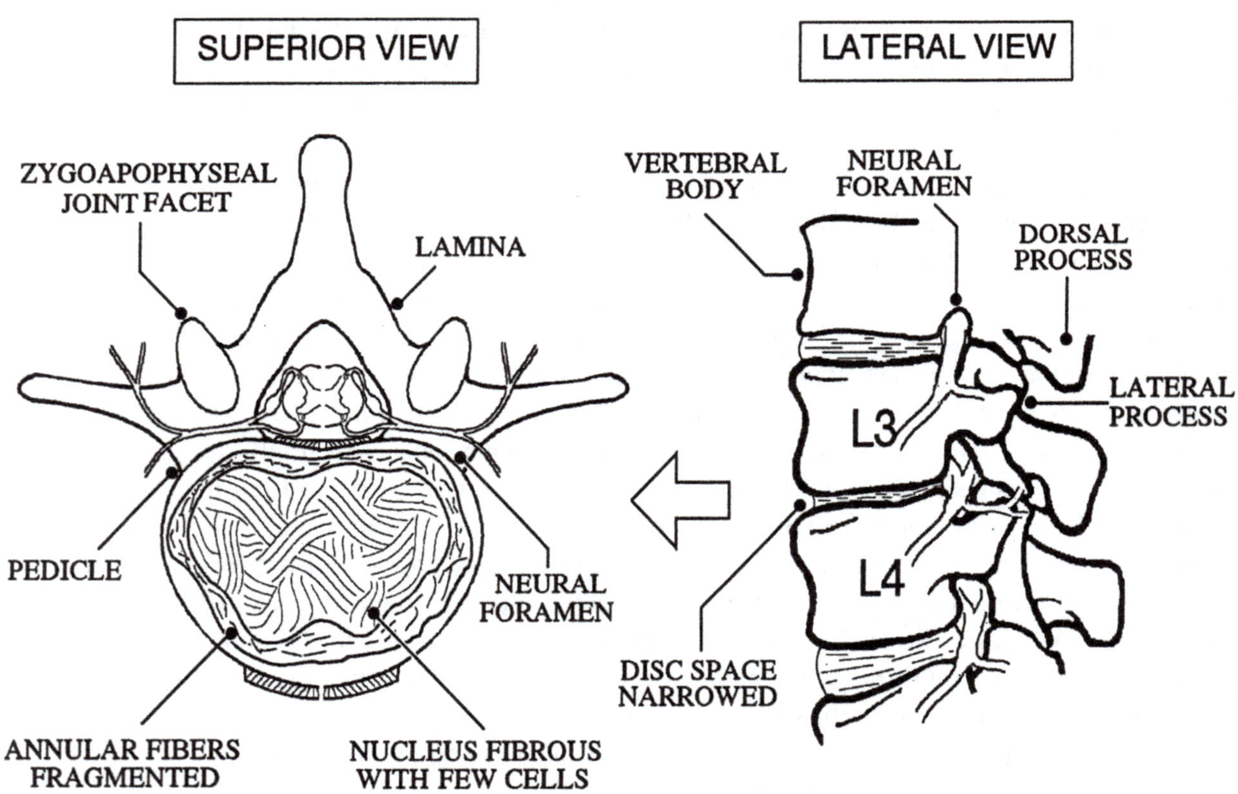

Fig. 5-17 Degenerative disc disease

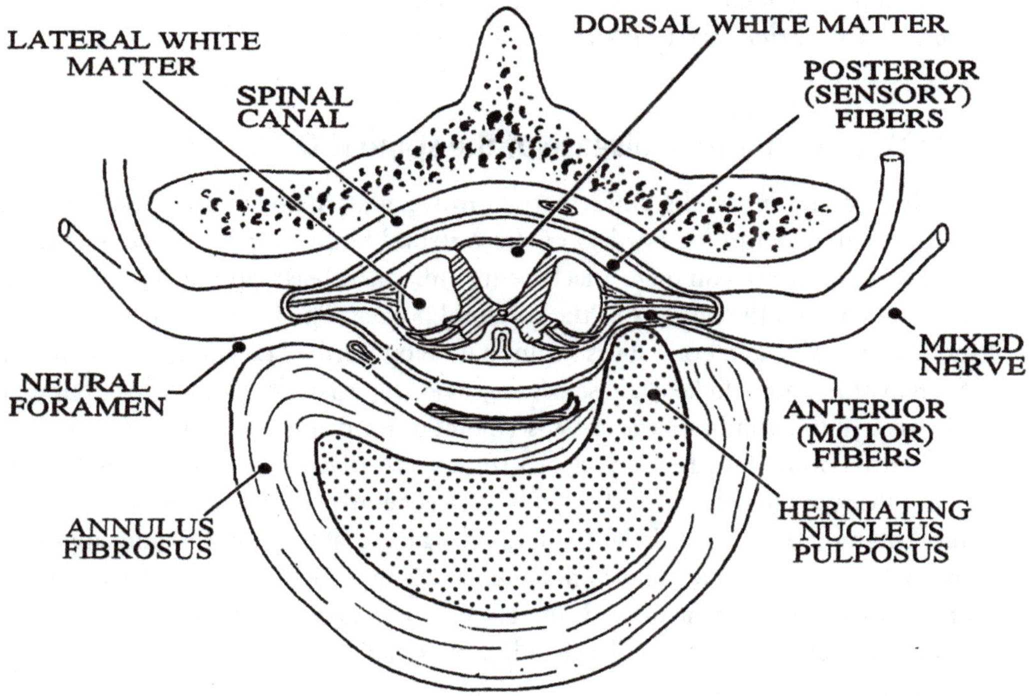

Fig. 5-18 Herniating nucleus pulposus with nerve root impingement

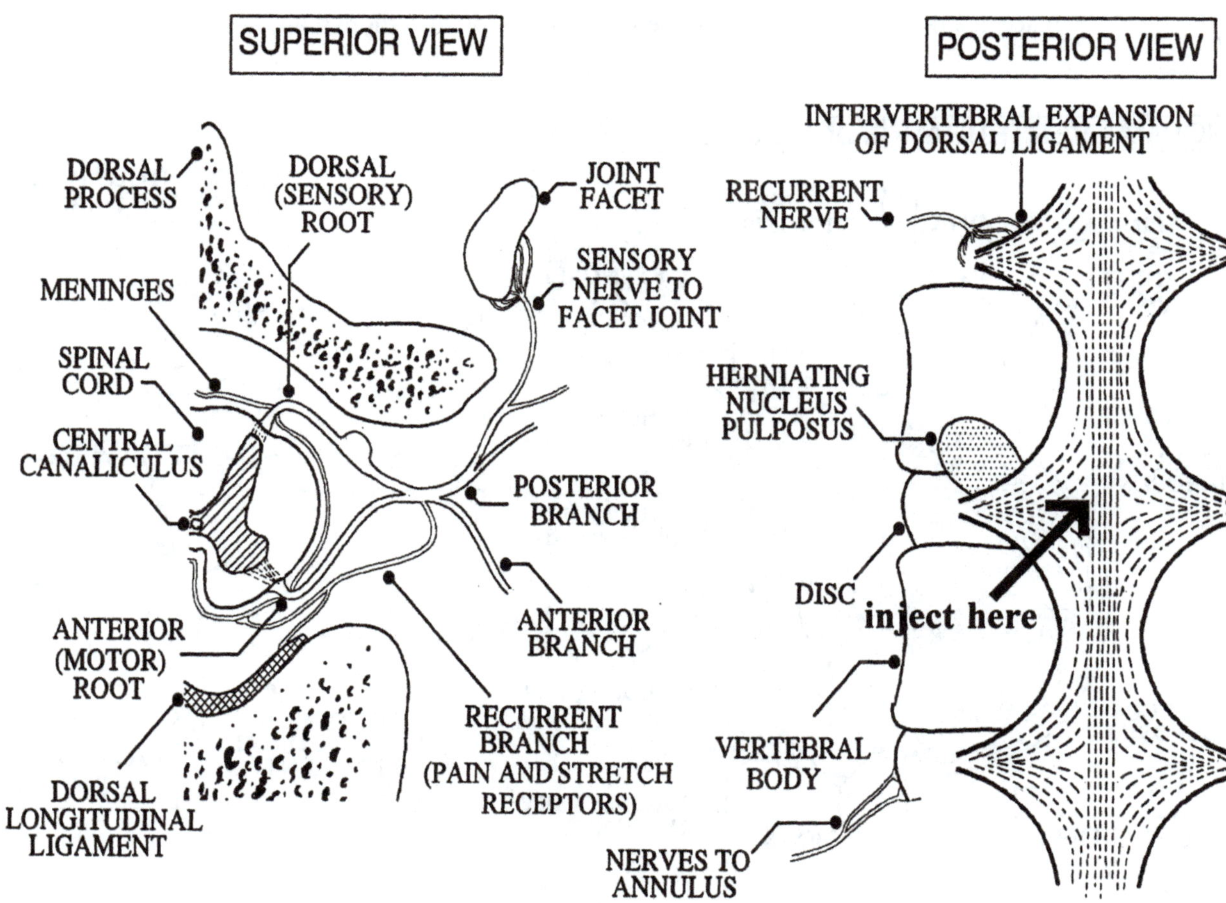

Fig. 5-19 Neural mechanisms of chronic low back pain

longitudinal ligament, may impinge on and injure the nerve roots, producing the clinical picture of the *acute disc syndrome.* [See Fig. 5-18.]

§ 5:21 Degenerative disease of the spine (DDS)

The changes in the discs necessarily involve adjacent structures. [See Fig. 5-20] The discs are attached to the borders of the vertebral bodies above and below them and, as they shrink, they tug on these attachments. Inflamed areas begin to appear at critical sites, especially round the borders of the vertebral bodies. The inflammatory process activates bone formation, and bony spurs begin to develop (termed *exostoses).* Bony spurs can also form in other musculoskeletal diseases too, especially *ankylosing spondylitis* (Marie-Strumpel disease). In this condition the exostoses point upward and downward, eventually meeting to fuse the bones together (ankylosis). In degenerative disc disease (DDD) on the other hand, the spurs tend to point straight out. Degenerative changes are obvious on X-ray and very common. And it should be emphasized, again, that they can exist and appear crippling in a patient who has few or no complaints. An X-ray of the spine with narrowed disc spaces and exostoses all over the place, is therefore poor evidence of disability, if it is not accompanied by well established evidence of low back pain, or some other clinical entity relating to the spine.

The shrinking disc, as was mentioned earlier, allows more movement between the vertebral bones. The upper bone tends to move forward on the lower one and this shift often takes place in a rotatory fashion, with one side moving forward more than the other. These move-

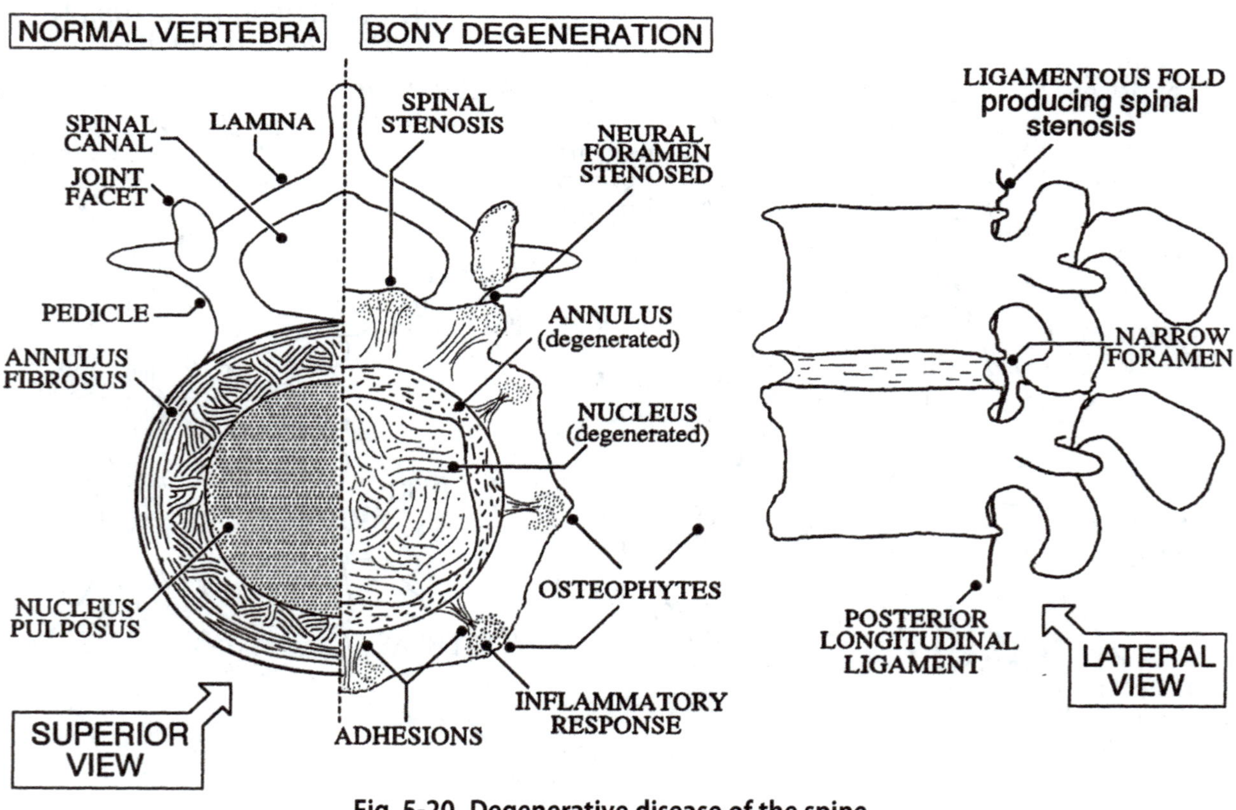

Fig. 5-20 Degenerative disease of the spine

ments affect the small zygoapophyseal joints (*facet joints*) in the bony ring which surrounds the spinal canal. Inflammatory changes are then initiated at the margins of the facet joints and the *inflammatory cytokines* again stimulate bone osteogenesis to produce bony spurs. These spurs may point into and narrow the neural foramina, where the nerve roots leave the spinal canal. These three changes (forward subluxation of the facet joints, the bony spurs emanating from their borders and backward pointing spurs coming from the borders of the vertebral bodies) can all combine to squeeze the nerve roots in the neural foramina and give rise to *nerve root compression syndromes*. The entire spinal canal, indeed, can be narrowed (*spinal stenosis*). When this happens above the level of L1 (where the cord is still solid) *cord compression syndromes* may result. Cord compression in the lumbar spine usually presents with pain in the legs. This is like the claudication pain of vascular insufficiency, and the condition is called *neurogenic claudication*. The difference is that it comes on with standing rather than with walking. However, spinal stenosis is more likely to occur in the cervical spine (where the spinal canal is narrower) rather than in the lumbar area. Here it does not usually present with pain, but with weakness of the lower extremities (LEs) and with complaints relating to the pelvic organs such as the bladder.

§ 5:22 The clinical presentation of lumbar disc disease

There are two basic presentations of disc disease, acute and chronic. *Chronic disc syndromes* are largely the symptoms produced by slow progression of degenerative changes [See § 5:20]. Patients experience episodes of pain in the low back which occasionally gets worse. Exacerbations are often precipitated by lifting something awkwardly, driving long distances in a car, or by some other kind of stress to the lower back. The pain may radiate into the hip on one side or the other, but does not, as a rule, shoot down the leg as *sciatic pain*. This kind of problem is very common. It is estimated that 85% of people will have significant episodes of this nature at one time or another in their lives. Yet even those who have chronic back trouble in some degree of severity, usually manage to live with it. They modify their activities and go about their business despite the problem.

Acute disc syndromes are different and are often brought on by an injury such as lifting a weight at an inappropriate angle, or by an automobile accident. The pain is severe, is made worse by standing or sitting, radiates into the hip, and may indeed radiate down the back of the leg into the foot (sciatic pain). In severe cases there may be numbness of the foot or muscle weakness (*foot-drop*). The patient is likely to be completely incapacitated, and it may take several weeks of rest to recover sufficiently so that they can go about their business. If they are so unfortunate or so unwise as to have another lifting episode or injury, they are likely to have a recurrence of the problem.

§ 5:23 The explanation of low back syndromes

The events which underlie these syndromes are somewhat controversial, but the following account at least makes sense of them. The inflammatory changes of degenerative disease of the spine are clearly capable of producing the symptoms of the chronic low back syndrome. Movement of the facet joints would tug on the sensory nerve endings in the joint capsule

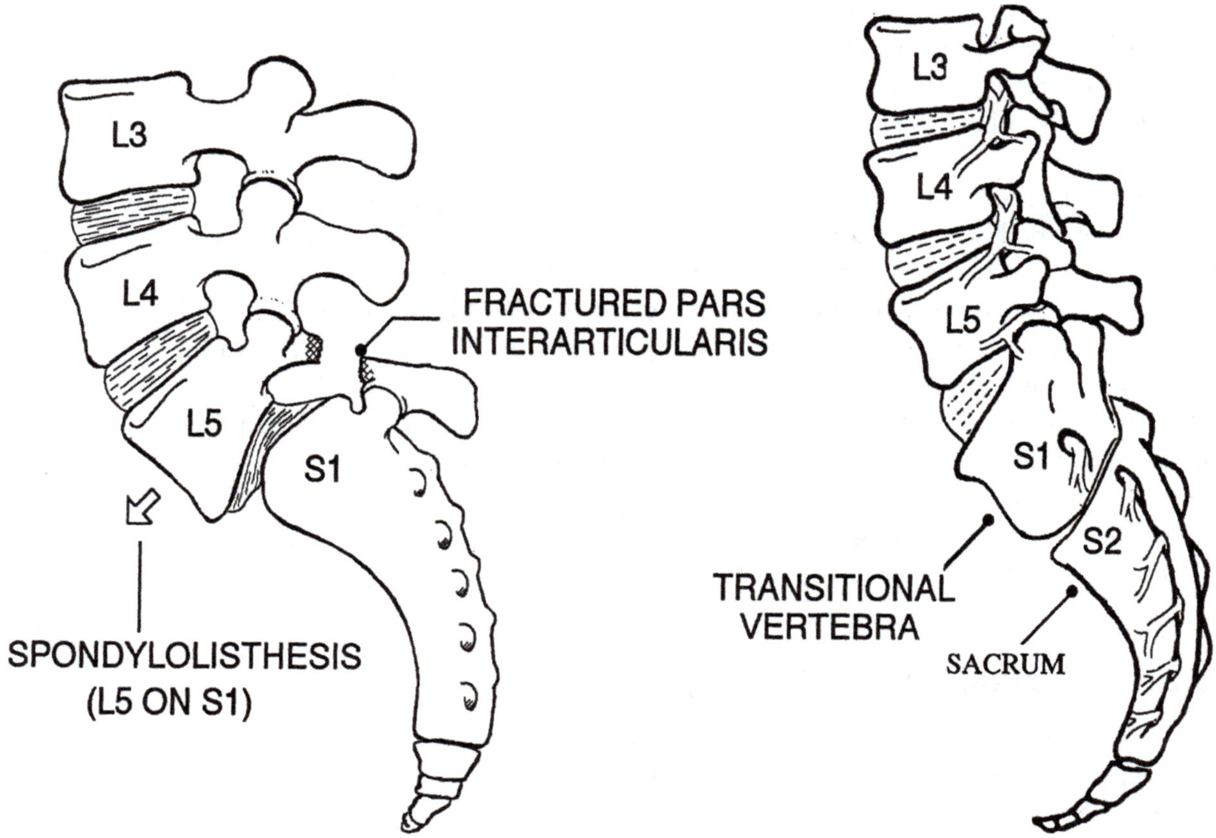

Fig. 5-21 Congenital defects of the spine

and produce pain. If these little joints subluxated once in a while, and stuck in an abnormal position, this would produce an acute exacerbation with back pain (but no radiation into hip or leg). Abnormal expansion or distortion of the degenerated disc might also press on the lateral expansions of the *posterior longitudinal ligament.* These lateral expansions, which are directly opposite the disc spaces [see Fig. 5-19], contain sensory nerve endings. Some of these are stretch receptors functioning in the maintenance of proper tension in the muscles which support the spine. Others however are clearly pain endings, and activating them could account for some of the pain experienced in chronic disc disease.

In the acute severe episode, however, it is likely that the nucleus pulposus has ruptured out through the anulus fibrosus and is pushing past the posterior longitudinal ligament to exert pressure on the nerve roots on one side or the other. This is the true *herniated nucleus pulposus* (HNP) or slipped disc. If the disc space involved is L5-S1 (as is commonly the case), pressure will be exerted on the sciatic nerve roots, and the typical sciatic pain (down the back of the leg into the foot) will result.

§ 5:24 Congenital defects of the spine—transitional vertebra

There are a number of relatively common congenital abnormalities of the spine which may be associated with low back complaints. [See Fig. 5-21.] In some people (approximately

1% of males of Irish descent), the first sacral bone does not fuse with the rest of the sacrum but becomes in effect an extra lumbar vertebra. This condition has been given a number of names in the past (e.g., a sixth lumbar vertebra) but is currently termed a *transitional vertebra*. It was thought, at one time, that people with transitional vertebrae had a predisposition to back trouble, since the extra lumbar bone would presumably make the spine over-mobile. Persons applying for jobs in the construction business, or other occupations which required lifting, were screened with X-rays, and those found to have a transitional vertebra were not hired. The current view is that, if they are asymptomatic, they have no more risk of lumbar disc problems than anyone else. So X-ray screening of applicants for such jobs has been discontinued.

§ 5:25 Congenital defects of the spine—pars defect

The bone in between the two zygoapophyseal processes of each vertebral bone is called the *pars interarticularis* (the part in between the joints). It is laid down as a cartilaginous matrix during embryological development, and later calcified and transformed into true bone by the actions of the active cells in bone tissue (osteoblasts which lay down bone and osteoclasts which reabsorb it). These cells line the little cavities which honeycomb cancellous bone and by their activities continually remodel it. In some people (again about 1% of the population) the transformation from cartilaginous matrix into true bone is not completed properly. In these persons the bone of the zygoapophyseal processes (the pars interarticularis) is abnormal and tends to fracture rather easily with minor trauma. If the defect is bilateral, affecting both sides of the neural ring of bone behind the vertebral body, the fracture may effectively separate the bone above from the one below. One vertebra may then subluxate forward on the other, a condition known as *spondylolisthesis*. This generally affects the L5-S1 joint so that the last lumbar vertebra subluxates forward on the first sacral bone. [See Fig. 5-21] Significant subluxation means that these patients have great difficulty in reaching for their toes, in some cases being unable to get their hands much past their knees. Patients with a *pars interarticularis defect* who are not symptomatic (like those who have a transitional vertebra), are no longer considered to be at much greater risk of having back trouble than anyone else, but, if their condition is known, they may be wise to avoid jobs involving bending and heavy lifting.

§ 5:26 Familial back problems—defective collagen

The anulus fibrosus and the posterior longitudinal ligament are both fibroelastic structures, and hereditary conditions exist in which fibrous tissue is in some way abnormal or laid down in an abnormal manner. These persons can, indeed, have a greater risk of disc disease, and may rupture one intervertebral disc after another, following very slight trauma or stress on the back. Enquiry as to a family history of back trouble is therefore very relevant, but is not always conclusive. Low back problems are very common, so that everyone is likely to have some family history of such complaints. The absence of a family history is likewise not conclusive, for a genetic defect relating to fibrous tissue can appear *de novo* in a family. It is likely that DNA probes will be developed in the future, which will allow definitive diagnosis of such conditions. In the meantime, proof of a genetic predisposition to back trouble may be difficult, and will seldom be conclusive, although a very strong family history may be persuasive.

Part III.
The Diagnosis of Low Back Problems

§ 5:27 Clinical diagnosis of lumbar disc problems

The findings on examination of a patient with a chronic disc problem may be unremarkable; but once the disc truly herniates, a more positive clinical picture tends to emerge. Typical items which should be sought in the record are:

1. The back is tender when pressure is applied between the dorsal spines over the appropriate disc space.

2. Scoliosis (lateral deformity) of the spine is visible in the appropriate area. It is normally convex (bulging) to the side of the disc lesion. This deformity is due to spasm of the paraspinalis muscles, which can also be seen or palpated. This spasm is in itself painful but it may take pressure off the herniating disc by opening up the intervertebral disc space on the opposite side. Muscle spasm then will usually be found on the side opposite to the herniation, but this is not always the case. Occasionally, herniations occur underneath the nerve root, instead of in the usual position on top of it. These are called *axillary herniations* since they appear to be tucked under the arm of the nerve, instead of pressing down on top of it, as is usually the case. Axillary herniations are relieved by spasm on the same side, which rotates the nerve root downward and away from the herniating disc. In these cases clinical opinion as to the location of the lesion are likely to be in error; the findings will suggest that the HNP is one space above the real level of the problem. These considerations make it clear that while the location of the muscle spasm, and the side on which the scoliosis is convex, are normally good indications as to the spinal level and side of the lesion, this is not necessarily so. The clinical findings then, are usually confirmed, if possible, by diagnostic imaging of some kind. This is especially desirable if surgery is being considered in order to identify more accurately the proper operative site.

3. There is fixation of the lumbar spine on flexing the back. [See Fig. 5-22.] Normally, when someone bends down to touch their toes, the spine can be seen to flex normally throughout its entire length (like bending a bow). In patients with a herniated disc, the lumbar spine remains stiff and straight (loss of lumbar lordosis). It is virtually impossible to fake this sign. One can voluntarily stiffen the entire back but not one part of it.

4. Straight leg raising causes pain, ideally sciatic pain. This is *Lasegue's sign*. Normally when the patient is lying supine (flat on their back), straight leg raising can be carried out to approximately 85° from the horizontal plane. With nerve root irritation, they may not reach 60° before the typical pain of sciatica is felt. [See Fig. 5-23.] This sign is due to stretching of the sciatic nerve over the obtruding disc, and so it will not occur when the herniating disc is higher up than L4-L5. Most lumbar disc problems (over 90%), however, are below this level, most commonly at L5-S1.

The clinical picture may then be atypical and puzzling, but where the appropriate signs are present, the diagnosis of an HNP can be made with some confidence from the history

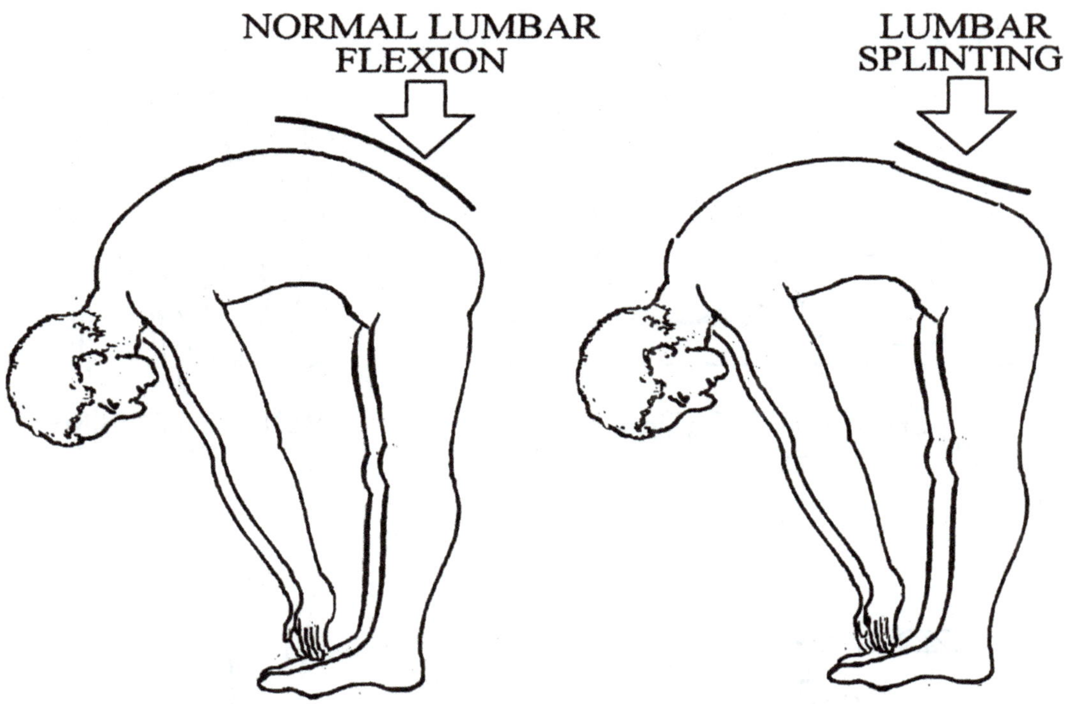

Fig. 5-22 Findings in acute disc syndrome—loss of lumbar flexion

and physical examination (H&P). Orthopedic surgeons will, if the case is urgent, operate in reliance on the clinical picture when the objective tests (CT scan, etc) are equivocal.

§ 5:28 Investigating disc problems—diagnostic imaging

1. Ordinary X-rays of the lumbar spine are not normally helpful in the diagnosis of a disc problem. The finding of bony spurs, and even narrowed disc spaces, may suggest degenerative disc disease [See § 5:21] but since these findings can be present in people who appear to have no back problems at all, they are not very helpful. Nevertheless, in the presence of positive clinical findings, abnormal findings in routine X-ray studies of the spine may provide supportive evidence.

2. *Lumbar myelogram* is a contrast X-ray study where a bolus of radiopaque dye is injected into the subarachnoid space (into the CSF). [See Fig. 5-25] The table (with the patient strapped to it) is moved around to maneuver the dye past and around the disc spaces. A herniating nucleus pulposus (HNP) may be seen as a *filling defect* (dye moves round the herniation). Sometimes a piece of nucleus pulposus will break off and lodge in one of the sleeves of dura mater, which accompany the nerve roots for part of the way out through the neural foramina. The dye may then fail to enter that pocket, and the report will record that "the sleeve was not visualized" (*sleeve defect*). Approximately 75% of disc herniations can be diagnosed by lumbar myelogram. This is considered a good percentage in a test; and it is even better when one realizes that some of those test results considered to be false negatives were really cases where the herniation was too small to show at the time, but enlarged to give a positive test later.

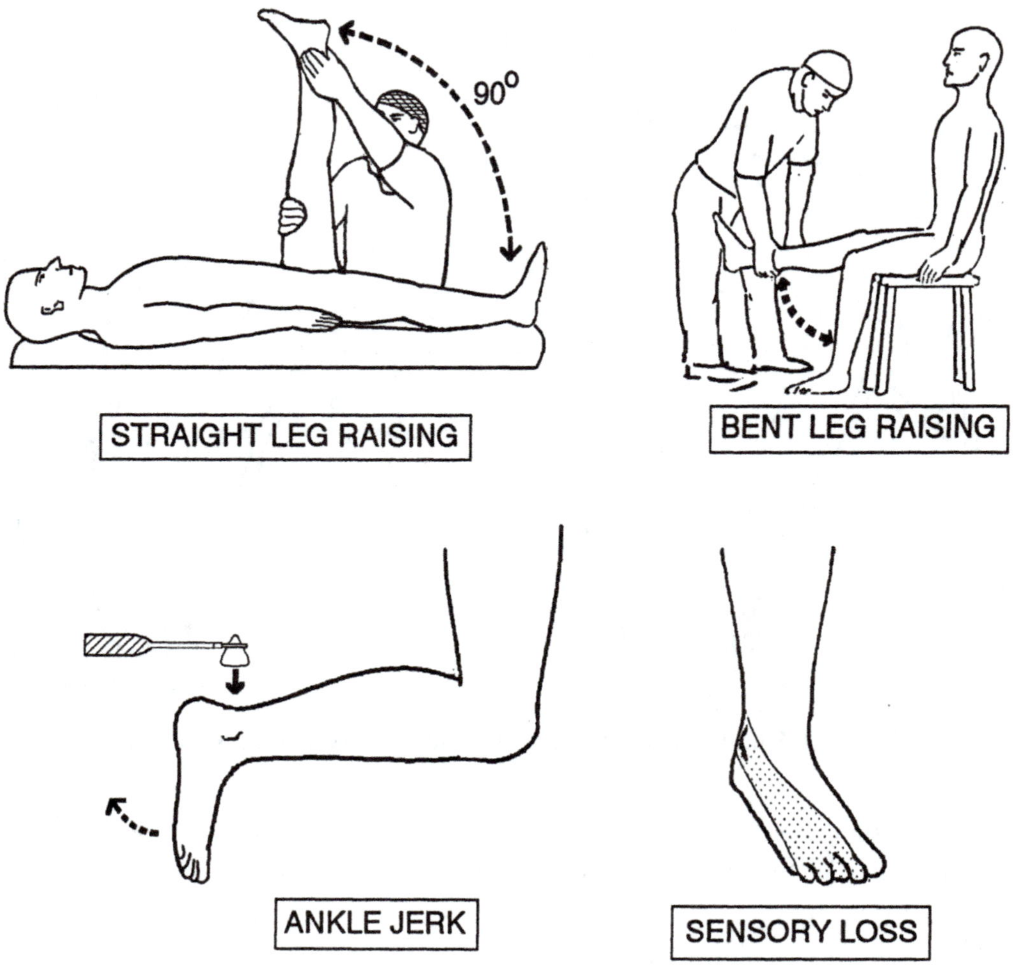

Fig. 5-23 Neurological findings in acute disc syndrome

3. *Air myelogram*, using air or some other gas as a contrast material, is almost obsolete, since it is liable to produce a very nasty headache following the test. It has, however, one remaining virtue which may, very occasionally, be an indication for its use. It is very valuable in detecting folds of dura and other such obstructions which tend to be obscured by ordinary contrast dyes. An air myelogram may then be ordered in the investigation of a spinal stenosis when all other test results are equivocal. This is likely to be a rare event, since MRI normally produces excellent views of spinal stenosis.

4. *CT-scan* is now widely available for imaging intervertebral disc spaces and surrounding tissues. CT is considered as reliable as lumbar myelogram in the diagnosis of disc herniations and it is certainly more convenient for the patient. CT is superior to MRI in imaging bone so that it may be the modality of choice where a fracture or compression of nerves by bony exostoses was suspected.

5. *Magnetic resonance imaging* (MRI) is now widely available for use in diagnosing disc problems. Currently available machines are much faster, less expensive and generally more convenient than the earlier versions. *Multi angle oblique* (MAO) software, enables a lateral scout film of the spine to be taken which notes the angles of the various

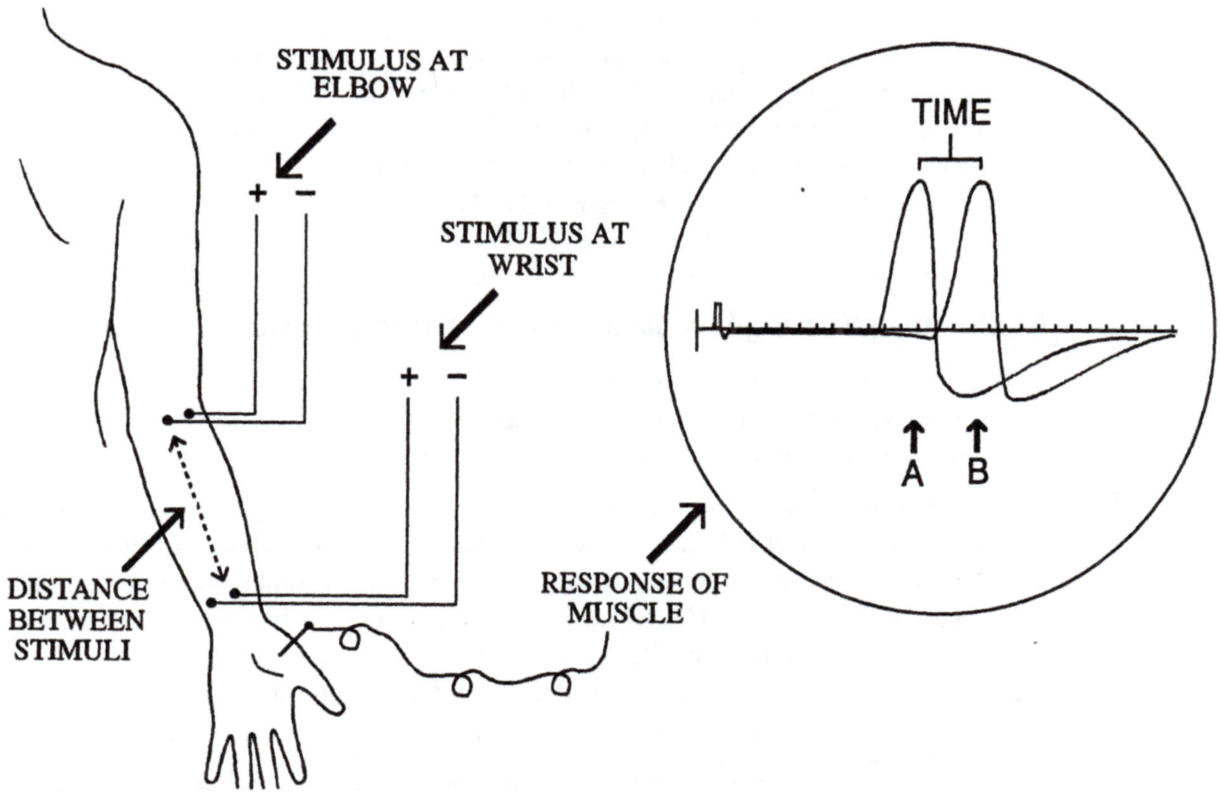

Fig. 5-24 Nerve conduction studies

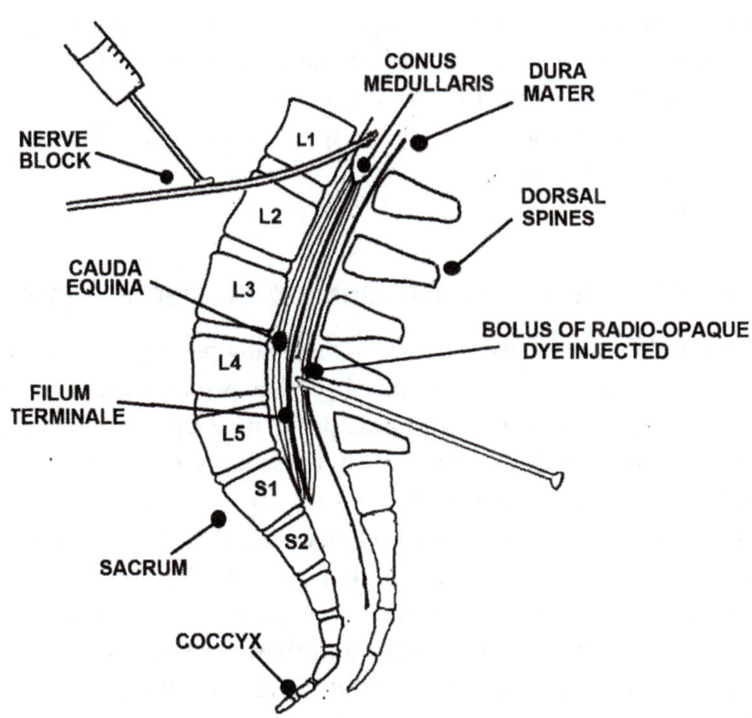

Fig. 5-25 Nerve block and differential spinal block

intervertebral disc spaces. The machine then uses this information to automatically line up the machine on these spaces and images them in very short time so that several spaces can be examined in approximately 10 minutes. MRI has not replaced CT in the work-up for an HNP, but it is superior to CT in distinguishing different tissues from one another and so is particularly indicated where there is any suspicion of a cord lesion such as a cyst or tumor of the cord.

§ 5:29 Investigating low back pain—electrodiagnostic studies

The general term electrodiagnostic studies, in the context of low back problems, refers mainly to *nerve conduction studies*, accompanied in most cases by an electromyogram. EDS are indicated when damage to nerve roots is in question.

In a nerve conduction test, a tiny electrical stimulus is applied proximally to the nerve; the time taken to travel a measured distance distally is noted; and the rate at which the impulse is conducted is calculated. [See Fig. 5-24.] A delay in conduction, even though it is only a few milliseconds, can be detected and indicates nerve dysfunction. There are many possible reasons why a nerve should not conduct signals properly but, in the presence of a history of sciatic pain, a positive nerve conduction test will be almost diagnostic of nerve root compression by the disc, and surgical decompression may well be indicated.

An *electromyogram* is similar to a nerve conduction test and, indeed, is often conducted at the same time. Again, an electrical stimulus is applied to the nerve, but this time it is the response of the muscle that is studied. Where either the muscle or the nerve supplying it is defective, there will be an abnormal electromyographic trace. The appearance and characteristics of the trace, along with a suggestive history, may again be diagnostic of sciatic nerve involvement in a disc problem. Unfortunately myography using a surface electrode over the muscle is not very satisfactory, and it is usually deemed necessary to insert a needle into the body of the muscle. This, especially when coupled with electrical stimulation, is not very popular with patients.

§ 5:30 Other tests—discogram, lumbar venogram and spinal block

Some rather specialized tests are occasionally performed. [See Fig. 5-26.] A *discogram* is an X-ray study done after the disc itself has been injected with a small quantity of radiopaque dye. A *lumbar venogram* is performed by introducing dye into the plexus of veins which surround the spinal cord. These are sensitive tests but require some skill to carry them out. Consequently they are seldom ordered unless the results of the usual investigative modalities have proved equivocal, and it is really necessary to know whether there is a disc problem or not. Another test used for this purpose (especially when it is suspected that the patient is hysterical or malingering) is a *differential spinal block*, [See Fig. 5-25] where first normal saline and then local anesthetic are injected into the subarachnoid space (into the CSF). If the saline cures the problem, or the local anesthetic fails to cure it, the complaints will probably be considered to be factitious. An *individual nerve block* is also occasionally used to diagnose nerve root compression syndromes. [See Fig. 5-25.]

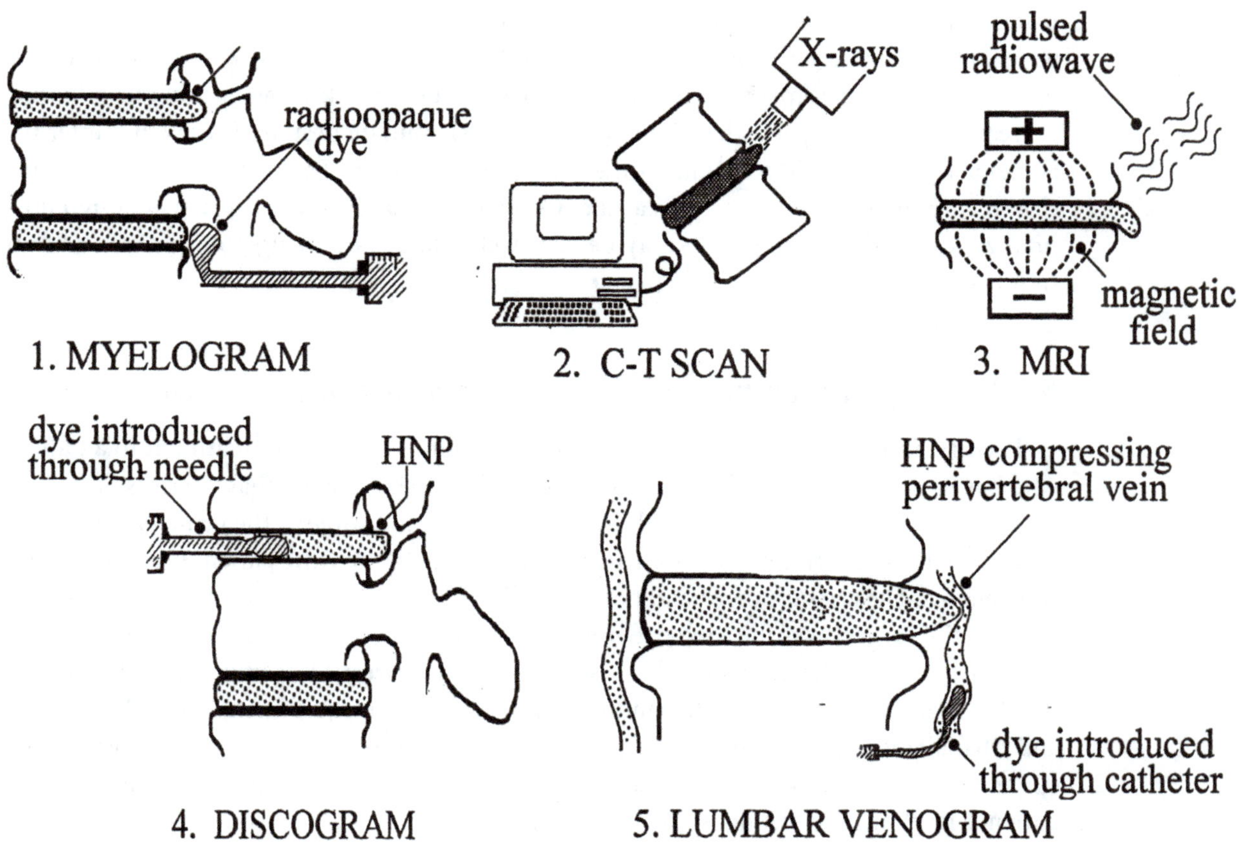

Fig. 5-26 Imaging of the intervertabral disc

Part IV.
Treatment and Prognosis in Low Back Conditions

§ 5:31 Conservative treatment

This should perhaps be called non-surgical treatment, for it has been pointed out that in certain circumstances, the least dangerous and, therefore, the most conservative thing that one can do is to operate. Nevertheless, more than 85% of low back patients can be managed during the acute phase with a medical regime of rest, analgesics, muscle relaxants, etc., and surgery is not required. A small percentage of these patients are hospitalized to control pain. Those hospitalized are usually put in pelvic traction, with weights slung over pulleys, stretching their back in the direction of the long axis of the spine. Theoretically, this is supposed to draw the nucleus back away from the spinal nerves and into the intervertebral space (by suction); but it is unlikely that pelvic traction could generate enough negative force to do this (hanging by the heels upside down might help). Nevertheless, it appears to do some good. Skeptics claim that it works by immobilizing the patient. If they are not moving around, their back hurts less. Most of these hospitalized patients get well without recourse to surgery.

When the acute phase has passed and the pain has eased so that the patient can move around, active rehabilitation begins. This used to be continuation of the physical therapy using heat packs, high energy ultrasound, infrared lamps, etc., (all of which are generally lumped together as *modalities* by therapists). But the consensus among orthopedists at present, is that modalities may help in the acute phase, but have little or no part in rehabilitation thereafter. Studies suggest that the patients who rehabilitate best are those who, after the acute phase, learn to do rehabilitation exercises on their own. Patients who want someone else to cure them do not do well as a rule. Cooperative patients, even if they required hospitalization in the acute phase, may be very well and even playing golf in three or four months.

§ 5:32 Surgical treatments—laminectomy/discectomy (L/D)

The first indication for surgical intervention is failure of medical treatment in a patient who has so much pain, or who is so limited in their level of activity, that the risks of surgery become acceptable. Besides the usual risks of anesthesia and surgery, the principal unwanted result is that the operation will not help and perhaps even leave the patient worse than they were before. The classical representation of the likelihood of the various outcomes following lumbar disc surgery was that one patient in four would get a good result, one in four would be worse, and that the others would be somewhere in between. It is now generally thought that this view is a little pessimistic, and that improvements in equipment, surgical technique and rehabilitative methods, have improved the odds in favor of a good outcome. Nevertheless, surgeons are still not likely to recommend surgery until medical means have failed, and the patient's level of functioning is unacceptable.

Laminectomy/discectomy (the posterior approach) has been, until recently, the favored procedure. The anterior approach through the abdomen avoids the spinal canal and its contents, but it involves working in a very deep wound (especially in obese patients) and consequently has few, if any, advocates at present. In the posterior operation [see Fig. 5-27], laminectomy (removal of the lamina) exposes the spinal canal; the nerve roots are then drawn aside with a nerve retractor; and the disc material is nibbled out, a piece at a time, with a bone rongeur. A number of prostheses were developed to take the place of the removed disc (the Swedish orthopedists used ball bearings for a time) but none of these seemed to offer much benefit, and it is usual now to simply allow the upper vertebral body to settle down on the lower one. Scar tissue develops between them which partially fills the space but it still looks narrower on X-ray. This may not seem physiological and it may put additional stresses on the facet joints posteriorly, but it does not appear to create any serious problems (that are known). Newer prostheses have been designed to replace the removed disc and have been favorably reviewed, but it is too early to say if they will come into universal use.

§ 5:33 Surgical treatment of disc disease—spinal fusion

In the '70s and early '80s it was common to carry out a posterior fusion operation at the same time as laminectomy /discectomy, or later as a second procedure. This could be done anteriorly using the abdominal approach, but was usually carried out posteriorly along with the L/D. The dorsal processes were clamped together between metal plates, and various spaces in between the two vertebral bones were packed with bone chips. The metal clamps provided temporary stability till the grafted bone fused the two vertebrae together. It was

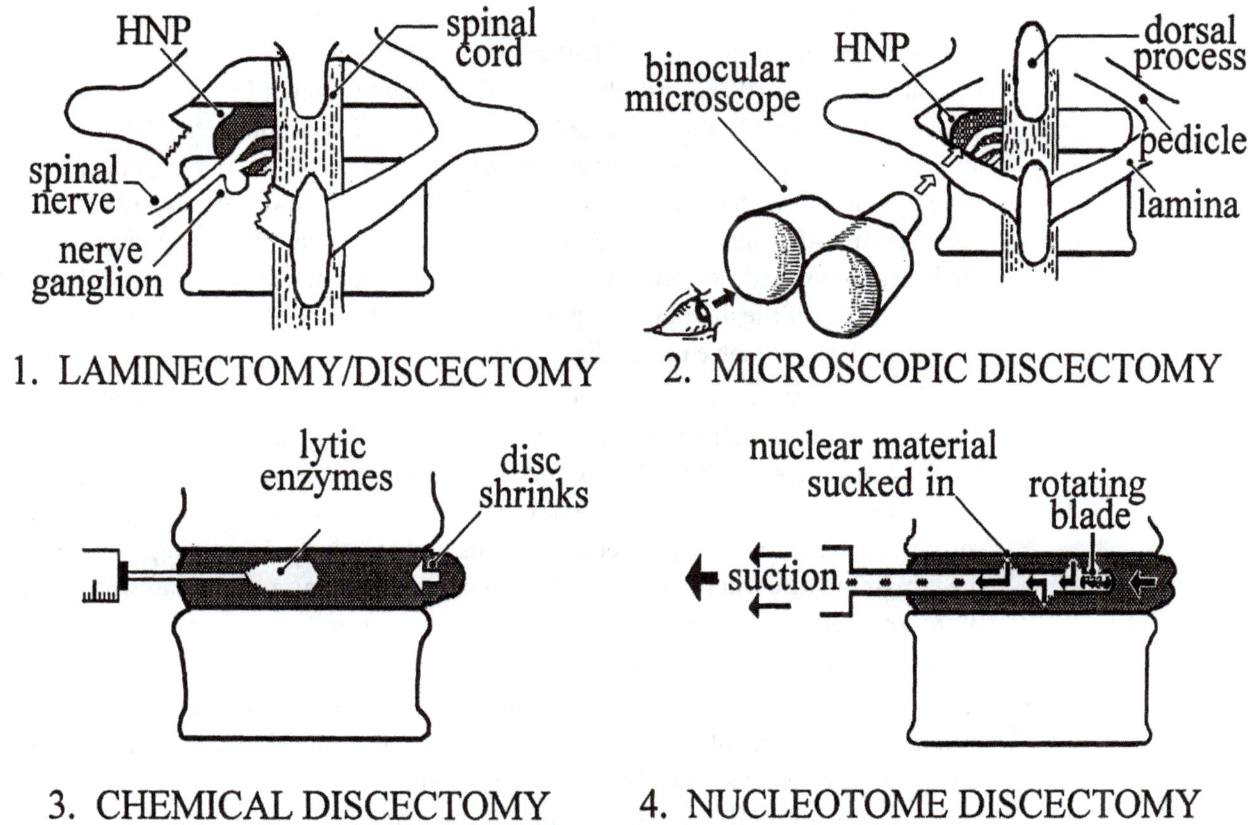

Fig. 5-27 Surgical treatments of herniating nucleus pulposus

thought that stabilizing the spine in this way would have a number of benefits, including less pain and therefore more ability to exercise. There appears to be very little evidence that spinal fusion does confer any significant benefits; and it has been found that in over 25% of cases there is overgrowth of the grafted bone with consequent narrowing of the spinal canal. This combination of doubtful benefit and serious risk has made spinal fusion a relatively rare procedure, though it is still indicated in certain cases where excessive mobility of the spine is creating problems. A procedure is currently being evaluated in which the pedicles are fused together by plates and screws; no bone chips are needed, and the operation has been favorably reported.

§ 5:34 Newer surgeries for degenerative disc disease (DDD)

Laminectomy/discectomy involves a sizable incision and recovery time is measured in weeks rather than days. Most of the effort and much of the surgical trauma was related to exposing the disc, and several ingenious and less destructive ways of getting to and removing disc material have been devised.

1. *Chemical discectomy* (CD) is carried out by injecting *chymopapain* or some other lytic enzyme into the disc [see Fig. 5-27]. These digest the disc material, which is then absorbed into the body. Unfortunately, some operators accidentally injected the enzyme into the CSF, and it was claimed that it damaged the nerve roots (this claim has been

disputed). More seriously, a number of patients had anaphylactic reactions to the enzymes, and some of them died. Neither of these things are real contraindications, and several series report large numbers of patients being treated in this way with good results and few complications. Nevertheless, chemical discectomy declined in popularity and was largely replaced (as an alternative to open operation) by microscopic surgery. Recently, however, there has been a revival of interest in CD, partly because the new enzymes are safer, but mainly because of the increasing number of discograms that are being performed; for once the needle is in place to inject the dye into the disc, it is not difficult (if the discogram is positive) to substitute a different syringe and inject lytic enzymes to dissolve the nucleus pulposus.

2. *Microscopic discectomy* can be performed through a very small (2") incision, and does not usually require a laminectomy. [See Fig. 5-27.] The operating microscope can be maneuvered past the bones and nerves, and placed adjacent to the extruded disc material, which can then be removed by means of special instruments. It is now considered better to remove the entire nucleus, not merely the herniating part, because the remaining disc will herniate again in an unacceptable number of cases. When this more complete removal of the disc is performed, the results are said to be comparable to those in laminectomy/discectomy.

3. *Suction discectomy* is an adaptation of a procedure used to remove atheromatous plaques from peripheral arteries. [See Fig. 5-27.] A tiny tube (2 mm internal diameter) is inserted through a skin incision only slightly larger than the tube, and introduced under X-ray control through the anulus fibrosus into the nucleus. Nuclear material is sucked into the lumen of the tube through openings in the sides, sliced off by rotating blades, and the fragments removed by suction. This procedure is almost an outpatient surgery; most patients are discharged home after an overnight stay in hospital, and may be back to work in a few days. A great many suction discectomies have been carried out in the San Francisco area, and it is recognized by Blue Cross /Blue Shield of California for purposes of reimbursement, i.e., it is an established procedure.

All these alternative procedures have become very popular, especially microscopic discectomy, which is now offered in most centers. They are not, however, suitable in all cases. Patients who have disc fragments free in the spinal canal, may require open surgery to retrieve this material. Similarly, those who have scarring from previous back surgery are poor candidates for any of these new techniques, since scar tissue makes the use of an endoscope or a long needle very difficult. The older open operation may therefore still be indicated by the special circumstances of the case.

§ 5:35 The prognosis in low back cases

The outcome, with or without surgery, for most patients with low back problems is good. Only a small fraction, perhaps less than 5% of those who seek medical help, become disabled. It has been found however that this tiny fraction are responsible for more than 80% of the costs, direct and economic, of this condition, and this could be 80% of 20–40 billion dollars each year. A good deal of research effort has been devoted to identifying these people and either educating them to avoid injury, or diverting them to tasks where they are less likely to hurt their backs. None of these objectives are easily obtainable, The main common factors which these patients have appear to be psychological and social rather than physical (e.g., unhappy in their work). Reports on this project tend therefore to be pessimistic at present.

Part V.
Neck Problems

§ 5:36 The differences between low back and neck problems

The cervical spine has a number of anatomical peculiarities, and its functions are quite different from the lumbar spine. The spine in general, and the lower parts of it in particular, need to be stable to bear the strains of moving about (leg movements) and lifting, etc,. (arm movements). The cervical spine on the other hand must move the head around to investigate the environment. They also differ a good deal in the causes and kinds of injury they are likely to suffer, and so merit special treatment, although the same general outline can be retained.

1. The vertebral bones (and the intervertebral discs) are smaller than those in the dorsal or lumbar spine. Consequently, the usual degenerative changes are completed sooner, so that the discs become replaced by fibrous tissue. A disc herniation is therefore less likely in older persons, since fibrous tissue, unlike the jelly like substance of the nucleus pulposus, does not herniate.

2. The neck is less well protected than the rest of the spine. There is no bony support as there is in the chest (the rib cage) and the muscles in the neck are relatively small compared with the massive paraspinalis muscles of the lumbar spine. The soft tissues of the neck are thus much more likely to be badly damaged in an accident than those in the dorsal or lumbar areas.

3. Finally, neck problems are usually caused by automobile accidents, especially rear end collisions. Low back problems, on the other hand have more varied causes, and are commonly work related.

§ 5:37 The anatomy of the cervical spine—the cervical vertebrae

There are seven vertebral bones in the neck. The lower five are similar in a general way to those in the rest of the spinal column, but there are differences. [See Fig. 5-28.]

1. The vertebral bodies, intervertebral discs, etc., of the cervical spine, as was earlier mentioned, are smaller than those lower down, since they have less weight to carry.

2. The surfaces of the cervical facet joints are angled upward and outward in such a way that flexion and extension are maximized. Little rotation is possible in these joints. Rotation is accomplished by the head moving round the odontoid process of the axis.

3. There is an opening in each lateral process called a *foramen transversarium*. The foramina transversaria (left and right) surround and protect the vertebral arteries.

4. The upper two vertebral bones in the cervical spine, the *atlas* and *axis*, are quite different from the other vertebral bones. [See Fig. 5-29.] The *atlas* lies directly under the skull (hence the name, as the mythical giant Atlas was supposed to carry the world

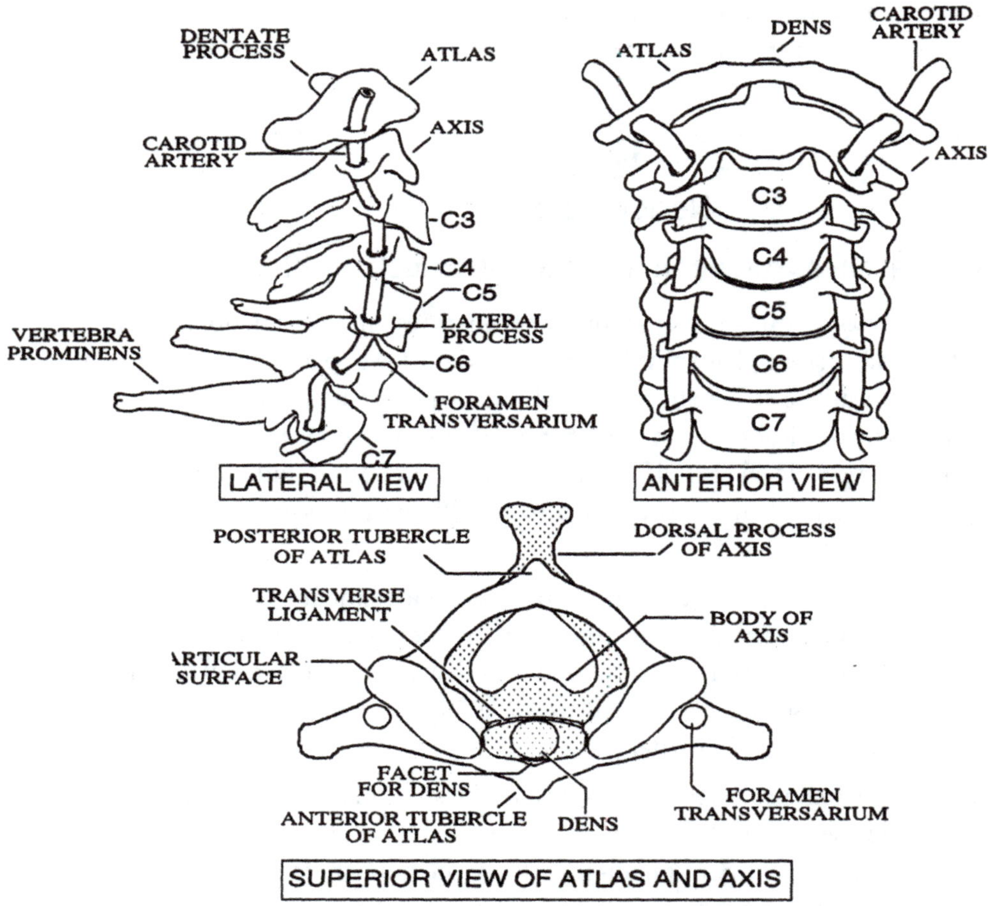

Fig. 5-28 The cervical spine; anterior, lateral, and superior views

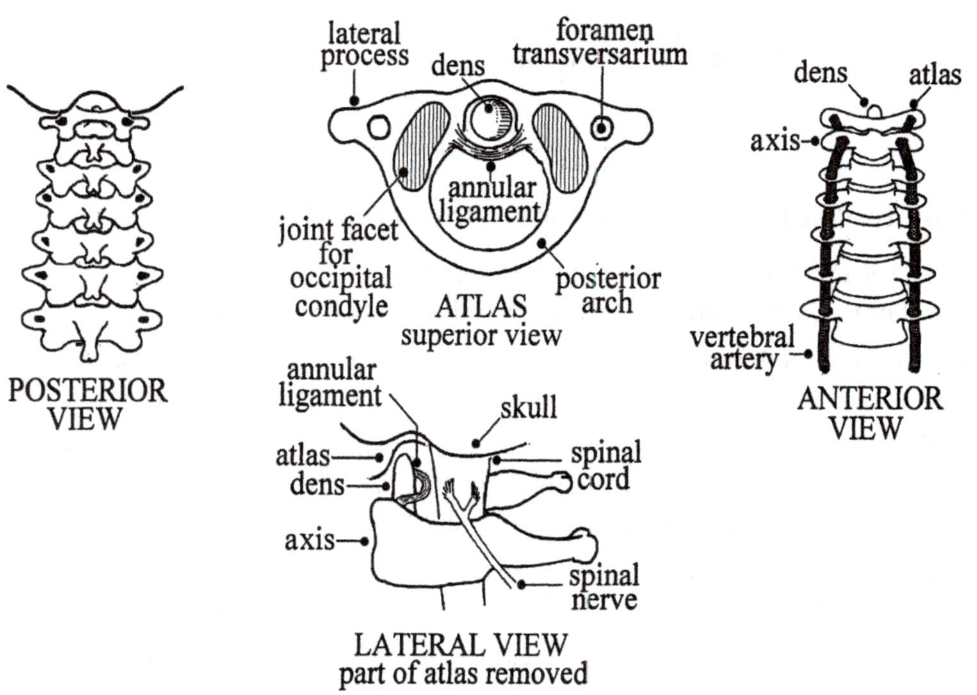

Fig 5-29 The atlas and axis bones

on his back). Its distinctive features are that it has no vertebral body and has two large joint facets on its upper surface which articulate with the *occipital condyles* of the skull. This *atlanto-occipital joint* allows the head to flex and extend (nod) on the neck. In the *axis* the vertebral body is replaced by the *odontoid process*, which looks like a canine tooth (hence the name). This projects upwards into the bony ring of the atlas. Here it articulates with a joint surface on the anterior arch of the axis. It is held in place against this joint surface by a powerful fibrous band, the *cruciform ligament* (transverse ligament). Most of the rotation of the head takes place at this joint, with the head and atlas together turning round on the odontoid process like a wheel on its axle. The cruciform ligament also protects the *brain stem* which lies directly behind the odontoid process. If this ligament breaks with trauma or degenerative change (or a combination of both), the odontoid process can press back against the brain stem with fatal consequences.

§ 5:38 Soft tissue injuries of the neck

The intervertebral discs in the cervical spine (as was mentioned earlier) are smaller and, in consequence, become fibrous much sooner than those in the thoracic and lumbar regions. One researcher, indeed, who has studied a great many cervical discs during autopsies on young patients, reports that very few of them who were over 25 years of age had any recognizable nucleus pulposus, has concluded that they are therefore incapable of having an HNP. This conclusion does not square with the fact that a herniated nucleus pulposus is found from time to time in patients much older than this, and that cervical discectomies have been reliably reported on elderly patients. It is, however, probably true to say that a disc herniation is uncommon in the neck region and that the most likely result of neck trauma is injury to ligaments and tendons, the so-called *soft tissue injury of the neck.* Conversely a low back injury which does not clear up readily with rest and conservative treatment is likely to be a disc problem, since the muscles in this region are so massive that great force would be required to tear the ligaments and tendons. There will no doubt be occasional exceptions to this rule also.

§ 5:39 Life threatening neck injuries—neck fractures

Direct trauma to the neck is classified as either blunt or penetrating. Penetrating injuries can sever the arteries and blunt trauma can damage the larynx and other vital structures. Such injuries may require prompt expert attention if the patient is to survive.

Neck trauma usually occurs in front or rear end collisions, or occasionally through violent shaking. Very violent shaking can cause bony fractures. Neck fractures, unlike skull fractures, are always taken seriously, for they can be immediately life threatening or leave the patient paralyzed. If the fracture is in the upper cervical bones the injury is likely to be rapidly fatal. The lower brain stem lies in the spinal canal of the upper two cervical bones and fracture here, unless the patient is very fortunate, will press on the vital centers of the medulla oblongata so that death follows almost immediately. Fractures involving the third, fourth and fifth cervical vertebrae may result in ventilatory failure and death since the spinal nerves emerging at these levels are motor to the diaphragm, the principal muscle involved in breathing ("C 3, 4, and 5 keep the diaphragm alive"). Damage to C6 and C7 may produce quad-

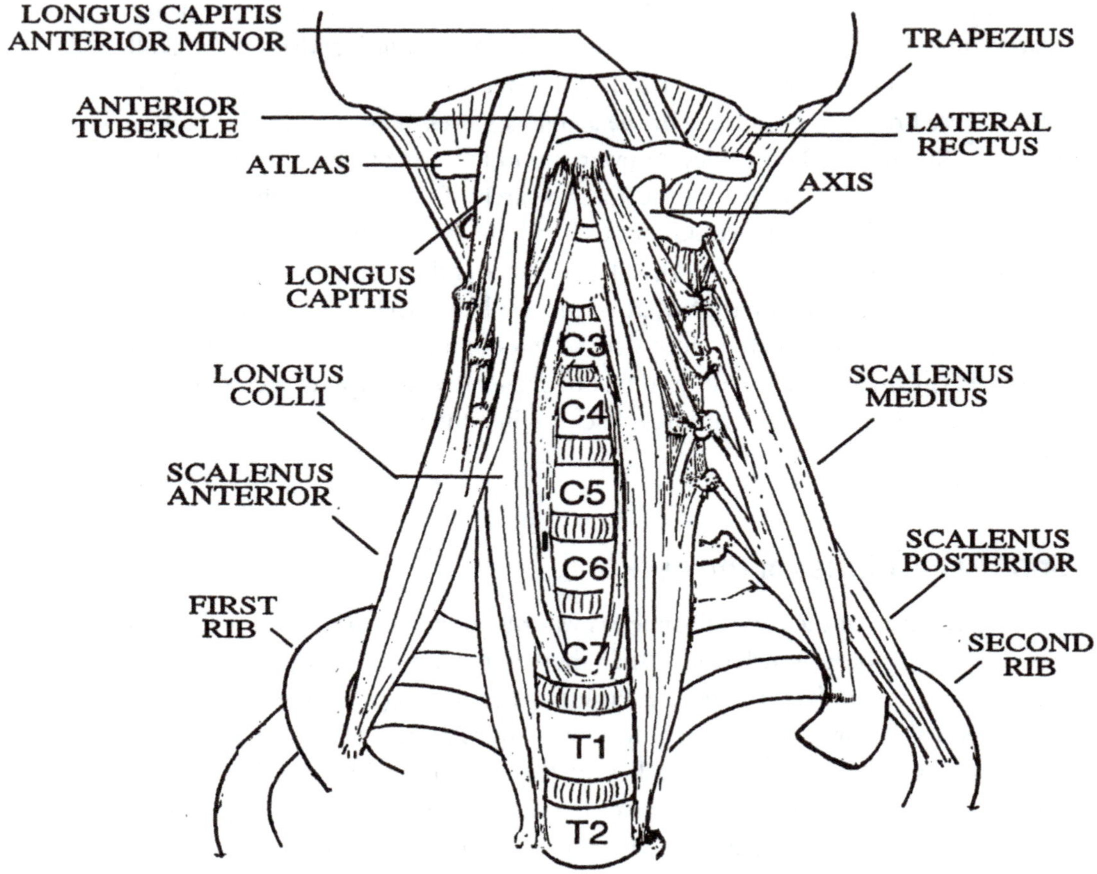

Fig. 5-30 Deep muscle layers of the neck, anterior view

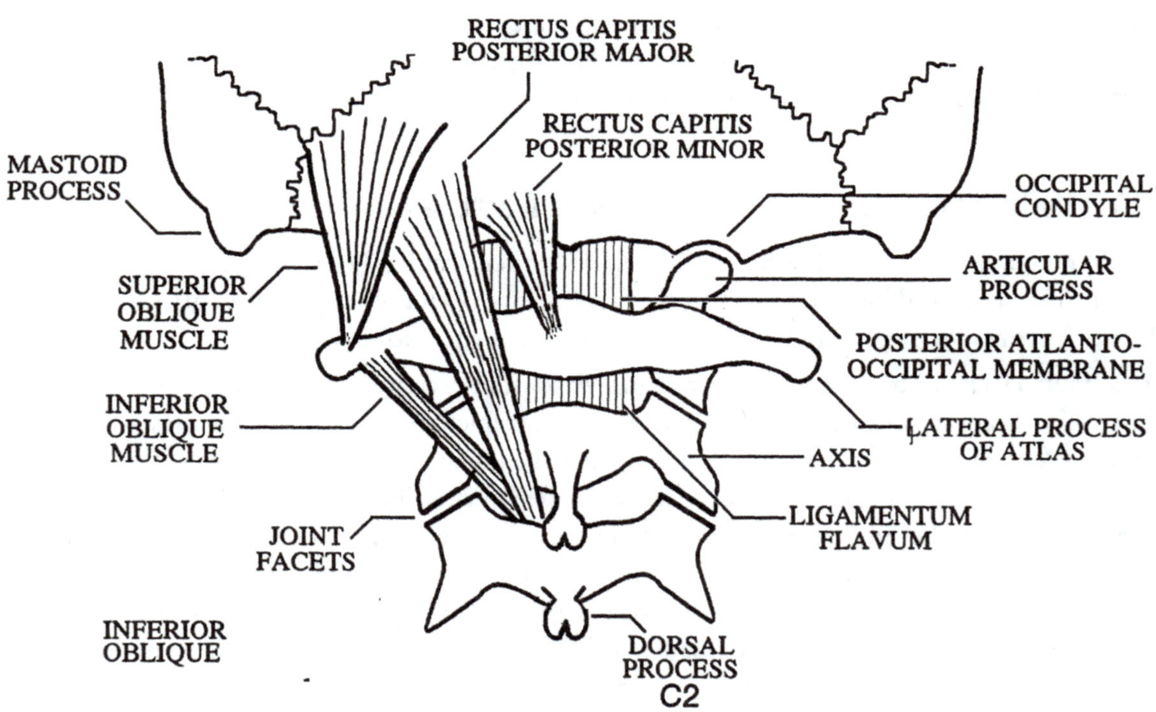

Fig. 5-31 Deep muscle layers of the neck, posterior view

riplegia. The higher the fracture in this region the more likely it is to be fatal, though much depends on the extent of the associated injuries to the spinal cord. If cord damage is very localized or milder, a patient may retain ventilatory function and survive with only C3 intact. A patient who survives spinal cord injury may well be quadriplegic or paraplegic (depending on the level of the cord damage). Some very resourceful and determined patients have learned to live with their disabilities, and some of them have even been able to work. It must be acknowledged, however, that achieving meaningful existence following such injuries requires much mental fortitude and a good outlook on life. Considerable family resources are also probably needed.

Small children are particularly likely to have high neck fractures since the head is relatively large and much more mobile on the neck at the *atlanto-occipital joint* than it is in the adult. The muscles of the neck are likewise less robust. It is not surprising then that the fatality rate with neck trauma in small children is high.

§ 5:40 Non-fatal neck trauma—whiplash injuries

The typical neck injury occurs during forceful hyperflexion or hyperextension. Both of these movements are involved in the so-called "whiplash" injury, where an automobile is struck from behind and accelerated forward. The head of a passenger or driver is therefore suddenly jerked backward. Reflex actions of the neck muscles stop this backward movement and then pull the head forward again into the normal position. Commonly the car is suddenly braked or stopped just after the rear-end collision so that the head is suddenly jerked forward and the process repeated in reverse (forward jerk followed by backward compensatory movement). In the most serious forms of this accident, severe whiplash injuries, the brain moves suddenly also, so that the brain stem suffers traction damage and the brain itself is rotated, bumped, squeezed and generally pulled around inside the skull. In the less severe cases (the great majority) the only injury is to soft tissues; the muscles, tendons, and joint surfaces of the neck.

Whiplash injuries can also be found in abused children who have been taken by the shoulders and shaken, so that their heads move violently forward and back. These, like rear-end collisions in automobiles, may damage the brain stem and spinal cord, cause fractures of the neck bones or merely damage the neck muscles. Because of the relatively large head and weak neck muscles of little children, these injuries tend (as was mentioned earlier) to be more severe than in adults.

§ 5:41 A typical neck injury case

In the typical neck injury complaint which is seen by a lawyer, the claimant has been involved in an accident (e.g. a rear end collision) and seen shortly thereafter at a hospital emergency department, where X-rays of the cervical spine were taken and read as negative. A soft cervical collar was supplied, medication was prescribed (analgesics and perhaps muscle relaxants), and the patient instructed to be seen for review in one week by their family physician (or sooner if symptoms became worse). If the pain was still severe one week later, X-rays may well be repeated (hair line fractures show up better after a week or so), and physical therapy perhaps ordered. If complaints continued, consultation with an orthopedist may have been arranged or the patient, on their own, may have begun to visit a chiropractor where further X-rays were probably made.

Such cases are notoriously troublesome to lawyers. They present a number of problems, two of which merit discussion here. These are:

1. What is the nature of the injury? and
2. How can the severity of the damage be demonstrated?

§ 5:42 The nature of soft tissue injuries

The term "soft-tissue injuries" is much bandied about by both lawyers and doctors, and it is something of an "omnium gatherum" expression. It literally means non-bony injuries, and in this sense it lumps together a number of things that are quite different from one another, and which probably should be discussed separately. Thus nerve fibers, intervertebral discs and blood vessels are all soft tissues, strictly speaking, but they are never so described. In both medical and legal usage, the term is confined to muscle, tendon and ligament damage. These are somewhat different entities, but they have important features in common. Tendons (joining muscle to bone) and ligaments (joining bones together) are similar in that they are both fibroelastic tissues. The fibrous element prevents over stretching, and the elastic fibers allow some movement and absorb energy. Fibroelastic tissues are also like one another in that they both have a poor blood supply. They are said to be *bradytrophic tissues* because they do not use much energy, nor do much work. Because of their poor blood supply and relatively few cells, these tissues heal poorly and slowly. If they are torn they also difficult to repair. Sutures must be inserted in a special way to prevent them from tearing

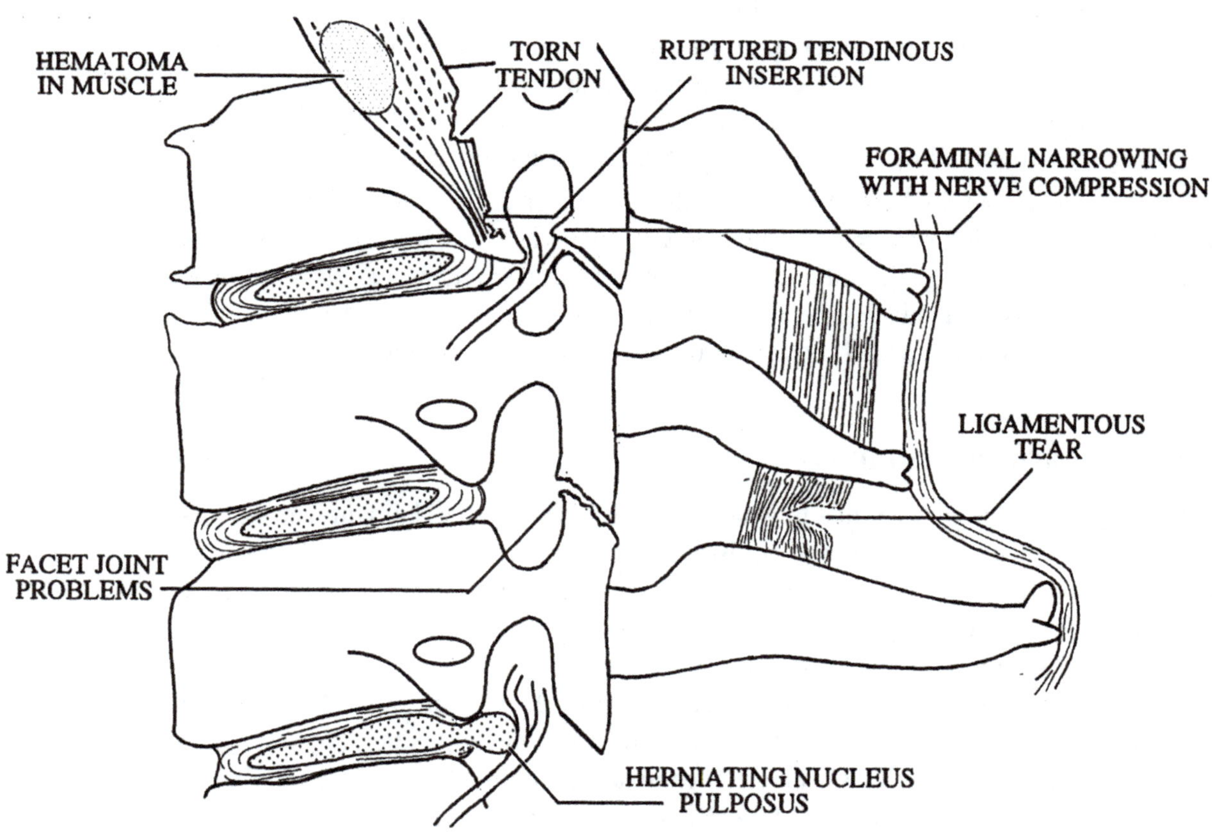

Fig. 5-32 Diagram representing soft tissue injuries in the neck

through the ligamentous or tendinous tissue. Injury to muscle fibers is quite different since they have a good blood supply and so should heal well. But it must be remembered that muscles contain fibroelastic supporting tissues throughout their entire bulk, and these connective tissue supports, if damaged, will behave as bradytrophic, not as vessel-rich, structures.

Muscles, ligaments, and tendons which are injured, but not obviously torn, are said to be *sprained*. Connective tissue sprains may be mild or severe. Mild sprains heal eventually. Severe ones may be very slow to heal or may never do so. The diagnosis of a sprain, based on clinical examination alone, tends to be in the nature of an educated guess. Unfortunately, soft tissue injuries and their severity can only be shown by imaging in a few special cases, e.g., damage to structures as small as the temporo-mandibular joint can be imaged by MRI, using a magnetic coil placed locally over the injured part, and tears in the glenoid cartilage can be shown using ultrasound imaging. But for most soft tissues, imaging will not be helpful, since its results are not verified by open operation. Thus having no verification of their results, such studies are generally not admissible in evidence

§ 5:43 Late-developing cervical arthritis

The bony surface of a joint is covered with a layer of cartilage. This smooth layer of cartilage is lubricated by the secretions of a thin, shiny, synovial membrane which encloses the joint at its margins. So effective is this system that human joints would never wear out in the absence of severe trauma or disease. There is really no such thing as "wear-and-tear arthritis"; damage is more likely to be the result of pathological processes such as viral infections. Cartilage itself has no blood supply and few cells. It receives its nourishment and gets rid of its metabolic waste by diffusion to and from the capillaries of the adjacent tissues, especially bone. The paucity of its cells and the nature of its vital supply lines have an unfortunate consequence—if seriously injured, cartilage repairs itself slowly, if at all.

The mechanisms by which trauma eventually leads to arthritic changes in joints is not really known. It has been thought that it was due to scar tissue replacing cartilage and then rubbing against the opposing joint surfaces eventually extending the damage to and fro in this way till the entire joint surfaces were destroyed. It is unlikely that this is the whole explanation, even if it is partly true. More recent accounts tend to implicate inflammatory processes with the release of cytokines by white blood cells or even negative pressure effects generated by thick inspissated joint fluid. But whatever its pathogenesis, the destructive processes somehow extend to destroy the entire joint surface and stimulate wild uncoordinated growth in the underlying bone. This process takes time—from four to ten years as a rule—by which time the compensation process is completed or else the Statute of Limitations has taken care of the matter. The possibility of post-traumatic arthritis must then be considered for compensation purposes before the problem surfaces—a difficult and doubtful process.

Delayed onset neck pain, starting four to ten years after the original accident, is likely to be due (if it is not a delayed disc problem) to an injury to the small joints of the neck: Whatever its causes may be, the destructive process proceeds, until the joint surfaces are destroyed. The underlying bone grows in an uncontrolled manner when thus exposed, making the joint surfaces irregular and producing bony spikes around the joint margins. These bony *exostoses* may impinge on exiting spinal nerves and produce nerve compression problems.

By one mechanism or another, then, the ultimate disability is likely to be substantial. Difficulty in turning the head interferes with many things, including driving an automobile: but the principal problem is pain. Not only is there pain on the slightest movement, but there is irritation and spasm of the muscles of the neck, probably due to nerve entrapment. Involvement of the first and second cervical nerves, which control the muscles of the scalp, can lead to "muscular headaches" which may be severe enough to be disabling. Headaches starting in the neck and spreading to the front of the head are a common finding in cervical arthritis. To control this pain, aspirin or other anti-inflammatory drugs may be required in sizable amounts. The stomach is commonly affected by these drugs, sometimes to the point of producing significant peptic ulcer disease (PUD). In some cases large amounts of *non-steroidal anti-inflammatory drugs* (NSAIDS) may affect the kidneys or other organs. This is especially likely to occur in older patients.

One of the worst sequelae of cervical arthritis is *compression neuropathy* (a pinched nerve) affecting the arms and hand. This term is used loosely to describe any ache or pain, but in its true significance, it is a serious affliction. The neural foramen is narrowed by arthritic bony spurs (*osteophytes*). These may grow to press on the nerve roots. The result is maddening pain, and eventual damage to the nerve. Individual fingers become numb (a tell-tale sign), and muscle wasting may begin. Treatment is commonly surgery to relieve pressure on the nerve.

The effect of all of these things on the patient's ability to do effective work or indeed to enjoy any other activity whatever, can hardly be imagined. Yet it must be very rare indeed if compensation for future cervical arthritis is included in a settlement.

Part VI.
Proving Damage in Neck Injury Cases

§ 5:44 Proof of neck injuries in general—severe and milder damage

Serious neck injuries with bony fractures are usually not difficult for compensationists to manage. If the spinal cord is damaged the resulting neurological problems should be obvious, e.g., a paraplegia or damage to the cervical plexus of nerves, which should manifestly impair movements of the arm or hand. Probably the most likely error of omission in these cases would be to miss minimal brain damage from concomitant *diffuse axonal injury* (DAI).

The cases which cause most difficulty to lawyers involve soft tissue injuries, and the remainder of this chapter will largely be devoted to proof of soft tissue damage.

§ 5:45 Proof of soft-tissue injury in the neck using medical records

The medical record in a neck injury begins at the scene of the accident. The ambulance attendants (rescue squad, paramedics or whatever) make out a report, which can be most useful in evaluating the severity of a cervical injury. It will generally state if the patient complained of neck pain at once, or only later. It is unlikely (although not impossible) that someone will have a serious neck sprain and not complain of pain at once. An important exception to this, will be when there are serious injuries elsewhere. A broken arm or leg, generating extreme pain, reduces the patient's awareness from pain elsewhere, and such pain may not be noticed until later. Important records which should be considered are:

1. A copy of the *ambulance report* may be found in the emergency departmental records or can be sought in the records of the ambulance service.

2. The *police report,* if available, should not be ignored. This will normally include some details about the accident which may be useful. The type of collision (rear end or frontal), the condition of the vehicles (totally wrecked /relatively intact), the position of the vehicles (upright, turned over, nose down in the ditch etc.), the directions, weights and speeds of the vehicles (judged from skid marks etc.), can all be important pieces of information which can give some idea as to the magnitude of the forces involved and whether they would be likely or not to whip the neck around. Serious injuries can occur with low speed impacts but the physical features of the accident are part of the total picture and should be reviewed.

3. The *emergency room record* should also be consulted. This contains evaluation by nurses as well as by physicians, and both should be read: the more detailed history may indeed be provided by the nurses. The important points to note are whether complaints about the neck were immediate, and whether they were mild or severe. Slight neck pain or pain which only began the day after the accident are likely to represent, *prima facie,* a mild neck sprain, which should normally heal quickly and completely. The record of the physical examination may note any muscle spasm present; the precise site of any tenderness present; and whether or not there were any marks on the skin such as bruises or abrasions. A severe neck injury is not of course necessarily accompanied by bruising or complaints of pain, immediate or otherwise. But these things are part of the total picture and should be noted.

4. The *office records* of treating physicians may need to be consulted to see how the problem developed following the accident. A most important finding, which should be sought out if possible from these records, is whether or not there was spasm of neck muscles present. Spasm of a group of muscles (as opposed to stiffening of the whole neck) cannot normally be accomplished voluntarily and therefore cannot be faked. The office records of physicians are also useful for details about pain medications. The amounts and kinds of analgesic prescribed may be due to the demands of the patient (addiction rather than pain) but potent analgesics and muscle relaxants, liberally and freely prescribed, are *prima facie* indications that the pain problem was perceived by the treating physician to be serious. The office records of the treating physician may, in addition, provide a bonus so far as lawyers are concerned; they may contain reports from referral physicians such as orthopedists, rheumatologists and rehabilitation specialists. They may also contain important radiological reports.

5. The departmental records of *physical therapy departments* should also be consulted. They often contain records of very thorough physical examinations by the physical therapists. These reports can, indeed, be more detailed than those of physicians and can be very useful indeed to compensationists. Comments by the therapist as to the genuineness and appropriateness of the complaints of pain may well be entered in the record, when there is a serious possibility of malingering or compensationitis. It is especially compelling if there is inconsistency in the patient's story. The physical therapy records also contain notes about treatments given and comments on their effectiveness. The number of treatments and the period of time over which treatments were continued may be of some importance. A record describing prolonged treatment and slow re-

sponse is *prima facie* evidence of a serious injury, while a short course of treatment suggests (again *prima facie*) a relatively mild injury. Conclusions about the severity of the injury should not, however, be reached by considering the duration of treatment only, without examining the record carefully. Prolonged treatment may merely indicate a poor attitude on the part of the patient or inadequate cooperation with the therapist. It may even be due to somatization (hysteria) or be fraudulent. Conversely a short course may merely mean that the patient was discouraged by slow progress or could not afford the treatments. The short course may, indeed, have been explicitly ordered by the treating physician. Orthopedists tend now to think that prolonged physical therapy may slow recovery rather than hasten it. Patients like to be passive, letting the therapists do things for them, rather than be responsible for the exercise programs which are currently viewed as the most important part of a rehabilitation program.

§ 5:46 Physical examination of the cervical spine

Deformity and malposition of the neck can be easily seen. The commonest is probably *torticollis* (wry neck), a painful spasm of the deep musculature of the neck on one side or the other. This may be due to underlying disc disease, but is often the result of a viral infection or a draft of cold air (from a car window) irritating the neck muscles.

Active movements of the neck are examined by asking the patient to turn the head sideways and attempt to touch each shoulder with the ear (to test lateral flexion); to put their chin on their chest (which tests forward flexion); and to bend their neck back to test extension. Rotation is tested by asking the patient to look round over their shoulder as far as they can on either side without turning the body. Variable patient responses in these tests suggests that the injury may not be genuine or is being exaggerated.

Passive range of motion can be carried out in much the same manner, but should be performed very carefully (if at all) in patients with neck injuries. If there is any suspicion of a fracture of the neck, X-rays are ordered first, and the movements are examined afterwards when the possibility of an unstable spine has been ruled out. The necks of patients with severe rheumatoid arthritis also merit gentle examination. Ligaments can be involved and weakened in the rheumatic process, and avulsion of a compromised annular ligament in the first cervical bone can allow the *odontoid process* of the *axis* to press on spinal cord or the lower brain stem with disastrous consequences.

Abnormalities in lateral flexion are found in the earlier stages of degenerative disease of the cervical spine. Pain and tenderness on forward flexion or backward extension suggests more advanced disease or even a herniated cervical disc.

Complete immobility of the cervical spine (commonly in the flexed position) is found in the latter stages of ankylosing spondylitis.

Clinical examination in a neck injury case should include examination of the arm and hand since the cervical plexus of nerves, deriving from cervical nerves 5-8 and T1 (the first thoracic nerve) control the upper limbs and extremities. *Power*, *tone*, *coordination* and *sensation* should all be tested. Weakness and wasting of muscle and sensory loss will be particularly significant in association with a neck injury. Muscle power is first tested by asking the patient to carry out active movements of all joints and then to repeat these against increasing resistance. Muscle power is graded on various scales (O-IV or 0-VI) but the scale used should be indicated and perhaps explained. Zero in any scale means complete paralysis and grade IV or grade VI, the upper limits of the scale, will indicate full power. Grades in between these extremes represent some intermediate degree of power [See § 7:55]

The clinical examination of sensation should test all types of sensation (pain, temperature, vibration, light touch and pressure sensation). It is usually enough, however, in order to demonstrate nerve root damage in a neck injury, to test the ability to feel pinprick (using a needle point) or to distinguish blunt from sharp sensation (B/S) using the hub and the point of the needle alternately.

§ 5:47 Evaluating neck injuries using diagnostic imaging

1. Ordinary *X-rays* of the cervical spine are rarely helpful in evaluating neck sprains. They will often show chronic degenerative changes which are not usually important (they can be present in patients with no neck or back complaints whatsoever). But they can sometimes show narrowing of the neural foramina (this normally requires oblique 45° angle pictures). This finding may be important in cases where there is clinical evidence of nerve compression syndrome (pinched nerve). In acute neck injuries, however, provided no bones are broken, they are commonly non-contributory.

2. *Diagnostic ultrasound* (U/S) is potentially helpful. Ultrasound does not penetrate bone well and it also performs poorly in the presence of pockets of air (e.g. bowel gas); but it can distinguish different tissues well and the pictures can be color coded. Computerized ultrasound is used by orthopedists to evaluate torn *glenoid cartilage* round the shoulder joint (prior to operative repair following repeated dislocations). Potentially U/S could be used to show tears in tendons and ligaments and also hematomas and ruptures in muscles. All of these findings would be valuable evidence as to the seriousness of a neck injury. Unfortunately this modality has not been used much in imaging soft tissue injuries, possibly because it is not perceived as influencing treatment decisions. Sprains, even severe ones, are generally treated conservatively and for the most part get better. So there is no point, from the medical point of view, in identifying the contusions, minor tears and inflammatory changes that might definitively make the diagnosis of a sprain. Unfortunately this approach, although justifiable from the therapeutic and administrative (cost control) point of view, is not helpful to compensationists who are trying to determine whether a claim relating to a neck injury is genuine or not. Special ultrasound studies could be ordered for compensation purposes, but until U/S is more extensively utilized in soft tissue imaging, protocols and interpretative guidelines cannot be properly established and the results are unlikely to be considered reliable.

3. *Computerized tomography* (CT) is currently capable of distinguishing different tissues, and also of differentiating normal from damaged tissue. As with U/S, this modality has not been used much in the study of soft tissue injuries, and probably for the same reason. It is not that the machine will not do the job, but that such studies are not generally perceived as being clinically important. This in turn means that they have not been validated in soft tissue injuries.

4. Probably *magnetic resonance imaging* (MRI) is the most promising modality currently in use so far as soft tissue injuries are concerned. It can penetrate bone to image joint cartilage, and the resolution is sufficiently good to permit even small joints to be viewed. The surfaces of the tiny temporomandibular joint can be imaged by means of MRI to investigate facial pain and rule out the *temporomandibular joint* (TMJ) syndrome. MRI is also extremely useful in evaluating knee injuries. The classification of injuries of the knee has indeed been altered completely due to the availability of MRI. When only clinical examination was available (unless the knee was being opened surgically) knee injuries were described as instabilities (medial, lateral or cruciate) depending on how much abnormal movement of the joint was found. Since MRI became more readily available, they are now described by the extent of the tears in the various ligaments, measured as a percentage of the breadth of the ligament. If the anterior cruciate is torn half way across (and this can be shown non-invasively by MRI) the injury will be described, very precisely, as a 50% tear of the anterior cruciate ligament.

There is no reason why MRI should not be used to distinguish serious injuries of the neck, which have produced significant disruption of the various tissues, from those which merely show a small tear or hemorrhagic spot here and there. But again since such studies are not routinely carried out on sprains and strains, they cannot be introduced in evidence since the images have not been compared to operative findings to establish reliability, and rule out the possibility of artifacts. Whether it would be worth while, in appropriate cases, to request an MRI for legal purposes, is a nice question. The MRI showing of a severe tear in a ligament or tendon might be so obvious that the possibility of artifact could be ruled out. And it is to be hoped also that the ability of MRI to image small joints might be extended to study the zygoapophyseal joints of the neck (and lower back). But present practice is against the use of imaging in soft tissue injuries.

§ 5:48 Demonstrating soft tissue injuries of the neck using thermography

Until MRI, CT and U/S are more regularly used to evaluate soft tissue injuries clinically, the mainstay of the compensation lawyer is likely to be *thermography*. This is imaging using body heat as the signal. Inflamed areas, such as joints or tendons, give off heat which can be detected if they are not too far below the surface of the body. If muscles are in spasm, the blood vessels will be squeezed, blood flow reduced and the area will be cooler than normal. If a nerve is being irritated (e.g. by an HNP) the sympathetic fibers contained in it may initiate vasospasm in a limb and lower temperature (by reducing blood flow).

There are two systems of thermographic imaging, liquid crystal thermography and infrared thermography. *Liquid crystal thermography* is carried out using thin envelopes which contain heat sensitive crystals. The crystals are selected so that they change color within the usual ranges of skin temperature with a temperature difference of about 1° Celsius. They are simply applied to the body part being studied, and the resulting color pattern recorded with a Polaroid camera. Thermography using an *infrared camera* is more expensive, but more suitable for showing damage, since the record is stored on magnetic tape and so is easily reproducible. Thermography is still a somewhat controversial topic in

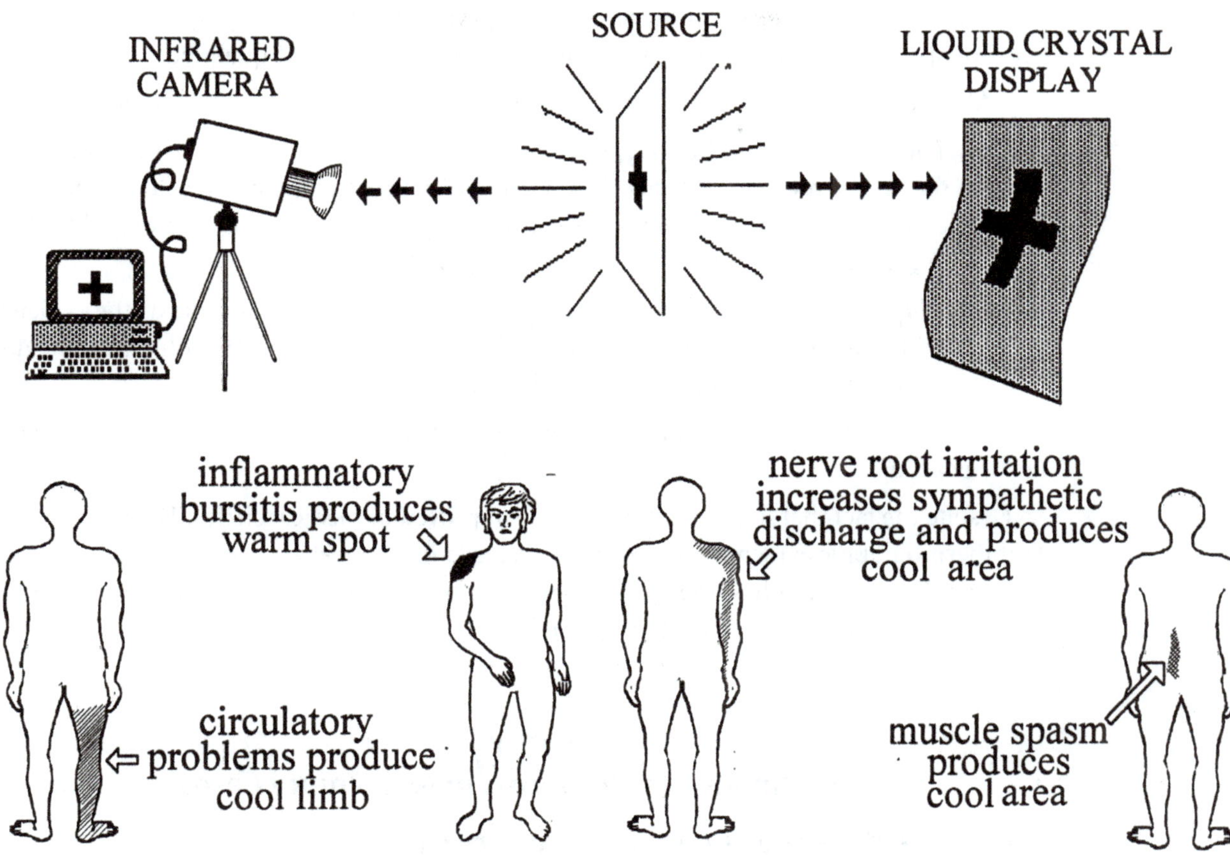

Fig. 5-33 Principles underlying thermography and some typical findings

orthodox medicine. Orthopedists have little experience of it and little use for it, since it does not convincingly show the nature of the damage, but only that some damage exists. Lawyers, on the other hand have more need to know that there really is some damage than the exact nature of it. But outside hospitals. thermography is a well established modality, with learned national societies (whose members include neurologists, rheumatologists and orthopedists) involved in developing its use and in training and accrediting technicians.

Thermography, strictly speaking, merely shows that the surface of the skin in some area was either cooler or warmer than normal (the other side of the body is often used as a reference). Expert opinion is required to interpret these findings in terms of the underlying causes (inflammation, muscle spasm or nerve root irritation) and this opinion may well be challenged. The undoubted value of thermography, however, is that if the temperature of the skin over an allegedly injured area is abnormal, whatever the cause, this suggests that there is a real problem, i.e., the claimant is not malingering or neurotic.

§ 5:49 Using thermographic evidence to show soft tissue injury

Dr. Harry Rhyne, an orthopedic surgeon and well known author on this subject, stresses the importance of carrying out the test according to strict protocols and presenting thermographic evidence properly. The most important requirements are:

1. The test should be conducted by a properly certified thermographer: a researcher or specialist physician, if not certified as a technician, is not qualified.

2. Room conditions and room temperature should be stable (no drafts, no sunlight).

3. The patient should be stripped and their skin temperature allowed to equilibrate to that of the room for a period of at least twenty minutes (more on cold or hot days). The skin temperature should be monitored with sensors to be sure that equilibration with the ambient temperature has been achieved.

4. If liquid crystal sheets are used (not recommended in the legal context) the evidence should state that they were properly applied. An area of apparent coolness can be due to the fact that the sheet was not touching the skin at that point.

5. If an infrared camera was used the proper standardizing procedures should be evidenced.

Despite the fact that it is not yet universally approved in medical circles, Dr. Rhyne states that thermographic evidence has never been refused in an appellate court when it was properly presented. When it has been refused, one or other of the above standards, and generally more than one, has been violated or ignored.

Part VII. Treatment and Prognosis in Neck Injury Cases

§ 5:50 Treatment of serious neck injury cases

The treatment of serious neck problems which are life threatening or associated with risk of spinal cord damage, is a complex matter, the details of which hardly concern us here. Serious neck trauma may well require transfer of the patient as quickly as possible to a trauma center. An experienced team may need to conduct evaluation, diagnostic imaging and treatment more or less simultaneously. The airway may need to be secured with a rapid tracheostomy if intubation would mean moving and so endangering the cervical spine. Surgical decompression of the spine may be required or the spine may need to be immobilized in a head and neck brace screwed into the skull. Spinal cord injuries need to be diagnosed quickly because medical treatment can limit and reduce the extent of cord damage if it is begun early enough. Trauma seldom completely transects the cord and it has been found that much of the damage is produced by secondary release of interleukins and free radicals around the nerve fibers. High dose intravenous steroids and other medications, which block interleukins or scavenge free radicals, can prevent this secondary damage. In some cases the nerve fiber bundles will be left intact and the patient will be more or less normal. And even when the cord damage is severe, medical treatment may make a difference in the outcome. To reduce cord damage by even one segment may mean the difference between the patient walking with calipers instead of being confined to a wheel chair.

§ 5:51 Treatment of degenerative disc disease in the neck

The treatment of degenerative disc disease in the neck does not really differ much from that of DDD in the lumbar spine. Cervical disc herniations are relatively uncommon, but when they do occur they are diagnosed and treated exactly as they would be anywhere else in the vertebral column [see § 5:31-§ 5:34 above]. If medical treatments should happen to fail, *laminectomy /discectomy* or *microscopic discectomy* may be indicated, and will not differ substantially from the same operation in the lumbar region. The development of bony spurs around the neural foramina are more likely to compress emergent nerves in the cervical region than elsewhere in the spine, and *decompression surgeries* may be needed to deal with related problems (muscular headaches in the scalp and numbness and weakness in the arms and hands). *Spinal stenosis* is more common in the cervical region (due to the smaller diameter of the spinal canal). This presents somewhat differently from the same condition in the lumbar region of the spine [see § 7:21 above] and is difficult to treat, but if surgery is indicated, it will be essentially the same procedure, i.e., by surgical decompression of the cervical spinal cord.

§ 5:52 Prognosis in soft tissue injuries of the neck

Follow up studies on patients with soft tissue injuries of the neck vary somewhat in their findings, but most report that the majority of these patients will be more or less back to normal in six months (the time varies somewhat in the different reports). It has also proved difficult to find any features which accurately predict prolonged disability, although generally this is associated with high energy trauma. A more sinister finding, rather like the findings in studies of low back injuries, is that the disabled group of patients resemble one another more in features of their MMPI scores and in results on other social and psychological inventories and tests, rather than in their physical findings. Consequently, as in the case of low back injuries, all claims, including those that are genuine, may be viewed initially with some suspicion by insurance adjustors and others representing payor agencies.

Part VIII.
Clinical Examination of the Musculoskeletal System

§ 5:53 General organization of the clinical examination of the musculoskeletal system

Like all examinations, the M/S exam is made up of the basic elements of looking, listening, palpation, and testing. Listening, of course, is not so important as it is in the cardiovascular or respiratory exam. In fact the only abnormal things that you could expect to hear would be the creaking of joints and tendons (crepitus) or perhaps the sound of the patient's footsteps before they enter the examination room. Observation, palpation and clinical maneuvers are all important. The record of the M/S examination may be very complete, or cursory, or even sketchy. But it should not be concluded that a very brief report implies an incomplete examination, or that an incomplete examination is inadequate. The physical examination here, as elsewhere in the body, follows and depends upon the history—the patient's story and responses to questions. If a patient has sprained an ankle and denies pain or injury elsewhere (waving all his sound limbs around to prove it) one can hardly complain if the examining doctor concentrates on the ankle and only perfunctorily examines the rest of the body.

§ 5:54 Inspection

This begins as the patient enters the room and continues all through the examination. The patient's gait, posture, etc., may be specifically tested, but are often evaluated automatically out of the corner of the physician's eye. Gait is very revealing. An *antalgic gait* is one produced by pain. It is characterized by a rapid step on the affected side which minimizes the time spent on the sore leg. The antalgic gait has even a characteristic sound which can be recognized by the experienced ear before the patient appears at all. The *Trendelenburg gait* is another very characteristic one found in patients with one leg shorter than the other, or with weakness of the hip muscles on one side. The sound of the footstep is the same on both sides but one side (with the longer leg or the weak muscles) has to be lifted up past the other so that the second step is delayed. Other typical walking patterns are the so-called *scissors gait* (typical of spastic patients) where the knees rub past one another, and the slapping *ataxic gait* of advanced CNS diseases such as tertiary syphilis. Abnormalities of muscle tone and the positioning (set) of the body can also be observed, as can deformities or other gross abnormalities. Redness (erythema) over a joint, or obvious swelling of a joint, may also be seen. Observation of the face is important for evidence of pain (painful facies), and also for concomitant or related mental disorders, e.g., anxiety and depression (common following accidents).

§ 5:55 Examination of muscles

The various muscle groups can be observed for size and symmetry. Dislocation of the head of the humerus, for example, alters the appearance of the deltoid muscles, changing the outline of the shoulder from the normal smooth round shape to a sharp angular one. Wasting or hypertrophy of any muscle group can also be noticed. If the median nerve to the hand is being compressed in the region of the wrist, as in the carpal tunnel syndrome, the muscles of the hand will eventually become wasted.

Wasting of a limb should not be merely described in general terms, but quantified with a tape measure. Forearm muscle wasting, for instance, may be standardized by measuring the diameter of the forearm ten inches above the wrist on the affected side, and comparing the result to the measurement of the other arm at the same point. There is usually a difference between the dominant and non-dominant arm but allowance can be made for this. The difference between the two sides is normally less than an inch (except in professional tennis players, etc.).

The *power* of each muscle group can then be tested. Power is measured in standard terms clinically. A typical system of measurement would be:

Power 0 = inability to move the limb

Power I = slight movement of the limb is possible when the limb is supported (removing the force of gravity)

Power II = ability to move against gravity

Power III = ability to overcome slight resistance

Power IV = ability to move against moderate resistance

Power V = full power

The conventional units may vary some from place to place, but the meaning is made clear by declaring the number of units that denote full power. In the example just quoted, for example, the ability to move against gravity might be described as power II/V where normal power (the highest category) is grade V. Rehabilitation specialists may quantify muscle weakness more precisely than this by seeing what weight the limb can move or lift, or even by making the patient push and pull against fixed resistances and recording their performance electronically. Fatigue is measured, e.g., by moving a weight repetitively until the muscle tires.

§ 5:56 Examination of the joints and joint movements

The joints are observed for deformity, swelling, redness or bruising, and palpated for tenderness or any sign of heat. They are then tested for range of movement (ROM). Active range of movement (AROM) and passive range of movement (PROM) are both tested. In *active range of movement* the patients put their own joints through all the standard movements and the examiner notes the angles obtained (and any associated pain). *Passive ROM* means that the examiner does the moving. The ROM of a joint can be measured fairly precisely by using a *goniometer* (a simple device for measuring angles) but it is often calculated (perhaps guessed) approximately by looking at the movement with an "educated eye." The normal ranges of motion for each joint can be found in books, such as those published to aid doctors doing evaluations for Workers' Compensation purposes. A rough estimate of normal ROM can, however, be obtained by observing ones own movements in a mirror, or taking those of some other person (presumably healthy) as normal. It is important to observe if there is pain at any point in the range of motion of a joint and, if so, at what angle in the arc it appears. The pain of bursitis in the shoulder, for example, characteristically appears at 90° of abduction.

§ 5:57 Examination of the cervical spine

Deformity and malposition of the neck can be easily seen. The commonest abnormality found in clinical practice is probably *torticollis* (wry neck), a painful spasm of the deep musculature of the neck on one side or the other. This may be due to underlying disc disease but is often due to a viral infection or cold air (from a car window) irritating the neck muscles.

Active movements of the neck are examined by asking the patient to attempt to touch each shoulder with their head and to bend the head down unto the chest or back. These movements test lateral movement, forward flexion and backward extension. Rotation is tested by asking them to look over each shoulder as far as they can without turning the body.

Passive range of motion can be carried out in much the same manner, but should be performed very carefully (if at all) in patients with neck injuries. If there is any suspicion of a fracture of the neck, X-rays are ordered first, and the movements are examined afterwards when the possibility of an unstable spine has been ruled out. The necks of patients with severe rheumatoid arthritis also merit gentle examination. Ligaments can be involved and weakened in the rheumatic process, and avulsion of a compromised *transverse ligament* in the first cervical bone can allow the *odontoid process* of the axis to press on the spinal cord or the lower brain stem with disastrous consequences.

Abnormalities in lateral flexion are found in the earlier stages of degenerative disease of the cervical spine. Pain and tenderness on flexion or extension suggests more advanced disease such as a herniated cervical disc.

Complete immobility of the cervical spine (commonly in the flexed position) is found in the latter stages of *ankylosing spondylitis* (*Marie-Strumpel disease*).

§ 5:58 Examination of the lumbar spine

The spine is first observed for deformity. It may be deformed by disease of the bones (e.g. tuberculosis of the dorsal spine); or muscle spasm (in a disc problem) may cause a *scoliosis* (abnormal lateral curvature).

Forward flexion of the spine is tested as follows. [See Fig. 5-22] The patient is asked to stand with the knees straight and, bending the back, slide the palms of the hands down over the front of the legs. Two things are worth noting here; first how far the back can be flexed without pain and second, whether the lumbar spine flexes properly. Normally the lumbar spine flexes in every part as the patient attempts to touch their toes (like the bending of a bow). Patients who have lumbar disc problems, however, keep the lumbar spine straight as they bend. It is splinted by the muscles in order to minimize pain. This loss of flexion in the lumbar spine cannot easily be faked if it can be faked at all. Malingerers tend to hold the whole back stiff, not the lumbar part only. Lateral flexion of the lumbar spine is also tested.

Palpation of the spine is important to detect pain, deformity and muscle spasm. The dorsal spines and the interspinous spaces are palpated (usually with the thumb). The L3-L4 interspace is roughly opposite the iliac crest in the pelvis (which can easily be identified). Vertebrae can be counted upward and downward from this point so that an approximate estimate of the level of any pain or tenderness can be made. It is important to palpate the *sacroiliac joints* at the bottom of the spine. Sacroiliac joint pain can mimic disc pain, as it can be felt down the side of the leg even to the calf. Sacroiliac strains can, however, be secondary to low back problems, as the low back spasm tends to put the spine in an abnormal posture and throw stress on one or other of the sacroiliac joints.

Straight leg raising (SLR) is usually carried out with the patient lying supine (on their back). Each leg in turn is raised to the point where there is pain (preferably sciatic type pain running into the leg). The angle at which this occurs should be roughly estimated. Normally the legs can be raised to 85° or 90° without difficulty. A patient with significant disc disease may hurt at 45° or even less. The results of straight leg raising can be confirmed by bent leg raising (BLR). [See Fig. 5-23] The test begins with the hip and knee both flexed to 90°. The flexed knee joint is then slowly straightened out and the angle at which pain appears is noted. If pain appears, it should occur at about the same angle as in the straight leg raising. Malingerers will get the angle wrong, unless they are able to gauge the proper angle with their eyes or by joint position sense, both of which can easily be confused by the examiner asking them to close their eyes and pressing in a variable manner on the soles of their feet.

Bent leg raising can also be performed while the patient sits with their knees flexed over the edge of the examination table. The lower leg can then be moved up and down, almost without the patient noticing it.

Finally the *deep tendon reflexes* are tested as in the neurological examination. If one of the ankle jerks is diminished or missing on the same side as the radiation of the pain, this will be very suggestive of a nuclear disc herniation, probably a considerable one.

§ 5:59 Examination of the hip-joint

The hip area is observed in the usual way but the hip joint is surrounded by bulky muscles which conceal its contours and make it difficult to examine. Observation of the hip is usually only revealing when the patient is walking. This joint, for the same reason, requires deep palpation and it is necessary to know exactly where to find it. With the hip joint flexed and laterally rotated, a point is found half way between the *anterior superior iliac spine* and the *pubic tubercle* (a little bump on the upper surface of the body of the pubic bone near the mid-line). The inguinal ligament runs between these two points, and its mid-point can be identified by palpation. If a line about two inches long is drawn downward (distally) at right angles to the mid point of the inguinal ligament, the end of it should lie directly over the head of the femur. Similarly, pressure on the side of the leg at a point about four inches below the iliac crest will find the greater trochanter. If there is inflammation in the hip joint, pressure in either of these two places will produce pain.

The movements of the hip are tested in turn. *Rotation* can be tested by flexing the hip, holding the knee in place with one hand and moving the foot from side to side with the other. *Flexion* and *extension* are checked by moving the knee up and down, and *abduction* and *adduction* by moving the knee in and out from the midline. If these movements can be performed reasonably fully without pain, there is probably nothing wrong with the hip joint, but one must be sure that the muscles are relaxed, or else a muscle strain will cause pain. Even then the examiner can usually pick out a true hip problem since, in a muscle strain, there may be at least some direction in which movement is painless (unless all the muscles are injured, which is unusual).

§ 5:60 The examination of the knee

The first part of the examination of the knee is *inspection* for deformity, swelling, asymmetry or discoloration. A red swollen knee on one side only suggests a septic arthritis or pseudo-gout. Bilateral warm swelling would be more characteristic of rheumatoid arthritis. Gross bony deformity of both knees is typically found in long standing osteoarthritis. The knees should be inspected while the patient is standing . During weight bearing it is easier to see if the patient is knock-kneed (*genu valgus*) or bow-legged (*genu varus*). Atrophy of the quadriceps muscles in the thigh, a common concomitant of knee problems, is also more easily seen when the patient is standing.

The *popliteal fossa* behind the knee should be inspected for the presence of a Baker's cyst or an aneurysm. A *Baker's cyst* is an out-pouching of synovial lining from the knee joint. It is the equivalent of a ganglion on the wrist.

Palpation of any swelling of the knee should determine whether the problem is in the skin over the knee (as in cellulitis) or due to fluid in the knee itself. The swollen boggy synovial membranes of rheumatoid arthritis can also usually be recognized on palpation. The presence of fluid in the knee is confirmed by the method of *ballottement*. In this maneuver, fluid is displaced anteriorly in the knee joint by squeezing all round and behind the patella. If there is excess fluid in the joint, the patella will be floating free and can be made to bounce back and forward against the underlying bones. This is done by rapping on its anterior surface with one or two fingers. In the presence of excess fluid the patella will be felt to tap against the bones of the knee joint behind it. The record will read, if the test was positive, "patellar tap present." The *bulge sign* is present when the excess fluid is squeezed to one side of the knee and the swelling rapped sharply. The other side of the knee is watched for bulges appearing when the fluid is thus percussed. The bulge sign is said to be more sensitive than the patellar tap in the hands of someone who knows how to elicit and interpret it, but equivocal results may be obtained by less experienced persons.

Active and passive *range of movement* are both tested because patients with rheumatic diseases of the knee often have weakness of the quadriceps muscles and are unable to extend the knee against gravity. Passive movement may be carried out with one hand on the patella to feel for crepitations (grating sensations). Thus, the sensation (or even sound) made by the patella scraping on the underlying bones may be described as "patellar grating." *Crepitations* are found in any kind of rheumatic or degenerative disease of the knee, but minimal crepitations may also be heard in the normal knee, so that some care must be exercised in interpreting this finding.

The knee is tested for the presence in the joint space of foreign bodies or torn pieces of cartilage, by holding the joint with one hand and flexing and extending the knee with the other..This is done with the foot forcibly turned first inward and then outward, to bring additional pressure to bear on the meniscal cartilages at each side of the knee joint. The joint may then lock in in one position or a "clunk" may be felt as the joint surfaces move across the torn piece of cartilage. The occurrence of this "clunk" is known as "*McMurray's sign*."

The integrity of the ligaments of the knee is then tested. The collateral ligaments, medial and lateral, are examined by bending the lower leg inward and outward with the knee extended. If the ligaments are intact very little movement in either direction should be possible. If one or other is torn, the joint may open up rather easily and widely on that side.

The cruciate ligaments inside the knee joint are tested by laying the patient supine, flexing the hip and knee, and putting the foot flat on the examining table. This fixes the hip and the foot, but permits gliding movements at the knee joint. The tibia is then pushed backward and pulled forward. If the cruciate ligaments are intact very little movement backward and forward should be possible. If even one of the internal ligaments is torn, gliding movement will be appreciable. If the ligaments are not completely torn through but stretched or partially torn, there may be no increased mobility but there should be pain.

Short Working Vocabulary of Musculoskeletal Terms

V: Extension

Λ: Flexion

AA: Active/assisted exercises (order to physical therapist)

add.: Adduction

Acute disc syndrome: Low back problem problem of sudden onset.

Ankle jerk : The achilles tendon reflex

AFROM: Active full range of motion (physical therapy order)

Anatomical position: Standard positioning of the body for descriptive purposes, with the feet slightly apart, the arms to the sides and the palms (thumb outward) facing forward.

Ankylosing spondylitis: An systemic rheumatic disorder (like RA or SLE) which particularly affects the spine. Bony spurs eventually unite to fix the spine, commonly in a typical hyperflexed position. This condition is also sometimes called Marie Strumpel disease.

Annulus fibrosus: The fibrous and elastic covering of an intervertebral disc.

Anterior longitudinal ligament: A strong fibroelastic ligament, about an inch in width, which lies anterior to the intervertebral bodies. It mainly functions in stabilizing the spine but can, like the posterior longitudinal ligament, absorb force when the intervertebral discs expand under compression.

Anterior nerve root irritation: Cause of a number of problems such as spasm and weakness of muscles (the anterior nerve roots are motor in function). It is typically, caused by a herniating nucleus pulposus (HNP) but can have other causes.

AROM: Active range of motion (exercises or testing).

Austin-Moore prosthesis: A device used to replace a defective femoral head e.g. following a fracture high up on the surgical neck of the femur.

BJ: Biceps jerk.

BLR: Bent leg raising,

Bone rongeur: Surgical instrument used to remove pieces of bone.

BTx: Buck's traction. Technique for immobilization of a broken leg. Often used as a first aid measure during transportation for definitive treatment.

BWP: Body whirlpool (physical therapy treatment modality)

C: Cervical /chronic

Callus: Bony material (not true bone) which forms in a healing fracture. The expression "good callus formation" in an X ray report means that healing is proceeding satisfactorily.

Chemical discectomy: Removal of nuclear disc material by dissolving it with lytic enzymes.

CDS: Chronic disc syndrome.

Chronic disc syndrome: A symptom complex characterized by grumbling low back pain related to chronic degeneration of the intervertebral discs and surrounding structures. See acute disc syndrome

Crystalline arthritis: Where the cause of the problem is crystals of one sort or another laid down in the joint such as the uric acid crystals (gout) or calcium pyrophosphate crystals (pseudogout).

Cervical traction: System of pulleys and weights used to treat disc herniations in the neck.

D1-D12: The twelve dorsal vertebrae

DIP: The distal interphalangeal (joint of the finger)

DTRs: Deep tendon reflexes, the "ankle jerk"

Entrapment neuropathy: A condition where a nerve is being squeezed, such as when bony spurs compress a nerve root in the neural foramen.

Ext/extn: Extension

Extension: Opening up of the anterior angle of a joint (posterior angle in the knee joint). [See also *Lateral flexion.*]

FCA: Functional capacity assessment

Flexion: Narrowing of the anterior angle of a joint (posterior angle in the knee joint)

Functional capacity assessment: Computerized system used particularly to evaluate injured workers. The physical activities involved in their occupation are simulated by the machine, and the performance of the patient is compared with that of the spectrum of "normal" workers. If the patient is placed in the (top) 25th percentile, they are rated as having no disability. If they fall into the bottom 25, they are considered totally disabled.

Fx: Fracture

Giant cell arteritis: A systemic inflammatory arthritis characterized (like polyarteritis nodosum) by nodular lesions in the walls of medium to small arteries. It can affect arteries in any part of the body, but typically the temporal arteries are the prominent area of involvement. The usual complaint is headache; the characteristic clinical findings are a painful spot in the left temporal area and diminished pulsation in the temporal artery. Diagnosis is by biopsy of the arterial wall, and treatment is similar to that for PAN and SLE, i.e., steroids or some other treatment aimed at damping the immune response. If the diagnosis is missed, the eye on the side involved may become blind.

Gouty arthritis: Disease characterized by deposits of uric acid crystals in joints. In its later stages it can resemble rheumatoid arthritis.

gt: Gait

HNP: Herniated nucleus pulposus, i.e., a herniated intervertebral disc

HP: Hot pack (to treat muscle spasms)

IBTx: Intermittent Buck's traction

ICS: Intercostal space (the space between the ribs)

ICTx: Intermittent cervical traction

Intertrochanteric fracture: Where the fracture line runs between the greater trochanter (lateral and superior) and the lesser trochanter (medial and inferior). These are bony protrusions at the top of the shaft of the femur which act as attachments for muscles.

Intervertebral foramen (pl. **foramina**): The "windows" between the intervertebral bones through which the peripheral nerves exit from the spinal canal into the body.

IPTx: Intermittent pelvic traction

KJ: Knee jerk (the quadriceps reflex)

Laminectomy/discectomy: Surgical procedure for herniated intervertebral discs

L/S: Lumbosacral

L: Lumbar/left/liter

L4 5: Lumbar four/five (interspace)

Lat.: Lateral

Lateral rotation: Where the anterior aspect of a bone moves laterally as it turns.

Lateral flexion: Movement where the head and neck are bent left or right.

LBP: Low back pain.

LDD: Lumbar disc disease.

LEs: Lower extremities

LLE: Left lower extremity (strictly the left foot but is used to describe the leg).

LOM: Limitation of motion

LUE: Left upper extremity (strictly the left hand but used to describe the arm).

M/3: Middle third (e.g. of 4 bones).

Medial rotation: Where the anterior aspect of a bone moves medially as it turns.

Median: A midline plane running from center of the head to a point between the feet in the anatomical position.

M/S: Musculoskeletal (system)

Nucleus pulposus The central jelly-like part of an intervertebral disc

Osteoarthritis: Arthritic condition which is characterized by osteophyte (bony spur) formation around the larger joints. It is sometimes called "wear and tear" arthritis but is almost certainly due to other things. Another term for this type of joint problem is degenerative arthritis. The causes are unknown. Medical treatment is supportive and palliative. Surgical treatment is joint replacement, which is now becoming very sophisticated.

Osteotomy: Surgical cutting of a bone to correct a malalignment or other deformity.

PAN: Polyarteritis nodosum (panarteritis nodosum)

PFROM: Passive full range of motion

PIP: Proximal interphalangeal (joint of the finger)

Polyarteritis nodosum: A systemic arthritis characterized by inflammatory lumps which form in the walls of small arteries. A very high eosinophil count (cells found in allergic conditions) is characteristic of this disease and suggests that a hypersensitivity reaction may be involved, but this is an educated guess; the causes are not really known. The heart and any organ in the body may be affected (especially the kidneys). Treatment is similar to that for SLE, high doses of steroids or antimitotic drugs (normally used to treat cancers).

Posterior longitudinal ligament: The 1" wide strip of fibrous and elastic material running down behind the vertebral bodies from the base of the skull to the top of the sacral bone.

It absorbs force transmitted from the intervertebral discs and also helps to prevent damage to the spine and nerve roots as the discs expand when being compressed.

PRE: Progressive resistive exercises

PROM: Passive range of motion (examination or exercises)

PT: Physical therapy

R: Right /resistive

RA: Rheumatoid arthritis as in RA test or RA factor (test)

Residual functional capacity (RFC): Term used in Social Security Regulations (SSRs). A disabled person who does not meet the standard conditions for disability, is evaluated under RFC to see if (given their age, education, skills, and work opportunities) they should nevertheless be considered totally disabled.

Right lower extremity: Strictly the right foot but often used to describe the leg

ROM: Range of motion of a joint (studies or exercises)

rot.: Rotation

Rotation to the left: Turning movement of the head to the left (other joints rotate medially and laterally)

Rotation to the right: Turning movement of the head to the right

Rotation: Turning movements of one of the bones in a joint. See also *medial rotation; lateral rotation; rotation to the left; rotation to the right.*

RROM: Resistive range of motion (studies or exercises)

RUE: Right upper extremity (strictly the right hand but used to describe the arm)

S: Sacral

SBWP: Sterile body whirlpool

SEWP: Sterile extremity whirlpool (physical therapy treatment)

SLE: Systemic lupus erythematosus

SLR: Straight leg raising, Lasegue's test

Soft-tissue injuries: Injuries to tissues other than bone. The term is generally used, however, to describe injuries to muscles, tendons and ligaments.

Spinal stenosis: A syndrome characterized by pain on standing rather than when walking. The pain is caused by insufficiency of the small vessels supplying the spinal cord. It has been described as the spinal cord equivalent of claudication pain in the legs. It is caused by pressure on the cord and is commonly due to narrowing of the spinal canal in the lumbo-sacral region. The same condition (narrowing of the canal) can be found in the cervical spine where it produces numbness and weakness of the legs and bladder complaints rather than pain.

Subcapital fracture: Fracture just below the femoral head (usually requires a prosthesis)

Suction discectomy: Operation to remove herniating nuclear discs using a suction nucleotome, a tiny tube with rotating blades which remove nuclear disc material drawn into the lumen of the tube by suction. A similar device is used by vascular surgeons to remove atheromatous plaques from the walls of arteries.

Systemic lupus erythematosus: A systemic arthritis characterized by a rash over the nose and face (butterfly rash) which is brought on by exposure to sunlight. It is an autoimmune disease where antibodies are produced against the patients' tissues including their own antibodies. Very characteristic test findings, such as the presence of antinuclear antibody (ANA), can be used to make the diagnosis with some reliability. SLE has indeed been found, by means of these tests, to be a fairly common disease, but fortunately it often occurs in milder and medically manageable forms which produce little or no disability. Severe forms, however, are associated with organ damage, especially kidney failure, and may require high doses of steroids. The treatment usually controls the condition but may carry its own hazards.

Systemic arthritides: General term for arthritic conditions due to conditions which affect other parts of the body also (e.g. autoimmune diseases or hypersensitivity). In general these diseases involve medium to small joints and also affect skin, kidneys and other organs. [See also *Ankylosing spondylitis*; *Giant cell arteritis*; *PAN*; *SLE*.]

T: Thoracic

TJ: Triceps jerk

UEs: Upper extremities (strictly speaking the hands but often used to refer to the arm

Specimen Handwritten Note on MS Patient

1/CC. 49 y.o. W♀ c/o #1. LBP x 7/7
#2. arthritis x 2 yr.

H.CC #1. S&F 1 yr ago when carrying a heavy box →
LBP then, CB x 7/7, LMD Rx'd meds.
RTW in 3 weeks. Recurrent episodes of LBP since,
approx q 1 mo. responds to HR & A, ō OOW, ō CBR.
1/52 ago while pulling weeds in garden exp'd
severe acute pain in LB → L hip. "barely
able to walk into the house". ō sig+ improvem+
c̄ usual txs (heat, rest, muscle relaxants & analgesics)
Pain now → (L) foot c̄ c/o numbness (L) foot.
ō previous X-rays.
#2. Pains x 2yr off and on, in hands mainly.
stiff in a.m. gets a little better as day goes on.
Has not previously seen M.D. for this.
No definite dx.

PMH:- N/C No meds other than above. NKDA

FH:- Both parents have had back trouble
-3 sibs, all older than pt. A & W.

SH:- Secretary, gardens a little. Unmarried.
Lives with her sister.

PH:- ō smokes, ō ETOH.

O/E WDWNWF A≐SA. Sl. antalgic limp
favoring LLE. Some fusiform swelling of
MP & PIP joints. DIP joints nl.

Translation of Handwritten Report on the MS H&P

Identification and chief complaints: 49 year old white female complaining of:

#I Low back pain for one week

#2 Arthritis for two years

History of chief complaints:

#1 Slip and fall (accident) one year ago when carrying a heavy box. Low back pain then, confined to bed for one week. Local medical doctor prescribed medications. Returned to work in three weeks. Recurrent episodes of low back pain since, approximately once a month, (which) respond to heat, rest and non steroidal aspirin without (needing to be) out of work or requiring complete bed rest. One week ago while pulling weeds in garden, patient experienced severe acute pain in lower back radiating into the left hip area, (she was) "barely able to walk into the house'. Has not significantly improved with usual treatments (heat, rest, muscle relaxants and analgesics). Pain now radiating to the left foot with complaints of numbness in the left foot. No previous X rays.

#2 Pains for two years off and on, in the hands mainly. Stiff in the morning, gets a little better as the day goes on. Has not previously seen doctor for this. No definite diagnosis (ever made on this problem).

Past medical history: Non contributory. No medications other than above,no known medical allergies.

Family history: Both parents have had back trouble, 3 siblings all older than patient are alive and well.

Social history: (Works as a) secretary, "gardens a little". Unmarried, lives with sister.

Personal history: Does not smoke or use alcohol.

PHYSICAL EXAMINATION

Well developed, well nourished, white female with appearance approximately equal to stated age. Slight antalgic limp (due to pain) favoring the left lower extremity. Some fusiform swelling of the metacarpophalangeal and proximal interphalangeal joints bilaterally. The distal interphalangeal joints are normal.

Back :- ↓ lumbar flexion, unable to reach much below knees due to pain. Splinting of LS ++. Lumbar scoliosis cx to (L), spasm of (R) P/S muscles visible and palpable.

Tender +++ L5-S1 interspace

SLR. 80°+ (R) 45° (L) pain → L leg

BLR 85°+ (R) 50° (L) "

C-spine :- AROM & PROM full & s̄ pain.

Ext:- All mts full and ō pain other than above.

CNS:- ō wasting, ō weakness of LLE

? dull to PP over dorsum (L) foot.

DTRs :-

	(R)	(L)
BJ	++	++
TJ	++	++
KJ	++	++
AJ	++	?+/-

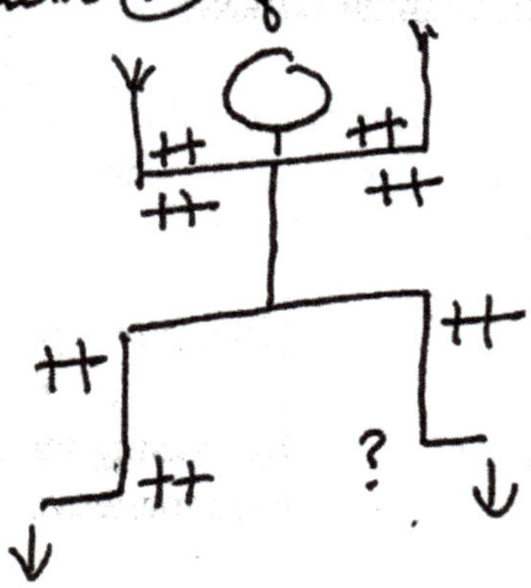

A:- #1. R/O HNP ? L5/S1.

#2. Arthritis R/O RA

P:- #1. XR LS c̄ PA & O views

#2 CT of LS in a.m.

#3. Screening for arthritis by lab in am RF, ANA etc

Back: Decreased lumbar flexion (on attempting to touch toes) unable to reach much below the knees due to pain, splinting of lumbar spine obvious. Lumbar scoliosis convex to the left. Spasm of the right paraspinalis muscles visible and palpable. Very tender (on compression over the) interspace between the fifth lumbar and first sacral vertebrae.

Straight leg raising: to more than 80° on the right, 45° on the left (flexion of the hip on the left limited by) pain radiating into the left leg.

Bent leg raising: to more than 85° on the right, 50° on the left (again with flexion limited by) pain radiating into the left leg.

Cervical spine: Active range of movement and passive range of movement full and without pain.

Extremities: All movements full and painless other than (the) above.

Central nervous system: No wasting or weakness of the left lower extremity. Possibly a little dull to pinprick over the dorsum of the left foot.

Deep tendon reflexes:	Right	Left
Biceps jerk	++	++
Triceps jerk	++	++
Knee jerk	++	++
Ankle jerk	++	?+

[Diagram represents the above table showing all DTRs normal and symmetrical except the left ankle jerk which is questionable even with reinforcement introduced by causing the patient to lock the hands together and then attempt to pull them apart (this maneuver augments the force of the DTRs]

ASSESS:

#1 Rule out herniated nucleus pulposus of ? L5 S1

#2 Arthritis, rule out rheumatoid arthritis

PLAN:

1 X ray lumbar spine with posterior/anterior and oblique views

#2 Computerized tomography of lumbar spine in the morning

#3 Request to lab for arthritis panel in the a.m. (test for) rheumatoid factor, antinuclear antibodies etc.

Chapter Six

Injuries to the Nervous System

§ 6:1 Introduction — what lawyers need to know about neurological injuries

Injuries involving the central and peripheral nervous systems are very common. Estimates vary, but it has been calculated that there may be 300,000 significant head injuries each year from automobile accidents alone. The mortality and permanent impairments will vary with the seriousness of the injury. The commonest deficits are mental (psychological). It has been estimated that approximately 80% of significantly head injured patients will have psychiatric problems related to their trauma. Of these, only three in ten will seek out or be referred to a psychiatrist, psychologist or mental health facility. An even smaller group (about one in ten) will have mental harm included in their compensation. It is the business of the compensation system in general, and the plaintiffs' attorneys in particular, to make sure that all genuine harms are compensated. Awareness of psychiatric harm is increasing among health care providers, administrators and even lawyers. Social Security Disability administrators now require a psychiatric evaluation as part of every disability determination, whether the claimant mentions it or not. Scrutinizing each head injury case for cognitive and psychiatric sequelae may be viewed by critics as the attorneys shaking every possible branch on the tree and encouraging compensationitis on the part of the head injured plaintiffs. But the fact is that subtle psychiatric impairments are quite commonly missed by medical providers. A recent large study reports that while 80% of the new admissions to nursing homes (a notoriously inadequately treated group of patients) have serious psychiatric problems, such as depressive illnesses, these are generally overlooked by their medical attendants.

Another sequel to a head injury which may be overlooked is *minimal brain damage* (MBD), a term applied when mental harm is present but not obvious. Unfortunately these kinds of deficits may seriously interfere with functioning. Patients pronounced normal or well recovered by their medical attendants may be found on more careful review to have subtle impairments which interfere significantly with their personal and working lives. It is most important that lawyers be aware of this problem and know how to spot it and handle it. These subtler forms of brain damage are, indeed, the main focus of attention here, for it is in these kinds of cases that more detailed knowledge of neurological medicine is required. It takes no great medical expertise to handle major head trauma that leaves the plaintiff totally disabled; and if they are really fully recovered, no medical knowledge at all is needed. It is not these black or white situations, but the gray areas between them, that try the mettle of compensationists and require them to venture into the unfamiliar world of medicine.

We will consider here:

Part I. Relevant anatomy and physiology

Part II. How the brain is injured and responds to injury

Part III. Impairments (especially subtle forms of brain damage)

Part IV. Proof of neurological impairments

Part I.
Basic Anatomy and Physiology

§ 6:2 Anatomy and physiology—the skull

There are a great many bones in the skull. Fortunately, lawyers (and for the most part even doctors), do not need to know the names or locations of most of them. However, a few items of information about the skull are worth learning, since they provide a broad map on which to locate things.

The skull [see Figs. 6-1 & 6-2] can be roughly divided into the *vault* (the thinner bones which roof over the cranial cavity), and the *base* (the thicker bones which form its floor). The bones of the vault comprise three pairs which are (from front to back) the *frontal*, *parietal* (side) and *occipital* (posterior) bones. The *temporal bones* lie laterally and inferior to the others, in the region of the ear and the temples. Time invested in learning the names and locations of these bones is well spent, since they are used to localize other things. The underlying lobes of the brain take their names from them, and head injuries will generally be described by reference to the nearest bone, e.g., a wound at the junction of the parietal and temporal bones will be described as *parieto-temporal.*

The base of the skull is composed of a number of bones which (fortunately) one seldom needs to identify by name. More important is the division of the skull base into *fossae* (ditches). [See Fig. 6-4.] The base of the skull can in fact be considered as a set of three descending steps. The upper one is the *anterior fossa,* and the frontal lobe of the brain lies in it. The next, the *middle fossa,* contains the temporal lobes of the brain. The middle fossa is divided into right and left compartments by a raised area in the midline called the *sella turcica* ("Turkish saddle"), which indeed it resembles. In the center of this is a tiny depression which contains the *pituitary gland.* The *posterior fossa* contains the brain stem and the *cerebellum.* The posterior fossa is roofed over by a thick layer of fibrous tissue called the *tentorial membrane.* This is an important structure which helps to protect the underlying brain stem. It also features in medical records, where the term "*supratentorial*" can be found with some frequency. This is usually employed, not in its anatomical sense, but to indicate that the problems of the patient are "in their mind," (imaginary or factitious). There is an opening in the anterior part of the tentorial membrane (*the incisura*) which allows the brain stem to pass through. When intracranial pressure rises high, a little nubbin of brain may be pushed through this opening to press against the brain stem with fatal results. This is an *incisural hernia* or a *tentorial herniation.*

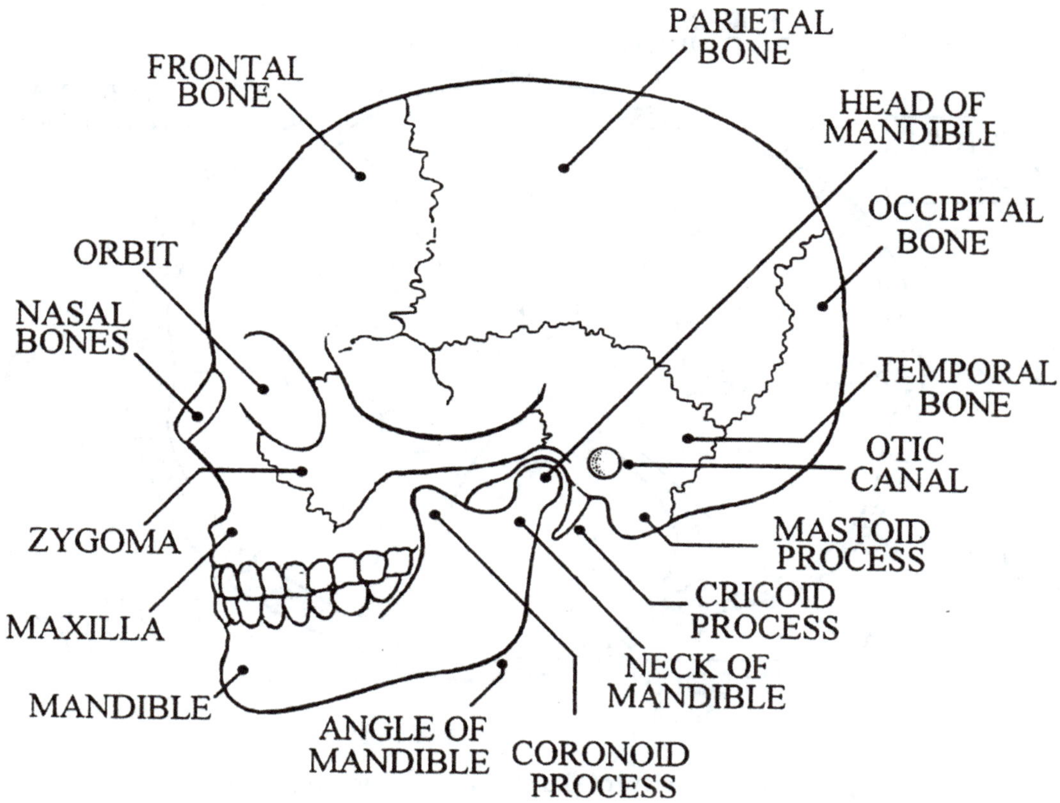

Fig. 6-1 Lateral view of the skull

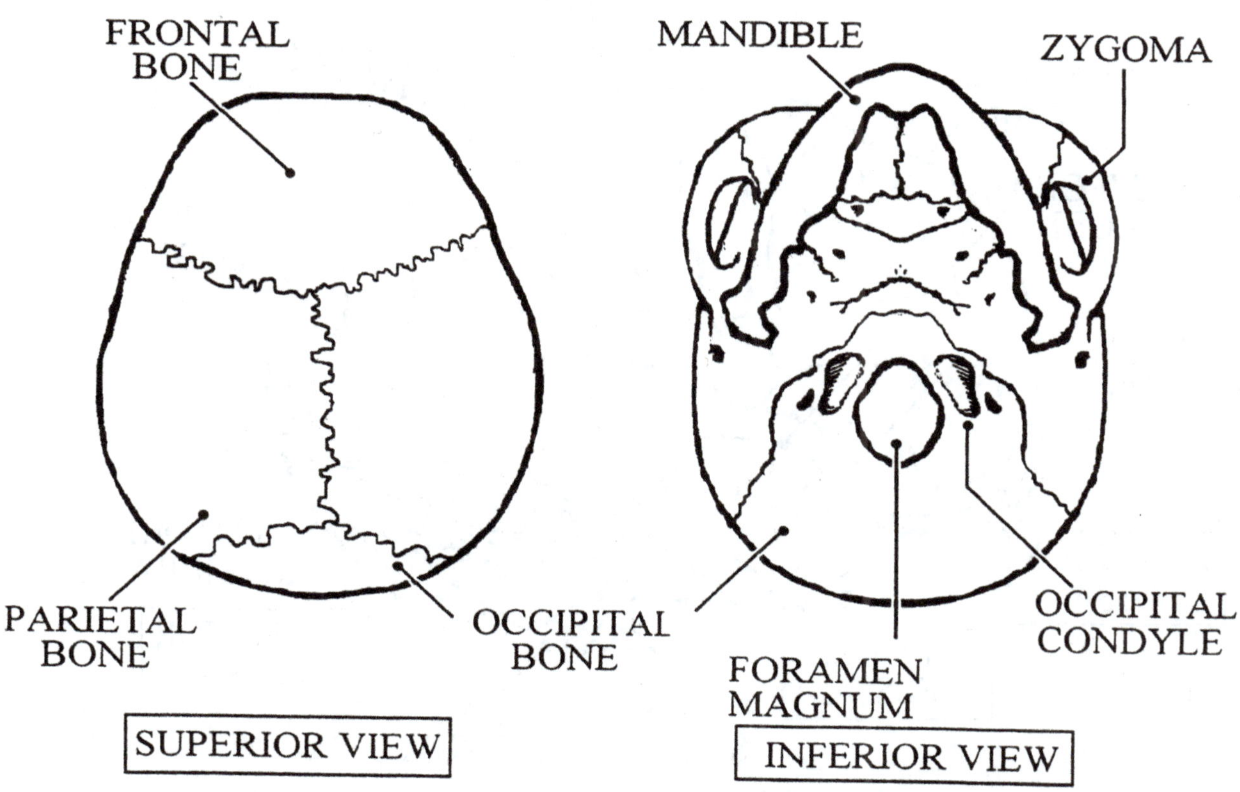

Fig. 6-2 Superior and inferior views of the skull

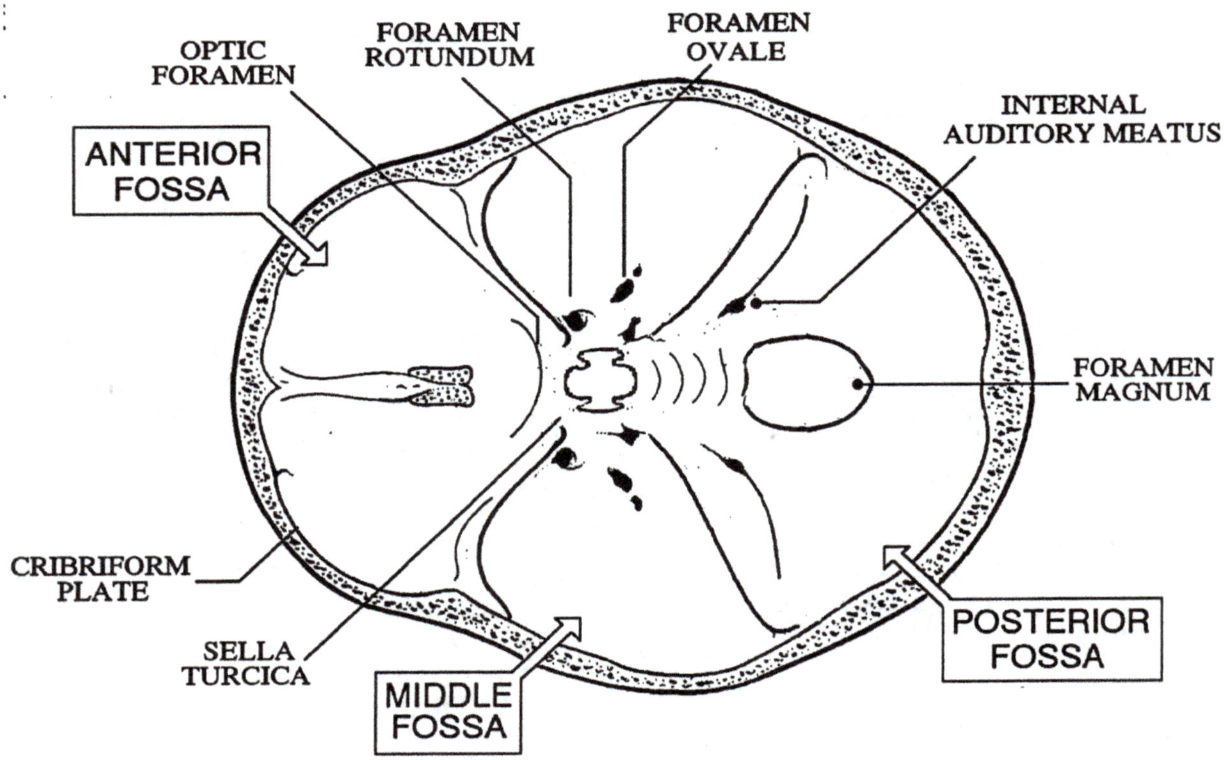

Fig. 6-3 Superior view of skull fossae — transverse section

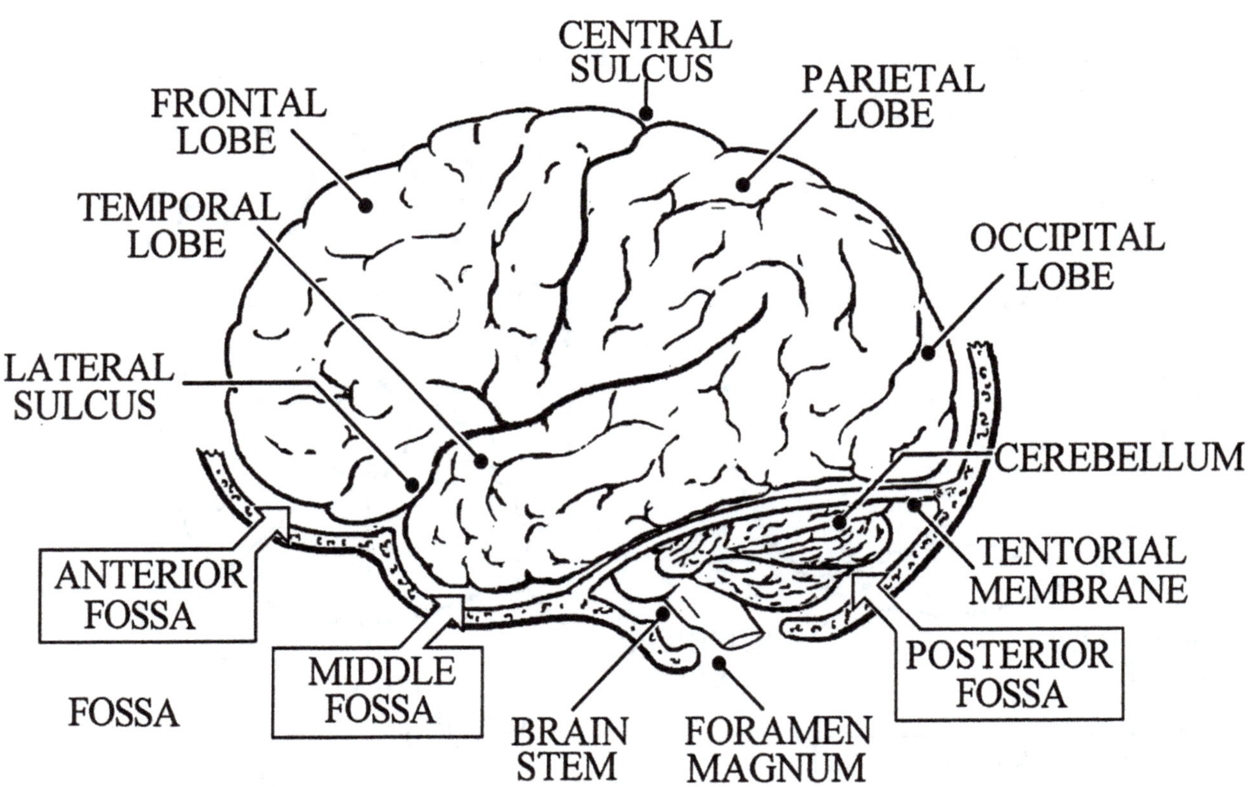

Fig. 6-4 Lateral view of skull fossae showing contents — sagittal section

§ 6:3 Anatomy and physiology — general outline of the nervous system

The nervous system is broadly divided into:

- The central nervous system and
- The peripheral nervous system

The distinction is artificial in that all parts of the nervous system function together and cannot be understood in isolation from one another. Nevertheless, dividing it up into sub-systems is useful for organizational and learning purposes. The central nervous system (CNS) consists of the *brain, brain stem* and *spinal cord* (the parts inside the skull and vertebral column). The peripheral nervous system lies outside the skull and spine. It comprises the cranial and peripheral nerves, and also certain ganglia and nerve plexuses which process information and so act like little brains outside the brain.

The central nervous system is divided, as has already been mentioned, into the brain, brain stem and spinal cord, and each one of these is subdivided further. The principal parts of the brain are:

- The cerebral hemispheres;
- The diencephalon (the part in between the hemispheres which joins them together);
- The brain stem; and
- The spinal cord.

These will be discussed later but a few observations may be appropriate at this point,

1. First, it is worth noting that all of these structures (not the brain only) process information and issue instructions. Much of what we do is monitored and controlled at levels below the brain.

2. The nervous system generally, and the brain in particular, is in communication with other parts of the body but is isolated from them in a number of ways. One of these is the so-called *blood /brain barrier* (BBB). The nature of this protective system is not fully known, but some of the *glial cells* [see § 5:4].are considered to play an important role here. The BBB will facilitate entry of some things into the brain, and tend to exclude others. Lipid-soluble substances are more easily taken up than those that dissolve primarily in water. Certain antibiotics enter easily into the brain, while others only do so with difficulty. The BBB tends to be less effective during infections, so that some of these less preferred antibiotics (such as cephalosporins) may enter well enough when the covering membranes of the brain are inflamed, as in meningitis. Nevertheless, it is considered wiser in dealing with CNS infections to use medications which cross easily into the brain.

3. The central nervous system floats in liquid, the *cerebrospinal fluid* (CSF). This is produced in cavities inside the brain known as the *cerebral ventricles* (little stomachs). [See Figs. 6-5 & 6-6.] There are four ventricles: the *lateral ventricles*, one in each hemisphere; the *third ventricle* in between them; and the *fourth ventricle* behind them in the posterior fossa (between the cerebellum and the brain stem). CSF is produced in special bunches of capillaries in the roof of each ventricle, flows through the ventricles, exits from the fourth ventricle to bathe the brain and spinal cord, and is finally reab-

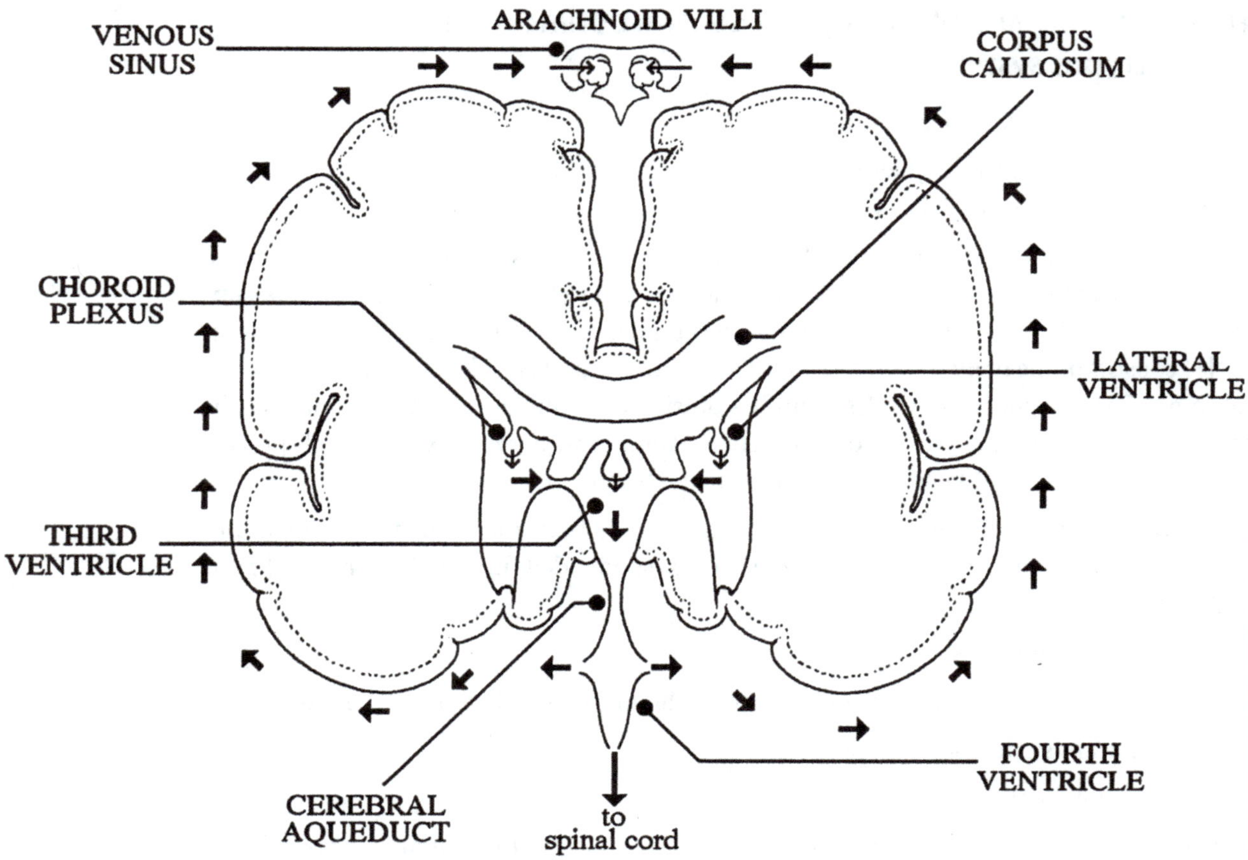

Fig. 6-5 The production, distribution, and reabsorption of cerebrospinal fluid

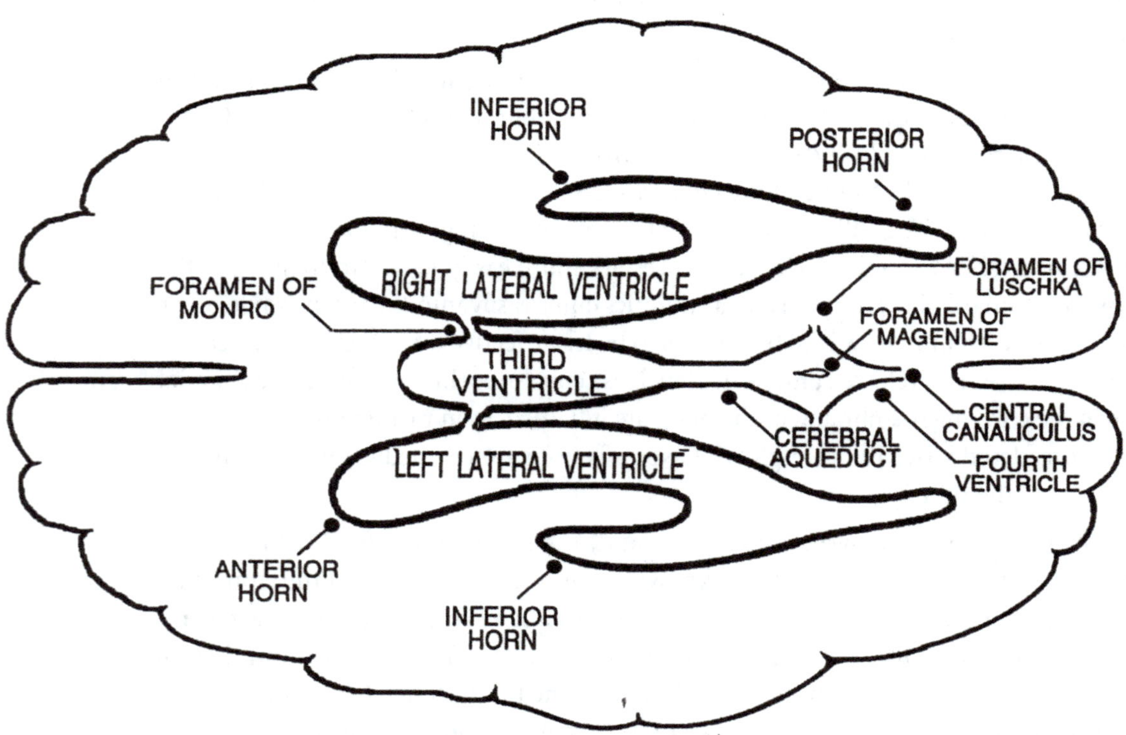

Fig. 6-6 The cerebral ventricles

sorbed in the *arachnoid* villi (special clusters of blood vessels) in the *superior venous sinus* which lies above the brain. This system has a number of functions, but it principally reduces the weight of the brain (like a whale in water) so that it does not need a stiff structural supporting system. It also buffers and slows down movement, so that the brain is not bumped as we move; this is a valuable protective device which reduces brain damage in traumatic events such as automobile accidents.

4. The focus here (from the legal perspective) will be on the brain and on injuries to the brain. This is not because the other parts of the nervous system may not be injured and require compensation; spinal injuries are very frequent and commonly devastating. The reason for the present emphasis is that injuries to the brain, especially the subtler ones, require more medical knowledge on the part of compensationists. Injuries in the brain stem, spinal cord and peripheral nerves tend to be more obvious and are normally well documented in the medical records. The main skill required for compensation purposes is turning these gross deficits into disabilities and the disabilities into money compensation terms; these are legal rather than medical procedures.

§ 6:4 Anatomy and physiology—the brain cells

There are two basic types of cells in the CNS. [See Fig. 6-7.] *Neurons* are the cells which receive, process and transmit signals in the CNS; they are the true brain cells. There are also several kinds of supporting cells, which are generally referred to as *glial cells*.

The neuron or nerve cell is the processing and communicating cell of the CNS, and there are astronomical numbers of them in the brain and spinal cord. Neurons come in many shapes and sizes, but all of them have basically the same structure. The nerve cell body (*soma*) is like that of other cells, with a nucleus and a cytoplasm (like the yolk and white of an egg). The neuron differs from other cells in its appendages (nerve fibers), which enable it to receive and transmit signals to other cells. These special fibers are called dendrites and axons.

Dendrites (little branches) receive incoming signals, and each neuron can have as many as 200 dendrites. The *axon* is the transmitting fiber, and there is normally only one main axon to each nerve cell, though there can be two or more terminal branches. There are also special *internuncial neurons* which link cell to cell and multiply the intercommunications between them.

Glial cells, which make up a considerable percentage of brain cells, provide physical support for the neurons and assist them in other ways. There are several kinds of glial cells. *Astrocytes* have a number of functions, both in normal brain activity and response to disease or injury. They function like the fibrocytes in the rest of the body, producing scar tissue to repair defects. There are also *oligodendrocytes,* which help insulate the axons and dendrites of the nerve cells. *Microglia* are phagocytic cells which engulf invaders and initiate immune responses. Ep*endymal cells* line the ventricles and produce CSF, and they may function in the blood /brain barrier, preventing all sorts of things (including certain drugs) from entering the CNS. Glial cells also occasionally give rise to brain tumors.

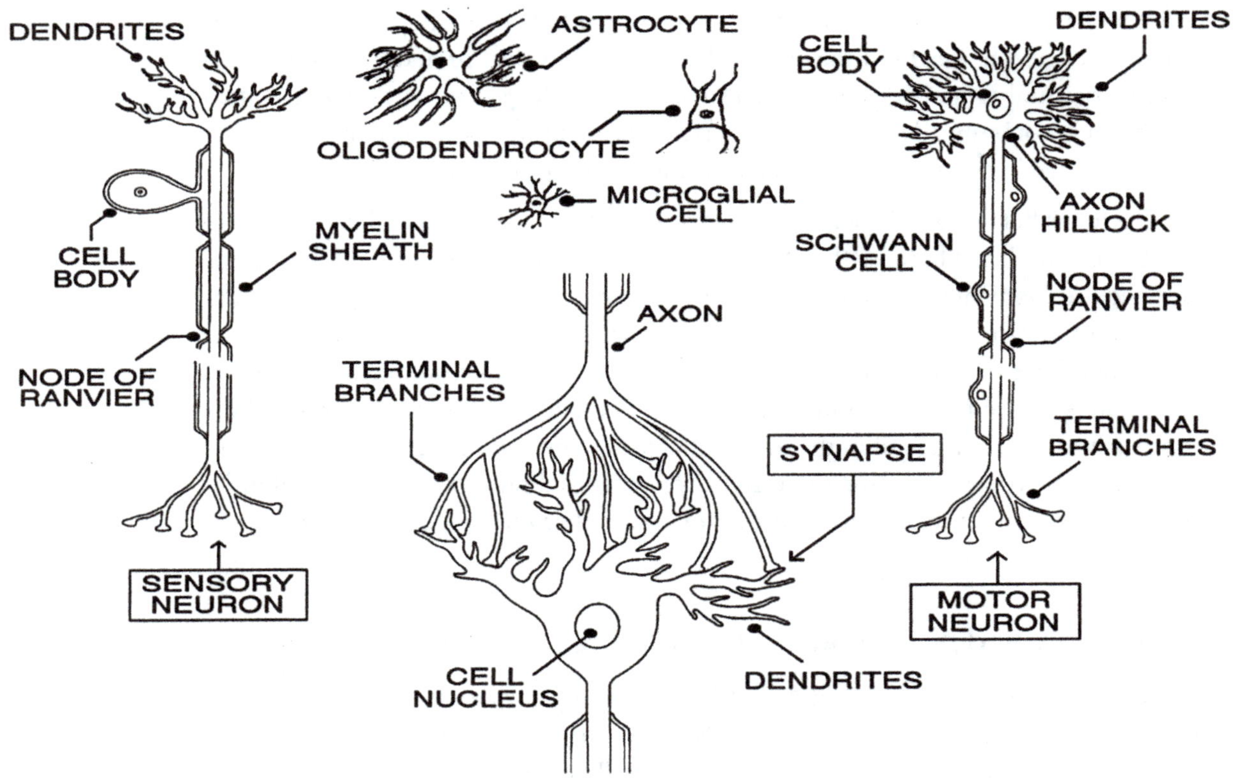

Fig. 6-7 Neurons and supporting cells

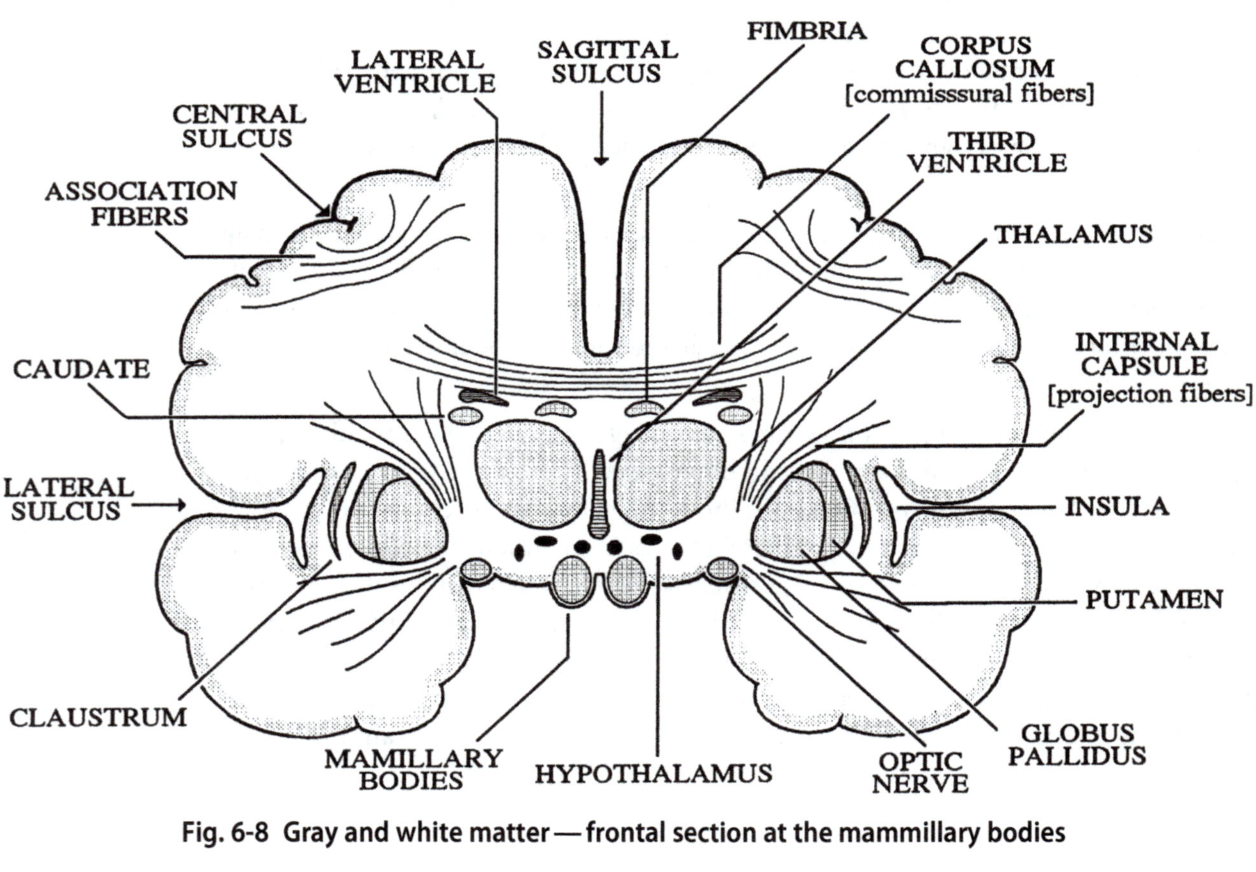

Fig. 6-8 Gray and white matter—frontal section at the mammillary bodies

§ 6:5 Anatomy and physiology—gray matter and white matter

The cell bodies are concentrated in certain areas of the CNS substance. These areas appear gray when the brain is preserved and sectioned. They are therefore called the *gray matter* of the brain, even though their normal and natural color is pinkish due to a rich blood supply. Axons, on the other hand, remain shiny and white even when stained, since they have a fatty insulation covering which protects them, and are therefore called the *white matter* of the brain. [See Fig. 6-8.] The gray matter, where the cell bodies are found, is concentrated in a number of places in the CNS. The layer of gray matter, about half an inch thick and which lies on the surface of the brain, is called the *cerebral cortex* (cortex means the rind of an orange or some other fruit). There are other gray matter areas inside the cerebral hemispheres, called the *deep gray matter* of the brain [see Fig. 6-10], and the various nuclei and groups of nuclei which compose it have separate names (which are not usually very important for lawyers). In the brain stem, the gray matter is broken up into smaller nuclei by the ascending and descending columns of white fibers passing through it. In the spinal cord, the gray matter is concentrated in the middle and so is known as the *central gray matter* of the spinal cord.

These collections of gray cells are like microprocessors in a computer. In each of them, large numbers of individual cells are linked together at tiny connecting points called *synapse*s to form, in effect, little computers. Incoming information is processed in one way or another, and commands are issued to other CNS centers and to the organs of the body.

The white matter consists of communicating bundles of axons linking gray areas with one another, like cables in a computer network. [See Fig. 6-8]. If they link two parts of the same hemisphere together, they are called *association fibers.* If they cross from one hemisphere to the other, they are called *commissural fibers.* If they run down to the deep gray matter of the brain or beyond to the spinal cord, they are called *projection fibers.* The *corpus callosum* is a major collection of commissural fibers which forms the main link between the two cerebral hemispheres. There are two other smaller groups of connecting fibers between the two sides of the brain, known as the *anterior commissure* and the *posterior commissure.* These integrate several gray matter areas, controlling more primitive behaviors such as emotion, smell and automatic functions. They are known collectively as the *archipallium* (old brain).

The *anterior white matter of the cord,* i.e., lying anterior and antero-lateral to the central gray matter of the cord, consists largely of descending columns of white fibers, which carry signals from the brain or brain stem to motor neurons in the anterior gray matter of the cord. These are, as was mentioned earlier, *projection fibers.* Some of these are long axons, two or three feet in length, extending from the cerebral cortex to the *anterior horn cells* of the lumbar and sacral spinal cord. The *posterior columns* of white matter consist of large diameter fast-conducting axons which carry sensory signals from the periphery to the brain. They do not directly communicate with the cerebral cortex, but synapse in intermediate centers at the upper end of the spinal cord which in turn connect with the *thalamus.* The thalamus receives and processes most of the sensory input from the various parts of the body, and relays the information so obtained to the appropriate part of the cerebral cortex. Pain, however, is thought to be directly sensed in the thalamus, since thalamectomy will relieve intractable pain, whereas severing the connections between the thalamus and the cerebral cortex will not.

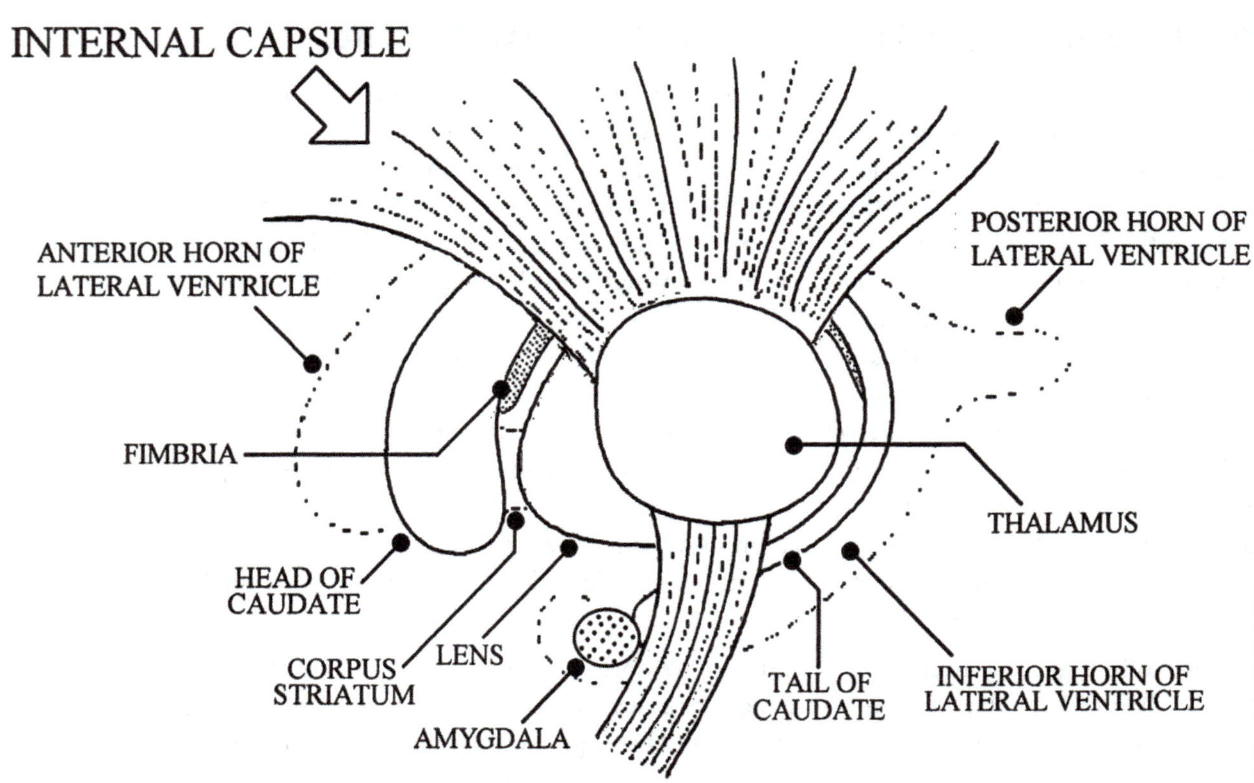

Fig. 6-9 White fiber bundles — the internal capsule

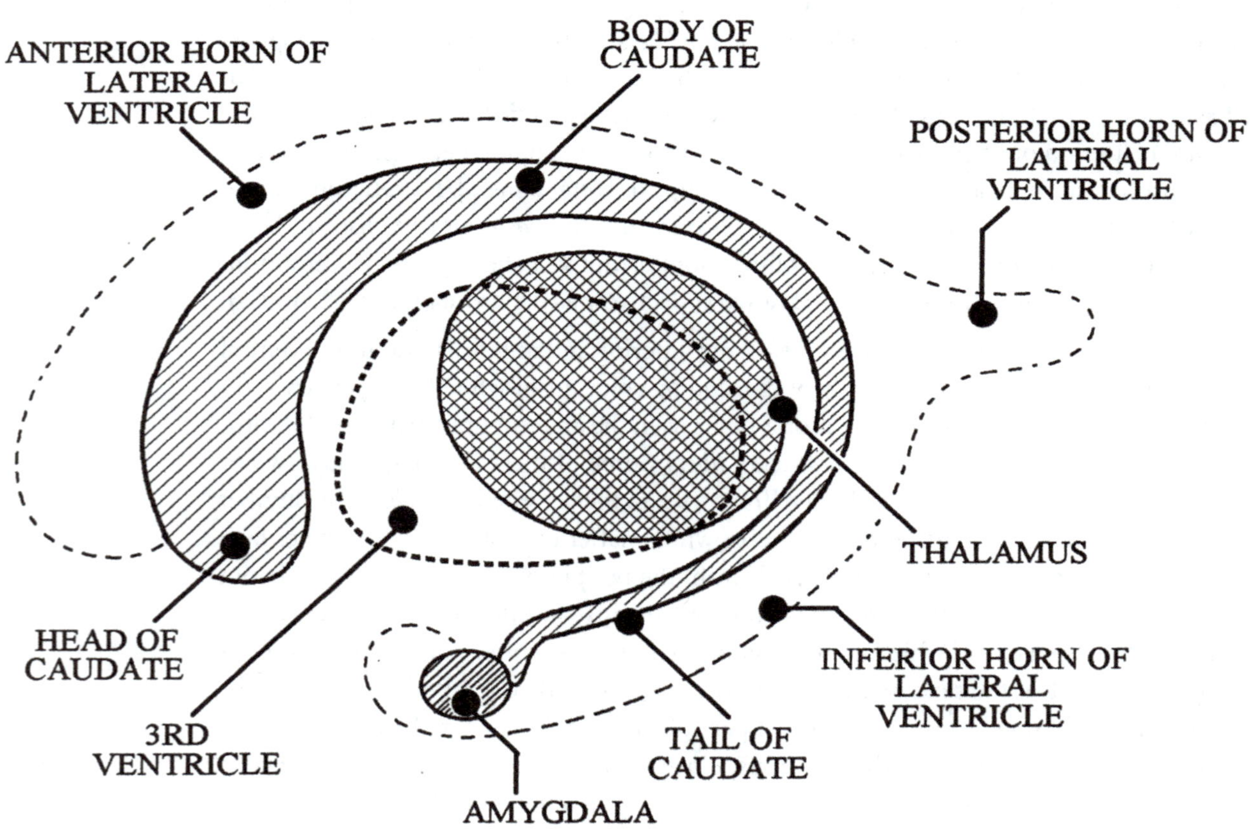

Fig. 6-10 The gray matter nuclei of the brain — lateral view

Collections of white fibers in the spinal cord and brain stem have various names such as *fasciculi*, *bundles* and *lemnisci*, but these are really only synonyms.

§ 6:6 Overview of structure and function in the brain and brain stem

Different functions and activities in the central nervous systems tend to be centered in particular parts of the nervous system. However, it must always be remembered that the brain, stem, spinal cord and even the peripheral nerves, operate as an interconnected system. Thus the *cochlea* (inner ear), brain stem nuclei and cerebral cortex all play a part in hearing.

Generally speaking, the cortical surface of the cerebral hemispheres contains the higher association areas, processing information and programming activities at the "top level," so to speak. Many of these activities are voluntary; they are performed with our knowledge and are under conscious control. Others are not. A more detailed review of the workings of the cerebral cortex will be given in the following section [§ 6:7].

The *basal gray matter* includes a number of structures [see Fig. 6-10] such as the *caudate nuclei* (a pair of C-shaped structures closely associated with the roof and floor of the lateral ventricles); the *thalami* (paired nuclei on either side of the third ventricle); the *lenticular nuclei* to name a few. These function together with certain parts of the cerebral cortex, and with gray nuclei in the brain stem in a number of ways, but they are particularly involved in the control of resting muscle tone and also with emotion and mood. The white fiber pathways which link them together are being intensively studied, since malfunction here is a cause of well-known diseases. There are four known separate pathways here which use the neurotransmitter *dopamine*. [See Fig. 7-1.] Malfunction in one of these pathways is associated with Parkinsonism, while schizophrenia is linked to an excess of dopamine in another. The *thalamus*, mentioned earlier, monitors all sensation travelling to the brain and, as was noted then, is especially involved in the sensation of pain.

The gray nuclei of the brain stem are way-stations (processing centers) in the ascending or descending white fiber paths. Vital centers such as the *respiratory center* are located here so that pressure on the brain stem tends to produce instant death. The *reticular formation*, which functions importantly in the arousal response, is also mainly located in the brain stem, so that a sudden twisting movement of the brain stem, perhaps due to a punch on the jaw, renders the victim unconscious. [See Fig. 5-18.]

The spinal cord not only transmits signals to and from the brain, but also processes information and issues motor signals to the body on its own. Data is thus processed and commands are issued by gray matter nuclei in the spinal cord, brain stem, basal gray matter and cerebral cortex. The higher centers, generally speaking, have a more general influence and tend to control lower ones. The brain, for instance, exercises an inhibitory influence on the spinal reflexes so that damage to the cerebral cortex causes them to be overactive and produces a spastic tone in the muscles.

§ 6:7 Anatomical features of the cerebral cortex — brain mapping

The cerebral cortex is roughly divided up into the *frontal*, *parietal*, *occipital* and *temporal* areas. These correspond to the overlying bones of the skull which have the same names.

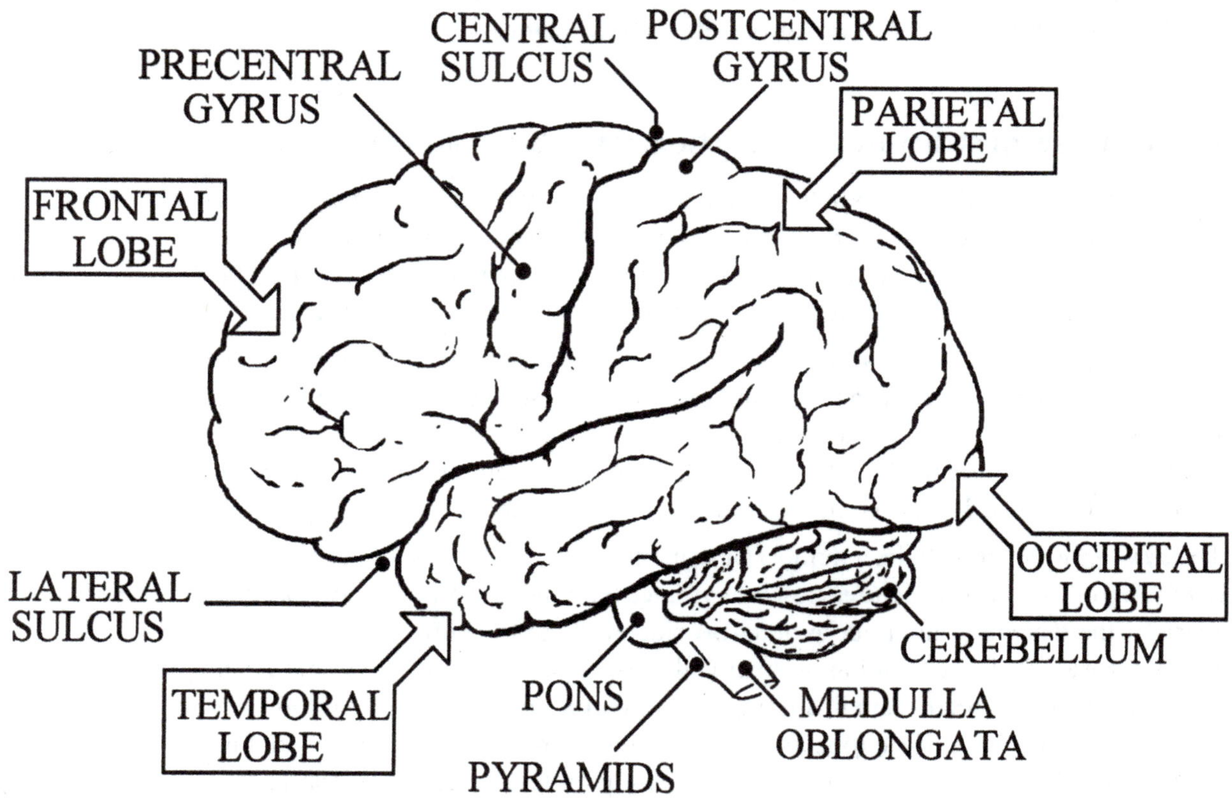

Fig. 6-11 Brain and brain stem — lateral view

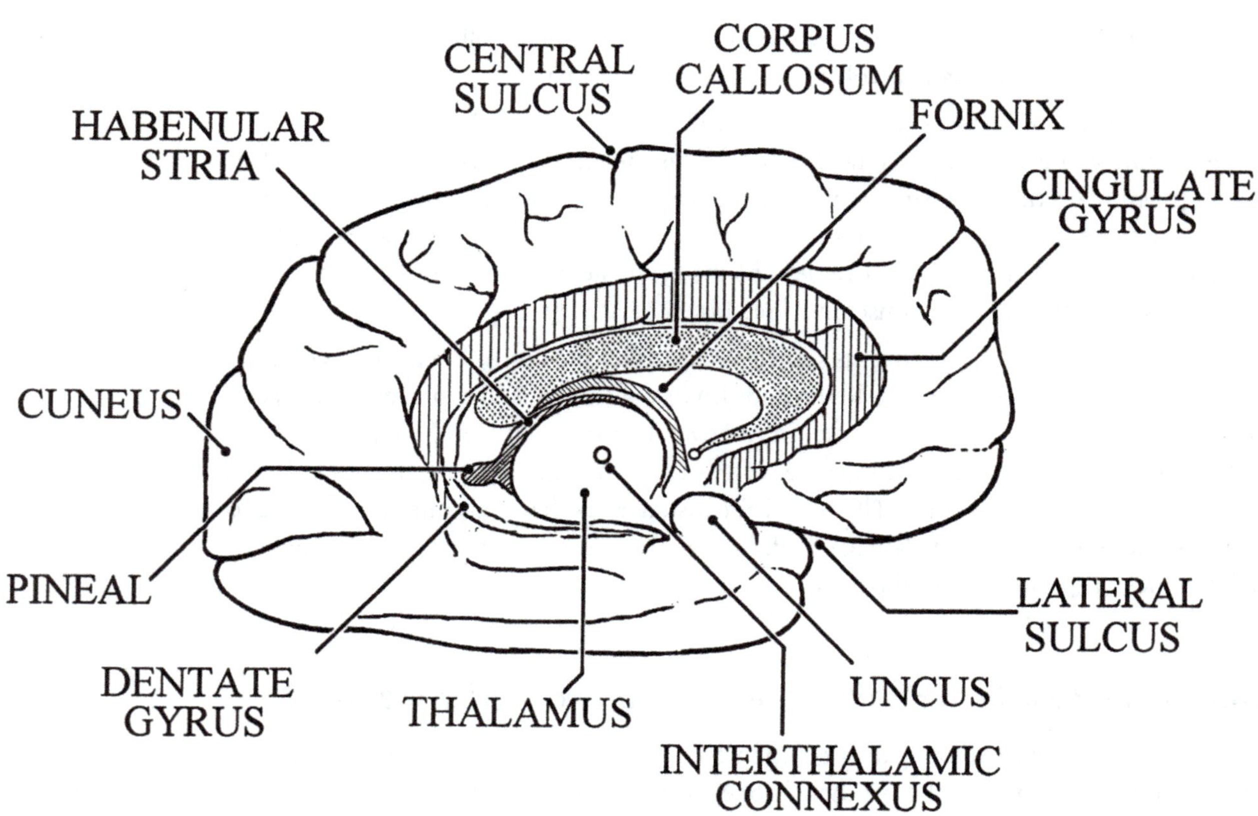

Fig. 6-12 Medial surface of the brain — midline sagittal view

[See Fig. 6-1.] This division is useful for locating things on the brain, but has no great functional significance. These areas are mainly demarcated by the three major fissures (*sulci*) of the cerebral cortex. [See Fig. 6-4.]

The surface of the brain is convoluted and wrinkled to provide greater surface area. The raised ridges are called *gyri* and the fissures between them are called *sulci*. Each of these gyri and sulci are named, but most of these names are never needed by doctors, much less lawyers. The two most important named sulci are the *central fissure of Rolando* which separates the frontal from the parietal cortex, and the *lateral fissure of Sylvius* which lies between the frontal and parietal lobes above and the temporal lobes inferiorly. [See Fig. 6-4.] There is also the longitudinal (*sagittal*) sulcus that separates the two cerebral hemispheres.

It had long been suspected that different parts of the cortex had different functions, but Professor Wilder Penfield of Montreal (1891–1976) showed that it was possible to produce a functional map of the brain. He applied tiny electrical stimuli to the surface of the brain of a person who was awake during neurosurgery, and was able to show that different parts of the body moved when certain parts of the cortex were stimulated. The strip of cortex, less than an inch wide, that showed this activity lies anterior to the central sulcus (*precentral gyrus*) is therefore called the *precentral motor area*. Penfield, indeed, was able to trace the outline of a little man (homunculus) on this part of the precentral cortex. [See Fig. 6-14.] The mannikin's legs are hung over the rim of the longitudinal fissure at the knees, and the rest of the body hangs head down along the precentral gyrus. The cortical motor homunculus does not have the same proportions as the human body. Certain areas are grotesquely large because they are important and require a lot of "computer space." The mouth and the hand, especially the thumb, thus loom disproportionately large on the brain map of the motor cortex, whereas the trunk, which does not carry out very intricate movements, is represented by a relatively small area. A similar little man, the sensory homunculus, can be traced on the narrow strip of cortex behind the central sulcus (*the postcentral gyrus*). If a part of the body (for example the nose) is stimulated electrically, a particular part of the postcentral area can be made to show electrical activity. It is interesting that the index finger has a larger representation on the sensory cortex than the thumb (we feel with the index finger but work with the thumb). For convenience, the various functional areas in a brain map are usually labeled with numbers rather than their given names. [See Fig. 6-13.]

§ 6:8 Visual and speech centers

There is a cortical region on the posterior tip of each cerebral hemisphere, called the *visual cortex*, which integrates visual signals coming from the eye on the opposite side of the body. If the cortex here is damaged, the subject will see perfectly well, but not be able to recognize what they are seeing. They will not be able, for instance, to identify or distinguish different shapes or different faces properly. In this instance, the cortex on the non-dominant side (normally the right hemisphere) controls the total integration.

Broca, a French anatomist, studied the brains of twelve people who were unable to speak following brain injuries of various kinds. He identified an area of damage common to them all, located on the dominant hemisphere just anterior to the motor cortex, where the mouth and tongue are represented. This is called *Broca's area* or the *motor speech center*. If the cortex here is ablated, the patient may understand speech and wish to say something, but

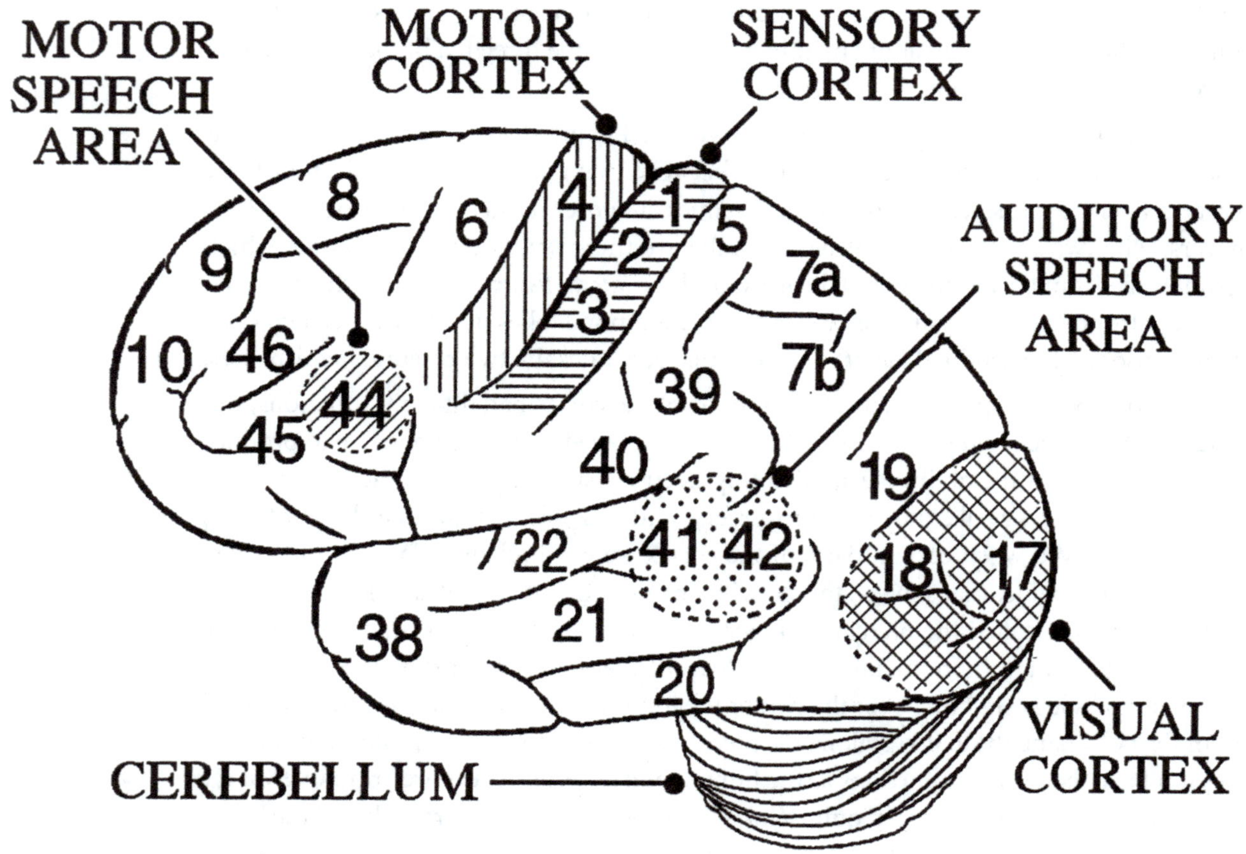

Fig. 6-13 Brain mapping — the Brodman number system

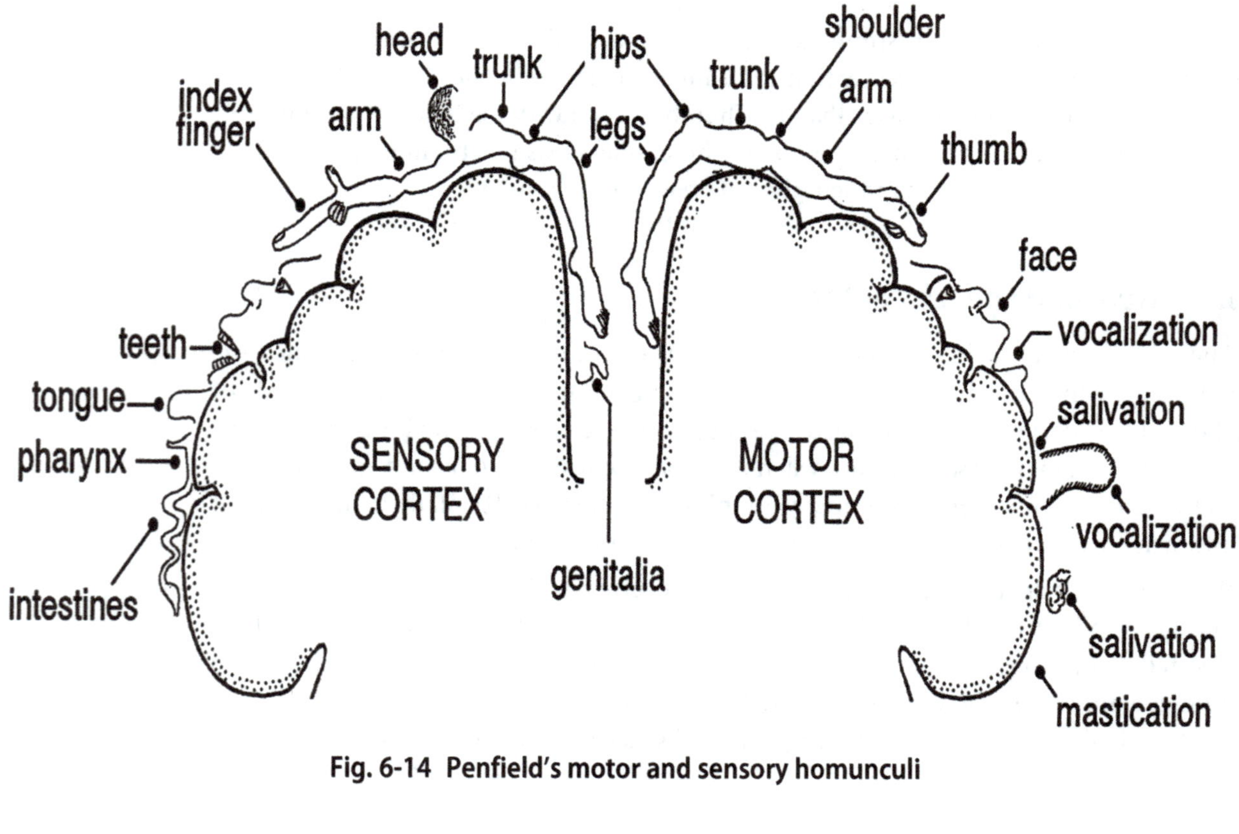

Fig. 6-14 Penfield's motor and sensory homunculi

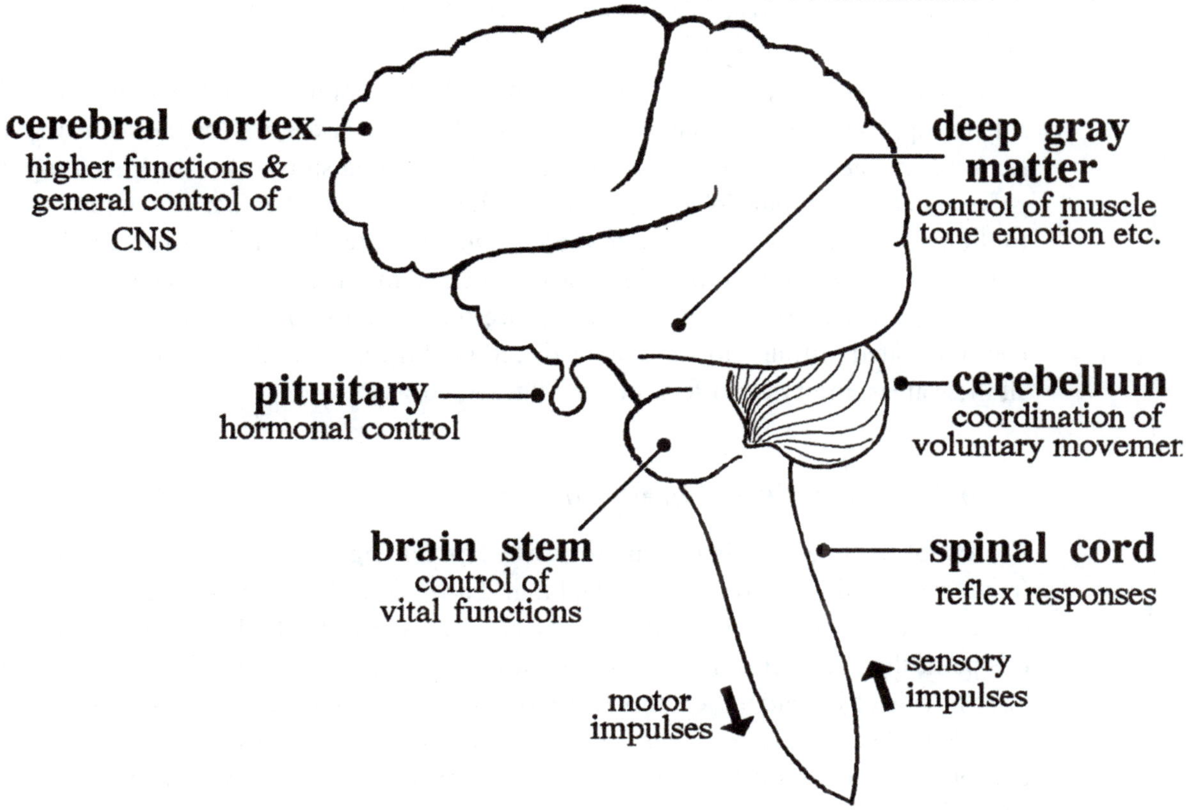

Fig. 6-15 Functions of various parts of the CNS

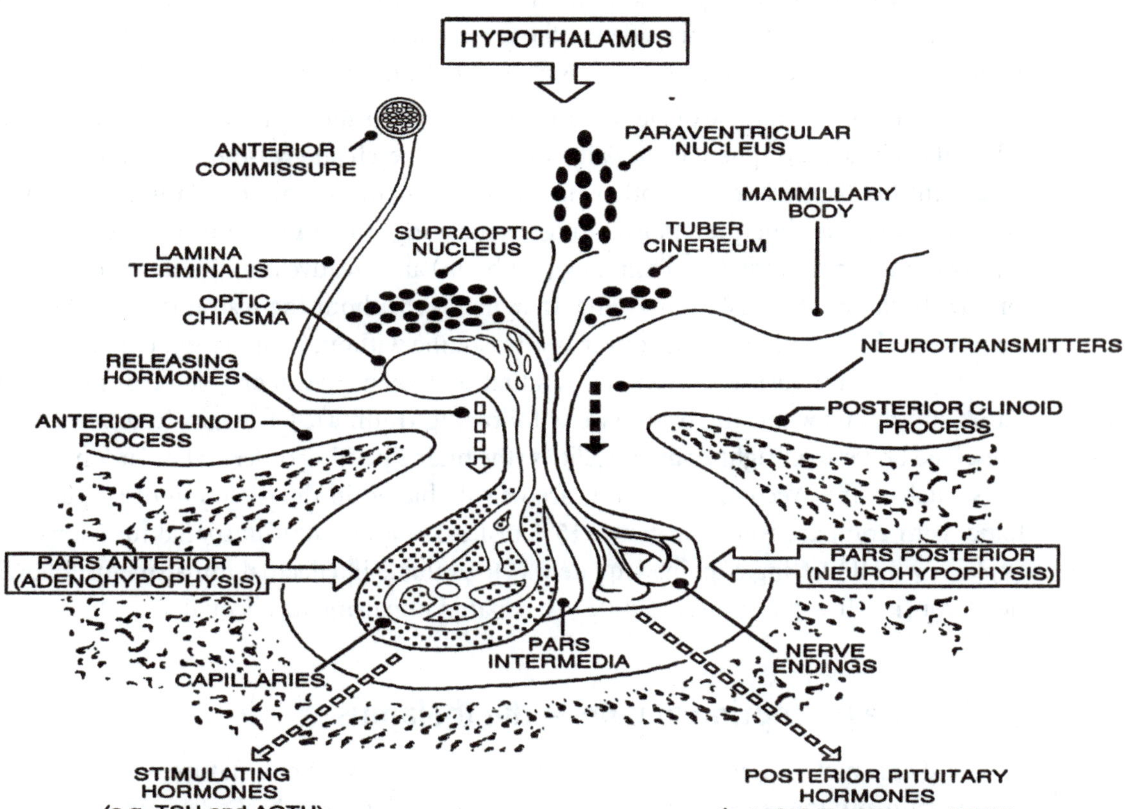

Fig. 6-16 The pituitary gland

is unable to put the words together and express themselves in uttered speech. This kind of deficit is called *motor aphasia.*

Another small area, posterior and superior in the temporal lobe on the dominant hemisphere (appropriately adjacent to the ear) is called *Wernicke's area* or the *sensory speech center*. Damage here leads to difficulty in understanding spoken words. Visual input is processed in the occipital lobe, at the posterior tip of the brain. Another center, just anterior to the visual cortex, is specialized to understanding written language. An area in between the sensory speech and motor speech areas, effects communication between these two. Auditory speech and written words are thus processed in the appropriate areas, and the results communicated rostrally (forward in the direction of the nose) to the motor speech area. In all these areas, injury can affect speech. [But see § 6:30.]

§ 6:9 Lateralization of brain functions

Most of the fibers leaving the motor cortex, or coming to the sensory cortex, *decussate* (cross over) to the opposite side of the brain. Each hemisphere then is largely responsible for integrating input from or output to the opposite side of the body. It is worth noting at this point that, as a general rule, activities which are functions of the whole body, and not just one side of it, tend to be ultimately and finally controlled from a center located in one or other of the hemispheres. Thus the *dominant hemisphere* (the left side of the brain in 95% of people) integrates and controls most body movements, including speech. This arrangement has nothing to do with right or left handedness. Left handed people are not right brain dominant for speech. Each total body response is finally programmed in the cortex of one or other of the cerebral hemispheres. From here the instructions travel to the same side of the brain directly and to the other side via the *corpus callosum.* The two hemispheres then act together to control the appropriate muscles on the contralateral side of the body.

The best known example of lateralization of function is the left brain /right brain concept. The left cerebral hemisphere is specially involved in speech and reasoning (language /math). The right hemisphere, on the other hand, is dominant in matters relating to shape and form (*visuospatial interpretation*). Roughly speaking, these functions can be considered equivalent to formal structured thinking (left brain) and creative intuitive imagination (right brain). Both are obviously important. Imagination without the restraint of the left brain leaps to wild conclusions; and, conversely, reasoning without imagination is a rather sterile and unproductive business. In a scarcity situation (when oxygen or glucose or blood are in short supply, or when the brain swells following trauma), left brain functions will be preserved better than right brained abilities (the brain's pecking order). Standard intelligence tests, such as the Wechsler II IQ test, are heavily biased in the direction of language and logic, with comparatively few items (15% or less) relating to visuospatial functions. This explains why IQ testing is an inadequate way to evaluate intellectual impairments following head injuries. It will not reveal subtle visuospatial impairments adequately.

§ 6:10 The perception of pain—the thalamus

There are many other localizations, of a more or less precise nature, on the cerebral cortex. Pain and the response to pain have a relatively large cerebral reference area, though the actual sensation of pain is, as was mentioned earlier, "felt" in the thalamus, in the deep gray matter of the brain. The thalami are a pair of lozenge-shaped collections of gray matter, located one on each side of the third ventricle (lying deep in the brain in the midline). [See Fig. 6-18.] There are many subnuclei in the thalamus, with various functions, mostly relating to the processing of incoming signals from sensory end organs, such as pain and fine touch receptors in the skin. The thalamus, as was mentioned earlier, feels pain and also passes on sensory information to the appropriate parts of the cerebral cortex.

§ 6:11 The limbic system — emotion and memory

The limbic system is a term used to describe a number of interrelated gray association areas, partly cortical and partly in the deep gray matter. [See Fig. 6-12.] The main parts in the limbic system are the cortex of the *cingulate gyrus* on the medial surface of each cerebral hemisphere; the *isthmus* (a smaller cortical area on the medial surface of the brain); the *hippocampus* (in the floor of the lateral ventricle); and the *amygdala* (amygdaloid nuclei), which lie in the deep gray matter of the brain. These areas receive olfactory (smell) signals and are responsible for establishing basic levels of emotional functions (emotion and smell are commonly inter-related in the CNS). They also appear to be important in memory functioning. Damage to the limbic cortex on the medial surfaces of the brain is likely to be followed by psychic disturbances, especially anxiety and depression. Amygdaloid damage is associated with profound emotional disturbance, characterized by episodes of deep depression and fits of violent temper.

The *hippocampus* is an important part of the memory circuits. Short-term memories (which last about 45 seconds) are located in various parts of the cerebral cortex and communicate their data to the hippocampus. The hippocampus processes these items and selects some of them for transfer into long-term memory in the cerebral cortex (the location of permanent memory on the cerebral cortex is a disputed matter). One famous patient following bilateral removal of the hippocampal cortex (as a treatment for intractable temporal lobe seizures) could only thereafter remember anything new for about half a minute, but could, of course, recall things stored in long-term memory before the operation. [See Fig. 6-33.]

§ 6:12 The pyramidal and extrapyramidal systems

Involuntary (resting) muscle tone, regulating the length and tension of each muscle group, is controlled by a system of integrative areas deep in the brain called the *extrapyramidal system*. [See Fig. 6-17.] The extrapyramidal system gets its name from the fact that the axons which transmit the signals from these nuclei to the motor cells of the spinal cord travel outside the pyramids. The *pyramids* are two bumps on the front of the brain stem made up of large fiber bundles which carry impulses directly from the motor cortex in the precentral area to the anterior horn cells of the spinal cord, and so control voluntary movement. [See Fig. 6-19.] The extrapyramidal system controls background position and tone, the environment, as it were, in which a voluntary act takes place (it can indirectly initiate movements also). The *basal ganglia*, a group of nuclei deep in the brain that are closely related to the lateral ventricles, are the principal integrative centers of the extrapyramidal system. Major components here are the head of the *caudate nucleus*, the lentiform nucleus (*lens*) and the *claustrum*. The head of the caudate nucleus and the lentiform nucleus, together

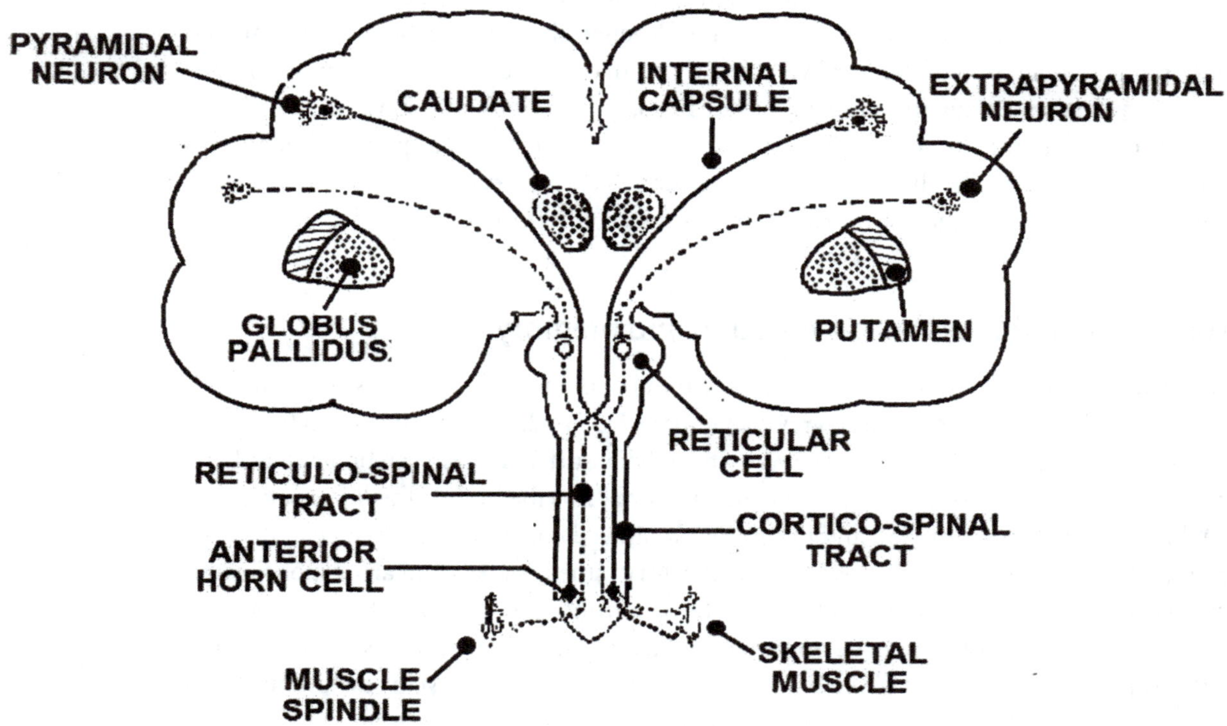

Fig. 6-17 Pyramidal and extrapyramidal pathways

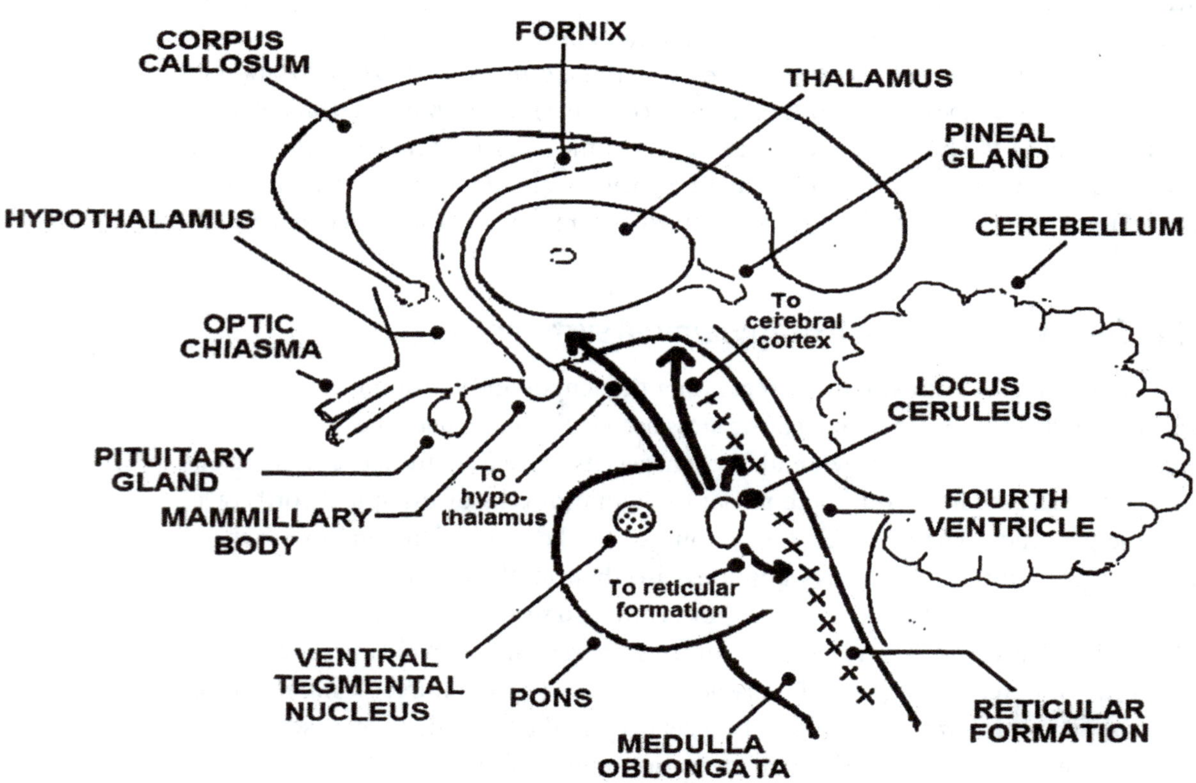

Fig. 6-18 The reticular formation and the arousal system

with scattered nuclei and white matter between them, are also called the *corpus striatum* since this area has a striped appearance when viewed under the microscope (due to bundles of white fibers piercing the various gray nuclei). If the extrapyramidal system is injured, the patient develops abnormal tone and tremors at rest. *Paralysis agitans* (Parkinsonism) is a disease of the basal ganglia. This condition is characterized by *hypertonia* (stiff muscle tone) and a typical shaking *tremor* (pill rolling tremor). Extrapyramidal disturbances are quite common sequelae to severe head injuries.

§ 6:13 Reticular formation — alertness and hypervigilance

The *reticular formation* [see Fig.6-18] is a collection of many small groups of nerve cells (nuclei) in the brain stem that controls wakefulness or arousal from sleep. These nuclei receive signals from the ears and eyes and also from other parts of the body. They process this information and may then communicate a wake-up call to the cerebral cortex. Thus when light strikes the eye, or an unusual sound reaches the ear, this message is relayed to the reticular formation which can quickly arouse the whole brain. Shaking of the brain stem (as from the twisting movements in a whiplash injury) disturbs this mechanism and thus rapidly produces unconsciousness. Damage to the cerebral hemispheres or to the *hypothalamus* [see Fig. 6-16] which are other important functioning units in the arousal response) will have the same effect. Alertness is closely associated with vigilance and with fear responses. The *locus ceruleus,* a center in the brain stem which is linked to the reticular formation, initiates the *stress response*, a physiological reflex system which alerts the organism for fright, flight or fight responses. Interference with this system by brain damage or by an extremely frightening experience, can produce *stress disorders* where there is a more or less continuous arousal state (sometimes called *hypervigilance*). These give rise to dysfunctional anxiety, sleep disorders and other anxiety related problems which will be discussed in Chapter 7.

§ 6:14 The hypothalamus and the pituitary gland (hypophysis)

The *hypothalamus,* as the name suggests, indicates that part of the brain which lies below the thalamus. [See Fig. 6-16.] This area has numerous nuclei controlling the various animal functions and appetites of the body. Hypothalamic lesions affect the level of activity, basic emotional set and sexual interest. In animal studies, some lesions in the hypothalamus will produce a placid, amorous animal, and others a very aggressive and irritable beast.

The hypothalamus lies above the *pituitary gland,* the great hormonal controller of the body. [See Fig. 6-16.] The *pars anterior* of this tiny organ produces hormones which control the thyroid gland, the adrenal glands, the gonads, lactation, and several other things as well. The *pars posterior* principally produces *antidiuretic hormone* (ADH) which keeps the water content of the body constant. The pituitary gland (hypophyseal gland) is thus the chemical controller of many body functions; and the pituitary itself is controlled by the hypothalamus.

§ 6:15 The cerebellum

The cerebellum, which lies in the *posterior fossa* of the skull below the *tentorial membrane* (*tentorium cerebelli*) [see Fig.6-14], controls the voluntary movements of the body. The cerebellum programs the actual voluntary movement (e.g., the movement of the arm in delivering a blow to an assailant), relaxing some muscles and contracting others at the correct speeds to make the movement smooth. It also adjusts the positioning of other parts of the body, moving a limb or the trunk or the head into a new position, in order to counterbalance the effects of the movement. If this were not done, we would become unbalanced with each significant bodily action. The cerebellum has numerous connections with both the ascending and descending fiber bundles in the brain stem. These keep it informed as to positions and movements in the rest of the body. This information allows it to integrate each movement with what is going on in the rest of the body, and vice versa.

§ 6:16 The cerebellum and the extrapyramidal system compared

The cerebellum controls voluntary active movements. The extrapyramidal system controls involuntary tone and posture, the background environment of the active movements. Injury to either system produces abnormal tremors, movements and postures, but the abnormalities are different. Thus cerebellar damage produces *action tremors*, which begin or get worse with voluntary movements; whereas extrapyramidal damage is associated with *tremors at rest*, which actually improve when voluntary movement brings the cerebellum into play. Another difference is that extrapyramidal lesions are generally associated with hypertonias (spastic tone), whereas cerebellar disease tends to produce hypotonia (flaccid tone). It is interesting that the cerebellum acts on the ipsilateral, not (as is the case in most other brain centers) on the contralateral side of the body, since its fibers do not decussate.

§ 6:17 The brain stem

The brain stem, which connects the brain to the spinal cord, is conventionally divided into three parts. The middle part is the *pons*, meaning bridge, for it resembles a little hump-backed bridge lying on its side. The hump is caused by bundles of fibers running back and forward between the great fiber tracts and the cerebellum. These keep the cerebellum informed as to motor and sensory activity, and also carry instructions from the cerebellum back to the motor tracts. The part above the pons, lying between it and the base of the brain, is called the midbrain (*mesencephalon*). The part below the pons, between it and the spinal cord, is called the *medulla oblongata*. These divisions are more formal than real; in other words, they are useful to localize things but do not represent a real structural or functional division in the CNS. In general, the brain stem contains the centers for the automatic control of the important (vital) functions such as arousal, respiration, heart rate, blood pressure, and so on. It also contains the nuclei of ten of the twelve *cranial nerves*.

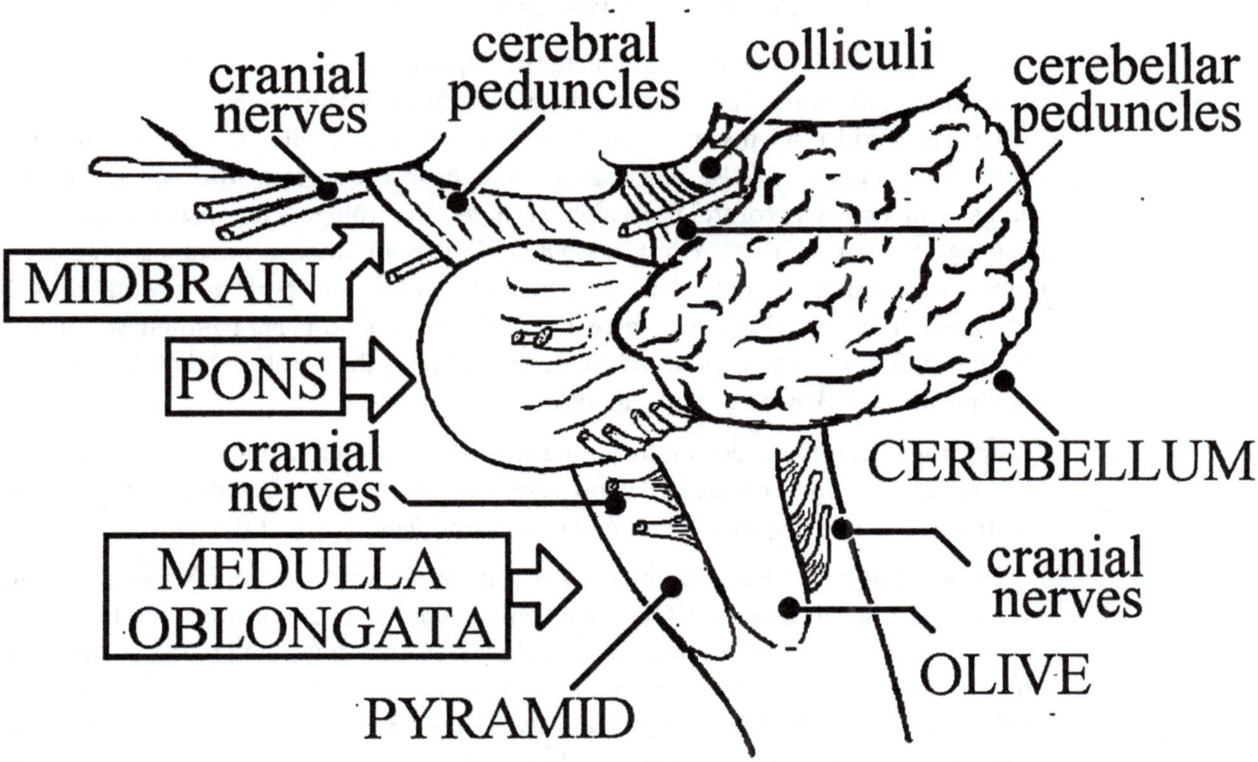

Fig. 6-19 Structures of the brain stem — lateral

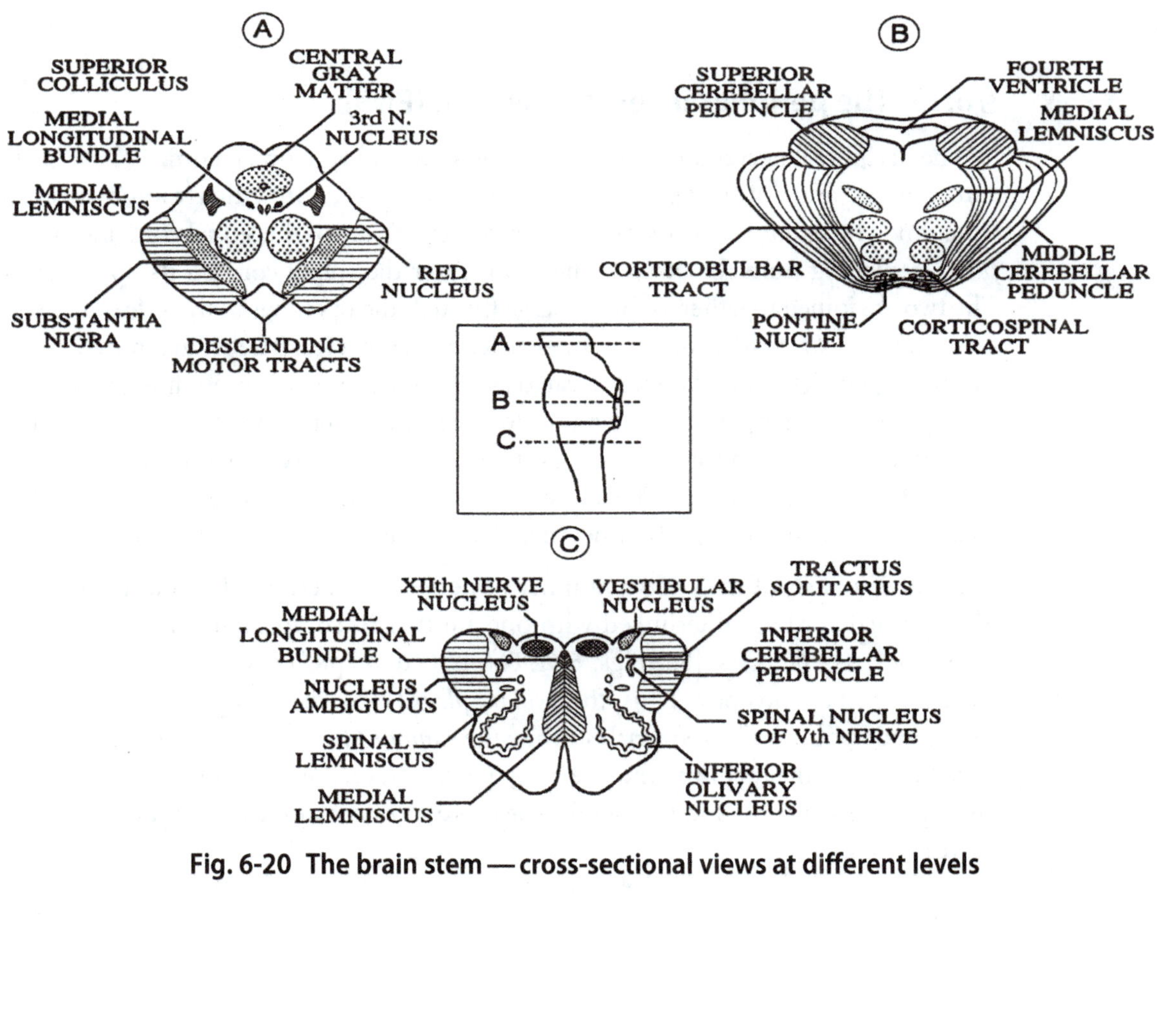

Fig. 6-20 The brain stem — cross-sectional views at different levels

§ 6:18 The spinal cord—reflexes and fiber tracts

The spinal cord is not a mere conductor of impulses to and from the brain. It is also a processor of information, and controls many body functions and activities by reflex movements. The bladder, for instance, functions mainly by spinal reflexes, although voluntary control is exercised on it, also. The *knee jerk* and *ankle jerk* are also processed in the spine (though moderated by control from higher centers). Neurologists use these reflexes to test the integrity of various parts of the CNS, but in life, they are automatic methods of adjusting limbs to the pushes and pulls that take place when we walk or perform any other bodily movement. *Withdrawal reflexes,* where a limb draws back on being painfully stimulated, are spinal reflexes. They are protective in function, taking the burnt part rapidly away from the fire without us having to think about it.

Motor impulses travel downward in the anterior and anterolateral spinal tracts. A few of these fibers originate on the ipsilateral (same) side of the brain, but 95% of them, as was mentioned earlier, cross over (*decussate*) to the contralateral side of the body.

Sensory information travels up in the dorsal (posterior) white columns of the spinal cord. Most of these signals cross over (decussate) either at or a segment or two above the level of entry into the spinal cord. Some sensations, however, (fine touch and vibration sense) do not cross over until they reach the brain stem. So if there is cord damage at a particular level, a unique complex of motor and sensory clinical findings will appear on both sides of the body. These will enable clinical neurologists to localize lesions, with some precision, in particular parts of the spinal cord or brain stem.

§ 6:19 The peripheral nervous system (PNS)

The peripheral nerves are those outside the skull and vertebral column. They are divided into somatic and autonomic nerves. The somatic nerves are either motor or sensory in function. The *motor fibers* emerge from the anterior part of the spinal cord and the *sensory fibers,* returning from the body to the CNS, enter the spinal cord on its posterior aspect. The two are joined together as they emerge through the openings in the side of the vertebral column (*neural foramina*), and are then called mixed nerves. The cranial nerves (emerging through openings in the skull) are treated as a separate category, even though they function exactly like the other peripheral nerves. Most peripheral nerves are mixed nerves, and many of them also contain autonomic nerves (treated in the next section). Even those which are primarily motor (such as the facial nerve) or mainly sensory (like the trigeminal nerve) usually contain all three kinds of nerve fibers (motor, sensory and autonomic).

In certain parts of the body a number of nerve roots deriving from different segments of the spinal cord are interlinked with one another in complex arrangements which are known as *nerve plexuses.* [See Figs. 6-22 & 6-23] Nerve plexuses are generally sequestered and protected by the body. Thus, the *axillary plexus* is tucked under the arm and protected before and behind by large muscles; while the *lumbar plexus* and the *pelvic plexus* are protected by the spinal column and the bony pelvis. Nevertheless, plexus injuries can occur (as in pelvic fractures), and they tend to be more serious matters than injuries to individual nerves.

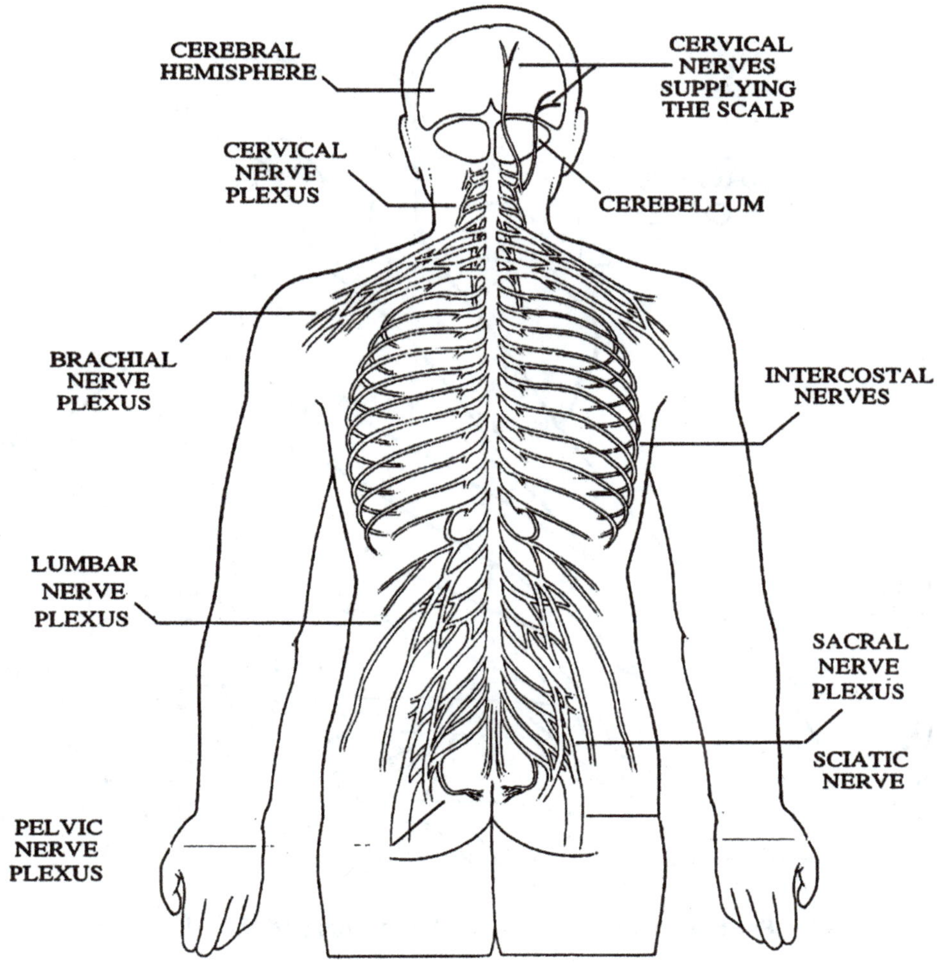

Fig. 6-21 The peripheral nervous system

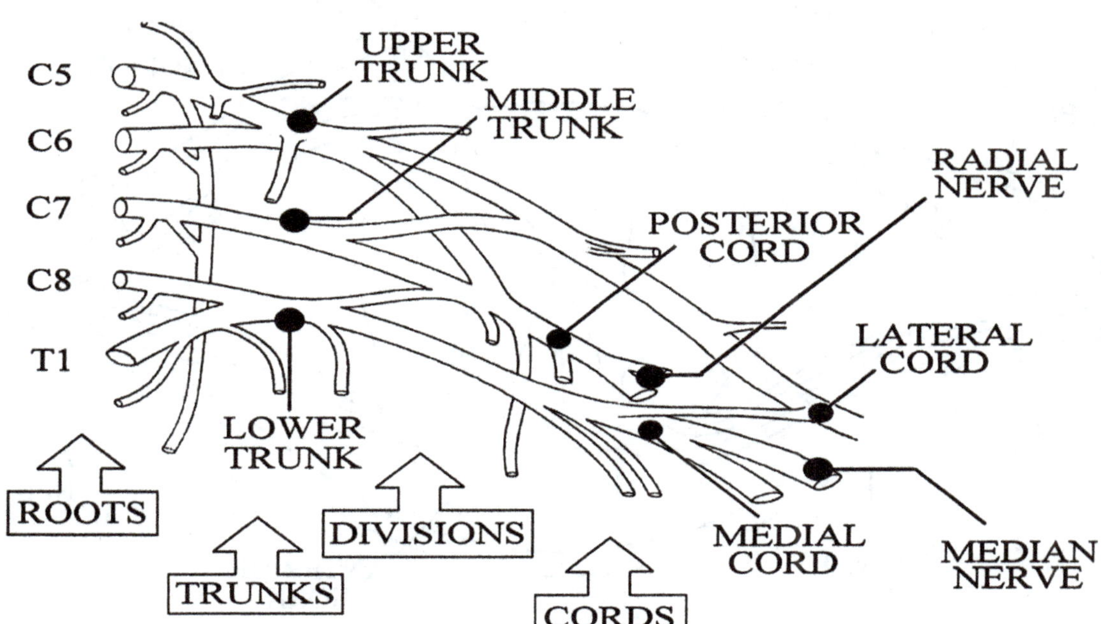

Fig. 6-22 The brachial plexus

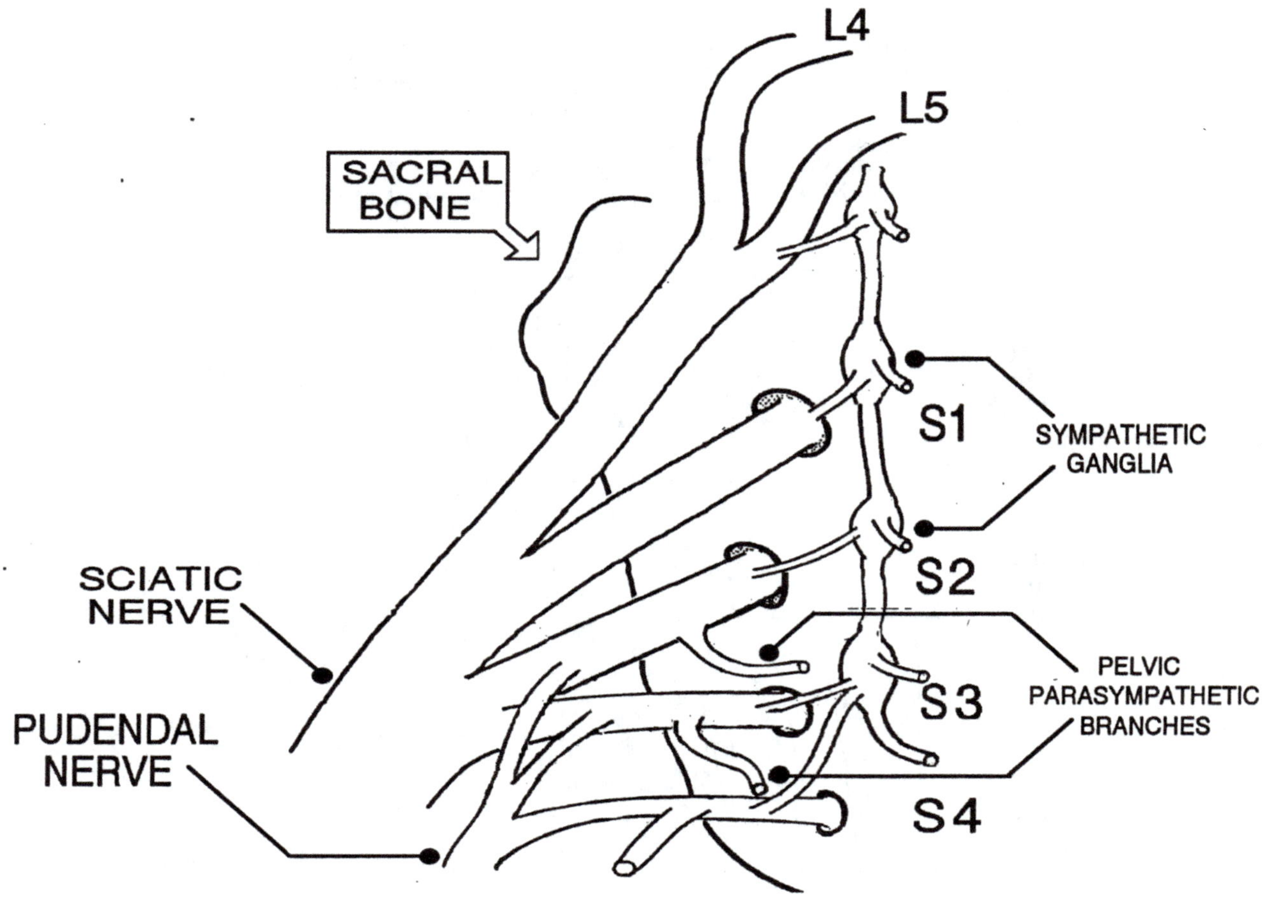

Fig. 6-23 Peripheral nerves — the lumbar plexus and the sciatic nerve

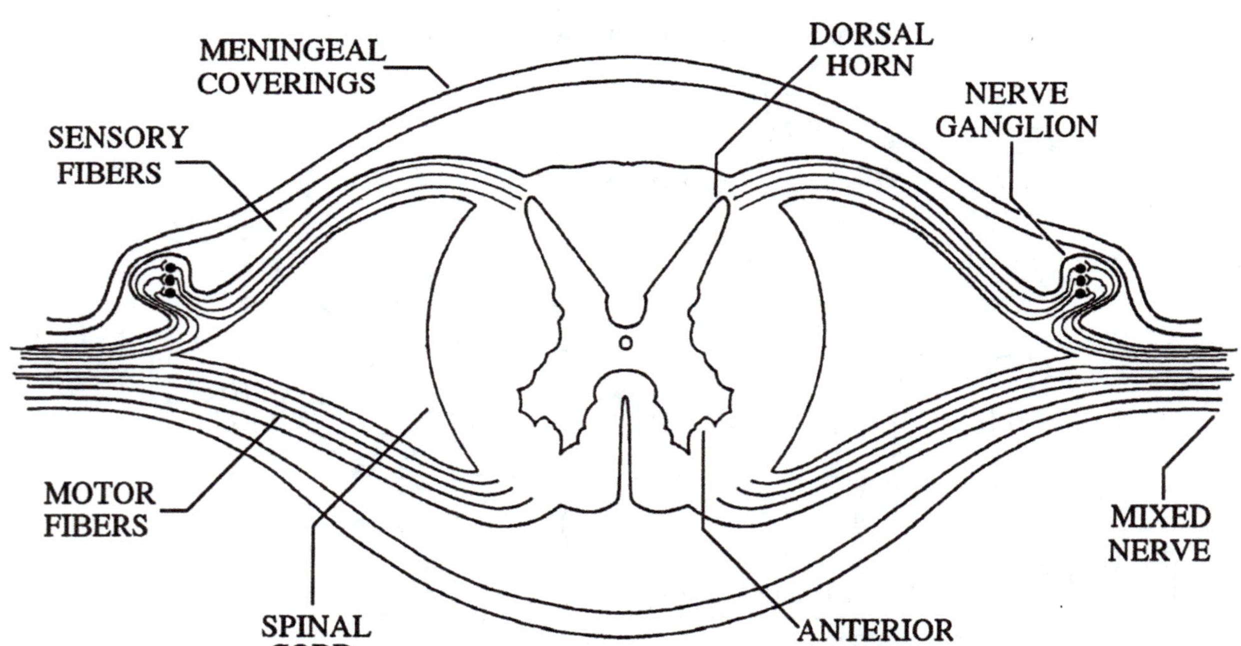

Fig. 6-24 Spinal cord with emerging peripheral nerves — cross section

§ 6:20 The autonomic nervous system (ANS)

The autonomic nervous system automatically controls such things as intestinal activity, breathing, dilatation and contraction of the pupils in the eye, heart rate, blood pressure and the flow of blood to various organs. The ANS is divided into the sympathetic and parasympathetic nervous systems. The *parasympathetic system* originates at both ends of the spinal cord [see Fig. 6-26]. There are also parasympathetic centers in the brain and brain stem (such as the *Edinger-Westphal nucleus* in the midbrain which controls the pupillary reflex). There is also a cervical parasympathetic outflow which affects the heart and lungs and the intestines down to the midpoint of the colon. The pelvic parasympathetic outflow (largely composed of fibers from the S1 and S2 level of the cord) controls the distal parts of the colon, the bladder and the sexual organs. Any injury to the lower end of the cord (such as spinal trauma) may produce very severe disability, not only involving movement of the lower legs but also bowel, bladder and sexual function.

The *sympathetic nerves* [see Fig. 6-25] emerge from the cervical, thoracic and lumbar spine between the sources of the parasympathetic outflow. They form a chain of nerve complexes on each side of the spinal cord (*the sympathetic chain*), with processing stations (ganglia) more or less opposite each intervertebral space. Sympathetic nerve fibers then tend to travel along the arteries to their target organs.

The sympathetic and parasympathetic nerves generally oppose and balance one another. The sympathetic nervous system is particularly concerned with the stress response, sometimes described as the "fright, fight or flight" reaction. Sympathetic tone is also important in maintaining blood pressure and in preventing blood from pooling in the peripheral veins. It is the active agent in maintaining blood supply to vital organs such as the brain and heart, following severe acute hemorrhage or a heart attack. Absence of sympathetic tone in these circumstances produces circulatory collapse known as "shock." Sympathetic activity can also persist when the occasion is past. This can occur in susceptible people following mental trauma (e.g., being held hostage in life threatening conditions or observing a horrible event). This is the basic impairment underlying *post-traumatic stress disorder* [considered in Chapter 7].

The sympathetic nerves have sensory functions including pain. Sympathetic pain syndromes typically occur after severe crush injuries to a limb, where the circulation to the damaged body part is left permanently impaired. The severe chronic burning pain which may occur in these situations is very disabling and likely to be compounded by addiction to narcotic pain killers. The notion that such pain is of sympathetic origin is supported by the fact that it may be relieved by blocking the sympathetic nerves to the limb. Critics, however, consider the effect of sympathectomy to be vascular, increasing blood flow to the damaged tissues. Blocking the *stellate ganglion* (a sympathetic ganglion in the neck) is quite commonly performed in order to deal with arm pain deemed to be of sympathetic origin (called *reflex sympathetic dystrophy*).

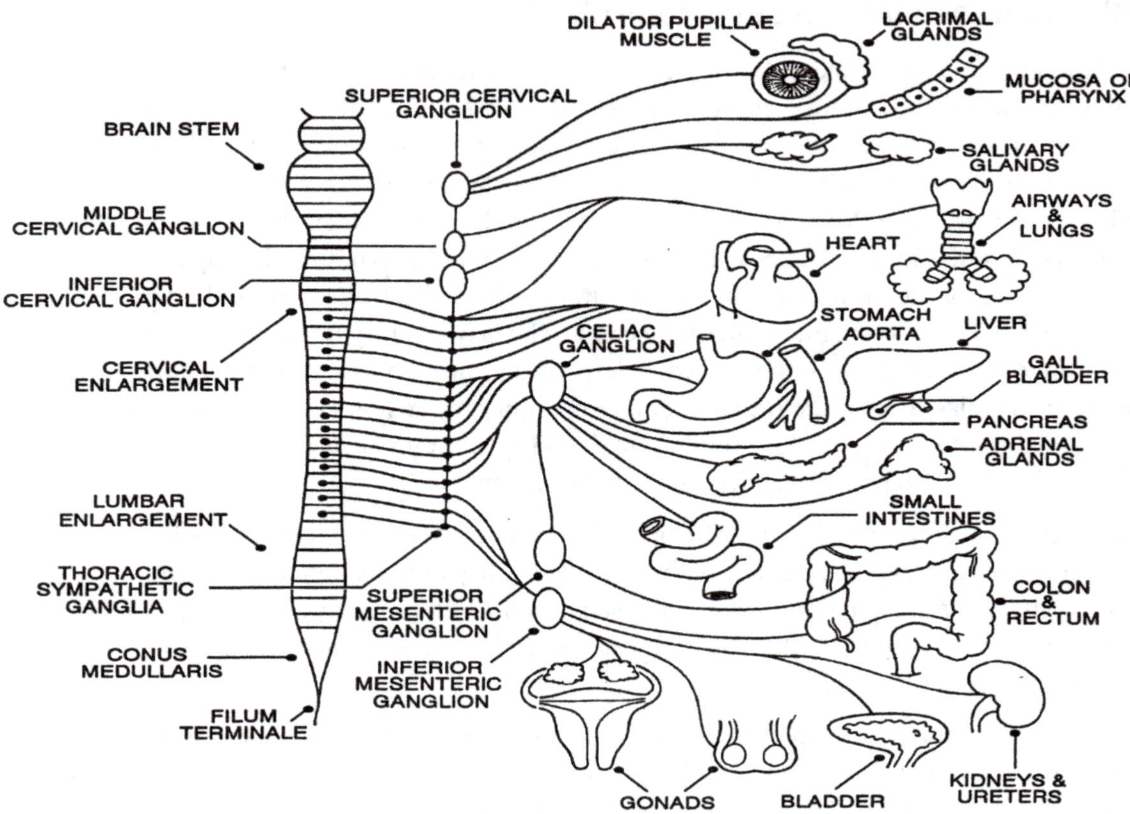

Fig. 6.25 The sympathetic nervous system

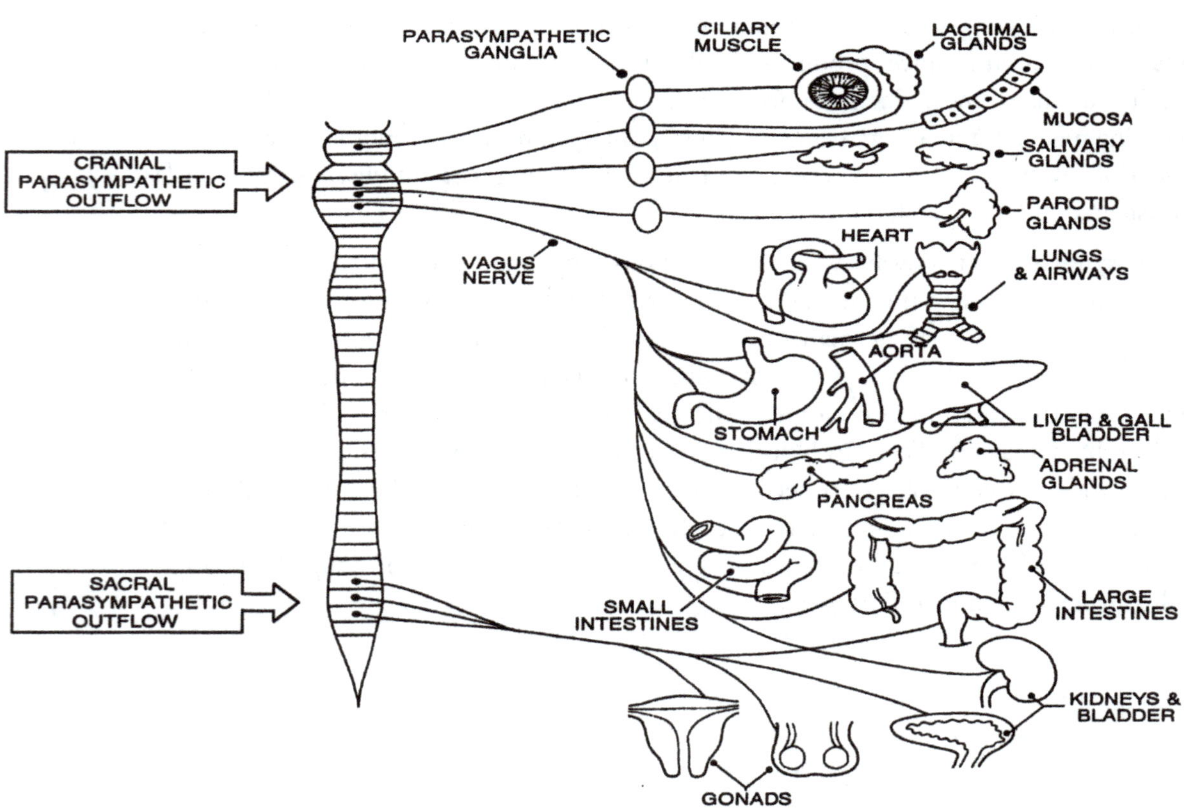

Fig. 6.26 The parasympathetic nervous system

Part II.
Brain Disorders

§ 6:21 Injuries to the brain — concussion and brain contusion

Injuries to the brain are classified in several ways. *Concussion* is defined as *temporary* neurological dysfunction following a head injury. This may occur in a torsion injury where the head and skull (or the brain inside it) is rotated rapidly so that the brain stem is twisted. In the mildest cases, there is only a period of confusion, following which the patient seems to be fully recovered. More severe injury, besides rendering the victim unconscious, produces a period of profound confusion with *retrograde amnesia* (RA) which is loss of memory for events which preceded the injury. There is frequently *post-traumatic amnesia* (PTA) also, where the patient moves around (somewhat drowsily perhaps) and carries on with their business, but has no memory afterwards of what they did or what was happening. In some cases there may be no loss of consciousness (LOC). In *classical concussion,* however, loss of consciousness is immediate and retrograde amnesia and post-traumatic amnesia are usual findings. Recovery appears to be complete, but subtle mental, emotional and personality deficits can follow this kind of injury and should be ruled out. The term, *cerebral contusion,* literally means that there is a bruise on the brain and, properly speaking, it is defined by the presence of small scattered hemorrhages (seen at operation or autopsy). This term is often used when the patient is slow to recover from the head injury, when something more than a bump (i.e. a bruise) is then presumed to be present.

Focal injuries are those which mainly affect one part of the brain, leaving the others relatively intact. *Diffuse (generalized) head injuries* on the other hand, produce widespread (*global*) damage. Generally speaking, focal injuries produce less dysfunction and are, therefore, less important to lawyers than generalized brain injuries. Hypoglycemia and hypoxia produce diffuse (generalized) cortical damage. Rapid rotatory movements of the head (such as occur in whiplash injuries) also tend to produce widespread damage to the white matter of the brain, stretching and tearing the axons and the little blood vessels which supply them. These results of rotational trauma (*diffuse axonal injuries*—DAIs) will be discussed later [see § 6:23].

§ 6:22 Types of head injury — skull fractures

Head injuries are classified and described in various ways, most of which are not important for compensation purposes. If a pointed implement (like a bullet or an ice pick) penetrates through the skull tables to enter the brain cavity, this will be called a *penetrating injury.* Penetrating head injuries are unfortunately becoming quite common and are usually the result of intentionally inflicted trauma. If brain damage occurs without a penetrating wound or even a fracture, this will be termed a *closed head injury.*

There is no particular term for head injuries associated with a fracture, since the presence or absence of fractures does not correlate well with the occurrence or severity of brain damage. There can be serious brain damage with no fractures, and nasty looking skull fractures with no sign of brain damage. A fracture can, of course, be clinically important by ,virtue of its location. In the region of the ear it can nip or tear the middle meningeal artery and result in an epidural hemorrhage. Or, a linear fracture in the floor of the anterior fossa can damage the olfactory nerves so that the patient loses their sense of smell; it can also tear the meninges here, so that CSF flows down the nose and creates some risk of ascending infection, like meningitis. Fractures are generally more important to lawyers than to doctors. To begin with, they can be used to show a causal connection between an accident and a brain injury. Fractures, especially linear fractures, also provide important evidence as to the magnitude of the forces involved in trauma. Linear fractures are produced by rapid deformation movements of the calvarium. [See Fig. 6-27] When the bony plates whip out and in again during such movements, they may fracture, and the resulting fracture line is likely to occur on the side of the skull opposite to where the original deforming force was applied. The presence of a linear fracture, running down into the thick bone at the base of the skull, is thus evidence of significant applied force.

Vigorous shaking movements of the head can damage the brain. This kind of brain injury is sometimes found in child abuse cases, but most often occurs in automobile accidents, in a rear- or front-end collision producing the so-called *whiplash injury.*

§ 6:23 Whiplash injuries

The expression "whiplash" is often used loosely to describe a simple neck strain, the sort of thing that occurs when a car is hit from the rear and the occupant's neck is jerked a little. Properly speaking, the term, whiplash injury, means that the head is jerked back and forwards violently, as in cracking a whip. This may injure the neck (a topic discussed in the previous chapter), but can also cause brain damage. The brain is only really firmly attached to the skull in the posterior fossa, around the foramen magnum where the brain stem begins. If the brain rotates in the calvarium, as it does in a whiplash injury, the applied forces are concentrated and focused in places where it is attached to the base of the skull (corresponding to the junction of the handle and the lash in a whip). Very violent whiplash injuries may interfere with the vital centers in the brain stem and can, therefore, be instantly fatal. Structures at the base of the brain (close to the brain stem) may also be affected in severe whiplash injuries. If the patient should survive the brain stem insult, damage in the basal ganglia can lead to extrapyramidal problems with tremors and muscle spasms and abnormal postures. More commonly, the cerebral hemispheres merely twist round inside the skull (rotatory injury) stretching and tearing the white fibers and their associated capillaries. This can produce the subtle kind of brain damage which tries the mettle of compensation lawyers—the common whiplash brain injury.

Brain stem injuries need not concern us much here since the patient either dies or recovers completely, and in either event the compensation problems require little or no knowledge of medicine. Damage to the basal gray matter is likewise simple from the compensation viewpoint, since the resulting damage, if significant, is obvious, and disability is likely to be complete (spastic paralysis). More subtle forms of whiplash brain injury produce mild cortical dysfunction with less obvious impairments, which are much more difficult to evaluate for compensation purposes. These non-obvious deficits are sometimes called *minimal brain damage,* but the disabilities may be far from minimal in their effects on the victim's functioning.

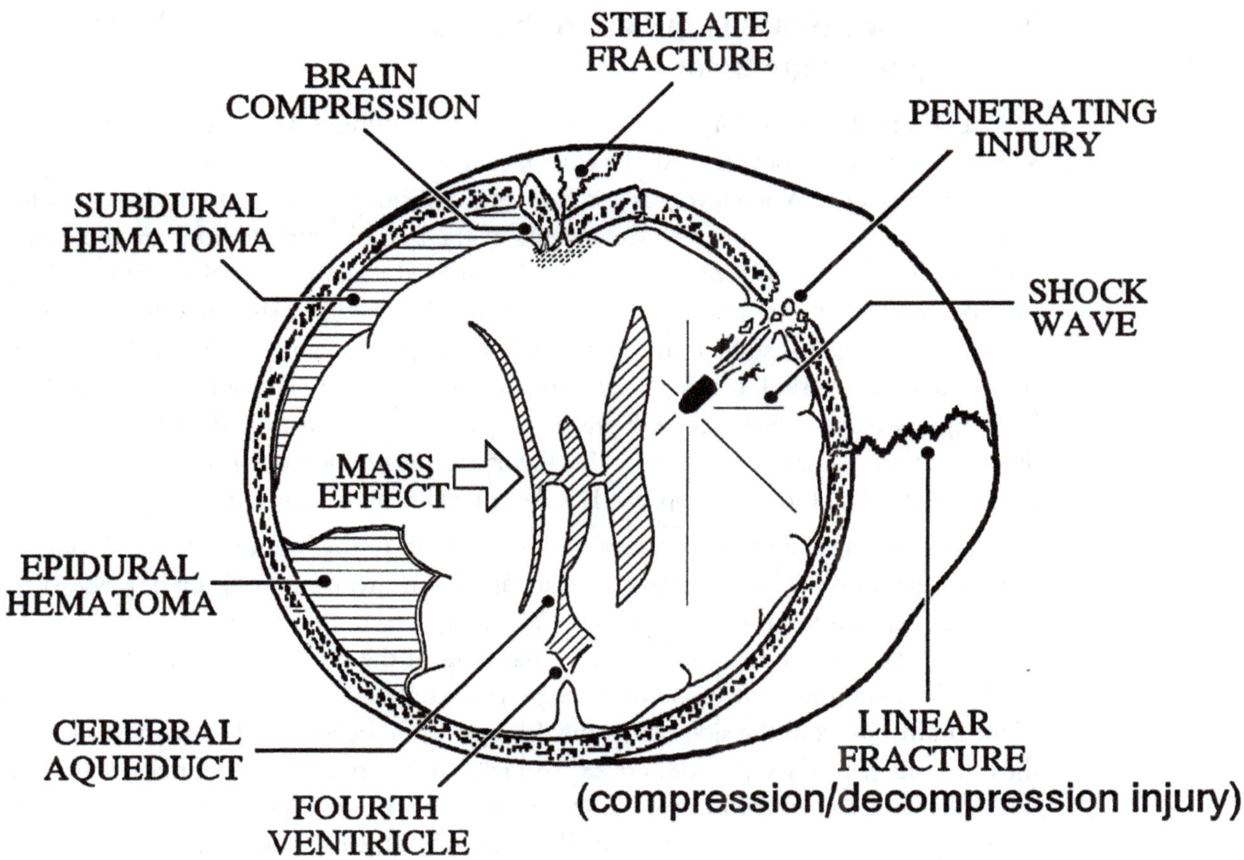

Fig. 6-27 Mechanisms of brain damage

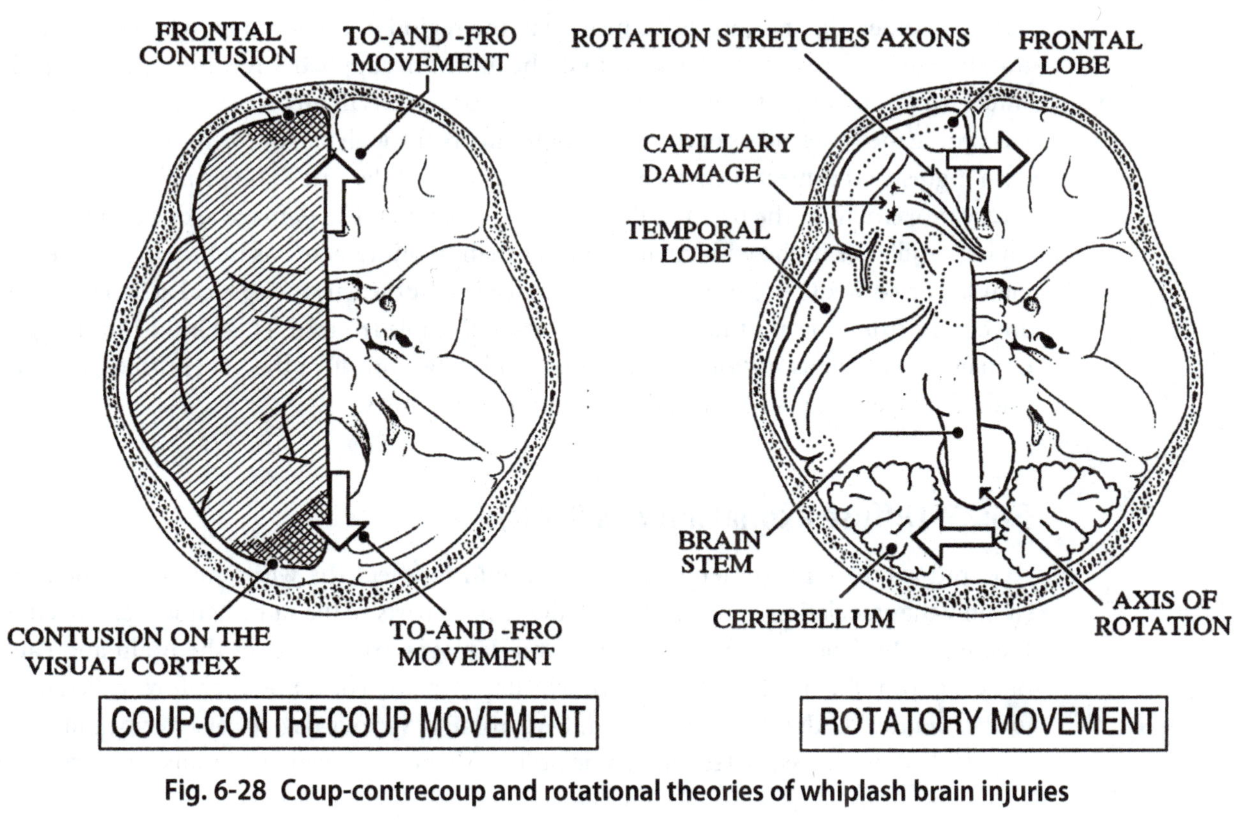

Fig. 6-28 Coup-contrecoup and rotational theories of whiplash brain injuries

§ 6:24 How whiplash injuries produce cortical damage — the coup-contrecoup theory

Until relatively recently, it was thought that whiplash injuries damaged the cerebral hemispheres by backward and forward movement, *coup* and *contrecoup*. The injury was supposed to occur as follows. When force (as in a front end collision) is applied to the head and neck (coup), the head jerks forward. Movements of the brain inside the skull are buffered by cerebrospinal fluid (CSF). So when the head is moved rapidly forward the brain follows, but does so more slowly, since it is moving through the CSF like a ship in water (which protects the brain against sudden movements). If the applied force is sufficient, however, the brain will meet the skull coming back again and bump into it. The brain surface will then be compressed and these forces will presumably damage the cortex and underlying tissues. Since the brain damage envisaged by this theory occurs on the side of the head opposite to where the original force was applied, it is described as *contrecoup*. [See Fig.6-28.]

Understanding the mechanisms of whiplash injury to the brain in terms of coup and contrecoup may describe some part of what happens in a rear-end collision or a side-swipe. As a total explanation it is, however, clearly inadequate. It does not explain, for instance, why the worst damage is always in the frontal areas of the brain, even when the force was applied from on front (when one would expect the contrecoup damage to occur at the back of the brain); or from the side (when the damage would be expected to be most severe on the other side). Likewise, it does not explain why the functions of the damaged cortex are not reallocated to some other part of the brain. However, the most serious defect of this notion is that it fails to account for what happens when the head and neck are jolted in any direction. Physicists have pointed out that the brain inside the skull should act like a liquid in a container, since it is soft and moveable, only loosely attached to the skull by blood vessels and nerves, and mostly at the base in the region of the foramen magnum. It would not then move forward and back again in the line of the applied force, but rather *rotate* like water, when the bucket containing it is kicked or shaken in any way. Animal experiments (recording the movements of the brains of monkeys through perspex windows in their skulls with high speed cameras) showed that this was indeed the case. The principal effect of rotatory movement of the brain in the skull is to stretch and so damage axons and their supplying capillaries in the white matter, rather than to injure neurons in the cortex (the older view). The consequence of this axonal damage is that the various cortical association areas are cut off from one another, like computers with cable trouble. This kind of white matter damage is known as *diffuse axonal injury,* and it can produce the generalized and subtle brain damage that is so troublesome to compensationists.

§ 6:25 Diffuse axonal injuries (DAIs)

Rapid rotatory movements of the head tend to affect the white matter of the brain, (mainly the association fibers which link the various parts of the same hemisphere together). [See Fig.6-29] The movement stretches and damages axons all over the brain and causes bleeding from the tiny blood vessels which supply them. These are, therefore, called *diffuse axonal injuries* (DAIs). Like concussion, DAIs come in various degrees of severity, but almost invariably they are associated with some period of unconsciousness (because the brain stem

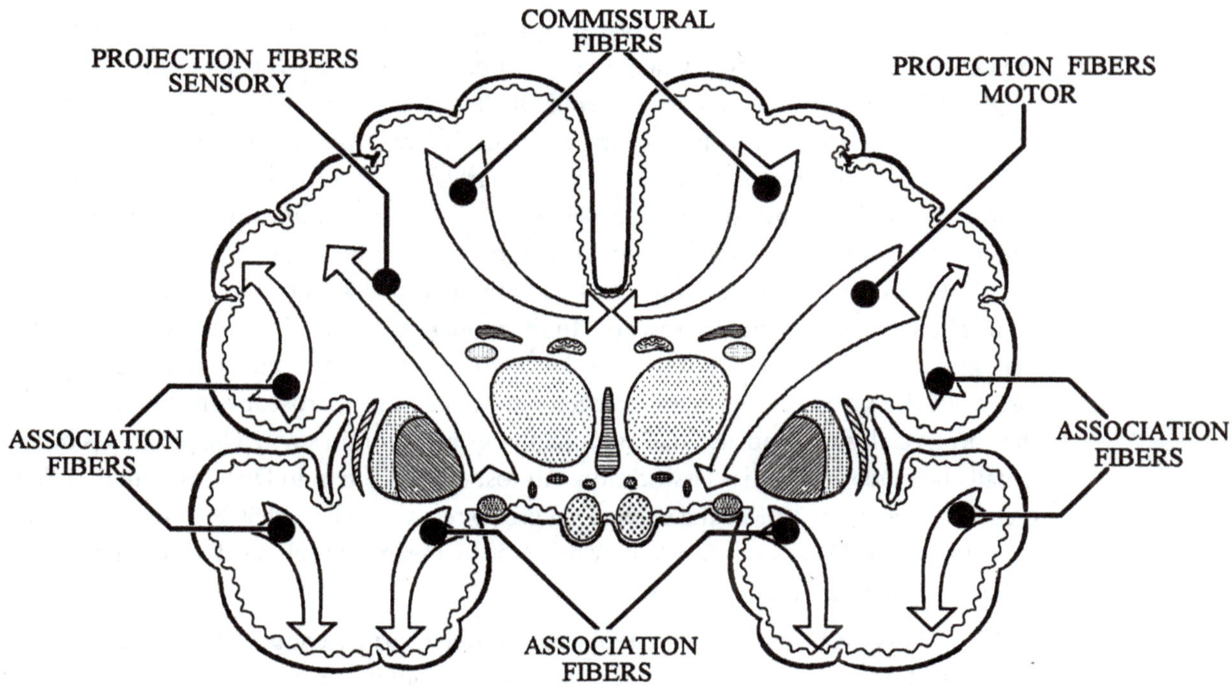

Fig. 6-29 White fiber connections in the brain

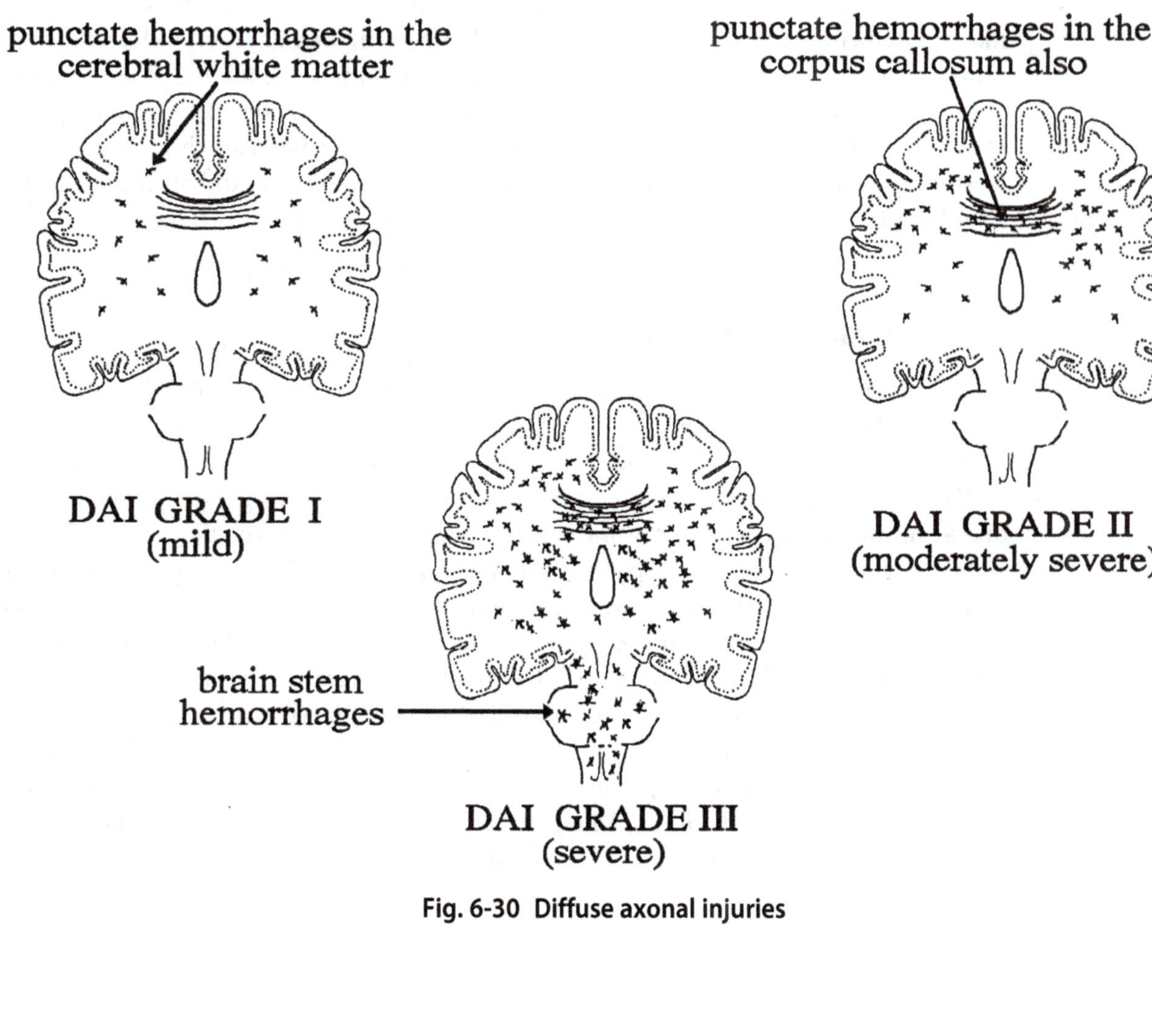

Fig. 6-30 Diffuse axonal injuries

is twisted). They are now considered to be the main way in which the brain is injured in automobile accidents. DAIs are classified as mild, moderately severe and severe. Mild DAIs are defined clinically as those where Loss of Consciousness (LOC) persists for 6–24 hours. Moderately severe DAIs are those where LOC lasts for more than 24 hours, but there are no persistent abnormal involuntary movements. Severe DAIs are those where LOC exceeds 24 hours and involuntary movements (particularly *decerebrate rigidity*) persist. This classification has been found to correlate well with the clinical findings in head trauma cases, and also with the pathological findings on autopsy when these have become available. [See Fig. 6-30.] In the mild cases only a few scattered hemorrhages can be seen in the cerebral hemispheres with the light microscope. In the moderately severe DAIs, there are more hemorrhages and they are seen not only in the cerebral hemispheres but also in the *corpus callosum.* In the severe group, hemorrhages can be seen on microscopy in the hemispheres, the corpus callosum, and also in the white matter of the brain stem. The prognosis can also usually be made using this classification. Almost 80% of the mild DAI group make a "good recovery." Less than 20% of the severe DAI group recover well, and 50% of them die. In the near future, the DAI classification may be made by means of high resolution CT scans, imaging the tiny point hemorrhages directly.

The DAI concept has virtually replaced the older terms, coup and contrecoup, which were used to describe the injuries produced when frontal or rear-end force was applied to the head. It is more in accord with general physical principles, and it is clinically valuable as it relates well to prognosis. It also explains, as the older theory did not, why the worst injuries tend to be frontal and limbic. Twisting movements are particularly likely to produce more movement in the frontal region, since the brain stem, the axis around which the brain moves, is not central but *posterior* (at the foramen magnum in the middle of the posterior fossa). Frontal areas will, therefore, move relatively farther and more rapidly than those at the back; the frontal axons and the blood vessels which supply them are thus more likely to be stretched and damaged. Furthermore, the less severe damage in the other areas of the brain may be enough to prevent relocation of functions from the frontal parts.

§ 6:26 Intracranial bleeding

A penetrating wound, a fracture, or even blunt trauma can cause bleeding inside the skull. [See Fig. 6-31.] The term, *hemorrhage,* is used to describe the active bleeding, while a *hematoma* is the blood clot which results from it. A *subdural hemorrhage* or *hematoma* (SDH) is one which lies between the *dura mater*, the outer covering of the brain, and the middle membranous covering, the *arachnoid mater* (CSF flows between the arachnoid mater and the *pia mater.* which directly covers the brain and spinal cord). SDH is usually the result of a torsion injury of the brain inside the skull, when little veins in the subdural space become torn. An *epidural hemorrhage* or *hematoma* (EDH) is caused by bleeding outside the dura. It is most often due to a tear in the middle meningeal artery in the epidural space (occasionally one of the venous sinuses is involved); and it is usually caused by direct trauma to the skull, a blow or a fall, rather than torsion. *Intracerebral hemorrhage* (ICH) is bleeding into the brain substance. Its important causes include rupture of deeply placed aneurysms or *arterio-venous malformations* (AVMs). It can also be produced by penetrating injuries, especially intentional trauma (gunshot wounds).

Subdural and epidural hematomas have distinctive appearances on CT scan. Since SDH involves venous blood at low pressure, the problem generally develops slowly (over 12–24 hours or more) and has a diffuse flattish appearance on CT scan. The dura tends to be strongly attached to the inner table of the skull, and so epidural hemorrhage (which comes from tearing of the little arteries between the dura and the skull) does not spread out so widely (is more circumscribed). It also tends to make more of an indentation into the brain substance due to the higher pressure of arterial blood. [See Fig. 6-31.]

A chronic subdural hematoma develops 10–21 days after the original injury. These are thought (with some authorities, however, dissenting) to be due to a semipermeable membrane developing round the clot, which draws water in by osmosis to produce late swelling and neurological signs. A *subdural hygroma* is a collection of cerebrospinal fluid (usually blood tinged) under the skull tables. It is most commonly due to a leak of CSF into the subdural space and it can press (*mass effect*) on the brain. A hygroma can often be treated by making an oblique hole through the skull with a *twist drill* and inserting a needle through the dura to withdraw the fluid.

§ 6:27 Raised intracranial pressure (RICP)

The way in which the clinical picture emerges in intracranial bleeding is interesting. Venous bleeding is low pressured and so the ICP rises slowly. Compensatory mechanisms, therefore, have time to work. CSF is squeezed out of the ventricles into the subarachnoid space surrounding the brain and cord, and even a little venous blood may be displaced to make space for the clot and reduce intracranial pressure. There is a limit, however, to this kind of compensation, and when no more CSF can be expelled from the ventricles, the pressure inside the closed box of the skull starts to rise, and the brain begins to be compressed. The clinical signs of rising intracranial pressure are all processes and so characterized by the suffix "-ing." They are:

- Rising blood pressure
- Falling heart rate
- Slowing respirations
- Increasing vomiting
- Diminishing level of consciousness

The vomiting is rather characteristic and is called *cerebral vomiting.* It tends to be very violent, even explosive, and is therefore sometimes called *projectile vomiting.* The signs of arterial bleeding inside the skull are essentially the same as in SDH, but since arterial blood is at much higher pressure than venous blood, the clinical picture emerges more rapidly, often within 30 minutes, so that permanent brain damage may occur before treatment can be given.

§ 6:28 Intracranial bleeding — diagnosis and treatment

When bleeding inside the skull is suspected, a craniotomy may be indicated to stop the bleeding and relieve the pressure. If possible, of course, the bleeding site should be located first by imaging of some kind. Where a hematoma is suspected and there is no urgency in the situation (the patient is not deteriorating and has remained stable for some time), nuclear scanning can be ordered using radio-labeled dyes, which will remain in the blood clot but wash out of the healthy brain. Usually the bleeding has to be present 24 hours or more to show up in RNI. RNI is thus not suitable for acute intracranial bleeding where urgent treatment is required. The investigative modality of choice in the first 24 hours is computerized tomographic scanning (CT scan). If CT scan is not available locally, the patient should be transferred, if possible, to a facility with a CT scanner. CT shows up fresh blood well. MRI cannot distinguish fresh blood from brain tissue reliably. After 24–48 hours, decomposition of blood makes it different from brain substance so that magnetic resonance imaging can detect it.

Surgical management (when indicated) consists of exposing the bleeding site by opening up the skull cavity (*craniotomy*). An overlying flap of bone is mobilized to allow removal of the clot and treatment of any bleeding. A little pressure sensor is often left under the skull flap to detect any recurrence of raised pressure inside the skull. When a clot is removed, the swollen brain can bulge right out through the craniotomy opening. Sometimes this brain tissue must be extensively excised to close the craniotomy opening. One would think that serious impairments would follow; but a considerable part of the temporal lobe can be removed in this manner, without apparently ultimately interfering with brain function. Months later, neurological examination, electrodiagnostic testing, imaging and neuropsychological studies may all be unremarkable. Any functions lost can be relocated elsewhere in the brain (provided there are white fibers to carry them and intact cortex to receive them).

§ 6:29 Observation of head injured patients

If the injury seems mild and the patient is alert, it is perfectly proper to allow her to go home, provided there is someone present there to observe her. It is usual to instruct the family to rouse the patient every two hours until the next day, and to seek medical help at once if she is hard to rouse. Cerebral vomiting is, of course, another indication for return to the hospital. More serious head injuries should be observed in the hospital. Usually clinical observation every hour is adequate, but more frequent checks may be needed if the patient's condition is fluctuating or changing in any way. If there are neurological signs, the patient will probably be admitted to an intensive care unit. The ICU nurses' head injury observation record (HI obs.) is a most valuable record in evaluating the seriousness of the injury, the progress of the patient in hospital, and the likelihood of permanent deficits. In critical cases a sensor (a *subarachnoid bolt*) can be inserted through the skull under local anesthetic, or a catheter may be placed in the spinal canal. These can be connected to a pressure transducer and the signal watched on an oscilloscope, thus providing continuous monitoring of intracranial pressure (ICP).The fact that a subdural clot has shown up on CT scan does not mean that the patient needs an operation. The bleeding may stop and the clot resolve. It is the clinical picture that determines whether surgical intervention is needed or not.

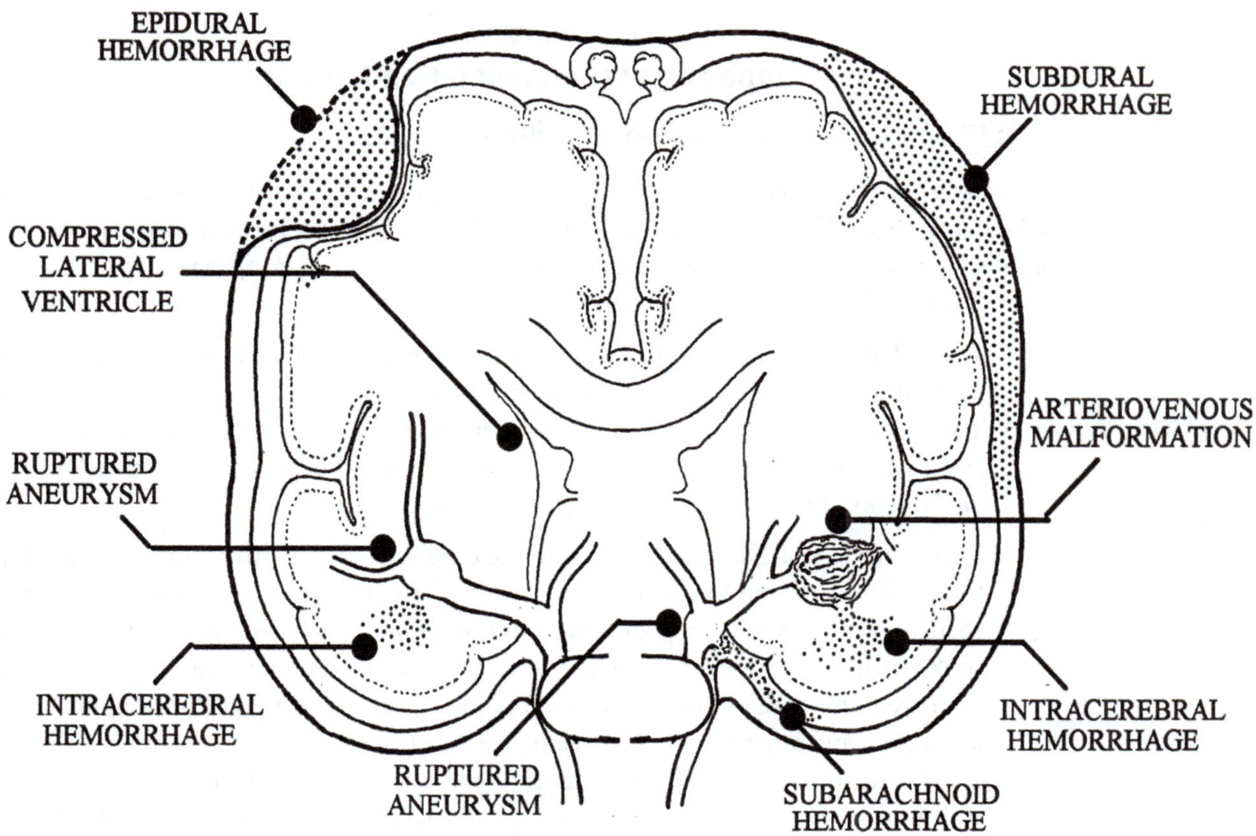

Fig. 6-31 Various intracranial hemorrhages — frontal sectional view

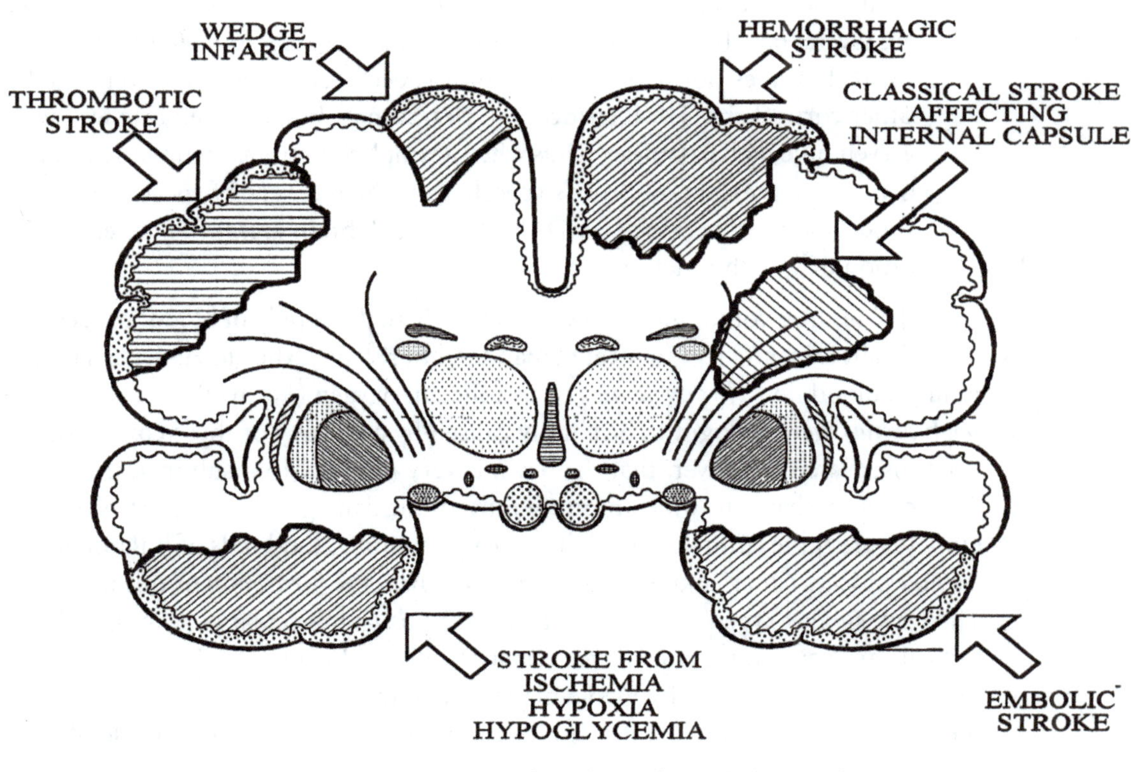

Fig. 6-32 Various types of stroke — frontal sectional view

Part III. Impairments Following Head Injuries

§ 6:30 Global injuries and local injuries

Damage to a particular part of the cerebral cortex or to a particular cranial nerve is called a *local injury* (focal injury), while one which affects the entire cerebral cortex will be termed a *global injury.* Global injuries are much more important than local injuries so far as lawyers are concerned for two quite distinct reasons:

1. Local injuries of any significance, involving cranial or peripheral nerves or particular parts of the spinal cord, are generally very obvious (anyone can see a facial paralysis). They will also, almost certainly, have been picked up on neurological examination and noted in the medical records. Very little medical knowledge is required on the part of compensationists to manage such cases.

2. Damage to specific areas on the cerebral cortex are also relatively unimportant but for a different reason. It is true that all sorts of functions are carried out in particular cortical regions, such as motor speech in Broca's speech center and interpretation of spoken words in Wernicke's sensory speech area. However, if one of these areas is destroyed, this does not mean that its function is lost. It is simply relocated and transferred to some other processing area of the brain. Thus if Broca's motor speech area is ablated, the patient will immediately be unable to speak. In time, however, the ability to speak will return, and the function will be found to have relocated itself elsewhere, e.g., on the parietal cortex, or even in the deep gray matter of the brain. So, immediately following a major stroke which affects the dominant side of the brain, the patient is usually aphasic, but gradually recovers the ability to speak. There are several possible reasons for this. Cortex that was only stunned may have recovered, or, if that does not happen, the motor speech center may have relocated in some other cortical site. Local cortical injuries cannot, however, relocate well when there is even mild global damage. Thus when a whiplash injury is complicated by a subdural hematoma pressing on Broca's speech area, the recovery of speech might not be so good as in a stroke, since the DAI (affecting all brain areas) may interfere with relocation of speech function.

Global injuries commonly follow episodes where the supply of blood, oxygen or glucose to the brain is insufficient to meet demand. Until recently, the global deficits that followed reduced blood flow (*hypovolemia*) or insufficient oxygen (*hypoxia*) or lack of glucose (*hypoglycemia*) were thought to be simply caused by a scarcity of these commodities. It has been discovered, however, that the brain is very resistant to insult in scarcity situations. The actual mechanisms which produce most of the damage following a stroke or a cerebral embolus are quite complex, involving release by white blood cells of inflammatory agents called *cytokines* (interleukins) and, in consequence, the formation of free oxygen radicals. These are single oxygen atoms (O) replacing the usual molecular oxygen (O_2). Free oxygen radicals are very active substances metabolically and cause much of the tissue damage that follows hypoxia and hypovolemia in ischemic organs. Substances which "scavenge" these free radicals or block interleukins can reduce tissue damage considerably.

§ 6:31 Impairments following head injury

Many kinds of impairment can follow brain damage. These may include:

1. *Paralysis* (complete inability to move a muscle group) or *paresis* (weakness of muscles). A head injury or stroke can leave a patient paralyzed down one side of the body or with *paralysis* or weakness (*paresis*) in any group of muscles, such as the muscles of the face (in Bell's palsy). *Hemiplegia* is weakness or paralysis on one side of the body. *Paraplegia is* weakness or paralysis affecting the lower half of the body; it may affect bladder and bowel function as well as the lower limbs. *Quadriplegia is* weakness or paralysis affecting all four limbs.

2. *Disorders of movement or tone.* Excess movement is called *hyperkinesia,* reduced activity *is hypokinesia* and absence of activity (not paralysis) is described as *akinesia. Dyskinesia* is abnormal movement, which may take the form of tremors, spasms or *tics* (sudden spasms) of muscle groups. Involuntary writhing movement is called *athetosis. Dystonias* are broadly classified into *hypotonias* (diminished tone) or *hypertonias* (increased tone). Prolonged recurrent spasms are described as *clonus.* Prolonged hypertonia is commonly called *rigidity.* There are a number of named types of rigidity, such as "clasp-knife" rigidity and "lead pipe" rigidity; each of these tends to be characteristic of certain disease conditions.

3. *Loss of sensation or abnormal sensation. Loss* of sensation is called *anesthesia;* diminished sensation is *hypesthesia;* and odd or unpleasant sensation is *dysesthesia. Paresthesias* are tingling or burning sensations (pins and needles). *Acroparesthesias* are tinglings or numbness in the hands or feet.

4. *Lack of coordination.* Damage to the extrapyramidal system or to the cerebellum (especially the latter) may lead to difficulty in coordinating movements. Inability to perform movements well, in a smooth coordinated way, is called *dystaxia.* When they cannot be performed at all, this is called *ataxia.* The ability to perform rapid repetitive movements, like clapping hands, is called *diadochokinesia.* Inability to perform them well is *dysdiadochokinesia. Adiadochokinesia* is inability to perform them at all.

5. *Cognitive impairments.* Global cortical damage produces a number of intellectual disabilities, generally classed as cognitive impairments. These include poor memory (not loss of memories), difficulty in learning new things, following arguments, and generally reduced capacity to process information. Inability to concentrate and lack of interest in former pursuits are common complaints following a head injury; their presence suggests that there is something wrong with the frontal lobes. *Frontal lobe syndrome is* characterized by loss of interest in things which were formerly enjoyed, and a short attention span, like that of a child.

6. *Emotional impairment.* Nervousness, amounting to an anxiety state, frequently follows head injury, and can last for a year or much longer. Sometimes these complaints are due to the fright itself (*post-traumatic stress disorder*). Sometimes, however, they are caused by subtle damage to the limbic cortex, which can produce anxiety and depression in a previously normal person (*limbic lobe syndrome*). Injuries involving the deep gray matter (amygdaloid nucleus) can produce profound emotional disturbance.

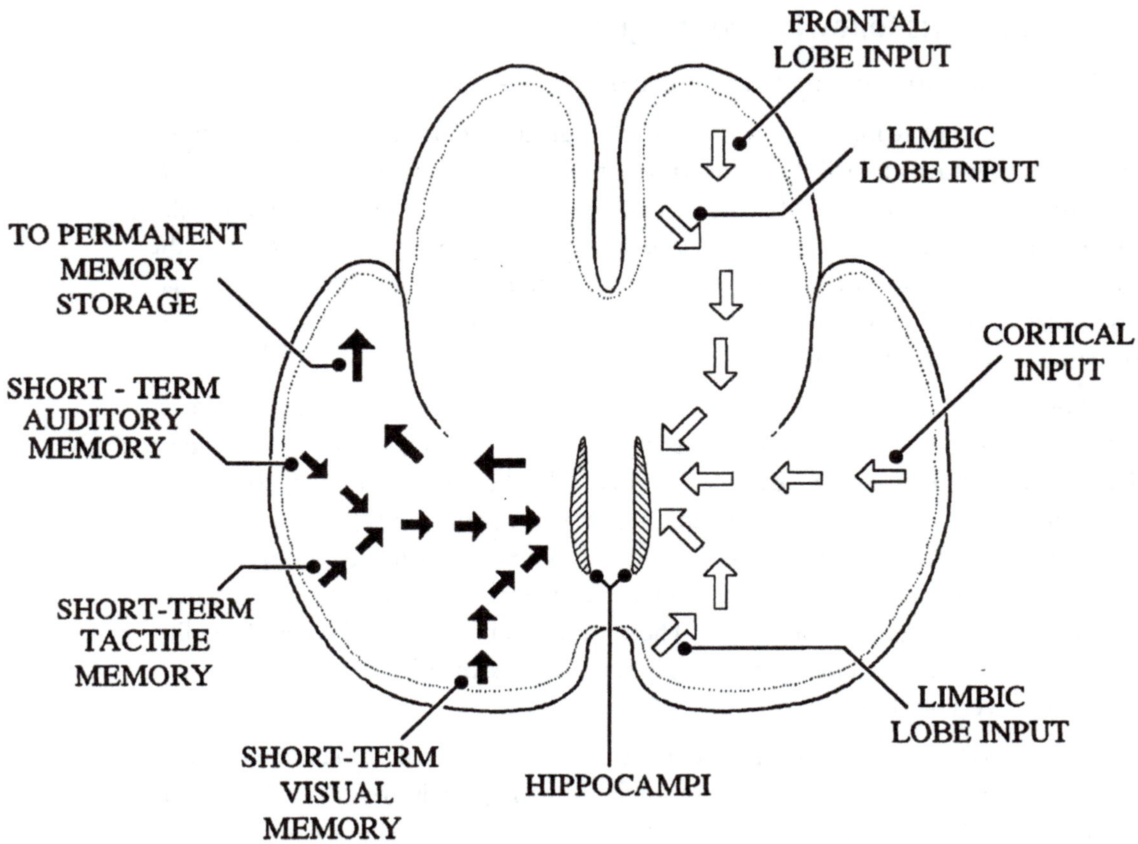

Fig. 6-33 The pathways of memory

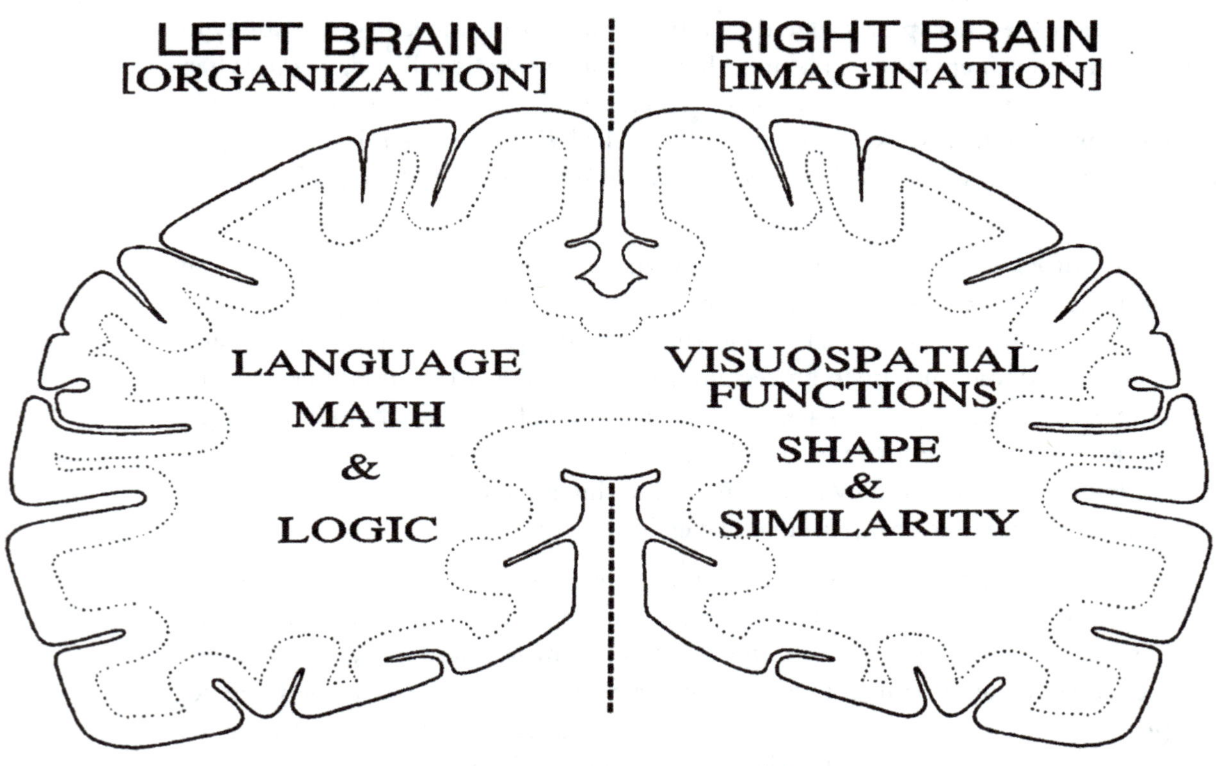

Fig. 6-34 Lateralization of function in the brain

7. *Behavioral or personality problems.* Frontal lobe damage just above the eye (*supra-orbital damage*) can produce a condition where the patient loses much of their social sense and behavioral restraint, so that they act very inappropriately (to the embarrassment of friends and family). Temporal lobe damage can produce *temporal lobe epilepsy* (TLE) and *schizophrenia spectrum disorders.* It can also produce cyclic changes in behavior which are marked by increasing unpleasantness which culminates in an explosive temper tantrum. This is followed by a contrite super-sweet phase which, however, only lasts for a little while and then the cycle begins again. This kind of behavior pattern is sometimes known as the *temporal lobe personality.* All three of these problems, occurring together, are termed the *temporal lobe syndrome.* But it should be noted that all three need not be present. They can occur separately from one another.

§ 6:32 Subtle and gross neurological and mental changes

When abnormalities are gross enough to be noticed by anyone, they are not very difficult for compensation lawyers to handle. But with subtle deficits, the patient may even be normal to neurological examination and yet have intellectual, emotional and personality problems. These, though not obvious, can be serious in terms of their effects on the lives of patients and their families. Such deficits need to be ruled out in all cases where there has been a significant head injury. Complaints about memory or the ability to concentrate, or loss of interest, should be taken quite seriously and followed up; for these apparently trivial complaints are often the tip the of the iceberg, the presenting symptoms of serious mental impairments. If there is suspicion of subtle mental losses, the patient may need referral for *neuropsychological evaluation* (N/P). N /P can demonstrate deficits which were not apparent on clinical examination [see Part IV infra].

§ 6:33 Complications of head injury—epilepsy

Epileptic seizures are a common accompaniment of the acute severe head injury, and those who survive such injuries often need to remain on antiepileptic medication for extended periods, or even for life. Some of these seizures, however, are temporary in nature, secondary to reversible problems such as acute blood loss, or a traumatic pneumothorax producing hypoxia. In these cases, correction of the underlying cause will commonly take care of the seizures, and there should be no further recurrence of the problem. Seizures may also be due to cerebral edema which can develop between the third and tenth day following a head injury. These patients may remain on antiepileptic drugs for some time after they have recovered; but if given a trial period off their medication, they may not need to be put back on medication again. Late developing epilepsy is a serious problem when it occurs, since it is a future complication, and one, moreover, which may not appear for 8–10 years following the injury. Consequently it may be deemed speculative damage, which is difficult to make compensable.

§ 6:34 Complications of head injury — Parkinsonism

Parkinson's shaking paralysis (*paralysis agitans*) *is* generally considered to be due to a deficiency of or a resistance to the neurotransmitter *dopamine* somewhere in one of the dopamine pathways of the brain. The problem is commonly believed to be located in the *lenticular nucleus* (lens) in the deep gray matter of the brain. Some researchers, however, are of the opinion that the problem is overactivity of an inhibitory center elsewhere acting on the dopamine pathway, and have accordingly treated it by producing deletions in this area.

Parkinsonism may appear for no known reason, or be due to physical causes, such as hydrogen sulfide poisoning in sewer workers. There is a good deal of controversy as to whether it can follow trauma. The issue is a difficult one, since apparently spontaneous onset of the disease is relatively common among elderly people. Even if, as is probable, head trauma involving the lenticular nucleus does cause Parkinsonism, it is likely to be considered speculative damage and not compensable, unless the condition develops immediately or very shortly following trauma, which is not usually the case. It may, however, be the result of serious, more widespread brain damage, in which case it should be deemed compensable.

Part IV.
Proof of Neurological Impairment

§ 6:35 Evaluating CNS damage — clinical examination

Neurological examination by a competent physician should be sufficient to establish cranial or peripheral nerve damage, motor weaknesses, abnormal sensation and ataxia, the so-called neurological findings. It is less likely to reveal cognitive or mental impairments. The neurological examination, it is true, begins with a brief review of mentation (memory and general fund of information) and mood; but this is far from the full *mental status examination* used to show mental impairments. Neurologists and neurosurgeons may even be of the opinion that if there are no abnormal neurological findings, there can be no significant mental impairments. For both these reasons, an adequate evaluation of mental impairments of the more subtle kind may require evaluation of the patient by a psychiatrist or clinical psychologist.

§ 6:36 Evaluating brain damage — electrodiagnostic studies (EDs)

Electrodiagnostic studies is the general term for tests which interpret electrical activity, whether spontaneous or in response to a stimulus. These include such things as the *electroencephalogram* (EEG), which studies brain waves, and *nerve conduction testing* (NCT), which studies the rate of transmission of electrical impulses along peripheral nerves. There are all sorts of electrodiagnostic studies. The simplest kinds merely record the actual electrical activity in the brain. More sophisticated modalities use the effects of special stimuli (a light in the eye, a sound in the ear or a stimulus applied to the skin) on the brain. Most of these latter are computerized and they can, in many cases, provide a map of cortical electrical activity showing normal and damaged areas.

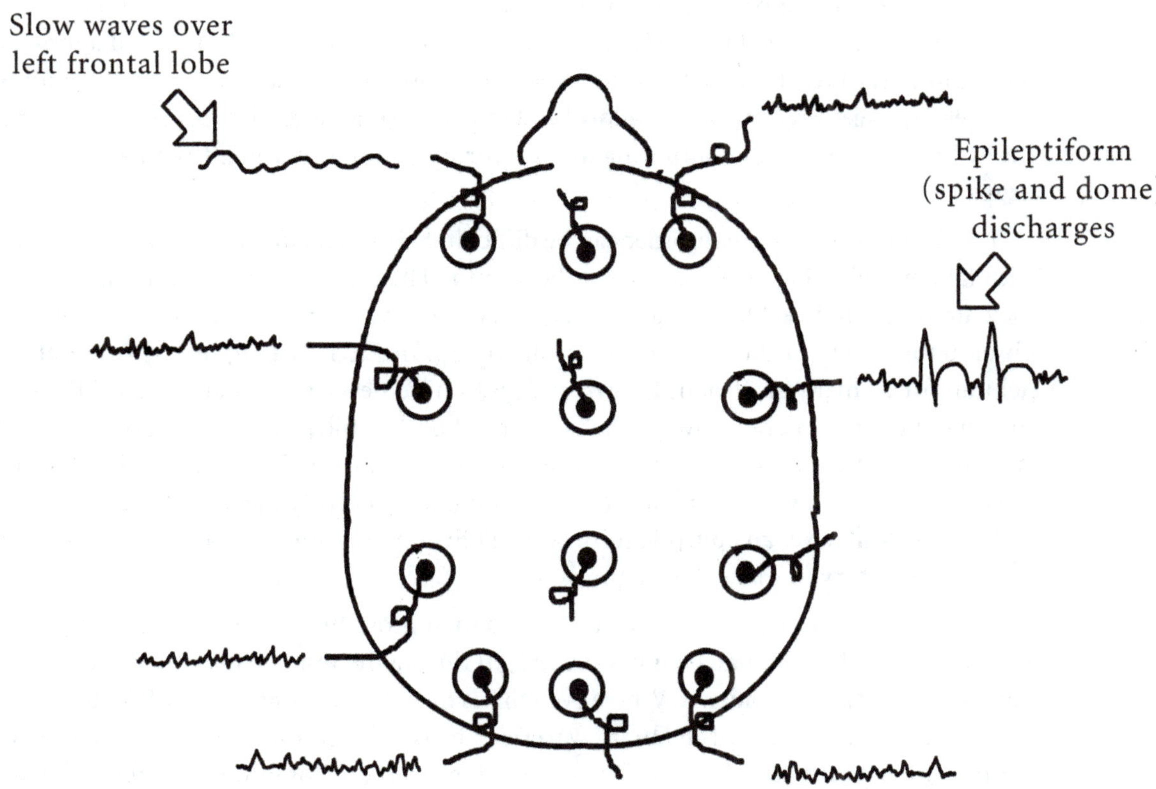

Fig. 6-35 Abnormal findings in electroencephalogram

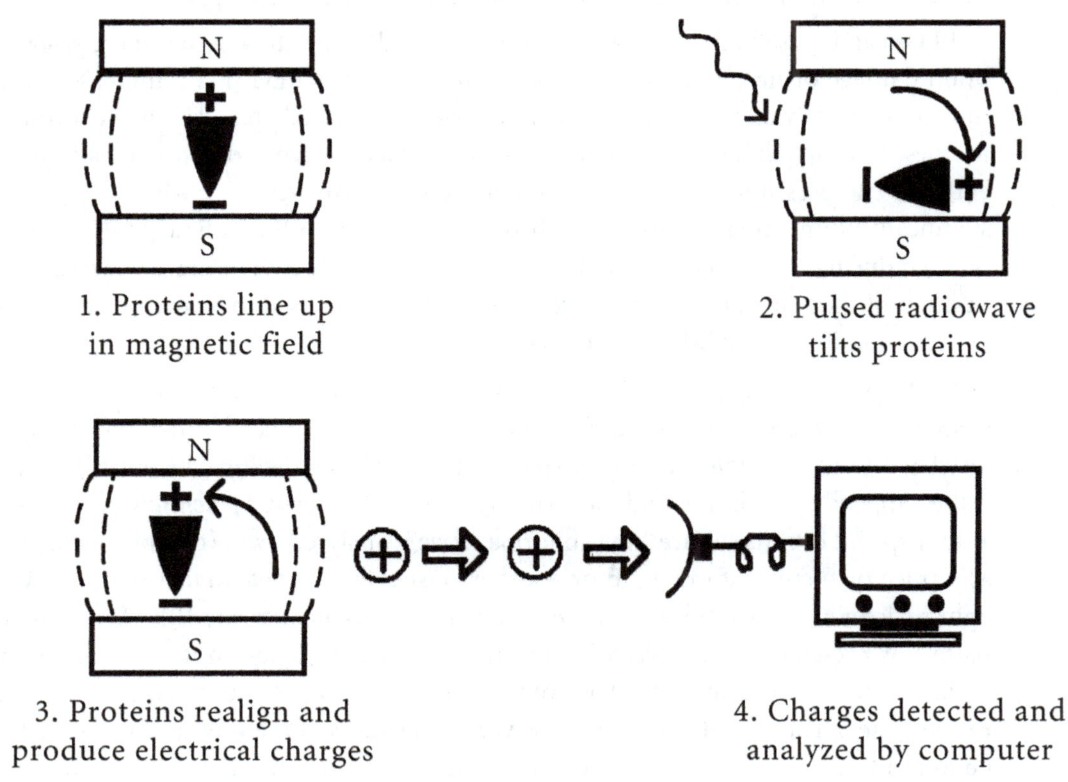

Fig. 6-36 The principle underlying magnetic resonance imaging

The simplest and most commonly used form of electrodiagnostic testing in the brain is the ordinary EEG. [See Fig. 6-35.] It is most frequently used to help in the diagnosis of epileptiform seizures, though it has at least one other use which is helpful to compensationists [see below]. Seizures commonly follow head injuries, sometimes disappearing as the brain heals, but in other cases continuing and requiring lifelong treatment with antiepileptic drugs.

The diagnosis of seizure disorder can be difficult. Seizures are not always dramatic affairs with falling, twitching, and foaming at the mouth. They can be so mild and transient that they are barely noticeable, or they can take place during sleep when no one is around to observe them. The ordinary electroencephalogram or EEG [see Fig. 6-15] is not always helpful; for as many as 25% of known epileptics have never had an abnormal EEG trace showing the *spike and dome waves* that are typical of the epileptic seizure. A negative EEG is therefore not conclusive nor even strong evidence of normality. Positive findings, too, must be interpreted with some caution. They do not necessarily mean that the patient has had, or ever will have, an epileptic seizure. The EEG findings must be viewed together with the clinical history to make the diagnosis.

A number of techniques have been developed to improve the diagnostic yield of the EEG. The patient can be stimulated with a *strobe light* during the test, as this will induce seizure activity in a number of patients. Where even this is not enough, continuous EEG monitoring with electronic recording of the brain waves can be continued throughout the night while the patient is asleep (*sleep EEG*). Seizures during sleep are common, and the abnormal traces may show up during this time. A video camera can be synchronized with continuous EEG monitoring (*video EEG*). Abnormal traces can then be matched up with seizure-like movements, and the two together will be strong evidence of epilepsy.

EEGs can be useful in cases where there is some doubt as to whether there is significant brain damage or not. Brain damage will show up on the EEG in a number of ways, but most importantly as *slow waves* in the leads over the injured area. The most common site for these in whiplash head injury cases is in the frontal leads (consider frontal lobe syndrome) and they can persist for one or two years or even be permanent. So, where the presence of significant brain damage is in doubt, it is wise to check on the ordinary EEG (commonly ordered during the hospital stay in head injury cases) to see if there are slow waves over one or other of the frontal leads. This objective finding can be used to provide credibility to the experts' opinion that subtle brain damage is present.

Sophisticated computerized EEGs are now widely available and may be used to evidence CNS injuries where the usual traces of the EEG are stilled and converted into straight lines by what is termed *computer averaging* (popularly described as "stilling the pond"). A stimulus is then applied to the brain, and the resulting wave forms (*evoked potentials*) can be detected as they spread over its surface. Any abnormal wave is analyzed by the computer and recorded as a trace or picture of one kind or another. *Visual evoked potential studies* (VEPs) use a light or icon as the stimulus. In *brain electrical activity monitoring* (BEAM), a picture or pattern is presented to the eye, which initiates a wave of depolarization beginning in the region of the visual cortex at the back of the brain and proceeds anteriorly across the surface of the cortex. The rate of spread and the various features of the wave are analyzed and will be found to be abnormal in areas of the cortex which are damaged. These deficient areas can be color coded on a map of the brain (*brain mapping*). BEAM is fairly widely available and available to lawyers for compensation purposes, though it has been relegated to the back burner by the wider availability of PET scans. Auditory *evoked potential studies* (using a sound as the stimulus) are used to prove or disprove damage to the inner ear and acoustic nerves. They can also evaluate the function of the brain stem, since that is the site of a number of way stations in the auditory pathway, so in this context, they are described as *brain stem evoked potential studies* (BSEPs). *Somatosensory evoked potential studies* (SSEPs), where the stimulus is heat or a pinprick applied to the skin, are used as monitors during surgery to the spine. A continuous or repetitive stimulus is applied to the foot or hand and picked up at the brain. If this signal is not reaching the brain, the surgeons are warned that they may be pulling too hard on the retractors or damaging the spinal cord in some other way. *Nerve conduction studies* (NCSs) may be needed to demonstrate damage to peripheral nerves, such as in evaluating damage to the median nerve in the *carpal tunnel syndrome* (CTS). An electrical stimulus is applied to the median nerve at the elbow, its arrival in the hand, and the time required to reach the hand, are noted. This allows the calculation of the nerve conduction time, which is prolonged (transmission of wave of depolarization slowed) when the nerve is damaged [see Fig. 5-25].

§ 6:37 Contrast angiography

This term covers any X-ray study of arteries using radio-opaque dye as a contrast agent. Traditional cerebral angiography required significant sedation and commonly required a general anesthetic, since the carotid arteries were punctured with a large bore needle (to get rapid flow of the dye); and bleeding afterwards could be a problem. It was also only possible to inject the two anterior arteries (the *common carotid arteries*) as the *vertebral arteries* are tucked inside bony canals in the lateral processes of the cervical vertebrae and so unavailable. Long catheters with flexible tips have made cerebral angiography safer, more adequate and more acceptable to patients. The catheter is inserted through a needle into a peripheral vein, where bleeding can be more easily controlled. It can be manipulated at the tip and introduced (under radiographic guidance) into all four cerebral vessels, not just the carotid arteries. Since there is not a nasty needle sticking in the neck, only light sedation is all that is usually needed.

Cerebral angiography can demonstrate even small *berry aneurysms* and *arterio-venous malformations* (AVMs), and this remains the main indication for its use. It can also show an embolus blocking a cerebral artery, or asymmetry and distortion of the blood vessels can show the existence and location of brain tumors, subdural hematomas, and other injuries and malformations.

Retinal artery plethysmography (RAP) uses a dye (such as indocyanin green) which can be injected into a peripheral vein and viewed with an opthalmoscope as it flows through the retinal vessels in the eye. Measured pressure can be applied to the eyeball; the amount of pressure needed to reduce retinal blood flow to zero can be used to give a measure of retinal artery pressure and to show the adequacy of the blood flow in the internal carotid artery.

The use of contrast angiography of one sort or another has been considerably reduced by the advent of computerized tomography (CT) and magnetic resonance imaging (MRI). However, it is still the best imaging modality for small cerebral aneurysms and arteriovenous malformations (AVMs).

§ 6:38 Structural imaging — CT scanning

A tomogram is an X-ray study where only the images deriving from a thin slice of tissue are in sharp focus, the rest are more or less screened out. Tomograms are produced by moving the X-ray source and the film in opposite directions to one another while the picture is being taken. The section at the axis of rotation of these movements does not move and so remains in sharp focus; sections at all other levels are blurred. The blurred sections can be recognized and removed by computer processing. By altering the relative speeds of the source and film, the level of the focused section can be raised and lowered, providing a series of thin sections through the tissue. State of the art machines can integrate these sections to produce three dimensional images, or produce artificial sections at right angles to the original ones. Contrast materials are commonly used to help distinguish the various tissues from one another more clearly.

The computerized tomogram is currently the method of choice for evaluating acute brain injuries, since it distinguishes fresh blood from other tissues better than MRI. It will also demonstrate aneurysms and arteriovenous malformations of reasonable size, though it is still not so sensitive as contrast angiography in detecting smaller ones. Hematomas and tumors will show up as a rule, especially when contrast dyes are used. Higher resolution machines are now becoming available which, it is hoped, will even be able to show the small hemorrhages characteristic of diffuse axonal injuries (DAIs). Fast CT (cine-CT) machines can show cerebral blood flow and blood flow in the carotid artery. In spiral CT, the source and receptors are made to rotate around the body. Spiral CT can image the entire body in less than ten minutes. It is already in use for some special purposes and further extensions of its use may be expected. CT scanning in its simpler forms is currently available in many community hospitals and is adequate to show subdural and subarachnoid hemorrhage (SDH).

§ 6:39 Structural imaging — magnetic resonance imaging (MRI)

MRI uses intermittent pulsed radio waves impinging on a constant magnetic field produced by electrical coils (formerly by large, fixed magnets). [See Fig. 6-36.] Charged molecules, such as the proteins of the body, are lined up and rotate in the fixed magnetic field like spinning tops. When bombarded by pulsed radio waves, they move out of their normal axis of rotation and then return to it again when the impacting radio wave is switched off. This is essentially like tapping a spinning top which tips over and then returns to its vertical axis. The movements of the charged particles in a magnetic field produce small electrical currents which are picked up by detectors on the surface of the body; their size and point of origin is calculated, and this information is used by the computer to produce images of the tissues. Variation in the forces applied (called T1 and T2 weighting) can be adjusted until the different tissues being imaged are clearly distinguishable. MRI produces images of the brain which are superior even to those made using CT. MRI was formerly confined to large research centers but has now become available in most referral hospitals and is even appearing in some of the larger community hospitals. Its main limitation is that it cannot reliably distinguish fresh blood from normal brain tissue (CT is better here). It is also poor at imaging bone, and so CT would be preferred in any case where bony detail was required (as where a piece of a stellate fracture might be impinging on the brain).

§ 6:40 Structural imaging — ultrasound imaging (U/S)

Gross displacement of brain tissues may be shown by *A-wave ultrasound* (*U/S*) which operates rather like the fish finder on a boat. A-wave U/S is not generally used for this purpose any more, having been largely replaced in the United States by CT. *B-wave U/S* which can image tissues in sections through an organ, produces excellent pictures of the brain. Unfortunately it does not easily penetrate bone, and so can only be used for this purpose on very young children whose fontanels are still open, or at operation when a skull flap has been raised to expose the brain. It is also affected adversely by air pockets, as in the lungs or in bowel.

Ultrasound imaging is very valuable in medical malpractice cases relating to labor and delivery ("bad baby" cases), where poor obstetrical management is blamed for the later development of cerebral palsy. Damage to brain cells eventually produces loss of white fibers which are replaced by little cysts. These are most commonly seen in the vicinity of the cerebral ventricles and so are called *periventricular cysts*. The presence of these cysts can be shown in newborn babies by placing the ultrasound probe on the open fontanel; this can even be done during the delivery process as soon as the baby's head begins to appear. It takes two or three weeks for periventricular cysts to develop and so, if they are seen during the first week of life, the damage which produced them must have preceded labor and delivery; thus, obstetrical mismanagement, even if clearly present, was not the cause of the problem. On the other hand, if the cysts do not develop until three weeks following delivery, the obstetrical management may have been responsible for the brain damage. The commonest cause of cerebral palsy is now thought to be maternal infections during the course of the pregnancy, although, occasionally, obstetrical causes may be responsible. It would seem that the matter could generally be decided using ultrasound. Unfortunately, the U/S study may not have been carried out in time. Various parties, indeed, may deliberately avoid ordering U/S for fear of what it may show.

§ 6:41 Radionuclear imaging (RNI) — brain scans

Radionuclear imaging (RNI) is carried out with markers which emit radiation in some form or another. These enter into the target tissues, and the emerging radiation is detected by a scintillation detector or a gamma camera, allowing an image to be developed. Radionuclear brain scans can be used to reveal cerebral tumors or intracranial hematomas. The size and shape of the ventricles of the brain can also be shown, since the radionuclear dyes persist in the CSF of the ventricles for some time after they are gone from the other brain tissues. Abnormalities of blood vessels such as *angiomas* or small *aneurysms* would not show up on currently available machines. Research and development (using computer analysis of results) is still being done on RNI, but presently available systems are too slow to be used in emergency situations, and so RNI has been generally replaced by CT and MRI in such cases. However, some forms of functional imaging are essentially RNI.

§ 6:42 Functional imaging — PET scans and SPECT

CT and MRI are structural imaging modalities, in that they show the shape and size of tissues. Functional imaging also shows if the tissues are working properly. *Proton emission tomograms* (PET scans) use special radionuclear pharmaceuticals with unstable nuclei, which emit positively charged electrons (*positrons*). The positrons soon collide with negatively charged electrons (*negatrons*) orbiting the nucleus. The two then fuse and disappear, producing two photons of energy that fly off at an angle of 180° to one another. These discharges can be picked up by detectors on the surface of the body, and the data is analyzed by the computer to produce a picture. PET scans commonly use glucose or water molecules which have been rendered unstable by proton bombardment in a cyclotron. Unfortunately the decay rate in positron emitting substances is very rapid, and they become normal again within an hour or so after removal from the cyclotron. PET scanning has therefore, until recently, been limited to the small number of research hospitals with immediate access to a cyclotron. But more long lasting positron emitters have been developed, which have made PET more widely available. It is very popular with physicians who appreciate the wealth of information that the PET scanner can provide. Where it is available, it is a very sensitive way of demonstrating nonfunctional areas in the cerebral cortex. These do not take up the unstable sugars or water as well as normal cortex and appear on the PET scan as "dim" spots.

The developer of PET later devised a similar imaging system known as *single proton emission computerized tomography* (SPECT). This uses modifications of adrenergic drugs as dyes instead of unstable substances (water or glucose). These preferentially enter the brain cells (as one would expect since they are related to psycho-active substances). They can be labeled using Technetium 99m, are injected into a peripheral vein and find their way to the brain. These radioactive marker substances will enter cells, especially healthy brain cells. Radiation emitted from these cells can be picked up and processed by the computer to produce good images, and show dim spots. The resolution is not quite so fine as in PET (1.5 mm instead of 0.5 mm) but quite satisfactory for most purposes. PET scans were originally mainly used by researchers, as they are relatively inexpensive (the poor man's PET scan), but they are more and more coming into clinical use both in neurological and cardiac medicine.

§ 6:43 Functional imaging — magnetic resonance spectroscopy (MRS)

BEAM (already mentioned) is a form of functional imaging. *Magnetic resonance spectroscopy* (MRS) is now being used in functional imaging. This is a revival of the original biochemical function of magnetic imaging, to measure the amounts of certain molecules present in living tissues. By assaying the numbers of molecules (such as phosphorus) which are released during tissue metabolism, MRS can detect damaged areas of the cortex, where metabolic activity and phosphorus release is low. These areas will thus show up as "dim spots" that can be color coded and entered on a map of the brain. MRS is now being used to show dysfunctional areas in the cerebral cortex or in heart muscle.

§ 6:44 Neuropsychological evaluation (N/P)

In 1935, Ward Halsted, a psychologist, began to work in a Chicago hospital carrying out performance tests on patients with brain pathology of one kind or another. He found that his results measured up well against both clinical examination and the diagnostic tests then available. He could usually determine not only whether a patient had brain pathology or not but, as a rule, tell approximately where the lesion was sited. He was later joined by his pupil, Ralph Reitan, and between them they developed batteries of tests that have proved most useful in a number of ways, particularly in picking out the subtler forms of brain damage. A subspecialty known as *neuropsychology* has developed out of this work, and most major universities have at least one neuropsychologist on their staff. The type of injury where neuropsychology is most helpful to a lawyer is where there is generalized cortical damage but no definite neurological signs. The most obvious neurological signs come from damage to the large columns of motor or sensory fibers in the brain or cord, or centers in the deep gray matter of the brain, or the nuclei of the brain stem. Yet the cortical cells on the surface of the brain can be rendered dysfunctional by white fiber damage in rotatory head injuries (DAIs). It is possible in these cases to have no neurological signs, and yet have such widespread damage to the axons leading to or from the neurons, that the patient is less capable in many ways than before.

The cortex of the *dominant hemisphere* also tends to be spared in global injuries, in comparison with the non-dominant hemisphere. [See Fig.6-34.] IQ tests predominantly focus on dominant hemispheric functions such as language and calculation, with less than 15% of the tasks relating to visuospatial (non-dominant hemisphere) functions. This means that a patient who is neurologically normal and has a normal or even fairly high score on IQ tests may be told that their perceived deficiencies are imaginary or due to nervous anxiety following the accident. Yet when they are evaluated with a neuropsychological battery, it may become apparent that they have a marked loss of *visuospatial* abilities. Visuospatial perceptions enable us to see patterns, trends and the expressions on faces; they also function in imaginative, creative thinking (lateral thinking), and these abilities may be much more important in business affairs than the language /logic capacities of the dominant hemisphere. A neuropsychological assessment can be given to anyone over the age of four years old. It takes about five to six hours to administer in an adult (two hours or so in a child), and is generally much less expensive than imaging. It is also helpful in rehabilitation, since neuropsychologists see themselves primarily as rehabilitation consultants, rather than as specialists in diagnosing brain damage.

Part V.
The Neurological Examination

§ 6:45 Clinical evaluation of the CNS — evaluating mentation

The neurological examination begins with a review of the mental capacity of the patient. This resembles the mental state examination of the psychiatrist, but is generally much more brief. The *alertness* of the patient is first tested by asking if they know where they are, etc. This is called orientation and, if normal, is commonly recorded as "oriented to time, place and circumstances," more cryptically stated as "oriented x 3," even symbolically as "Ox3."

Knowledge is usually perfunctorily tested to see if the usual fund of common information is present or not. The patient may be asked, "Who is the current President of the United States?" and a few other simple questions of this nature. Emotion also merits a brief enquiry such as "How do you feel in your spirits?" and "Are you ever depressed?" Social orientation, the way the patient relates to their associates and to the world in general, can be crudely tested with such questions as "how do you get along with people?" or "do you think people like you?" The patient's *ideation* (thinking) should be evaluated both as to content and form. Very abnormal ideas may show up in answer to the question, "Do you have any ideas which other people think are peculiar?" or the patient may be asked, "Do you ever hear voices?" and if so "What do they say to you?" An apparently normal individual can surprise the examiner at this point, by remarking in the most matter of fact manner, that God speaks to him out of the vacuum cleaner. Formal impairment of ideation can be seen in disassociated patterns of thought where there is no proper linkage between one idea and the next (salad speech). *Intellectual functions* such as memory, use of language, ability to calculate, and the ability to recognize shapes and patterns are also rougly tested. Memory is commonly tested by asking the patient to remember a couple of telephone numbers since we are supposed, normally, to be able to recall seven digits forward and four in reverse order. There is no reason why neurologists should not examine every aspect of the patient's mentation quite thoroughly, and sometimes they do. Usually, however, only a brief overview is undertaken to screen for these kinds of defects. If a significant deficit is uncovered or there is a real indication for working up someone's mental state or mental capacity in detail, the patient will usually be referred to a neuropsychologist who has had special training in performance tests.

§ 6:46 Clinical evaluation of the CNS — the first cranial nerve

The first cranial nerve (cn i) is the *olfactory nerve.* [See Fig. 6-37.] The sense of smell can be tested by covering the patient's eyes and holding coffee or tobacco under each nostril in turn while blocking the other. Doctors do not carry these substances around with them as a rule, and so they often omit the examination of the first cranial nerve. They will then write (if the other nerves are normal) "cranial nerves ii–xii grossly intact" or more cryptically "cnn ii-xii GI."

Loss of a sense of smell is not taken very seriously by most people, but it can be significant. One third of taste is actually smell, the other two parts being on the tongue (sweet, bitter, salt and acid) and in the eye or the mind (response to the appearance of the food). This explains why food tastes so insipid when we have a cold and why the appearance of food is important. Olfactory loss can also be serious in a number of occupations and critical in a few. It should always be sought out in head injury cases. Olfactory sense is especially likely to be affected in fractures of the base of the skull in the frontal area, where the olfactory nerves pass through the cribriform plate to the olfactory bulb on the underside of the frontal lobes.

§ 6:47 Examination of the cranial nerves — the second cranial nerve

The *ophthalmic nerve* is the second cranial nerve (cn ii) [see Fig.6-39]. A patient who is being seen for a routine visit, or for some problem remote from the CNS, may simply be asked if there is anything wrong with his vision. If he replies that it is 20/20, vision may only be very perfunctorily tested or not tested at all. In suspicious circumstances, however,

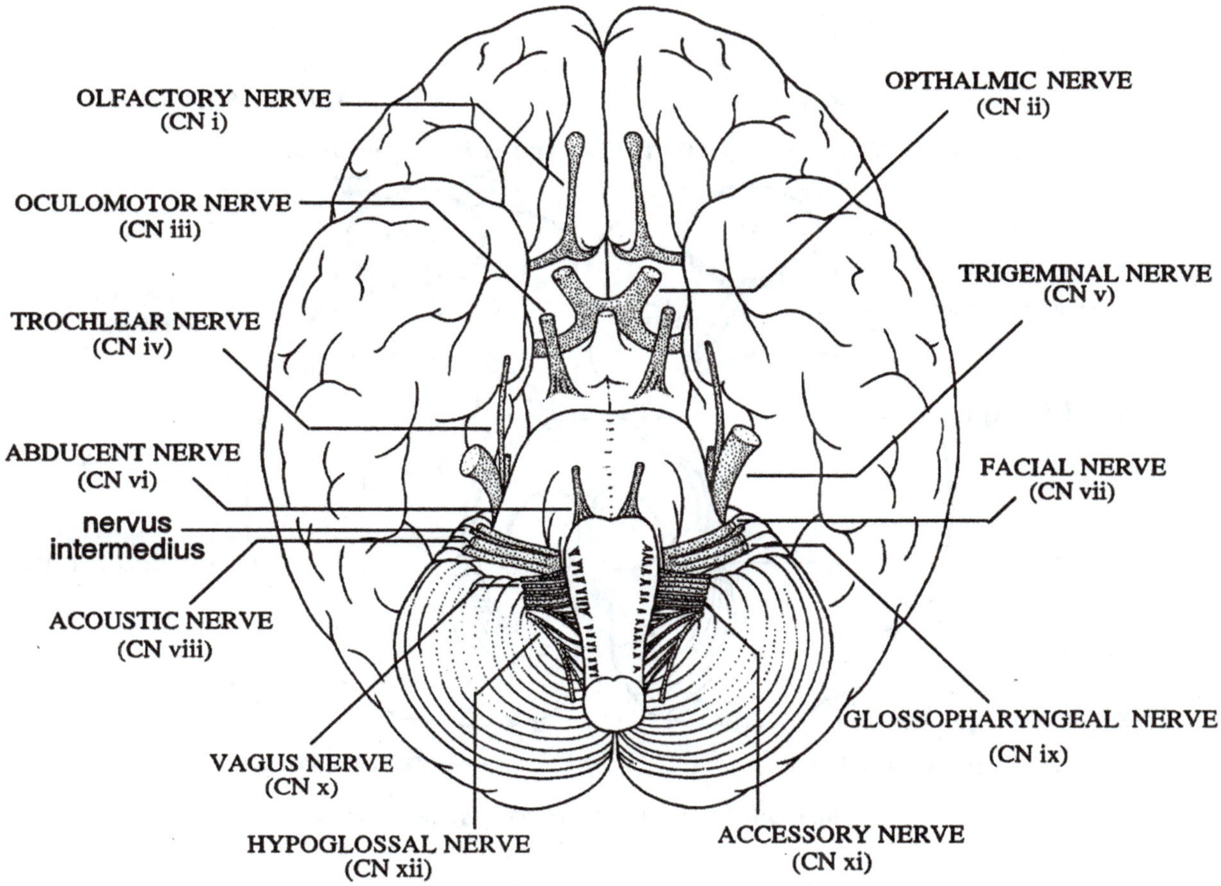

Fig. 6-37 The cranial nerves—inferior view

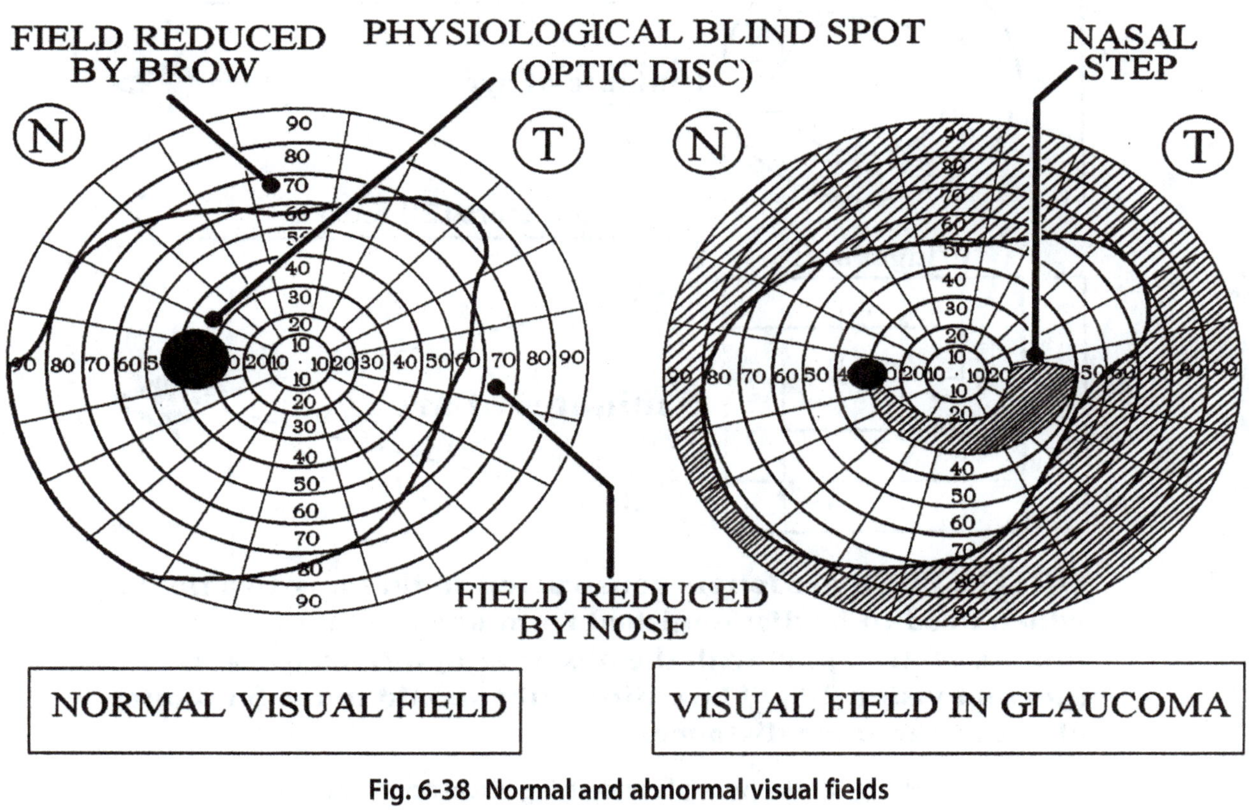

Fig. 6-38 Normal and abnormal visual fields

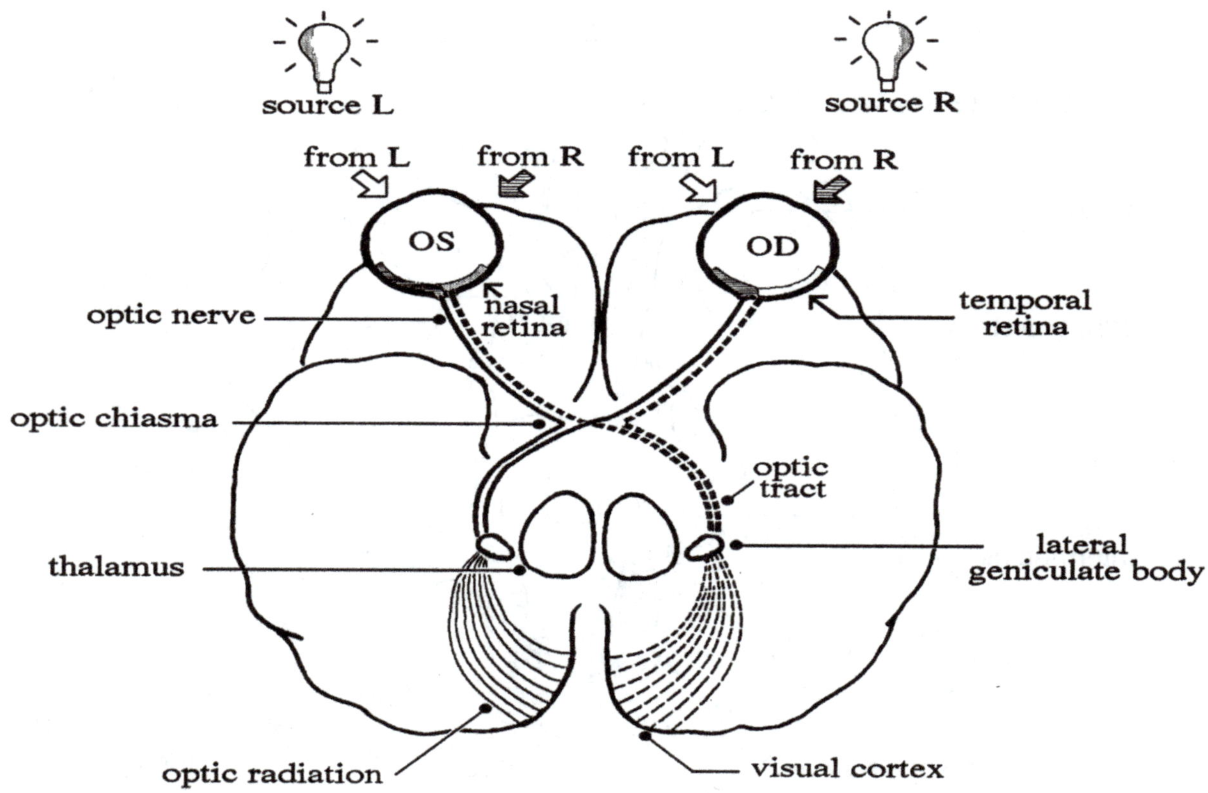

Fig. 6-39 The optic pathways—superior view

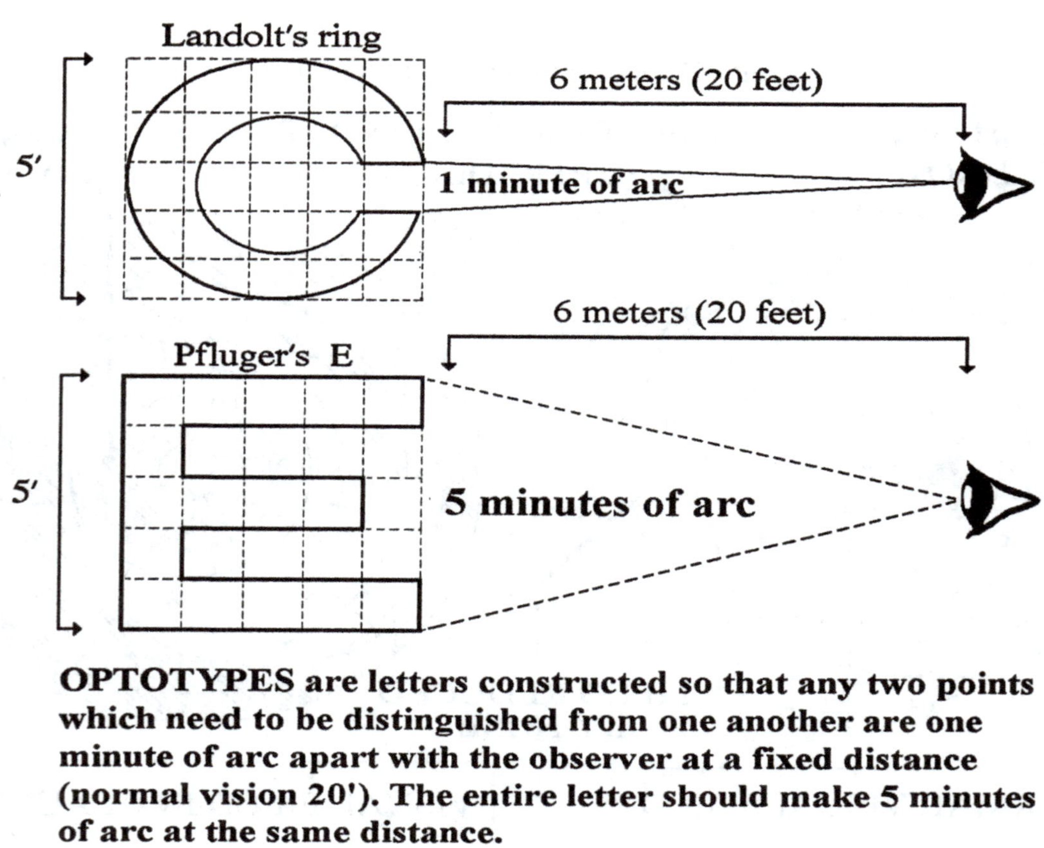

Fig. 6-40 The principle underlying visual acuity testing

it may need to be evaluated very carefully. Someone with very poor vision may be described as "blind," but it is usually necessary for legal purposes to define and describe visual impairment more precisely. Complete blindness means that light cannot be distinguished from darkness. A lesser degree of *visual impairment* would be that the patient notices bright light but cannot see a hand moving in front of his face. Further evaluation of vision requires assessment of *visual acuity* (the ability to distinguish two points near one another) and *visual field* (peripheral vision). Visual acuity can be crudely tested by asking the patient to read a newspaper. A *Snellen's Chart* or a similar device enables the patient's visual acuity to be tested quantitatively. Normal visual acuity is 20/20. The term, *legally blind,* normally means that visual acuity is 20/200 or worse, i.e., the person can only see at 20 feet from the chart what someone with normal vision would see at 200 feet. [See Fig. 6-40.]

Visual field is tested crudely by the method of *confrontation,* where the patient looks straight ahead and is asked to notice and point to movements of the examiner's finger in the periphery of their field of vision. This will detect gross field defects such as a *hemianopsia* where the patient is only able to see things on one side of the body or *quadrantopsias* where the patient is blind in one quarter of the visual field. A patient with advanced *retinitis pigmentosa* may have tunnel vision, with little or no peripheral vision.

To examine the visual fields properly, a perimetry device (called a *campimeter*) should be used. This is a dish, or disc shaped field, where point sources such as little lights are made to appear at different points in the field, and the patients, looking straight ahead, are asked to press a button when they see them. The field of vision is normally automatically recorded in these machines and printed out on a standard card which contains the normal visual field already marked on it for comparison. Even quite small blind spots in the visual field, called *scotomas,* can be detected by these devices. [See Fig. 6-38.]

§ 6:48 Examination of the cranial nerves — third, fourth and sixth nerves

The third (*oculomotor*), fourth (*trochlear*) and sixth (*abducent*) cranial nerves control the extraocular muscles (eye movement) and the muscles which control the iris and lens (accommodation). The patient, with the head in fixed position, is asked to follow the examiner's fingers with their eyes. If the left eye cannot move laterally, this may mean that the abducent (VI th) nerve to that side is inoperative. If this examination is normal, the report may read EOMI, "extraocular muscles (or movements) intact."

The motor component of the pupillary reflexes (the efferent arc of the reflex) is controlled by the third cranial nerve (the *oculomotor nerve*). The sensory part, the afferent arc, is in the ophthalmic nerve. The *light reflex* is first tested by flashing a light into the eye. The pupil in the eye which is illuminated should constrict (*direct light reflex*), and the pupil of the other eye should also be seen to narrow (*consensual light reflex*).

Accommodation is tested by asking the patient to look at a distant object and then quickly focus the eyes on a finger held a few inches from the nose. As the eyes focus on the finger, the pupils should constrict. Normal findings may be recorded as PERRLA (pupils equal, round, react to light and accommodation). This mnemonic will be found in most history and physical reports [see Chapter 4 and specimen handwritten H&Ps].

§ 6:49 Examination of the cranial nerves — the fifth cranial nerve

The Vth cranial nerve (cn v) is known as the *trigeminal nerve* because it has three major divisions, namely the *ophthalmic, maxillary,* and *mandibular* nerves. It supplies sensation to the face and the anterior part of the head, and so is tested by asking the patient to close her eyes while the examiner touches her lightly with a piece of cotton on each side of the forehead, on the cheeks, and on the two sides of the jaw. This really only tests light touch and so is only a screening test. For a full examination, other sensory modalities, such as deep touch, pain and temperature and two-point discrimination should be tested also. Full testing of sensation is, however, time consuming, and will only be carried out in the examination of the trigeminal nerve in very suspicious circumstances. The statement that the trigeminal nerve is intact may, therefore, occasionally need to be evaluated further, and some questions asked about the details of the examination.

The trigeminal nerve has some motor fibers which control the *muscles of mastication* (chewing). These are tested by asking the patient to clench their jaw and feeling the large masseter muscles to determine if they contract properly and symmetrically on both sides.

§ 6:50 Examination of the cranial nerves — the seventh cranial nerve

The VIIth cranial nerve (cn vii) is the *facial nerve,* and it controls the muscles of the forehead, periorbital muscles, and the ring of muscles around the mouth; in short, the *muscles of facial expression.* It contains some *secretomotor fibers* which control the tear glands of the eye and salivary glands. It also contains motor fibers to the tiny muscles that "damp" the vibrations of the eardrum, and even sensory fibers which carry taste sensation from the anterior two thirds of the tongue. The motor functions of the facial nerve can be crudely and partially tested by asking patients to frown, squeeze their eyes closed, puff out the cheeks, and so on. In addition, a little salt or sugar on a Q-tip may be placed on each side of the tongue to see if the substance can be identified by taste or not. The full examination of the VIIth nerve can indeed be quite time consuming, and may only be carried out completely when a neurologist is evaluating a patient who has a VIIth nerve lesion such as *Bell's palsy.* The statement that the seventh nerve was examined and found intact may, on occasion, merit a little further investigation.

§ 6:51 Examination of the cranial nerves — the eighth cranial nerve

The VIIIth cranial nerve (cn viii) is the acoustic or more properly the *vestibulo-acoustic nerve,* as it contains fibers from the vestibular apparatus in the inner ear (which functions in maintaining balance) as well as those relating to hearing.

A simple clinical test of hearing is to stand six feet away from the patient and whisper numbers. A card or envelope is held in front of the examiner's face so that the patient cannot lip-read. The examiner gradually moves closer and closer until the patient can repeat most of the numbers correctly. The distance at which this is accomplished is written in the chart. Hearing can also be crudely assessed by moving a wristwatch (if you can find one that ticks) in and out from each ear or (more usual nowadays) by rubbing the finger and thumb together

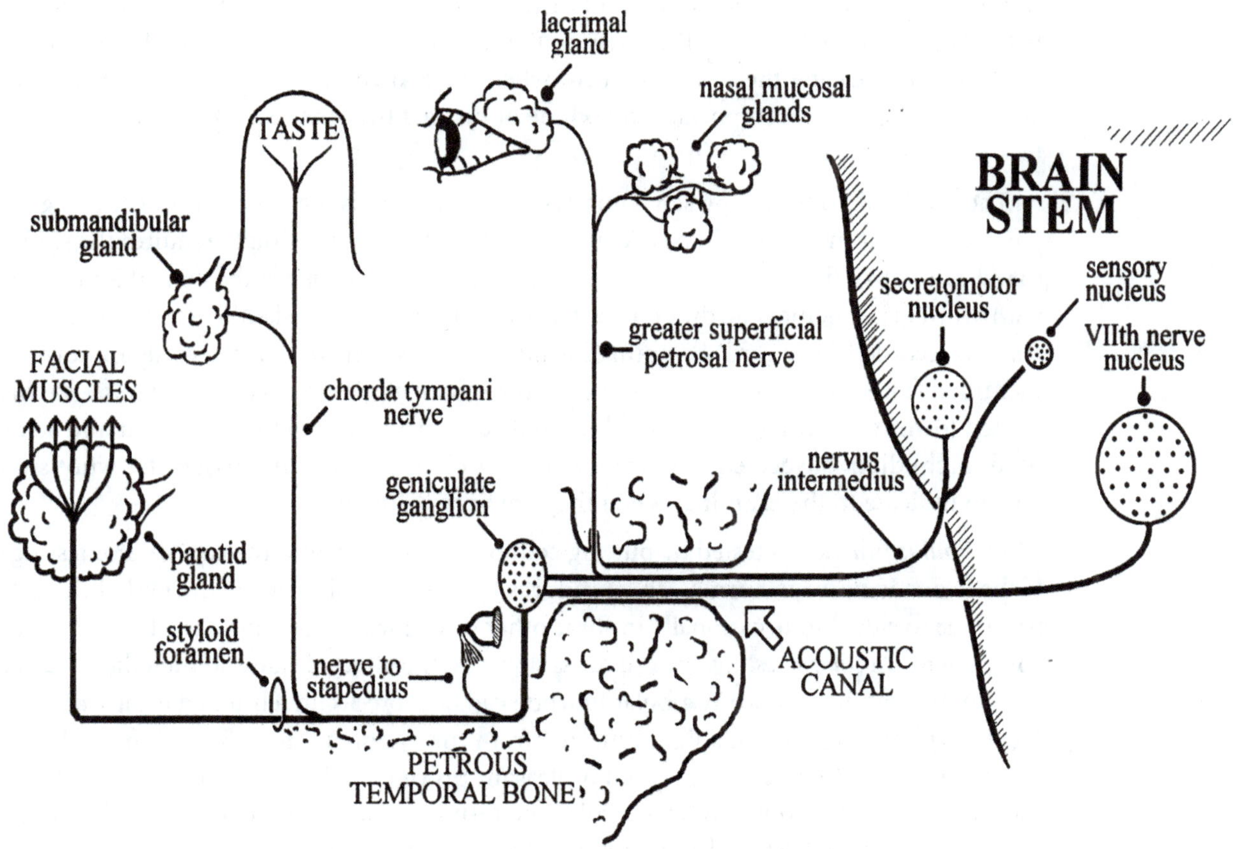

Fig. 6-41 Branches of the facial nerve

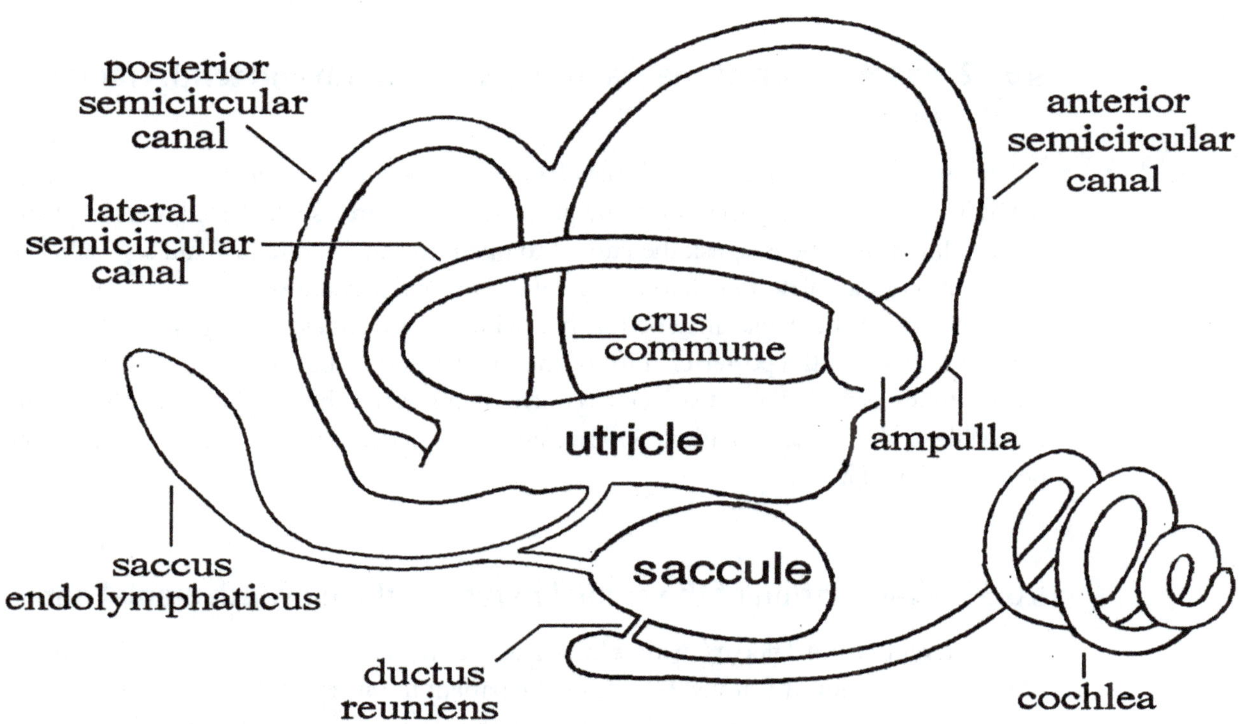

Fig. 6-42 The vestibulocochlear apparatus

to produce a rustling sound at different distances from each ear. The distance at which the patient can hear the ticking of the watch or the rubbing of the fingers with each ear is noted. With normal hearing these will be heard when the source of the sound is about two feet away from the ear. It is important to occlude or distract the other ear while performing this test.

These are, of course, only screening tests and, if there is any suspicion of hearing impairment, audiometry should be ordered. *Pure tone audiometry* simply requires the subject to indicate with a finger when a "beep" is heard. In *speech audiometry,* the patient is presented with words (phonemes) at different intensities of sound and asked to repeat them. The result is recorded (on a card) by noting the intensity at which 50% of the words are correctly identified. *Impedance audiometry* and *evoked response audiometry* (ERA) are more sophisticated forms of hearing testing which do not require a response by the patient and so are used in children, suspected malingerers, unconscious persons or anyone else who is not able to indicate to the examiner when they are hearing the test sound.

Vestibular function is tested by putting cold or warm water into the ear (caloric testing). If the acoustic nerve is normal, this produces *nystagmus,* a flicking of the eyeball, usually from side to side, but occasionally in some other direction. Nystagmus has a fast and a slow component. In *caloric testing,* the eye turns slowly to the affected side and then flicks quickly back to the central position. Vestibular function can be more accurately tested using *electronystagmography* (ENG) where a light reflected from the eye on a screen is used to display the eye movements. *Caloric testing* is not a pleasant procedure. If the nerves are normal and the water is a little too warm or too cold, the response may be over-brisk and the patient will develop severe *vertigo,* become nauseated and even vomit. So caloric testing is only carried out when it is really necessary to test the intactness of the vestibular apparatus.

§ 6:52 Examination of the cranial nerves — ninth and tenth cranial nerves

The ninth cranial nerve (cn ix) is the *glossopharyngeal nerve; the tenth* (cn x) is the *vagus nerve.* They function together for many purposes and so are usually tested together. Commonly all that is done is to ask the patient to open his mouth, swallow and say "aah." The movements of the palate and pharynx are noticed to see if they are asymmetrical (abnormal), and the back of the throat may be touched with a Q-tip to test the *gag reflex.* The ninth nerve is sensory to the posterior third of the tongue (taste), but this test is liable to evoke the gag reflex as well. These two nerves control items in the chest and GI tract that are not accessible to clinical examination. So since little is expected of it, it is often carried out very perfunctorily, if at all.

§ 6:53 Examination of the cranial nerves — the eleventh cranial nerve

The eleventh cranial nerve (cn xi) is known as the *accessory nerve,* and it controls a number of the neck muscles. It is tested by getting the patient to push with his head against the resistance of the examiner's hands forward (*anterior flexion*) and towards both sides (*lateral flexion*). The muscles of the neck are observed to see if they contract properly; they should stand out and be clearly visible and also palpable. These muscles can become weakened or paralyzed in a number of conditions, but especially in the severe and rapidly progressive form of *amyotrophic lateral sclerosis* (ALS) known as *progressive bulbar palsy.*

§ 6:54 Examination of the cranial nerves — the twelfth cranial nerve

The twelfth cranial nerve (cn xii) is the *hypoglossal nerve.* It controls glottal (tongue) movements and so is tested by asking the patient to stick out her tongue. The tongue is a pushing organ, and therefore deviates towards the weak side. Weakness of the tongue muscles can be tested by asking the patient to push forward and sideways with the tongue against a wooden spatula.

§ 6:55 Clinical evaluation of the peripheral nervous system

The peripheral nervous system (PNS) is conventionally divided into the examination of:

- Power,
- Tone,
- Coordination,
- Sensation, and
- Reflexes

It is obvious that some of the maneuvers included here are really tests (at least in part) of the central nervous system, since they involve associated areas of the cerebral cortex, the cerebellum, or even of the spinal cord. Reflexes, for instance, are markedly affected by brain damage when loss of cerebral inhibition will produce exaggerated reflexes. However, these items are traditionally included in the examination of the peripheral nerves, and there is no real harm in this; it is merely a conventional way of organizing the neurological examination in a convenient manner so that nothing of importance is overlooked. A deficit in any of these areas indicates something wrong somewhere, but not necessarily in the peripheral nervous system.

§ 6:56 Clinical testing of muscle power

Muscle power is graded clinically on a conventional scale reading from 0 to IV or in some similar way. A typical grading system would be the following:

Power 0 means that the limb (or head) cannot be moved even when the force of gravity is removed (e.g. by a water bath).
Power I means that movement is possible if the force of gravity is neutralized.
Power II means that movement is possible against slight resistance.
Power III means that movement is possible against moderate resistance.
Power IV means full power.

Since there are several possible schemes for classifying muscle power, the total number of grades should also be indicated, for example, by saying that the muscle group is "power III /IV." In a full examination, each muscle group should be examined in turn. In a particular case where there seems to be no real problem with the muscles, only entire limbs may be examined in this way, and the medical record may read "power 4/4 AE," or "full power in all extremities."

§ 6:57 Clinical testing of muscle tone

Muscle tone is commonly described as the background "set" of the muscles, or the context or environment of voluntary movements. It is mainly controlled by the extrapyramidal system and is distinguished into two forms, resting tone and tone maintained during voluntary movements. Only resting tone is directly tested during clinical examination, although voluntary movements can be observed to see if they proceed smoothly, without jerking or hitching. Resting tone is tested by passively moving the limbs, with the patient (hopefully) relaxed.

Several types of abnormal tone are described. *Flaccid tone* (hypotonia or in extreme cases *atonia*) is the complete floppiness that is found in a limb for the first few days after a stroke. *Spastic tone* (hypertonia) is the general term applied to the stiff feeling, the resistance to passive movement, that is the general hallmark of *upper motor neuron lesions,* where the damage is above the level of the anterior horn cells in the spinal cord. There are some descriptive terms used to describe particular types of spastic tone. *Clasp-knife rigidity* is a term used to describe a type of spasticity which develops in a limb shortly after a stroke. The limb is at first resistant to passive movement and then suddenly gives way just like a clasp-knife suddenly closing. *Cogwheel rigidity* is found in Parkinson's disease. The limb yields in increments just like a cogwheel. *Lead pipe rigidity* presents a constant smooth resistance throughout the entire movement, just as a lead pipe does when you bend it. Somatizing patients or malingerers often present with some kind of rigidity, but their pattern of resistance to passive movement is distinctive. It increases as the movement progresses. If the examiner moves the limb suddenly, tone is normal. Then, when the patient realizes that the limb is being moved, resistance begins and increases with movement.

A good way to examine tone is to pick up a limb and drop it. In a normal patient it will automatically come to a smooth stop. In the paralyzed patient the limb will crash on to the bed as a dead weight. In someone with spastic tone, the movement will look and feel distinctive.

§ 6:58 Clinical testing of coordination

Coordination testing really examines central nervous system functions such as the activities of the cerebellum and the extrapyramidal system; but since the testing involves asking the patient to do certain things with the limbs, these routines are included among the PNS tests. The usual clinical testing of coordination involves the following:

1. *Observing the performance of repetitive acts,* such as hand clapping, patting the left hand with the right as fast as possible, and then patting the right as fast as possible with the left. Alternately pronating and supinating the hands is another repetitive act often tested. This kind of rapid repetitive movement is called *diadochokinesia.* Abnormality or deficit in this activity is called *dysdiadochokinesia* (performed with difficulty) or *adiadochokinesia* (if the movements cannot really be performed at all).

2. *Pointing tests.* The patient is asked to use the index finger of the right (or left) hand, to touch first the tip of his own nose, and then the tip of the examiner's index finger. The test is then repeated with the other hand. The examiner can make the task more difficult by moving his /her finger around. A defect in coordination will lead to *past pointing,* where the patient will not be able to hit the target. A normal test will be recorded as "no past pointing" or "finger/nose normal" or simply "FN nl." A similar test is performed by asking the patient to rub the heel of one foot up and down the shin of the other leg. This will be recorded as "heel/shin normal" or "H/S nl." Coordination tests (like sensation tests) are rather simple screening tests. More precise testing of the patient's ability to coordinate movements may require examination by a psychologist with training in psychometric testing.

3. *More complex coordination testing.* Coordination can be further tested by assigning various tasks to the patient. A common test is to put several coins on the table and ask the subject to lift them one at a time with one hand without letting any of them go. Normal performance here would be three or four coins (depending on the size). Failure to hold more than one is said to be a useful indicator of subtle brain damage. Hand-eye coordination can also be tested by asking the subject to draw a shape, such as a square or a circle or a flower, or even to copy a simple picture drawn by the examiner. It is obvious that this kind of testing relates to brain functions as much as to coordination. Tasks of this kind are an important part of most neuropsychological batteries testing brain functioning.

§ 6:59 Testing sensation

There are a number of varieties of sensation, other than the special senses, vision, hearing and smelling. For example:

- Light touch
- Deep touch or pressure
- Temperature sensation
- Pain sensation
- Vibration sense
- Position sense (of joints)

To test all of these modalities in every part of the body is a formidable task. A general screening of the main sections of the body is often all that is warranted. If study of a particular part, for example the arm, is indicated, this can be examined in some detail.

Sensation is further assessed by discrimination testing which assesses the patient's ability to recognize things placed or drawn on his hands. The usual discrimination tests are:

1. *Blunt/sharp discrimination.* This is often performed using the two ends of a pin or the hub and point of a needle. The patient must be able to tell whether his skin is being touched by the hub or the point.

2. *Two point discrimination.* This is most accurately performed with a set of draftsman's compasses, but two pins can be used as a rough screening test. Two points an inch apart can barely be distinguished on the skin of the back, but two very close together should be distinguishable on the tip of the index finger.

3. *Shape discrimination.* Keys or other objects can be placed in the patient's hands, or numbers can be drawn on the tips of the fingers, and the patient is then asked to identify them.

There is no reason why a neurologist should not go beyond these simple tests. In practice, a fuller examination by a neuropsychologist can be arranged if indicated.

§ 6:60 Clinical testing of reflexes

Reflex arcs are usually centrally processed in the spinal cord, although some modification and control of them is exercised by higher centers in the CNS, and even by the cerebral cortex. Reflex movements in real life are automatic protective actions or mechanisms which adjust muscle length and tone in accordance with the body's needs, balancing oneself or avoiding painful stimuli. In neurological practice, a number of reflexes are used as pointers to different kinds of pathology and to pinpoint the location of pathological defects.

The following reflexes are commonly used by clinicians:

1. *The withdrawal reflex.* The soles of the feet or skin of the arm are pinched. If the limb does not withdraw, the patient is decidedly unconscious. The advent of the withdrawal reflex in a previously completely comatose patient is a step in the right direction.

2. *The plantar (Babinski) reflex.* The lateral side of the sole of the foot is rubbed (using the thumbnail or the point of a key) from heel to toe. The toes should bunch together and flex downward. If they "splay" upward, this will be described as a positive Babinski's sign. A positive Babinski's test indicates an upper neuron problem (one high in the cord or even in the brain, not in peripheral nerves).

3. *The deep tendon reflexes.* The *biceps reflex* is tested by tapping the biceps tendon where it inserts into the head of the radius. The *triceps reflex* is tested by tapping the tendon of the triceps muscle where it inserts into the olecranon process of the ulna behind the elbow. The *brachioradialis reflex* is tested by tapping the radial side of the wrist. The hand should jerk laterally. The *finger reflexes* are tested by flicking the fingers into extension, whereupon they should flex. The *knee jerk* is tested by tapping the infrapatellar tendon. The *ankle jerk* is tested by tapping the Achilles tendon. Each of these reflexes is associated with a particular segment (or related segments) of the spinal cord. The ankle jerk, for example, is associated with the segment which issues in the spinal nerve roots at the S1 level, the knee jerk is associated with L3-4, and so on. Weakness or absence of a particular deep tendon reflex can be used by the clinician to localize a lesion at a particular location in the spinal cord.

Glossary of Anatomical Terms Relating to the Nervous System

[This item is for reference purposes only]

Anatomical names crop up in neurological reports more than in any other kind of medical document. It is often possible to evaluate disability without knowing what they mean, but they puzzle lawyers (who like to understand what they read and worry if they cannot do so). A short glossary of these somewhat difficult terms is therefore included here, for reference purposes rather than for detailed study.

Amygdala: The amygdaloid nucleus lies at the tail of the caudate nucleus, deep to the *olfactory cortex* on the underside of the brain. It has important emotional and memory functions. [See Fig. 6-10.]

Archipallium: The old brain, the primary overgrowth of the uppermost part of the embryonic neural tube, the *prosencephalon.* It includes the *diencephalon* and certain parts of the cortex but not the *basal ganglia* which are part of the *neopallium.* The archipallium in each hemisphere is connected with that of the other side by the anterior and posterior *commissures.* The *corpus callosum* represents the commissural fibers of the neopallium, the full development of the cerebral vesicles which overgrows and buries the archipallium.

Association fibers: Axons connecting different parts of the cortex of the same hemisphere. These fibers are those primarily affected in DAIs.

Cerebral peduncles: These are a pair of columns of white matter (they are projection fibers) which connect the cerebral cortex to the brain stem and spinal cord. [See Fig. 6-19.] They contain both incoming sensory (*afferent*) fibers carrying information to the brain and *efferent* fibers carrying signals which ultimately reach the large motor neurones in the anterior horns of the spinal cord. Between the base of the brain and the upper border of the pons, they are seen as two thick cords of fibers which meet in a V-shaped junction just above the *pons,* properly called the *pons cerebelli,* which is in the middle part of the brain stem. The *superior cerebellar peduncles* similarly connect the cerebellum at the back of the brain stem to the brain. Tucked in between the cerebral peduncles lie (from lower to higher), the two *mammillary bodies,* the *infundibulum* (the stalk of the pituitary gland) the *posterior perforated substance* and, anteriorly, the *optic chiasma* and the *anterior perforated substance* (part of the olfactory cortex). Posteriorly on the brain stem, in between the cerebellar peduncles [see Fig. 6-19] lie the *superior and inferior colliculi* and the *pineal gland.*

Corpus callosum: The large bundle of commissural fibers connecting the two cerebral hemispheres. [See Fig.6-8.] They connect the neopallium. The smaller *anterior* and *posterior commissures* connect the philologically older parts of the hemispheres, the archipallium.

Corpus striatum: Part of the deep gray matter of the brain. Some of the fibers of the *internal capsule* run through the basal gray matter, splitting the caudate and lentiform nuclei apart. Gray matter is, therefore, scattered between the fiber bundles in this area giving it a striped appearance, hence its name.

Choroid plexus: A collection of large capillaries protruding from the roof of the lateral and third ventricles. Blood is strained through the walls of these capillaries into the ventricles to become the cerebrospinal fluid (CSF).

Claustrum: A thin strip of gray matter (part of the basal ganglia) which lies between the *lentiform nucleus* and the *insula* (the piece of cortex tucked into the lateral sulcus). [See Fig. 6-8.]

Commissural fibers: Bundles of axons joining the two cerebral hemispheres. Most of them are in the corpus *callosum*, but some are in the *anterior* and *posterior commissures* and the *habenular commissure.*

Diencephalon: This means the "between brain" and, as the name suggests, it lies tucked in between the cerebral hemispheres connecting them. It consists of the thalamic nuclei and its associated areas, the hypothalamus, metathalamus, and so on. It does not include the *basal ganglia.*

Fornix: A prominent bundle of fibers on the medial side of each hemisphere. [See Fig. 6-12.] The *body* of the fornix is a single bundle of fibers in the midline of the brain just above the roof of the *third ventricle.* Posteriorly it divides into two branches (which diverge out into the two hemispheres) called *the crura* which run anteriorly. Between the two crura run *commissural fibers* connecting the hippocampi of both sides. These are called the *hippocampal commissure.* The crura proceed down to end in the *cingulate gyrus* (on the medial sides of each hemisphere). Anteriorly the two columns of the fornix end in the *mammillary bodies* (on the inferior surface of the brain just anterior to the brain stem). From here impulses are relayed to the anterior nucleus of the thalamus, which receives all kinds of sensory input. Most of the fibers of the fornix originate in the hippocampus. The fornix is thus an association and commissural pathway in the limbic system (emotion and memory).

Habenular commissure: A bundle of fibers running between the cerebral hemispheres at the posterior part of the thalamus. The fibers curve forward to the *piriform area* of the brain and are (like the anterior commissure) probably olfactory in function. Behind lies the *pineal gland.*

Hippocampus: Twin collections of gray nuclei (one in each hemisphere). [See Fig. 6-33.] They lie at the medial side of the base of the brain (bulging into the floor of the lateral ventricles). They are really the infolding of the hippocampal sulcus. The hippocampus functions as an emotional center and also as a processing station for putting short-term memories into long-term storage in the anterior poles of the temporal lobes (or wherever).

Hypothalamus: The hypothalamus is essentially the floor of the *third ventricle.* [See Fig. 6-33.] It contains many nuclei which, in general, function as way stations in the *autonomic nervous system* (ANS), just as the basal ganglia are way stations in the extrapyramidal system. Projection fibers from the hypothalamus pass down in the spinal sympathetic tract to the autonomic effector cells in the lateral horns of the spinal gray matter. The hypothalamus also controls the secretion of hormones by the pituitary gland. Hypothalamic nuclei affect the level of activity of many body systems by putting out releasing substances which cause the pituitary to put out its hormones. The hypothalamus is also connected to the *nucleus ceruleus* in the brain stem (which mediates the stress response).

Indusium grisium: A thin layer of gray matter on the upper surface of the *corpus callosum.* It is part of the *limbic system* (i.e. it is related to olfaction, emotion, and so on).

Insula: A part of the cortex which is tucked into the depths of the *lateral* sulcus. It can be exposed on dissection by removing overlying cortex above and below the lateral fissure. It has visceral functions.

Internal capsule: Bundles of projection fibers which connect the cerebral cortex to lower centers. [See Fig. 6-9.] As they pass between the *lentiform nucleus* and more midline structures such as the head of the *caudate nucleus* and the *thalamus,* these fibers are called the internal capsule. Bleeding here causes the classical form of a "stroke."

Interventricular foramen: Otherwise known as the *foramen of Monro.* These foramina (there are two of them) connect the third ventricle to the lateral ventricles on each side. They lie anterior to the thalamus.

Lateral geniculate body: A small rounded nucleus of gray cells on the posterior surface of the thalamus. It is a complex structure having six layers of cells which make synaptic connections with the fibers of the optic nerve. The axons of this nucleus project to the visual cortex in the occipital area of the brain. These nuclei act as waystations in the visual pathway.

Lateral ventricle: Ventricle means "small stomach." The lateral ventricles, one in each hemisphere, are cisterns filled with CSF (cerebrospinal fluid). [See Fig. 6-6.] The CSF is produced in the *choroid plexus* (grape-like clusters of capillary tubules which protrude from the roofs of all the ventricles). CSF flows from the lateral ventricles through the *foramen of Monro* into the centrally located third ventricle (the lateral ventricles are the first and second) and from there through the *cerebral aqueduct* into the fourth ventricle (which lies between the brain stem and the cerebellum).

Limbic lobe: A ring of gray matter on the medial side of the cerebral hemispheres and in the deep gray matter of the brain. It functions in emotional and visceral matters and has important connections with the *hippocampus* (thus influencing memory). [See *limbic lobe syndrome* §6:31]

Medial geniculate bodies: A pair of nuclei (one on each side of the brain) located behind the pulvinar (the posterior part of the thalamus). They act as waystations in the auditory pathway.

Medial longitudinal bundle: These are major fiber tracts (one on each side) of the brain stem. Each of them runs from the region of the third ventricle down to the upper cord and connects together the nerves which move neck muscles with those which control the movements of the eye. It also has vestibular (balance) and auditory connections as well. Eyes, ears and vestibular apparatus are thus connected to the neck, as they all need to be to function, i.e., the head needs to turn in order for the eyes to look or the ears to listen in a certain direction.

Neural tube: The brain develops in the embryo from a groove, the *neural crest,* which folds over to become the neural tube. The front end of this tube is a thin plate of gray matter which is called the *lamina terminalis* (end plate). The neural tube develops three swellings. The most anterior swelling is termed the *prosencephalon* which produces the cerebral hemispheres and the diencephalon. The *mesencephalon* behind this develops the midbrain. The most posterior, the *rhombencephalon,* develops into the rest of the brain stem and the cerebellum. Many congenital defects of the CNS are described as *neural tube defects* (NTDs).

Lentiform nucleus: The lentiform nuclei (one in each hemisphere) are part of the *basal ganglia.* They are roughly in the shape of a crude lens or prism with the more pointed pole angled medially and slightly forward. Each lies lateral to the thalamus posteriorly and the head of the caudate nucleus anteriorly. They have two parts: the *putamen* (the outer or lateral part) and the *globus pallidus* (the inner or medial part). The lentiform nucleus is closely connected with the head of the *caudate nucleus.* Together they form the corpus *striatum* and function in the extrapyramidal system. Parkinsonism appears to be a defect in the lentiform nucleus.

Nucleus ceruleus: A small gray nucleus in the posterior part of the brain stem (in the floor of the fourth ventricle). It is a major center in the *stress response,* releasing adrenaline into the circulation and triggering the alerting response in the reticular formation of the brain stem. Prolonged or excessive stimulation of this center can lead to stress syndromes.

Pathway, tract, bundle, fasciculus and lemniscus: All these are synonyms for collections of axons linking two sets of nuclei in the cord or the brain e.g. the *rubrospinal tract* joins the *red nucleus* in the brain stem to centers in the gray matter of the spinal cord.

Piriform area (of the cerebral cortex): This is part of what is called the *archipallium* (the old brain). It lies on the inferior surface of the brain, anterior to the brain stem, and has olfactory and emotional functions.

Pretectal nuclei: These are each a small group of cells lying in the tegmentum (in the anterior part) of the midbrain, above and lateral to the *superior* colliculi (visual way stations on the back of the midbrain). Each of these transmits impulses to another nucleus, the *Edinger-Westphal nucleus,* which mediates the pupillary response to light. Damage here (which sometimes occurs in tertiary syphilis) produces an unreactive pupil.

Projection fibers: These are axons which connect the gray matter of the cortex with lower centers such as the thalamus or the spinal cord. They can be motor or sensory.

Red nucleus: A major gray nucleus of the midbrain. It functions along with the basal ganglia in regulating muscle tone, as part of the *extrapyramidal system.*

Reticular (network) formation: Islands of tiny nuclei scattered throughout the white matter of the brain stem. [See Fig. 6-18.] The reticular formation continues down into the cord and also up into the brain. In the brain stem, its major part, it can be shown to have connections with almost every part of the brain and cord. The functions of the reticular formation are many. It is involved in motor tone via the reticulospinal tracts and so it is no surprise that it connects with the basal ganglia and with the cerebellum. One of its important functions is the *arousal reflex.* It has connections with the eyes, ears, and sensory inflow. So we waken when it is light and become alert when we hear unusual noises or experience painful stimuli. The reticular formation is also involved in blood pressure and breathing. It even has visceral functions. In the legal context, it is mainly important because of its association with stress disorders.

Septum pellucidum: A thin membrane separating the two anterior horns of the lateral ventricle. The septum pellucidum also acts as a supporting curtain which suspends the body of the fornix from the corpus callosum above it.

Substantia nigra: Gray nuclei in the midbrain associated with the basal ganglia in the control of muscle tone (part of the extrapyramidal system).

Superior brachium: A small bundle of fibers in the optic tract with reflex functions connected with seeing. They connect the eyes with reflex centers in the tectal area (in the posterior part) of the midbrain. The axons arborize in the *superior colliculum* (a little bump at the back of the brain stem) and further connections run from here (in the *tectobulbar* and *tecto-*

spinal tracts) to motor nuclei in the brain stem and spinal cord to mediate reflexes of the eye such as blinking and withdrawing from bright light. The pupillary reflexes do not arborize in the superior colliculi but travel direct to the pretectal nuclei of the brain stem.

Tectum: The dorsal part of the midbrain lying behind an imaginary line drawn transversely through the cerebral aqueduct. The tectum principally contains the four colliculi. The colliculi, two superior and two inferior, lie just below the *pineal gland* and function as way station nuclei in the visual and auditory tracts respectively.

Tegmentum The midbrain anterior to the tectum.

Thalamus: The thalami are two bodies of gray matter lying on either side of the third ventricle. They develop out of the walls of the neural tube. The medial (and developmentally older) part of the thalamus sends projection fibers to the hypothalamus, thus connecting it with the hormonal control of the body. As the cerebral hemispheres are blossoming forth from the neural tube during the embryological development of the brain, new cells develop in the lateral part of the thalamus which project afferent fibers to the sensory cortex behind the central sulcus. The two thalami usually fuse or stick together across the third ventricle, but there is no direct communication between them; the *interthalamic connexus* is not a commissure. The thalamus is wedge shaped, being broader in its posterior end and also broader inferiorly. In short, it is large and blunt at the back and on the bottom, and narrower and smaller on the top and at the front. The large posterior part bulging outward is called the *pulvinar.* Two nuclei that are developmentally part of the thalamus become separated from it and form the lateral and *medial geniculate bodies.* The medial geniculate bodies are quite separate from the thalamus and are part of the auditory pathway. The *lateral geniculate bodies* bulge down from the lateral part of each pulvinar; they are waystations in the visual pathway.

Uncus: This means "the hook." It is really the anterior end of the *parahippocampal gyrus* (part of the olfactory cortex). [See Fig. 6-12.]

Short Working Glossary of CNS Terms

ALS: Amyotrophic lateral sclerosis

Amyotrophic lateral sclerosis: Otherwise known as Lou Gehrig's disease or motor neuron disease. It is characterized by progressive destruction of motor neurones in the brain stem and spinal cord. As brain stem centers become involved, patients cannot hold their heads up properly. When vital functions such as the ability to breathe become affected, the condition becomes terminal. Causes are unknown; there is no definitive (only supportive) treatment.

Anterior nerve roots: The two sets of nerve bundles emerging from the anterior aspect of the spinal cord which carry motor signals to the body.

Anterior fossa: The most anterior of the three basal compartments of the cranium. It contains the frontal lobes of the brain.

BSEPs: Brain stem evoked potential studies

Brain stem evoked potential studies: Computerized electroencephalograms (EEGs) where a pure sound or some other auditory stimulus is presented to the ear in order to study the intactness of the auditory pathways in the central nervous system. Since the auditory nerves synapse at nuclei in the brain stem, this also tests the intactness of that part of the CNS. BSEPs are, therefore, sometimes used by neurologists to evaluate severely head-injured patients. They are also used for various purposes by otologists, to expose malingerers who are claiming to be deaf. [See also *VEPs* and *SSEPs.*]

Cerebellopontine angle: The angle made by the apposition of the cerebellum and the pons (the middle part of the brain stem). Tumors occurring in this area (e.g., acoustic neuromas) will be referred to as cerebellopontine tumors.

CN: Cranial nerve(s)

cn's: The (twelve) cranial nerves. They are numbered i through xii.

CNS: Central nervous system

CSF: Cerebrospinal fluid

CT: Computerized tomogram (cat scan)

DAIs: Diffuse axonal injuries

Diffuse axonal injuries: The current descriptive term for whiplash brain injuries. They are mainly injuries to the white fibers in the brain, which occur particularly with sudden violent movements of the head leading to rotatory movements of the brain inside the skull. They are classified into severe, moderate and mild types, each of which are identified by fairly precise criteria. The types and severity of disabilities following such injuries can be predicted to a large extent by considering the class of DAI to which the injury has been allocated.

Dorsal nerve roots: The two sets of posterior nerve bundles which carry sensory signals into the spinal cord. [See also *anterior nerve roots.]*

DTRs: Deep tendon reflexes, the "knee jerk"

EDH: Epidural hematoma, usually an arterial bleed under the skull tables. [See also *ICH* and *SDH.*]

EEG: Electroencephalogram

Electrodiagnostic studies: General term for all investigations involving electrical activity in the body. These include electroencephalograms (EEGs), evoked potential studies(EPS), nerve conduction testing (NCT), and electromyography (EMG).

Electromyogram: Electrodiagnostic study of the response of muscles to electrical stimuli, either of the muscle or the nerve controlling it. EMGs are specifically used to diagnose muscle diseases (myopathies) but also demonstrate the intactness of the associated nerves. EMGs are commonly carried out along with nerve conduction studies to demonstrate nerve root involvement in a disc herniation.

EMG: Electromyogram

Encephalitis: Infection or inflammation in the substance of the brain.

EP: Evoked potential (EEG) [See *EPs.*]

EPS: Evoked potential studies [See *evoked potential EEG.*]

Evoked potential EEG: A general term for studies where the wiggly traces of the various leads on the EEG are first stilled, by computer averaging, so that they appear as straight lines. A peripheral stimulus (a light flashing in the eye, a noise in the ear or a tiny electrical shock to the skin) is then administered and the resulting brain wave activity recorded. EPs are used by ophthalmologists, otologists, neurologists, and neurosurgeons to demonstrate problems in the various sensory pathways to the brain. [See also *BSEP, SSEP,* and *VEP.*]

Extrapyramidal lesion: One which affects motor nerves originating in the deep gray nuclei of the brain and in the brain stem, rather than in the cerebral cortex. The extrapyramidal system, in general, controls posture and tone, but can also be used to initiate voluntary movements. It is so called because its efferent fibers run outside the pyramids (bulging structures on the anterior surface of the brain stem. [See Fig. 6-19.]

Fissure of Sylvius: The *central fissure* dividing the parietal from the frontal lobes.

Fissure of Rolando: The *lateral fissure* separating the temporal lobe below from the frontal and parietal lobes above.

Frontal lobe syndrome: A constellation of behavioral symptoms found in patients who have injuries or diseases involving the frontal lobes of the brain. There are two main presentations of frontal lobe problems, depending on the location of the damage. If the lesion is in the anterior part of the frontal lobe just above the orbit (supraorbital type), there is loss of inhibition, and behavior is exaggerated and socially unacceptable. If the problem relates to cortex posterior and superior to this, high up on the sides of the frontal lobe (high convexity type), the principal finding is a short attention span and a general lack of interest in things, with an inability to complete tasks, especially those which are of a complex nature. [See also *frontal lobe syndrome* § 6:31.]

GCS: Glasgow coma scale.

Glasgow coma scale: A system for evaluating the neurological status of head injured patients. Speech, eye movements and muscle movements are used to provide a total score of 15. The GCS was mainly designed as a communication system for medical researchers, but serial GCS scores can also be used as a prognostic indicator of the sort of recovery which a head injured patient is likely to make. A persistent score of 5 or less indicates little likelihood of survival, or recovery only with serious neurological and mental deficits.

Gyrus: Literally the elevated part of a plow furrow. In relation to the CNS, it signifies the elevations on the convoluted surface of the brain which lie in between the sulci (fissures). [See also *sulcus.*]

HA: Headache

Herpes simplex virus: Common term for a number of species which produce serpentine (herpetic) lesions in skin and mucous membranes. Herpes A virus mainly affects the lips and face, Herpes B virus mainly affects the genital regions, but they are not necessarily so limited, as sexual practices can affect the distribution. Herpes simplex infections of the cornea of the eye are very serious conditions which can cause blindness. Herpes viruses can assume a dormant form inside peripheral nerve cells, and periodically erupt into an active phase to cause typical blistering lesions on the skin (cold sores) or the typical painful erosions of shingles (Herpes zoster).

HSV: Herpes simplex virus

HVA: Herpes simplex virus type A

HVB: Herpes simplex virus type B

ICH: Intracerebral hemorrhage or bleeding into the brain substance. [See also *EDH* and *SDH.*]

IEIR: Ischemic event of incomplete resolution

Ischemic event of incomplete resolution: A term used to describe a mild stroke-like event which did not completely clear up, but left some slight residual neurological deficits; something more than a TIA but something less than a stroke.

LOC: Level of consciousness /loss of consciousness

LP: Lumbar puncture

LT: Light touch, "sensation normal to light touch"

M&S: Motor and sensory (systems), as tested in the neurological examination.

Meningitis: Infection or inflammation of the brain coverings (meninges) and CSF.

Middle fossa: The compartment of the floor of the skull which lies between the anterior and posterior compartments of the cranium. It contains the temporal lobes of the brain and also, in the midline, the *sella turcica* (turkish saddle) which contains the *pituitary gland.*

Mixed nerve: One containing both motor and sensory (and probably also autonomic) fibers.

MRI: Magnetic resonance imaging

MS: Mental status

Nerve conduction testing: Where a tiny electrical stimulus is applied proximally to a nerve, and the distal response noted and timed. Slow conduction or no conduction indicates nerve fiber damage. Since most nerves include sensory and other fibers as well as motor axons, a normal nerve conduction test is often taken to indicate that all nerve fibers in the bundle are intact. This may be a fair assumption in most instances, but in doubtful cases, other types of nerve fiber may need to be tested, as sensory fibers by SSEPs.

neuro.: Neurological (examination)

O x 3: Oriented as to time, place and person (or circumstances).

Poliomyelitis: Viral disease involving the anterior (motor) horn cells of the spinal cord and (more rarely) the motor centers of the brain stem (the bulb). It often leaves residual weakness with muscle wasting. The virus has been known in some cases to reactivate (some authorities preferring other terms) after many years and cause further disability.

Posterior columns: Bundles of white fibers in the posterior part of the spinal cord which carry light touch and vibration sense. Posterior column dysfunction (loss of vibration sense) is characteristic of certain diseases, such as *neurosyphilis* and *subacute combined degeneration of the cord* (due to prolonged vitamin B 12 deficiency). It can also be found in old age and in patients with diabetic neuropathy and a number of other conditions.

SDH: Subdural hematoma, or venous bleeding under the dura mater [See *EDH* and *ICH.*]

SEEG: Sonoelectroencephalogram (ultrasound study of the brain)

Sella turcica: An elevation in the midline floor of the middle fossa which contains and protects the pituitary gland. There are bony prominences on its anterior and posterior ends (the clinoid processes) which produce its distinctive outline on X-ray (hence the name).

SSEPs: Somatosensory evoked potential studies.

Somatosensory evoked potential studies: Electrodiagnostic testing where a stimulus is applied to the skin and the resultant brain waves detected and studied. They are used by neurosurgeons during operations (e.g., on the spinal cord) to give early warning of damage to conducting bundles due, perhaps, to too much tension on retractors [See also *BSEPs, EPSs* and *VEPs.*]

Sulcus: Literally "a ditch," one of the linear indentations (fissures) separating the gyri (elevations) of the surface of the brain. This wrinkling effect greatly increases the surface area of the cortex.

Supratentorial problem: Literally a problem where the lesion lies above the tentorium cerebelli (the fibrous sheet which covers the posterior fossa). Commonly, however, this term is used in medical parlance to refer to an imaginary (factitious) illness, either malingering or a somatiform disorder (conversion hysteria or hypochondriasis). A factitious illness is one manufactured by the patient.

Temporal lobe syndromes: Collective term for abnormalities associated with temporal lobe brain damage. These include temporal lobe epilepsy (TLE), schizophrenia spectrum disorders and also a group of behavioral patterns (temporal lobe personality) characterized by progressive irritability directed at family and associates, culminating in a stormy outburst which is followed by a temporary period of solicitous and penitent behavior. These three forms of temporal lobe problem can be associated with one another, but a patient can have one of them and it does not follow that they will develop any of the others.

TIA: Transient ischemic attack

TLE: Temporal lobe epilepsy

Transient ischemic attack: Formally defined as a stroke-like illness which lasts less than 24 hours and clears without residual neurological deficits. It is unlikely, however, that such illnesses lasting more than six hours will clear up completely without deficits; most of them are very brief (less than one hour).

Visual evoked potential studies: Computerized EEG testing where a light or some other visual stimulus, is presented to the eye, and the resulting brain waves detected and studied. They are used by ophthalmologists to study the intactness of the visual pathways in the CNS. [See also *BSEPs, EPSs* and *SSGPs.*]

VEPs: Visual evoked potential studies

Zoster: Common abbreviation for herpes zoster virus (HZV) which causes chicken pox and also (in adult life) shingles. [See also *Herpes simplex virus.*]

Specimen Handwritten Note on CNS Patient

68 y.o. ♂ adm. per amb. p̄ MVA. 10[30] PM

CC: HI c̄ LOC. 12/3/0?

HCC: Pt involved in AA while operating a motorscooter "struck from (L) side by a truck & thrown against sidewalk." LOC reported by rescue squad at site of accident but A & O on arrival @ ER 15 mins later.

P.M.H. (informant pts wife) ō hx of HA, ō PMH of head tx "slight stroke a few years ago" but "good recovery in less than 1/52 maybe a couple of days".

F.H.: N/C.

SH: Semiretired but still self employed as accountant does tax returns. Married c̄ 4 children none LAH all A & W.

PH: ō smokes ō ETOH ō cont. meds. NKA. Plays the piano at home & also @ social fnctns.

ROS: N/C

PE: H&N: - 6" curvilinear lac" on (L) temp. region. skull exposed. ō fx palpable. Neck moves easily s̄ pain

Sensorium: A & O x3 but a little drowsy speech nl. not slurred - responds approp'y. to commands Moves AE s̄ c/o pain & approp'y.

EENT: VA not tested (glasses missing) Fy report "sees OK with glasses" appears to be sighted.
EOMI - ō nystagmus
Hears whispered speech (R) 6/6 (L)? (hearing aid missing)

Translation of Specimen Handwritten Note on CNS Patient

10:30 PM 12/3/05

68 year old male admitted via ambulance following a motor vehicle accident

Chief Complaints: Head injury with loss of consciousness

History of Chief Complaints: Patient involved in automobile accident while operating a motor scooter. "struck from left side by a truck and thrown against sidewalk." Loss of consciousness reported by rescue squad at site of accident but alert and oriented on arrival at Emergency Room 15 minutes later.

Past Medical History: (informant patient's wife) No history of headache, no past medical history of head trauma. "slight stroke a few years ago" but "good recovery in less than a week, maybe a couple of days."

Family History: Nil (nothing) contributory

Social History: Semiretired but still self employed as accountant, does tax returns. Married with 4 children, none living at home, all alive and well.

Personal History: Does not smoke or use alcohol, no continuing medications. No known allergies. Plays the piano at home and also at social functions.

Review of Systems:

Physical Examination: Head and neck – 6" curvilinear laceration on Left temporal region, skull exposed. No fracture palpable. Neck moves easily without pain.

Sensorium: Alert and oriented to time place and circumstances but a little drowsy. Speech normal, not slurred, – responds appropriately to commands. Moves all extremities without complaints of pain and appropriately.

EENT (Eyes ears nose and throat): Visual acuity not tested (glasses missing) Family report "sees O.K. with glasses", appears to be sighted.

Extraocular muscles (movements) intact, no nystagmus

Hears whispered speech in right ear at 6 feet/ six feet (what would normally be heard at six feet). Left ear – (hearing aid missing)

EAC s̄ blood. TMs seen easily c̄ otoscope. TM's intact
ō perforation ō hemotympanum.
RS: chest wall intact s̄ tenderness, moves easily.
AE ✓✓ BS AA s̄ RR/R (ō AS).
CVS: (Cor) RRR HR 80 vol ✓ PMI (AB) 5ICS MCL
HS nl S1 S2 nl, ō Ⓜ Ⓡ or Ⓖ. BP 115/80
Pulses: radial, good volume bilat.

	Ⓡ	Ⓛ
FEM	++	++
POPL	+	+ ?
DP	++	+
PT	++	+ ?

MS: NAD.
CNS: CNs ii–xii g.l.
i can smell perfume (daughter's) well.
ii NAD.
iii iv & vi AOMI.
V i ii iii } all intact to FT
vii All facial mts. intact.
viii Normally wears hearing aid Ⓡ Hears well
c̄ Ⓡ ear ō nystagmus.
IX & X. Palate moves symmet^y, gag reflex intact
ix/Xii SCMs intact. Tongue protrudes symmet^y 4/4.
PNS : P- 4/4 all groups ? sl. weakness Ⓛ LE
T. WNL. ∴ KJ & AJ ↑ LLE
C F/N nl ō PP. H/S not done.
ō dysdiadochokinesia but L < R.
S. FT, DT, B/S P & T° all intact
V.S. Intact

External auditory canal is without blood. The tympanic membranes are easily seen with otoscope. Tympanic membranes intact without perforation, no hemotympanum (blood

Respiratory System:– Chest wall intact without tenderness, (it) moves easily. Air entry good bilaterally, breath sounds in all areas, without rales, rhonci or rubs (no adventitial sounds)

Cardiovascular system (cor is the Latin for heart): – Regular rate and rhythm, heart rate 80 (beats per minute), volume (of pulse) good. Point of maximal impulse (apex beat) at the fifth intercostal space and the mid-clavicular line, heart sounds normal, first and second heart sounds normal, no murmurs, rubs or gallop (heard), blood pressure 115/80 (mm Hg)

Pulses – radial (pulses) good volume bilaterally

	RIGHT	LEFT
Femoral	Normal	Normal
Popliteal	Normal	Normal
Dorsalis pedis	Normal	Normal
Posterior tibial	Normal	Normal

Musculoskeletal – No abnormality detected.

Central Nervous system – Cranial nerves ii–xii grossly intact

i Can smell daughter's perfume well

ii. No abnormality detected (see above)

iii, iv & vi (the nerves that control eye movements) All ocular movements intact

vii Facial movements intact

viii Normally wears hearing aid in left ear. Hears well with right ear, no nystagmus

ix & x Palate moves symmetrically on swallowing, gag reflex intact.

xi. Sternocleidomastoids (muscles of the neck) intact

xii. xii. Tongue protrudes symmetrically with full power.

Peripheral nervous system

Power – Full power all groups, possible slight weakness in left leg.

Tone – Within normal limits, knee jerk and ankle jerk brisker in left leg.

Coordination – Finger/nose (test) normal, no past pointing. Heel shin not done, no dysdiadochokinesia (difficulty in performing rapid repetitive movements) but (performance) on left is worse than on the right.

Sensation – Fine touch, deep touch, blunt/sharp, pain and temperature (sensation) all intact. Vibration sense intact

DTRs

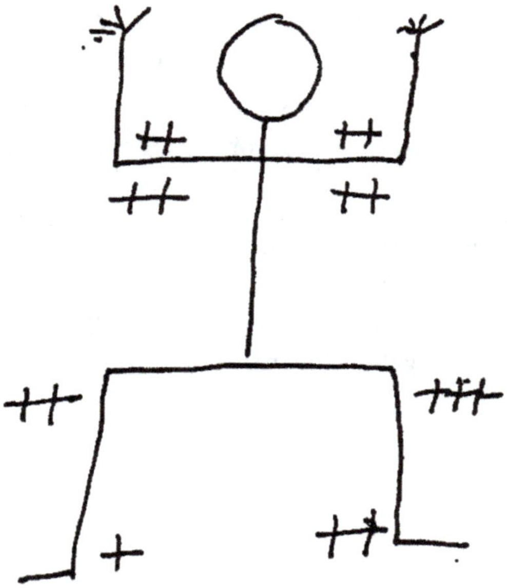

ASSESS:

#1. HI c̄ LOC, now lucid but ? a little drowsier than on adm. to ER.

#2. 6" scalp lac" → skull in (L) temporal region

#3. Signs of UMNL on (L) ↑ DTRs in KJ & AJ. etc. ? 2° to TIA/IR

PLAN: #1. Suture laceration scalp

#2. adm. R/O developing SDH, SAH, or ICH — on HI obs.

#3. CT if LOC ↓ further

#4. Skull X-RAY series in a.m

J. Wills M.D.

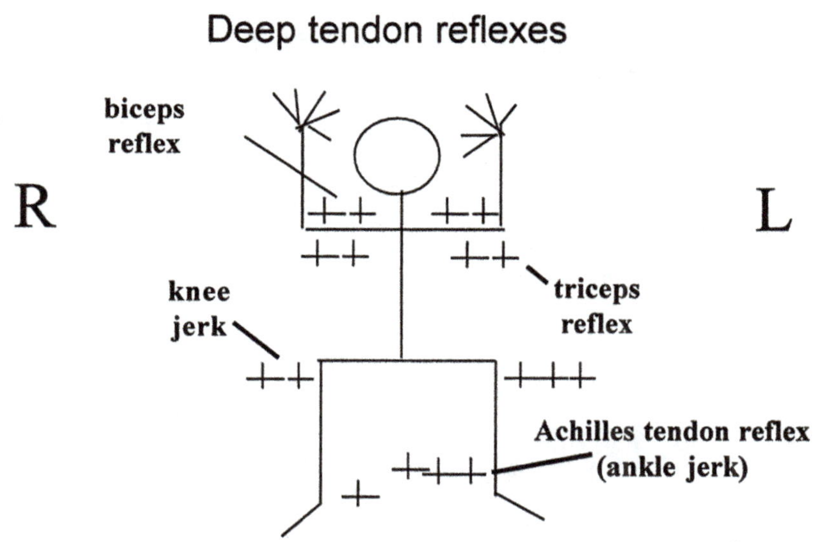

[*Diagram indicates increased reflexes in the left leg as compared with the right (knee jerk +++) Also reduced response in right ankle jerk.which may not be significant*]

<u>ASSESS</u>:

1 Head injury with loss of consciousness, now lucid but possibly a little drowsier than on admission to the Emergency Room

#2 Six inch scalp laceration (right down to) the skull in the left temporal region

#3 Signs of an upper motor neuron lesion on the left (with) increased deep tendon reflexes in the knee jerk and ankle jerk etc. These (findings) may be due to (previously mentioned) transient ischemic attack with incomplete resolution.

<u>PLAN</u>

1 Suture scalp laceration

#2 Admit (to) rule out developing subdural hematoma, subarachnoid hematoma or intracranial hemorrhage—(to be) on (routine) head injury observations.

#3 Computerized tomography if level of consciousness deteriorates further

#4 Skull X-ray series in the morning.

J.Wills M.D.

Chapter Seven

Psychiatric Disorders and Disability

Part I.
Introductory Matters

§ 7:1 The legal importance of emotional and behavioral harm

Knowledge of psychiatric problems is becoming more important for lawyers for the following reasons:

1. The old artificial legal rules which restricted compensation for mental harm are rapidly disappearing. Psychiatric impairments can now be shown just as objectively as physical disorders and are no longer regarded as areas where plaintiffs can easily pretend to be ill and receive unmerited compensation.

2. It is becoming clear that mental harm is a common sequel to head injuries. It was estimated, in a 1986 study, that there are some 300,000 serious head injuries in the United States each year (loss of consciousness more than 24 hours) due to automobile accidents alone, and that 70% of these had significant psychiatric impairments, i.e., lasting more than six months. It was also reported that less than one third of these were referred for psychiatric evaluation, and that only a few consulted a lawyer or sought compensation.

3. People exposed to a very terrifying situation (especially when they are unable to do any thing about it) may also suffer significant mental harm (stress disorders of one sort or another), even though they have not suffered any physical insult to the brain.

It is, therefore, important that compensationists should be aware of the various kinds of psychiatric disorders, how they may arise (especially in trauma) and how they may be proved.

§ 7:2 Overview of the topics to be discussed

The field of mental disorders and their treatment (psychiatry) is now too large to be treated in a single volume, much less a chapter. Attention will, therefore, be focussed on three topics which are of particular interest and importance for lawyers. These are:

1. The nature and qualifications of the various professionals who work in the mental health field.

2. The concept of mental disorder in general and a brief introduction to the major types of mental problems (neurosis, psychosis, personality disorder, etc.). This will provide the background and context for the next and principal item.

3. An introduction to the Diagnostic and Statistical Manual (4th edition) published by the American Psychiatric Association in 1996.

Part II.
Mental Health Professionals

§ 7:3 Psychiatrists and clinical psychologists

A *psychiatrist* is a medical doctor with postgraduate training in the diagnosis and treatment of mental illnesses. Being physicians, psychiatrists are licensed to use drug therapies. A *clinical psychologist* is not a medical doctor, but someone with doctoral and post-doctoral training in clinical psychology. They require a state license to practice and may treat patients without medical supervision, but cannot prescribe drugs. They, therefore, tend to work with other forms of treatment, such as counselling and group therapy. By virtue of their training, they are very comfortable with the use and interpretation of psychological inventories and other tests. The distinction between psychiatrists and clinical psych ologists is far from absolute, especially since they commonly work together in mental health clinics and hospitals. Psychiatrists commonly focus on drug therapy and /or psychoanalytic consultation. But by virtue of associating with psychologists on a daily basis, they are becoming increasingly likely to use group therapy or aversion therapy, and may routinely order a battery of psychological tests. Psychologists likewise are very aware of the benefits of medication. In fact, the common view at present among mental health professionals is that the best results are achieved by a combination of psychopharmacy and psychological methods of treatment, and therefore, ideally, by psychiatrists and psychologists working together.

Psychiatrists and psychologists, thus, tend to function as partners in team therapy in hospitals and clinics and to complement one another. If a psychologist seeing a patient thinks that drug therapy is needed, they can be referred to the psychiatrist with the suggestion that an antidepressant or sedative would help. Similarly the psychiatrist is likely to refer the patient to a psychologist when psychometric evaluation is indicated.

In the legal context, there is no significant difference between psychiatrists and clinical psychologists. Each is equally competent to provide a psychiatric diagnosis and generally to evaluate mental harm. The expert selected in any case may simply be the one who was mainly responsible for treating the patient. Or, the choice may turn on the specific circumstances of the case. If there has been extensive psychological testing, a psychologist may be needed either as the sole expert, or to supplement the testimony of a psychiatrist. A psychiatrist is competent to interpret psychological testing, but someone with a good background in psychometrics will probably be more authoritative. In most cases, in short, the particular training and experience of the individual psychologist or psychologist is more important than the professional hat that she happens to wear.

§ 7:4 Other mental health professionals

Psychiatric social workers (PSWs) are specially trained social workers who assist psychiatrists or psychologists in a number of ways. They investigate and work with the families of patients, arrange job placements or nursing home admissions, and carry out home visits after psychiatric patients have been discharged from hospital. They usually have some training in counseling and may help in therapy sessions. Indeed, when a psychiatric consult is ordered in a medical or surgical unit, the first person to arrive may well be a psychiatric social worker. The PSW will interview the patient and write a note in the patient's medical chart, a note which will probably contain an opinion as to the diagnosis. A psychiatric social worker functions in some ways like a district nurse and nurse practitioner rolled into one. Psychiatric social workers (like district nurses) do a great deal of the home health care connected with the mental health clinic or hospital outpatient clinic. Their records can be very valuable to the compensation lawyer. The note of the psychiatric social worker on a patient who was just wakening up in the intensive care unit may be the most valuable item (from the legal perspective) in the whole chart.

Psychiatric nurses are ordinary nurses who have taken additional training in a psychiatric hospital and passed a state examination to qualify them for a license in psychiatric nursing. They commonly work in hospital psychiatric units where (due to the nature of the patients admitted) there is a heavy emphasis on drug therapy. The familiarity with pills and needles which they have acquired in their ordinary nursing training is most useful in this setting. They are also helpful when, as is often the case, psychiatric patients have physical complaints as well. They make entries in nursing notes just as their counterparts in the medical and surgical units do, but their observations relate to mood and behavior rather than vital signs. In addition to looking after the patients' medications, they share in counselling or group sessions and generally provide the same kind of twenty-four hour supportive presence that may well be the nurse's greatest contribution to any kind of therapy.

Psychiatric technicians of various sorts are commonly used nowadays to administer routine questionnaires and tests. It is uneconomical and generally wasteful of time and resources to have a clinician administer tests. It is, indeed, becoming one of the main characteristics that clinicians look for in a test, that it can be administered by a technician or, better still, be taken by the unaided patient. Psychological technicians have formal training as required for a state license, and many of them have learned a great deal more "on the job." But their training only qualifies them to administer tests, not to interpret them. They may be considered experts as to whether a test was properly given or not. They are not competent to interpret it.

Part III.
Mental Science and Mental Disorders

§ 7:5 Controversies and schools of thought

Psychology and psychiatry are rapidly expanding branches of learning, and it is only to be expected that there will be varieties of approach and differences of opinion. There are a large number of viewpoints and perspectives, but three will be mentioned here.

1. The mental science approach, using introspection and interview

2. The behaviorist approach, emphasizing observables such as behavior and speech
3. The psychoanalytic school associated with the name of Sigmund Freud and his associates

§ 7:6 The notion of mental science

The classical notion of mental science derives from the teachings of the French philosopher, Rene Descartes, as developed in the eighteenth and nineteenth centuries by Hume and Hamilton. In this tradition, mental events (thoughts, feelings, imaginings, etc.) are taken to be quite different from physical events. The work of the psychologist then is to describe and systematize these ideas. These internal mental events can, according to this school of thought, be directly experienced by introspection, and indirectly known as other persons describe their feelings and thoughts during interview. Internal ideas can also be linked up with observed behavior. This approach is no longer fashionable, though by no means defunct, seeming ghostly and imprecise to contemporary researchers who may tend to prefer dealing with events which are publicly observable.

§ 7:7 Behaviorism

The opposite approach to the mental science is to discount or ignore hidden mental events and concentrate on observable behavior. This approach, associated with the names of Crick and Watson, is known as *behaviorism* and represents an effort to bring psychological research in line with the methods and presuppositions of the physical sciences. This is sometimes known as the "hard science" approach. In its more extreme forms it is open to the criticism that it is ignoring a fact of life, namely that we do have internal ideas and that they are important. Nevertheless, behaviorist methodology has proved workable as, indeed, one would expect it to be, since behavior, like anything else which has a measure of regularity about it, is clearly capable of being studied by observation and experiment. Whatever the merits and demerits of behaviorism may be from the perspective of psychological theory, this approach is clearly valuable for lawyers who likewise emphasize observables and behavior. It is true that legal theory uses concepts like *motive* and *intent* which are mental events, but these are proved and evidenced by behavior and frequently will be defined in terms of observable acts and recorded speech. DSM-IV, which will be discussed later [see § 7:18 and § 7:19], has been largely influenced by the St. Louis School of psychiatric opinion, which emphasizes public observables in the description and study of mental disorders. It is a most useful reference book from the legal perspective.

§ 7:8 Psychoanalytic theory of mental disorders

The reputation of Sigmund Freud has become somewhat tarnished of late, and psychoanalytic notions about the nature and treatment of mental disorders have likewise been criticized in recent years and are no longer center stage in psychiatric opinion. Nevertheless, Freud focussed the attention of researchers on the disorders of the mind as opposed to its normal function, and many of his ideas and terms are still found in psychiatric literature, even if they have become considerably modified to conform with more recent thought. A good example is his distinction between a neurosis and a psychosis. Freud defined a *neurosis* as a functional problem, where thinking had become warped and messed up during early development; whereas a *psychosis* represented something wrong with the brain. The importance of this distinction, for Freud, was his view that neuroses could be treated by psychoanalytic therapy (untangling the mess) whereas psychoses could not be treated by these means.

Freud's broad distinction between these two types of mental disorder still stands, but the definitions have changed. It has been found that most serious neuroses are not merely functional problems but, like psychoses, are associated with biochemical or structural changes in various parts of the brain. The distinction is now based on the clinical feature that, in neuroses but not in psychoses, the patient is still in touch with reality. A depressed patient may hallucinate but be aware of the fact (he knows that in actual fact there are no green Martians in the vacuum cleaner).

Freud's treatment methods and the underlying theory upon which they are built are no longer highly esteemed in the general psychiatric community, and psychoanalysts in the Freudian mold have, indeed, become rather scarce. Nevertheless, his emphasis on interpersonal therapy is still very much in evidence, despite the advent of drug treatments for most mental disorders. Indeed, psychotherapies of all sorts are being emphasized again. It has become appreciated that the underlying structural and biochemical lesions in mental disorders are generally compounded by personal and social factors. So, while drug therapies may be used to treat underlying neural and neurochemical problems, the patients generally fare much better if they are helped at the personal level as well (e.g., depression responds better and is less likely to recur if psychotherapy is given in addition to drug treatments).

§ 7:9 Mental disorders of particular importance to lawyers

The *Diagnostic and Statistical Manual of Mental Disorders,* 4th edition (DSM-IV), which will be described later [see § 7:18], lists a very large number of mental disorders. These include all kinds of *substance use disorders* (listed now by the substance involved), and even conditions peculiar to certain cultures. Any of these may somehow concern some lawyer sooner or later; however, only a few of them are of such recurring importance that they should be considered in advance. Those singled out for special attention here, due to their legal importance, are *anxiety disorders* and *stress syndromes.* Anxiety (often accompanied by depression) is the commonest mental harm following head injuries; while stress syndromes, such as *post-traumatic stress disorder,* are associated with very frightening experiences, including accidents of various kinds. Schizophrenia, personality disorders, and dementias will also be briefly mentioned.

§ 7:10 Anxiety and depression

An anxiety disorder is defined as chronic dysfunctional anxiety. The term *dysfunctional* means that the condition must interfere with the patient's work or lifestyle to a significant extent, and it must last at least six months to be considered *chronic.* The most characteristic. features of these conditions are:

1. The anxiety is extremely intense, much more than the anxieties of everyday life.
2. There is *avoidance behavior.* The patient does things designed to avoid anxiety creating circumstances or thoughts, or to reduce the stress in some way or other.

A number of particular anxiety conditions are described such as *panic attacks* and *phobic disorders.* In panic attacks, there is an episode of intense fear, which comes on suddenly and for no good reason. This is usually accompanied by shortness of breath, palpitations, sweating, choking, and even a feeling on the part of the patient that he is dying. Phobias are experiences of fear associated with particular objects or situations, such as *claustrophobia* (fear of being shut up in a closed space). Phobic attacks often take the form of panic attacks, and this is especially the case with *agoraphobia,* where there is a fear of open spaces. However, phobic episodes may not amount to panic attacks, and panic attacks may not be associated with particular phobias. Agoraphobia, the commonest phobic disorder, is also the most disabling since the patient is afraid to go out of the house and into public places. *Social phobia,* where there is fear of meeting people, especially in crowded places, can also be very disabling.

§ 7:11 Obsessive compulsive disorders (OCD)

OCDs are classified as anxiety states, the obsessive/compulsive aspect being considered avoidance behavior. Obsessive/compulsion disorder is formally defined as an overwhelming need to do or say things or to carry out rituals, even though they are perceived to be pointless, silly or even morally wrong. Thus, the compulsion may be to shout out rude or obscene words, to count up to a hundred, or to dwell on certain thoughts (*compulsive ruminations*). Obsessive rituals are sometimes described as *secondary obsessional behavior* when they are performed to ward off the primary obsession, such as counting to a hundred to avoid recurring obsessional thoughts.

OCD patients will often be found to have shown odd mildly obsessive traits prior to the development of the disorder, e.g., an obsessive personality trait with an extreme preoccupation with orderliness. Approximately a third of OCD patients go on to develop other mental disorders such as *depression* (30%) and even *schizophrenia* (5%). It has also been noted that the obsessive personality, and even full-blown obsessive/compulsive disorder, can develop following head injuries or severe encephalitis (viral, bacterial or hyperimmune).

The premorbid obsessional trait is not disabling, and may even make the patient a good employee (though rather hard to live with). However, once OCD develops, the condition is likely to be disabling, with dysfunction affecting both occupational and home life. If OCD is complicated by the development of depression or a psychotic disorder, disability is likely to be total.

§ 7:12 Post-traumatic stress disorder (PTSD)

PTSD is an anxiety-related syndrome which follows an extraordinarily frightening or distressing experience. It is more likely to occur when the person involved is passive and helpless at the time of exposure, as when watching people being burned to death; or where an individual has been taken as a hostage and been physically/mentally tortured, or forced to watch others suffer. This observation is in line with animal experiments, where rats developed comparable behavior when they were exposed to electric shocks with no way to predict when they would recur, and no way to escape them. It is also said to be more likely to occur when the frightening event was the intentional horrible and cruel act of another human being (e.g., a rape or a beating) rather than an impersonal thing like a mass accident. PTSD is characterized by nightmares during sleep, or mentally reexperiencing the frightening episode while awake (flash-backs) and can be induced by seeing things which remind the patient of the original horrible event. Victims may also develop a feeling of remoteness from things and events around them (*detachment*) and a lack of emotion known as *psychic numbness* or *emotional anesthesia* (negative symptoms). They may also be very emotionally unstable and irritable, liable to "flare up" at the slightest annoyance. Similar presentations can be found following head injuries, but the term PTSD is usually reserved for cases related to psychic trauma only, without any suspicion of traumatic brain damage.

§ 7:13 Mechanisms involved in stress syndromes

A good deal of knowledge has accumulated in recent years about the stress response and about the things which happen when it goes wrong. The central nervous system processing area, which becomes active in stress, is a tiny gray nucleus in the upper brain stem, called the *locus ceruleus* [see Fig. 6-18]. This, together with another brain stem center called the *ventral tegmental nucleus*, is activated by sounds and sights which are deemed threatening. This leads to the release of both *adrenaline* (epinephrine or EPI) and a closely related substance called *noradrenaline* (NE). These neurotransmitters have direct actions in the body and also activate other brain centers, especially the limbic structures [see § 5:13] and the hypothalamus. When the limbic system is activated, the animal becomes aroused, vigilant, fearful and ready for either fight or flight [see § 6:14]. If the locus ceruleus is ablated in an animal, it loses all fear and becomes inappropriately rash, even attacking animals from which it would normally run away. On the other hand, stimulation of the LC by drugs such as yohimbine (used in cultic manhood rituals in certain tribes), produces extreme, almost unendurable fear.

The actions of EPI and NE on the hypothalamus produce *corticotrophin releasing factor* (CRF) which makes the pituitary release corticotrophin, which in turn causes the adrenal glands to put out steroids [see § 6:15]. *Steroids* carry out a number of functions which are helpful to the stressed animal, and without them, stress can prove fatal. Thus, if supplementary steroids are not given to surgical patients with adrenal suppression, they may succumb to the stresses of the operation.

The way in which these mechanisms become involved in the *post-traumatic stress disorder* has been elucidated by animal studies, using all sorts of induced and prolonged stress. When there is no way of escape *(inescapable stress* or IS), the animal becomes very passive and indeed numb. This may be a mechanism which produces a sort of anesthesia when taken by a predator, and it has obvious links with negative symptoms found in PTSD.

Some of the biochemical findings in animal studies are interesting and probably important to lawyers. In acute stress, as one would expect, levels of both adrenaline and corticosteroids rise. In prolonged stress, however, especially inescapable stress (IS), the animal adapts and the whole stress response system alters. The activity of the LC appears to be damped, and levels of corticosteroid fall (steroid levels tend to be normal or high in depressive disorders).

Prolonged stress also reduces the number of NE receptors on brain cells (damping the effects of the stress response), and this can also be found in other cells, including platelets, which can be made available by simply drawing a little blood from the patient. If the number of adrenergic receptors on platelets is found to be reduced, this will confirm the diagnosis of PTSD. There is some dispute about the reliability of adrenergic receptor findings, and clinicians are by no means unanimous in proposing to rely on them. But if platelet studies have been carried out for any reason, there seems no reason why they should not be offered in evidence; the results may be helpful to lawyers on both sides. They provide *some* evidence that there is a real problem. Whether such evidence would be admissable or not is perhaps another question.

Animal experiments also confirm that individuals in certain families are more likely to develop post-traumatic stress disorder; which argues for genetic predisposing factors. Previous frightening experiences will similarly increase the likelihood and severity of PTSD following a later one. Moreover, PTSD is more likely to occur and to be prolonged in animals who have suffered mother deprivation in infancy. Studies of populations of Vietnam veterans have suggested that these same factors are to be found in humans. The presence of other psychiatric disorders (such as depression) does not, however, seem to predispose to the development of PTSD.

Animal experiments relating the effects of stress on alcohol consumption are interesting. While they are in the frightening environment, the animals show no particular need for alcohol. However, once they are released from the stressful environment, they do tend to seek out and overdose on alcohol if it is made available to them.

§ 7:14 Schizophrenia spectrum disorders (SSDs)

This is a group of *psychotic* conditions (defined by a loss of contact with reality) characterized by a dissociation of one aspect of personality or mental life from others, or dissociation of patients from their environment. There are a number of presentations of schizophrenia. Some are characterized by detachment, with lack of interest in other persons or in things. In extreme cases, the patient may even be *catatonic*, remaining fixed and unmoving in one position for long periods of time (*negative findings*). There also may be dissociation of affect (mood) from its usual concomitants. Thus, the patient may be unafraid in frightening circumstances or happy in sad happenings. The expression of mood may also be inappropriate, with laughter representing anger or anger indicating pleasure. *Paranoid schizophrenia* is characterized by inappropriate suspiciousness, interpreting events and other people's actions as hostile and threatening. This can be a very dangerous condition if the patient decides to take drastic action to protect herself and remove the threat.

Schizophrenic disorders are classified into a number of types (usually including a catch-all category for cases that do not fit into the usual boxes). The older names for some of these still linger and are not inappropriate. Thus the term *hebephrenia* was used to describe an early onset type of schizophrenia with florid hallucinations and generally a bad prognosis, while paranoid schizophrenia, already mentioned, was more likely to have a later onset and (although dangerous) to have a better prognosis. The present trend (represented by DSM-IV) is to divide schizophrenic disorders up into a larger number of types and subtypes (paranoid, disorganized, catatonic, undifferentiated and residual types), with very precise and specific markers for each.

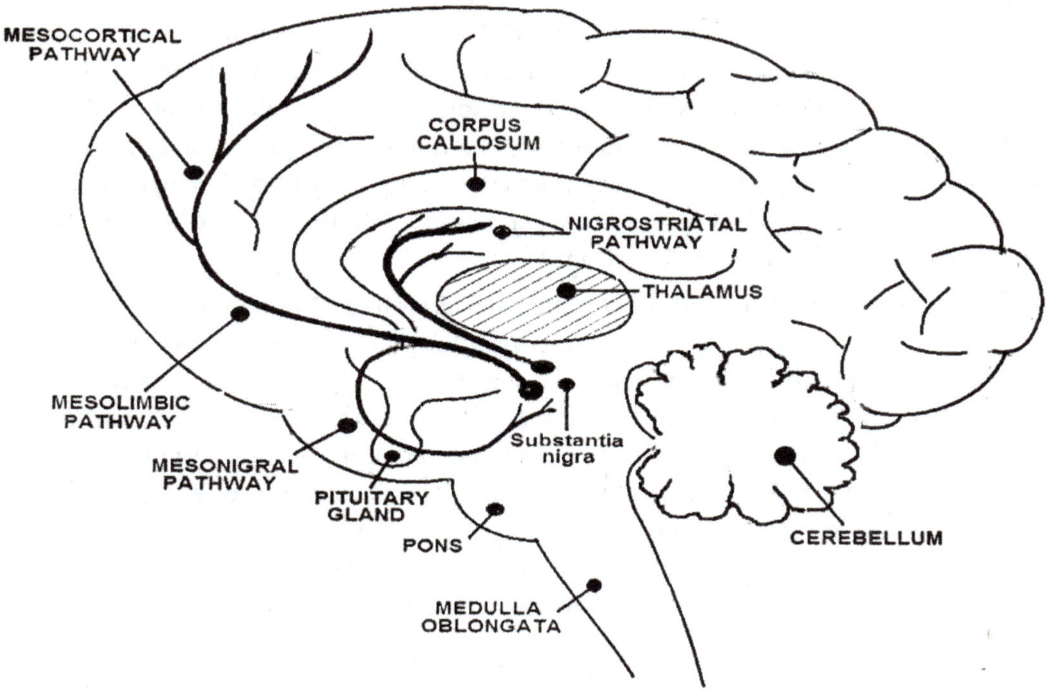

Fig. 7-1 Sagittal section of the brain and brain stem showing main dopamine pathways

It is virtually certain (with a few psychoanalysts dissenting) that there is an organic basis for schizophrenic disorders. Twin studies (using identical and non-identical twins separated at birth living in different homes) suggest that a genetic factor is involved on occasion, but this is probably not the explanation in all cases. Birth trauma is a frequent concomitant, and this too may be familial, since certain mothers tend to have difficult births. Schizophrenia can also appear following trauma. Computerized electrodiagnostic studies (using BEAM) have identified abnormal areas in the cortex of schizophrenic patients. One study reported lesions in the left temporal lobe in schizophrenic patients, with right temporal lobe abnormalities associated with manic depressive disorders (bipolar disorders). Others have identified lesions in the frontal cortex. Indeed, it is probable that the term schizophrenia covers a number of separate conditions with varying underlying brain lesions.

The underlying biochemical causes of schizophrenia are still somewhat controversial. The florid episodes of the disorder are associated with excessive activity of the neurotransmitter dopamine, and the odd behaviors which persist in between the active episodes (negative symptoms) appear to be due to other neurochemical abnormalities.

Treatment for schizophrenia is largely drug therapy, which is helpful with the florid symptoms, but tends to be relatively ineffective in treating the negative behaviors. Until relatively recently, only drugs of the phenothiazine group (especially thorazine) were available, and they are still the mainstay of treatment. Unfortunately they have a number of side effects, notably *dysphoria* (the patient doesn't feel well). There is also a serious associated spastic muscular condition known as *tardive dyskinesia,* which may not be reversible upon stopping the drug and can on occasion be fatal. Alternative drugs, known as *atypical antipsychotics,* are now available, but each has its own drawbacks. The original atypical antipsychotic was an old drug which had been marketed as an antidepressant, but discontinued when it was found to produce bone marrow suppression in some patients. It was later found to have beneficial effects in patients with schizophrenia. The patients feel well on this drug (as one would expect since it is an antidepressant) but the possibility of a fatal bone marrow dysplasia developing mandated periodic white cells counts for early detection and treatment of that condition. This added to the treatment costs and did not always prevent a dysplasia from developing. A number of other atypical antipsychotic drugs have been developed since and are thought to carry less risk of bone marrow suppression. But they can have other problems, notably that patients tend to put on weight.

The prognosis for patients with schizophrenia is very varied. Not only are there different presentations, but also differences in the severity of the presentation. In some cases a single episode, even with florid hallucinations, may pass and leave the patient relatively normal. In others, there is a progressive downhill course. The expression *schizophrenia spectrum disorders* (SSDs) is a general term sometimes used to cover all these cases. Even in the severe progressive types, the condition may burn itself out, the hallucinations cease, and the patient becomes more or less stable (though far from normal). In short, the diagnosis of schizophrenia does not necessarily spell total disability (they may be able to work in a sheltered environment), and each patient must be evaluated individually.

§ 7:15 Dementias

Dementia is loss of mental powers, such as memory and the ability to understand and think. It can be temporary, as when it is caused by drugs, reversible brain insults, and deficiency diseases, to name a few. It can also be permanent (residual effects of a head injury or birth trauma) or progressive. When the progressive type is associated with old age, it is called *senile dementia,* whereas in younger persons it is termed *presenile dementia.* Two basic patterns of dementia occurring before the senium are described and are known as *Pick's disease* and *Alzheimer's disease.* There are similarities between the two, but Pick's disease tends to involve the frontal cortex and so affects personality more. The definitive diagnosis of Alzheimer's disease is made at autopsy by microscopic finding in the brain known as *senile plaques* and *fibrillary tangles.* There are also clinical indications and psychological tests which can help in making the diagnosis while the patient is still alive, but these are not always reliable, especially in the early stages. There is commonly then a measure of doubt about the diagnosis, and cautious clinicians may prefer to describe the condition as a dementia of the Alzheimer type (DAT).

The causes of Alzheimer's disease are not completely known, though all sorts of things (from aluminum to vitamin A) have been proposed as causal factors. Some studies have suggested that there may be a genetic predisposition involved somewhere. The course is usually progressive, and no treatment has been shown to be effective. One positive item which is receiving a good deal of publicity at present is the effects of *mental activity* in preventing, or at least slowing, the progression of dementia. It has been shown that although we lose neurons with aging, mental activity stimulates the remaining ones to sprout new dendrites and make new connections with other brain cells (which increases brain power). Current policies in nursing homes, and in dealing with aging persons generally, emphasize mental stimulation and the importance of encouraging mental activities of any and every kind.

§ 7:16 Personality disorders

Personality disorders are patterns of thinking and behavior (traits) which have become maladaptive. They are not really susceptible to treatment, and so payor agencies will not reimburse for therapy where a personality disorder or mental retardation is the sole diagnosis. They can, however, be reported as important concurrent problems which affect the course and management of other treatable mental disorders. All sorts of personality types and subtypes are described in DSM-IV and ICD-10 (e.g., paranoid, schizoid, schizotypal, antisocial and obsessive-compulsive personalities). These have some importance for lawyers, in that personality can affect employability in certain occupations; and a change of personality, like that following a head injury, should then be taken into account in determining disability.

Part IV.
Standard Classifications of Mental Disorders

§ 7:17 DSM-IV and ICD-10

It is very desirable generally that there should be standard ways of describing mental disorders, as there are for other diseases. There are at least two important reasons for this. Payor agencies need to identify each disease precisely in order to know if treatment was appropriate and effective, so that the therapist should be paid. Standard communication is also necessary for researchers, who must be sure that they are talking about the same thing when they are reporting on the reliability of tests and the effectiveness of treatments.

There are basically two standard classifications of mental disorders, the Diagnostic and Statistical Manual of Mental Disorders, 4th edition (DSM-IV), and the psychiatric volume of the International Classification of Diseases, 10th edition (ICD-10). DSM was initiated because of American dissatisfaction with the preparation of the psychiatric sections of the original ICD. It was felt that the work was parcelled out to various "experts," and so did not present a common nomenclature with clear objective criteria to be met in order to include a disorder in a particular category. The validity of this objection has been acknowledged by the World Health Organization (WHO), which produces ICD, and successive versions of its mental disorders classification have brought it more and more into line with the requirements laid down by the American Psychiatric Association (APA).

It was indeed proposed by WHO that the American Psychiatric Association should join with them in the preparation of ICD-10. However, this suggestion was rejected by the APA, who went ahead with the development of DSM-IV (published in 1996; ICD-10 was published in 1991). [See Kendall RE, *Relationship between the DSM-IV and the ICD-10.* 100 (3) Journal of Abnormal Psychiatry 297-301 (Aug. 1991)] It is perhaps unfortunate that APA and WHO are still going their separate ways, but relationships between the two organizations appear to be reasonably cordial; a committee of the APA has been established to keep in touch with those working on revisions of ICD-10. Furthermore, and perhaps most fortunate of all from the point of view of compensation lawyers, there now appear to be no major differences between the two systems. The methodology of production (using field studies to test the usefulness of proposed classifications) is the same and the results do not differ on major points.

Indeed, each includes tables which indicate the equivalent term in the other. One can skip back and forth between the two if necessary. We will focus on DSM-IV here, as it is almost universally used in the U.S. (outside of hospitals, which used ICD for billing purposes).

§ 7:18 The DSM-IV reporting system.

A number of tools are provided in DSM-IV to allow reports on mental disorders to be made in a common language and standardized form. At the same time, it is recognized that some cases may not easily fit into such forms. In these circumstances, the reporter is allowed to select the nearest fit and add a note explaining any qualifying comments that appear to be needed. This is particularly likely to happen when the findings do not quite fulfil all the listed criteria for a condition, but the treating psychologist /psychistist nevertheless feels that it is the correct diagnosis in the case.

The reporting system is axial, that is to say the case is linked to five separate categories of information.

Axis I describes the particular mental disorder (or disorders) identified. These should be further identified by their coding numbers. There are literally hundreds of these, each accompanied by major and minor criteria, so that not only the diagnosis, but the grounds for making it can be explicitly stated.

Axis II reports personality disorders or mental retardation if they are present. These are not considered to be treatable, but may be reported as complicating factors in another disorder.

Axis III reports physical diseases present (e.g., diabetes mellitus) when they affect the mental condition in any way.

Axis IV reports psychosocial and environmental factors. These are important since the presence or absence of support by the family and the social environment makes a great deal of difference to management strategies, and even to outcome.

Axis V provides for global assessment of functioning (GAF). This is assessed on a percentage scale, with 100% representing normal or near-normal functioning in both occupational and social environments, while 0–10% represents cases where the patients are in danger of harming themselves or others, or are unable to manage minimal standards of self care. Eight other grades are described in between these two extremes.

Another important reporting device is the use of severity indices along with each diagnosis. A condition may be described as mild, moderate, or severe. It should also be indicated if the disorder appears to be in partial remission, or full remission. In some cases a prior history of a different but perhaps related disorder (e.g., a different kind of anxiety disorder) may be relevant.

§ 7:19 The use of DSM-IV by lawyers

The introductory sections of DSM-IV contain warnings about mechanical applications of DSM-IV in the legal setting; it is not designed to act as a statutory disability system. This warning is well taken, yet nevertheless, the DSM-IV categories with their accompanying criteria are a most useful instrument for lawyers trying to evaluate mental impairments. Establishing medical disability in mental disorders (or any other kind of disease) requires three things:

1. An accepted diagnosis
2. An estimate of the severity of the condition
3. An assessment of its effects on occupation, social function and on personal life

The DSM system helps in all these items. It allows compensationists evaluating a case to look at the psychiatrist's or psychologist's report and use it to meet compensation requirements. It also provides an opportunity to question experts further about the evidence upon which their opinions are based. A psychiatrist who has given an opinion that a claimant has a major depressive disorder, or suffers from post-traumatic stress disorder, can be asked which items in the patient's medical record were used to meet the DSM criteria and make the diagnosis. The expert can hardly claim to have ignored DSM-IV in the process, since reimbursement depends on its use. At the very least, he should have made some statement explaining why he was varying from the DSM system. This is permitted, since one cannot expect every patient to fit neatly into a little box. But although variance from the DSM schema is permitted, the clinician must explain why the patient has been assigned to a particular diagnostic category, even though the patient did not fit all the criteria.

§ 7:20 The use of psychological tests and inventories — the MMPI

Psychological tests commonly take the form of lists of questions *(inventories)* which subjects may answer on their own, or with the assistance of a technician or psychologist. *Performance tests* require subjects to carry out some task, e.g. calculate with numbers or some such. There are also *projection tests,* where subjects interpret drawings or blots (the Rorschach test) or tells a story interpreting a picture card (Thematic Apperception Test). These performances are used to provide insight into patients' mental conditions. Projection tests have been generally viewed with some suspicion in the legal setting, taking the view that ten psychologists could have ten different interpretations of these tests. But this may change, since scoring protocols have been developed, which make interpretation much more uniform (rater /rater reliability), and performance tests are acquiring a much better reputation among mental health professionals.

There are now thousands of psychological tests, and there is at least one for any condition that one might encounter. It is important in presenting test results for legal purposes to be sure that the tests in question have been well validated and are considered reliable in the scientific community. One of the best known of these is the *Minnesota Multiphasic Personality Inventory* (MMPI). This consists of over five hundred questions which the subject answers (yes /no) unaided. The questions and responses are then separated out into a number of *scales*, representing all sorts of categories such as *paranoia*, *schizophrenia*, *depression*, and *mania,* to name a few. There are usually about 13 clinical scales, but as many as two hundred may be used. There are also *reliability scales* which determine whether the subject was answering the questions honestly, or malingering or answering at random (*joy riding*). The data can be analyzed by the psychologist (using a scoring protocol) or processed by a computer. The latter does not replace expert evaluation. It is simply an alternative tool. But

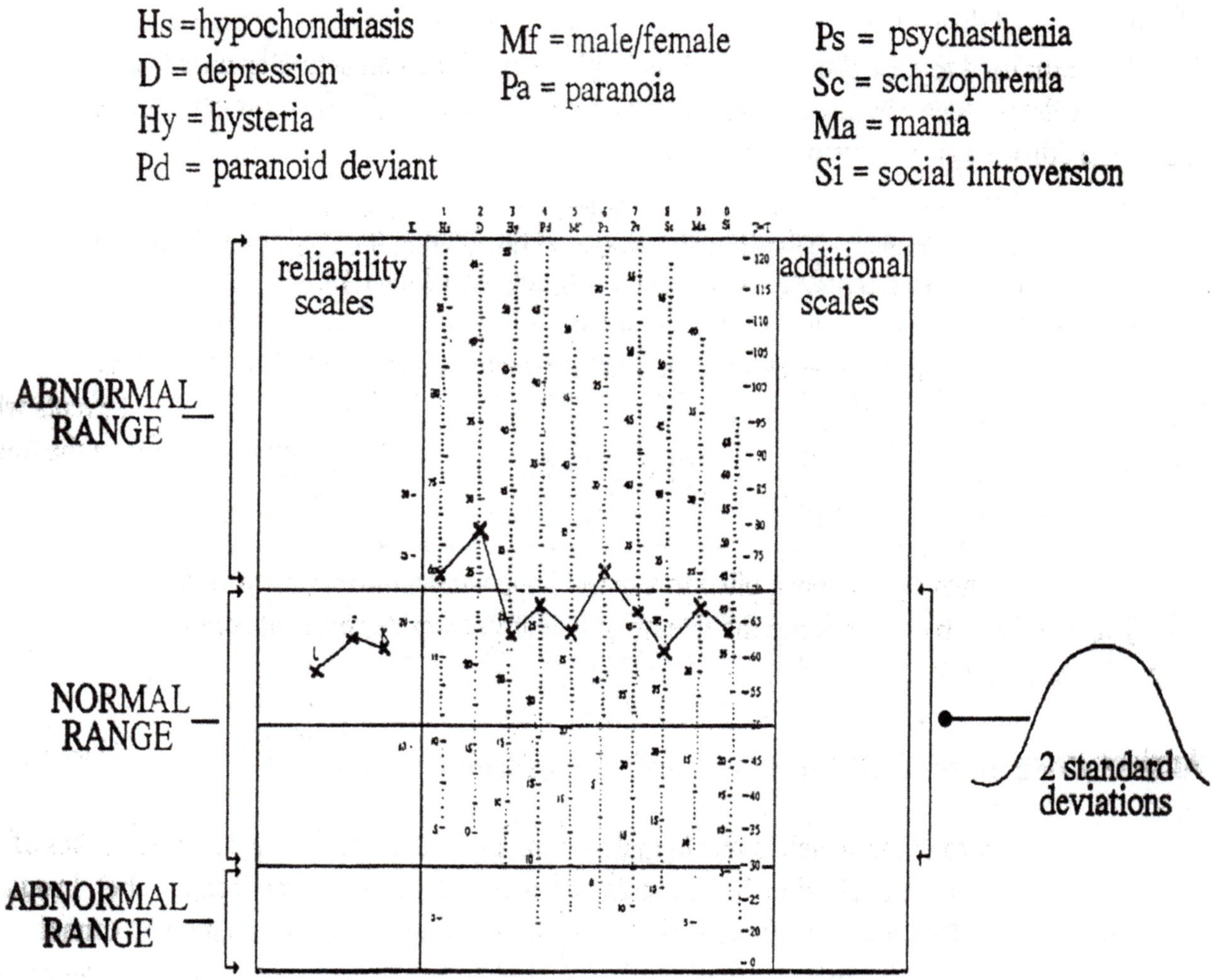

Fig. 7-2 Diagrammatic representation of an MMPI test result

computer analysis is now considered very reliable and has obvious features which would recommend it to lawyers. The results of an MMPI test are presented in the form of a linear graph [see Fig. 7-2].

It is important to remember a few things in interpreting an MMPI result.

1. A single scale cannot be used on its own to reach a conclusion. An elevated paranoia (Pa) score does not mean that the subject is paranoid, or even that he /she has a paranoid personality trait. They simply may be a strong critical thinker. The results in all the scales must be put together, using a scoring protocol, before the diagnosis is made.

2. The MMPI is not intended to be used independently of clinical opinion, but rather to support it. The clinician must incorporate the MMPI results into what is known about the general condition of the patient.

3. The MMPI is a screening test (like the serum multianalyzer in the biochemistry lab). Any diagnoses that it suggests should be confirmed with other more specific tests, like the Beck Depression Scale or the Hamilton Anxiety Scale.

§ 7:21 The objectivity and reliability of psychiatric opinion

It is often stated that if you have two psychiatrists or psychologists, you would have two opinions. If this was ever true, it is no longer so. An opinion, accompanied by DSM criteria and supported with objective testing, is likely to be at least as reliable as any medical opinion. One small study, which used only a few psychiatrists and a few "patients," found agreement as to the diagnosis between the clinicians in only 35% of the cases. This sounds like a very low level of inter-rater reliability. However, further analysis showed that some of the "patients" (who were actors) had changed their story between interviews, and this was held to account for 5% of the discrepancies. It was also found that a number of the differences were merely verbal, with different clinicians using different names for much the same diagnosis. When all these errors were taken into account, the level of agreement was almost 70%, and few medical diagnoses are made with greater reliability ratings than this. If it is further remembered that this rather odd study was carried out using only 20-minute interviews, with artificial subjects and without the benefit of confirmatory testing, it seems to support the view that good psychiatric opinion compares well with medical diagnostic opinion in physical ailments.

Short Working Vocabulary of Psychiatric Terms

Abstraction: The ability to think abstractly, seeing connections and resemblances between separate things. Concrete thinking, with loss of the ability to abstract, is found in schizophrenic disorders.

Affect: Feeling or emotion. Generally used for more fluctuating rather than steady emotional states (See also *Mood).* Affect may be described as restricted (reduced level of feeling); or blunted (very much reduced level of feeling); or flat (poverty of emotion), where there is little or no sign of emotion at all. This latter is found in severe depressive states and in some kinds of schizophrenia and schizophrenia spectrum disorders. Rapidly changeable emotional responses may be termed *labile affect.*

Agitation: Excess motor activity associated with anxiety or tension. Movements are rather random and non-purposive in type, like moving around rapidly, wringing the hands, fidgeting, or blinking.

Agonist: Term used to describe a muscle which directly performs an action or movement; it can a be applied to a drug which directly activates a body function (by releasing a neural transmitter substance or in some other way). [See also *Antagonist.*]

Alogia: Term used to describe reduction or absence of the amount of speaking (poverty of speech), or in the quantum of information that is contained in it (poverty of ideas).

Amnesia: Loss of memory for events which were experienced and noted at one time. It is a common event following a significant head injury. *Anterograde amnesia* is loss of memory about events which followed a traumatic episode. *Retrograde amnesia* involves events which happened before the traumatic episode, when the patient was alert and conscious.

Antagonist: Term which may be applied to a muscle opposing a movement or to a drug which abates a body function, e.g., by suppressing the release of a neurotransmitter or its attachment to a receptor on a neuron. [See also *Agonist.*]

Anxiety: Inappropriate degree of apprehension accompanied by negative behavior (avoidance).

Aphasia: Inability to speak which is due to malfunctioning of the brain rather than the organs of speech. It is termed *motor aphasia* when the problem is in Broca's motor speech center (in the frontal lobe). In *auditory aphasia* Wernicke's auditory speech center in the temporal lobe is involved; patients cannot respond with speech because they do not understand what is said to them. The ability to understand written speech is located in the occipital cortex, and problems here are termed *alexia* (inability to read words) or *dyslexia* (difficulty in reading words).

Catalepsy: A condition where the body is maintained immobile in the same position for a significant period of time.

Catatonia: Often used to describe the fixed postures of catatonic schizophrenia, but may be a general term for abnormalities of motor behavior including purposeless motor activity and inappropriate behavior such as negativism (refusing to follow instructions or doing the opposite of what is ordered).

Conversion: A neurological impairment (deafness, blindness, etc.) which is not due to physical causes, but is an unconscious response (or at least not deliberate) to psychological problems.

Defense mechanisms: Mental ploys designed to mitigate or otherwise deal with unpleasant experiences, e.g., by suppressing or denying the presence of an illness in oneself or a near relative.

Delirium: A state where consciousness and cognition are both impaired. It must be distinguished from *dementia* where consciousness is generally preserved. Delirium may be due to all sorts of causes, such as high fever, drugs (or withdrawal from drugs), and certain medical conditions especially *encephalitis.*

Delusion: A false but unshakable belief (not affected by contrary evidence) based on an incorrect interpretation of events that are actually presented to the subject, like the notion that everyone knows what the subject is thinking (thought broadcasting). If the false notion is not irresistible but open to doubt, it many be called an *illusion.* Where the subject is able to entertain the idea that the belief may be false, it may be called merely an *overvalued idea.* [See also *Hallucination.*]

Dementia of the Alzheimer's type: Term used when Alzheimer's disease is strongly suspected, but not known with certainty to be the diagnosis.

Dementia: Condition characterized by cognitive impairments, especially memory loss.

Derealization: Where the world and events taking place in it somehow seem unreal, as if they were a dream.

Dipolar mood disorder: One characterized by both mania (or hypomania) and depression. Both may be present together, one or other may be predominant, or they can follow one another in succession.

Disorientation: Unwarranted confusion as to time, place or circumstances.

Dissociative identity disorder: The current DSM-IV term for what was formerly called multiple personality disorder.

Distractibility: Where attention is easily turned from one object or topic to another.

Dysarthria: Difficulty in articulating speech (the problem is in the mechanics of speech, not in the brain). Cerebral causes of speech problems are called **dysphasia.**

Dyssomnias: Disorders of sleep.

Echolalia: Where patients repeats everything that is said to them.

Echopraxia: The patient imitates every action done by another person.

Flashback: Vividly reliving a past (unpleasant) event while still awake.

Flight of ideas: A pattern of speech, typical of mania, where one phrase or expression is followed by others which are inappropriate but not totally disconnected. Thus the key word in a sentence or phrase may rhyme with a word in the preceding expression, or resemble it in some other way.

Gender identity: Belief on the part of persons that they are male (or female).

Gender dysphoria: Feeling uncomfortable about one's sexual orientation.

Grandiosity: Inappropriately exalted view of oneself or one's personal abilities. Very bizarre and persistent ideas (despite contrary evidence) are described as *grandiose delusions.*

Hallucination: A false idea that has no basis whatsoever in reality; it is not a misperception of something (which would be a delusion). Hallucinations may be sounds (auditory hallucinations) sights (visual hallucinations) touches (tactile hallucinations) or tastes (gustatory hallucinations). Notions about one's body (e.g. that there are no internal organs) are called *somatic hallucinations.*

Hypomania: A less severe form of mania where there is expansive mood, grandiose ideation, and pressured speech, but without delusions.

Ideas of reference: The notion that unrelated incidents and statements are directed at the patient. "The newscaster is speaking about me." When such notions are firmly and unshakably believed, they may be called *delusions of reference.*

Ideation: Mental contents or thoughts, like paranoid ideation, or suicidal ideation.

Insomnia: Difficulty in sleeping: difficulty in falling asleep is *initial insomnia*; *middle insomnia* is wakening in the middle of the night but later falling asleep again; *terminal insomnia* is wakening early and being unable to go back to sleep.

Magical thinking: The belief that one can do miracles by means of words or ritual acts.

Mania: A serious disorder characterized by expansive mood, grandiose delusions and pressured speech. [See also *Hypomania.*]

MAST: Michigan Alcohol Screening Test.

MMPI: Minnesota Multiphasic Personality Inventory.

MMPI-2: Second edition of the Minnesota Multiphasic Personality Inventory. It is shorter and therefore less expensive than MMP-1. It is essentially an improved version of MMPI-1. By virtue of its newness, it lacked the extensive validation of MMPI-1 and there was for a time some hesitancy about using it. However, it is now generally held to be as reliable as MMPI-1.

Mood congruence: Term used to describe delusions or hallucinations which, though odd, nevertheless fit in with or are appropriate to an abnormal mood (e.g., depression or mania) that is present. When they are not appropriate to the dominant mood, they are called *mood incongruent* delusions or hallucinations.

Mood: Sustained and persistent emotional feeling that colors all activities and thoughts like depressed mood, anxious mood, feeling excessively good (euphoria), feeling poorly about things (dysphoria), feeling over-optimistic and bold (expansive mood), and so on. Normal mood is called *euthymia,* and unhappy mood is *dysthymia.*

MSE: Mental status examination. The psychiatric equivalent of the history and physical in medical practice, but employing only observation and interview. Like the H&P, the questions and observations are reported in due order so that nothing may be left out or forgotten.

Mutism: Where the patient, although capable of speech, does not speak at all.

Neologisms: Newly created words; production of neologisms is found in certain kinds of schizophrenic disorder.

Neuroleptic malignant syndrome: General term covering a group of serious side effects that occur with phenothiazine tranquilizers, especially in high doses. These include tardive dyskinesia (especially with a stiff face and tongue) and anticholinergic effects (where the parasympathetic system is blocked). These latter are the most dangerous effects and in severe cases, patients can develop hallucinations, seizures and cardiac arrhythmias and may die. The problem will sometimes, but not always, resolve on discontinuing the medication.

Neurosis: A general term for a dysfunctional mental condition where the subject remains in touch with reality; this term is still used on occasion but not considered very useful.

Obsessive compulsive disorder: Disorder characterized by repetitive acts (movements or speech) which patients feels obliged to carry out, although aware that they are senseless and in some cases (as with obscene language) repugnant to them.

NMS: Neuroleptic malignant syndrome.

OCD: Obsessive compulsive disorder.

Paced Auditory Serial Addition (test): A form of standardized psychological testing which is particularly useful in detecting subtler forms of intellectual impairment. Standard numbers are presented to the test subject to be added together, and this is done with increasing complexity and varying speeds. The number of errors at each speed is noted, and this information is used to produce a combined numerical result for the test. This is considered a very sensitive way to detect minimal brain damage following a head injury.

Panic attack: Term used to describe an episode where the subject suddenly experiences an inappropriate sensation of intense fear. This is usually accompanied by other things such as palpitations, chest pains, sweating and a feeling of impending death.

Phobia: Irrational fear linked to specific objects or situations, e.g., *acrophobia* (fear of heights), *claustrophobia* (fear of enclosed spaces) or *agoraphobia* (fear of the open).

Pressured speech: Where words pour out of the subject, very rapidly and emphatically (like water under pressure). As with flight of ideas, this is a very characteristic finding in mania.

Prodromal: A period before and leading up to a full-blown illness. Many mental conditions, like schizophrenic episodes and obsessive compulsive disorders, are preceded by a prodromal phase. The full blown disease state which follows is called the *active phase* (florid phase) and the remaining (still abnormal) condition, when the active phases has blown over, is called the *residual phase.*

Psychomotor retardation: Where motor activity is slowed down, as happens in depressive disorders (e.g., it takes all day to make the breakfast).

Psychomotor agitation: [See *Agitation*]

Psychosis: General term for a mental state where subjects are out of touch with reality, i.e., they are having hallucinations or delusions, and they are not aware that they are false.

Schizoid personality disorder: A condition, usually appearing in early adulthood, characterized by detachment from other persons and emotional detachment generally (patient has very few emotions). These patients are loners and rarely marry. They have difficulty making decisions (poor responders) and this may affect their ability to be gainfully employed. It can be associated with *temporal lobe epilepsy* which in turn may be the result of head trauma.

Schizophrenia spectrum disorder: A general term used to cover the entire spectrum of schizophrenia-like illnesses, ranging from fulminant schizophrenia with hallucinations and delusions, to odd aloof personality traits.

Schizotypal personality disorder: A personality disorder which becomes apparent in childhood, characterized by aloofness, odd ideas (strange fantasies) and idiosyncratic language. Only a very few of these children go on to develop schizophrenia; they just remain odd.

Stressor: A life event (e.g., the death of a loved one or loss of one's job) likely to initiate or produce a mental disorder such as *anxiety* or *depression*.

Temporal lobe syndrome: General term covering the three presentations which (separately or in combination) are associated with temporal lobe damage. These are temporal lobe epilepsy (TLE), schizophrenia spectrum disorders, and personality changes (temporal lobe personality).

Trait: A persistent pattern of behavior. Thus a personality trait is a persistent pattern of perceiving, interpreting and responding to one's environment.

Dictated and transcribed report of psychiatric history and physical examination

Patient's Name: William Walton

Date of Service: 1/1/2005
Date dictated: 1/1/2005
Date typed: 1/1/2005

PSYCHIATRIC EVALUATION:

IDENTIFICATION: Patient is a 36-year-old single white male who lives with his brother and sister-in-law. Patient was originally referred to us by his family physician who has persuaded him to return here for evaluation and treatment.

CHIEF COMPLAINT: Patient expresses a desire to resume his medications.

PSYCHIATRIC HISTORY: Patient was seen here four years ago (2001) and treated for schizophrenia. Patient missed a scheduled appointment three months ago as he felt he was improving and did not need his medications any longer. Since that time his auditory hallucinations have returned i.e., voices calling his name, and telling him to do bad things, such as to harm himself and destroy things. He does not recognize the voices as belonging to anyone that he knows. He now realizes his problems have returned and are not likely to get better so that he needs to get back on his medications. He has had difficulty maintaining male/female relationships and is currently living with his oldest brother and his brother's wife. He has been unable to work due to the voices telling him to do things he realized he should not be doing, but he was not willing to particularize the auditory hallucinations at this time. Patient had been started on medications the last time he was here, but cannot remember the names of any of them. He states that one of them was helpful for his depression. He thought the other medications were for the hallucinations, ? Haldol and one other, but he could not be sure of the names. He has a past history of substance abuse but denies using any illegal substances in the past several years.

FAMILY HISTORY: Patient has three brothers and one sister who are all in good health. Patient is the youngest of the four siblings. His mother is alive, aged 56, his father, aged 60 is also alive. Both parents are in good health. He denies any family history of mental illness or substance abuse. He denies current legal problems although he has had at least one DWI conviction in the past.

MENTAL STATUS EXAMINATION: This young adult male was alert and cooperative, neatly dressed and well groomed, though with gait somewhat slowed. Mood appeared depressed and affect was congruent. Facies was flat and expressionless and mannerisms likewise as he relayed his symptoms. Patient denies paranoid ideations or delusions of grandeur. Insight and judgment are impaired but denies suicidal/homicidal ideation or plans.

DIAGNOSIS/IMPRESSION:

Axis I:	Schizophrenia, recurrent.
Axis II:	Personality disorder, not otherwise specified.
Axis III:	History of migraine headaches.
	No known drug allergies.

Axis IV: Stressors - difficulty maintaining employment and relationships.
Axis V: GAF: current 45; best in past year 55.

PLAN: 1. Start patient on an atypical antipsychotic medication. We will provide samples for a trial period. If this works well for him we will give him a prescription on his next visit. We will restart his SSRI antidepressant as this apparently has worked well for him in the past.

2. Patient will schedule an appointment one month from now to see me for reevaluation of his medications and in the meantime will need to see his therapist/social worker (appointments already arranged).

Willard I. Heal MD

FOLLOW UP APPOINTMENT

Date of service: 1/1/05
Date dictated: 3/3/2005
Date typed: 3/3/2005

IDENTIFICATION: Patient is a 36-year-old Caucasian male with a history of schizophrenia and personality disorder NOS. Patient states he has been compliant with his medication during the last month with no side effects, and that he is doing well. He has no problems with appetite, sleep, constipation, or gait.

MENTAL STATUS: Patient is alert and oriented times three. He is well groomed with good eye contact, and his speech is normal in volume and tone. There is no thought disorder, hallucinations, delusions, or paranoia. In particular his auditory hallucinations have ceased. Patient denies suicidal/homicidal ideation or plan.

PLAN: We will continue patient on his current regimen of medications: Haldol 5 mg p.o. h.s. and Cogentin 1 mg p.o. h.s. Patient is given prescriptions with two refills. He will continue to see his psychiatric social worker and will make a follow up appointment for three months.

Willard I. Heal MD

Chapter Eight

The Heart and Cardiovascular Disability

§ 8:1 Introduction — the meaning of the term *cardiovascular*

The principal item in the cardiovascular system is, of course, the heart itself, yet the heart is not an isolated organ, but ultimately related to every other part and aspect of the body. It is, however, in direct communication with the blood and lymph vessels and their contents; all these together (heart, vessels and their contents) are described as the cardiovascular system.

In considering the cardiovascular system, the following topics will be discussed.

- The *anatomy and physiology* of the heart itself.
- The *circulatory system in general*, dealing with how blood and its contents are carried and distributed throughout the body.
- *Local circulatory systems*; discussing important subsystems such as the cerebral circulation, the renal circulation, and the coronary vessels (supplying the heart).
- *Fluid dynamics*. The circulatory fluids, blood and lymph (the vascular space), are in dynamic equilibrium with the other fluid compartments of the body (the intracellular and extracellular spaces) [see Fig. 8-1]. The interrelationships of the contents of these compartments are a vast topic on their own, far beyond the scope of a work such as this. However, there will be some discussion of blood and fluid replacement under the topic of "shock" [see § 8:28 infra].

§ 8:2 The legal importance of the cardiovascular system

Lawyers mainly encounter cardiac and cardiovascular problems in relation to disability questions, such as Social Security. Since, however, the heart is a vital organ of the body, cardiac problems can enter into and affect any compensation question. The disability resulting from any injury will be greatly increased if there is a heart disorder as well. It is important, then, to know how cardiovascular conditions present, and how they interact with other injuries and illnesses.

Cardiovascular conditions can affect virtually any organ in the body in several ways. Tiny blood clots, accretions on the heart valves, or on the intimal surface of large vessels, can break loose and float (embolize) to the brain or the lung or any other organ, to cause injury or even death. Very low blood pressure, such as can occur in severe acute hemorrhage or in shock, can reduce blood flow in the brain to produce a cerebral infarct. Conversely, the

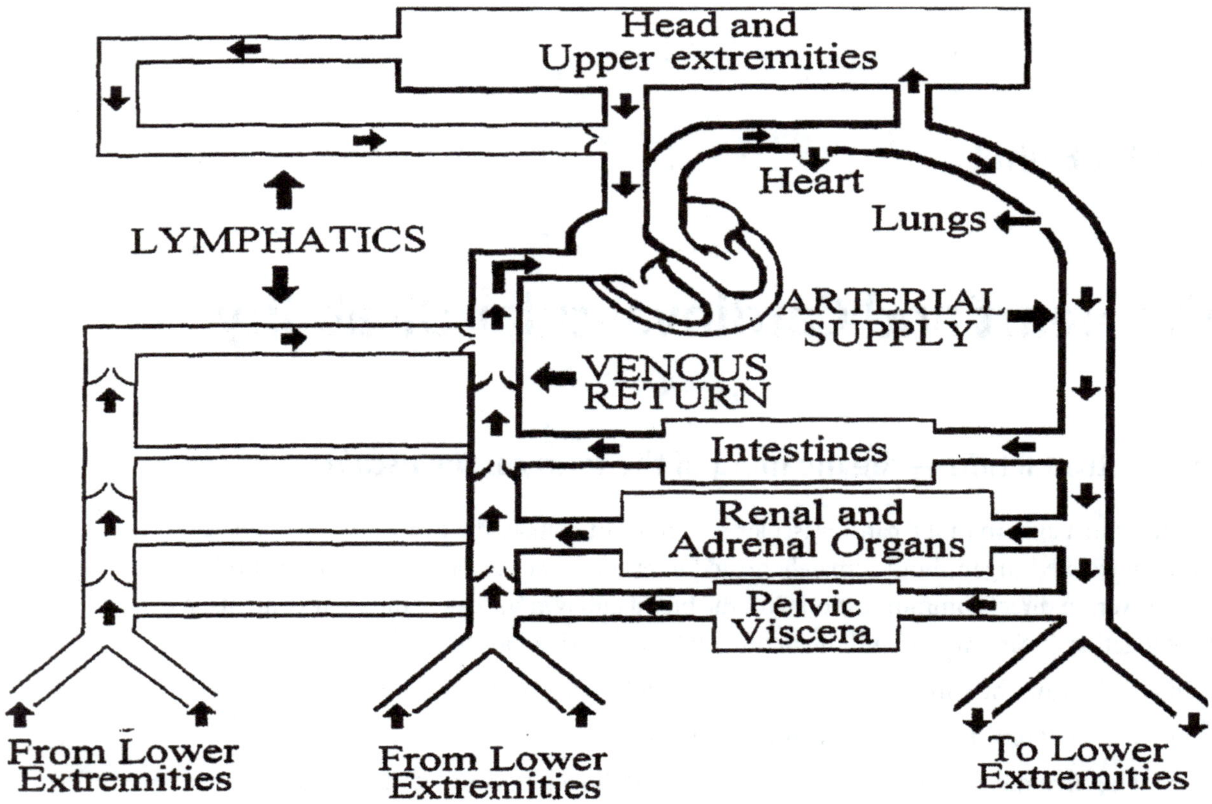

Fig. 8-1 Diagram of the circulatory system

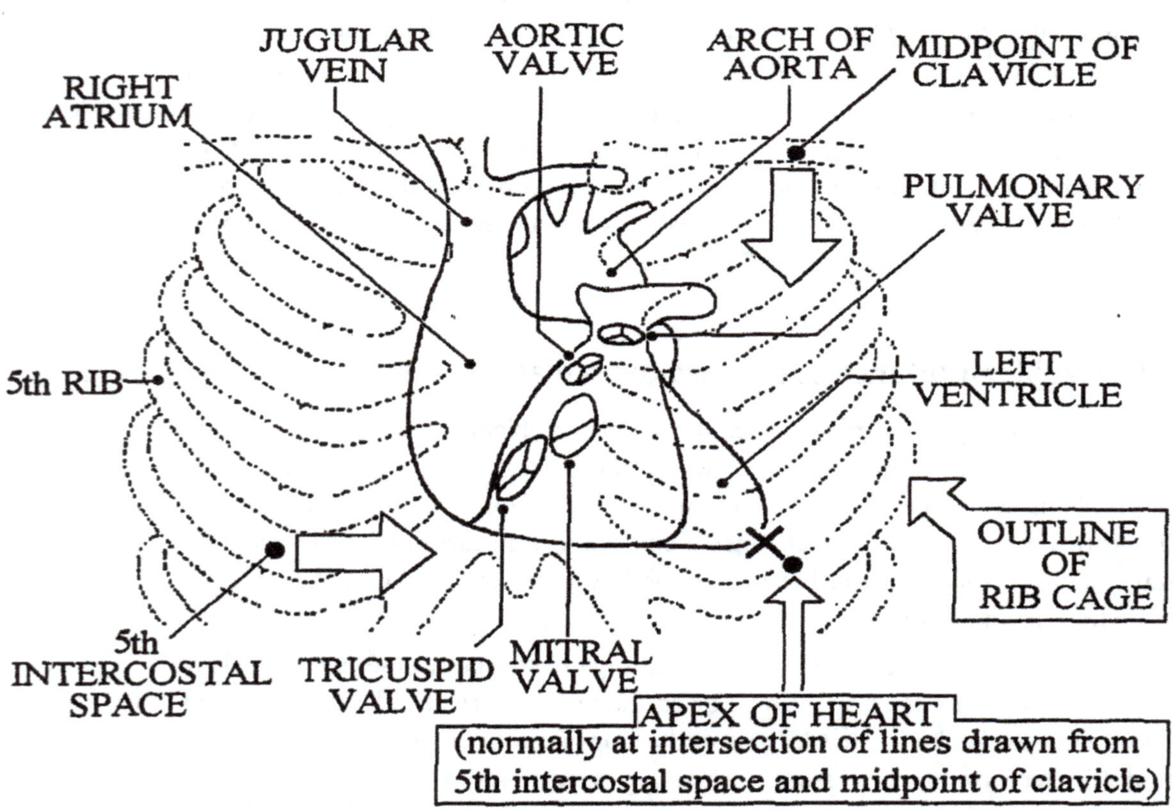

Fig. 8-2 The precordium — approximate site of important cardiac organs

cardiovascular system can itself be affected as the result of injuries elsewhere in the body. The clotting mechanisms of the blood can be affected by serious trauma so that the patient hemorrhages in all sorts of places in the body, a condition which is called *disseminated intravascular coagulation* (DIC). Cardiovascular complications such as these can accompany or be precipitated by other injuries. Thus even where the heart and circulatory system are not directly involved, it can be difficult or even impossible to understand what is happening, without some understanding of cardiovascular medicine.

§ 8:3 Cardiac diseases and cardiac disability

Almost any kind of heart disease process can produce cardiac malfunction, but there are three recognized categories of cardiac disability. These are associated with:

- Cardiac arrhythmias
- Cardiac pain
- Heart failure

1. Cardiac arrhythmias may be occasional and asymptomatic, e.g., the occasional ectopic beat. When they are frequent enough or severe enough to be noticeable, they can be disabling, even though cardiac output is reasonably well maintained. Runs of atrial (supraventricular) *tachycardia* produce dizziness, and some ectopics produce such a forceful contraction that it can be felt in the chest. The awareness on the part of the patient that the heart is malfunctioning can cause severe anxiety, and commonly a visit to the doctor or an emergency room. However, proof of disability requires more than showing an abnormal EKG rhythm strip. It must be evidenced that the episodes were frequent, at least once a week, and that they occurred despite optimal treatment. This requires a showing that the patient was taking her medications properly, and blood levels of these drugs may be needed to see if they were being properly absorbed into the body. Arrhythmias, however, seldom give rise to disability. The reason for this is that they can be very effectively treated in most cases. A pacemaker can be inserted, which can both diagnose the problem, e.g., a run of tachycardia or atrial fibrillation, and also deal with it by taking over the pacing of the heart or directly administering shock treatment.

2. Pain of cardiac origin is a more subjective matter, and the suspicion that it is factitious (due to somatizing or malingering) may need to be overcome. Confirmatory evidence of cardiac ischemia (especially stress testing) will be important here. The pain must be "too frequent" and also have persisted despite optimal treatment. But cardiac ischemia is not usually disabling since it can be corrected surgically. [See § 8:17.]

3. *Heart failure* (cardiac decompensation) is commonly involved in disability determinations because, unlike arrhythmias and cardiac pain, it is difficult to treat. Heart failure is defined as a condition where cardiac output cannot meet body requirements, and it is distinguished accordingly into two kinds, high output and low output failure. *High output failure* is where body metabolism is in overdrive, so that even a normal heart cannot keep up with its demands. This occurs in such diseases as *hyperthyroidism* or in *malignant hyperthermia* (a nasty complication of general anesthesia) where metabolic processes are accelerated with exorbitant oxygen and fuel requirements and enormous generation of waste products (like carbon dioxide and waste acids). Faced with

such impossible demands and an unfavorable environment, the normal heart fails. *Low output failure* is much more common, and more often found in legal disability determinations. This is where the heart is not putting out enough blood to meet the ordinary demands of the normal body. Low output failure is usually the result of atherosclerotic heart disease, especially following a myocardial infarction, when all sorts of mechanisms may reduce cardiac output. These include arrhythmias of various kinds, ventricular aneurysms which produce to-and-fro movement of blood in the left ventricle, and incompetence of the heart valves from damage to the chordae tendineae which tie down the valve cusps. Most commonly, however, it is simply due to loss of functioning heart muscle. Heart failure may also be caused by left ventricular enlargement. The ventricles enlarge naturally when it is necessary to improve performance, for as heart muscle fibers lengthen they contract more forcibly. But beyond a certain point, this mechanism fails (the muscle fibers become too long to contract properly) and cardiac output then declines (low output failure). *Dilated hypertrophy* of the heart is commonly due to prolonged overwork, as in untreated hypertension, but idiopathic types (cause unknown) occur. Some of these are familial (hereditary), and it is expected that the others will in time prove to be genetic in origin. When the idiopathic enlargement is due to increased thickness of the heart wall, this is called *idiopathic hypertrophic cardiomyopathy*. When it consists mainly of dilatation of the chambers it is termed *idiopathic dilated cardiomyopathy*. These idiopathic (hereditary) myopathic heart diseases are the commonest conditions requiring heart transplant.

Part I. Anatomy and Physiology

§ 8:4 General description of the heart

The human heart is a four chambered vessel (a frog's heart has only three). Two of these are receiving chambers called *atria* (a Latin term for "the porch" or "entry room of a house") and the others, the main pumping chambers, are called *ventricles* ("little stomachs" in Latin). [See Fig. 8-3.] The *right atrium* receives venous blood from the head and arms via the *superior vena cava* and from the rest of the body through the *inferior vena cava*. This venous blood, low in oxygen and high in carbon dioxide, flows (with a little assistance from the right atrium) into the *right ventricle*, whence it is propelled through the pulmonary artery into and through the lungs. The *left atrium* receives the freshly oxygenated blood from the lungs and transmits it into the *left ventricle*, the main pumping chamber of the heart. From here it is propelled with considerable force into the *aorta* (the main vessel in the arterial tree) and to the rest of the body.

Abnormal openings in the partitions between the chambers are called *septal defects* (popularly known as "holes" in the heart), and they can affect cardiac function in several ways. If the defects are large enough they can cause *shunts* where venous blood is diverted out of its normal course through the heart and lungs so that it is not reoxygenated. This may produce all sorts of problems which will be discussed (briefly) later in this chapter. Collections of fibrin and other materials can collect round the margins of septal defects and are known as *vegetations*. Bacteria can grow in these vegetations, producing *endocarditis*; pieces of the vegetations can break off and embolize to the lung, brain or some other part of the body.

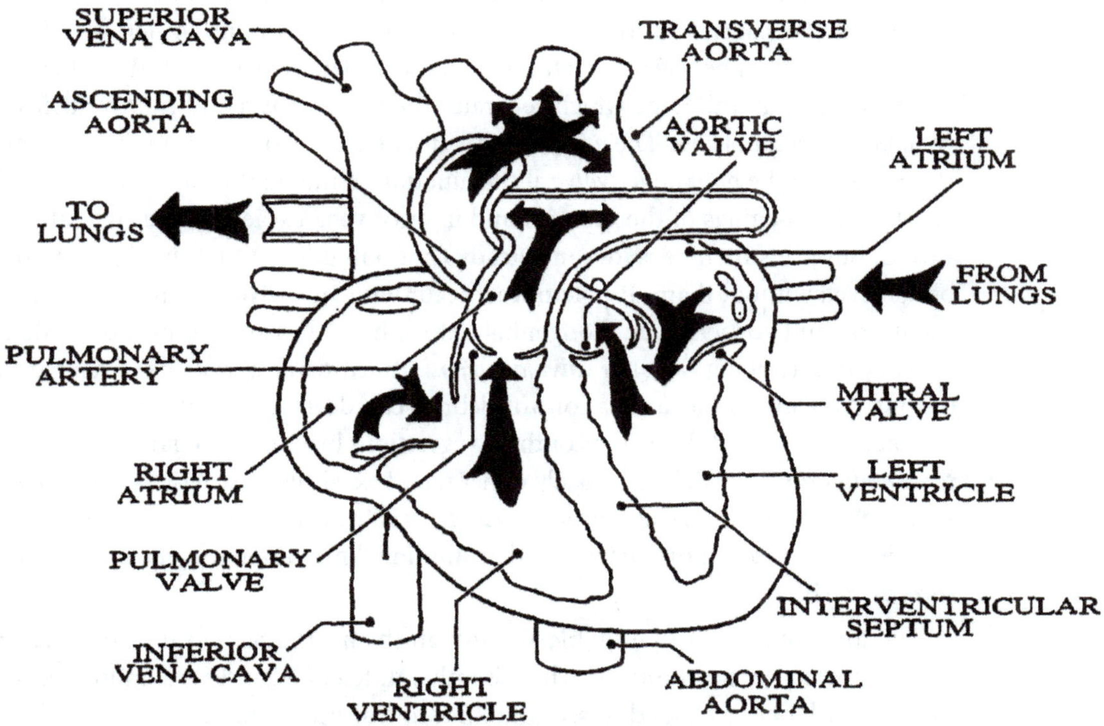

Fig. 8-3 Blood flow through the heart and lungs

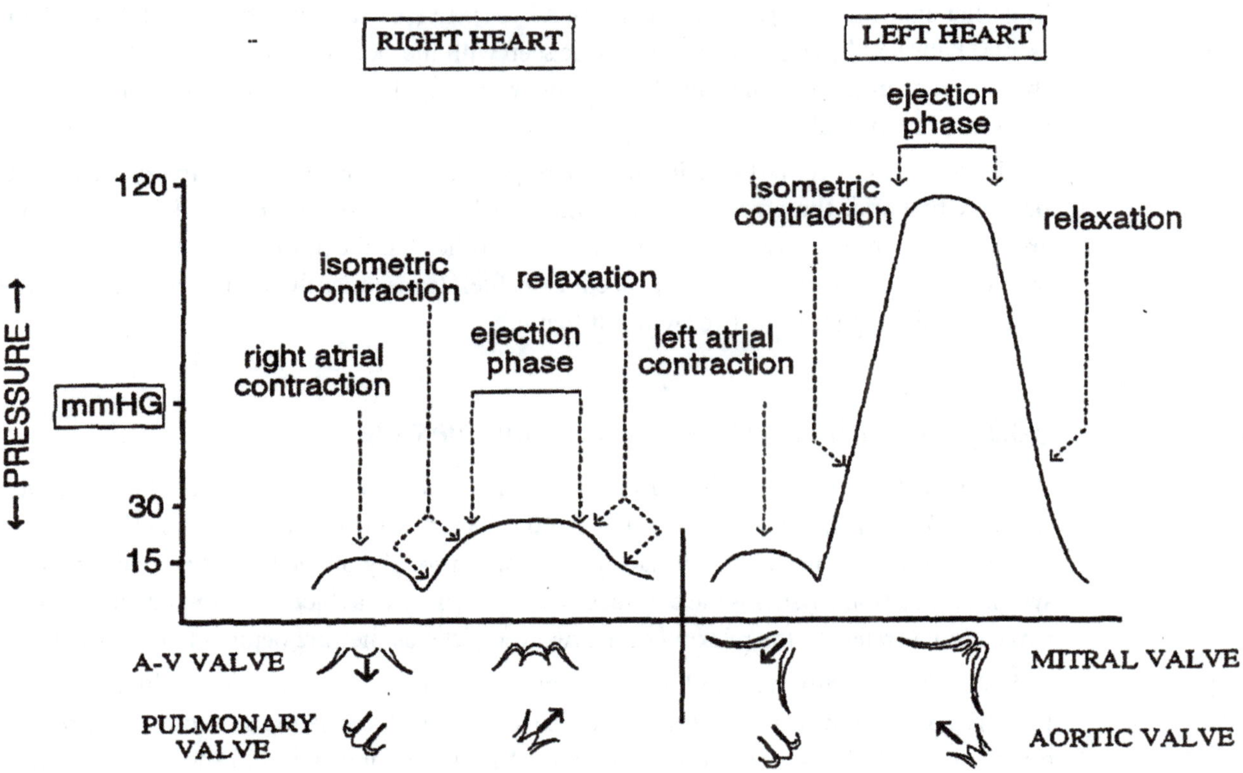

Fig. 8-4 The cardiac cycle

The forward flow of blood through the heart is controlled by valves. [See Fig. 8-3] The *mitral valve* (so called because its two leaves intruding down into the left ventricle resemble a bishop's hat) lies between the left atrium and the left ventricle. All the others have three leaves (cusps), and the one which separates the right atrium and right ventricle is in fact called the *tricuspid valve.* The *aortic valve* is situated at the outlet from the left ventricle into the aorta, and the *pulmonary valve* at the junction of the right ventricle and the pulmonary vessels. The openings of the superior and inferior vena cavae into the right atrium are not valved, but pressure here is low and steady (not pulsatile) so that the direction of flow can be achieved without them. Problems can occur with any valve, but are most common with the mitral and aortic valves. Congenital deformity or disease can produce either *valvular incompetence* (leaking valve) or *valvular stenosis* (narrow valve) both of which reduce cardiac output. *Vegetations* (accumulations of debris) can develop on deformed valves and these may become infected. Infections of these vegetations by virulent organisms cause *acute bacterial endocarditis* which is fortunately rather rare. Less virulent bacteria (such as Streptococcus viridans), can colonize on abnormal valves, especially during dental or urological procedures, and these produce a more chronic and grumbling illness known as *subacute bacterial endocarditis* (SABE).

The force required to pump blood through the heart and into the body is supplied by the *myocardium* or heart muscle; which is rather different from skeletal muscle or the smooth muscle which lines the blood vessels, intestines and airways. The various cells which comprise the heart muscle are intimately linked together and seem to be a single multinucleated muscle cell when viewed by the ordinary light microscope. The heart was indeed termed by earlier anatomists a *syncytium* (compound cell). In fact, however, there are fine divisions (septa) between the cells which can only be seen with the electron microscope. Nevertheless, the different units of heart muscle act synchronously, like a single cell, so that the older view was functionally correct.

Heart muscle is remarkable in another respect, also. Skeletal muscle uses glucose as its primary fuel and, therefore, tires and functions badly as metabolites build up within and around it during exercise. Heart muscle on the other hand can use the waste products of the body's metabolism (e.g. lactate /acetate) as fuel. Consequently, it can keep working day and night throughout our lives without tiring.

§ 8:5 The cardiac cycle — systole and diastole

The repeated relaxing (filling) and contracting (emptying) of the heart is known as the *cardiac cycle* [see Fig. 8-4], and each time that the heart fills and empties again may be regarded as one turn of the wheel. The cardiac cycle is conventionally divided into two major phases, systole and diastole. *Systole* is the contraction of the ventricles as blood is pumped out of them, while *diastole* refers to the relaxing of the two ventricles as they are being refilled with blood.

Systole begins with the simultaneous contraction of the two ventricles, right and left. At first this contraction acts against the closed valves and produces increased ventricular pressure but no flow. Then, as pressure within the ventricles rises above that in the vessels distal to them (the pulmonary artery and the aorta), the valves passively open and blood flows through them into the large vessels beyond. Retrograde flow from the ventricles back into the atria during systole is prevented by the closing of the *atrioventricular valves* (A-V valves).

The tricuspid and mitral valves are in fact tied to the ventricular walls by *chordae tendineae* (tendinous cords) which prevent them from ballooning up into the atria during systole. So restrained, the surfaces of the valve cusps come together during systole and effectively prevent regurgitation into the atria. The chordae tendineae are supplied with tiny muscles which adjust their length and tension appropriately as the heart chambers contract. One of the serious complications of a *myocardial infarction* (MI) is that these little muscles may infarct and rupture. The mitral valve cusps may then be pushed too far upwards into the left atrium during systole, or even float free, with serious and even disastrous effects on cardiac output. As the ventricles contract in systole, flow is at first very rapid but later slows. When pressure in the ventricles drops below that in the outflow vessels, the pulmonary and aortic valves will close again, and blood will flow into the ventricles from the atria; systole ends and diastole begins.

Diastole is at first a passive affair, as the relaxation of the ventricular walls reduces pressures below those in the atria so that the valves open and filling of the ventricles begins. Part way through this process, however, the atria contract and push an additional bolus of blood into the distending ventricles—the active phase. This additional atrial contraction is important. When it is lost, as in atrial fibrillation, the ventricles do not fill completely, and cardiac output will drop by approximately 25%.

Pressures rise and fall in the heart with each relaxation and contraction of the heart muscle, and there is a good deal of difference between the ranges of pressure found in the different chambers. Since the atria only have to push the blood a few inches into the relaxing ventricles, they have a very thin muscle wall and generate very little pressure, commonly only 5 to 10 cm of water pressure during atrial contraction (atrial systole). The atria can, if need be, work up to 20 cm H_2O pressure, but beyond that they go into failure (decompensate). The right ventricle pushes blood through the lungs (a low resistance system) and so this likewise does not need much pressure, 25 cm H_2O during ventricular systole is usually enough. The right ventricular muscle is, therefore, thicker than that of the atria but still relatively thin. The left ventricle must push blood to all parts of the body against a good deal of vascular resistance. Systolic pressures of 100 to 120 mm of mercury (mm Hg) are required to do this, and so the left ventricular muscle is relatively thick. The units of pressure used in medicine are somewhat peculiar. One millimeter of mercury (mmHg) is approximately equal to 1.3 cm of H_2O pressure. The smaller mmHg pressure units are used for left ventricular pressures since these are measured with a cuff compressing the arm, attached to a mercury column. The H_2O pressure units are conventionally used for the low pressures found on the right side of the heart. This is because these have, until recently, been measured with a column of water in a glass tube open to the air, connected up to a catheter which has been inserted into the superior vena cava. This simple and direct way of measuring central venous pressures is still in use in clinical medicine; but other more sophisticated methods are becoming available which use the mmHg units of pressure measurement. As these become more widely used, it is likely that pressures in the jugular veins, right atrium, right ventricle and pulmonary artery will be given in the mmHg notation.

§ 8:6 The arterial tree — systolic and diastolic blood pressures

Blood from the heart enters the aorta, and is distributed from there to the rest of the body. The first part of the aorta, the *ascending aorta*, almost immediately gives off the two coronary arteries which supply the heart muscle [see Fig. 8-9]. It then turns horizontally at the top of the thoracic cavity, becoming the *transverse aorta* where it branches to the arms and head. Turning downward, it becomes the *descending aorta* (thoracic aorta) and branches here supply the chest wall and lungs (the *bronchial arteries*) [see Fig. 8-1]. Passing through the diaphragm, it becomes the *abdominal aorta* which supplies the kidneys by the *renal arteries* and the abdominal viscera (liver, intestines etc.) by means of a number of *mesenteric arteries*. In the pelvis, it divides into the two *iliac arteries* whose branches supply the bladder and other pelvic organs. The iliac arteries pass under the inguinal ligament at the top of the legs to become the *femoral arteries* supplying the lower limbs. This whole system is called the *arterial tree* [see Fig. 8-3].

Pressure in the various chambers of the heart rises and falls as their muscular walls contract and relax, so that blood flow out of them is discontinuous (in separate spurts). This is especially obvious in the aorta where high pressures are generated, but the arterial walls modify and smooth out this pulsatile character of the cardiac output. The aorta distends as the heart pushes blood into it, and elastic fibers in the media (the muscular part of the arterial wall) absorb energy. Later the arterial walls contract, using the acquired energy to propel blood forward through the arterial tree during diastole, acting in fact like a second heart beating out of phase with the first one. This alternating thrusting of heart and aorta causes blood flow to become more or less continuous, although pressures still rise and fall, and flow is, to some extent, pulsatile (so that the radial pulses can be palpated). Arterial blood pressure is conventionally measured at the highest and lowest levels, which are described as the *systolic* (highest) and *diastolic* (lowest) blood pressures.

§ 8:7 Capillaries and capillary beds

A capillary is a tiny tubule with walls which are composed of a single layer of flat cells. Fluids and gases are able to pass through the thin walls in either direction. The capillary leaving a small arteriole quickly divides up into a number of branches which indeed form a maze of intercommunicating canaliculi. Ultimately these converge to become one or two venules which eventually come together to form veins. The complex collections of capillary tubules are called *capillary beds*, and they supply the needs of the surrounding tissues in an interesting way [see Fig. 8-6]. Fluids and small particles (e.g., sodium or potassium) can leak out of the capillaries into the tissues, but the large proteins of the blood can not. These, remaining in the blood vessels, exert a negative pressure known as osmotic (encotic) pressure, which later draws fluid from the tissues back into the capillaries. In the proximal part of the capillary, fluid pressures are higher and osmotic pressures generated by the serum proteins will not be sufficient to hold fluid in the capillary. Fluid rich in oxygen and nutrients, therefore, flows out and is distributed to the tissue cells. In the distal part of the capillary bed, however, after fluids have been lost to the tissues, osmotic pressures will be relatively higher and be sufficient to draw a good deal of this lost fluid back into the circulation. Fluid thus leaves the capillaries at their proximal end to bathe and supply the tissues, but returns from them at the distal part to carry waste products back into the circulation.

Some of this fluid is not returned to the capillaries but enters another system of tiny tubules called the *lymphatic system* [see Fig. 8-1]. These are valved (like veins) and ultimately connect up with large veins, so that this fluid is returned to the circulation. While travelling

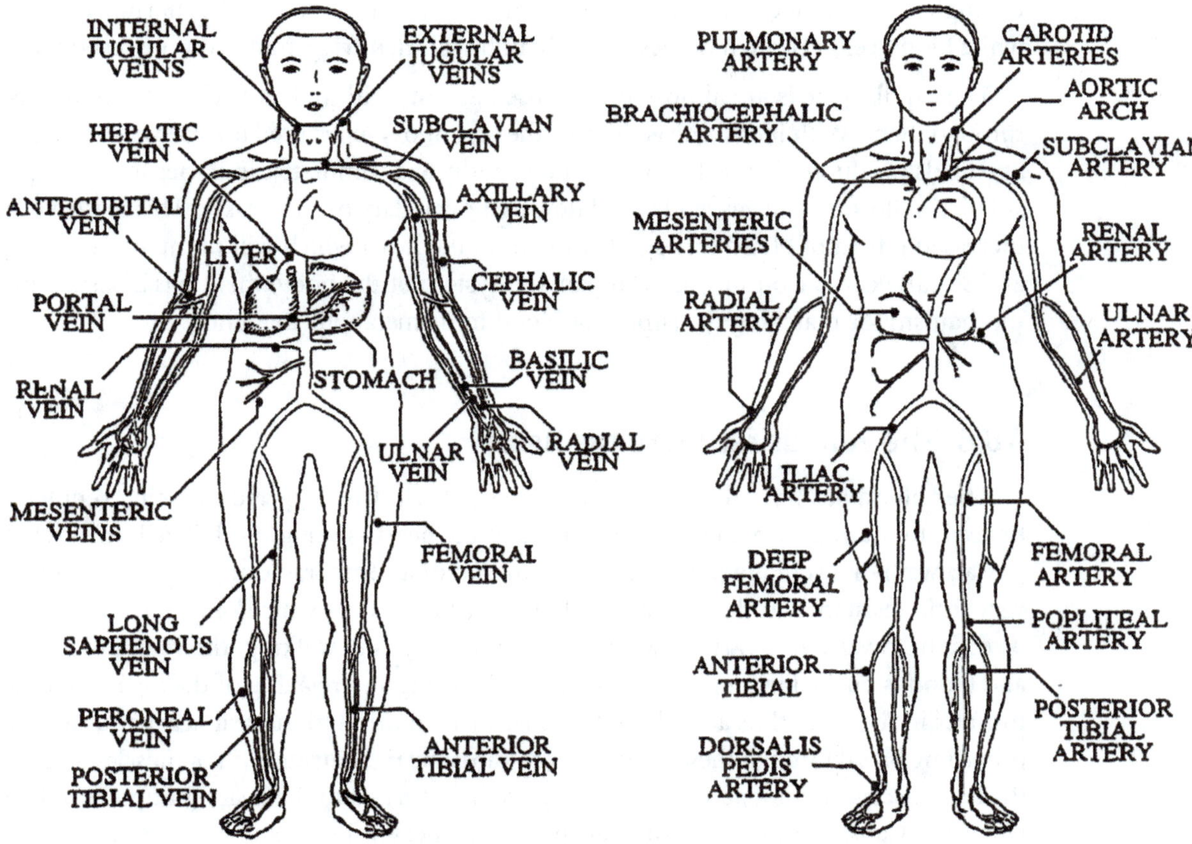

Fig. 8-5 Overview of the arterial and venous systems

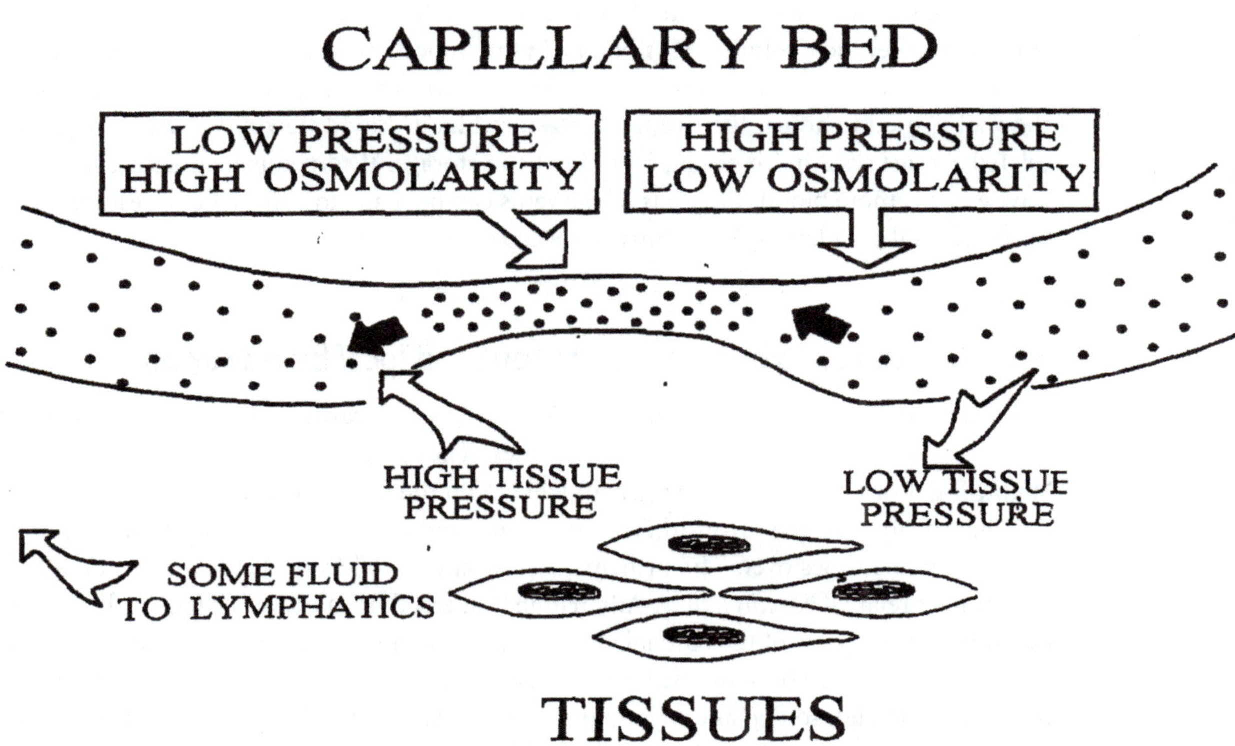

Fig. 8-6 Fluid exchange between capillaries and tissues

through the lymphatic system, fluids encounter lymph nodes, which harbor numerous white blood cells. Foreign bodies in the lymph will then trigger an immune response.

The capillary beds are almost 100% closed at rest, with only a trickle of blood passing through them. With increasing activity of the organ, oxygen is used up and waste substances and acids produced. These hypoxic, acidic conditions stimulate capillaries to open up, resistance to flow then drops, and blood flow in the capillary bed increases. This in turn causes increased return of blood through the organ to the heart which will pump out this blood, and so raise cardiac output. Each organ and system of the body, then, has a basic built-in mechanism for matching the supply of blood to its metabolic demands.

§ 8:8 The venous return to the heart

After blood has flowed through the capillary beds, it is delivered into tiny venules and hence into the veins which return the blood to the heart [see Fig. 8-1]. The lumen (central passageway) of a vein is generally larger than that of a comparable artery, and so they offer very little resistance to flow. They do, however, have valves which only allow flow in one direction, toward the heart. As we move our muscles, as in walking, the veins are squeezed and blood is pushed through these valves. The tensing and relaxing of the ordinary skeletal muscles in the body thus acts like a third heart (in addition to the real heart and the aorta) propelling blood through these valves back towards the right atrium. If the muscles, especially the leg muscles, are not active, blood may not be returned to the heart, but pool in the peripheries. Cardiac output will then drop, and the person in question may even faint. This is why guardsmen on duty must periodically march up and down.

The walls of veins are very thin, but they do contain a little muscle which can relax and contract to alter their volume. Muscle tone in the smooth muscle fibers in the arteries alters resistance to flow, and so controls blood pressure. In the veins, however, muscle tone in the wall is used to adjust their capacity to store blood. Blood flowing slowly through the dilated venous system can be considered to be in storage. If someone hemorrhages or otherwise needs more blood, the walls of the veins can be made to contract and restore blood to the general circulation. Veins thus act as capacitance vessels.

§ 8:9 Central control of cardiac output and local blood supply

In times of stress and excitement, a sudden increase in cardiac output can be achieved by CNS stimulation or by release of hormones. The *sympathetic nerves* (which facilitate "fight, flight or fright" in an emergency) will act on the heart itself, raising heart rate, increasing the force of the myocardial contractions, and generally multiplying the output of the heart many times over. The principal chemical controllers of the heart are *adrenaline* and its near relative *noradrenaline*. Adrenaline is released from nerve endings and from the medulla (central part) of the adrenal glands (sitting on the kidneys) during exercise and in times of stress. It acts both on the heart muscle itself and also on the muscle in the walls of the smaller arteries, so that as cardiac output is stimulated, peripheral resistance is increased and, as the result of both of these changes, blood pressure rises. The *vagus nerves* on the other hand (which are part of the opposing parasympathetic nervous system), act on the atrial pacemaker of the heart (discussed later) to slow the heart rate and damp down the activity of the heart muscle. By either increasing or lowering sympathetic tone in the veins, the walls of the veins can be dilated so that blood can be put into storage, or contracted, returning blood into the system. The autonomic nerves supplying a particular organ can thus be used to alter the blood supply to that organ. In a crisis, increased sympathetic tone on the supplying arteries diverts blood from one organ (e.g., the kidneys) to some other part of the body which needs it more urgently. Conversely, increased parasympathetic activity can reduce the metabolic needs of an organ or body part, like the gastrointestinal tract (GI tract) and, reducing blood flow though it, frees up blood which can be transferred to more needy areas, like the muscles. Noradrenaline (mainly produced in the adrenal medulla) has some effect on cardiac contractility, but mainly acts by increasing tone in the walls of the smaller arteries, thus increasing peripheral resistance to blood flow and raising blood pressure. The actions of the sympathetic system on the heart and blood vessel resistance greatly improve blood supply to vital organs during acute stress, e.g., hemorrhage or vigorous exercise.

Under ordinary circumstances, as was briefly mentioned earlier, neural or humoral agencies will not be needed to any great extent to control either the activities of the heart or local blood flow. A little vagal tone to slow the heartbeat is normally present, but for the most part, as was mentioned earlier, simple mechanisms operating in the tissues themselves are sufficient to regulate both local blood flow and the output of blood by the heart to the body as a whole. These operate (as was mentioned earlier) on the principle of supply and demand. If any tissue in the body (e.g., the muscles of the legs or the digestive tract) becomes active, fuel is turned into energy and metabolic waste substances are produced. Many of these waste products act chemically on the local capillaries causing them to dilate. Local resistance drops and blood flow to that tissue is increased. This increased local blood flow is also returned to the heart and will tend to increase cardiac output; the heart will normally put out whatever blood is returned to it. Thus, the output of the heart and the supply of blood to various tissues can be adjusted to match both local needs and the requirements of the body as a whole.

§ 8:10 The electrical activity of the heart

It is important that the atrial and ventricular chambers of the heart pump in sequence and not against one another. The two atria contract (more or less) together to fill the ventricles and, a little later, the ventricles contract synchronously to pump blood to the lungs (from the right ventricle) and to the body (from the left ventricle). The correct sequence: atria contracting first, then after a pause (to allow the ventricles to fill) the contracting of the ventricles is achieved by the controlled spread of electrical activity in the heart muscle [see Fig. 8-7]. Heart muscle cells, like nerve cells, are kept electrically charged by ion pumps in the cell membrane. Positively charged sodium ions are actively extruded from the cells, so that the outside is positively charged relative to the inside; the cell membrane is polarized. If any part of the cell membrane becomes depolarized, Na^+ ions rush across the cell membrane into the cell. When this happens, the membrane surfaces adjacent to this spot will also be affected in the same manner, and so a wave of depolarization will spread across that cell and on to the next one. When this occurs in heart muscle, special

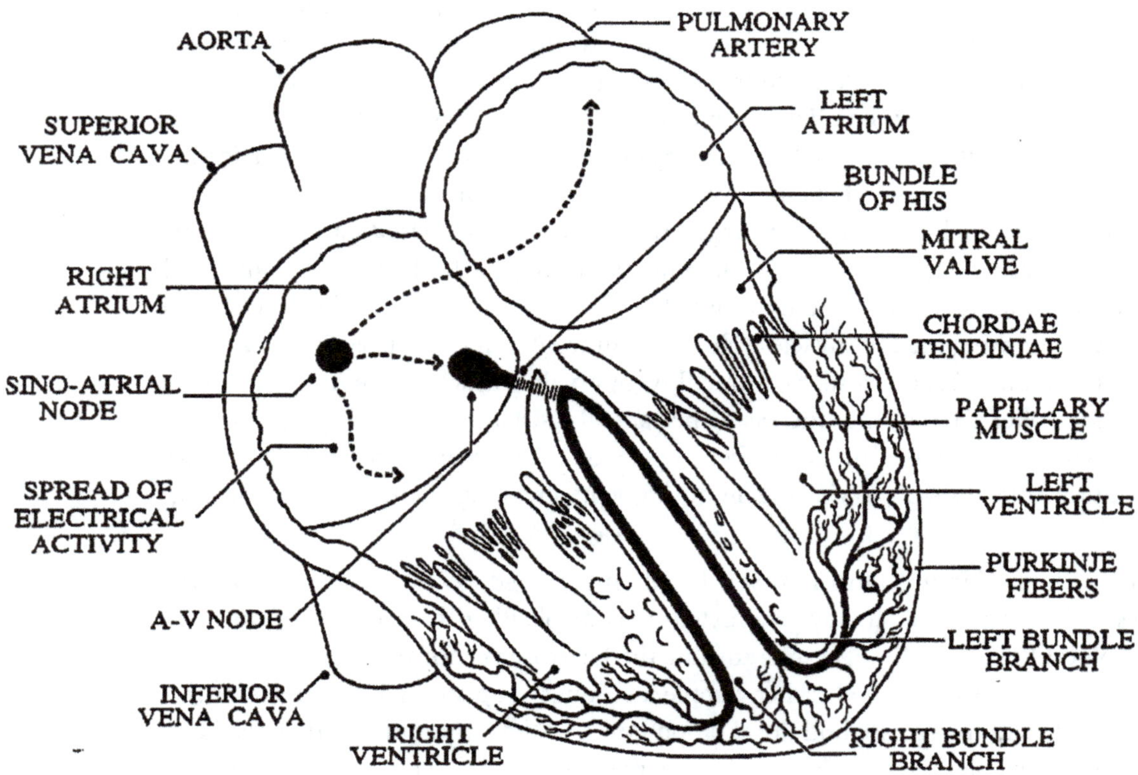

Fig. 8-7 The electrical activity of the heart

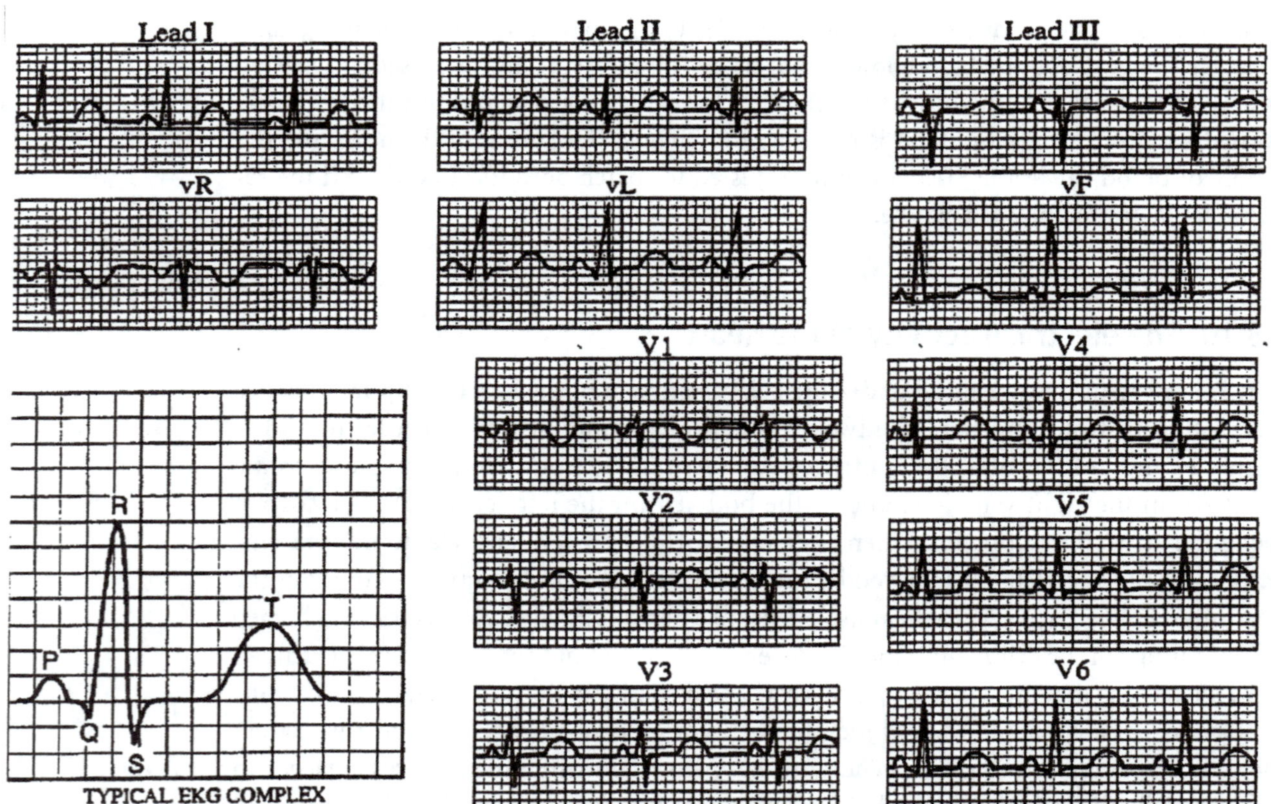

Fig. 8-8 The EKG complex and normal EKG trace

protein fibers inside the cell shorten, and the muscle cell contracts. Thus, if any part of the heart muscle becomes stimulated electrically, a wave of depolarization will spread across the whole muscle mass, and it will contract. Each heart cell, left to itself, will depolarize and contract periodically on its own, and each type of cell has its own intrinsic rate. The natural rate at which atrial cells contract is approximately 60 beats per minute. The idiopathic ventricular rate is around 40 contractions a minute. These natural firing rates are occasionally seen in pathological conditions, as when the ventricles contract at 40 b.p.m.(beats per minute) in complete heart block. Under normal circumstances, however, the two atria depolarize together at a rate of approximately 80 b.p.m., with the entire ventricular mass depolarizing a brief time later. The mechanisms by which this happens are complex, but they can be simply described as follows [see Fig. 8-7].

There is a special group of cells in the right atrium which naturally contract about 100 times a minute. These are the cells of the *sinoatrial node* (*S-A* node). This node is under the control of the vagus (xth cranial) nerve which normally damps its rate of firing down to about 80 depolarizations a minute. When the S-A node depolarizes, a wave of electrical activity spreads out over both atria and causes them to contract, but it cannot spread to the ventricles because they are separated off from the atria by a plate of nonconducting tissue called the *fibrous ring*. There is normally only one way through this fibrous ring. A second group of cells in the right atrium just above the interventricular septum is stimulated by the atrial depolarizing wave, and retransmits it through the fibrous ring to the ventricles. This node is called the *atrioventricular node* (A-V node) and its function is to delay the contraction of the ventricles until the atria have time to pump them full of blood. From the A-V node, after a brief delay, the wave of depolarization is carried through the fibrous ring to a special set of conducting fibers called the *bundle of His*. This is rapidly conducting tissue, and it divides into right and left branches (branch bundles). The right bundle transmits electrical activity to the muscle of the interventricular septum which forms part of the wall of the left ventricle. The left branch bundle links up with very rapidly conducting *Purkinje fibers*. These conduct the depolarizing wave very rapidly to all parts of the left ventricle which then contracts as a whole, virtually at once. Fractionally later, the wave of depolarization circles back around to the wall of the right ventricle which then contracts slightly out of phase with the major muscle mass of the left ventricle.

The electrical activity of the heart muscle, even though it is very low voltage, can be picked up by sensitive electrodes on the skin [see Fig. 8-8] and used to produce a trace, the *electrocardiogram* (EKG).There are now all sorts of electrocardiography systems, some of which will be briefly mentioned later in this chapter. Computerized EKGs can be used to produce maps of the heart surface, (like the brain maps described in Ch. 6). These are used to identify arrhythmic foci (in order to ablate them surgically) when an arrhythmia is resistant to medical treatment.

§ 8:11 Blood flow in the various organs and body systems

The circulation to each part of the body has special features. Each organ regulates its own local blood supply by its own peculiar structure and mechanisms.

The first organ to be supplied from the aorta is the heart itself [see Fig. 8-9]. The two *coronary arteries* come off the proximal aorta just beyond the aortic valves. The *right coronary artery* usually circles around posteriorly between the atrium and the ventricle and there

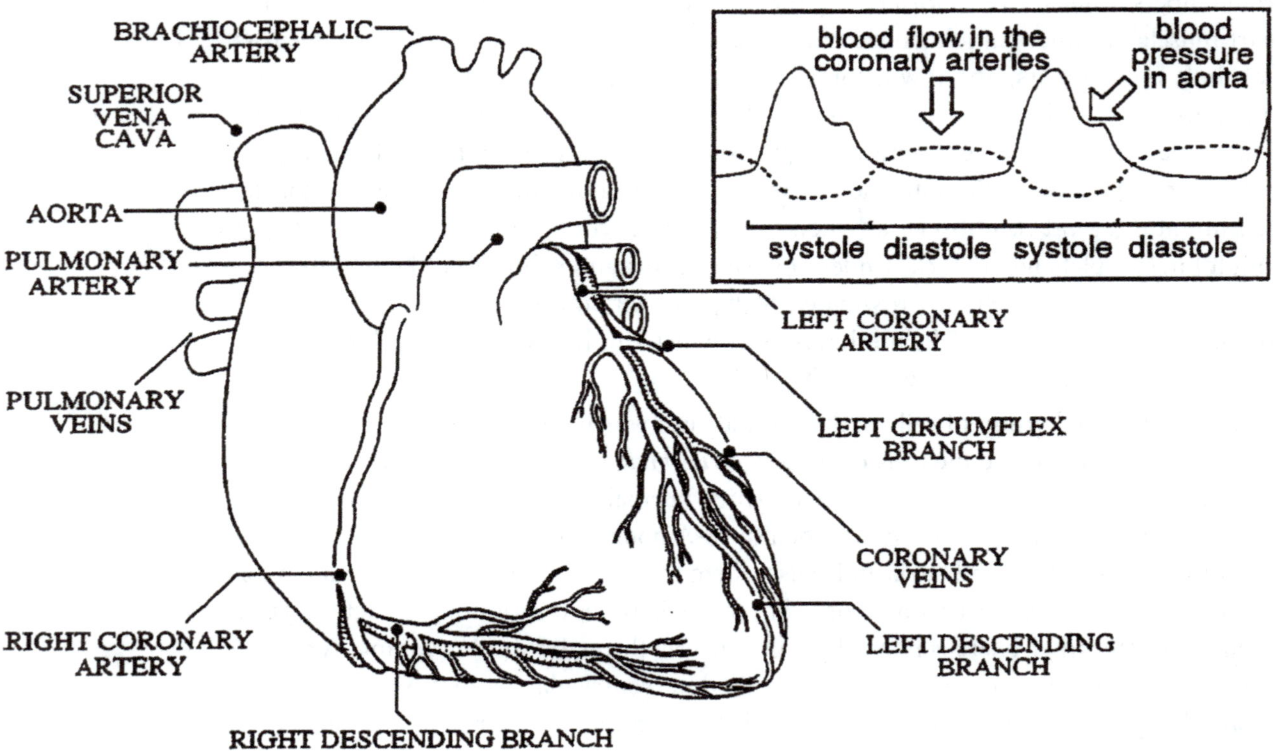

Fig. 8-9 The coronary arteries and coronary artery blood flow

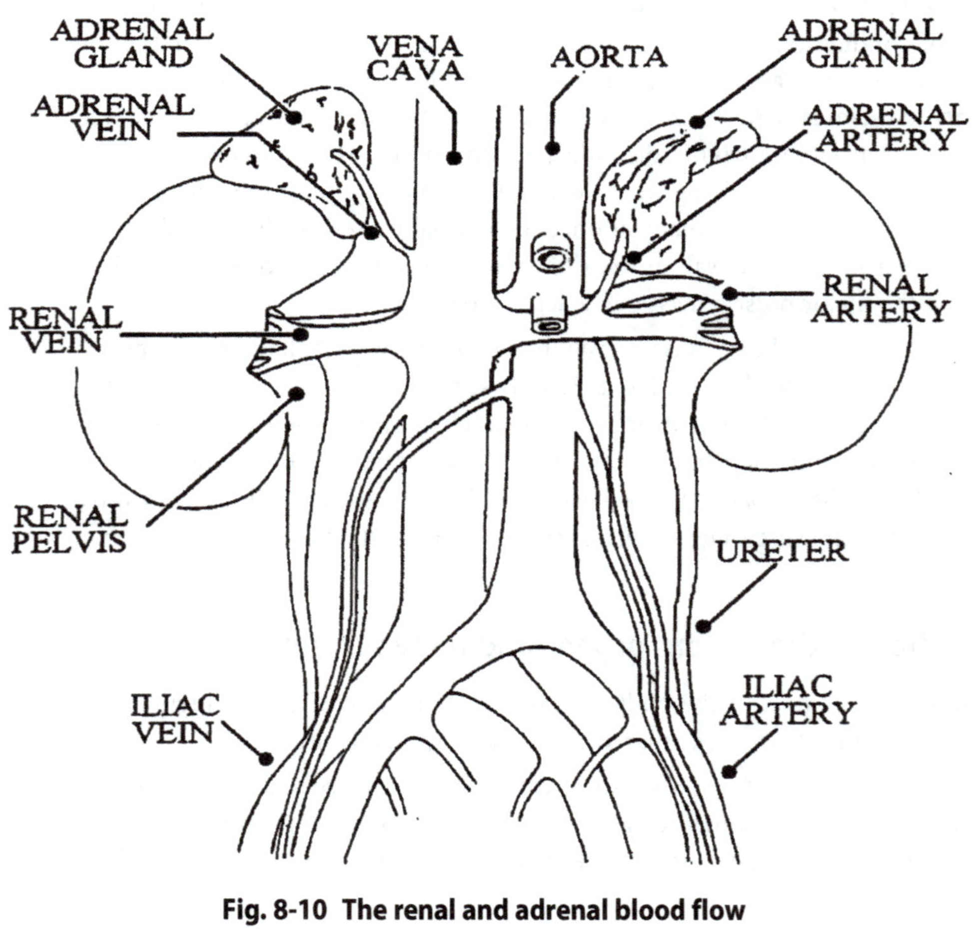

Fig. 8-10 The renal and adrenal blood flow

gives off a *posterior descending branch* which runs down the posterior surface of the heart. The *left coronary artery*, which supplies most of the heart muscle in the majority of people, gives off the *anterior descending branch* and then continues left around to the back of the heart as the *circumflex branch.*

It is obvious that heart muscle cannot efficiently take in blood while it is contracting (during systole). The capillaries are being squeezed, and little if any blood can flow through them. The blood flow to the heart muscle must therefore take place during the relaxation of the heart muscle (in diastole) [see Fig. 8-9—inset]. The coronary blood flow depends then on an adequate blood pressure in the proximal aorta during diastole. The *aortic diastolic counterpulsion balloon pump* (sometimes used following open heart surgery) works on this principle. The device consists of a set of balloons introduced into the aorta by means of a catheter. The balloons remain uninflated during systole so that blood can get past them to the kidneys and other organs. In diastole, however, the balloons can be briefly inflated and a wave of pressure is delivered back to the proximal aorta which increases the blood flow through the coronary arteries. This device can support a failing heart in a sick cardiac surgery patient for days, to buy time until definitive treatment can be provided.

The *cerebral circulation* has a number of special features. There are four main arteries supplying the brain. The two *carotid arteries* anteriorly, each divide to become the *anterior cerebral artery* and the *middle cerebral artery*. The *posterior cerebral arteries,* supplying the posterior parts of the brain, derive from the *basilar artery,* which is produced by the joining together of the two *vertebral arteries* which lie posteriorly in the neck. The vertebral arteries are protected throughout most of their course through the neck by the fact that they pass through small foraminal openings in the lateral processes of the cervical vertebral bones (the *foramina transversaria*). Anastomotic (connecting) branches between these four main arteries supplying the brain provide a protective device known as the *circle of Willis.* If any one of the supplying arteries should become occluded for any reason, blood can make its way around from the other three, via the circle of Willis, to supply the deficiency.

The renal circulation is also worthy of special mention [see Fig. 8-10]. To begin with, it is self-regulating; within considerable limits of blood pressure, the renal blood flow will remain constant. Also, one of the main mechanisms for regulating blood pressure in the rest of the body is located in the cortex of the kidneys. Here tiny organelles in the region of the glomeruli (*the juxtaglomerular apparatus*) monitor blood flow and regulate arterial blood pressure by releasing (or withholding) a substance called *renin.* Renin splits a protein called *angiotensinogen* to produce another substance called *angiotensin.* This in turn is split by further enzymes, *angiotensin converting enzymes* (ACEs) to produce *angiotensin II.* This substance acts locally to constrict blood vessels and raise blood pressure. It also acts on the adrenal glands to stimulate the release of *aldosterone,* a hormone which retains salt in the kidney and so elevates blood pressure. Substances which inhibit the actions of angiotensin-converting enzymes are called ACE inhibitors. ACE inhibitors are particularly important for a number of reasons:

1. They are very effective in treating hypertension.

2. There are concerns about the safety of antihypertensive drugs, especially thiazide diuretics, which have been associated with increased mortality in hypertensive patients.

3. They have been found useful in treating heart failure and some forms of renal failure.

Part II.
Diseases of the Cardiovascular System

§ 8:12 Cardiovascular diseases which are important to lawyers

The list of diseases which affect the heart and the circulation is long. It includes alcohol and heavy-metal poisoning, autoimmune diseases, trauma, cancers (both primary and secondary) and even neurological processes, which can involve the heart both on an acute and on a long-term basis. However, many of these diseases are uncommon, and most of the cardiovascular cases that come to a lawyer's attention are concerned with two or three kinds of problems.

- Atherosclerotic coronary artery disease (ASCAD) which is often called simply atherosclerotic heart disease (ASHD).
- Cerebrovascular disease (of atherosclerotic origin).
- Peripheral vascular disease (of atherosclerotic origin).

§ 8:13 Coronary artery disease (CAD)

Coronary artery disease (CAD) is a major cause of death in this country. It is also (more importantly for our purposes here) a common cause of disability and a contributor to disability from other causes. Coronary artery occlusions can be caused by a number of disease processes, such as the inflammatory arteritis found in *systemic lupus erythematosus* (SLE), or *periarteritis nodosum* (PAN). However, atherosclerotic heart disease (ASHD), together with its various associated problems, is by far the commonest cause of cardiac disability.

It must be said right away that no one is sure of the ultimate causes of atherosclerotic vascular disease. Many studies have been carried out, and a number of factors, such as diabetes, high cholesterol and hypertension, have been implicated as contributing to the condition, but the ultimate causes are not really known. Confessions of ignorance of this nature by cardiovascular researchers are therefore common. It should, nevertheless, be remembered that a great deal of knowledge about atherosclerotic coronary artery disease has been accumulated. The clinical pictures are known, and improvements and refinements in the methods of evaluating and treating the condition are developing apace.

The coronary circulation, like most others, has anastomotic vessels (joining one major blood vessel to another) which are not normally patent, but which can open up to create a way around an obstruction. Several major arteries or branches can, therefore, be almost or even completely occluded without any complaints on the part of the patient, since the deficit is being supplied circuitously by anastomotic connections. Eventually, however, a vital supply line becomes narrowed just a little too much, and symptoms may then begin to appear.

Angina or cardiac pain is typically felt in the central part of the chest and is described as a squeezing pain or a discomfort rather than the sharp pain of a muscle sprain or arthritis. In its classical form, the pain comes on with exercise and is relieved by rest or by trinitroglycerin (TNG) tablets placed under the tongue. Sometimes, however, the pain can come on at rest or with psychological stress. In other cases, a patient can have angina and even suffer a myocardial infarction with spasm in apparently normal coronary arteries. This is called *Prinzmetal's variant angina.* These variations are probably due to the fact that angina has two components. The first is a fixed obstruction in the coronary artery. The second is spasm of the coronary vessels, which narrows them and reduces flow. If the problem is mainly obstruction, the angina will take its classical form. The presence or superimposition of spasm will produce the variant pattern of symptoms. If the coronary circulation is moderately compromised, the EKG trace at rest may be normal, but signs of ischemia (shortage of blood) may appear with exercise. The patient with suspicious chest pains is usually investigated by exercise stress testing (EST) using a treadmill (*exercise treadmill testing* or ETT). [See Fig. 8-60] The speed and slope of the treadmill can be increased in a measured and precise manner, using one or other of the standard protocols. Coronary artery disease is best shown by the typical EKG changes of ischemia, especially S-T depression with a characteristic down-sloping appearance. The positive reliability of the ordinary stress test is around 75% but it can be improved by adding in more sensitive measures of ischemia than the EKG, such as radionuclear imaging with gallium, or some other tracer that adheres differently to normal and abnormal heart muscle. Heart wall movement studies using *sonocardiography* are in common use. Less expensive monitors of heart wall movement are also available, such as the electroseismograph (ESG) which uses a miniaturized earthquake detector, or a miniaturized metal detector (invented and favored in Israel). These simple devices, being inexpensive, are mostly used by researchers who have limited funds. They have, however, promise for use in mass screening projects, since abnormal heart wall movement is a very early sign of myocardial ischemia.

If the stress test is suggestive of coronary artery disease, a cardiac catheterization may be ordered. A tiny catheter is introduced into the left and right coronary arteries via the aorta, contrast dye is injected and X-ray pictures taken. The occluding lesions can be demonstrated, and they are usually measured by the percentage of the cross-sectional area that is obstructed. Two-dimensional obstruction of 50% or less is generally considered normal, and 80% or more is viewed as serious. Current practice (unless contraindicated for some reason) is to introduce a small amount of a vasoconstricting drug into the blood at some time during the test. This causes some spasm of the coronary arteries and tests the response to the vessel walls to emotional stress. Vasoconstrictor challenge adds little additional risk and provides important information. Contrast angiography is invasive and carries some risks, though they are slight and it is, therefore, only used when clearly indicated. It is particularly useful when some kind of interventional therapy (such as balloon angioplasty or bypass surgery) is being contemplated. It is hoped that new generations of high speed CT and MRI scanners will have sufficiently high resolution to be able to image coronary arteries without catheterizing them.

§ 8:14 Myocardial infarction (MI)

If the coronary arteries are occluded long enough, some heart muscle will necrose (die). This is myocardial infarction (MI). The presenting classical symptoms are a little different from the anginal pain which results from simple ischemia.

1. The pain is more severe and may be described as a "crushing" pain (as if someone was standing on the patient's chest) rather than the squeezing pain of angina.
2. Pain lasts longer (typically 30 minutes or more) and is not relieved by rest or TNG.

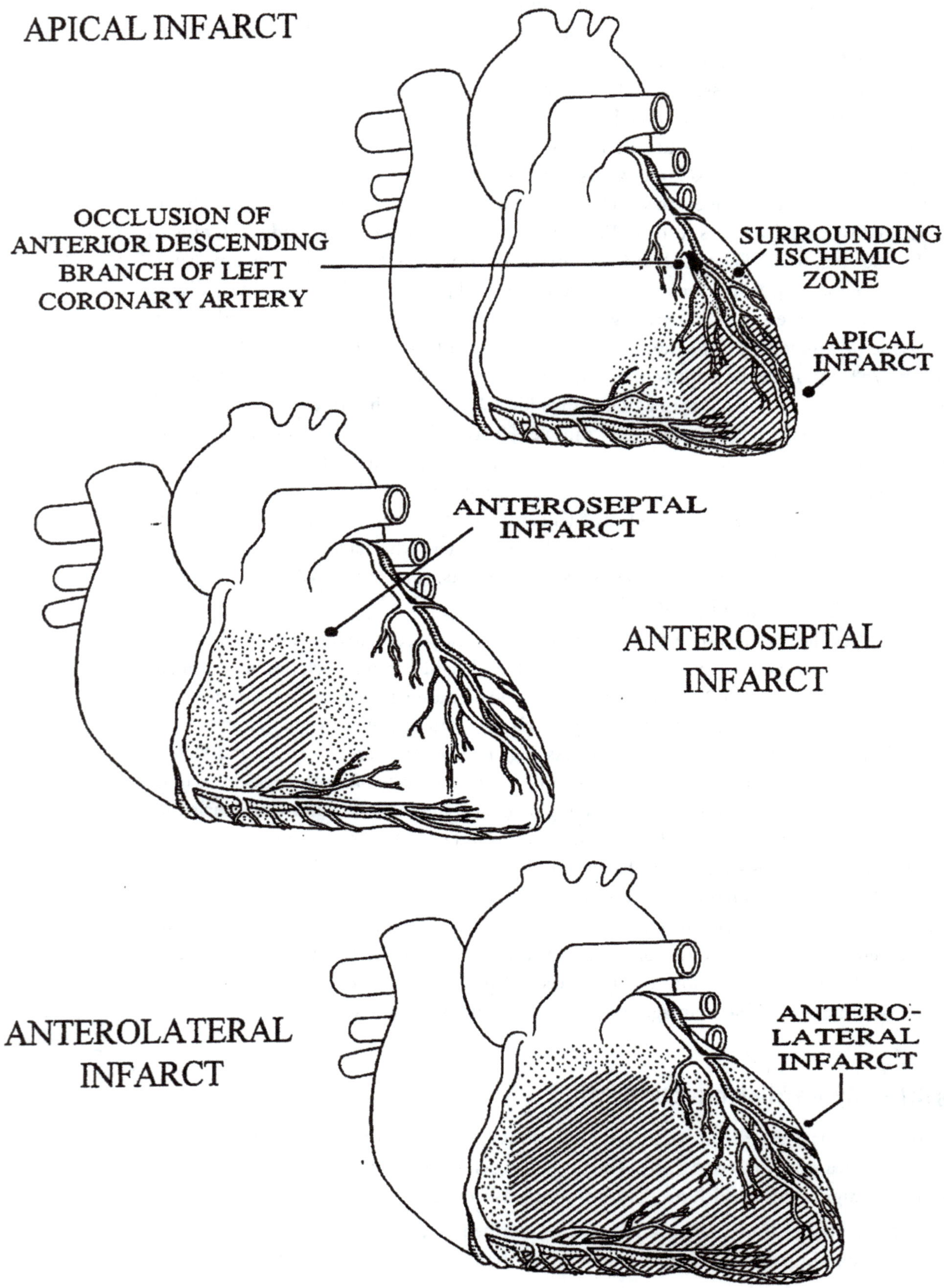

Fig. 8-11 Common sites for myocardial infarctions

3. The patient often experiences strange mental symptoms (extreme anxiety sometimes described as " a sense of doom"). Psychometric testing may even show mental changes months before the MI.

4. If damage to the heart muscle is sufficient to seriously reduce cardiac output, the brain will put the sympathetic nervous system into overdrive. This adrenergic activity "flogs" the heart into increased activity, squeezes the peripheral vessels to increase blood pressure, and diverts blood to the heart from other organs, including the skin, where it also causes sweating. The patient who has had a severe heart attack is then likely to have a faint rapid pulse and pale, cold, sweaty skin, which is often described in the records as being "cold and clammy."

These are the classical signs of a myocardial infarction but, as in all areas of clinical medicine, the atypical may not be uncommon. A myocardial infarction may present with no chest pain at all (silent MI), with only epigastric pain and vomiting so that it mimics an intestinal problem, or with pain in the arm only or pain in the jaw. The physician requires a high index of clinical suspicion in dealing with patients in the age groups most at risk for coronary artery disease, or in dealing with "high risk" patients who have predisposing conditions such as diabetes mellitus, hypertension or a bad family history of heart disease. It is also important to remember that some people, especially the elderly and diabetics, have defective pain sensation and may have few or minimal complaints of pain. These two groups are, in fact, the ones most likely to have a silent MI; they may also have fewer complaints of pain in other conditions, e.g., appendicitis. In short, clinicians need to be particularly suspicious in dealing with the elderly and diabetics (and some patients are both).

§ 8:15 Tests used to diagnose myocardial infarction

When someone is suspected of having a heart attack, two standard tests are carried out to help make the diagnosis. These are:

1. *The twelve lead EKG* [see Fig. 8-8]. There are six standard leads: the bipolar leads (I, II and III) and the limb leads (VR, VL and VF). The bipolar leads record the potential difference between two points on the body: lead I between the right and the left arm, lead II the difference between the right arm and the left leg, and lead III between the left leg and the left arm. The limb leads are *unipolar leads*; they record the potential difference between a neutral (averaged) point and the right arm (VR), the left arm (VL) and the left foot (VF). The six chest leads (VI–V6) are also unipolar leads. These are attached in standard positions across the front of the chest from right to left and they record signals from the anterior aspect of the heart. They are, therefore, called the *anterior chest leads.* In the first 4–6 hours following a coronary artery occlusion (beginning of the MI), there may be no EKG changes. The earliest change in an acute MI is S–T elevation which normally lasts for 18–24 hours [See Fig. 8-12]. Then S–T depression appears, with deep V-shaped inversion of the T-waves. This change can last for 48 hours or more. The T-wave gradually returns to the isoelectric line, but the deeply inverted T-waves may remain for months. In the following months, the ST depressions slowly return to their normal configuration, but a rounded saucer-shaped inverted T-wave may remain. Such rounded inverted T-waves are the least reliable sign of a previous infarction since they can be due to other causes, such as

digitalis therapy and hypertension. They can even be present in a healthy heart as a normal variation. Nevertheless, in the presence of an appropriate history, like other abnormal EKG findings, rounded invented T-waves can be used not only to diagnose an infarction, but also to provide some idea as to when it took place and what part of the heart muscle was mainly affected.

2. *Cardiac enzyme estimations* [see Fig. 8-13]. Heart muscle cells, like any other cell, contain enzymes, the chemical tools which carry out their biochemical processes. When the cell is damaged, these enzymes are released into the blood and can be detected there, even when they are only present in minute quantities. A number of these enzymes are used to test for a recent MI, but especially *creatinine phosphokinase* (CPK) and *lactose dehydrogenase* (LDH). The CPK appears first, normally after 4–6 hours, and has usually returned to normal in 18–24 hours, provided a second infarct has not taken place. The LDH on the other hand does not usually begin to rise until after 18 hours and remains elevated for 2–5 days. Unfortunately, striated muscle cells contain CPK, and red blood cells and liver cells are plentifully supplied with LDH. Consequently, it was formerly difficult to be sure, on the basis of increased enzyme levels, whether the patient had really suffered an MI or not. Chronic alcoholics, for instance, can have markedly elevated CKP levels from falling down on the ground and bruising their muscles and a raised LDH from liver disease. Fortunately, however, these enzymes are not homogeneous; there are several different types of each of them, known as *isoenzymes,* that can be separated out from one another by electrophoresis. There are three distinct kinds of CPK: known as BB, MM and MB. BB is found predominantly in brain tissue and MM in striated muscle. All but a tiny percentage of MB is in heart muscle, so that the statement in a medical record that the MB fraction of the CPK was elevated makes it most likely that the patient has very recently suffered a myocardial infarction. There are five fractions in LDH (labeled I–V), two of which are used to diagnose a myocardial infarction. Normally fraction I is smaller than fraction II, but following an acute MI this ratio is reversed, and such a finding is commonly known as "I–II flip." This finding (again in appropriate circumstances) indicates that an MI took place one or two days earlier. New cardiac enzymes are continually being studied, e.g., *treponins* (especially treponin I or treponin T). These are present in cells, including myocytes, and are leaked out into the body and found in the blood following a myocardial infarction. They are said to be more sensitive indicators of myocardial damage than CPK and LDH, though their presence is not diagnostic and may be elevated in persons with no myocardial damage. The amounts in the blood can be quantified and are reported to be proportional to the seriousness of the heart damage. More importantly, they are apparently good indicators of outcome. Large amounts of treponins following a heart attack are generally linked to a bad prognosis (further heart attacks and cardiac problems).

§ 8:16 Initial treatment of acute myocardial infarction

The treatment of an MI has several phases:

- Emergency treatment aimed at stabilizing the patient. This may or may not include emergency surgery to improve the coronary artery circulation

- Close observation of the patient (usually in a cardiac intensive care unit) to detect and deal with early complications, especially arrhythmias which can be lethal.
- Evaluation of the patient's post-MI condition in order to plan rehabilitation.
- Patient education in lifestyle to reduce risk factors for coronary disease.

Emergency treatment is to stabilize the patient and then (by one means or another) to reopen the occluded coronary arteries and restore blood flow to the infarcting area of heart muscle. It is still generally accepted that accomplishing this early reduces myocardial damage. The main interventional treatments (antithrombotic drugs, angioplasty and bypass surgery) will be discussed in a later section.

Following emergency treatment of whatever kind, the patient normally will be admitted to a cardiac intensive care unit (CICU) for continuous EKG monitoring until deemed stable. The principal reasons for doing this are:

1. A small MI may be followed by a massive one.

2. The commonest cause of death following an MI is the development of a serious arythmia, (such as ventricular fibrillation) where the heart muscle cells contract asynchronously rather than together in concert as they should. Cardiac output virtually disappears, and the patient will die unless urgent resuscitative measures are undertaken at once. In many cases, this complication can be prevented from occurring by treating the earliest signs of cardiac irritability such as ectopic beats (heart beats originating in some site in the ventricle other than the proper atrial pacemaker, e.g., in the bundle of His). When these suspicious findings are detected by the continuous EKG monitors in the ICU, an alarm will normally go off and an intravenous bolus of an antiarrhythmic drug can be quickly given into the IV line. This may be followed by continuous administration of medication by intravenous drip to prevent the development of farther rhythm disturbances.

After a few days in intensive care (or earlier if stable) the post-MI patient will be evaluated. This is done in order to assess the extent of the cardiac damage, to identify risk factors, to institute measures to reduce them, and to estimate the patient's potential for rehabilitation. Researchers are using high speed MRI to determine the size of infarcts, but in the clinical setting, exercise treadmill testing (ETT) is the principal measure used, and it will be attempted as soon as it is deemed safe for the patient. A very gentle test, the ETT uses the "rehab" protocol: slow speeds, short exercise intervals and no elevation of the treadmill. This establishes the baseline against which future progress can be assessed. Depending on the results of ETT, together with the clinical picture, the decision can then be made whether to continue with medical management or to schedule cardiac catheterization with a view to surgical treatment.

§ 8:17 Interventional treatments of coronary artery disease

In the not too recent past, patients who had suffered heart attacks were only treated supportively, with rest, careful monitoring, treatment of complications and rehabilitation. Optimum medical treatment (OMT) with aspirin, statin drugs to reduce cholesterol, and ACE inhibitors, to reduce vascular resistance are the basic forms of medical treatment, and surgical and other interventions have not been shown to markedly improve outcomes. But nevertheless, intervention to restore or improve the coronary circulation is common. There are basically three ways of going about this task:

- Dissolving the clot with thrombolytic drugs such as streptokinase or recombinant (genetically engineered) thromboplastin activator (rTPA).
- Balloon angioplasty (or some variation of it) to enlarge the stenosed lumen.
- Coronary artery bypass surgery to restore the circulation beyond the blockage.

1. *Thrombolytic therapy*. Most heart attacks are caused by the sudden development of a blood clot on the surface of an atherosclerotic plaque. Usually this event begins with rupture of a soft plaque and exposure of the blood to tissue thromboplastins (substances which initiate a clotting response). The plaque need not be occlusive for this event to happen; indeed the causes of plaque rupture are largely conjectural. This explains why heart attacks happen to people with relatively good coronary artery blood flow and normal EKGs. Removal of the clot by thrombolytic drugs was at first accomplished by catheterizing the coronary arteries and releasing the drugs at point blank range. It was later discovered that it was safe and effective to introduce the drug in larger amounts via a peripheral vein. This was exciting news since an MI could be managed by a simple interventional treatment in a local hospital with no facilities for cardiac catheterization. The main complications were bleeding (especially intracerebral) and nasty arrhythmic episodes as ischemic (stunned) myocardium was reperfused. There are two other limitations:

i. Thrombolytic therapy, in order to be effective, must be administered early (preferably within four hours of the first signs of the MI).

ii. It is now known that other interventional procedures have much worse outcomes if they are performed on patients who had previously (within a few days) had thrombolytic therapy.

2. *Angioplasty*. Angioplasty is enlarging the lumen of an artery. It is usually accomplished by inserting a tiny inflatable balloon on a catheter over a guide wire into the narrowed or occluded segment. The balloon is then inflated, so that it tears open the atheromatous plaques and squeezes them back into the wall of the artery. Atheromas are not elastic and do not spring back into place again, so this procedure enlarges the lumen (to at least 50%) and restores the circulation. The main complication of angioplasty is late restenosis of the vessels, which may occur weeks to months latter in anything from 25% to 40% of cases. The patient then requires a second angioplasty or bypass surgery (sometimes as an emergency procedure). Late restenosis is not due to clotting, but to the proliferation of *non-contractile muscle cells* in the wall of the artery. Attempts to prevent restenosis by creating a larger lumen using rotating blades, laser beams, or dental burrs, have not so far been notably successful. The use of stents (little tubes made of wire mesh to hold the vessel open) for the same purpose has reduced the incidence of restenosis but not removed it entirely. Stents have a few problems of their own, especially early occlusion by clotting, so that patients must normally be treated with anti-clotting medications. Stents coated with anti-mitotic substances to inhibit the development of the unwanted muscle cells are called *drug-eluting stents*, and are currently being evaluated; stents without such drugs are called *bare stents*. Initially it was felt that angioplasty was contraindicated if there were more than two oc-

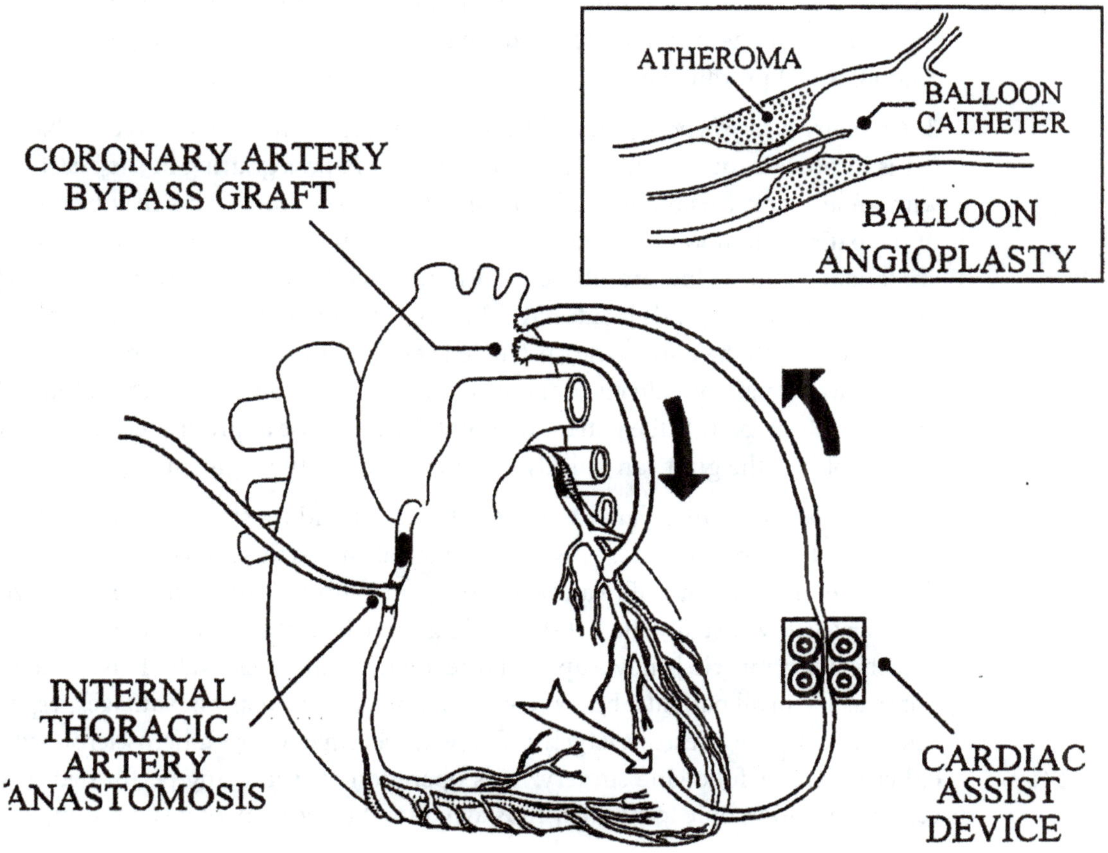

Fig. 8-14 Surgical procedures used to treat coronary artery disease

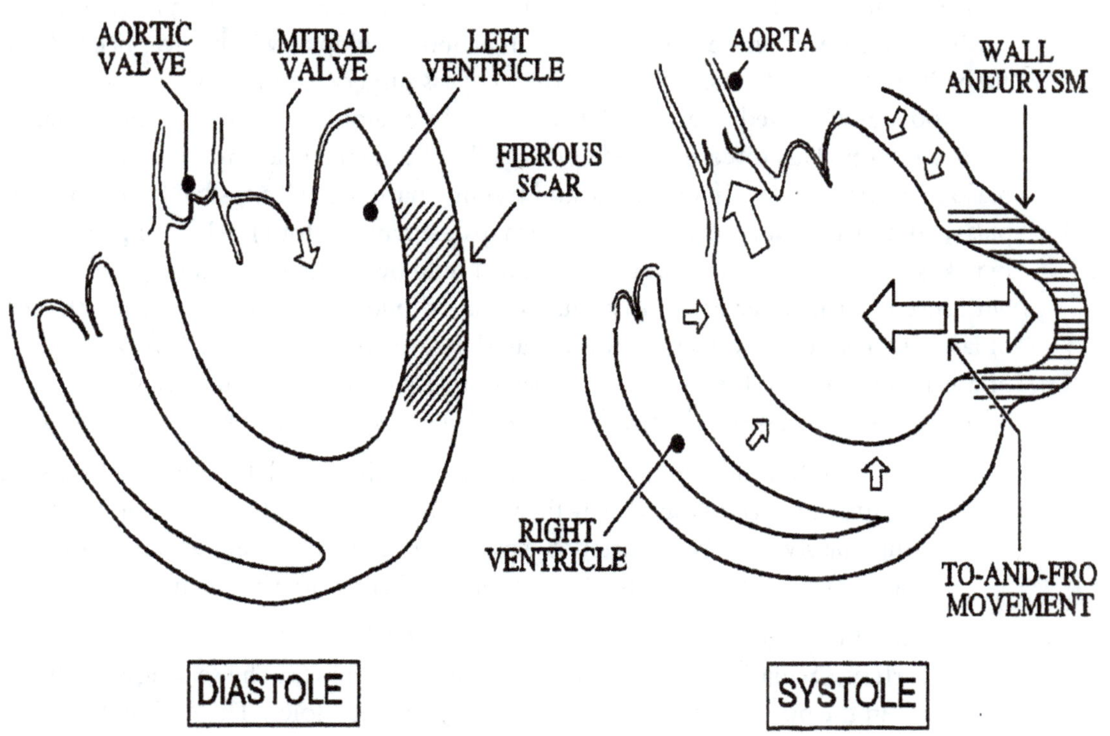

Fig. 8-15 Ventricular aneurysm following a myocardial infarction

cluded arteries, but this is no longer the case. It also has been found that when a number of arteries are badly stenosed, enlarging one or two of the larger ones (partial angioplasties) produces just as good a result as reopening all of them.

3. *Coronary artery bypass graft.* CABG can be undertaken on an emergency basis if an MI is in process, but has not actually developed. Bypass grafting in the heart is done with an autograft, using tissue from the patient's own body. This may be a segment of the patient's femoral vein, but arterial grafts are being increasingly used, since they are longer lasting. One end of the graft is attached beyond the obstruction, and the other (the supplying end) is sutured either to a proximal unoccluded part of the coronary artery or to the aorta. The obstructed vessel is left in place and may indeed open up later as the patient adheres to the strict postoperative regime which is required following such surgery. If the patient does not diet, exercise appropriately, and above all stop smoking, the graft can quickly become as bad as the segment bypassed.

4. *Internal thoracic artery anastomosis* is the latest and most favored form of bypass treatment for coronary artery disease. The distal end of this artery, which runs down the inside of the chest wall, can be freed up and sutured into (anastomosed with) a coronary artery (usually the left descending branch) just beyond the obstruction, so that the heart muscle is now supplied directly from the chest wall. This procedure is not possible in all patients, but where it is feasible, it has many advantages, especially since this artery, for reasons largely unknown, seldom develops atherosclerotic plaques either before or following surgery. This operation is even being performed in some centers by endoscopic technique, thus avoiding the necessity of a stemotomy.

There has been a good deal of controversy as to the place of each of these treatments. Earlier protocols suggested a stepwise arrangement in which thrombolytic therapy was given first to remove the blood clot causing the occlusion; then, when the patient was stable, cardiac catheterization was carried out with balloon angioplasty if that was needed to open up badly stenosed arteries. Coronary artery bypass surgery would only be indicated if there were too many blocked arteries to be dealt with by angioplasty, or if angioplasty had failed for any reason. This three-pronged approach has been largely abandoned for a number of reasons. Improvements in technique and training have made it possible for balloon angioplasty to be used on several arteries (perhaps as many as four). Also, improvements in bypass surgery have made it arguable that it should be the first treatment given to patients with severe coronary artery disease and angina or following an MI. Above all, the reports of large international outcome studies of all these treatments have made it clear that many of the assumptions of the stepwise approach, described above, are not tenable. The smoke of battle has not yet quite cleared, but the emerging consensus appears to as follows:

i. Thrombolytic therapy, although effective, has a deleterious effect on surgical treatments carried out shortly thereafter. It should only be used in situations where angioplasty or coronary artery bypass are not available locally and the patient could not be transferred in a timely manner to a facility offering them.

ii. Either angioplasty or bypass surgery are equally effective in restoring the coronary artery circulation and have much the same outcomes. The selection of one rather than the other would then be a matter of patient choice. The problem with angioplasty, mentioned earlier, is that anywhere from 25% to 40% restenose in the weeks and months following the procedure so that the procedure must either be repeated, or the patient may need bypass surgery. The problem with bypass surgery is that it is a major operation with a longer recovery time.

Research continues and the pros and cons for each treatment will change with new findings and new developments. CABG surgeries, for some reason or other, have been reduced in number, while percutaneous angioplasty remains at a constant (high) rate. The new coated stents may reduce the incidence of early and late reocclusion with angioplasty; and endoscopic bypass surgery with anastomosis of the internal thoracic artery to the coronary arteries (without stemotomy) may make the surgical option more attractive.

The other controversy is whether any of these treatments are any better than medical management, featuring reduction of risk factors and handling complications such as arrhythmias and heart failure. The general consensus here is that, while outcomes with medical treatment are much the same as with angioplasty or bypass surgery, there are more deaths from reinfarction in the nonsurgical group (and also more hospital admissions and doctor visits). These features are generally tilting the balance in favor of active surgical treatment, but not enough to take it out of the realm of patient preference.

§ 8:18 Other surgeries to improve cardiac performance

Cardiac surgery is a rapidly developing field; and new procedures and improved procedures are continually being reported. Interventional procedures to remove ventricular aneurysms and to ablate or remove troublesome arrhythmic foci are discussed elsewhere. [See § 8:31.] Surgery to correct congenital abnormalities of the heart is not new but is becoming more sophisticated, so that formerly untreatable conditions can now be corrected, or at least modified to make the heart more functional. In severe congenital conditions, palliative operations can be undertaken which allow the child to develop and grow. A definitive procedure can be carried out later with a better chance of success.

The most recent developments in cardiac surgery involve the treatment of the hopelessly damaged and failing heart. Heart transplants using donor organs are now virtually routine in large centers, and the "success rate" is high, but these procedures are far from ideal. Donor hearts, like transfused blood, must be carefully matched to the recipient, and the supply of hearts is very limited. Even when a suitable one is found, the patient usually requires continuous immune suppression of some kind to prevent rejection of the transplant by their body. Finally, the graft only lasts for a limited time, although some quite long survivals have been reported. Replacing the heart altogether with a mechanical pump, or *total artificial heart* (TAH), is possible but clumsy, and only currently recommended as a means of keeping the patient alive until a donor heart can be found for transplantation. Simpler, less expensive ways of treating the hopelessly damaged heart are clearly desirable. The most promising new developments are *cardiac assistive devices* (CADs) of various sorts [see Fig. 8-15]. Many of these are tiny mechanical pumps which, unlike the total artificial heart, do not replace but only supplement the efforts of the heart. Usually they take blood from the left ventricle after it has been oxygenated in the lungs and pump it, during diastole, into the aorta. Assist devices are being rapidly developed in a number of centers, and a good deal of effort is being directed to miniaturizing them and making them convenient for patients, so that they can move around relatively normally without being tied to an external

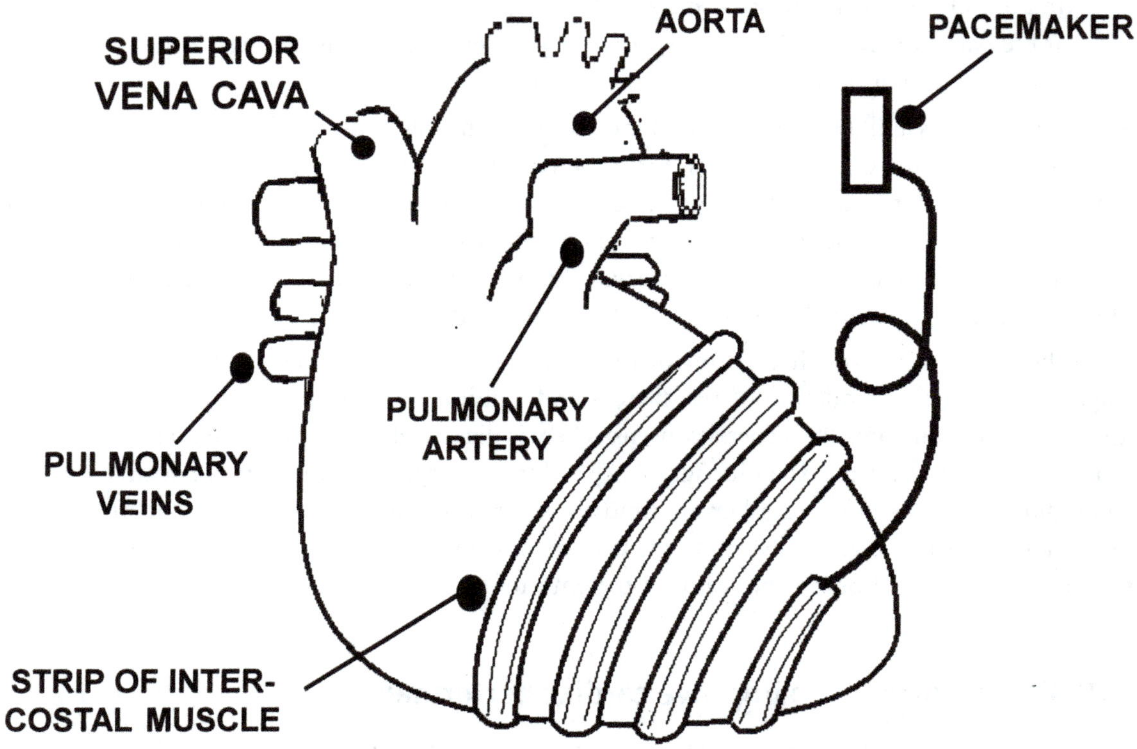

Fig. 8-16 Dynamic cardiomyoplasty

power source. More hopeful still, and even nearer to a normal physiological solution, are surgeries which use the patient's own muscles as an assist device (*dynamic cardiomyoplasty*) [see Fig. 8-16]. Intercostal muscle, complete with its nerve and blood supply, is detached from the chest wall and wrapped round the ventricles. It is then stimulated by a pacemaker to contract in time with the patient's own heart and so assist its efforts. Striated muscle [see § 8:4] is quite different from heart muscle (it tires easily); but over a period of weeks it appears to take on the properties of heart muscle (fatigue-resistant muscle). Some hundreds of dynamic cardiomyoplasties have been reported worldwide, mostly favorably, although there are some contraindications which may limit its use in severely damaged hearts; it is major surgery.

The ultimate treatment option for severely damaged hearts is likely to derive from the growth of new hearts (and other organs) from the patient's own tissues. This would avoid the necessity of both anticoagulation and immune-suppressive treatments, since the new heart would not be foreign to the patient and should not stimulate blood clotting. The organs have already been grown, usually from fetal tissue, but recently from tissue from the patient's skin, and used in a few transplant operations. Reports are encouraging but much work lies ahead before such treatments would be widely available.

§ 8:19 Estimating the prognosis following a heart attack

When someone has a heart attack, various interested parties may wish to know if the MI was a "big one." Certainly, persons evaluating them for disability purposes will wish to know what the likely outcome will be. The prognosis for a patient following a heart attack is not commonly an item found in the medical records. It must usually be specifically sought from the physicians, who may indeed be reluctant to commit themselves on this subject. They are aware that a small MI strategically placed can give rise to severe rhythm disturbances, and also that a small MI can be the prelude to a larger one happening days or even months later. Nevertheless physicians can usually give some useful information as to the likely course of events, once they are made aware of its legal importance. The following are important factors to consider:

1. *The initial findings in the admission history and physical and the early progress notes.* A sizable infarct produces a cold clammy and profusely sweating patient. If blood pressure has also dropped (e.g., to below 100 mm Hg systolic) this suggests that a significant amount of myocardium has been involved. This does not mean that the patient's condition will not improve. Some of the heart wall may not be really infarcted but only "stunned." With improvement of the coronary artery circulation, this heart muscle may recover and the patient do surprisingly well. Nevertheless, the initial clinical picture is a factor to be considered in determining the prognosis.

2. *The timing, extent and type of the EKG findings.* The early appearance of EKG changes (in one or two hours after the onset of chest pain) generally indicates a more serious MI with a good deal of heart muscle involved. S–T elevations also tend to be higher in a significant MI and also to involve more leads. The anterior chest leads are particularly suggestive in this regard. If the changes are seen all across the chest leads, this is described as an *anterolateral infarct* and represents impairment of a large amount of left ventricular heart muscle. If the changes are confined to the right chest leads, (*anteroseptal infarction*) or to leads V5 and V6 (*lateral infarction*), then the amount of muscle involved is likely to be less, although the MI may still produce significant impairment in other ways, such as rhythm disturbances. Deep Q-waves are generally considered (some authorities dissenting) to be evidence of a *transmural infarction*, i.e., one which extends right through the heart wall from outside to inside, and so likely to represent a significant MI, and the possibility of a heart wall aneurysm developing might need to be considered [see fig. 8-15]. Changes in the inferior leads, leads II, III and VF, all of which represent a "left foot" component, i.e., "looking up" at the undersurface of the heart, are associated with a greater incidence of rhythm disturbance, but less likelihood of heart failure, whereas involvement of the anterior wall leads (the chest leads) is associated with a greater incidence of heart failure.

3. *Clinical findings relating to recovery from the MI in hospital.* Several studies have identified patients at high risk of having a second heart attack or developing other problems in the year following their first MI. These include patients who (after stabilization) required intravenous medications (such as dopamine) to maintain satisfactory blood pressures; who had repeated or persistent rhythm disturbances; or who had complaints of chest pains throughout their hospital stay.

4. *Test results after stabilization.* Patients who have significantly reduced *left ventricular ejection fractions* (poor cardiac output), or who have performed poorly on the treadmill, are also more likely to have cardiac problems in the months and years following.

Patients who have had one heart attack are aware that they may have another, and this fear adds to, and indeed may be an important part of their disability. It may or may not be important for compensation purposes to know whether these fears are reasonably related to a heart attack or not. If, however, one or more of these poor prognostic indicators are present, then this question is moot: the patient's fears are reasonable and there is indeed some likelihood of further heart attacks or other cardiac problems. The patient's psychological reactions are contributing to the disability.

§ 8:20 Cerebrovascular disease

The brain is supplied by four main arteries, the two carotid arteries anteriorly, and the two vertebral arteries which unite to form the basilar artery and divide again to produce the posterior cerebral arteries. The four cerebral arteries communicate with one another at the base of the brain, forming in effect a traffic circle from which the smaller arteries to the brain branch off. This intercommunicating ring, mentioned previously, is called the *circle of Willis*. Narrowing, or even the complete occlusion of one of these arteries, need cause the brain no embarrassment. The other three can supply the circle of Willis, which can then deliver blood into all the arteries going on into the brain from there. Some people manage very well with three occluded arteries or serious narrowing of all four. As long as enough blood gets through somewhere, the system will work. However, there can be additional stenoses in the smaller 2nd and 3rd order blood vessels which complicate the picture. The blood supply to some area may be marginal. Any fall in the overall blood supply to the brain may reduce blood flow in that critical area below the survival level, and some kind of *cerebrovascular accident* (CVA) will result. This is why an occlusion in the left carotid artery may result in damage to some other apparently unrelated part of the brain.

§ 8:21 Cerebrovascular accidents (CVAs)

If an occlusion is large enough to affect the blood supply to the internal capsule, where motor axons pass down between the thalamus and the caudate nucleus to the brain stem and spinal cord [See § 5:8], a classical stroke is produced [see Fig. 6-32], with the patient paralyzed and numb down one side of the body . If the problem is in the dominant hemisphere (normally the left) the speech centers may be affected, and the patient becomes unable to speak (aphasic). If there is involvement of the central arousal areas of the brain stem, the patient will also become unconscious. The more widespread and severe the damage, the greater the ultimate disability, and the less likelihood that the patient will make a good recovery or recover at all. But not all CVAs are classical strokes. The descending bundles of white matter may not be affected, and the patient may speak and move all limbs. All that may be noticed is that they are not quite themselves, and perhaps a little "out of it" for a few days. What has happened in these cases is that a smaller area of the brain is affected or else, if the trouble is widespread, the occlusion is not complete and the area of brain is only rendered sick, not dead. Or arterial spasm, triggered by bleeding or a minor occlusion, may be an exacerbating factor, so that when the spasm wears off the patient will improve.

A brief cerebrovascular occlusion is called a *transient ischemic attack* (TIA). A TIA is classically defined as a stroke-like illness which clears up completely within 24 hours (though it may be the herald of a major stroke). But most of these attacks last for a much shorter time, in some cases only for a few minutes. If they last more than six hours, it is likely indeed that there will be some residual deficits. Such incidents (where recovery is not total) are sometimes described as *ischemic episodes with incomplete recovery* (IEIRs).

TIAs can result from a number of causes. Quite commonly, they are caused by small emboli coming from the right atrium (especially when the patient has atrial fibrillation); or by thrombi breaking off an atheromatous plaque on the wall of the carotid artery, or even the proximal aorta. These problems were formerly managed by giving the patient a little aspirin each day to inhibit the activity of platelets and so prevent clots from forming. Several studies have reported that outcomes with anticoagulant drugs (keeping the prothrombin time 2.5 times above normal) are superior to those using platelet inhibition alone. Anticoagulation is, however, expensive, more bothersome to the patient (periodic blood clotting tests), and it carries the risk of hemorrhage, especially brain hemorrhage. Moreover, it appears that it is only superior to antiplatelet agents (such as low dose aspirin) in some but not all cases. The current policy is to anticoagulate these patients unless there are contraindications to such treatment. Meanwhile research continues in the hope of identifying those groups of patients who can be managed on aspirin alone.

§ 8:22 Shock

The term *shock* is used very loosely by the general public, and even in medical circles. Someone who appears confused following a bad experience or severe fright may be described by their friends, or even by ambulance attendants, as being in a "state of shock." In clinical medicine, this term has a very specific meaning which has nothing to do with emotional responses to situations. It refers to a condition where the normal mechanisms for maintaining blood pressure in the body have broken down and can no longer function. Strictly speaking, it means a serious deficiency in the relationship of blood volume to the vascular space. This can be due to blood loss (too little blood) or too rapid expansion of the vascular beds as in a severe allergic reaction (too much vascular space).

Severe shock has a characteristic presentation with a cold sweaty patient, rapid thready pulse, low blood pressure and narrow pulse pressure, e.g., a pressure of 80/60 mmHg (pulse pressure 20) instead of 120/80 (pulse pressure 40). The typical example of this is an acute catastrophic hemorrhage, where the patient is losing blood externally from a wound or internally from a bleeding ulcer or a ruptured spleen. A shock syndrome can also be the result of severe multiple trauma (or a devastating illness), even though there has not been drastic blood loss. This can set in when the patient has been stabilized and seems to be improving. It is commonly associated with and proceeds to decompensation of other body systems, such as the lungs, brain, liver and heart. This event is known as *multiple organ failure* (MOF). The causes of the shock syndrome following trauma are not really known, but few patients survive once it has become established, and no treatments have significantly improved outcomes.

During serious acute hemorrhage or a severe allergic reaction (*anaphylactic shock*), the body will try to maintain blood flow to vital organs (e.g., the brain and heart). Several mechanisms come into play to effect this.

§ 8:23 The response of the body to acute blood loss

The first response of the body to severe acute blood loss is often that the patient faints and falls down, which puts the brain on a level with the rest of the body and allows blood to reach it more easily. This occurs typically in the ordinary *vasovagal attack* (fainting spell) or an anaphylactic reaction where the capacitance vessels of the body open up and divert blood away from the brain and heart. Sitting a fainting person up is thus working against nature. They should be allowed to lie down till they recover, so that blood does not drain away into the veins of the lower body.

The next protective reaction is that blood flow to less important organs is restricted by the action of the sympathetic nervous system. Adrenalin is released, which causes the heart to beat faster and more forcefully. Adrenalin also produces arteriospasm, which diverts blood from other tissues to the brain and heart. In this situation, the body observes a sort of pecking order. The first part to be deprived of blood is the skin. Sympathetic tone squeezes blood out of the skin and, since the sympathetic nerves also control sweating, the patient becomes pale and clammy. A similar mechanism comes into operation on a limited scale on a cold day to prevent heat loss from the extremities. A pathological form of this response, where the blood vessels to the hands close down in response to the slightest exposure to cold, is called *Raynaud's disease* (or Raynaud's phenomenon if it is secondary to some other disease process such as scleroderma).

If acute blood loss continues and the blood withdrawn from the skin is not sufficient to compensate for it, then the blood supply to the intestines is cut off. The body can tolerate this well since we do not need to digest all the time. A similar mechanism comes into operation with patients in severe pain, or with pregnant women in labor. This is the reason why patients come to an anesthetic with full stomachs, even six to ten hours after their last meal. The sympathetic tone that keeps their blood pressure up, for instance after a fracture, slows down digestion. One cannot conclude then that a trauma patient, or a woman in labor, who has not eaten for four to six hours, has an empty stomach. It is necessary to enquire how much time occurred after the last meal before they had the fracture or went into labor. If it was one hour afterwards, she probably still has a full stomach.

The renal circulation is the next to suffer and it is much more sensitive to blood deprivation than the skin or intestines. If severe deprivation goes on for more than an hour or so, renal failure is likely. At first only the tubules in the renal medulla (the central part) necrose. Fortunately these tubules are usually able to recover. If severe ischemia is prolonged much over an hour, the cells in the cortex of the kidney may necrose (cortical necrosis) and these can not reconstitute themselves. Irreversible renal failure may result, and the patient will then require renal dialysis and perhaps kidney transplant.

§ 8:24 Treatment of acute severe hemorrhage

Experience in the Korean war made it plain that blood transfusion is not necessary, even in cases with major blood loss, in order to avoid shock. Rapid and generous intravenous fluid replacement will restore blood volume, pending more adequate treatment, and avert most of the problems, especially renal failure. This experience has been applied in all sorts of other conditions, such as bleeding during surgery or following shark bites, and the results have been good. Survival rates have been greatly increased, and the renal dialysis rate greatly reduced by these measures.

Volume replacement can be more efficiently carried out using solutions containing large molecules which stay in the blood compartment, rather than redistributing in the body as electrolytes do. Low molecular weight dextrans (sugar like molecules) are commercially available and are widely used for this purpose. Pooled human plasma can also be used and works very well, but carries a high risk of infection. Albumin is a normal human protein and albumin solutions are available. These carry a low risk of infection, but they are expensive and the supply is limited. Genetically engineered human albumin solutions (r-HA) are now available and carry no risk of infection, but they too are expensive and have other problems, so that they are seldom used for volume replacement.

Blood replacement does not need to begin at once in blood loss; a patient at rest who is breathing 100% oxygen can survive on almost pure electrolyte provided that blood volume is maintained. Eventually blood transfusion will be required following severe bleeding. Donor blood is a very dangerous substance. Even when it is of a type which is compatible with the recipient (type O or the same ABO and Rh grouping as the patient), a transfusion reaction can take place, since there are a number of other antigens on the surface of human red cells besides the Landsteiner ABO and Rhesus groups. Furthermore, and more significantly, there is a risk of infection. Blood collection agencies screen donors and donor blood very carefully, but an occult infection can still be present. For these reasons, donor blood is only given when really needed. If bleeding has stopped, patients will only be given blood if their hemoglobin after dilution has dropped to 9 grams % or less (hematocrit approximately 27). With hemoglobin values greater than these, they will be given iron supplements and allowed to make their own blood. If blood is needed, packed red cells are usually given instead of whole blood, since the infectious agents are mainly carried in the protein fraction.

The dangers associated with donor blood, even when drawn and administered with due care, have stimulated efforts to find alternatives to it. One of these is to use the patient's own blood where possible. There are two ways of doing this. When an elective operation has been scheduled, several units of the patient's blood can be drawn in the weeks prior to surgery and stored. An additional unit can be drawn on the day before surgery and replaced with electrolyte. Three or four units can easily be made available in this way. If catastrophic blood loss occurs during operation, the patient's blood can be "scavenged" fresh from the wound, filtered, put into sterile packs and returned to the patient via an IV line. Scavenging machines which can process the patient's blood in a few minutes are now available at larger medical centers, and can be expected to become more generally available in the near future. Finally *blood substitutes* have been and are being developed The best known of these are the carbon compounds produced originally in Japan and now available in other countries. These have been somewhat disappointing in their performance, as they do not carry oxygen very well. More efficient types are under development. More promising are encapsulated hemoglobin solutions. Hemoglobin, freed from the surrounding envelope of the red cells, is not normally an allergenic substance, and its supply is abundant from donor blood which has not been used and has become outdated. It can be artificially encapsulated by mixing it into a foaming solution of a synthetic material which forms bubbles containing hemoglobin. These can be harvested and used to transfuse patients. The characteristics of these synthetic red cells are said to be similar to those of normal erythrocytes, both in their oxygen transportation and other properties (they last about 100 days in the blood just like red blood cells). Some animal experiments have reported that hemoglobin can even be administered as a free solution, without producing the renal problems associated with hemolytic anemia in humans. However, there may be differences between animals and humans in this matter, and it is unlikely that free hemoglobin transfusion would be considered safe at the present time. Human hemoglobins are also being developed by genetic engineering but these too, besides being very expensive, have had their problems. In short, blood substitutes, while promising, have not yet lived up to expectations. Hemoglobin substitutes can be useful, however, in situations where oxygen must be delivered through narrowed arteries. The carbon substances can slip easily through where red cells would stick; and they have been used to buy time in ischemic situations until definitive treatment can be arranged.

Certain patients, such as those who suffer from *hemophilia*, require periodic transfusions with clotting factors derived from human plasma proteins. These special proteins are present only in small amounts, and the blood of many donors may be required to give someone with hemophilia a single treatment. The risk of infection is therefore high, and a number of these patients have acquired AIDS, hepatitis and other diseases. Specially purified plasma protein derivatives (PPDs) are in use, and these reduce the risk of infection. Genetically engineered plasma proteins are also available, though expensive. They also have the drawback that the body may develop antibodies to the genetically engineered proteins and render them ineffective. The reason for this is that many kinds of hemophilia are due to defective, rather than absent, factor VIII; the immune system will thus consider normal factor VIII a foreign substance and take action to destroy it.

§ 8:25 Peripheral vascular disease

Advanced atherosclerotic disease in the femoral vessels does not then mean that there will necessarily be problems like coronary artery problems or cerebrovascular disease elsewhere. Peripheral vascular disease was well known and its clinical aspects were accurately described in ancient times. It normally affects the legs—the term peripheral vascular disease will usually be taken to refer to a problem in the lower extremities unless otherwise stated. The most prominent symptom, calf-pain following exercise, is called *claudication*, after the Roman Emperor Claudius who suffered from it. Claudication is a very distinct clinical entity, as the pain characteristically begins after a measured amount of exercise such as walking one block or climbing 27 stairs. Until recently, the only way to investigate peripheral vascular disease was by *contrast angiography*, such as a femoral arteriogram, which involves introducing a needle or a catheter into the femoral artery at the top of the leg, injecting radiopaque dye, and taking X-rays. Digital subtraction angiography (DSA), which was mentioned earlier [§ 8:17], can be used as a screening technique, but is being increasingly replaced by other modalities, especially ultrasound imaging which is now being utilized a good deal in the workup of peripheral vascular disease. High resolution CT and MRI imaging are also capable of imaging arteries, and may become more important in the near future. DSA, indeed, is now more or less on the back burner, and many major centers like the Mayo Clinic no longer offer it.

The only surgical treatment of occlusive arterial disease, until recently, was bypass grafting of the occluded segment of the artery. This involved a significant operation (including a vein stripping to provide the graft). These grafts may only work for a few years, and there is a limit to the amount of vein available for repeat operations. Arterial grafts are in common use, as they last longer. Balloon angioplasty is commonly used, and various laser systems and techniques using rotatory cutters and drills have been developed to evaporate, excise and otherwise remove the plaques and reopen the arteries. These new catheter techniques are still basically investigational tools. They do produce a larger and more adequate lumen, but still do not seem to improve outcomes or reduce the incidence of reocclusion, the principal problem with angioplasties at present.

Part III.
Tests Used In Determining Cardiac Functioning

§ 8:26 Cardiac imaging — X-rays, contrast studies, CT and MRI

This topic, touched on previously, will now be considered in greater detail. After the acute problems have settled down, the patient will usually be evaluated further, either to deal with specific problems that have occurred during recovery, such as persistently low cardiac output, or to see whether further treatment such as angioplasty or bypass surgery would be helpful to them.

A variety of imaging techniques can be used to review the state of the heart following an MI.

1. A simple anteroposterior (A-P) X-ray will show heart size, but only if it is considerable.

2. *Fluoroscopy* (where the X-ray image is viewed continuously on a fluoroscopic screen in a dark room) has been used to directly observe the beating of the heart and detect any abnormal movement of the ventricular walls. But there are now better ways of doing this, especially cardiac ultrasound, and so this modality [electrokymography) is more or less obsolete.

3. *Coronary artery angiography* (cardiac catheterization), inserting a fine catheter into the coronary arteries and injecting radio-opaque dye into them to show up the lumina of the vessels on X-ray, may be used. The concentrated dye used in angiography may irritate the heart, so it is usual to wait until the heart has settled down after an MI before this kind of investigation is attempted.

4. *Digital subtraction angiography* (DSA) is a technique (described earlier) which delineates arteries by X-raying them with and without contrast dye. DSA was an interesting technological device and is still being developed; but it has been relegated to the back burner by the advent of cardiac ultrasound imaging (sonocardiography) to be described in the next section.

5. *Computerized tomography* (CT scan) is capable of imaging most tissues and structures in the heart (CT-angiography or CT-A). Ultrafast machines can even study blood flow and estimate cardiac output. Helical (spiral) CT is a new modality where the source and receptors are rotated during the study. It rapidly produces multiple sections of

the whole body which can be processed into three dimensional images. Helical CT is being used in the diagnosis of arteriovenous malformations in the brain, and its uses are likely to be extended.

6. *Magnetic resonance imaging*, like CT, is now both sophisticated and fast enough to image heart structures and even blood flow. It is hoped that imaging of blood flow in the coronary arteries will be possible using fast MRI. But the place of MRI in cardiac imaging, as is the case with CT, is largely speculative, since most of the things that it can do are more easily and less expensively accomplished by cardiac ultrasound.

§ 8:27 Cardiac imaging — sonocardiography

Early diagnostic ultrasound machines were simple devices, rather like sonic fish finders (*A-mode sonocardiography*) which were used in the diagnosis of brain pathology. More complex U/S instruments are now standard equipment in gynecological /obstetrical practice and also in cardiology. *M-mode* sonocardiogaphy produces a moving strip (rather like an EKG strip) filled with wavy lines representing the movements and thicknesses of various structures in the heart [see Fig. 8-17]. A contemporaneous continuous EKG trace is included in the strip. M-mode echocardiograms are not easy to read, but the significant aspects of these traces can be pointed out and made plain to lay persons. Sonocardiography is now usually real time, like a movie presentation. It is a easier to read than M-mode and can demonstrate virtually any structural abnormality in the heart. The shapes, positions and movements of the heart valves can be seen, as can abnormal movements or unusual thickening of the ventricular walls. Accumulations of pericardial fluid, provided they are sufficient in amount, can also be seen. Real-time imaging has replaced M-mode echocardiology, which is mainly used by researchers since it is relatively inexpensive. It is also used by neonatologists as a quick way to evaluate neonatal heart functioning in suspicious cases.

"Real time" ultrasound machines, working like a moving camera, show the movements of a thin section through the heart. The location of the section can be altered by moving the probe. The ultrasound data is processed by the computer and put in phase with the EKG trace, so that the electrical activity and the movements of the heart walls and valves are presented together on the same screen. The volumes of the chambers, the patency and shape of the valves, the thickness of the chamber walls, distortion of the valve leaves, and abnormal movement of any structure, can all be seen. The images are recorded on magnetic tape which can be played over repeatedly by the clinician interpreting them. They can also be analyzed by the computer, and measurements of various components in the picture can thus be made and recorded. Computer derived three-dimensional presentations of the multiple thin U/S sections through the heart can also be produced.

Sonocardiography (cardiac ultrasound) has many uses. It is the principal way of showing and evaluating *cardiomegaly*, especially the hereditary types (hypertrophic and dilated cardiomegaly) which can produce angina, arrhythmias, or heart failure. *Subaortic stenosis* (one type of hypertrophic cardiomegaly) is particularly dangerous during the induction of general anesthesia, when the slight loss of contractile power in the heart, produced by the anesthetic agents, can be enough to drastically reduce coronary artery blood flow and precipitate a cardiac arrest. This problem can now be definitively diagnosed in advance of surgery by a sonocardiogram. Cardiac ultrasound is also very useful in the diagnosis of valvular heart

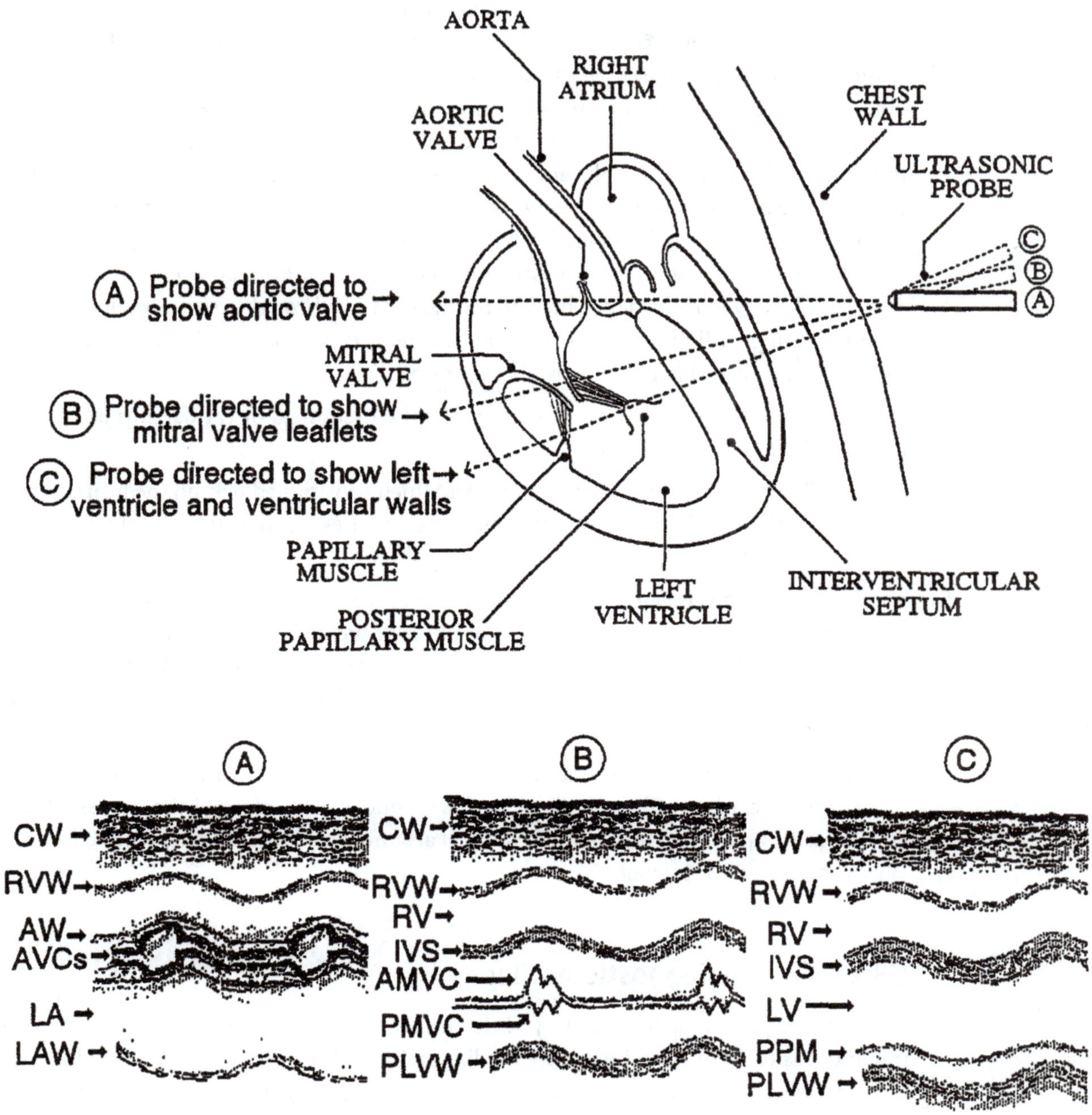

Key to Ⓐ

CW = Chest wall
RVW = Right ventricular wall
AW = Aortic wall
AVCs = Aortic valve cusps
LA = Left atrium
LAW = Left atrial wall

Key to Ⓑ

CW = Chest wall
RVW = Right ventricular wall
RV = Right ventricle
IVS = Interventricular septum
AMVC = Anterior mitral valve cusp
PMVC = Posterior mitral valve cusp
PLVW = Posterior left ventricular wall

Key to Ⓒ

CW = Chest wall
RVW = Right ventricular wall
RV = Right ventricle
IVS = Interventricular septum
LV = Left ventricle
PPM = Posterior papillary muscle
PLVW = Post[r] left ventricular wall

Fig. 8-17 The principle of M-mode echocardiography and normal M-mode strips

disease, *mitral valve prolapse*. Sonocardiology is commonly used during heart surgery to monitor the cardiac output and can even be used to calculate the *left ventricular ejection fraction* in ICU patients confined to bed. Current U/S machines have Doppler capability. Doppler technology is based on the observation that the pitch of the sound from a moving object (like a train whistle) coming towards the observer, changes when the object passes and starts to move away. This effect can be used to image moving things such as blood. If the sonic probe is pointed at the aortic valve or the root of the aorta, the Doppler machine can produce an image of the flowing blood. Cardiac output can be estimated in this way. Turbulent flow due to a deformed valve or *retrograde flow* from an incompetent one, can also be seen. These differences in direction and speed can even be color coded—normal anterograde flow may be made blue and retrograde flow through an incompetent valve colored red. Sonocardiography in short has become very sophisticated, and these advanced modalities are available in virtually all major hospitals.

Several new features have greatly improved the usefulness of cardiac ultrasonography, especially to lawyers. These are:

1. The availability of esophageal probes which (positioned behind the heart) produce much clearer pictures of more posterior structures, such as the mitral valve and the left atrium.

2. Newer software enables the computer to process the pictures, highlighting the most important features, such as the mitral valves or the movements of the ventricular wall, which are then much easier to read. Their evidence may even be clear to lay viewers; indicating whether an atheroma is "hard" or "soft" (likely to rupture and trigger blood clotting).

3. Finally, ultrasound probes can be introduced into the heart and coronary vessels through cardiac catheters. These can "see" under the surface of the tissues, showing the amounts of calcium in the heart wall around a valve that is to be replaced, or some other important detail.

§ 8:28 Electrodiagnostic studies

The principal use of the ordinary 12-lead electrocardiogram (EKG) in disability determination, is to identify and diagnose cardiac arrhythmias of various sorts. The EKG is, in fact, the gold standard in this matter. A clinician palpating and listening to an irregular heart beat may be convinced that it represents atrial fibrillation, but one cannot be absolutely certain without an EKG. The EKG will also show rhythm disturbances and conduction abnormalities that cannot be detected clinically. First degree heart block can only be reliably detected by EKG. The electrical activity of both atria and ventricles is normal in this condition, save that conduction is delayed too long in the bundle of His. This shows up as a prolonged P–R interval on EKG.

It is normally possible, using only the simple 12-lead EKG, to determine the type and the general location of an irritable focus which is giving rise to rhythm disturbances in the heart. Sometimes, however, it is necessary to go beyond this general kind of information and be more precise. If episodes of arrhythmia cannot be well controlled by medical means, surgical intervention may be considered; and this requires accurate localization of the

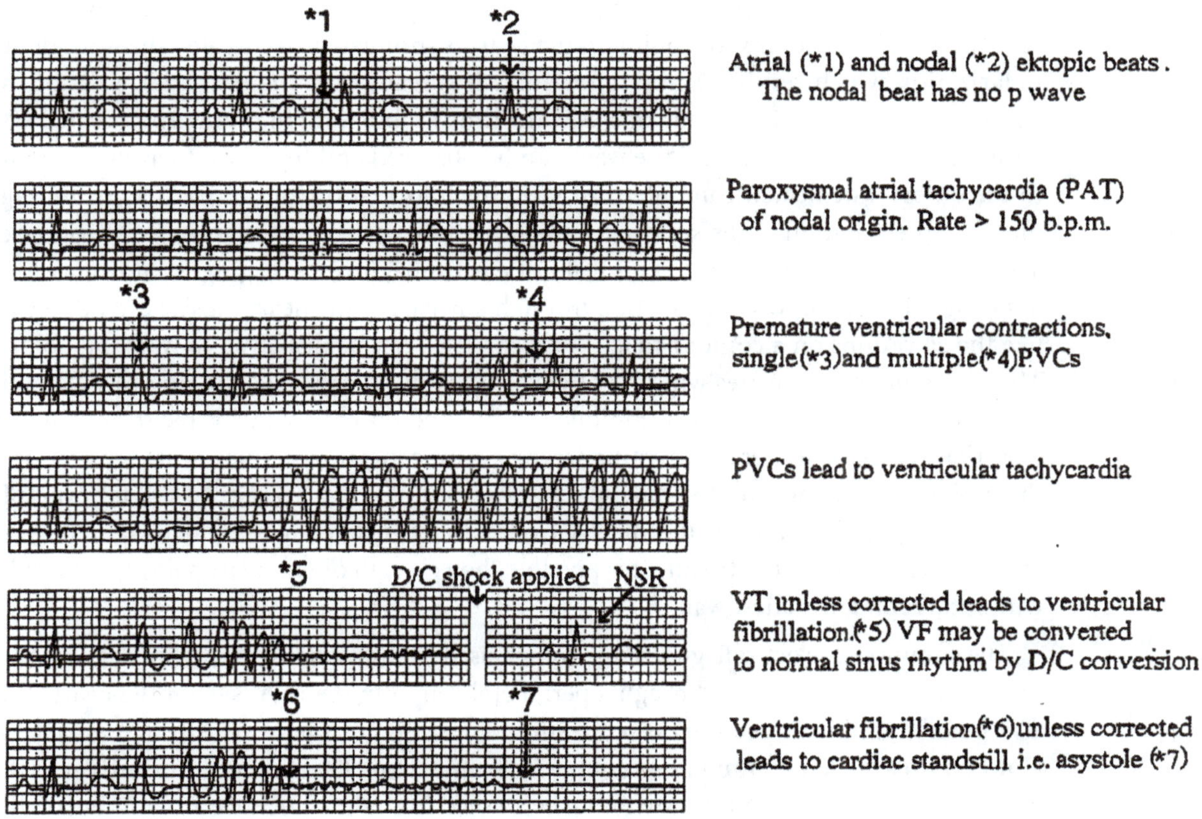

Fig. 8-18 EKG strips representing arrhythmias which may follow an MI

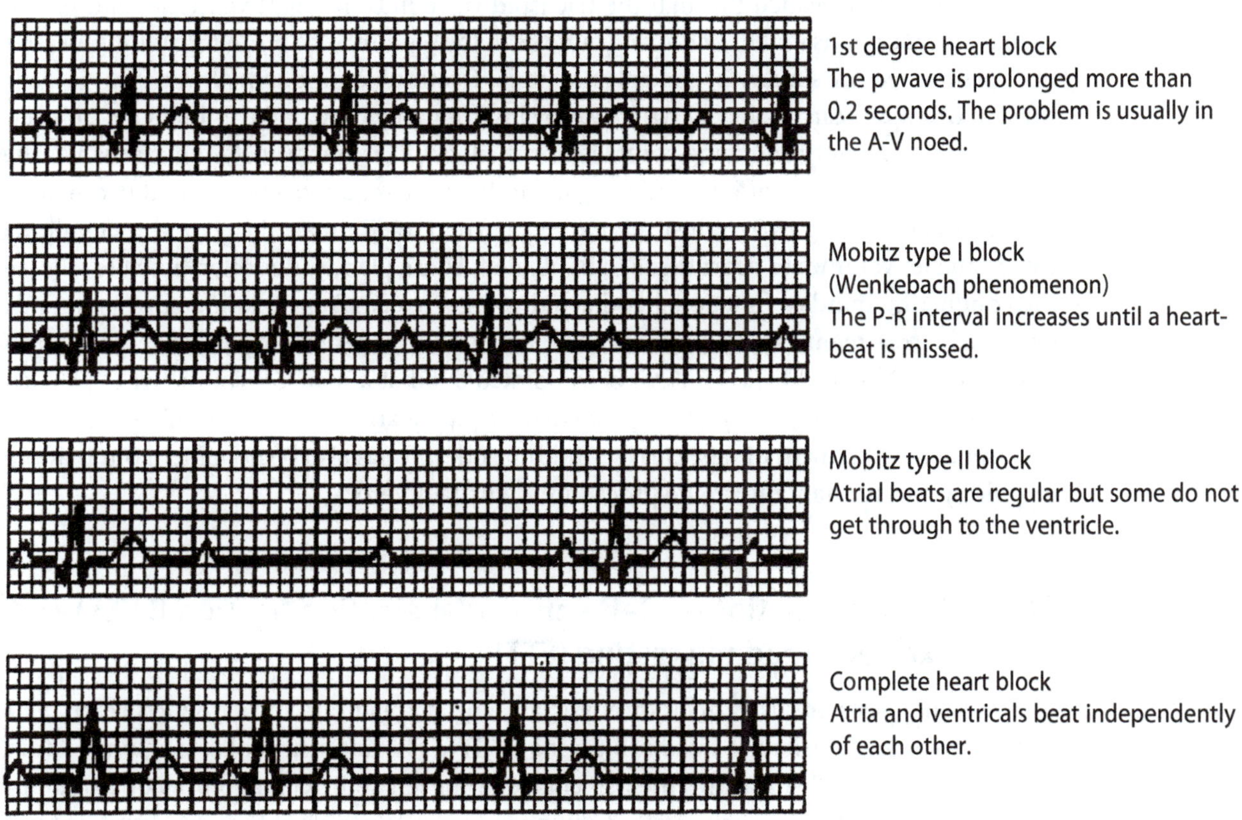

Fig. 8-19 EKG strips representing various kinds of heart blocks

lesion by means of special electrodiagnostic studies. The theoretical principle involved in such studies is simple. If some point on the heart is stimulated electrically, the wave of depolarization which results can be followed as it spreads over the muscular walls of the heart. In the ordinary EKG, only one lead at a time is observed. In more sophisticated systems, all are active at once and the wave can be observed and timed as it passes from one to the other. A dedicated computer can take this information and transcribe its findings on to a representation of the surfaces of the heart. The wave can be shown as it progresses across the surface of the heart. This kind of electrodiagnostic imaging is known as *EKG mapping*. The rate of wave conduction through any part of the heart muscle can be viewed like the elevations on a contour map. Different rates can be displayed in different colors. The end result is that an area which has slow conduction spread will show up as a differently colored area on the map. This technique can be used on patients with recurrent rhythm disturbances to see if there is anything wrong at some location in their heart muscle, or if the problem lies elsewhere. EKG mapping works best with the heart exposed, for example during an operation to find and excise a troublesome irritable focus which is causing arrhythmias resistant to treatment. It is possible, however, to obtain reasonably good results without opening the chest wall.

The commonest electrodiagnostic technique used to study and treat rhythm disturbances involves inserting a catheter through a peripheral vein into the right side of the heart. It is also possible to introduce the catheter into the left side of the heart through an artery. However, this is a less common procedure, since more than 90% of rhythm disturbances are in the interventricular septum, which can be studied from the right atrium. Working on the right side of the heart, the stimulating electrode is set near the A-V node, and the receiving electrode can be threaded through the tricuspid valve into the right ventricle, and placed against various points in the conducting bundles in the septum. The procedure is thus invasive but does not require surgery or general anesthesia. If a troublesome arrhythmic focus is identified in this way it can be ablated right away by inserting a thermal probe through the catheter. This formerly meant producing complete heart block if (as was usually the case when the lesion was in the bundle of His) and the patient therefore required a permanent pacemaker. The use of alternating current instead of direct current to eliminate the ectopic focus allows much smaller volumes of heart tissue to be ablated; consequently, it is often possible to leave the conducting bundles functional and avoid using a pacemaker. Ablation surgery sounds like drastic treatment, and it is—it is only indicated in cases that have not responded to more conservative measures. Yet it has been pointed out that it may seem attractive to patients who have been blacking out and falling due to intermittent arrhythmias, or needing admission to hospital for treatment of nasty arrhythmic episodes. It has also been pointed out that the morbidity and mortality from the procedure is virtually zero.

§ 8:29 Testing function — left ventricular ejection fraction (LVEF) and exercise treadmill testing (ETT)

Two major tests are used by both physicians and compensationists, the *left ventricular ejection fraction* and exercise treadmill testing (ETT). The left ventricular ejection fraction (LVEF) [see Fig. 8-20] measures the percentage of the left ventricular volume of blood put out with each heart beat. The blood remaining in the left ventricle at the end of systole (end systolic volume or ESV) is subtracted from the amount present when the heart is filled (end diastolic volume, or EDV). The LVEF is then calculated by the formula:

$$(EDV - ESV) = LVEF$$

The calculation is simple enough and the end systolic and end diastolic volumes can be obtained in a number of ways. The usual method is to introduce a bolus of radioactive dye (or radiolabeled red blood cells) into the left ventricle and measure the radioactivity before and after systole. The radioactivity in each case will be proportional to the amount of blood present and the ratio of the scintillation counts will represent fairly accurately the volume of blood present in the left ventricle at any one time. The EDV and the ESV can also be estimated by means of a high speed CT or MRI scanner. A quick approximate method, using an ultrasound scanner, is sometimes used in intensive care units, since U/S machines can be brought to the bedside of very sick patients without bothering them too much. The distance between the interventricular septum and the lateral wall of the left ventricle is measured at the end of systole and diastole, and these diameters are taken to represent the volumes of blood present.

In the healthy heart, the LVEF is approximately 0.5, meaning the heart can eject approximately 50% of the left ventricular contents in a single beat Challenged by exercise or some other need, the normal ventricle can put out 75% or more of the end-diastolic volume. The failing heart puts out less than 50% of its left ventricular contents at rest and is unable to increase its performance when challenged. An LVEF of 0.3 is generally considered to represent total cardiac disability.

Exercise treadmill testing (ETT) may be considered the work horse of cardiac disability determination. Indeed, Social Security disability determinations center on the exercise stress test (EST) on the treadmill almost exclusively; Social Security agencies will only pay for other tests under very unusual circumstances. However, any other tests which have been carried out for medical purposes can and should be presented as supporting (or rebutting) evidence, including coronary artery angiograms, even though they may not in themselves prove that the claimant has any heart problems or cardiac disability.

Exercise stress testing has become progressively more sophisticated and safer for heart patients. It is not so long since patients were asked to walk up and down a flight of stairs outside the doctor's office before they had a cardiogram made. The "Masters Two-Step" apparatus, essentially a small set of stairs, was an improvement on this and can still be found in the basement store room of many hospitals. These have been replaced by the treadmill [see Fig. 8-21] or the exercise bicycle (in Europe). The treadmill has many advantages: the handrails, which can prevent a fall; the speed of the rollers can be controlled; and the angle of the treadmill can be altered to simulate walking uphill. The resistance (braking) on the wheels of the exercise bicycle can likewise be adjusted to make the patient do more work. Telemetry monitoring allows the EKG complex and the heart rate to be continuously observed without the patient tripping on the wires. Blood pressure can be measured every few minutes (usually in between the stages of whatever protocol is being used). The measurement of blood pressure is important in this test. Normally blood pressure rises slightly with exercise. If it begins to fall, the heart is not responding to the exercise challenge. The test must be stopped at once, and the patient will probably be transferred rapidly to a coronary car unit for observation.

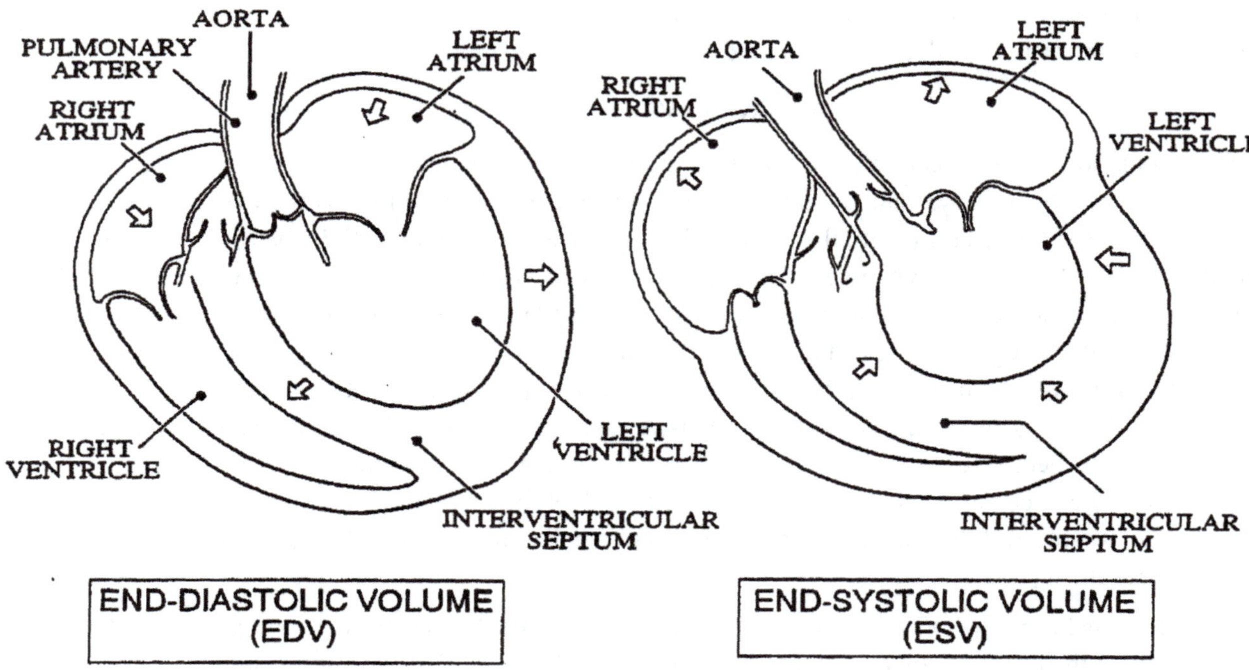

$$LVEF = \frac{(EDV - ESV)}{EDV}$$

Fig. 8-20 Measurement of the left ventricular ejection fraction

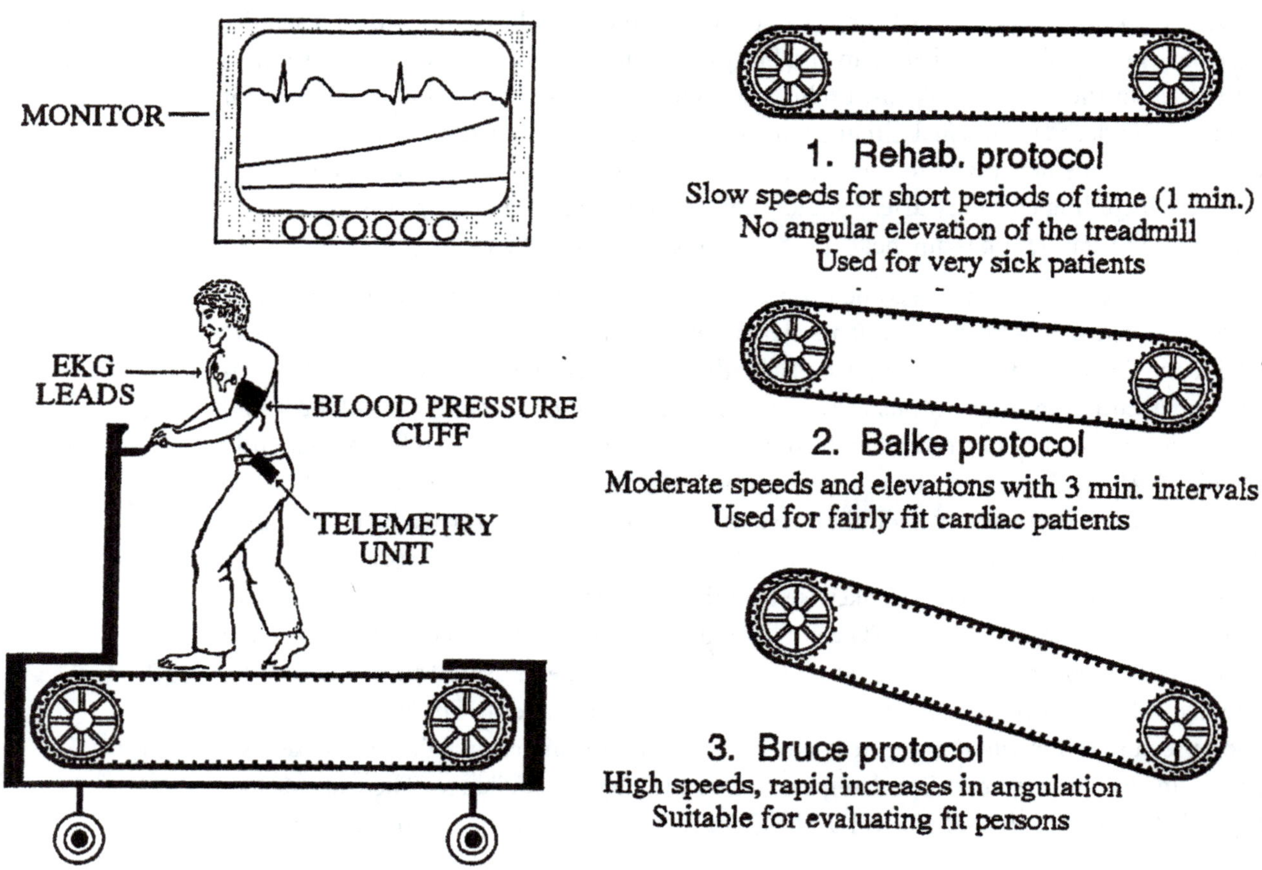

Fig. 8-21 Exercise treadmill testing

A treadmill test will be stopped at the first sign of trouble, but for disability purposes treadmill testing is only considered objective evidence, when one of the following proper *end points* has been reached:

1. Abnormal findings on the EKG trace indicative of myocardial ischemia, OR
2. The patient has reached their maximum allowable heart rate (HR_{max}) calculated as 90% of the difference between their age and the number 210 (allowing 135 b.p.m. for a 60 year old person), OR
3. The patient's blood pressure begins to fall. This last is a sinister sign, and the test must be promptly terminated, with the patient usually being transferred to an intensive care unit for observation and/or treatment.

The procedure will probably be discontinued if the patient complains of chest pain or tiredness, but the test will not be considered satisfactory for purposes of evaluating cardiac disability, since these complaints are subjective. But the test can usually be completed in some other way. If the patient cannot tolerate walking, an exercise bicycle may be used. If the patient can neither walk nor use a bicycle, the exercise may be provided by squeezing a rubber ball or spring loaded device with the hand. Even bedridden patients can be evaluated by dripping increasing amounts of a vasoconstricting agent into the IV to raise vascular resistance, and so incrementally increase the work load of the heart. Most cardiac patients, however, can be evaluated using the treadmill.

The measured work of the treadmill will produce an abnormal EKG in over 80 percent of patients with heart disease, and do so under much safer conditions than the older exercise tests. A treadmill test is usually declared positive for coronary arterial disease when a significant S–T segment depression more than 1 mm deep is found. The S–T depression is most significant when it is of the kind that "slopes down" into the T-wave. Treadmill testing can also be coupled to radionuclear imaging (using radioactive Thallium) that distinguishes abnormal from normal heart muscle. Studies using cardiac ultrasound or electroseismography (ESG) or some other test to show abnormal heart wall movement during the test, are much more sensitive indicators of heart dysfunction than the EKG.

Treadmill testing, taking patients up to their calculated maximum heart rate (HR max), can be used for a number of purposes. It is employed, for instance, to evaluate the exercise tolerance of athletes, to monitor the recovery of patients from heart attacks or other problems, and to measure cardiac disability. Patients who develop their maximum heart rate at stage I of a stress test (lowest speed, gentlest incline) have a poor cardiac reserve. Very fit persons on the other hand may go through all the stages of a demanding regime before reaching their calculated HR_{max}. It is customary, nowadays, to evaluate post-MI patients on the treadmill very soon after the heart attack, often within a week. A very gentle system known colloquially as "rehab" (mentioned earlier) will most likely be followed; this protocol uses very low speeds for short intervals with no elevation of the angle of the treadmill. Later, as the patient's condition improves, more demanding regimes such as the Balke protocol may be used to follow and document the patient's recovery and response to rehabilitation. The particular protocol used is unimportant from the point of view of determining disability, since the results of all treadmill tests are expressed in terms of METs (metabolic units), calculated by computer, which essentially represent the energy or work done by the patient (in Kilocalories) on the treadmill before the test had to be stopped. A very fit person may achieve

15 METs or more on the treadmill; a normal person should make it to 12; someone who has had a significant MI will normally only be able to manage 10 METs at most. Achieving less than 5 METs indicates total disability by any standards.

Part IV.
The Clinical Examination of the Cardiovascular System

§ 8:30 The clinical examination of the heart—observation

The color and general appearance of the skin are important. Pale, dry skin may be a normal finding in some persons. *Pallor* of the nail beds and of the epithelium on the inner surface of the eyelids is likely to represent anemia of some kind. It can be particularly important in a patient with chest pain to note whether, in addition to being pale, the skin is cold and clammy. Pale, cold, clammy skin in such a patient probably indicates massive sympathetic nerve activity. This means that the brain is running short of blood or oxygen or glucose, and is applying massive sympathetic drive to improve its supplies. In short, it implies that cardiac output is low. The same finding in a diabetic patient suggests hypoglycemia, and the cardiac output will be normal. A cold, clammy patient with a bounding pulse is likely to be a diabetic with too much insulin and too little food.

Cyanosis is the term used to describe skin that is blue where it should be pink. Cyanosis can be peripheral or central. *Peripheral cyanosis* is seen in the skin, nail beds, or lips. It can be caused by slow circulation in the skin so that the blood is robbed of a lot of its oxygen. Peripheral cyanosis may only mean then that it is a cold day and the circulation to the skin is shut down. Peripheral cyanosis, of course, may not be normal. Some people have an exaggerated response to cold (Reynaud's disease) to the point that they can even lose fingers because of bad circulation. Cardiac cyanosis is *central.* It is seen, for example, in the tongue and mucous membranes of the mouth. These are warm tissues, and cyanosis here normally means one of two things, serious heart problems or significant lung disease.

The fingernails should be observed for several things. The pallor of anemia may be seen here, and *splinter hemorrhages* under the nails are a sign of rheumatic valvular disease. *Finger clubbing* may also be found This is a thickening of the distal phalanges of the fingers until they look like little clubs. It may also be seen on the toes. Finger clubbing is found in advanced lung disease and in serious chronic heart disorders. In both of these conditions the patient is effectively hypoxic.

The feet and legs must be examined for swelling that might represent *dependent* (cardiac) *edema.* In its typical form this is called "pitting edema" since the impression of a finger pressed into it remains after the pressure is removed (like pressing a finger into soft butter). If the patient is bedridden, the pitting edema is more likely to be found in the lumbosacral area of the back, since this is the dependent area in these patients.

§ 8:31 Examination of the cardiovascular system — auscultation

Auscultation (listening) is normally carried out with the stethoscope. In the examination of the heart, as in that of the lung, it is important to listen to the lung *bases.* Fine crepitations (discontinuous sounds) are a sign of heart failure. The *precordium* (anterior chest wall over the heart) is next examined, initially in order to listen to the heart sounds. [See Fig. 8-2] The stethoscope is placed on the right side of the sternum at the 2nd intercostal space (near the pulmonary valve); then on the left side of the stemum at the 2nd intercostal space (near the aortic valve); then at the apex; and finally over the epigastrium where the tricuspid valve can best be heard. The heart sounds are related to the closing of the valves. The *first heart sound* (S1) represents the closing of the mitral and tricuspid valves at the beginning of systole, when the ventricles are contracting. The *second heart sound* (S2) is due to the closing of the pulmonary and aortic valves at the end of systole. At this time, the pressure is still high in the arteries, but falling in the ventricles so that the valves are slapped back shut and no blood can return to the heart. The second heart sound (S2) is commonly split. This is because the aortic and pulmonary valves do not close at exactly the same time. The reasons for this are complex and need not concern us here. The "split" can be narrowed by taking and holding a deep breath. In some congenital heart conditions the split is unusually "wide" and the deep breath does not narrow it, but instead either makes no difference or widens it still farther. This finding will be described in the records as "fixed wide splitting of S2" and it is a pathological finding. Third and fourth heart sounds (S3 and S4) are pathological and should not be present in the normal heart. The fourth heart sound precedes the first (that is, it happens in late diastole). It is thus synchronous with the contraction of the atrium. It is found in all conditions where the ventricle is stiff and fixed, as when the pericardium is fibrosed. It is caused by the vibration set up when the left atrium discharges a bolus of blood into a "stiff' chamber. The third heart sound (S3) follows S2, and coincides with blood rushing from atrium to ventricle in early diastole. A pronounced S3 or S4, accompanying S1 and S2, sounds like a horse galloping and so it is called "gallop rhythm"; it is a sign of severe heart failure or some other pathological condition.

Murmurs may be heard on auscultation. Murmurs are simply noises made by blood in turbulent flow. This can be normal, for example in high cardiac output states (exercise or pregnancy). In these conditions the blood flows faster through the heart and the resulting murmur is functional rather than pathological. Other causes of murmurs are stenosed or incompetent valves, holes in the heart, or a narrowed segment (stenosis) in the aorta. The murmur of a stenosed aortic valve is systolic in timing, harsh in character, mid-crescendo in form and radiates (with the blood flow from the aorta) to the neck. Because of its form when observed on a sonogram it is sometimes called a "diamond-shaped murmur." The regurgitant murmur of aortic incompetence *is* early diastolic in timing, soft in character, starting loud and then becoming softer (decrescendo murmur); it does not radiate but is heard best down the left side of the sternum. Mention of an "early diastolic decrescendo murmur on the left side of the sternum" indicates the presence of aortic incompetence. Both aortic incompetence and aortic stenosis may be found together in a deformed aortic valve. Deformity of the aortic valve was formerly due in most cases to rheumatic valvular disease, but this disorder is no longer so common as it was. Congenital malformations, e.g., where the valve is bicuspid instead of having three leaves, may well be the cause. The murmur of mitral stenosis is rumbling, mid-diastolic in timing, and is best heard at the apex. It is low pitched and the patient may have to be exercised, (or suddenly turned over on the left side) in order to hear it. Mitral incompetence produces a soft blowing pansystolic murmur which radiates to the axilla. A typical report of the auscultation of the normal heart will read "HS nl, 2AA, no m̄" (heart sounds normal, two in all areas, no murmurs).

§ 8:32 Examination of the cardiovascular system — palpation

The hand should be placed on the *precordium* (the area over the heart) to palpate the apex beat, and it is also possible to detect very loud murmurs in this way. The apex beat, a vibration caused by the forceful contraction of the left ventricle, should be palpable and it is normally located just below and medial to the left nipple (at the mid-axillary line and the fifth intercostal space). This may be recorded as "AB,5ICS,MCL" (apex beat in the fifth intercostal space at the midclavicular line). If a murmur can be felt with the palm of *the* hand (palpable murmur), it is a loud one. Murmurs are graded I–IV or I–VI. It is usual to indicate the convention in use by saying, for example, that a murmur is II / IV or III / VI. The I–IV classification, for example, defines type I as a murmur that can only be heard after exercising the patient. A grade II murmur is one that can be heard without exercise, grade III indicates a loud murmur and grade IV is one that can be felt with the hand on the precordium.

If the neck veins are distended, it is necessary not only to observe the fact, but to palpate them. The reasons for this become apparent when we consider the causes of jugular venous filling. The jugular veins act like a manometer measuring the pressure in the right atrium. If the heart is failing and the right atrial pressure rises, the blood rises up into the neck veins which become visibly distended. JVD means "jugular venous distension." JVP means "jugular venous pressure" and normal JVP should be 5 cm H_2O or less. The JVP can be roughly calculated by observing the height of the blood in the neck veins above the clavicle in centimeters (when the patient is sitting up at an angle of 45°) and adding 5 to it (since the veins do not visibly distend at a central venous pressure less than 5 cm H_2O). The statement "JVP = 0" (more accurately JVP = 0–5 cm H_2O) simply means that no jugulovenous distension was observed. The finding of raised venous pressure must be distinguished from the prominent neck veins which are caused by blockage of the venous drainage into the heart. This is a normal finding in most people at some time and is usually caused by the positioning of the head and neck. True raised venous pressure is shown by flattening the vein between two widely separated fingers and then lifting the lower finger. The upper finger, still in place, will prevent blood from flowing down into the vein from the head. If there is true raised right atrial pressure, blood will well up into the vein once the lower finger is lifted.

The carotid pulses in the neck should be felt and the stethoscope placed over them to listen for the harsh systolic murmurs of carotid artery stenosis. In the abdomen, the liver should be palpated (it gets congested and distended in heart failure). The veins of the abdomen should also be observed for varicosities, and one should listen for stenotic murmurs over the renal arteries. It may even be possible to feel a large *abdominal aortic aneurysm.*

The examination of the CVS is not complete without evaluation of the *radial* and *pedal pulses.* Palpation of the radial pulse *is* indeed the single most important procedure in the examination of the heart. It was almost the only item that the ancient physicians could examine, and they made something of a specialty of it. The rate, volume, regularity or otherwise, and the shape or form of the pulse were all noted. Many terms were coined to describe pulse forms. "Water-hammer pulse" and "plateau pulse" are two of these, describing the typical short-lasting pulse of aortic incompetence and the prolonged pulse of aortic stenosis respectively. It is important to compare the pulses on both sides of the body and to compare the radial pulses with those of the feet. In aortic stenosis the pulses at the wrists may have good volume while the pedal pulses are barely palpable. This is because the narrowing is beyond the takeoff point for the arteries to their arms, but the flow to the legs (beyond the stenosed segment) is markedly diminished. The volume and rate of the pulse are important in clinical medicine. In a pale, clammy patient, a slow thready pulse may mean that he /she has simply fainted. A rapid thready pulse, however, means shock, inadequacy of the circulatory volume due either to blood loss, sudden expansion of the vascular bed or poor cardiac output. A cold, clammy patient in a hypoglycemic attack usually has a good volume pulse and a good blood pressure because the blood volume and cardiac output are normal; the problem is a sugar shortage in the brain. A strong, regular radial pulse indicates good cardiac output and generally implies a healthy heart. An absent or diminished pulse in one leg normally only means arterial insufficiency in that limb. A notation in the medical record that the pedal pulse on one side was weak or impalpable may, of course, only mean that the examiner was palpating the wrong place on the dorsum of the foot. The finding of a discrepancy between the pedal pulses by a competent examiner in a patient with claudication pain on walking supports the diagnosis of atherosclerotic peripheral vascular disease.

Short Working Vocabulary of Cardiovascular Terms

A-fib: Atrial fibrillation.

ABMCL51CS: Apex beat (heard) at the mid-clavicular line at the third intercostal space, the normal location just below the left nipple.

AB: Apex beat.

ACBG: Aorto-coronary bypass grafting.

ALMl: Anterolateral myocardial infarction.

AMI: Acute myocardial infarction.

Angina: Cardiac pain without damage to the myocardium.

Angiogram: General term for a picture of a blood vessel, but generally used as a synonym for arteriogram, e.g., a coronary artery angiogram.

Angiography: General term for the process or kind of study used to obtain images of a blood vessel and its functioning, e.g., "contrast angiography showed 75% occlusion of the proximal part of the anterior descending branch of the left coronary artery."

Apex beat: The point on the chest where the heart sounds are most easily heard, normally just below the left nipple.

Apical pulse: The heart rate counted using the stethoscope placed over the point of maximal impulse (PMI). Nurses commonly check the heart rate heard apically against that palpated over the radial pulse in the wrist.

Arteriogram: Literally a picture of an artery, e.g. a carotid arteriogram. [See *Angiogram.*]

Arteriography: The process or kind of study used to obtain a picture of an artery, but generally used to describe the product itself, e.g., "arteriography of the coronary arteries was negative."

Arteriospasm: Contraction of the muscle walls (media) of arteries so as to reduce blood flow.

AS: Aortic stenosis.

ASCAD: Atherosclerotic coronary artery disease.

ASCD: Atherosclerotic cardiac disease.

ASCVD: Atherosclerotic cardiovascular disease.

ASHD: Atherosclerotic heart disease.

ASPVD: Atherosclerotic peripheral vascular disease.

Atria: The receiving chambers (left and right) of the heart.

AV: Atrioventricular, e.g., the AV node in the right atrium.

AWMI: Anterior wall myocardial infarction.

Bacterial endocarditis: Bacterial infection of the membranes lining the heart and covering the heart valves.

BBB: Bundle branch block, e.g., LBBB is left bundle branch block.

C.cath: Cardiac catheterization.

CA/cath: Coronary artery catheterization.

CABG: Coronary artery bypass graft.

CAD: Coronary artery disease.

cap.ref.: Capillary refill. A simple clinical test of perfusion of blood in the skin by pressing on skin and then watching the flow of blood back into the blanched area.

Cardiac tamponade: Where blood flows into the pericardial sac and exerts pressure on the heart. If this pressure is not released, the condition is normally fatal. Cardiac tamponade may be due to trauma or be a complication of a heart attack where part of the ventricular wall ruptures and allows blood under pressure to escape into the pericardium.

Cardiac failure: Any condition where cardiac output is insufficient to meet the demands of the body. In high output failure, e.g., in hyperthyroidism, the cardiac output may be normal or high but still insufficient to supply the excessive demands of the tissues. In low output failure the heart is not able to supply the normal requirements of the body.

cath.: Catheterization.

CCU: Coronary care unit.

CHD: Coronary heart disease.

CHF: Congestive heart failure; where the lungs are overloaded with blood backed up behind the left ventricle.

Circle of Willis: The system of interconnections between the major arteries supplying the brain which allows them to compensate for one another if one or more of them should be narrowed.

Constrictive pericarditis: Where fibrous scarring of the pericardial membranes has occurred which inhibits the ability of the heart to expand.

cor: The heart.

COW: The circle of Willis.

CPK: Creatinine phosphokinase (an important cardiac enzyme).

Crescendo/decrescendo murmur: One which rises to a peak and then falls away again, typically the "diamond shaped" murmur of aortic valve stenosis.

CVA: Cerebrovascular accident, i.e., a stroke.

CVD: Cardiovascular disease.

CVP: Central venous pressure.

CVS: Cardiovascular system.

Decrescendo murmur: One which starts loud and gradually fades away, typically the left parasternal diastolic murmur of aortic incompetence.

Diastole: The filling phase of the cardiac cycle.

DOE: Dyspnea on exertion.

Early diastolic murmur: One heard early in diastole, i.e., after the first heart sound (S1).

Eclampsia: Term derived from the Greek word for "lightning." It refers to a sudden onset of a particularly malignant form of hypertension (with typical blood pressures of

200/120) accompanied by seizures, which occurs in late pregnancy or even after delivery of the baby. It can be fatal for both mother and child if not treated vigorously. See also *Preeclampsia*.

Edema: Excessive fluid in any location or tissue. Cellular edema means that cells are distended with water, and interstitial edema refers to excess fluid in the interstitial compartment (outside the blood vessels and not inside cells).

EKG: Electrocardiogram.

Endocardium: The inner lining layer of the heart chambers.

EST: Exercise stress test, i.e., a treadmill test or exercise bicycle test.

Exercise stress test: The commonest performance test used to evaluate cardiac functioning. The EKG is monitored continuously and the blood pressure intermittently during controlled exercise. Other monitors, such as radioactive dyes, a sonocardiogram, or electroseismogram may also be used to check on wall motion.

Gallop rhythm: A term used to describe the presence of a third and fourth heart sounds together with the normal ones, S1 and S2. When all these are present together, the total sound resembles a horse galloping.

Hb: Hemoglobin.

HBP: High blood pressure.

HCM: Hypertrophic cardiomyopathy. See also *IHSS*.

HCO^-: Bicarbonate (ion).

Hct: Hematocrit.

HCVD: Hypertensive cardiovascular disease.

HR_{max}: The maximum allowable heart rate to be reached in an exercise stress test (EST). It is calculated by the formula 90% × (210 − age in years). HR_{max} is an important concept in cardiac disability, since it is one of the proper stopping points in an EST. Subjective complaints of pain and discomfort may stop a test, but the test is not usually considered valid for disability purposes.

HS: Heart sounds.

HSnl2AA$\overline{0}$m$\overline{0}$G: Heart sounds normal, two in all areas, no murmurs, no gallop rhythm.

HTN: Hypertension.

ICF: Intracellular fluid.

IHSS: Idiopathic hypertrophic subaortic stenosis.

ISF: Interstitial fluid (fluid outside cells but not in blood vessels).

IVC: Inferior vena cava.

JVD: Jugular venous distention.

K^+: Potassium ion.

LA: Left atrium.

LAD: Left anterior descending (coronary artery) or left axis deviation.

LAH: Left anterior hemiblock.

Late diastolic murmur: One heard in late diastole, just before the first heart sound (S1).

LBBB: Left bundle branch block.

LDH: Lactic dehydrogenase (a cardiac enzyme).

Left ventricular ejection fraction: The fraction of the volume of blood in the left ventricle which is put out with each contraction of the heart. If 50% of the left ventricular volume were ejected, this would give a LVEF of 0.5 (the normal value at rest).

LPH: Left posterior hemiblock.

LV: Left ventricle.

LVEF: Left ventricular ejection fraction.

LVH: Left ventricular hypertrophy.

LVI: Left ventricular ischemia.

Lymphogram: A representation of a lymphatic vessel or vessels.

M/S: Mitral stenosis.

M1: The first mitral sound.

MCL: Mid-clavicular line.

METs: Metabolic units (used in exercise treadmill testing).

MI: Myocardial infarction.

Mitral valve prolapse: Where the chordae tendineae, or the little muscles controlling them, are not functioning properly, so that the valve cusps balloon up into the left atrium during systole. This is a serious complication of a myocardial infarction, where the tiny muscles controlling the chordae have infarcted and ruptured (usually 5–10 days after the Ml). Mitral valve prolapse of a less catastrophic nature can be found without any heart damage in some young persons, where the valve cusps balloon up into the left atrium. The condition may asymptomatic, but is commonly associated with episodes of chest pain and the periodic occurrence of paroxysmal atrial tachycardia (PAT).

MVP: Mitral valve prolapse.

Myocardial infarction: Necrosis (death) of myocardium.

Myocardium: Heart muscle.

NSR: Normal sinus rhythm.

NSSTTW: Non-specific S–T and T-wave changes.

P: Pulse (rate) or passive.

P1, P2: The first and second pulmonic beat sounds.

PABs: Premature atria beats.

PAC: Premature atrial contraction.

Pansystolic murmur: One heard throughout systole.

Paroxysmal atrial tachycardia: Episodes of rapid heart beat (>150 per minute and typically 180–200 bpm). The condition may last a few minutes and remit spontaneously, or with carotid massage, but may be persistent and require IV treatment with drugs (such as verapamil) to terminate them.

PAT: Paroxysmal atrial tachycardia.

PCs: Packed (red) cells. [See also PRBCs].

Pedal pulses: The pulses in the feet, i.e., the *dorsalis pedis* pulse (on the top of the foot) and the *posterior tibial pulse* (felt just behind the medial malleolus (ankle bone).

Pericardial fluid: The lubricant fluid secreted into the pericardial sac which surrounds the heart.

Pericardial sac: Essentially the space between the two pericardial membranes, the visceral (inner) and the parietal (outer) pericardium.

Pericarditis: Inflammation or infection of the pericardium.

Pericardium: The outer coverings of the heart. There are two of them, the visceral and parietal pericardial membranes. Pericardial fluid is secreted into the space between them, thus enabling them to slip easily over one another, so as to allow the heart to expand and contract smoothly.

PMI: Point of maximal impulse, the apex beat of the heart.

PMV: Prolapsed mitral valve.

PND: Paroxysmal nocturnal dyspnea (a symptom of heart failure).

Point of maximal impulse: Where the heart beat can best be palpated or heard with the stethoscope on the chest wall. This point is normally just below and medial to the left nipple. The PMI is an equivalent expression for the apex beat.

polys: Polymorphonuclear leukocytes (white blood cells).

PRBCs: Packed red blood cells (used for blood transfusion).

Preeclampsia: A condition occurring during pregnancy (or just after delivery) which precedes and can lead to eclampsia. It presents as a clinical triad of hypertension, edema of the fingers, and proteinuria. Vigorous medical treatment, enforced rest (sometimes in hospital) can usually prevent the occurrence of eclampsia and enable the baby to be delivered live.

Proteinuria: Protein in the urine. It is a sign of renal failure, and one of the cardinal signs of preeclampsia.

PRWP: Poor R-wave progression. An EKG sign of an antaerolateral myocardial infarction.

PTT: Partial thromboplastin time (a blood coagulation test).

PVD: Peripheral vascular disease.

RA: Right atrium.

RAD: Right axis deviation.

Radial pulse: The heart rate counted by palpating the radial pulse at the wrist.

RBBB: Right bundle branch block.

RBCs: Red blood cells.

RCC: Red (blood) cell count.

Rh: The rhesus antigen on the surface of red blood cells, e.g., a patient may be described as Rh^+ or perhaps as Rh^-.

RV: Right ventricle.

S-A: Sinoatrial (node in the right atrium) which initiates the electrical activity of the heart..

S1: The first (normal) heart sound.

S1,S2: The first and second (normal) heart sounds.

S2: The second (normal) heart sound.

S3: A third (abnormal) heart sound heard in early diastole.

S4: A fourth (abnormal) heart sound heard in late diastole.

sed. rate: Erythrocyte sedimentation rate (ESR).

Serous pericarditis: Inflammation of the pericardium where excess inflammatory exudate (not purulent as in a bacterial infection) is secreted into the pericardial sac. Serous pericarditis is typically found in rheumatic conditions.

SGOT: Serum glutamic oxaloacetic transaminase (a liver enzyme also found in heart muscle); estimated in liver function tests (LFTs).

SKG: Sonocardiogram or sonocardiography.

SO_2: The saturation of hemoglobin with oxygen (expressed as a percentage). Note that this is not the same thing as the PaO_2. [See § 9:10]

Sonocardiogram: Image of the heart obtained using cardiac ultrasound (U/S).

Sonocardiography: Study of the heart using ultrasound (U/S).

SVC: Superior vena cava, as in "SVC syndrome."

SVT: Supraventricular tachycardia.

Systole: The emptying phase of the cardiac cycle.

Systolic blood pressure: The upper limit of pressure attained with each heart contraction.

TIBC: Total iron binding capacity (of blood proteins).

Tuberculous pericarditis: A complication of tuberculosis where spread of the infection from the lungs to the pericardium occurs.

V-tach: Ventricular tachycardia. A fatal cardiac arrhythmia unless stopped.

Vasospasm: Virtually an equivalent term for arteriospasm, an occlusive constriction of a blood vessel, whether artery or vein or capillary bed.

Venogram: A study or report of a study of veins, e.g. contrast venography.

Ventricles: The pumping chambers of the heart.

WBCC: White blood cell count.

WBCs: White blood cells.

WPW: Wolf / Parkinson / White (syndrome). A condition produced by an aberrant pathway through the fibrous ring between the left atrium and left ventricle, which allows electrical stimulation to reach the interventricular septum. This produces frequent ventricular arrhythmias which are difficult to manage and potentially very dangerous. It is now usually treated by inserting an electrode through a catheter and ablating the unwanted pathway.

Specimen Handwritten Note on a CVS Patient

47 y.o. HF c/o #1. Chest pain - acute onset
#2. DM x 15 yr.
#3. A/D x 1 yr.

HCC:- #1. Pt is HW who has been having episodes of epigastric & central chest pain x 2/12. attacks typically last 5–10 min, induced by exercise but also occur p.c. & at rest, sometimes when upset. Acute onset of more severe pain 2 hrs ago → jaw and LUE. Not helped by rest or TNG.

#2. Acute onset DM aged 20, not controlled by OHM's. Reasonably good control c̄ NPH 100. 50U NPH q/am & 20U reg. q/pm a.c.

#3. Anxiety c̄ depressive episodes beginning 1 yr ago. Not really related to stressors. Mild. controlled by Ativan 1 mg HS p.r.n.

PMH:- Hx of heart (m) noticed in childhood. Tx'd c̄ PCN to cover dental procedures. ō hx ASHD or HTN.

F.H.:- FH of HTN otherwise N/C.

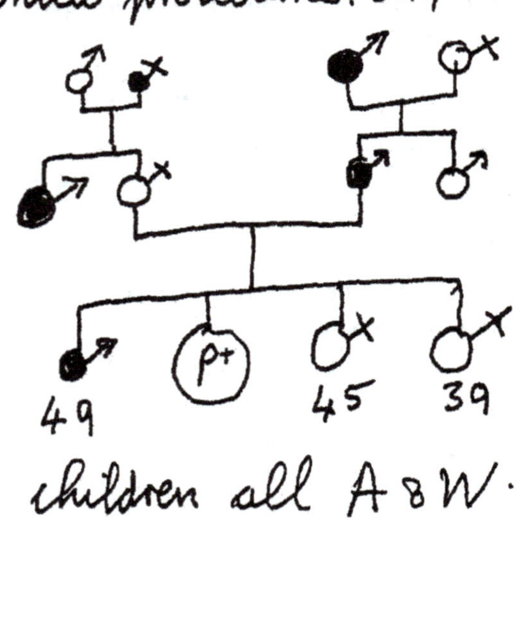

SH:- Married c̄ 3 children all A&W.

Translation of Handwritten Note on CVS Patient

IDENTIFICATION & CHIEF COMPLAINTS:

47 year old hispanic female complaining of-

#1. Chest pain - acute onset
#2. Diabetes mellitus for 15 years
#3. Anxiety/depression for 1 year

HISTORY OF CHIEF COMPLAINTS:

#1. Patient is a housewife who has been having episodes of epigastric and central chest pain for two months. The attacks typically last 5-10 minutes, are brought on by exercise but also occur after meals, also at rest sometimes when she is upset. Acute onset of more severe (than usual) chest pain 2 hours ago, radiating into the jaw and left arm. Not helped by rest or nitroglycerin.

#2. Acute onset of diabetes mellitus aged 20, not controlled by oral hypoglycemic (medications). Reasonably good control (achieved) on NPH U100 (a type and strength of injectable insulin with 100 units of insulin in 1 ml of solution) 50 units each morning and 20 units in the evening before food (the evening meal).

#3. Anxiety with depressive episodes beginning one year ago. Not really related to stressors (stressful events). (Episodes are) mild, controlled by ativan 1 milligram at bed time (hora somniae) as needed.

PAST MEDICAL HISTORY:

History of heart murmur noticed in childhood. Given penicillin to cover dental procedures. No history of atherosclerotic heart disease or hypertension.

FAMILY HISTORY:

Positive family history of hypertension (see diagram of family tree) otherwise nothing contributory.

> [Diagram shows four generations beginning with the patient's grandparents, then her parents, then her brother and sisters. Her children are not included since they are noted (below) to be alive and well]

SOCIAL HISTORY:

Married with three children, alive and well.

ROS:- CNS:- N/C

CVS:- ō PND, ō ankle swelling or other signs of dependent edema. ō hx of claudication or VVs.

RS:- N/C.

G.I.:- ō hx sugg^v of PUD or IBD. ō change of BHs.

IS:- N/C

Ob/Gyn - $G_3 P_3$, A & W.

P/E Sl. obese & short H ♀ A ≏ SA. Skin cold & clammy

CNS:- A & O × 3. Anxious facies.

RS:- Bases clear.

Cor:- HR 100/min, occ^l PVC, BP 100/60. HS nl, $S_1 S_2$ nl AA.
AB 5ICS MCL, ESM II/VI → neck, ō (r) or (g)

PPs:- Radial, femoral, pedal palpable bilat but thready.

Abd:- LKKS = 0, ō masses, ō tenderness

Ext:- s̄ CC or E.

Integ:- ō rashes.

A:- #1. Probable AMI 2° ASHD, R/O hypoglycemia
#2. DM ? Type I, tx'd c̄ insulin U-100
#3. A/D, mild, tx'd c̄ ativan. ? ∝ developing CAD.
#4. VSD probably N/C to PI

P:- #1 12 lead EKG → if nl. repeat in 2°
#2 Cardiac enzymes & repeat in 4°–6°
#3. Admit to CCU.

Allison Hart M.D

REVIEW OF SYSTEMS:

Central nervous stem: Non-contributory.

Cardiovascular system: No paroxysmal nocturnal dyspnea (sign of heart failure) no ankle swelling or other signs of dependent edema. No history of claudication or varicose veins. Respiratory system: Non contributory.

Gastrointestinal stem: No history suggestive of peptic ulcer disease or inflammatory bowel disease. No change in bowel habits (can be a sign of cancer).

Integument system: Non-contributory

Obstetrics/gynecology: Gravida 3/parous 3 (pregnant three times, delivered three live babies) (all) alive and well.

PHYSICAL EXAMINATION

Slightly obese and short Hispanic female with appearance approximately equal to stated age. Skin cold and clammy.

Central nervous system: Alert and oriented to time, place and circumstances. Anxious facial expression.

Respiratory system: (Lung) bases clear (to auscultation presumably)

Cor (heart): Heart rate 100 beats per minute, an occasional premature ventricular con traction, blood pressure 100/60 (mm Hg), heart sounds normal, first and second heart sounds normal in all areas. Ejection systolic murmur grade two out of a possible six, radiating into the neck, no rubs or gallop (murmurs) Peripheral pulses: Radial, femoral, pedal (pulses) palpable bilaterally but thready.

Abdomen: Liver, both kidneys and spleen not enlarged, no masses, no tenderness.

Extremities: No finger clubbing, cyanosis or edema.

Integumentary system: No rashes

ASSESS.

#l. Probable acute myocardial infarction due to atherosclerotic heart disease, but rule out hypoglycemia.

#2. Diabetes mellitus ? Type I, treated with insulin.

#3. Anxiety/depression, mild, treated with Ativan. Possibly related to developing coronary artery disease.

#4. Ventricular septal defect, probably non contributory to present illness.

PLAN.

1. 12 lead EKG, if normal order a repeat (EKG) in 2 hours.

#2. Order cardiac enzymes (estimation) and repeat in 4–6 hours.

#3. Admit to Coronary Care Unit.

Allison Hart M.D.

Chapter Nine

The Lungs

§ 9:1 Introduction — the legal importance of lung disease

Lungs principally feature — so far as lawyers are concerned — in disability determinations of one kind or another, but the respiratory system also crops up in all sorts of ways as a part of or factor in other legal problems. The asbestosis cases, for instance, are products liability suits, but much of the evidence relates to lung pathology. Furthermore, as was noted with the heart, lung impairments can enter into and complicate other problems. If an injury or deficit is accompanied by lung disease, it is likely to be more difficult to treat, slower to recover and to be more disabling. In short, some knowledge of pulmonary medicine is important for lawyers working in personal injury or disability areas.

Here again, as with hearts, the amount of knowledge that is absolutely necessary for compensation purposes is quite limited. Primarily the lawyer needs to know about lung function tests. But to really understand what one is doing, something should also be known about respiration in general and about the structure and functioning of the lung in particular.

Part I.
Anatomy and Physiology of the Lungs

§ 9:2 Basic anatomy

The lungs, if put together, would look like a beehive. Separately, each lung is like half a beehive with one half on each side of the heart. When sectioned, they look like sponges and this is no accident. Sponges relax after compression and passively take up water; the lungs expand to take in air which is presented to the blood passing through the lungs for gas exchange. The space between the two lungs is called the *mediastinum*, and the structures which are located in this space (the heart, the thymus gland and a few other things) are called the mediastinal contents or mediastinal structures.

It is not necessary to go into the minutiae of pulmonary physiology but it is helpful to have some idea about the mechanics of breathing and gas exchange.

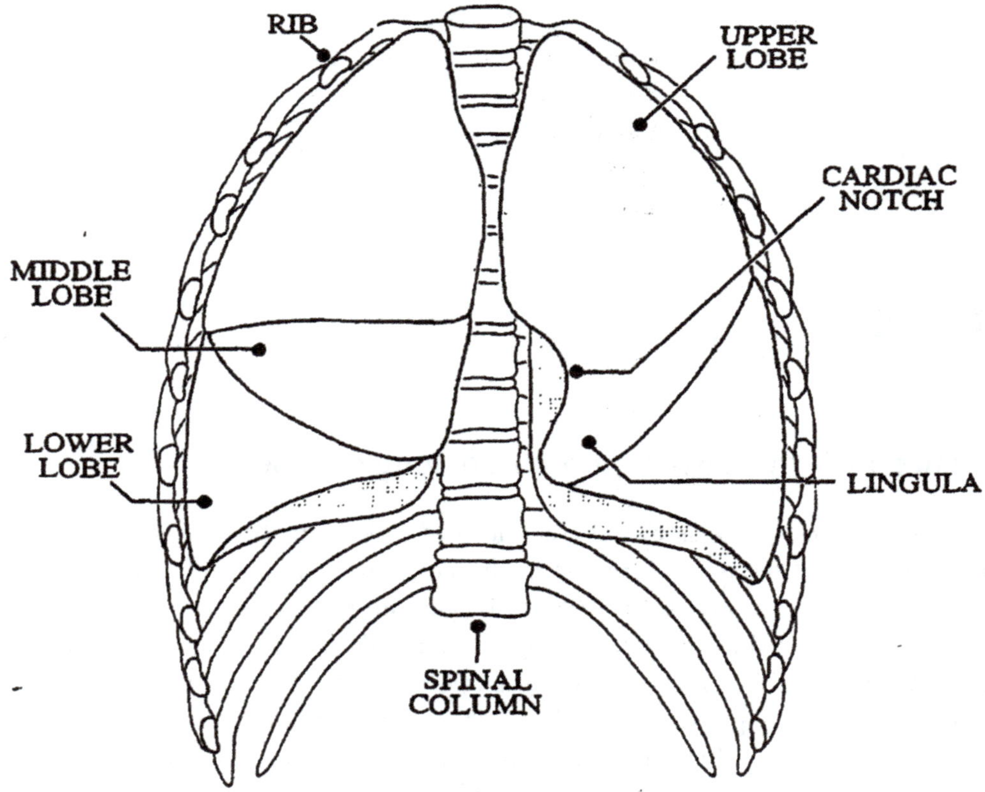

Fig. 9-1 The lobes of the lung—anterior view

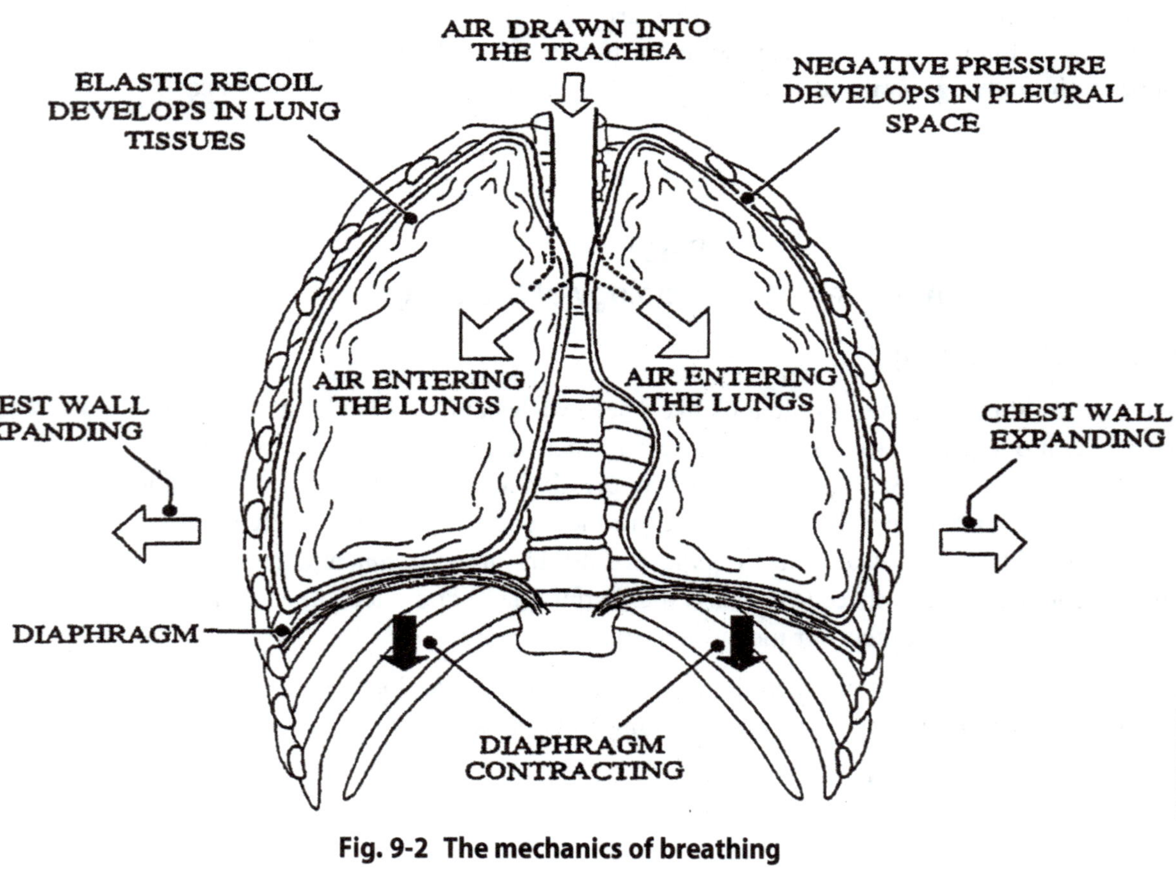

Fig. 9-2 The mechanics of breathing

§ 9:3 The mechanics of breathing — inspiration

The lungs are set inside a sealed cavity — the chest (thorax). [See Fig. 8-2] This cavity is sealed air tight by a double membrane, an inner layer covering the lung and the outer one lining the inside of the chest wall. These are called the *pleural membranes* or pleura, and the space between them is called the *pleural cavity*. The visceral pleura covers the lungs and the parietal pleura lines the thorax. These membranes produce a lubricating fluid which allows the lung to expand smoothly inside the chest as the two pleural surfaces slide easily over one another. An infection or inflammation of this pleural cavity is called a *pleuritis* (the old term was pleurisy). If there is too much pleural fluid for any reason, this is called a *pleural effusion*. When this sealed chamber is enlarged, air is sucked down from the mouth and nose into the expanding lung to fill the vacuum in the enlarged chest cavity. There are basically two (or three) mechanisms for enlarging the chest cavity and so drawing air down into the lungs.

1. The muscles of the diaphragm contract and pull downwards.
2. The ribs move forward and outward to expand the chest further.
3. For quiet breathing, only the diaphragmatic movement is needed; for more strenuous breathing, the chest wall moves also. For real emergencies, there are extra muscles running from the neck down inside the anterior chest wall — the *accessory muscles of respiration* — which pull on the ribs and expand the chest a little further. If the accessory muscles are seen moving in the neck, it is a sign of maximal respiratory effort. Patients with severe lung disease use these muscles to breathe even when they are sitting at rest in a chair. So a statement that the accessory muscles of respiration were moving at rest has sinister implications so far as the patient is concerned.

§ 9:4 The mechanics of breathing — expiration

Expiration in the normal lung is an entirely different process from inspiration. Unlike a sponge, the lung is supplied with elastic fibers. When the diaphragm is being drawn downward and the chest wall pulled outward, these elastic fibers absorb energy as the lung expands. At the end of inspiration when the muscles of respiration relax, the elastic fibers of the lungs contract and push the air out. So while we have to work to fill the lungs, they empty largely in this passive manner, as energy delivered to elastic tissues during inspiration is used to expel air during expiration. When these elastic tissues become fragmented and destroyed in advanced *chronic lung disease*, the patients, in addition to their other problems, have to work to exhale, pushing with the muscles of the abdominal wall to get the air out of their lungs. This abdominal expelling of air from the lungs is not efficient, and so precious oxygen is used up by a patient who can ill spare it.

§ 9:5 The upper airways

The air passages are distinguished into the upper and lower airways. [See Fig. 9-3] The upper airways, the part above the vocal cords, have several structures, each with peculiar functions. The *paranasal sinuses*, for instance, probably act as resonators when we speak or sing. However, the two main functions of the upper airway are:

1. To filter and generally condition the entering air [see Fig. 9-5].
2. To protect the airways while food is being swallowed.

The hairs of the nostrils remove larger dust particles, and the incoming air is also warmed and moistened as it flows over the complicated surface contours created by the *turbinate bones* in the nose. The *epiglottis* at the back of the tongue is a cartilaginous flap connected to the pharyngeal wall by muscles which contract reflexly and pull it down to cover the larynx during *deglutition* (swallowing). Impairment of the deglutition reflex by head injury or general anesthesia, or even too much alcohol, can lead to soiling of the airway with food which may produce *inhalation pneumonitis.*

The *immune response* of the airways begins in this area. The pharyngeal tonsils and the adenoids form a circle of lymphatic tissue at the back of the pharynx which is known as the *ring of Waldeyer.* Here, at the very entrance to the lungs, microorganisms and other foreign matter can be recognized, and the immune response to them initiated.

§ 9:6 The lower airways — the bronchial tree

The lower airway [see Fig. 9-3] begins with the vocal cords which are at the top of the *larynx.* Below the larynx is the *trachea,* the largest in diameter of the lower air passages. The trachea is also distinguished by the fact that it contains not only muscle but incomplete rings of cartilage which stiffen it and keep it from collapsing. The trachea divides at a point known as the *carina* into the two main-stem bronchi (left and right). The *carina* is a tiny cartilaginous ridge at the origins of the main stem bronchi which directs air preferentially into the right side of the lung. Further divisions produce the *segmental bronchi* which supply the ten or so main divisions of each lung. The bronchi all contain muscle and also some cartilage (a good deal less of the latter than is found in the trachea). Beyond the bronchi lie further divisions called *bronchioles* which contain muscle but no cartilage. The smallest of these lead into the air sacs and are called *terminal bronchioles.*

The mucosal linings of the lower airways are vascular and function importantly as a heat and fluid exchange system. Air coming into the lungs is warmed and moistened, while air that is being exhaled loses heat and moisture to the walls of the airways. The smooth muscle in the walls of the airways can be used to increase or decrease the diameter of the airways. Constricting these muscles and narrowing the airways reduces heat loss while dilating them increases it. This mechanism is very reactive in cold weather in order to preserve heat, which explains why asthmatic attacks can sometimes be triggered by exposure to cold air.

Small particles which escape the filtering mechanisms of the nose can be trapped and expelled in the mucus secretions delivered into the airways. A thin film of mucus is secreted from glands in the airway walls onto the surface of the *cilia* (little hairlike processes) which line the airways. The movement of the cilia propels this layer of mucus, like a moving carpet, upward towards the pharynx where it can be swallowed or coughed out. The *cough reflex is* triggered by large amounts of mucus, or by larger foreign bodies, or indeed by anything which a cough might clear from the airways. Movement of the cilia is slowed down even during the smoking of a single cigarette, and the cilia become fragmented and inactive with prolonged exposure to tobacco smoke and other airway contaminants.

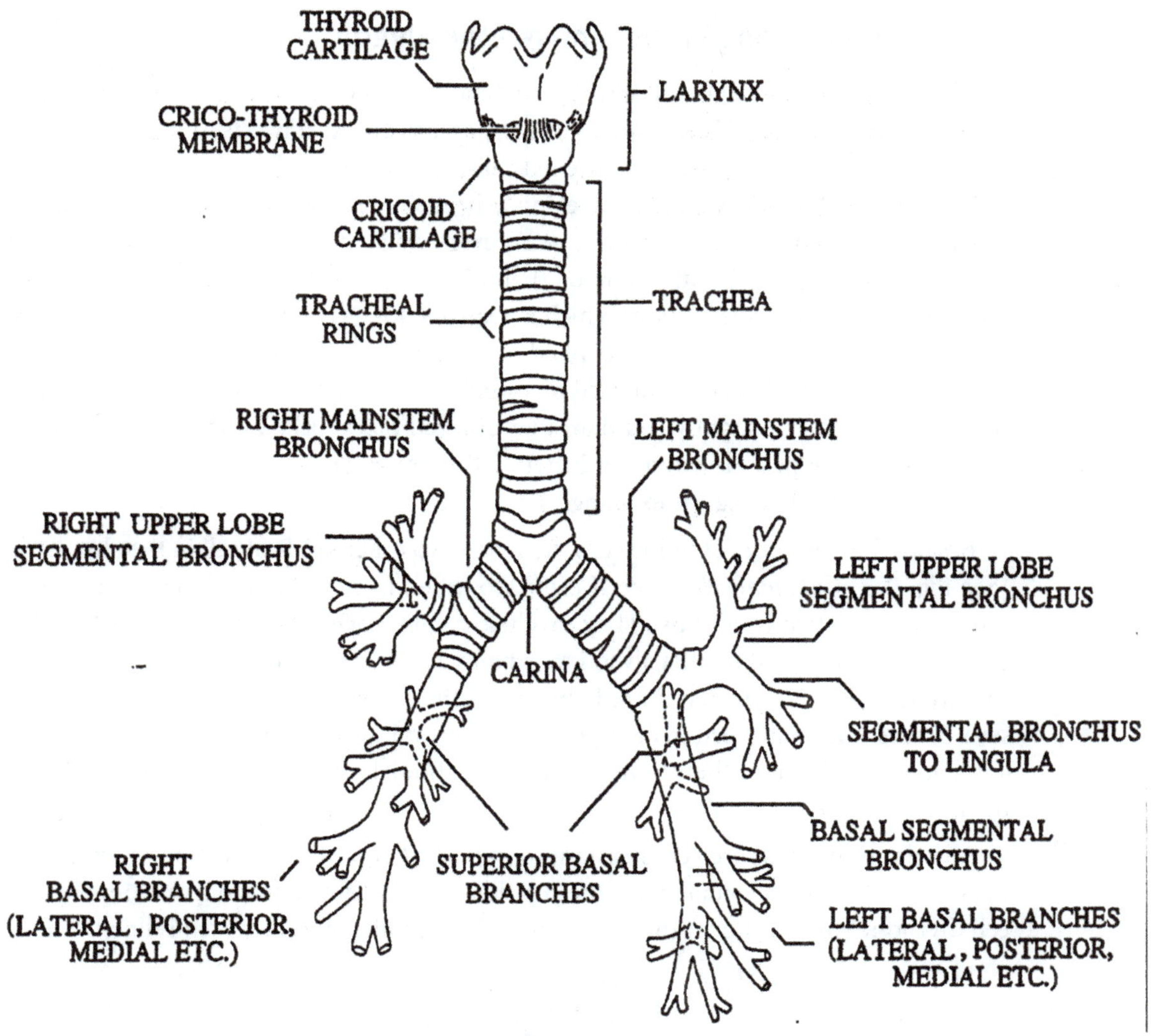

Fig. 9-3 The bronchial tree

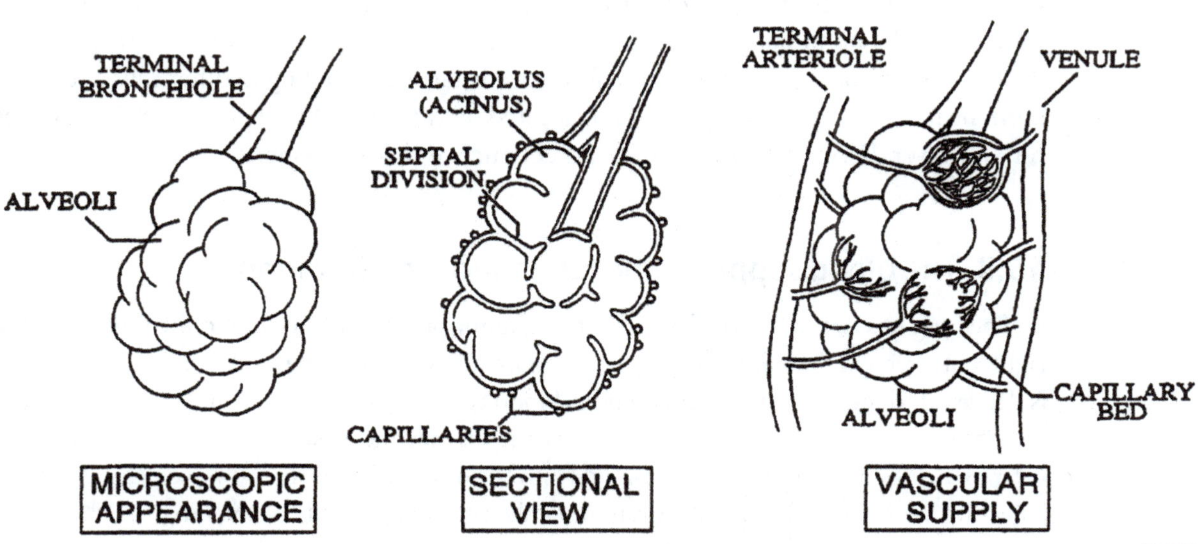

Fig. 9-4 The alveoli

§ 9:7 Gas exchange in the lungs — the alveoli

The air sacs or *alveoli* are the site of gas exchange, with blood coming into the lung from the heart. [See Fig. 9-4.] The alveoli (air sacs) are, in effect, tiny sets of balloons with walls which consist of a single layer of flattened cells. The shape of the alveolus is complex. The alveolar duct (which connects with a terminal bronchiole) leads into four subdivisions, each of which is a double V-shaped structure. At every stage there are smaller balloon-like protrusions with divisions (septa) between them. The net effect of all these convolutions is an enormous increase in surface area which is available for gas exchange. The capillaries of the pulmonary circulation are closely applied to the alveoli. They are tiny tubules whose walls, like those of the alveoli, are composed of a single layer of flat cells. The diameter of the pulmonary capillaries is slightly less than that of a red blood cell. Erythrocytes are therefore squeezed as they pass through, and their cell membranes are in close contact with the capillary wall, facilitating gas exchange.

Besides the ordinary flat lining cells, there are two other kinds of cell in the alveolar walls. [See Fig. 9-5] *Cuboidal cells* (type II cells), so called from their appearance under the microscope, have two functions. They produce a substance called *surfactant* which lowers surface tension and allows the alveoli to expand at lower pressures. These cells may not be mature in the lungs of premature babies who then have great difficulty in breathing. In severe cases, they may need to be supported by a respirator and have genetically engineered surfactant instilled into their lungs until their cuboidal cells mature to produce it on their own.

Alveolar lining cells are very resistant to injury, whether from infection or toxins. When the lining cells have been damaged, the cuboidal cells undergo a transformation, begin rapid cell division, and transform themselves into flat endothelial cells which reline the alveoli.

There are also *fixed phagocytic cells* in the alveolar walls. These are large white cells which engulf invading organisms and other foreign particles. Foreign materials are taken into vacuoles in the cytoplasm of these cells where all sorts of destructive enzymes are poured upon them in order to destroy and digest them. These fixed white cells may be considered the outposts of the pulmonary immune system, and they can trigger the immune responses of the body, recognizing the invader as a foreign substance and calling in other cells and other immune mechanisms to assist in neutralizing and destroying it. These protective mechanisms can, however, become over-vigorous and destructive of lung tissue.

§ 9:8 The blood supply to the lungs and lung filtration

The lung has two systems of blood supply. Venous blood is delivered to the lung from the right ventricle via the *pulmonary arteries*. Following gas exchange in the alveoli, this blood is delivered to the left atrium. This venous blood contains some oxygen and glucose, enough to supply most of the needs of the lung tissues. A second vascular system, the *bronchial arteries,* brings oxygenated arterial blood from the descending aorta. However, this is mainly a backup system supplying only approximately 20% of the needs of the lung.

The pulmonary vascular bed, in addition to its principal function of gas exchange, acts as a *blood filter.* It is particularly important in filtering out and dissolving blood clots from

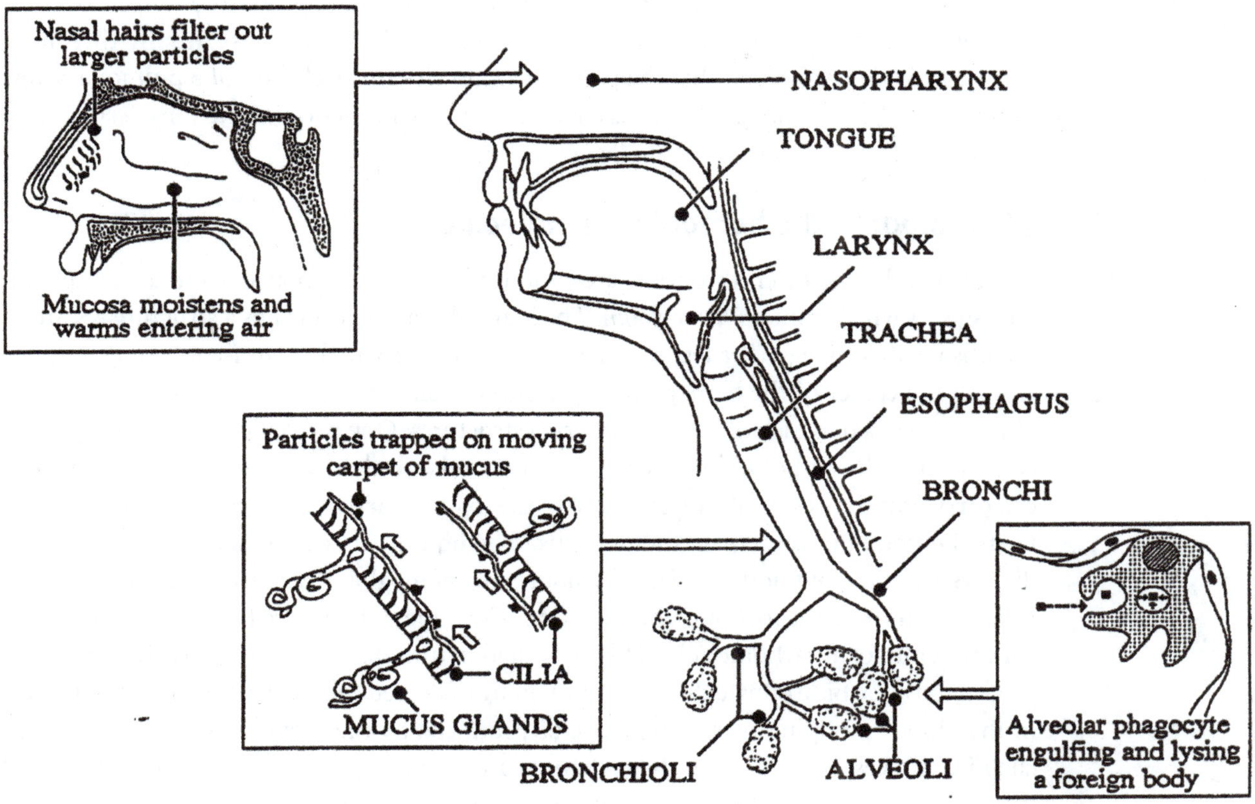

Fig. 9-5 The airway defenses

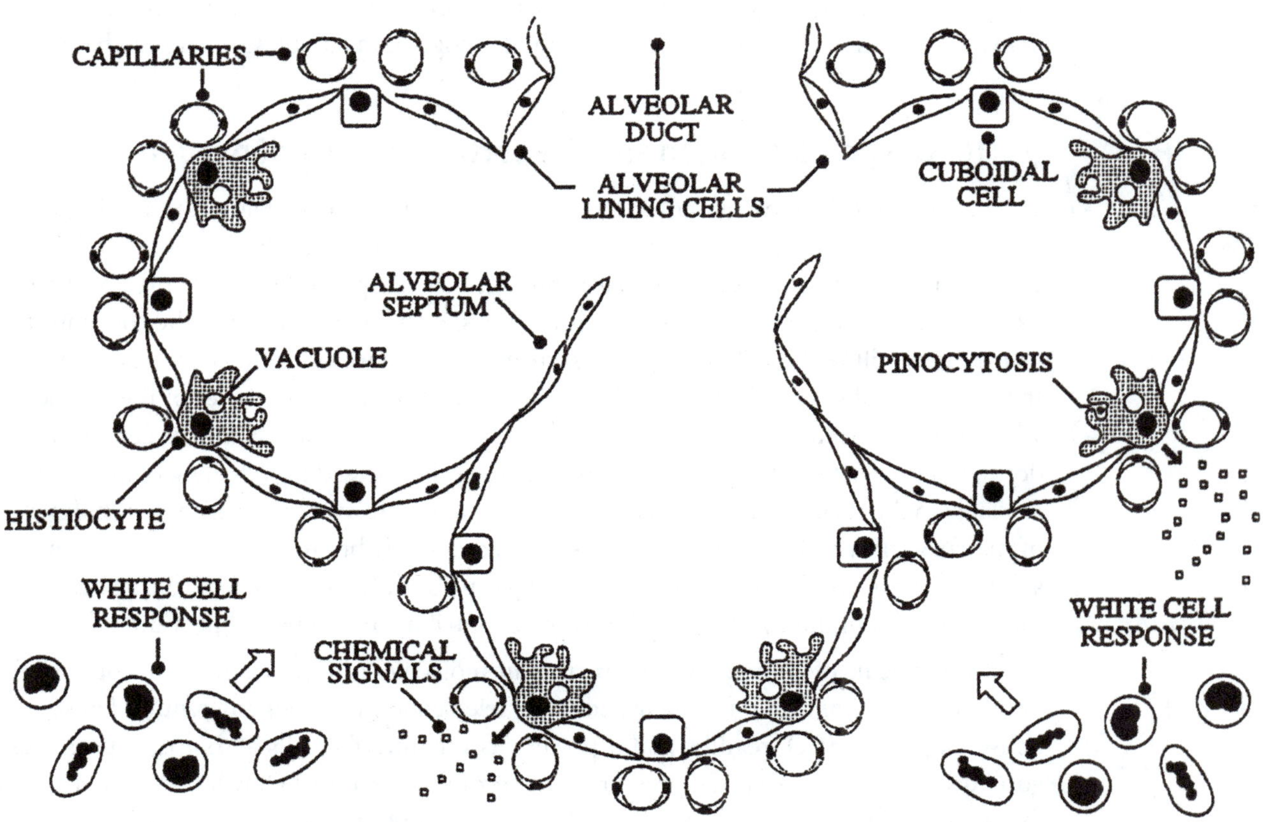

Fig. 9-6 The immune responses of the lungs

the circulatory fluids. Large blood clots from the veins of the pelvis and lower extremities can lodge in the pulmonary artery or its major branches, and these are life threatening events. Provided, however, that the patient can survive the occlusion of a pulmonary vessel in this way, the thrombus will be dissolved and normal function of the lung restored.

§ 9:9 Blood—the hemoglobin molecule

Red blood cells, or erythrocytes, are produced in the bone marrow and are simply little flattish sacs which contain *hemoglobin.* The hemoglobin molecule has a structure resembling a starfish with four legs. [See Fig. 9-7] There is a structure with four iron-containing porphyrin rings at the center of the hemoglobin molecules, (called *heme),* and a protein chain, called *globin, is* attached to each of these central ring structures. One molecule (two atoms) of oxygen can attach at the end of each of these globin strands, so that each molecule of hemoglobin can carry four molecules of oxygen. Most of the oxygen-carrying capacity of the blood resides in the hemoglobin present in the red cells. The liquid part of the blood can carry a little dissolved oxygen, but nothing like the amount that hemoglobin can deliver. Hemoglobin also functions in the transport of carbon dioxide. CO_2 enters the red cell and is there combined with water to form carbonic acid. This weak acid in turn dissociates into bicarbonate and hydrogen ions; the bicarbonate diffuses out again from the red cells and acts as a buffer substance in the blood, mopping up the excess acids produced by the metabolism of the body. The chemical processes involved in these changes are reversible, moving in one direction as the tissues to take up CO_2 and in the other direction as the lungs discharge it. Hemoglobin is indeed constructed so that in an *alkaline medium* such as in the lungs, it has an affinity for oxygen and discharges CO_2, whereas in an acid environment, such as exists in metabolically active tissues, the mechanism is reversed, and hemoglobin takes up CO_2 and discharges O_2.

§ 9:10 Oxygen saturation and the partial pressure of oxygen

The amount of oxygen present in blood can be measured in two ways, and it is important to be aware of the difference. *Oxygen saturation* (SO_2) measures the percentage of the full complement of oxygen molecules that is present in a sample of blood. If three of the four oxygen sites on the hemoglobin molecules in the specimen are occupied, the concentration (saturation) will be 75%. The *partial pressure of oxygen,* however, is the pressure exercised by the molecules of gas on the boundaries of its container or the boundaries of the solution in which it is dissolved. It does not represent all the oxygen present (as the oxygen saturation does), but only the active O_2 molecules that can easily be released from hemoglobin to become available to the tissues. Partial pressure (like barometric pressure) is measured in millimeters of mercury (mm Hg). Molecules of a gas which are tightly bound to a chemical present in a solution are part of the concentration of that gas present, but exercise very little pressure on the boundaries of the container and so do not contribute to the partial pressure.

Each molecule of hemoglobin can carry four molecules of O_2, one on each globin chain, but they are not bonded to it equally and so are released to the tissues differently. Hemoglobin delivers up the first O_2 readily, and it powers its way into the cells—that is, it possesses a good deal of tension or partial pressure. The second molecule of O_2 will only be released at lower oxygen tensions; the third at very low partial pressures, and it is very seldom indeed

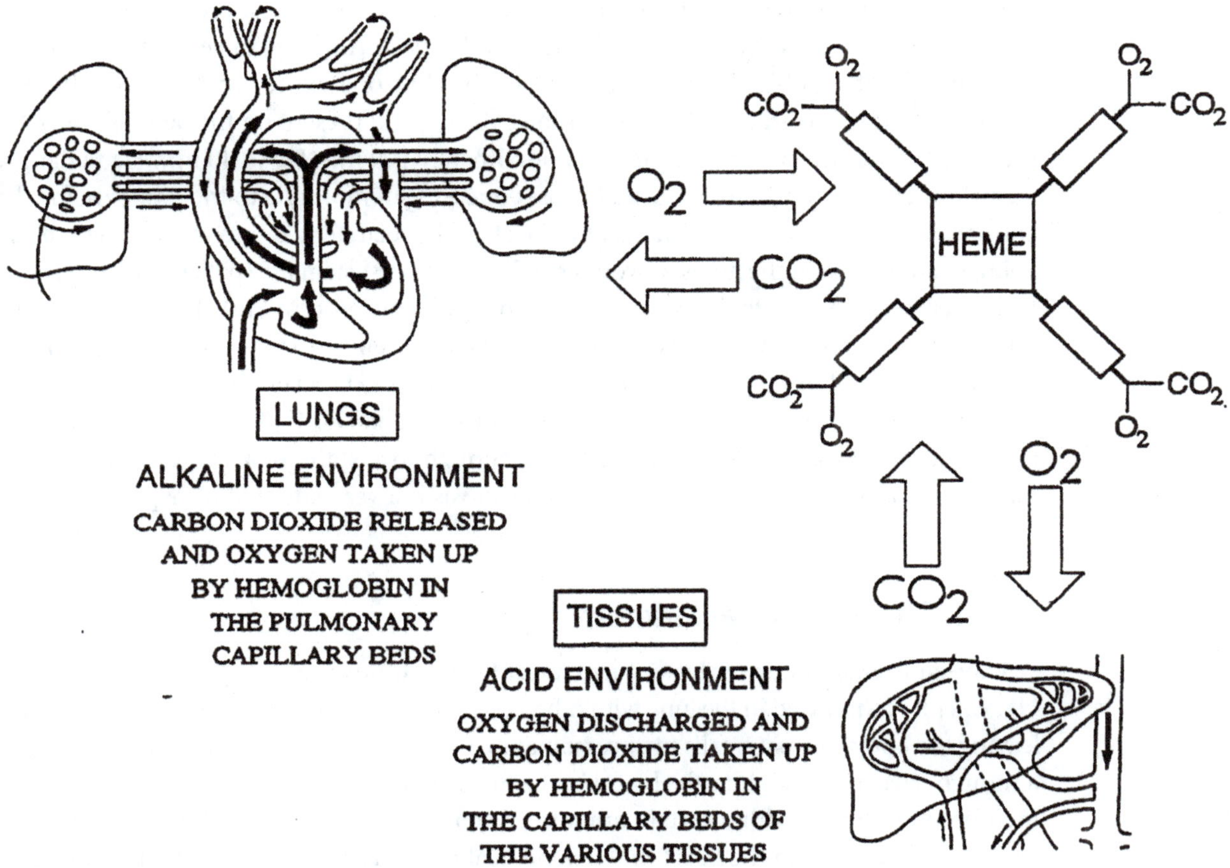

Fig. 9-7 Actions of hemoglobin in the lungs and at the tissues

UPPER AIRWAYS	150 mmHg	PARTIAL PRESSURE OF OXYGEN IN ATMOSPHERE
ALVEOLI	100 mmHg	OXYGEN DILUTED WITH CARBON DIOXIDE, NITROGEN & WATER VAPOR
PULMONARY CAPILLARY BED	95 mmHg	CAPILLARY O2 VIRTUALLY EQUAL TO ALVEOLAR O2
ARTERIAL BLOOD	85 mmHg	ARTERIAL paO2 REDUCED BY SHUNTING
CAPILLARY BEDS	40 mmHg	O2 RELEASED FROM HEMOGLOBIN IN CAPILLARY BEDS IN TISSUES
TISSUES	20 mmHg	p02 IN THE TISSUES
MITOCHONDRIA	5 mmHg	p02 AT THE MITOCHONDRIA INSIDE THE CELLS

Fig. 9-8 The oxygen cascade

that the last one can be released. It follows from this that the partial pressure of oxygen in the blood may be a great deal less than one would expect from the concentration of oxygen molecules on the globin. If every Hb molecule has lost one oxygen molecule, the blood is still 75% saturated (three of the four O_2 molecules are still present on the hemoglobin), but the oxygen pressure has dropped from approximately 100 mm Hg to 40 mm Hg, a dangerously low level. Arterial blood normally loses one oxygen molecule to the tissues before becoming venous blood. If this venous blood were to be recirculated into the arteries without being reoxygenated in the lungs, it would barely be able to sustain life (patients are transferred to intensive care when their oxygen tension drops below 50 mm Hg). Hemoglobin turns blue (cyanosis) when two molecules of oxygen have been lost (50% saturation), and the partial pressure of oxygen at this stage is less than 30 mm Hg, even though half the oxygen sites on the hemoglobin are occupied. A patient with a paO_2 of 50 mm Hg is critically ill, and a partial pressure of 30 mm Hg is barely enough to sustain life when the body is completely at rest. It can be seen from this that cyanosis is a very late sign of hypoxia.

§ 9:11 The oxygen cascade

Oxygen is taken in from the ambient air at a partial pressure of approximately 120 mm Hg. After it has mingled in the lung with other gases (water vapor, nitrogen and carbon dioxide leaving the body) the paO_2 falls to approximately 100 mm Hg. Another reason for this is that although oxygen crosses into the blood in the lungs with very little loss of partial pressure, it then becomes mixed with a certain amount of venous blood. Some of this comes from the coronary circulation in the heart, but a good deal of it is simply blood that has managed to bypass the air sacs of the lung without being oxygenated. Ideally one would think that this should not happen, but in fact it does; a certain amount of shunting is normal in the lung. In the upright position the upper parts of the lung are being well ventilated with air but very poorly perfused with blood. This is known as physiological shunt (it is not due to disease) and it explains why a paO_2 of 75–90 mm Hg is considered to be within normal limits. Pathological shunting is more properly termed *ventilation/perfusion* mismatch (V/Q mismatch), but is commonly described as shunt. The percentage of blood bypassing the lungs in this way can be estimated (or guessed). Some lung patients may have as much as 50% shunt (the equivalent of the blood to one lung being totally shunted) which means that they are very sick.

After oxygen has diffused from the capillaries into the extracellular fluids at the tissues, the partial pressure of oxygen will be 20 mm Hg or less. In the *mitochondria*, the little organelles inside cells where fuels are burned to produce energy, the pO_2 may well be less than 4 mm Hg. This fall in the partial pressure from its highest value in the inspired air to its lowest value inside the tissues is sometimes referred to as the *oxygen cascade*. [See Fig. 9-8.] It is clear that there is not much margin for error allowed in the body. Any drop in the inspired oxygen pressure is likely to affect the tissues. The reason for this is that oxygen, although needed in order to produce energy, is also toxic to cells. All cells, especially those in the lung, have enzyme systems which chemically reduce all oxygen not immediately needed to produce energy. Overgenerous oxygen therapy in the intensive care will damage the lungs, and oxygen tensions are therefore kept as low as possible in ventilated patients. Oxygen overdose is also very toxic to the developing optic retina of premature children, who often need supplemental oxygen to assist their immature lungs. Neonatologists, therefore, must walk a fine line, providing sufficient oxygen to make up for the inefficiency of the premature babys' lungs, but at the same time trying to avoid damaging their retinas.

§ 9:12 The respiratory quotient

Carbon dioxide and water are produced when glucose is metabolized in the presence of oxygen to produce energy. Some of this CO_2 is dissolved in water to form carbonic acid, but the major part of it is carried on hemoglobin and discharged into the alveoli in the lungs. The amount of CO_2 produced should in fact bear a fairly constant relation to the amount of oxygen taken up in the lungs and used in the tissues. This ratio is known as the *respiratory quotient.* Since the body at rest produces about 200 ml of CO_2 and uses approximately 250 ml of O_2 each minute, the normal respiratory quotient is of the order of 0.8. Alterations in the respiratory quotient are significant. A person who is "brain dead" produces very little CO_2 and the respiratory quotient falls. The partial pressure of CO_2 in the expired gases is therefore a very valuable piece of information for anesthesiologists, and the CO_2 monitor (capnometer) is today used during general anesthesia in even quite small hospitals in the United States. The respiratory quotient is also taken into consideration in deciding when a head injured patient is brain dead, so that extraordinary supportive measures can be discontinued.

Part II.
Lung Diseases

§ 9:13 The legal focus on certain lung diseases

Lung diseases represent every kind of pathology: traumatic, infectious, neoplastic, immune, toxic, etc. However, not all of these are of major interest to lawyers, and only a few of them need to be dealt with in any detail. This discussion will mainly center on a few topics such as traumatic injuries to the lungs, chronic obstructive pulmonary disease (COPD), and occupational lung diseases, though other matters may be mentioned also.

§ 9:14 Lung trauma

Trauma to the chest is one of the major causes of death in automobile accidents and gunshot wounds. Sometimes the heart or great vessels are torn and the patient bleeds to death, but trauma to the lungs can also cause injury or death in several other ways. In some cases, penetrating wounds or maximum force applied to the chest render the lung completely nonfunctional. For example, there may be lacerations of the major airways or they may be flooded by blood. In many of these cases there is little that can be done to save the patient's life (unless a heart/lung machine is immediately available). The lungs can also be damaged by shock waves from an explosion or, most commonly, from a high-velocity bullet. If a high-velocity bullet penetrates the chest, the energy released will be such that virtually all the lung tissues will be affected. The alveolar lining cells will not be able to prevent salt and water from entering the air sacs from the interstitial space so that the lungs will be inundated with plasma from the blood and the patient will be fortunate to survive. So even when a high-velocity bullet entering the chest cavity does not damage the heart or great vessels or the spine, the mortality approaches 100 percent.

Death can also result from penetrating injuries of the chest that do not do much damage to the lung substance. The functioning of the lungs depends on an intact chest wall. If the seal over the lung is broken, then when the diaphragm descends, expanding the chest, air is sucked through the hole in the chest wall into the pleural space, instead of being drawn down the airways into the lungs. Fortunately the two halves of the lung operate separately to a great extent, and the patient can sometimes survive on one lung until they get to a hospital.

The most dangerous kind of chest trauma is a penetrating injury where the lung is ruptured, but the chest wall seals over the wound. In some of these cases the lung keeps pumping out a little air into the pleural cavity with each breath. This air cannot escape out of the chest cavity, and a volume of air under pressure is produced which expands with each breath, pushing the heart gradually over to the other side. This is a *tension pneumothorax,* and unless the tension is released by a chest drain, the heart will be compressed until it cannot function and the patient will die.

§ 9:15 Chronic obstructive lung disease (COLD)—the basic pathological processes

There are many names for this disease. It is sometimes called chronic bronchitis or chronic obstructive lung disease (COLD), but is most commonly referred to as *chronic obstructive pulmonary disease* (COPD). These various names are nowadays more precisely defined:

The term *chronic bronchitis is* used to refer to the effects of this disease in the airways (damage to the cilia, glands, and other structures). *Emphysema* indicates the destruction of the alveoli (acinar damage), and *chronic obstructive pulmonary disease* (COPD) or *chronic obstructive lung disease* (COLD) are general terms to cover the entire condition.

COPD is perhaps an inappropriate term, since the obstructive aspect, though very characteristic, is only one facet of the disease. Destructive lung disease might be a more inclusive name [see Fig 9-4], but the term COPD is so well established in common usage that no one cares to change it. COPD is related to a number of causes including industrial pollution, certain kinds of coal mining and, above all, to cigarette smoking. The way in which the noxious agents affect the lungs is not really known (the activities of metalases and other enzymes are suspected), but every part and every aspect of the lung is affected.

1. There is *destruction of the alveolar membranes.* The septa dividing the alveolar sacs from one another disappear so that a large number of tiny sacs become a single large one. The result is a considerable loss of the area of lining cells available for gas exchange. The paO_2 therefore begins to fall. Since, however, CO_2 is exchanged in the lung much more efficiently than O_2, the $paCO_2$ does not alter significantly until very late in the progression of the disease. The body attempts to deal with this crisis by *hyperventilating.* Overbreathing exchanges more gas with the ambient air and tends to raise the alveolar oxygen paO_2. The paO_2 can be kept above 60 mm Hg. in this way even when the alveolar damage is quite advanced. There are, of course, limits to what can be accomplished by hyperventilation. In the first place, it lowers the CO_2 tension in the blood, which tends to make the patient dizzy. Furthermore, as the disease progresses, the work involved in the extra ventilation may not produce enough additional oxygen to make it worthwhile.

2. *Elastic tissue* is also destroyed in this disease process, so that the lungs will not exhale passively as is normally the case. [See § 9:4.] The muscles of the abdomen must be used to help push the air out of the lungs. The patient not only has difficulty in getting enough gas exchanged in the lungs, but must also waste precious oxygen on the increased work of expiration. Destruction of the elastic tissue in the lungs also means that the lungs tend naturally to expand, causing the chest cavity itself to expand, pushing the diaphragm downward and the ribs outward. Typical X-ray findings in a case of advanced COPD are, therefore, flattened diaphragms and horizontal, widely spaced ribs. COPD patients are therefore commonly described in medical records as being "barrel chested."

3. *Airway damage is* a prominent feature of the disease as it progresses. The *cilia* (little hairs lining the airways) become fragmented and abnormal in appearance and no longer move synchronously. The lungs, therefore, are unable to clear foreign particles out of the airways normally, and the mucus produced, since it is not removed efficiently, tends to collect in the trachea and bronchi and must be coughed up. Poor removal of foreign materials and the accumulation of mucus in the airways make infections inevitable, and chest infections are a frequent complication of chronic bronchitis. With such patients, upper respiratory infections tend to sink into the chest, so that a head cold, which would only be an embarrassment and an annoyance to a normal person, is likely to be a serious illness in someone with COPD. Frequent acute infections lead to chronic infection and irritation of the mucus glands in the airways. These eventually become enlarged and produce thick abnormal mucus in amounts which are difficult for the patient to expel. The production and accumulation of these quantities of thick, inspissated mucus further increase the likelihood of infection.

4. *Bronchospasm* is a common component of emphysema, especially in its later stages. Frequent infections tend to make the airways irritable and provoke contractions of the muscles in the walls of the bronchi (*bronchoconstriction*), leading to wheezing. This bronchial asthma is indeed the feature which gives this disease its most common name, *chronic obstructive pulmonary disease.*

5. The pulmonary vasculature is involved in the destructive processes, as one would expect since the pulmonary capillary beds are so closely approximated to the alveoli. The massive destruction of capillary pathways in the lungs that is found in advanced emphysema can be compared to the closing of five out of the six lanes in a highway leading into a city. Just as traffic backs up on the highway, blood becomes backed up in the pulmonary vessels. Pulmonary artery pressure rises, and the right ventricle must enlarge and hypertrophy to generate the extra pressure needed to drive blood through the diseased lung. Eventually, as the disease progresses, the right heart muscle will begin to fail. This right-sided heart failure which results from chronic pulmonary disease is known as *cor pulmonale.*

§ 9:16 The clinical picture in emphysema

The clinical picture in these patients is what one would expect from the underlying pathology. They are very short of breath (SOB) and have to get more air into the lungs to make up for the fact that less of it is exchanged in their alveoli. So they breathe rapidly even at rest, and the accessory muscles of respiration may be seen moving, even when they are sitting still. However, the actual breaths are shallow. The emphysematous patient is classically barrel-chested, and the chest does not move much during inspiration since it is already almost fully expanded before they start to take a breath. They also have to work with their stomach muscles to exhale; they cannot let the lung relax and empty itself, as it does in a normal person. Abdominal exhalation is not as efficient as the normal process, so that expiration is prolonged. This may be described in the medical record as E>I (expiration exceeds inspiration). This is especially the case if bronchospasm is present—expiration will not only be prolonged but accompanied by an expiratory wheeze.

Up to a certain point in the development of the disease, these patients can compensate fairly well by hyperventilation, increasing the amount of air entering the lungs. Patients in this condition used to be called "pink puffers" by the old clinicians, and it is a good name. Their color is quite good, and they are able to get around fairly well, but they have to puff all the time (hard work) to maintain this level of functioning.

In the last stages of emphysema, the effort of puffing uses up more oxygen than it brings in. In these circumstances, the adaptive mechanisms change and the body no longer attempts to keep the paO_2 above 60 mm Hg. It is allowed to fall below this level, and the enzyme systems of the body must learn to manage with less oxygen, more carbon dioxide and generally a more acid environment. These patients are no longer pink and, since they are often in heart failure (*cor pulmonale*), their ankles swell up. They were therefore called "blue bloaters" by the old clinicians. Modern physicians object to putting patients into such simple boxes, but these two distinct clinical pictures are apt descriptions of two important stages in the disease, and they also illustrate the characteristic pathological and adaptation processes that are taking place.

One last item associated with emphysema is worth mentioning, namely mental changes. Many patients with advanced emphysema are being treated with steroids, which in themselves will alter mood and mentation, generally making the patients somewhat manic, but occasionally causing depression. Withdrawal from steroids is also associated with psychological changes, some of them quite bizarre. Consequently, when steroids are being discontinued, it is important from the psychiatric point of view, as well as for other reasons, to reduce the dosage in a gradual manner. But psychiatric problems are associated with chronic lung disease, even when steroids have not been used. The reasons for this are not clear, although it is hardly surprising. It would be natural to expect that low oxygen tensions would affect the emotional centers of the brain to create psychiatric problems or perhaps activate problems that were already present, but latent.

§ 9:17 Typical findings in the medical records in COPD cases

COPD is such a common disease in the disability setting that it is worthwhile to mention typical findings in the medical records that should be sought out in evaluating a claim.

1. The admission history and /or the discharge summary should indicate the diagnostic features of the condition, and the past medical history (sometimes called the history of previous, or present, illnesses or HPI) may well note the various doctor visits and hospital admissions that mark the typical stages of the progression of the disease.

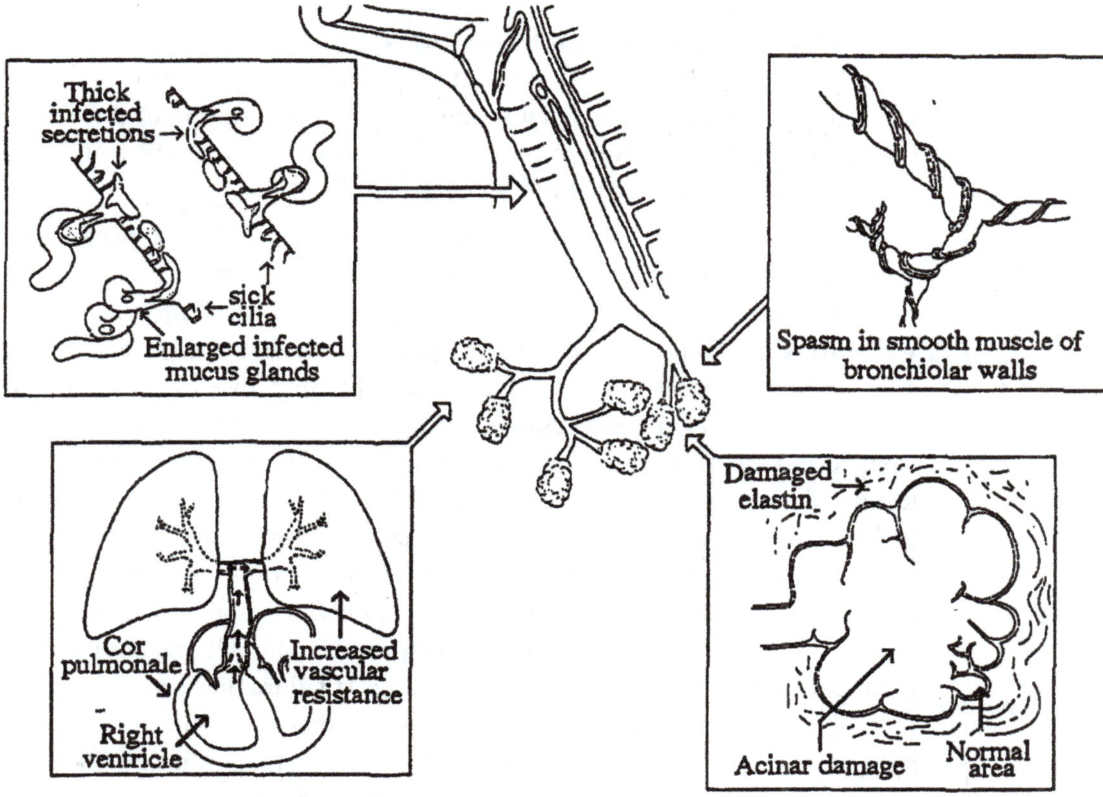

Fig. 9-9 Destructive mechanisms present in COPD

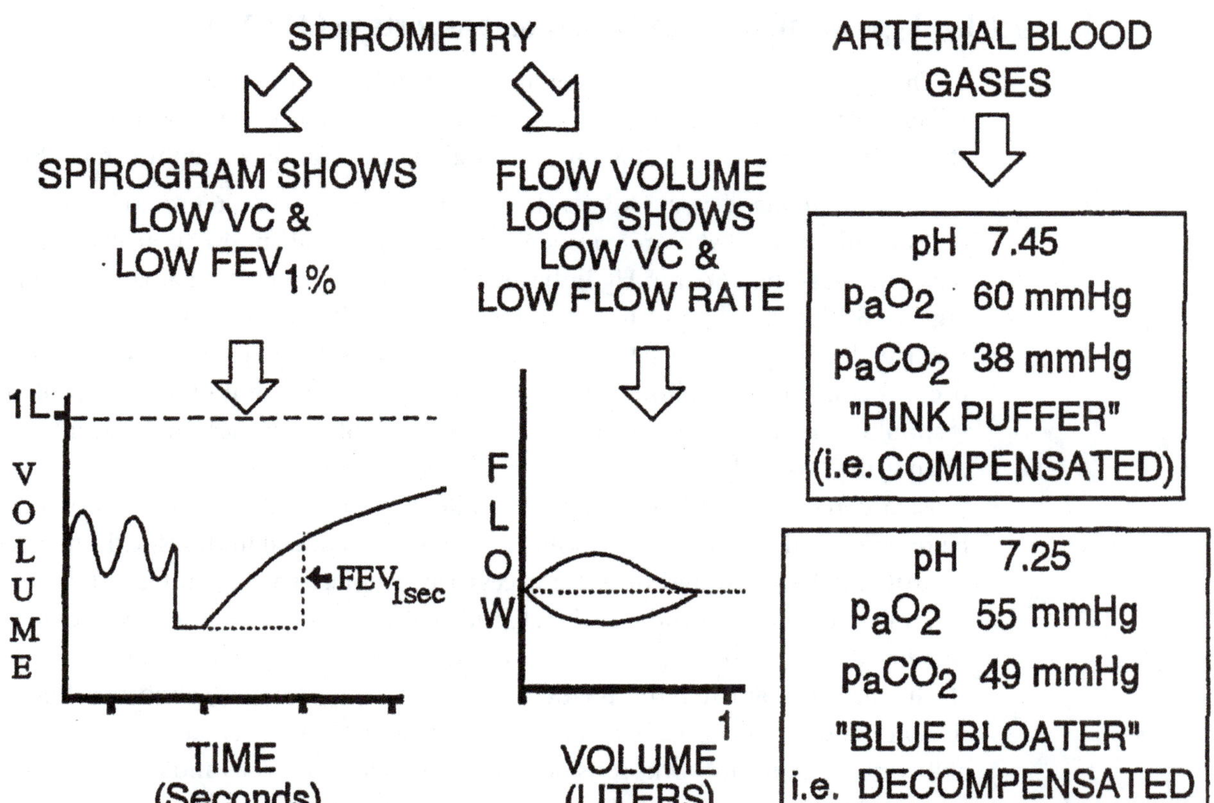

Fig. 9-10 Typical pulmonary function test results in COPD

2. The patient may or may not have been a smoker (the number of packs per day and the calculation of pack/years will normally be noted). Shortness of breath (SOB) on exercise and the persistence of a productive cough with clear colored or white sputum following a chest cold are the first symptoms. With progression of the disease, there is shortness of breath, even at rest, and a persistent, productive cough where the sputum is yellow (infected) at times.

3. The physical examination (P/E) should show a barrel-chested person, breathing rapidly (tachypneic), with difficulty in breathing (dyspnea) and with little or no movement of the chest wall during breathing. Absence of any lateral movement in the chest wall during breathing is a particularly significant finding. The accessory muscles of respiration in the neck [see § 9:3] may be noted to be active, even at rest, and this is an important finding suggesting severe impairment. The color of the mucus membranes (tongue and insides of the mouth) will probably be normal except during a chest infection when the paO_2 may drop to very low levels, and the patient probably needs to be hospitalized. Auscultation of the chest should show a prolongation of the time needed for expiration, and there may well be an expiratory wheeze. The heart rate will rise rapidly with slight exercise if anyone bothers to test this fact, but it is not necessarily a sign of cardiac involvement. The presence of ankle edema (pitting edema) is an early sign of heart failure. Right-sided heart failure may show up as distension of the jugular veins [see Chapter 8]. Unless it is very gross, the enlargement of the right ventricle is unlikely to be detected by percussing the cardiac outline to the right of the sternum, but may be seen on X-ray or by other imaging methods.

§ 9:18 Typical imaging and other test reports in COPD cases [See Fig. 9-10]

1. The typical right-sided cardiac failure (*cor pulmonale*) of advanced COPD is most reliably shown by cardiac ultrasound. If it is very pronounced, it may also be demonstrable by ordinary A-P chest X-ray, or by right ventricular hypertrophy (on the EKG).

2. The *arterial blood gases* (ABGs) should show a paO_2 of 60–65 mm Hg in milder cases (pink puffers who are compensating by overbreathing). An arterial oxygen tension of less than 60 mm Hg indicates significant disease. With a paO_2 of 55 mm Hg, disability may be presumed to be complete. It should be noted that Social Security disability systems take little account of arterial blood gas studies, and seldom order them. They may, however, be used to support a claim if otherwise available. It should be remembered, however, that, for disability purposes, the relevant ABGs are not the hospital tests carried out during an exacerbation of the condition, but those ordered after discharge home and following maximal recovery. It should also be remembered that failure to completely match the clinical findings with the Social Security disability listings, does not necessarily mean that a claimant is not disabled. Equivalent impairment and functional residual capacity can be considered. *Equivalent impairment* refers to cases where the findings under one category do not quite meet the listing requirements, but the deficiency may be made up by abnormal findings in other body systems. *Functional residual capacity* (FRC) evaluation considers the ability of claimants to work, considering all their circumstances and not merely their impairments. Thus, provided some compensable disease and some significant im-

pairment are shown, the claimant's age, education, skills, and available work opportunities may be taken into consideration to see if she is capable of working, and if there is suitable work for her to do. But abnormal findings during emergency room visits or hospital admissions may be used to show that the patient was having very frequent exacerbations and admissions to hospital, to the point that no one would give her a job.

3. The ordinary *chest X-ray report* is valuable, not only in making the diagnosis of emphysema, but also in roughly estimating the severity of the condition. The flattened diaphragms and horizontal, widely spaced ribs are typical findings which indicate significantly severe disease. Numerous enlarged air spaces (representing *bullae*) likewise suggest advanced disease. The typical finding of *cor pulmonale* (right ventricular enlargement in the X-ray report) indicates very severe impairment indeed.

§ 9:19 Spirometry reports in COPD

For legal compensation purposes, spirometry is the most important pulmonary function test [see § 9:27 & Fig. 9-10]. The lungs of COPD patients are already expanded (loss of elastic tissue), and the vital capacity is reduced to 2 liters or less (normal values 3.5–4.5 L). Forced expiration will also be very prolonged, taking five seconds or more to breathe out the inspired air. This characteristic is best expressed in a calculation known as the $FEV_1\%$ which is the percentage of the vital capacity (VC) which can be expelled during maximal expiration in one second [see § 9:27]. Normally 75% or more of the VC can be pushed out in one second. In COPD this figure will be less than 50%, and in severe cases may drop to 30% or less. [See Fig. 9-10.]

§ 9:20 Occupational lung diseases

The usual industrial and occupational lung diseases are classified into *hypersensitivity diseases* and *pneumoconioses.* Pneumoconioses are caused by inorganic particles such as silica dust. Hypersensitivity diseases on the other hand, are due to organic matter such as fungal spores or linen. According to this terminology *asbestosis is* a pneumoconiosis while *byssinosis* is a hypersensitivity disease. The distinction between pneumoconioses and hypersensitivity diseases is well known and well established, but it is unimportant for present purposes, because the disease mechanisms appear to be almost identical and the end result is certainly similar regardless of the cause. Deposits of some substance are laid down in the lungs. White cells migrate to these deposits and, in the process of dealing with them, release large quantities of destructive enzymes, which injure the lung and cause scarring (fibrosis). It is therefore simpler to include all of these diseases under the heading of hypersensitivity since they all seem to be caused by an overresponse of the immune mechanisms.

§ 9:21 Hypersensitivity reactions in the lungs

The allergic response of the body is meant to be protective, to destroy foreign invaders of various kinds. When a process is described as being a "hypersensitivity response," we are saying that this process can become dysfunctional at times, and destroy body tissues as well as the foreign substances. The exact reasons and mechanisms involved are not well known. The process is sometimes picturesquely described as being like a bouncer dealing with a bunch of tough customers in a bar. The police are called in to help and in the ensuing rumble, the room and furniture are wrecked. Translated into terms of known immunological processes, this means that particularly tough substances, such as *asbestos fibers* or *cotton dust* or the *tubercle bacillus,* are resistant to destruction by the lytic enzymes which the wall macrophage cells (histiocytes) release into their vacuoles. The histiocytes therefore put out chemical signals and attract other kinds of white cells in large numbers to the area (*chemotaxis*). These white cells, in turn, release their destructive agents in an attempt to deal with the foreign substances. These powerful inflammatory responses lead to tissue destruction and stimulate the production of scar tissue, especially in the interstitial space which lies between the capillaries and the alveolar sacs. Scar eventually contracts and produces the *limitation of chest expansion* which is the peculiar characteristic of these diseases. They are therefore commonly described as *restrictive lung diseases* although they have other characteristics as well.

§ 9:22 Clinical characteristics of fibrosing lung disease

The clinical course of industrial lung disease can be quite different from that of COPD. [See Fig. 9-11.] In *farmer's lung,* a disease caused by hypersensitivity to Aspergillus fungi found in grass products, the only symptoms following initial exposure may be a mild respiratory illness characterized by fever, cough, and shortness of breath, which only lasts for a few days. Subsequent exposures produce fewer symptoms, but the disease may progress silently, even after all contact with the offending substance has ceased. The existence of a lung problem may not be suspected until shortness of breath at rest, or with slight exercise, (the usual complaints) has become marked. By this time impairment will be evident.

Different lung contaminants produce variations in the presentation. *Byssinosis,* caused by linen dust, was known as "Monday morning sickness," since the linen workers recovered from it over the weekend and got used to the dust by Tuesday. Asbestos fibers, like the Aspergillus of "farmer's lung," can likewise continue to be active in the lung tissues and produce fibrosis long after exposure has ceased. *Asbestosis* has a number of peculiar features. It produces scarring of the pleural coverings of the lungs as well as in the interstitial spaces, which may further restrict breathing. It also accelerates emphysema and is associated with two kinds of cancer: *bronchial carcinoma* and also a particularly malignant type of tumor known as a *mesothelioma.* Mesotheliomas resulting from asbestos exposure are typically found on the pleural surfaces of the lungs, but similar tumors can also be found in the intestines. The intestinal tumors may represent blood spread from the lung lesions, or may arise independently from asbestos expelled from the air passages and swallowed. One of the major problems in compensation hearings concerning asbestos exposure is obvious from this description of the disease. Since some of the damage resembles that caused by cigarette smoking and other industrial pollutants, it can be difficult to apportion the harm if the claimant smoked (which is often the case) or had been exposed to lung contaminants other than asbestos.

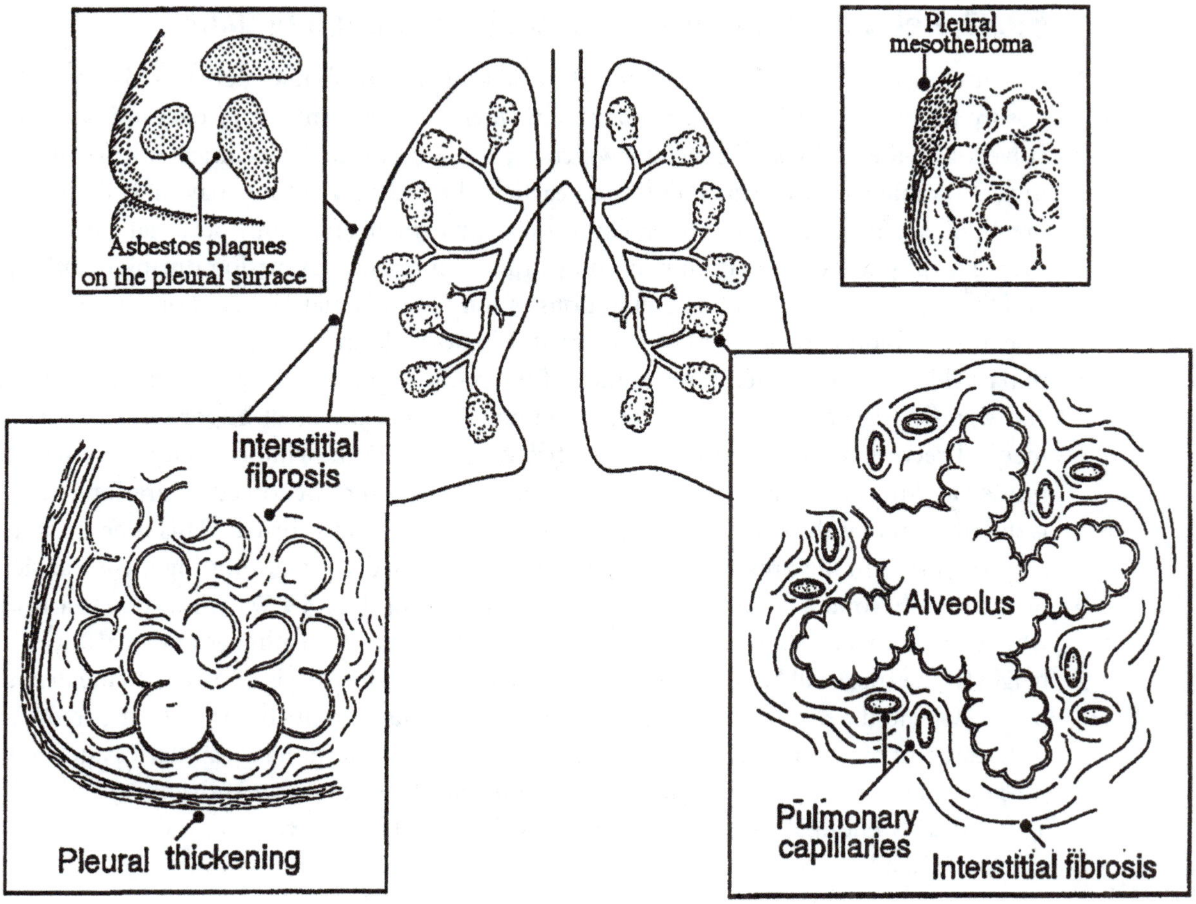

Fig. 9-11 The lung pathology found in asbestos

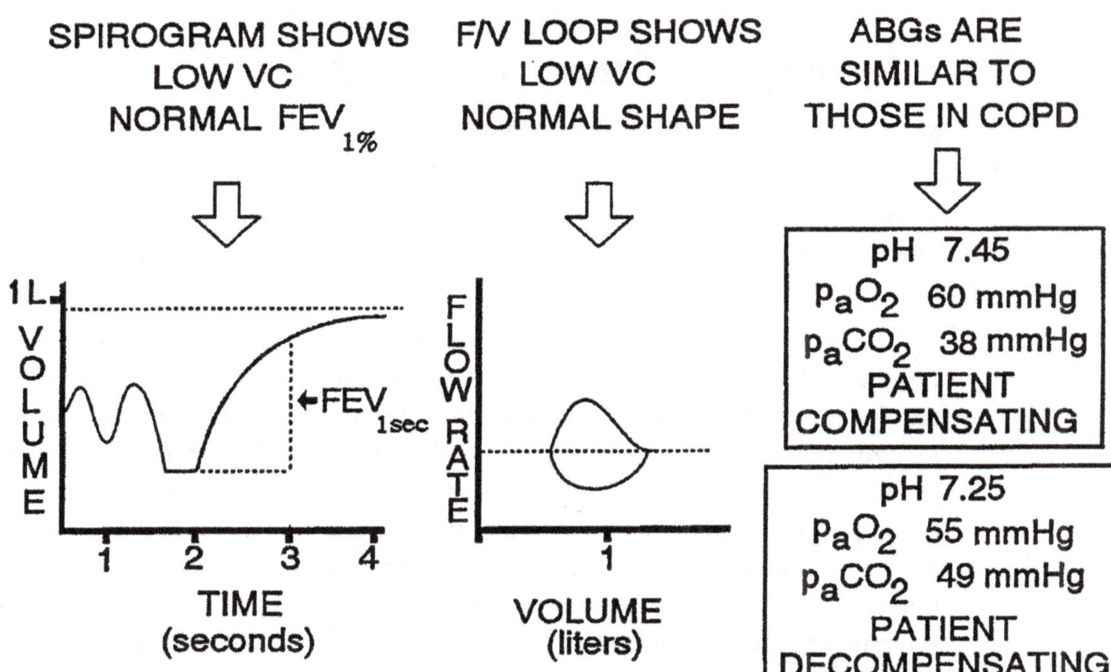

Fig. 9-12 Typical test findings in pulmonary fibrosis

§ 9:23 Relevant items in an industrial lung disability claim

The clinical findings supportive of industrial lung disease should include a history of exposure to the appropriate lung contaminant, including the amount of contamination involved, and the periods of time over which exposure occurred. The clinical history may be unremarkable since, as was mentioned earlier, the only complaint may be shortness of breath on slight exertion, and the most serious impairments may only occur late in the disease. The physical examination may show limitation of chest excursion during breathing, and the typical widespread fine crepitations of lung fibrosis may be heard on auscultation. The arterial blood gases at rest may be relatively normal, and the chest X-ray may not be remarkable. A "moth eaten" appearance of the X-ray is produced by widespread scarring and signifies significant disease. Here, as in emphysema, the most important item in the medical record is the report on spirometry. As in COPD the vital capacity (VC) will be limited and in severe cases may be one liter or less. However, the forced expiration pattern is different in that the early slope of the trace may be relatively normal. This is because the abnormality is in the presence of scar tissue which acts like a leash, limiting the expansion of the lung beyond a certain point. A flow/volume loop [see § 9:27] will produce a trace which has the usual sharp early upswing (since the form of breathing is normal) but the height of the trace will be reduced (since the excursion of the lung is limited). As the disease progresses and the scar tissues shrink and shorten, the vital capacity becomes further reduced until disability is complete. The scarring may involve the pulmonary capillaries and cause *cor pulmonale.* Treatment with steroids may prevent the disease from advancing if it is diagnosed early enough, but steroids have serious side effects which can produce their own kinds of disability. [See Fig. 9-12.]

Part III.
The Investigation of Lung Diseases

§ 9:24 The uses and limitations of the chest X-ray

Chest X-ray findings have been discussed earlier in relation to particular diseases. The uses of the roentgenogram in evaluating lung conditions will be treated more generally here.

Routine anteroposterior (A/P) chest roentgenograms are crude tests. Lung function can be severely impaired in the presence of a normal chest X-ray. The ordinary chest roentgenogram is useful however in demonstrating the following problems:

1. *Pneumonia and pneumonitis.* A sufficiently severe and extensive pneumonitis will cause an infiltrate (white patch) in some part of the lung. If the infiltrate surrounds the airway, so that the darker airway is outlined by the whiter infiltrate, those are called *peribronchial infiltrates.* Normally the smaller airways do not show up on a routine chest X-ray, but peribronchial infiltrates show up (on negative X-ray film) as opacities framing and outlining the airways. This appearance is sometimes called an "aerobronchogram" and it is the characteristic X-ray sign of bronchopneumonia. The visible infiltrate is simply fluid (edema of the tissues) produced by the inflammatory process. Widespread patchy infiltrates can be the sign of viral or mycoplasmal infection. Sometimes this appearance is also seen in heart failure. The involvement of a whole lobe

or area of a lung by an infiltrative process (white out) is characteristic of bacterial lobar pneumonia. It should incidentally be remembered that X-ray changes are slow to resolve. It may take a week or more to show any X-ray improvement even though the chest sounds clear and the patient feels well.

2. *Chronic obstructive lung disease.* By the time the patient is seeking disability evaluation, characteristic X-ray changes should be apparent. These are a widely spaced, horizontal appearance of the ribs and flattened diaphragms, both caused by the expansion of the lungs (loss of elastic tissue). If the destruction of the lungs is severe, there may be bulli visible. These are dark blobs which represent areas where the tissues separating the individual alveoli (septa) are destroyed thus producing large, distended, air-filled spaces. The enlarged right ventricle of *cor pulmonale* may also be evident.

3. *Gas or fluid in the pleural cavity.* This is called *pneumothorax* if air is present, *hemothorax* (blood present) and *hemopneumothorax* (both present). All these should show up on X-ray. Air from a torn bronchus can track up out of the thorax and advance under the skin of the neck, shoulders, and chest wall. It "crackles" under the fingers on palpation (*tactile fremitus*). Air under the skin is called *subcutaneous emphysema.* It shows up well on a chest x-ray.

4. *Collapsed (atelectatic) lung tissues.* The collapsed lung tissues will absorb the X-rays and so show up white on the usual negative film against the black background of the free air. Small areas of collapse (*atelectases*) may also be seen as white patches on the chest X-ray.

5. *Bony fractures.* Rib fractures and fractures of the dorsal spine may be seen on chest X-rays, but special X-rays of ribs and dorsal spine may need to be ordered in trauma cases, if such fractures are suspected but not seen on conventional X-ray studies.

§ 9:25 Investigation of lung diseases — arterial blood gases (ABGs)

Arterial blood gases (ABGs) measure a number of things, principally the following:

1. The partial pressure *of* oxygen in arterial blood (paO_2). This is normally between 75–95 mm Hg pressure. A low paO_2 is a sensitive indicator that something is wrong with the lungs. For example, when there is *shunting* (blood moving past the airways without gas exchange) the chest X-ray and the ventilation of the lungs can be unremarkable (at least for a time). A fall in paO_2 will, however, occur and show that something is wrong. In evaluating the report it is important to be sure (or as sure as possible) that the blood was drawn from an artery and not from a vein. If a glass syringe was used, it will be seen that arterial blood is at higher pressure than venous blood and pushes the plunger of the syringe back without any help from the technician; blood may also enter the container in a pulsatile fashion. A note to this or some such effect may be found in the medical records in cases where the arterial oxygen pressure was so low that the suspicion that the blood sample might have been venous crossed the technician's or the clinician's mind. Earlier replaceable plastic syringes did not show these features so well, but more recent types will show when the blood is entering the syringe with pressure and in a pulsatile manner.

2. *The partial pressure of carbon dioxide in arterial blood* ($paCO_2$) . This is normally approximately 45 mm Hg and is kept close to this value by the body. If it should rise a little, ventilation of the lungs will be increased to lower it and vice versa. The $paCO_2$ is therefore a good indicator of ventilatory function. If patients underventilate, their $paCO_2$ will go up. If they overventilate, it will fall. A rising arterial carbon dioxide tension which is approaching 50 mm Hg is normally a sign of ventilatory failure and an indication for transfer of the patient to intensive care for ventilatory assistance.

3. *Acid/base balance in the blood.* The acidity of the blood (pH) is normally 7.4. The explanation of this figure is a little complicated but it is worth knowing. Acidity can be described in several ways, but may be simply understood as the number of free hydrogen radicals (positively charged hydrogen atoms) present in a solution: it is these that produce the acidic effects. Water itself may be regarded as an incredibly weak acid, since some of its molecules dissociate and release an occasional positively charged hydrogen radical (H^+). If only one molecule of water in every million is dissociated in this way, then the dissociation can be represented logarithmically as 10^{-6}. If one molecule in every hundred is dissociated (a rather stronger acid), this would be represented as 10^{-2}. In the pH notation, the power 10 and the minus sign are removed for convenience sake, and thus the weaker acid is represented by the number 6 and the stronger one by the number 1. In ordinary chemistry 7.0, the pH of water, is taken as the neutral point; but in medicine the pH of blood (7.4) is regarded as neutral. Lower values will indicate acidosis and higher values will suggest alkalosis. The pH of blood is maintained within narrow limits by the body, since it affects the shape of enzymes, the chemical keys by which the body carries out its manufacturing and other processes. If pH varies much, enzymes will not work well and the patient will feel sick. If the pH falls to 6.8 or rises to 7.8 the patient will become moribund and may die.

4. *A serum bicarbonate estimation is usually included in the blood gas.* This can either be obtained by direct measurement, or indirectly, by calculating it from the results of a serum electrolyte determination. This is a valuable item along with the pH, since it is a measure of one of the main buffer systems of the blood which (like antacid powders) mops up excess acid. The serum bicarbonate level is normally approximately 25 milliequivalents per liter (mEq/L). In an acute acidosis (induced by, for example, aspirin poisoning or diabetic ketoacidosis when diabetes is developing) it may fall to a level of 2–3 mEq/L. Several other measurements appear on an arterial blood gases report, but these are derived numbers, the result of calculations made by the computer in the blood gas machine on the basis of the blood gas results, coupled with other data or standard assumptions.

§ 9:26 Typical arterial blood gas findings in various diseases

A patient with chronic obstructive lung disease (COPD) will (as a pink puffer) have a paO_2 of 60 to 65 mm Hg when in good health. His $paCO_2$ may be low, e.g., 38 mm Hg (N.V. 45 mm Hg) because the patient has to overbreathe in order to keep his paO_2 at a reasonable level. If such a patient catches a chest cold, this picture can change dramatically. The paO_2 can drop to 50 mm Hg or less, and this relatively well person will become very ill, requiring hospitalization and probably respiratory support. So in considering the disability of patients with COPD, one should consider not merely their blood gases when they are in relatively good health, but also the fact that they become very ill indeed when they get a chest cold. This kind of additional information may be needed to support a Social Security claim based on functional residual capacity. [See § 9:18.]

Another important point to remember in evaluating lung disability is that patients with even mild symptoms of chronic lung disease can have a heavy psychological overlay. This makes them difficult to employ (and sometimes difficult to live with).

§ 9:27 Evaluating lung diseases — spirometry

Respirometers are machines which measure the various characteristics of a patient's breathing. The traditional spirometer has an pen (marker) which impacts on a strip of graph paper rolling at a constant speed, and moves up and down on the page as the patient breathes in and out. [See Fig. 9-16.] In a typical examination the nose is held closed in a clip, the lips sealed tight around the mouthpiece, and the patient breathes through the measuring device. Before the paper strip is started moving, the patient is asked to breathe in as deeply as possible and then breathe out again completely. The needle moves straight up and down on the paper strip and draws a vertical line. This line represents the *vital capacity* (VC), the difference between full inspiration and full expiration (typical normal values would be 3.5 liters in a woman and 4.5 liters for a man).

The patient is next asked to breathe normally (*tidal breathing*) and the roll of paper is activated to move while the pen moves up and down with the breathing of the patient. The needle records this quiet respiration as a kind of sine wave. The difference between the peaks of these waves and the bottom of the troughs gives the amount of air that is breathed in (or out) with each ordinary breath. This is called the *tidal volume* (TV) and it is typically about 450 ml. About one third of this (150 ml) does not reach the alveoli but is simply moved in and out of the conducting airways without exchanging gas. This is called the *anatomical dead space.* It is important to remember this dead space and that its volume is fixed. If someone's tidal volume has dropped to 300 ml, one might think that the patient was getting two-thirds of the normal amount of air with each breath, and that this was relatively satisfactory. But if the dead space of 150 ml is deducted from the 300 ml, there is only 150 ml of gas actually reaching the alveoli. The exchangeable gas has dropped to one-half of normal, which may not be satisfactory.

Following the measurement of quiet respiration, the patient is instructed to take a deep breath and then (with the needle moving across the paper strip) to forcefully exhale, emptying the lungs as quickly and completely as possible. This produces a curve, steep at first and then leveling off. The amount of air breathed out in one second is called the *forced expiratory volume in one second* or $FEV_{I\ sec}$. Since the amount exhaled in this way will vary a good deal from person to person, according to the sizes of their lungs, it is usual to express this information as a percentage of the patient's vital capacity: $FEV_{I\ sec}$%. In a normal person, 75 to 80 percent of the vital capacity is breathed out in one second (i.e., their $FEV_{I\ sec}$% is 80). A patient with severe emphysema may only have an $FEV_{I\ sec}$% of 50 or less.

Finally the patient is asked to breathe in and out as deeply and rapidly as possible to measure the *maximum ventilatory volume* (MVV), which is the amount of air that can be breathed in one minute ventilating maximally. Ventilating in this manner is very difficult even for a normal person (it can make the subject dizzy) so it is only carried on for a few breaths and the results extrapolated to calculate the amount of air that could have been ventilated if the subject had breathed like this for one minute. Patients with very advanced lung disease may not even be able for this amount of overbreathing and it will be omitted.

The record of a spirographic test, the spirogram, is a strip of graph paper with wavy lines. [See Fig. 9-13] It is not difficult to learn to interpret them, and the time invested in doing so is well spent. A spirogram is in effect a picture of the lung function which can show the severity of lung disease and usually the diagnosis as well. The low vital capacity and poor FEV_1% of COPD is a good example. Modem machines are usually linked to a computer, which calculates and prints out the vital capacity, tidal volume, FEV_1% and a few other items as well, such as the FEV 25–75, a measure of mid-expiratory flow. The FEF is the *forced expiratory flow* and is further described by indicating the part of the slope represented. For example, the FEF 200–1200 is the slope of the expiratory flow line from 200 to 1200 ml, the early part of expiration.

§ 9:28 Evaluating lung disease — flow/volume loops

Computerized spirometry can show how the rate of air flow varies with lung volume. This is done during one complete inspiration and expiration. At the beginning of expiration, the flow rate rises rapidly to a peak and then falls away gradually until, at full expiration, there is no flow again. Inspiration then begins and is represented by a downward trace since it is in the opposite direction to expiration. Here, too, flow rate rises to an (inverted) peak and then falls away again until flow is zero at the same point where expiration began, since the volume in each direction is the same. The trace is thus a loop, and these are called *flow/volume loops* [see Fig. 9-14], since rate of flow is graphed against the volume of air that has been breathed in or out at any point, not against time. The loops have a distinctive appearance in different conditions. The loop in fibrosing lung disease for instance is normal in contour but very small in volume compared with the normal loop, since vital capacity is much reduced. The flow/volume loop in COPD, on the other hand, is likewise small in area, but the expiratory part is abnormal in contour, being low in profile, since expiratory effort is weak and often obstructed in this disease. The flow / volume loop in emphysema is not, however, elongated in the horizontal direction as it would be in an ordinary spirogram. since volume, not time, is being graphed against flow rate.

There are also characteristic loops for asthma and for obstruction of the large airways (as by a tumor). In asthma, there is a depression in the later part of expiration where the effect of spasm in the smaller airways is seen to reduce flow. An obstruction in the larger airways produces a depression in the early part of the expiratory trace; this finding raises the suspicion of bronchial carcinoma.

Flow/volume loops can be carried out more quickly than the traditional spirogram, and with less trouble to the patient. Only a single (in and out) breathing cycle is required, although the test may be repeated to verify maximum effort on the part of the patient. A test, including time spent in explaining it to the patient, can easily be completed in ten minutes, which is a much shorter time than it takes to carry out conventional spirometry. This saving of time translates into a saving of money, and flow / volume loops are thus not only

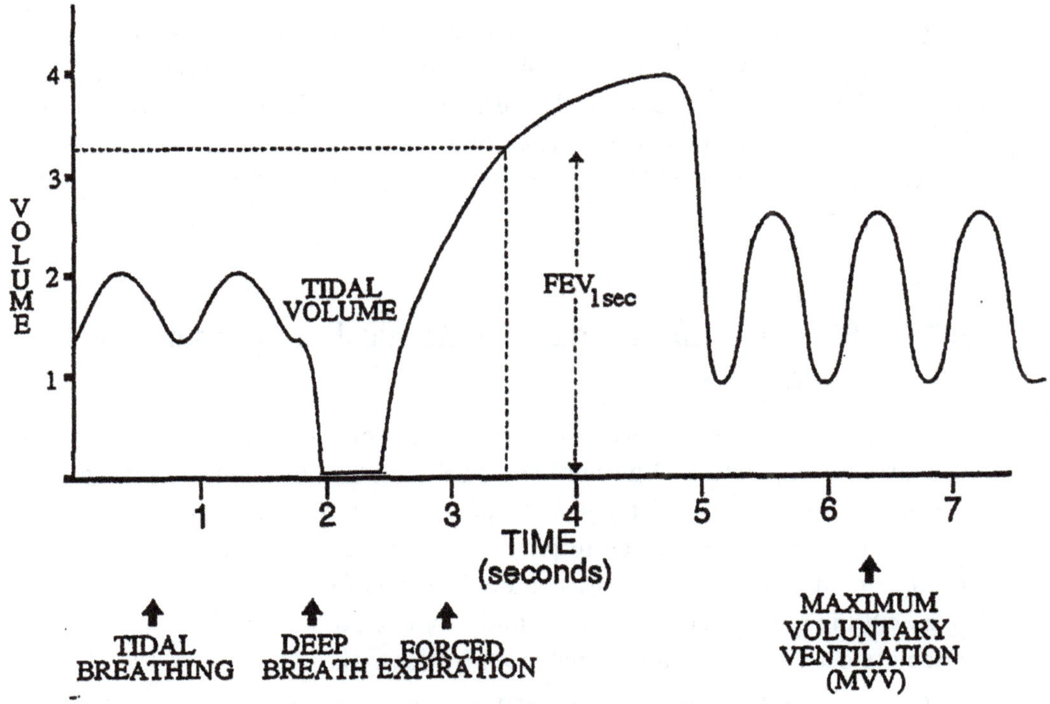

Fig. 9-13 The conventional spirogram—normal trace

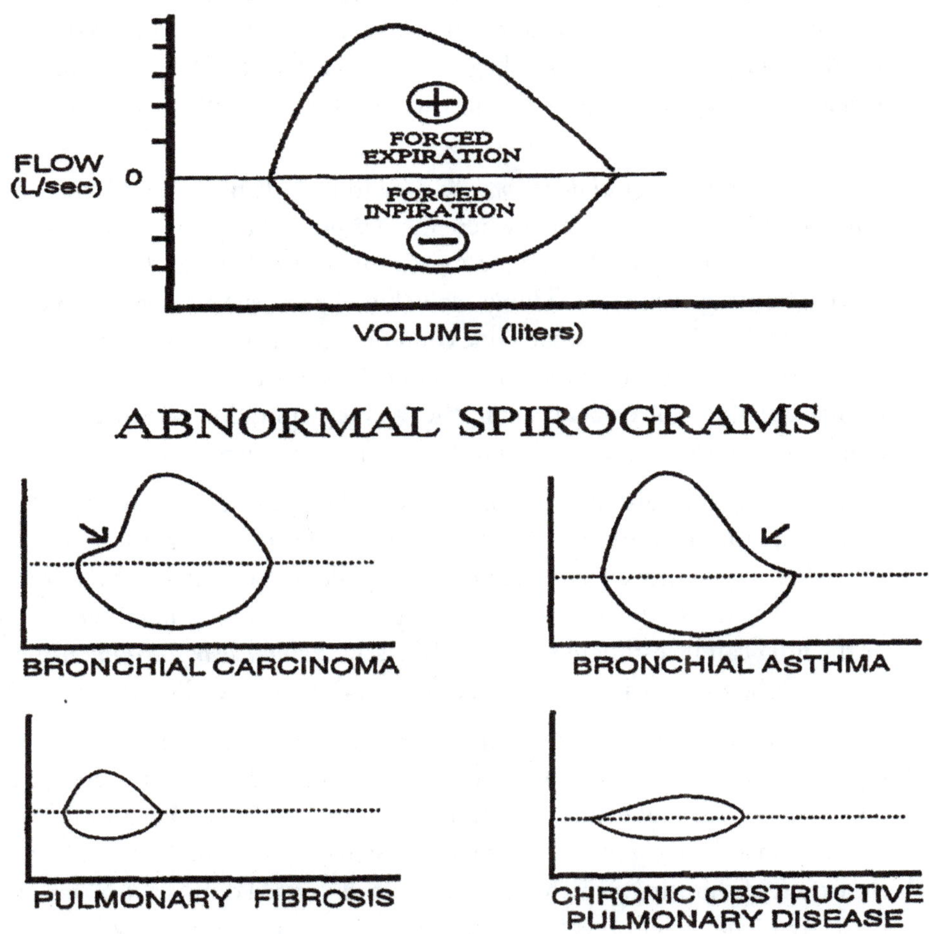

Fig. 9-14 Normal and abnormal spirogram traces—flow volume loops

more convenient for the patient but less expensive than ordinary spirometry. Almost all spirometry for clinical purposes is in fact carried out with flow/volume loop machines, however, if it is known that the test will be used for Social Security disability purposes, conventional spirometry is used. Social Security medical disability agencies do not accept flow/volume loops and require the older respirometry traces. This is because these agencies prefer the calculations, e.g., of FEV_1%, to be checked manually by their physicians rather than by a computer.

§ 9:29 Physiological testing — anatomical and physiological dead space

The measurements and tests discussed in the previous paragraphs are those commonly used in clinical practice. Other more sophisticated tests may, however, be required on occasion. These are often called *physiological tests* since they are more used in the physiology laboratory than in the hospital respiratory therapy department. There are a considerable number of such physiological tests and only a few of them will be described here. Others (e.g., closing pressures and closing volumes) are seldom ordered in clinical practice or for disability determination, and so will not be discussed.

The *anatomical dead space* consists of the conducting airways and is fixed in amount. It can be measured using the *single breath nitrogen test.* A single deep breath of oxygen is taken in and breathed out again through a nitrogen analyzer. At first, pure oxygen comes out (from the dead space). When nitrogen begins to appear, the air is beginning to come from an area where there is gas exchange — the air expired up to this point therefore represents the dead space.

The term *physiological dead space is* used to include not only the anatomical dead space but also other areas in the lung where there is no exchange of gas with the pulmonary circulation. This is in effect adding a measurement of *shunt* to that of the anatomical dead space. Shunting occurs in the lungs when blood goes past airways without receiving oxygen and enters the left atrium in the same condition as when it departed from the right ventricle. A 50% shunt can be a very serious matter. It is not the same thing as getting half of the normal amount of alveolar air to breathe. Oxygen saturation is reduced to 50% which means that oxygen tensions are very low indeed, barely sufficient to sustain life. [See § 8:10.]

If shunting is localized and cannot be cured otherwise, excision of the affected portion of the lung may be indicated. If, for instance, the shunt is mainly on one side, the patient may be greatly improved by a *pneumonectomy.* Before such an operation can be carried out, the extent and also the location of the shunt must be determined. Non-functioning areas of the lung can be estimated and identified by *radionuclear scanning* using Xenon^{127}. This can either be inhaled as a gas or injected intravenously as a liquid (or both).

The amount of blood being shunted past the lungs can be quantified in all sorts of ways. If a *Swan-Ganz catheter* (a tiny catheter with a little balloon on the end) is floated through the heart to lodge in the lung, the pulmonary capillary O_2 (wedge pressure) can be measured and used in a *shunt equation* to calculate the percentage of shunt. An older way of estimating the extent of shunting, which is still sometimes carried out, is a *nitrogen washout test.* [See Fig. 9-15.] The patient breathes pure oxygen until the nitrogen is washed out of her lungs.

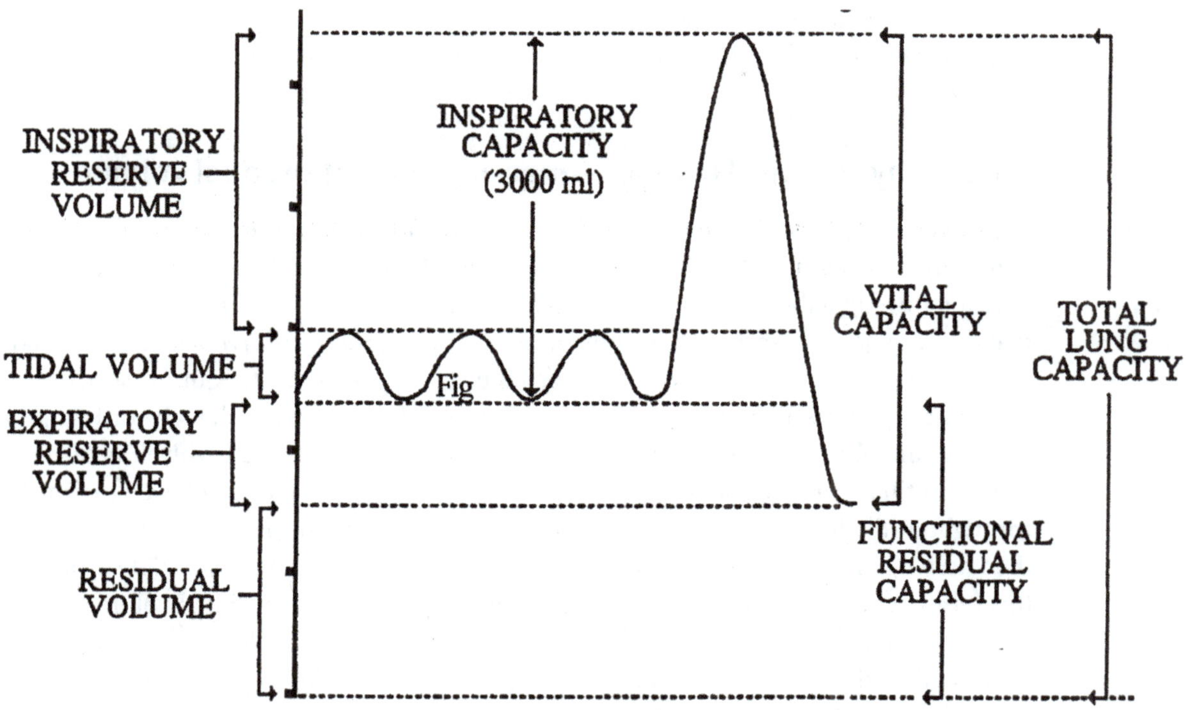

Fig. 9-15 Lung volumes and capacities

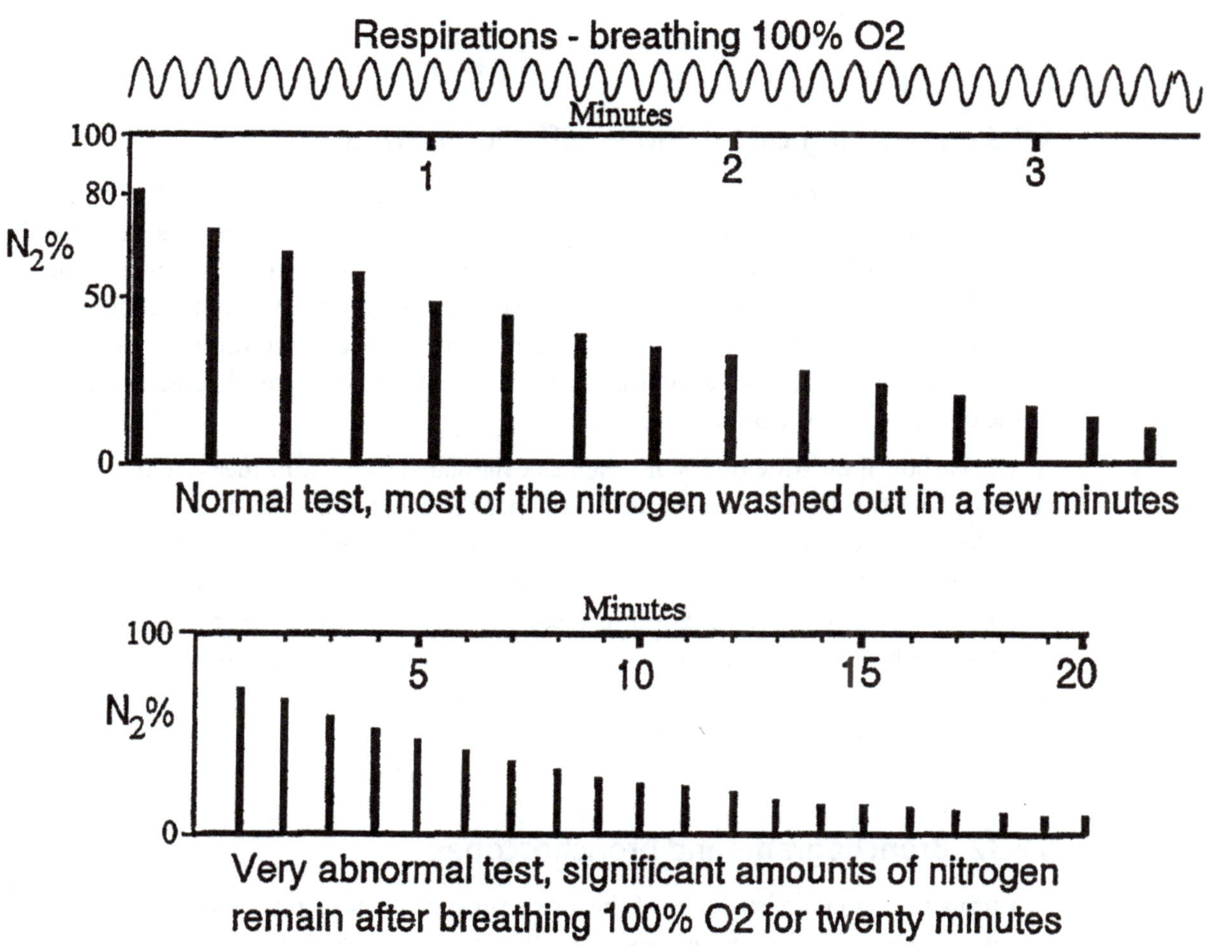

Fig. 9-16 Nitrogen washout test

The usual washout time for any gas in a healthy lung is only a few minutes. If the gas is still not well cleared out in 20 minutes, this is a sign of serious lung disease.

§ 9:30 Physiological testing — measurement of residual volume

The *residual volume is* the air that still remains in the lung at the end of full expiration. Normally it is about 15 to 20 percent of the total lung volume. Patients with emphysema have a reduced vital capacity and an increased residual volume, so much so in some cases that they can only perform tidal breathing; there is no *inspiratory reserve volume.* The residual volume was formerly very difficult to determine. The measurement requires estimating the total lung volume which cannot be calculated from information provided by ordinary pulmonary function tests. Dilution tests were sometimes used. These involved breathing in some identifiable gas or a small amount of radiolabeled gas, which was allowed to distribute throughout the lungs. A sample of expired air (with the added gas diluted through it) was then drawn, and a dilution equation used to derive the total lung volume. Not surprisingly, this measurement was not often ordered in clinical practice. The residual volume can now be measured quite easily using a body CT scanner, and since the calculation is made by the computer on the machine, it is likely to be done automatically if a CT scan of the lung is being carried out for any other purpose, for example, to exclude a cancer. If it is available, the residual volume is a useful item of information, confirming and measuring pulmonary disability.

§ 9:31 Physiological testing — diffusion testing

In the *carbon monoxide diffusion test* (DO), a small measured amount of carbon monoxide is breathed in and allowed to diffuse throughout the lung where it finds its way into the pulmonary circulation and becomes firmly attached to the hemoglobin in some of the red cells. These marked cells are allowed to mix evenly throughout the rest of the blood and a blood sample is then taken and analyzed. The percentage of carbon monoxide *which crossed* from the lung into the circulation can then be estimated and the result used as a measure of the diffusion of gas from lung to blood.

The carbon monoxide diffusion test was originally designed to measure the ability of gases to move through the alveolar walls and into the capillaries of the lung. It was thought that fibrosis or edema might interfere with this process by widening the distance between the lining cells of the alveoli and those of the pulmonary capillaries. In fact, oxygen moves almost as fast from alveoli to blood in these circumstances as it does normally. The real defect is shunt; alveoli are compressed or blocked by scar or fluid so that they do not ventilate properly. And since the carbon monoxide diffusion test is easy to perform, it is still sometimes used as a quick measurement of shunt.

§ 9:32 Bronchograms and bronchoscopes

A bronchogram is a visualizing of the airways using an endoscope or some other means. This was formerly carried out by passing a catheter via the nose through the vocal cords and injecting some radiopaque dye into the trachea. The patient was then allowed to cough and redistribute the dye throughout the lungs. X-rays taken at this point outline the air passages. This old technique gives fine pictures of the small airways and is still a good way to diagnose *bronchiectasis,* a chronic infectious condition where airways become dilated into large and usually pus-filled sacs. However, the larger airways are now normally directly viewed through a flexible bronchoscope, and the smaller passages can be more conveniently imaged using radioactive gases such as $Xenon^{127}$ and a gamma camera. This is much more acceptable to patients, and the old type of contrast bronchogram is rarely ordered nowadays. CT body scanners and MRI scanners can also visualize the bronchial tree and show bronchiectatic sacs, and detect other problems as well. *Bronchoscopy* used to be carried out with a straight, rigid, metal bronchoscopic tube under general anesthesia. The rigid bronchoscope is still used occasionally to remove foreign bodies from the large airways, but it has been largely replaced by the flexible fiberoptic bronchoscope, which can be passed down through the nose with only local anesthesia. It can get into smaller airways, and its tip can be turned around to peek into lung lobes that were formerly inaccessible. One of the important functions of a bronchoscope is to take lung biopsies in cases where an airway tumor is suspected.

Part IV. Examination of the Respiratory System

§ 9:33 Clinical examination of the respiratory system — generally

As always, the mainstays of clinical examination are the four methods of examination used in the evaluating function in any part of the body, namely:

- Inspection (I)
- Palpation (P)
- Percussion (P)
- Auscultation (A)

If all four of these show nothing unremarkable, the record may read "normal to IPPA."

§ 9:34 Clinical examination of the respiratory system — inspection

Under the heading of *inspection,* the patient's skin, fingernails and toenails, ankles and general appearance are examined, looking for much the same things as in the examination of the heart, i.e., cyanosis, clubbing of the fingers and toes, and swelling of the ankles (suggesting *cor pulmonale*). The emotional state of the patient may even be evident to inspection (e.g., an anxious facies). The distinctive things to be noted under the respiratory system are the following:

- Movement of the accessory muscles of respiration in the neck at rest
- Poor air entry, with shallow breathing
- Prolonged and difficult expiration
- A large, fully expanded barrel chest
- Working of the stomach muscles to accomplish expiration
- The absence or near absence of chest movement in breathing

§ 9:35 Clinical examination of the lungs — palpation and auscultation

Palpation essentially consists of putting the hands on the sides of the chest and seeing if they move laterally during breathing. The presence of some lateral movement of the ribs during breathing is a hopeful sign in a patient with COPD or pulmonary fibrosis (the lung is capable of some expansion). It is also sometimes possible to "feel" very loud harsh breath sounds resonating through the chest wall (palpable rales).

Percussion of the lung has been described as a skill that was important to physicians before the advent of the chest X-ray, but it still has its uses. Percussion is carried out by laying one or two fingers flat against the chest and rapping them sharply with the fingers of the other hand. A resonant sound (and sensation) is produced when this is done over normal lung which is described by saying that the chest wall was "resonant to percussion." A *pleural effusion* dulls the sound (and feel) of percussion. A collapsed lung is supposed to increase resonance, but this finding can be difficult to determine with any certainty. Percussion is dull over the heart and it is possible to draw an outline of the heart by percussion. If the heart is grossly enlarged, it can be detected by this means.

§ 9:36 Clinical examination of the lungs — auscultation

Auscultation is the most important item in the respiratory examination. The examiner listens to the breath sounds over each of the main areas of the lung using a stethoscope. The bell of the stethoscope is most useful for low-pitched sounds such as the low murmur of mitral stenosis. The diaphragm is better for high-pitched sounds, and most of the lung noises are high pitched. Abnormal breath sounds are called *adventitial sounds.*

There is some terminological confusion about abnormal lung sounds. The following are common, but not the only, conventions. The term *rale* is sometimes used to describe any abnormal sound but, strictly speaking, it refers to a discontinuous sound (rale is the French term for rattle). Discontinuous sounds are caused by fluid bubbling in the air tubes and are also called *crepitations.* Crepitations can be fine (as in heart failure) or coarse (as in bronchopneumonia). The term *rhonchus* is used to describe a continuous sound, and rhonchi are further described in terms of pitch and timing. High, whistling sounds are called *sibilant rhonchi,* and a low-pitched rhoncus may be called a *wheeze.* Bronchospasm is associated with an expiratory wheeze, whereas a spasm of the vocal cords tends to be inspiratory in timing and is usually called *stridor* or *croup.*

§ 9:37 Clinical examination of the lungs — testing lung function

Pulmonary function tests are usually laboratory tests carried out by respiratory technicians, but the older clinical tests may still be used occasionally since they are easy to perform. In the *match test,* the patient is asked to blow out a match held six inches from the mouth. Inability to do this implies considerable ventilatory impairment. The ability to speak (*phonation*) is greatly affected by lung disease and provides an obvious way to detect severe lung impairment. Someone who is complaining greatly about shortness of breath, but who is able to speak fairly clearly, must then be suspected (absent other explanations) of somatizing or being a malingerer.

Short Working Vocabulary of the Respiratory System

Adventitiae: Abnormal breath sounds.

Aerobronchogram: X-ray appearance where the smaller airways out in the periphery of the lung are outlined. This effect is produced by edema of the surrounding tissues and is a sign of pneumonia.

Alveolar ventilation: The amount of air reaching the alveoli in one minute (approximately 3.5 liters in one minute).

Anatomical dead space: Essentially the air taken into the airways (pharynx, trachea and bronchi) which does not reach the alveoli. This is normally 150 cc but can be increased by the volume of the tubing connecting a patient to ventilators or other devices used to assist respiration, e.g., during anesthesia.

Blunting of the angles: Term found in X-ray reports of chest X-rays. It refers to small amount of fluid in the lower corners of the pleural space in the angles between the rib cage and the diaphragm.

BS nl AA I=E 0 AS: Breath sounds normal in all areas, inspiration and expiration approximately equal, no adventitial (abnormal) sounds.

BS: Breath sounds (heard on auscultation).

Carboxyhemoglobin: Hemoglobin which has combined with carbon monoxide (CO).

cc: Cubic centimeter. [See also *ml.*]

Central cyanosis: Blueness of the tongue and mucous membranes. This is normally a sign of hypoxia indicating serious lung or heart disease.

CO: Carbon monoxide.

CO_2: Carbon dioxide.

Coarse rales: The loud rattling, bubbling sounds made by collections of fluid and phlegm in the larger airways

COHb: Carboxyhemoglobin.

Crepitations: Commonly a general term for discontinuous sounds. They can be described as fine, medium or coarse crepitations. Fine crepitations are heard in lobar pneumonia or other conditions where there are collections of fluid in the very small airways or alveolar ducts. Coarse crepitations are heard in conditions when fluid or mucus is bubbling in large airways, as in bronchopneumonia.

Dead space: The amount of air (in each breath) taken into the airways and expelled again without reaching the alveoli and taking part in gas exchange. [See also *Anatomical dead space* and *Physiological dead space.*]

Diaphragm: The muscle layer which separates the chest cavity from the abdominal cavity and the contractions of which operate normal quiet breathing.

Differential white cell count: The number of each different type of white cell found in 100 WBCs (thus it is a percentage). This figure is usually obtained, when it is not derived automatically by computer analysis, by averaging the numbers of each kind of white cell found over several counts of one hundred leukocytes under the microscope.

DWCC: The differential white cell count.

ERV: Expiratory reserve volume.

Expiratory reserve volume: The amount of air that can be exhaled following a normal quiet expiration.

FEF 25–75%: The average flow rate during mid-expiration (its middle two quarters).

FEF: Forced expiratory flow, the rate at which air is being expelled in forced expiration.

FEF100–1200: The average flow rate in the early expiration. [See also *FEF* and *FEF 25–75%.*]

$FEV_{1\,sec}$: The volume of air exhaled in the first second of a maximal expiratory effort following a full inspiration.

FEV_1%: The percentage of the vital capacity expelled from the lungs during the first one second of a maximal expiratory effort following full inspiration (normally 75% or more).

FIO_2: The fraction of oxygen in the inspired air. This is normally given as a percentage, e.g., the FIO_2 of room air is normally approximately 21%.

Forced expiratory flow: The rate at which air is expelled during forced expiration. Since this changes with time, being greatest in early expiration and then tapering off, it is usual to give the FEF as an average during a certain part of expiration. [See also *FEF 100–1200* and *FEF 25–75%.*]

Granulocytes: White blood cells whose cytoplasm appears granular under the microscope. This appearance is caused by the numerous collections of RNA in the microtubules of their cytoplasm used by these cells to manufacture circulating antibodies. Other types of white cells are called *agranulocytes.*

Hb: Hemoglobin.

Hb%: Hemoglobin percent, the amount of hemoglobin (in grams) present in one hundred cubic centimeters (cc) of whole blood.

Hct: Hematocrit.

Hematocrit: The percentage of the blood made up of packed red cells, normally 45%. The figure for the hematocrit should be roughly three times that of the hemoglobin (Hb).

Hemopneumothorax: Air and blood in the pleural space.

Hemothorax: Blood present in the pleural space.

Histiocytes: Large white cells fixed in tissues such as lymph nodes, liver and spleen. They are also present in the skin and in the alveoli of the lungs. They are related to monocytes (which are their circulating counterpart) and, like them, act as phagocytic cells (they ingest foreign particles) and initiate the immune response of the body.

Inspiratory reserve volume: The amount of air that can be breathed in following a normal quiet inspiration.

IRV: Inspiratory reserve volume.

MA-1: Trade name of a ventilator in common use in respiratory intensive care units.

Maximum ventilatory volume: The amount of air that can be ventilated in one minute breathing maximally, normally 50–60 liters. This is commonly calculated by extrapolating the amount ventilated breathing maximally for 10 seconds (or sometimes from the time required to take six quick maximal breaths).

ml: Milliliter, one-thousandth part of a liter, or one cubic centimeter (cc). It has become standard practice to use the milliliter (ml) terminology, but the cubic centimeter notation is still in common use.

Monos: Monocytes; large white cells which circulate in the blood.

MVV: The maximum ventilatory volume.

Oxygen saturation: The percentage ratio of the oxygen attached to hemoglobin compared to that which it could carry. Note that this is a measure of the oxygen carried in the blood, not of the blood available to the tissues. [See also *Oxygen tension.*]

Oxygen tension: The partial pressure of oxygen, as in arterial blood. It is the pressure exercised on the boundaries of the space that it occupies, and is therefore measured in pressure units (mm Hg). This is a measure of the availability of oxygen to the tissues, and is not the same thing as oxygen saturation.

$PaCO_2$: The partial pressure of carbon dioxide in arterial blood.

PaO_2: The partial pressure of oxygen in arterial blood, normally more than 75 mm Hg.

Parietal pleura: The outer covering membranes of the lung. [See also *Pleura.*]

Peribronchial infiltrates: X-ray appearance where there are white patches (in the negative film) in areas surrounding the bronchi. They highlight the smaller airways and so are often called aerobronchograms. They are caused by edema of the tissues and are a sign of bronchial pneumonia.

Peripheral cyanosis: Blueness of the lips and skin which may be a normal finding in cold weather or due to inordinate vasospastic response to cold, as in Raynaud's disease.

pH: A measure of acidity /alkalinity of a fluid: a pH of 7.4 represents the normal neutral point in blood (7.0 the pH of water is the normal chemical standard of neutrality).

Physiological dead space: The total amount of air in each breath which is ventilated but not exchanged with blood in the alveoli. This includes not only the air breathed in and out of the airways without exchange (the anatomical dead space) but also air which reaches alveoli which are not being perfused adequately (ventilation /perfusion mismatch).

Pleura: The membranes covering the lungs. There are two of them: the visceral pleura, which is attached to the lung surface, and the parietal pleura, which forms the outer cover. Between these lies the pleural sac (pleural space). Pleural fluid is secreted by the membranes into the sac as a lubricant. The two membranes thus glide smoothly over one another allowing the lung to expand easily and without friction (the pericardial membranes surrounding the heart function in the same way).

Pleural sac: The space between the parietal and visceral pleural membranes. [See also *Pleura.*]

Pleural effusion: Excessive fluid present in the pleural space.

Pleuritis: Infection or inflammation of the pleural membranes.

Pneumothorax: Air present in the pleural space. [See also *Hemopneumothorax.*]

Polymorphonuclear white blood cells: Cells with multiloculated nuclei (like a string of sausages). They function in the cellular immune responses of the body. [See also *Lymphocytes*]

polys: Polymorphonuclear white blood cells. See *segs* and *band cells.*

Q: The amount of blood flowing through the pulmonary bed in one minute. [See also *V/Q ratio.*]

Rales: Discontinuous abnormal breath sounds (the term "rale" in French means "rattle"). [See *Crepitations* and *Coarse rales*]

RBCs: Red blood cells.

Respiration: Term used to describe the entire respiratory cycle including the uptake and transportation of oxygen to the tissues, its utilization in cells there, the production of carbon dioxide (CO_2) at the tissues, its transport through the body and elimination in the lungs.

Respiratory quotient: The ratio of carbon dioxide production to oxygen utilization in the body. The normal figure is approximately 0.8.

Rhronci: Continuous (uninterrupted) abnormal breath sounds such as wheezes or stridor.

RQ: The respiratory quotient.

RS: Respiratory system.

Shunt: Where blood is bypassing alveoli without gas exchange. This is really only one form of ventilation /perfusion (V/Q) mismatch but the terms are used virtually interchangeably by most clinicians.

SO_2: Oxygen saturation (of hemoglobin).

Tidal volume: The amount of air ventilated (breathed in or out) during normal quiet breathing.

TV: Tidal volume.

V/Q ratio: The ratio of the alveolar ventilation of air to the flow of blood through the lungs (normally approximately 1).

V/Q mismatch: Where the air ventilated and the blood perfusing through the lungs are not meeting and exchanging gases. This can happen in two ways: due to no blood flow (or low flow) in the capillaries; or when alveoli are blocked so that blood is bypassing them without exchanging gas (shunting). A certain amount of shunt, due to the positioning of the body and other things, is normal.

V: The volume of air ventilated into the lungs in one minute. [See also *V/Q ratio.*]

VC: Vital capacity.

Ventilation: Term used to describe the movement of air into and out of the lungs. It should not be confused with respiration, which is a much more general term.

Visceral pleura: The inner coverings of the lungs. [See also *Pleura.*]

Vital capacity: The amount of air that can be expelled from the lungs following a maximal inspiration.

WBCs: White blood cells, or leukocytes.

WCC: The number of white cells present in one milliliter of blood.

Specimen Handwritten Note on Lung Patient

50 y.o. W ♂ C/O SOB x 1 yr

HCC:- Pt first noticed dyspnea 1 yr ago. DOE at first, later SOB at rest.

PMH:- AFD dx'd aged 25. TX'd c̄ INH & streptomycin. Several episodes of p'a → hospitalized x 2 & Tx'd c̄ I.V. PCN. No serious chest infections since aged 30 (occas^l URTI).

Meds:- No continuing meds. NKDA

S.H:- Worked in building construction. ? exposure to asbestos fibers over a period of 10 yrs. till aged 40. In present job (building materials sales) since.

PH:- ii p.p.d. (20 p.y's) till aged 30. None since

FH:- ō FH of lung disease – CF or asthma.

R.O.S.:- Gen N/C. ? LOW during last yr. but states was always thin.

O/E: Tall thin emaciated WM A ≥ SA
Color:- Mucosa pink.

R/S:- I & P: AMR's move at rest. SOB at rest
RR 30/min. Chest mt. poor – some lat. CW mt.
Auscultation:- air entry fair, BS nl AA I ≅ E
ō RR or R. Widespread fine creps, loudest at bases

Translation of Specimen Handwritten Note on Lung Patient

PATIENT HISTORY:

50 year old white male complaining of shortness of breath for one year.

HISTORY OF CHIEF COMPLAINT: Patient first noticed dyspnea 1 year ago. Dyspnea on exertion at first but later short of breath at rest.

PAST MEDICAL HISTORY: Acid fast disease (tuberculosis) diagnosed aged 25. Treated with isoniazid and streptomycin. Several episodes of pneumonia, hospitalized for this on two occasions treated with intravenous penicillin. No serious chest infections since aged 30 (occasional upper respiratory tract infection).

MEDICATIONS: No continuing medications.. No known drug allergies.

SOCIAL HISTORY: Worked in building construction, possible exposure to asbestos materials over a period of 10 years till aged 40. In present job (building supply sales) since then.

PERSONAL HISTORY: Smoked 2 packets (of cigarettes) a day for 20 years till aged 39, none since. No alcohol (use). No history of drug abuse. Married with 2 children (both) alive and well.

FAMILY HISTORY: No family history of lung disease (no cystic fibrosis or asthma).

REVIEW OF SYSTEMS: Generally non-contributory, no night sweats or fevers. May have had some loss of weight during the last year but was always thin.

ON EXAMINATION (PHYSICAL EXAMINATION)

Tall thin and emaciated (looking) white male with appearance greater than stated age. Color - mucosal membranes (inside the mouth) pink.

RESPIRATORY SYSTEM:

Inspection and palpation: Accessory muscles of respiration move (when the patient is) at rest and (he appears) short of breath at rest. Respiratory rate is 30 breaths per minute. Chest movement is poor but there is some lateral chest wall movement.

Auscultation: Air entry fair, breath sounds present all areas, inspiration approx. equal to expiration, no rules, rhonci or rubs. Widespread fine crepitations loudest at (lung) bases.

CNS :- Sl. anxious CN. ii – xii g.i.

PNS: PTCS & DTRs all nl.

CVS:- RRR, HS nl $S_1 S_2$ nl s̄ (m) (r) or (g)

BP 120/70, ō PVCs, ABMCL 5ICS.

Abd:- ō organomegaly, ō masses, ō tenderness any quad^T

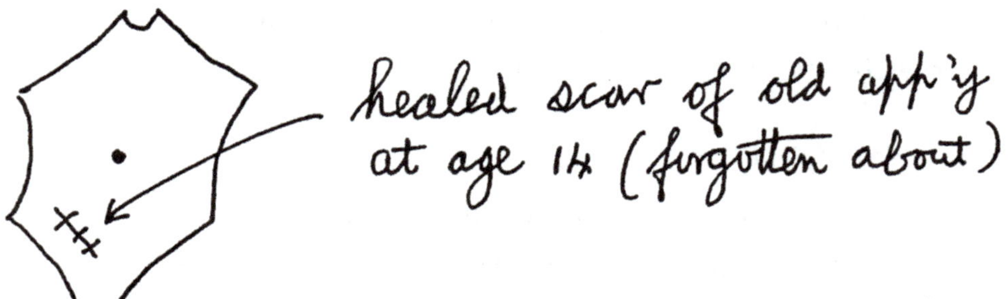

Integ:- ō rashes, ō lymphadenopathy

Asses:- #1. R/O COPD ? 2° smoking/asbestos

#2. R/O PF ? 2° asbestos or lung infections

#3. R/O reactivation of AFD.

#4 R/O Mitosis 2° smoking/asbestos

ie bronchogenic C/A or mesothelioma.

Plan :- #1. CXR

#2. ABGs

#3. Spirometry

#4. ?? Kveim test for sarcoid

#5. Consider bronchoscopy

Ray Spiro M.D.

CENTRAL NERVOUS SYSTEM: Slightly anxious. Cranial nerves two through twelve grossly intact.

PERIPHERAL NERVOUS SYSTEM: Examination covers power, tone, coordination, sensation and deep tendon reflexes, e.g., PTCRnl, i.e., power tone coordination and reflexes normal.

CARDIOVASCULAR SYSTEM: Regular rate and rhythm. Heart sounds normal, first and second heart sounds, normal, with out murmur, rub or gallop. Blood pressure 120/70 mm Hg, no premature ventricular contraction. Apex beat at the mid-clavicular line and fifth intercostal space.

ABDOMEN: No organomegaly, no masses, no tenderness in any quadrant.

[*Diagram is the traditional figure for the anterior abdomen showing the umbilicus in the middle, the lower borders of the rib cage above and the inguinal ligaments etc. below. A healed appendectomy scar is indicated in the right lower quadrant.*]

INTEGUMENTARY SYSTEM: No rashes, no lymphadenopathy (enlarged lymph nodes visible or palpable on the surface of the skin).

ASSESS:

#1. Rule out chronic obstructive pulmonary disease possible due to smoking or asbestos (exposure)

#2. Rule out pulmonary fibrosis possible due to asbestos (exposure) or to recurrent lung infections.

#3. Rule out reactivation of acid fast bacillus (tuberculosis).

#4. Rule out mitosis (cancer) due to smoking or asbestos exposure i.e. bronchogenic carcinoma or mesothelioma.

PLAN:

#1. Chest X-ray.

#2. Arterial blood gases.

#3. Spirometry.

#4. Consider (possible) Kveim test for sarcoidosis (a cause of pulmonary fibrosis).

#5. Consider bronchoscopy to rule out bronchogenic carcinoma.

Ray Spiro M.D.

Short Glossary of Symbols and Acronyms

↑ : Up, or raised

↓ : Down or lowered ("↓ temp" for fever has abated)

∨ : Flexion

∧ : Extension

> : Greater than

< : Less than

♂ : Male

♀ : Female

x : Times / for ("x3" would be "three times" and "x1 / 52" would be "for one week")

: Number ("#1")

(R): Rectal ("temp 99.60 (R)")

+ : Positive / plus / with ("Rhomberg's test +" or "episodes of chest pain + sweating")

– : Minus / negative / without ("episodes of arrhythmia – chest pain")

ō : Zero / none / without ("ō alcohol abuse")

1°: First degree / primary ("1° heart block")

2°: Second degree / secondary to ("weight loss 2° depression")

≙ :Approximately equal to

= : Equal to

? : Doubtful / possible ("? slight limp when walking")

@ : At / each ("apex beat @ mid-clavicular line")

ā : Ante, before or prior to

A: Assessment / active

A & O: Alert and oriented

A & P: Auscultation and percussion

A & W: Alive and well [See also *L & W.*]

AAF: African-American Female

AAM: African-American male

AF / A-fib: Atrial fibrillation

a.c.: Ante cibum, before food

AA: Automobile accident [See also *RTA*.]

AA: Active / assisted exercises, as in an order to physical therapist

abd.: Abduction / abdomen

ABGs: Arterial blood gases

ACLS: Advanced cardiac life support

AFB: Acid fast bacillus (euphemism for tuberculosis)

AD: Aurum dexter (right ear)

ad lib: As much as you wish ("out of bed ad lib")

add.: Adduction

AFROM: Active full range of motion (physical therapy order)

A / G: Albumin globulin (ratio)

alk.phos.: Alkaline phosphatase (enzyme elevated in several conditions, as in obstructive jaundice)

ALMI: Anterolateral myocardial infarction

amb.: Ambulation

AMI: Acute myocardial infarction

amt.: Amount

ant.: Anterior

AP: Anteroposterior (anteroposterior chest X-ray)

AROM: Active range of motion

AS: Aortic stenosis

ASA: Acetyl salicylic acid (aspirin)

ASAP: As soon as possible

ASCVD: Atherosclerotic cardiovascular disease

ASPVD: Atherosclerotic peripheral vascular disease

Ate / atel: Atelectasis

AU: Aura utra (both ears)

AV: Atrioventricular (the AV node in the right atrium)

AWMI: Anterior wall myocardial infarction

ax.: Axilla / axillary

BE / BaE: Barium enema

BBB: Bundle branch block (LBBB is left bundle branch block)

BM: Bowel movement

bil.: Bilateral

bid: Bis in die (twice a day)

BF: Black female (Current term is African-American female, i.e., AAF)

BM: Black male (Current term is African-American male, i.e., AAM)

BM: Bowel movement

BOE: Bilateral otitis externa

BOM: Bilateral otitis media

BP: Blood pressure

BPH: Benign prostatic hypertrophy

BR: Bed rest

BRBPR: Bright red blood per rectum

BRP: Bathroom privileges

BS: Blood sugar

BSC: Bed side commode

BS: Breath sounds / bowel sounds

BTL: Bilateral tubal ligation

BTx: Buck's traction; a technique for immobilization of a broken leg, often used as a first aid measure during transportation for definitive treatment.

BUN: Blood urea nitrogen (a biochemical blood test used to evaluate renal function)

BUS: Bartholin's, urethral and Skein's glands (noted during gynecological examination)

BWP: Body whirlpool (physical therapy order)

Bx: Biopsy

c̄: Cervical / chronic / cum, i.e., with

C&S: Culture and sensitivity

C / S: Caesarean section

c / o: Complaining of

Ca: Calcium / cancer

Ca^{+}: Calcium ion

CABG: Coronary artery bypass graft

caps: Capsules

cap refill: Capillary refill (test of perfusion of blood in the skin)

CAT / CT: Computerized axial tomography (CAT scan)

cc: Cubic centimeter (equal to one milliliter)

CCU: Coronary care unit

CHD: Coronary heart disease

CHF: Congestive heart failure

chr.: Chronic

Cl^- : Chloride ion

cm: Centimeter

CN / cnn: Cranial nerve(s)

CNS: Central nervous system

CO_2: Carbon dioxide

COLD: Chronic obstructive lung disease [See also *COPD.*]

comp.: Compound ("comp. fx" = compound fracture)

contr.: Contraction / contraception

COPD: Chronic obstructive pulmonary disease, emphysema

cor: The heart

CPK: Creatinine phosphokinase (an important cardiac enzyme)

CPT: Chest physical therapy

CRP: C-reactive protein. Considered a more sensitive test for inflammatory disease than the ESR.

CSF: Cerebrospinal fluid

CTx: Cervical traction

CVA: Cerebrovascular accident (a stroke)

CVD: Cardiovascular disease

CVP: Central venous pressure

Cx: Cervix

CXR: Chest X-ray

D&C: Dilatation and curettage ("gynecological D&C")

D5W: Solution with 5% dextrose in water

D5NS: 5% dextrose solution in normal saline

D5¼NS: 5% dextrose solution in ¼ normal saline

D5½NS: 5% dextrose in ½ normal saline

D10NS: 10% dextrose in (normal) saline

D&E: Dilatation and evacuation (a surgical abortion)

d.o.: Days old ("a 3 d.o. infant")

D / C: Discharge / discontinue ("pt. DC'd" means patient was discharged and "meds DC'd" means medications discontinued)

D / W: Dextrose in water

D1-D12: The twelve dorsal vertebrae

D50: 50% dextrose (i.e., 50 grams dextrose in each 100 cc of water)

DAT: Diet as tolerated

Dx / Dg: Diagnosis

diff.: Differential (the differential white cell count) [See also *DWCC.*]

DIP: The distal interphalangeal (joint of the finger)

DM: Diabetes mellitus

DNA: Desoxyribonucleic acid (basic biochemical unit in the genetic material of cells)

DOA: Dead on arrival

DOB: Date of birth

DOE: Dyspnea on exertion

dpm: Drops per minute

DPT: Diphtheria, pertussis and tetanus (combined injection used in immunization of children)

drs / drsg.: Dressing

DT: Delirium tremens

DTRs: Deep tendon reflexes

DW: Distilled water

E: Enema

ER: Emergency room

EAC: External auditory canal

ECF: Extracellular fluid, fluid in between cells [See also *ICF.*]

EKG: Electrocardiogram

EDC: Estimated date of confinement (in labor)

EEG: Electroencephalogram

EENT: Eye, ear, nose, and throat

EMT-P: Emergency medical technician, paramedic

ENT: Ear nose and throat

EOM: Extraocular movements / extraocular muscles

EOMI: Extraocular muscles (movements) intact

eos.: Eosinophils, eosinophilic (pink-staining) leukocytes seen in allergic conditions

Epith.: Epithelium

Eq.: Equivalent [See also *mEq.*]

ESR: Erythrocyte sedimentation rate (the rate at which RBCs settle in blood; an elevated ESR is a non-specific sign that something is wrong) [See also *CRP.*]

ETOH: Ethanol (ethyl alcohol)

ES: Endotracheal suction

Ex: Exercise

Ext/extn: Extension

Ext.gen.: External genitalia

F: Female (often represented by the symbol ♀)

F°: Degrees Fahrenheit

F/C: Fever and chills

F/U: Follow-up ("Pt. to be seen for F/U in one week")

FB: Foreign body

FBS: Fasting blood sugar

Fe: Iron

$FeSO_4$: Ferrous sulfate (used as supplemental iron to treat anemia)

FEF: Forced expiratory flow [See Vocabulary for the Respiratory System]

FEV: Forced expiratory volume [See Vocabulary for the Respiratory System]

FH: Family history

FHT: Fetal heart tone

FHB: Fetal heart beat

FIO_2: Fraction of oxygen in inspired air (see Respiratory vocabulary)

fl: Fluid

flex.: Flexion

Fm: Female ("28 y.o. HF" = 28-year-old hispanic female)

FMD: Family medical doctor

FS: Frozen section (for pathological examination, e.g., of breast tissue)

FSG: Finger stick glucose

FTB: Full thickness bum (bottom)

FTI: Free thyroxin index; a measure of the thyroid hormone free and active in the blood (i.e., not bound to the serum proteins)

FUO: Fever of unknown origin (a mysterious fever, usually low grade, which has persisted for more than three weeks [See also *PUO.*]

FVC: Forced vital capacity [See Vocabulary for the Respiratory System.]

Fx: Fracture

G: Gravida, Latin for pregnant

GA: General appearance ("GA=SA" means "general appearance equals stated age")

GB: Gall bladder

GC: Gonococcus (the organism responsible for gonorrhea)

GE: Gastroenteritis

gm: Gram

GSW: Gunshot wound

gt: Gait

gtt: Guttae, Latin for drops (of fluid)

GTT: Glucose tolerance test

GU: Genitourinary (system)

GYN: Gynecology [See also *Ob/Gyn.*]

H: Hypodermic (syringe or needle)

H&P: History and physical

h/hr: Hour, "h.s." is "hora somniae" (the hour of sleep, bedtime)

HA: Headache

H_2O: Water

HBP: High blood pressure

HCO_3^-: Bicarbonate (ion)

Hct: Hematocrit

HCVD: Hypertensive cardiovascular disease

HEENT: Head, eye, ear, nose, and throat

Hb: Hemoglobin

HisF/HF: Hispanic female

HisM/HM: Hispanic male

HIV: Human immunodeficiency virus (causing AIDS)

HNP: Herniated nucleus pulposus, a slipped disc

HPI/HOPI: History of present illness

HP: Hot pack (to treat muscle spasm, etc.,)

HPF: High-powered field, seen through a microscope ("30 white cells/HPF")

ht.: Height

HTN: Hypertension

Hx: History

Hx & PE: History and physical examination

hypo: Hypodermic (needle)

I: Iodine

I&D: Incision and drainage (e.g., of an abscess)

I&O: Intake and output (measurements to assess hydration of a patient)

I^{131}: Radioactive isotope of iodine used in thyroid studies

IBTx: Intermittent Buck's traction

ICF: Intracellular fluid, fluid inside cells [See *ECF.*]

ICS: Intercostal space (the space between the ribs)

ICTx: Intermittent cervical traction

INZ: Isoniazid (a drug used to treat tuberculosis)

IM: Intramuscular (an IM injection)

imp.: Impression

IMV: Intermittent mandatory ventilation

IPPB: Intermittent positive pressure breathing

IPTx: Intermittent pelvic traction

IS: Incentive spirometer (treatment) / Intermittent suction

ISF: Interstitial fluid (fluid outside cells but not in blood vessels) [See also *ICF*.]

IUD: Intrauterine (contraceptive) device

IV: Intravenous

IVC: Inferior vena cava

IVF: Intravascular fluid

IVP: Intravenous pyelogram

JVD: Jugular venous (jugulovenous) distention

K^+: Potassium ion

kg: Kilogram

KI: Potassium iodide

KJ: Knee jerk (the quadriceps reflex)

KUB: Kidneys, ureters, and bladder (urological X-ray study)

KVO: Keep vein open (giving just enough IV fluid to prevent blood from clotting in the IV catheter and closing it off)

L: Lumbar / left / liter

L&A: Light and accommodation (eye movement reflexes)

L&W: Living and well [See also *A / W*.]

L&D: Labor, and delivery

L / 3: Lower third, e.g., of a bone

L / S: Lumbosacral

L4-5: Lumbar four / five (interspace)

LA: Left atrium

lab.: Laboratory

LAD: Left anterior descending (coronary artery) / left axis deviation

LAH: Left anterior hemiblock

lap.: Laparotomy (i.e., surgical opening of the abdomen)

lat.: Lateral

LBBB: Left bundle branch block

LBP: Low back pain

LDH: Lactic dehydrogenase, an enzyme released from heart muscle in an MI

LE: Lower extremity

LEs: Lower extremities

LKKS: Liver, both kidneys and spleen

LLE: Left lower extremity

LLL: Left lower lobe (of the lung)

LLQ: Left lower quadrant (of the abdomen)

LMD: Local medical doctor [See also *FMD.*]

LMP: Last menstrual period

LOC: Level of consciousness / loss of consciousness

LOM: Limitation of motion

LP: Lumbar puncture

LPH: Left posterior hemiblock

lg.: Large

LT: Light touch ("sensation normal to light touch")

lt.: Left

LUE: Left upper extremity (literally the hand, but often taken to be the arm)

LUL: Left upper lobe (of the lung)

LUQ: Left upper quadrant (of the abdomen)

LV: Left ventricle

LVH: Left ventricular hypertrophy

LVI: Left ventricular ischemia

M: Male, often represented as ♂

M&S: Motor and sensory (items in the neurological physical examination)

MVV: Maximum voluntary ventilation (part of the conventional spirogram)

M / 3: Middle third (e.g., of a bone)

M1: The first mitral sound

MCL: Mid-clavicular line

meds.: Medications

mEq: Milliequivalent (serum electrolytes are normally measured in milliequivalents per liter)

mEq / L: Milliequivalents per liter

METs: Metabolic units (used as measurements of work done – kilocalories – in treadmill testing)

met.: Metabolic

Mg: Magnesium

mg: Milligram

mg%: Normally means the number of milligrams of a substance present in 100 ml of blood

mg / dL: Milligrams per deciliter, mg%

MI: Myocardial infarction

ml: Milliliter

mm: Millimeter

MMEF: Maximum mid-expiratory flow (the peak flow rate during a maximal expiratory effort)

MS: Multiple sclerosis

MS / MSE: Mental status / Mental status examination

MVS: Multiple vague symptoms

N: Nausea

N&V: Nausea and vomiting

N / C: Nasal cannula (for administration of oxygen)

NVD: Nausea, vomiting and diarrhea

N_2: Nitrogen

Na^+: Sodium ion

NAD: No acute distress

NB: Newborn

neb.: Nebulizer

neg.: Negative

neuro.: Neurological (examination)

NGD: No gross deformities

NKA: No known allergies

NKDA: No known drug allergies

nl: Normal

noct.: Nocturnal

NPO: Nil per os (nothing by mouth)

NSSTTW: Non-specific S-T and T-wave changes

NSR: Normal sinus rhythm (of the heart)

NS: Normal saline (solution)

NTND: Non-tender & not deformed (referring to a joint)

O&P: Ova and parasites (may be found in a stool specimen)

O x 3: Oriented as to time, place and person (or circumstances)

OR: Operating room

O / C: On call

OB: Obstetrics

OB / GYN: Obstetrics and gynecology

OD: Oculum dexter (right eye)

OOB: Out of bed ("OOB ad lib" means "out of bed as the patient wishes")

OP: Outpatient

OU: Ocula utra (both eyes)

p̄: Post (after)

P: Plan (i.e., part of S.O.A.P – Subjective, Objective, Assessment and Plan)

P: Pulse (rate) / passive

P: Phosphorus

Parenterally: Other than by mouth; by intravenous or intramuscular injection

P & A: Percussion and auscultation

P.C. / p.c.: Post cibum (after meals)

PD: Postural drainage

p.o.: Per os (by mouth)

PO: Post-operatively / post-operative

PT: Prothrombin time (often called pro.time)

P1, P2: The first and second pulmonic heart sounds

PA: Posteroanterior (a PA chest X-ray / pulmonary artery)

PAC: Premature atrial contraction

PAP: Papanicolaou smear test (for cancer of the uterine cervix)

P1, 2 etc.: Parous, i.e., having been delivered of one or more children. "G1, P1" means "gravida 1 parous 1"—a woman has been pregnant once and had one child.

PAT: Paroxysmal atrial tachycardia

PB: Piggyback (i.e., where one IV is delivered through another)

PCN: Penicillin

$PaCO_2$: Partial pressure (tension) of carbon dioxide

PCV: Packed cell volume (the volume of red cells in blood after centrifuging, usually given as a percentage)

PE: Physical examination

PEEP: Positive end-expiratory pressure

PEFR: Peak expiratory flow rate (the highest rate of air flow achieved during a maximal expiratory effort)

PEG: Pneumoencephalogram, i.e. an X-ray study of the spinal cord and surrounding structures using air as the contrast material (seldom if ever used nowadays)

p̄: Per, Latin for "through" ("Adm. p̄ ER" = "Admitted through the ER")

per: Through ("per os" is "by mouth")

PERRLA: Pupils equal, round, react to light and accommodate

PFR: Peak flow rate [See also *PEFR.*]

PFROM: Passive full range of motion

PFTS: Pulmonary function tests

PH: Past history

pH: System used to measure acidity/alkalinity

PI: Present illness, "HPI" is "history of present illness"

PID: Pelvic inflammatory disease

PIP: Proximal interphalangeal (joint of the finger)

PKU: Phenylketonuria (a congenital metabolic disease)

PMD: Private medical doctor

PMI: Point of maximal impulse (the apex beat of the heart)

PND: Paroxysmal nocturnal dyspnea (a symptom of heart failure)

PaO_2: Partial pressure (tension) of arterial oxygen, measured as millimeters of mercury, mm Hg. [See also *SAO_2.*]

PO_4: Phosphate

polys: Polymorphonuclear leukocytes (white blood cells)

pos.: Positive

p.p.: Post prandial (after a meal)

PPD: Purified protein derivative (a preparation made from killed tubercle bacillus organisms which is used in a skin test for TB)

PRBCs: Packed red blood cells (used for blood transfusion)

PRE: Progressive resistive exercise(s)

prn: Pro re nata (as needed)

PROM: Passive range of motion (used to refer to examination or exercises)

PRWP: Poor R-wave progression (an EKG finding suggesting anterior myocardial infarction)

PT: Pregnancy test/Physical therapy (therapist)

pt.: Patient

PTB: Partial thickness bum

PTT: Partial thromboplastin time (a blood coagulation test. See PT)

PTx: Pelvic traction

PUD: Peptic ulcer disease

Pulm.: Pulmonary

PUO: Pyrexia of unknown origin (equivalent expression for a fever of unknown origin) [See also *FUO.*]

PVC: Premature ventricular contraction

q: quomodo, Latin for "every" (q1h is every hour)

q1h: Every hour

qn: Quomodo nocte (each night)

qid: Four times a day (quattuor in die)

qhs: Each night at bedtime

qn: Each night

q.alt.d: Every other day

qod: Every other day

qns: Quantity not sufficient

qs: Quantity sufficient

qon: Every other night

R: Right / resistive

R: Respirations / respiratory

RA: Right atrium / Rheumatoid arthritis

RR: Recovery room

RAD: Right axis deviation (abnormality on EKG trace)

RBBB: Right bundle branch block

RBCs: Red blood cells

RCC: Red (blood) cell count

Rh: The rhesus antigen on the surface of red blood cells. A patient may be described as Rh+ or Rh– (rhesus positive or rhesus negative)

RLE: Right lower extremity

RLL: Right lower lobe (of the lung)

RLQ: Right lower quadrant (of the abdomen)

RML: Right middle lobe (of the lung)

R / O: Rule out (i.e., the diagnosis of exclusion)

ROM: Range of motion (studies or exercises)

ROS: Review of systems (part of the medical history—or systematic questions) **S / Q** (See §4:3)

rot. / rotn: Rotation

RRE: Round, regular and equal (pupils)

RROM: Resistive range of motion (studies or exercises)

rt.: Right

RTA: Road traffic accident (See AA)

RUE: Right upper extremity (strictly speaking the hand, but often used to indicate the entire arm)

RUL: Right upper lobe (of the lung)

RUQ: Right upper quadrant (of the abdomen)

RV: Right ventricle

Rx: Prescription

S: Subjective (part of the S.O.A.P. mnemonic)

S: Sacral

S-A: Sinoatrial (node in the right atrium)

Sl, S2: The first and second (normal) heart sounds

SAO_2: Saturation of arterial blood with oxygen [See also *SO_2*.]

SBWP: Sterile body whirlpool

sed.rate: Erythrocyte sedimentation rate (ESR), the percentage of red cells that will settle down in a tube in one minute; a non-specific test for something wrong in the body (it is elevated, for example, in systemic rheumatic diseases)

SEEG: Sonoencephalogram (ultrasound study of the brain)

SEWP: Sterile extremity whirlpool

SGOT: Serum glutamic oxaloacetic transaminase (an enzyme used in liver function tests (LFTs)

SH: Social history (part of the medical history)

SLE: Systemic lupus erythematosus

SO_2: Saturation of hemoglobin with oxygen. This is expressed as a percentage and must not be confused with the PaO_2 which is the partial pressure of oxygen expressed in millimeters of mercury or, mm Hg. [See also *SAO_2*.]

SOB: Shortage of breath / short of breath

SOBE: Short of breath on exertion

sos: Repeat if urgently needed

s.g.: Specific gravity

SR: Side rails ("SRU" is "side rails up" and "SRE" is "side rails elevated")

SSE: Soap suds enema

stat.: Statim, at once

STD: Sexually transmitted disease

STSs: Serology tests for syphilis

s.l.: Sublingually (under the tongue)

subQ / SQ: Subcutaneously

SVC: Superior vena cava, e.g., "SVC syndrome"

SVT: Supraventricular tachycardia

syn.: Syndrome

T: Thoracic

t / temp.: Temperature

T & A: Tonsillectomy and adenoidectomy

tid: Tris in die, three times a day

T3: Triiodothyronine (the active form of thyroid hormone)

T4: Tetraiodothyronine (a relatively inactive form of thyroid hormone, a precursor of T3)

TAT: Tetanus antitoxin

TB: Tuberculosis

tbs: Tablespoon

TCN: Tetracycline

TD: Tetanus and diphtheria (inoculation)

TENS: Transcutaneous electrical nerve stimulator

ther.ex.: Therapeutic exercises

TIA: Transient ischemic attack

TIBC: Total iron binding capacity (of blood proteins); a test used in iron deficiency anemia

TM: Tympanic membrane (the ear drum)

TP: Total protein (estimation)

TPR: Temperature, pulse and respirations

tsp: Teaspoon

TT: Tetanus toxoid

TUR: Transurethral resection (of prostate gland)

TURB: Transurethral resection of the bladder

TURP: Transurethral resection of the prostate

Tx: Treatment

U: Unit (ICU is the intensive care unit, SICU is surgical intensive care unit, NICU is neonatal intensive care unit, etc.)

U/3: Upper one third (e.g., of a long bone)

U/A: Urinalysis

UCD: Usual childhood diseases

UCG: Urinary chorionic gonadotrophin (hormone used to diagnose pregnancy)

UE: Upper extremity (strictly speaking the hand but often used to refer to the arm)

ung.: Unguentum, or ointment, defined as an oil-based topical medication; a cream is defined as a water-based topical medication.

URI: Upper respiratory infection

U/S: Ultrasound

USN: Ultrasound nebulizer (treatment)

ut: Uterus

UTI: Urinary tract infection

UV: Ultraviolet (radiation)

V tach: Ventricular tachycardia, a serious and often fatal arrhythmia

V / A: Visual acuity

vag.: Vagina

VD: Venereal disease

VDRL: Serological test for syphilis

vent.: Ventilation / ventilator

VFI: Visual fields intact

VS: Vital signs

W / C: Wheel chair

W&D: Warm and dry

W / D: Warm and dry

WM: White male

WF: White female

WBCs: White blood cells

WBCC: White blood cell count

WD: Well developed

WDWN: Well developed and well nourished ("WDWNWM" is "well developed, well nourished white male")

WFL: Within functional limits. See **WNL**

wk: Week ("FUc̄FD 1 / 52" is "follow up with family doctor in one week")

WNL: Within normal limits

WPW: Wolf / Parkinson / White (syndrome)

x̄: Except

y.o.: Year old ("5 y.o.WM" is "five year old white male")

Index

Page numbers in bold indicate pages with figures or images. Titles of books are in italics.